THE HANDBOOK FOR

Storytime

Programs

*ALA Editions purchases fund advocacy,
awareness, and accreditation programs for
library professionals worldwide.*

THE HANDBOOK FOR
Storytime
Programs

JUDY FREEMAN *and* **CAROLINE FELLER BAUER**

An imprint of the American Library Association

CHICAGO 2015

Caroline Feller Bauer (1935–2013) was a public librarian, professor of children's literature, radio personality, international speaker and performer, author of nineteen children's books and professional books about children's literature for adults, and tireless cheerleader for literacy and storytelling.

Judy Freeman (www.judyreadsbooks.com) is a former school librarian; an adjunct professor at Pratt Institute in New York City, teaching courses in children's literature and storytelling; an international speaker and performer for children, teachers, librarians, and parents; a children's book reviewer; and the author of more than a dozen professional books about children's literature and storytelling. She continues to work closely with librarians, teachers, and hundreds of students at several elementary schools to test out new books, ideas, and ways to incorporate literature into children's lives.

Both have developed and performed thousands of programs and workshops incorporating children's literature, storytelling, music, poetry, and drama to tens of thousands of children and adults across the United States and abroad.

© 2015 by Judy Freeman and Caroline Feller Bauer

Printed in the United States of America

19 18 17 16 15   5 4 3 2 1

ISBN: 978-0-8389-1265-2 (paper)

Library of Congress Cataloging-in-Publication Data

Freeman, Judy.
  The handbook for storytime programs / by Judy Freeman and Caroline Feller Bauer.
    pages   cm
  Includes bibliographical references and index.
  ISBN 978-0-8389-1265-2 (print : alk. paper)
    1. Children's libraries—Activity programs—Handbooks, manuals, etc. 2.
  Storytelling—Handbooks, manuals, etc. 3. Children's literature—Bibliography. I.
  Bauer, Caroline Feller. II. Title.
Z718.3.F74 2015
027.62'51—dc23   2014043687

Book design by Kimberly Thornton in the Charis SIL and Tisa Sans Pro typefaces.
Illustrations by Andere Andrea Petrlik/Shutterstock, Inc. Title lettering by Nenilkime/Shutterstock, Inc.

♾ This paper meets the requirements of ANSI/NISO Z39.48–1992 (Permanence of Paper).

To Caroline Feller Bauer, who had a magic touch with stories and children. Love and kisses.

Contents

Acknowledgments

I'd like to thank the following people for their help and support:

Izzy Feldman, my husband and best bud, who knows a good story when he hears one

Richard Freeman, for expert close reading, corrections, and many odd facts

Ann Guthrie, for general sagacity, for philosophies of teaching, and for allowing me to entertain her preschoolers at the Antioch School

Maren Vitali and Jennifer Fisher, two librarians extraordinaire, whose stream of clever ideas, projects, and book sense never failed to delight

Sasha Kleinman, for her keyboard wizardry and research acumen, online and off

Jessica Schneider, for intrepid searching skills

Margaret and Sam Feldman, for harboring the writing girl through many deadlines

Sharron Freeman, for daily chats and respites

Caitlin Freeman, for instructing me how to breathe correctly

Anita Silvey, for her exquisite taste in books and generosity in sharing it

Peggy Beck Haines, for general support and cheerleading

Michael Jeffers, for getting the ball rolling on this project

Jamie Santoro, acquisitions editor, for going to bat for this book

Stephanie Zvirin, editor, for reading, reorganizing, and fine-tooth-
   combing every chapter
The whole publishing team at ALA Editions, for taking on this set of
   books
And, of course, the inimitable Caroline Feller Bauer, whose books and
   ideas inspired a generation of creative storytellers

Introduction

By Judy Freeman

WHILE EACH HANDBOOK (*THE HANDBOOK FOR STORYTELLERS* and *The Handbook for Storytime Programs*) stands on its own, each complements and buttresses the other. The books contain scores of carefully compiled and annotated story lists, booklists, and website lists, plus hundreds of ideas and activities for using storytelling and literature with children.

When Caroline Feller Bauer's first *Handbook for Storytellers,* published by ALA, came out in 1977, there was nothing like it. Truth be told, there was no one like Caroline Feller Bauer in the library world back then—a book-mad sprite who not only advocated reading aloud and telling stories to children, but incorporated books, magic tricks, creative drama, reader's theater, puppetry, poetry, music, and technology in her books and presentations as part and parcel of what youth services librarians (both in schools and public libraries) and teachers could and should do with children. When she burst on the scene, she transformed the profession, giving us permission to fill our programs with delight and fun and joy. She revised her book in 1993, adding still more stories, poems, and songs, along with hundreds of new, useful, and innovative methods of storytelling and building a culture of reading with and for children.

Fast-forward a mere twenty-plus years and, at long last, we have revised, updated, reworked, rethought, and rebuilt Caroline's classic book—we've needed to break it into two large volumes to accommodate everything. Each book is filled to the brim with the best of Caroline's wonderful stories and ideas, plus an overflowing cornucopia of new stories, poems, songs, plays, and activities; a grand assembly of all-new annotated lists comprising thousands of the best stories, children's books, and professional titles; and a vast array of hundreds of related websites and technology tie-ins.

It's now an encyclopedic but very fun-to-read series of reference books that school and public librarians, teachers, and storytellers can use on a daily basis to support their programs and curriculums (tying in with the many educations goals of the Common Core State Standards, with their focus on "reading, writing, speaking, listening, and language"), and to supplement and strengthen their story hours.

The thousands of titles and stories listed in this book are the most exemplary ones of the hundreds of thousands I have read over the course of my career as a librarian, storyteller, reviewer, writer, and speaker to tens of thousands of teachers, librarians, and children. Inspired by Caroline's masterwork, I have mined my own material and stretched my knowledge of children's literature and storytelling to add practical ideas and inspiration on every page.

Each book contains:

- An eclectic and wide-ranging mix of folklore and children's books to develop innovative connections between storytelling and literature
- Practical, surefire suggestions for using storytelling and children's books together to create a literature-based and story-infused environment in schools and libraries
- Easy-to-learn storytelling techniques and read-aloud strategies to make each storytime session an enthralling experience for tellers and listeners
- The full texts of many dozens of stories just right for telling
- Scores of stories, poems, songs, chants, jokes, crafts, story scripts, magic tricks, and other literary delights to share with children
- Ideas, ideas, ideas, everywhere! The plethora of successful and invigorating ideas and activities can be used immediately in story hours, programs, booktalks, and lessons across the curriculum
- Hundreds of painstakingly selected and annotated folktale, children's book, professional book, and website bibliographies, all of which are the most up-to-date and comprehensive in scope in a storytelling and literature guide
- Comprehensive indexes by author, title, and subject

Here's what you'll find in *The Handbook for Storytime Programs.*

The first half of the book, "Part One: Interactive Storytelling," consists of individual chapters, each of which delves into one possible aspect of story programs, with a plethora of stories, books, songs, rhymes, plays, crafts, games, and other engaging material for building your repertoire as a cracker-jack storyteller. These chapters are:

- "Pictures and Objects in Storytelling"
- "Puppetry"
- "Creative Drama"
- "Storytime Fillers: Fingerplays, Tongue Twisters, Riddles, Jokes, Rhymes, and Other Nonsense"
- "Music"
- "Magic"

The second half of the book, "Part Two: Programs," ties all of those elements together and gives guidance on how to pull together a cohesive themed curricular unit or story hour. Those chapters are:

- **"Programs for Preschool and Primary School Children, from Birth to Age 7"**

   This chapter begins with descriptions of a range of story hour programs, from lap times for babies, to programs for toddlers, nursery school–age children, on up to grade 2. It includes a variety of participation stories, and two complete thematic units filled with stories, annotated booklists, and suggested activities: "Time for Bed" and "I'm Hungry."

   It ends with a "quicklist" of 150 thematic program starters for young children, ages 1 to 7, each containing a carefully selected list of exemplary read-alouds; a song, poem, or verse; and an activity and/or craft.

- **"Programs for Upper Elementary and Middle School Children, Ages 8 to 14"**

   This chapter is filled with more stories to tell for a tween audience, and includes story jokes, think stories, convoluted logic puzzlers, scary tales to make kids shiver, funny stories to make them laugh, and even a few well-chosen tales about love and death. Each type of stories is accompanied by an annotated list of related children's books to share.

The chapter ends with a "quicklist" of thirty-five thematic program-starters for tweens, ages 8 to 14, each comprised of two parts:

- **Program Description** (a brief description of a possible themed program)
- **Booklist** (a booklist of first-rate supporting materials to use, whether by reading them aloud, booktalking them, or simply having them on display for kids to check out after the session)

Pragmatically speaking, storytelling is all about language. When children listen and focus on a story told to them, they are developing listening, comprehension, and analytical skills. In terms of higher-level thinking skills, storytelling helps children recall details, summarize the plot sequence, and visualize and describe the settings and scenes. They can speculate on what will happen next in the story, and afterwards, cite the clues that supported their predictions. They can analyze the story structure; discuss plot elements; and evaluate, debate, and make their own judgments about why the characters behave the way they do. They can compare and contrast other similar stories. Finally, they can synthesize the experience in a creative way, perhaps acting out the story, writing a new story using the same structure, or retelling the story from another character's point of view. All the strategies that we use to analyze and evaluate other texts—both fiction and non-fiction—work just as well, if not better, when a story is told.

In this volume and its companion, *The Handbook for Storytellers*, you'll find countless stories to tell as well as songs, rhymes, jokes, crafts, puppets, and even magic tricks to use in your story-hour programming; and ways to use them with children. So many gorgeous and enticing children's books are published every year, and we have included our recommendations of more than a thousand irresistible titles to read aloud, tell, and share. There's a spectacular mix of brand-new and tried-and-true, all books we have read, adored, and, in more cases than not, tested out with the people for whom they are intended: actual kids.

Why should we waste our time reading or telling stories to children when there are perfectly good apps that do the same thing, when we have to worry about getting these kids up to speed before they take their standardized tests, and when everyone is so busy anymore? Why should parents take their kids to the public library for storytime or read aloud at bedtime when they can watch the same story on a device? Why should teachers use precious classroom time to act out a story or do a frivolous craft activity when we're supposed to be preparing these kids for life by analyzing texts for meaning and finding facts? Is there measurable data to prove that children who hear stories, songs, and poems do better in life?

You can find studies galore to support every thesis. Our main answer to the above questions is *because*. Because children love stories, respond to them, dream about them, live them, learn how to live their lives through them, laugh with them, and then grow up to read and tell stories to their own kids. Not everything needs to be measured, does it? We do it because it gives children intense pleasure and satisfaction to know that the world is a good place to be. We do it because we want our children to have wonderful lives, and playing with stories gives them (and us) compassion, companionship, and immeasurable pleasure.

part 1

INTERACTIVE STORYTELLING

RECITE A POEM. SING A SONG. TRANSFORM YOURSELF INTO A VEL-cro board. Have a conversation with a puppet. Put on a play. Turn a flower into a book. It's magic!

Now that you've begun to master the art and science of pure storytelling, (found in our companion volume, *The Handbook for Storytellers*), it's time to gather your resources—stories to tell, favorite read-alouds, poems, puppets, story scripts and drama activities, riddles, songs, and magic tricks—all of which will add another layer of enjoyment to your storytelling program. In this book, we two, Caroline Feller Bauer and Judy Freeman, offer even more of our favorite examples, stories, and booklists designed to help you promote the joys of storytelling and reading through a variety of activities. Not every storyteller will be captivated by these techniques, of course, but we encourage you to try at least a few of the interactive ideas offered here.

Do keep in mind that throughout this book there are many ideas that require props, patterns, and mechanical devices. In some cases, we've provided instructions for making a particular prop or storytelling aid. In other cases, we've simply tried to present enough of an idea of how things work so that you can start experimenting on your own. Should you find yourself intrigued by interactive storytelling, the many annotated booklists offer more detailed references.

As you would ascertain from the piles of props on our shelves, we love extending our own storytelling programs in this way. But beware: a prop should never outshine the material itself. After all, the story's the thing!

Whether you're preparing a thematic series of programs for children in the public library or looking for ideas for using exemplary titles in the classroom or school library, you will find many exciting, practical, and natural tie-ins here, and lots more stories that will enthrall and engage your kids and you.

Need some instant validation of this claim? Okay. Try this foolproof bit of zaniness with your children, ages five and up. The call-and-response chant, "Hello, My Name Is Joe" gets everyone up for a bit of movement.

Have your listeners do the first verse as a call-and-response, repeating each line after you recite it. Then say, "Now, try the whole thing *with* me, in unison, *not after* me." They'll catch on quickly and learn it by heart by the second time through, adding the cumulating motions as you demonstrate them.

Hello, My Name Is Joe

Hello,

My name is Joe

And I work in a button factory.

I have a house, and a dog, and a family.

One day, my boss said to me,

"Are you busy, Joe?"

I said, "No."

He said, "Push this button with your left hand."
> (*push out and back with palm of left hand*)

Continue pushing in and out with your left hand through the next verse and beyond, in time to the rhythm of the words. In the first two lines alone, you'll push in and out four times. You will be in perpetual motion throughout this chant, never stopping, but adding one more motion for each new verse to the actions you're already doing—a veritable ballet of movement.

Hello, my name is Joe
> (*continue pushing out and back with palm of left hand as you recite whole verse*)

And I work in a button factory.

I have a house, and a dog, and a family.

One day, my boss said to me,

"Are you busy, Joe?"

I said, "No."

He said, "Push this button with your right hand."
  (*add right hand and push out and back, alternately, with palm of left AND right hand*)

Repeat verse above, ending with each of these lines:

- He said, "Push this button with your left foot."
  (*all hand motions, plus step up and down with left foot*)

- He said, "Push this button with your right foot."
  (*all hand motions, plus march in place with both feet*)

- He said, "Push this button with your head."
  (*all hand and feet motions, plus push head forward and back*)

- He said, "Push this button with your tongue."
  (*all hand, feet, and head motions, plus stick tongue in and out as you speak the verse one last time*)

FINAL VERSE: (*doing all motions; it will be tricky to speak with your tongue going in and out, which will be supremely silly*)

Hello, my name is Joe

And I work in a button factory.

I have a house, and a dog, and a family.

One day, my boss said to me,

"Are you busy, Joe?"

And I said, "YES!"
  (*When you get to the shouted YES, stop all motions, put hands on hips and wait for your kids to break up in hysterical laughter.*)

———————

Adding a movement activity like this to your program makes the heart pump harder, the lungs take in more oxygen, and the brain go into gear. It can be done with all ages, including teens, even. (Come to think of it, adults love this chant, too, because it reminds them that when they are given one too many things to do, sometimes you simply have to put your foot down and just say "YES!") It's an icebreaker, a laugh inducer, and a way to warm everyone up for the fun to come. Add it to your repertoire, your treasure chest, and your box of tricks, and you'll thank us every time you pull it out.

Chapter 1

Pictures and Objects in Storytelling

There have been great societies that did not use the wheel, but there have been no societies that did not tell stories. —URSULA K. LEGUIN

WE LOVE USING VISUALS. WE KNOW THAT WE ARE SUPposed to use our imaginations to picture characters and events when we read, but wouldn't it be nice to have an illustration to break up, say, your tax forms? Let's look at ways to use objects, paper crafts, and pictures to enhance your storytelling programs. We'll begin, naturally, with a story.

The Miser and The Artist

Retold by Caroline Feller Bauer

The richest man in town was also the stingiest. Some folks thought he was rich because he never wanted to shell out any money for anyone's services. He did pay up eventually, but he always found a reason to complain and was so slow in paying that people didn't want to do business with him. However, since he owned many of the shops and even the fields around the town, many people had no alternative but to work for him.

One day an artist came to town and was summoned before this rich man. The artist had heard that the miser often found ways not to pay artists for creative work—by complaining about the finished product. The artist was reluctant to appear at the rich man's house, but he felt that he should see what the rich man wanted.

The wealthy man got right to the point. "I would like you to draw a colorful mural for me. Bring it to me on Thursday."

The artist wanted to say no to the request. He knew that since he was leaving town on Friday that the chances of being paid for the painting were slim. However, he accepted the commission and on Thursday he returned with a roll of paper.

"I've finished the mural. I'm sure you will be delighted with it since I have heard that you adore landscapes. The painting is called 'Cows in the Meadow.'"

The artist unrolled the picture. The miser stared at an empty space. "I don't see anything," he said. "Where is the grass?"

"It's gone," the artist said. "The grass has been eaten by the cows."

"But where are the cows?" the miser asked.

"Since there wasn't any more grass, the cows left."

The artist rolled up the picture and handed it over to the miser. "No charge," he said, as he walked out the door. "The mural is a gift."

As you near the end of the story, pull out a rolled up sheet of white paper, tied with a handsome ribbon. Unroll it with a flourish and show the blank page to your audience. When the artist says, "No charge. The mural is a gift," redo the roll and hand it to one of your listeners.

Object Stories

As with the story above, using objects mentioned in the story is a good way to involve your audience. When telling Ezra Jack Keats's *Jennie's Hat*, for example, ask a little girl in the audience to sit next to you and try out Jennie's headgear: a basket, a flowerpot, and a saucepan. For an after-story craft, ask children to each bring in an old hat or simply make new ones out of paper bags. (Cut the largest oval you can out of a large paper bag—12-by-10 inches or so. Then cut a cross or an X in the middle, about 8 inches long. Fold up the four resulting triangles and slide the new hat on a child's head. It looks pretty jaunty even before decorating.) Children can decorate their hats with found materials, crayons, and markers and have a hat parade.

Although Margaret Wise Brown's *Goodnight Moon* is traditionally used as a bedtime story, it also makes a tantalizing object story for a program. Use a dollhouse, and as each object is named, place it in a room. As the narrator says good night to each object, children can remove it from the house.

Before telling Marcia Brown's *Stone Soup*, pass out vegetables to the audience. As the citizens in the story contribute to the soup, your listening audience can place their vegetables into a large pot. If you have the facilities for cooking, add water, salt, and chopped parsley to the pot and make a simple vegetable soup with your group, and serve it as a snack.

ALPHABET BOOK STORY HOUR WITH PROPS

You could start off an alphabet story hour with one of the most innovative ABC books out there: *ABC3D* by Marion Bataille, a chunky little pop-up book with a graphically clever rendering of each letter of the alphabet. Show your kids the terrific little YouTube video of the book, complete with backup vocals of the Boswell Sisters singing "Roll On, Mississippi, Roll On" (www .youtube.com/watch?v=wnZr0wiG1Hg). Assemble a box of found materials (or ask parents to send in small objects they no longer need, like stray game pieces or plastic toys) for children to create their own 3-D ABC pages with the swag—an old toy harmonica for *H*, a leaf for *L*, popcorn for *P*, a straw for *S*. Use colorful heavystock cardboard, on which children can draw their alphabet letters, affixing their objects to each page. Use lots of tape, glue, or staples. Assemble the results alphabetically into a big, chunky book for all to read.

You know those old refrigerator magnet letters you have hanging around somewhere? You can use them to help children retell Judy Sierra's *Sleepy Little Alphabet: A Bedtime Story from Alphabet Town*, illustrated by Melissa Sweet. In a merry, rhyming, alliterative bedtime story, a tribute to each alphabet letter, it's "sleepytime in Alphabet Town," and each letter is procrastinating: "Uh-oh! a is wide awake. And b still has a bath to take." After children have laughed over the antics of each letter, you can read it again and have listeners fill in each rhyming end word. Hand out alphabet letter magnets for them to hold up in sync with the story. When you read, "U takes off his . . ." they'll shout, "UNDERWEAR!" as the kid with the U holds up the letter U. You'll be amazed at how many of the words they'll recall after listening just once. When you read the story yet again, without showing the pictures and leaving out words willy-nilly, ask them to fill in as many of the words as they can. Then have them stand up and act out the action of the story in narrative pantomime as you read it yet once again. Your children can write and illustrate new pages showing what will happen to those same letters when they wake up again in the morning, each picking a letter to personify and coming up with an alliterative a.m. activity.

In *Just in Case: A Trickster Tale and Spanish Alphabet Book* by Yuyi Morales, Señor Calavera ("Mr. Skull" in Spanish) gussies up for Grandma Beetle's birthday party and heads out on his bicycle. Along the way, he amasses an entire alphabet of birthday gifts for her, starting with *un acordeón* (an accordion), *un bigote* (a mustache), *un chiflido* (a whistle), and *dientes* (teeth). Pull out corresponding props to show as you read or as children retell the story. The *niños* can create a new alphabet book of the twenty-nine words, with each child picking a word or two to illustrate and label in English and Spanish.

SHOES AND OTHER CREATIVE CLOTHING

You can incorporate a prop into almost any story you read or tell, but you certainly don't need them for every story. It's just that sometimes the possibilities are too tantalizing to pass up. Greg Gormley's *Dog in Boots* was one such book for school librarian Janet Williams at Irving School in Highland Park, New Jersey. When Dog reads the book *Puss in Boots*, he sets off for the local shoe shop to get himself a pair of boots. He asks the salesman, "Have you got any footwear as splendid as this?" The man brings out four boots, one for each paw. "Bow WOW!" says Dog when he sees them. "I'll take them." Unfortunately, the boots turn out to be no good at all for digging, so he takes them back to the shop and trades them in for a succession of other footwear.

Janet not only brought in a pair of golden bedroom slippers as a prop, she brought in her Welsh corgi to help her read the story to her preschool classes. Now *that's* the ultimate prop—a real dog! (Want to get your students to improve their read-aloud skills? Bring in a dog so they can read to it! Studies show that reading to dogs will raise children's reading scores.)

No dog? That's okay. You could bring in all kinds of shoes and have children identify what they're for—such as ice skates, cowboy boots, sneakers, flip-flops, and sandals—and have children describe the functions of each.

PASS THE SHOE GAME

Next, you could play the Pass the Shoe Game. If you haven't tried this game, it's very cute. Go to www.youtube.com/watch?v=yvLNa6L7yi0 to see how it works and to hear the tune.

Here are the words:

> I will <u>pass</u> this <u>shoe</u> from me to you, to you,
> You will <u>pass</u> the <u>shoe</u>, and *do just like I do.*

Have children take off one shoe to use. Sit in a circle on the floor. As you sing the song, each person passes along his shoe to the person on his right each time you sing one of the underlined words above. When you get to "do just like I do," you simply wave the shoe you currently have in the air. Start very slowly—it's harder to do than it looks. Each time you sing the song, speed it up a fraction, until you're doing it very fast. Note that in the video, the children do it slightly differently. They tap the shoe twice on the floor and then pass the shoe to the right, meaning they pass the shoe only three times in a verse instead of six, which may be easier, and even more fun. Tapping twice is satisfying.

Finally, kids could write and illustrate a sequel to *Dog in Boots*. How about "Dog in Hats"? Kids could draw Dog in action with all types of hats.

One of Judy's favorite prop stories is Simms Taback's Caldecott-winning picture book, *Joseph Had a Little Overcoat*, an adaptation of an old Yiddish song and folktale. Joseph cuts down his "old and worn" overcoat to make first a jacket, then a vest, then a scarf, then a necktie, then a handkerchief. Finally, he's left with a button, which he loses. The enterprising fellow then has nothing—until he makes a book about what he did, which shows "you can always make something out of nothing." The collage-and-die-cut illustrations perfectly capture each of Joseph's sartorial creations, but the story is also tailor-made for using objects.

After *Joseph* won the 2000 Caldecott Medal, Judy wandered into a thrift store and found a child's jacket and snow pants made of heavy tweed, with the irresistible price tag of $2. From the pants, she cut out a scarf and the other smaller items and altered the jacket so the arms could be folded back to make it look like a vest as needed. After reading the book, she holds up the coat and has the audience retell the story with her while she shows each successively smaller item of clothing. Over the years, the little coat has gotten much use and has become more threadbare, which makes it seem even more authentic.

POEMS AND STORIES TO TELL USING OBJECTS

Poetry often lends itself well to the use of visuals. Here is a poem you might want to try with simple objects. You can collect multiple props or just one simple one: an old zippered sweatshirt or button-down sweater with side pockets (which also ties in perfectly with the clothing stories above). Say to your children, "I've got something interesting in my pocket. Can you guess what it is?" After they've suggested several things, say, "Okay, none of you has guessed it. Let me show you what it is." Fish around in the pocket and pull out a card upon which you have written the following poem.

Pockets

By Eve Merriam

Something's in my pocket,
What do you think?
It's nothing that goes down
The kitchen sink.

It isn't a penny,
It isn't a nail,
It isn't a cookie
That's nice and stale.

It isn't a whistle,
It isn't a stamp,
It isn't a toad
That's nice and damp.

It isn't an eraser
Or a ticket stub,
It isn't a piece
Of pocket flub.

It isn't a ring
Or string,
Or a stone,

It isn't a bead
Or a weed
Or a bone.

I won't give it to you—
Get a hole of your own.

On the last line, pull out your sweater pocket and show the nice big hole in it. As with all poems, do read it more than once so your listeners will get it. Wouldn't this poem be great fun to do as reader's theater? This is where you'll want to assemble all fifteen of the objects mentioned in the poem (including that kitchen sink—perhaps use a sink strainer—and a piece of "pocket flub" from your clothes dryer). If readers each place one or two of the items in their pockets, they can retrieve each listed item and hold it up as they read or recite it. Choreograph it so they're lined up in order, from left to right, There are sixteen items in all, so this would be great fun for a whole class to read aloud, or even memorize, and recite for an audience. At the end, they can all pull out their pockets and show the holes.

Now here are two good prop stories that will get everyone thinking.

Who Will Fill the House?

A Folktale from Latvia and Lithuania, Retold by Judy Freeman

There once lived a farmer who had three sons. The two older boys always belittled the youngest brother and boasted about how much stronger they were. When the boys grew up and were young men, they helped their father built a sturdy new house. He told his three sons, "Whoever can fill this entire house will inherit it from me."

The oldest son said, "Watch me fill this house." He brought in the horse, the cow, and the pig from the barn, but they only took up one small corner of the house.

The second son said, "Watch me fill the house." He brought in bales of hay, and then more bales, and then still more bales. He stacked them one atop another. The bales took up a fair amount of space, but they did not fill the whole house. In fact, they only filled half the house, and bits of straw were flying everywhere.

Now it was the youngest brother's turn. He pulled a small sack out of his pocket. His brothers laughed at him, but never mind. He took a candle out of the sack, lit it with a match, and handed it to his father to hold. Instantly, the whole house was filled with light. He pulled out a little flute he had carved from a willow branch and blew a tune on it until the house was filled with music. The father chuckled, filling the house with laughter, and said, "You, my youngest son and cleverest son, will inherit this house."

If you have a willow tree handy, try making your own willow flute. You can find instructions online at sites such as eHow (www.ehow.com/how_4812412_willow-flute.html). Pair it with the picture book *Mary's Penny* by Tanya Landmann, where the farmer's quick-thinking daughter wins the contest over her two brawny brothers.

Two Donkeys

Retold by Caroline Feller Bauer

Jake and Abe were friends. They each owned a donkey and often made the journey to market together. Jake always had trouble telling the two donkeys apart. "I wish that there was a way for me to tell which donkey is mine," lamented Jake.

One day, he had an idea. "I know what I can do. I'll cut a little hair off my donkey's tail. Now I will know that the donkey with the short tail is mine."

The next day Abe's donkey got his tail caught in a gate. When it was finally released, its tail was the same length as Jake's donkey's.

"Now I will not be able to tell which donkey is mine," wailed Jake. He thought for a moment. "I know what I will do. I'll just put a little nick in my donkey's left ear. Now I will be able to tell which donkey is mine."

The very next day Abe's donkey was passing under a low branch of a tree and nicked its left ear. "Oh no," wailed Jake. "Once again I will not be able to tell which donkey is mine."

The two donkeys were standing next to each other when suddenly Jake exclaimed, "Look! I never noticed before, but my donkey is taller than yours. Now I'll be able to tell your black donkey from my white one."

To make sure your listeners understand the punch line of this story, hold up a large picture of a white donkey and a large picture of an otherwise identical black one.

BOOKLIST: OBJECT STORIES

Aylesworth, Jim. *My Grandfather's Coat*. *Illus. by Barbara McClintock. Scholastic, 2014*. When Grandfather's coat—which he made when he came to America and got married—wears out, he snips, clips, stiches, and sews a succession of smaller garments. Based on the Yiddish folk song "I Had a Little Overcoat," this is a perfect companion to compare with *Joseph Had a Little Overcoat* by Simms Taback. Make your own little coat as described above, to help you retell both stories. (PreK–Gr. 2)

Bataille, Marion. *ABC3D*. *Roaring Brook, 2008*. A small, intriguing pop-up alphabet book that will beguile both kids and adults. You or your art teacher might want to explore making pop-ups. "Books About Paper Crafts" on page 27 can help. (PreK–Adult)

Baylor, Byrd. *Everybody Needs a Rock.* *Illus. by Peter Parnall. Scribner, 1974.* Decorate rocks as an after-story craft or hand out pet rocks for people to keep. (Gr. 1–6)

Brett, Jan. *The Umbrella.* *Illus. by the author. Putnam, 2004.* Carlos ventures into the Costa Rican cloud forest with his umbrella. When he leaves the upended umbrella on the ground, the rain forest animals climb in. (PreK–Gr. 2)

Brown, Marcia. *Stone Soup: An Old Tale.* *Illus. by the author. Scribner, 1947.* Make soup from a stone just as the soldiers did in this French folktale. (Gr. 1–4)

Brown, Margaret Wise. *Goodnight Moon.* *Illus. by Clement Hurd. HarperCollins, 1947.* The best baby bedtime story ever. Use toys when you tell this and if you have bunny slippers, wear them. (PreK–K)

Ehlert, Lois. *Leaf Man.* *Illus. by the author. Harcourt, 2005.* "A Leaf Man's got to go where the wind blows." Have kids collect fall leaves and arrange them into pictures. (PreK–Gr. 2)

Gormley, Greg. *Dog in Boots.* *Illus. by Roberta Angaramo. Holiday House, 2011.* "Bow WOW!" Dog exclaims when he buys boots like the ones he saw in Puss in Boots. Bring in different types of shoes. (PreK–Gr. 2)

Hest, Amy. *In the Rain with Baby Duck.* *Illus. by Jill Barton. Candlewick, 1995.* Baby Duck grumbles about walking through the rain and mud, but Grampa understands exactly how she feels. This just right story will get your preschoolers impatient to don their boots and umbrellas and go puddle-splashing on a rainy day. (PreK–Gr. 1)

Keats, Ezra Jack. *Jennie's Hat.* *Illus. by the author. HarperCollins, 1966.* Jennie's hat is entirely too plain until her friends, the birds, decorate it. Hold a hat parade. (PreK–Gr. 2)

Landmann, Tanya. *Mary's Penny.* *Illus. by Richard Holland. Candlewick, 2010.* A smart daughter proves that brains are better than brawn when she bests her brothers. Bring in a penny, a flute, and a candle. (PreK–Gr. 6)

Morales, Yuyi. *Just in Case: A Trickster Tale and Spanish Alphabet Book.* *Illus. by the author. Roaring Brook, 2008.* Señor Calavera ("Mr. Skull" in Spanish) gathers an alphabetical assortment of presents for Grandma Beetle's birthday party. Play an alphabet game, "I unpacked Señor Calavera's trunk and I found . . ." (Gr. 1–3)

Pellowski, Anne. *The Story Vine.* *Illus. by Lynn Sweat. Macmillan, 1984.* Pellowski demonstrates how to use a variety of story props, including dolls, string, and pictures. (Professional)

Sierra, Judy. *Sleepy Little Alphabet: A Bedtime Story from Alphabet Town.* *Illus. by Melissa Sweet. Knopf, 2009.* In this merry rhyming tribute to the alphabet, it's "sleepytime in Alphabet Town." Use magnetic alphabet letters to help children recall what each letter is doing before bed. (PreK–Gr. 1)

Taback, Simms. *Joseph Had a Little Overcoat*. *Illus. by the author. Viking, 2009.* Joseph turns his "old and worn" overcoat into a succession of smaller clothing. Distribute scissors and cut-out overcoat patterns for children to trim down as you retell the story. (PreK–Adult)

Zolotow, Charlotte. *Mr. Rabbit and the Lovely Present*. *Illus. by Maurice Sendak.* HarperCollins, 1962. When a little girl asks Mr. Rabbit to help her find a colorful birthday present for her mother, Mr. Rabbit picks some of his own favorite things: pears, bananas, apples, and grapes. Bring in a basket and fill it with fruit. Then prepare fruit salad to eat. (PreK–Gr. 2)

Paper-Craft Stories

Paper, especially scrap paper, is an inexpensive and readily available source of material for your book program. Try telling a few stories using paper folding and cutouts. Numerous books on paper crafts are available to help you and your young listeners learn techniques; you'll find some suggestions on page 27.

Wind and Fire

Retold by Caroline Feller Bauer

This is one of Caroline's favorite stories. After telling it, share Marguerite Davol's The Paper Dragon, *in which a humble scroll painter must complete three similar tasks when he volunteers to face a dragon. Robert Sabuda's remarkable paper-folded illustrations incorporate the art of Chinese paper cutting.*

Qwan and Ming Li were both young and silly girls. Young brides married to brothers, they lived in their husbands' home with their mother-in-law. Their own mother lived in a village a day's walk from their new homes. So after some time they became homesick for their own family.

"We want to go home and visit our mother," the girls said to their husbands. "Ask my mother," the husbands said. "If she says yes, then it is all right with us."

Ming Li and Qwan pleaded with their mother-in-law to let them leave for a visit. At last she said that they could go, so long as they brought back a present. "Of course," agreed the girls. "What would you like?"

"Bring me the wind in paper and fire in paper." The girls were appalled. How could they leave if they had to bring back something so impossible?

They decided to go on their trip anyway. Laughing and giggling all the way to their own village, the girls arrived home.

Their mother was overjoyed to see them. When she heard about the strange request from their mother-in-law, she told the girls to enjoy their visit. "I will see to it that you have wind in paper and fire in paper to bring back with you."

After several days Qwan and Ming Li were homesick for their husbands and even their mother-in-law. "We are ready to return to our husbands, but what shall we do about the present for our mother-in-law?"

"Have no fear," said their own mother. "I have prepared the gift. Have a safe journey."

Giggling and laughing all the way back, the two young brides enjoyed happy reunions with their husbands, and even their mother-in-law treated them with new respect when they returned with wind in paper—a fan—and fire in paper—a paper lantern!

At the end of the story, produce a fan and the paper lantern with a flourish. Asian grocery shops might carry fans and paper lanterns; you can also make your own.

CRAFT: ROSETTE FAN

Supplies: Newspaper or wrapping paper

Directions:
1. Pleat the paper in alternate folds of 2 inches each.
2. Open the fan by holding one end.

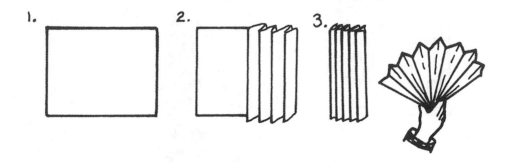

Supplies: A square of colored paper (12-by-12 inches); scissors; tape or glue

Directions:
1. Fold the paper in half diagonally (fig. 1).
2. Fold the triangular shape in half two more times (figs. 2, 3, and 4).
3. Cut into the two folded edges of the triangle, first from one side, and then from the other side, leaving about half an inch uncut (fig. 5).
4. Unfold the paper (fig. 6).
5. Bring the four outer corners of the paper together and tape or glue them in place and gently pull the center of the paper down. Use a string or ribbon as a handle for the lantern if you like. You can also shine a flashlight through the bottom to show how the "fire" might look.

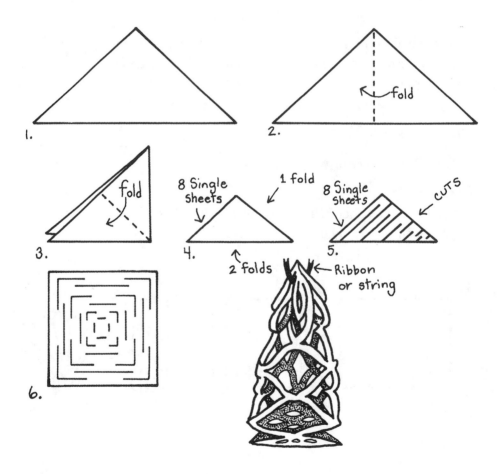

Origami

If you haven't tried origami already, get yourself a how-to book or simply look it up online. You'll find hundreds of demonstrations on YouTube showing how to make every conceivable shape or animal. A dexterous eight-year-old will be glad to show you a few clever tricks to keep under your belt.

A delightful book celebrating origami is *Fold Me a Poem*, written by Kristine O'Connell George and illustrated by Lauren Stringer, in which a young boy folds a collection of origami animals and offers haiku-like observations about them. You can find suggestions for writing and paperfolding activities on George's and Stringer's websites (www.KristineGeorge.com; www .LaurenStringer.com). George's site also links to a downloadable teacher's guide with directions for folding a simple dog—which your students will love doing—and a lesson on writing three different kinds of poems.

Knowing how to fold a paper crane will come in handy when reading or telling Rosemary Well's *Yoko's Paper Cranes*, featuring a young gray cat who makes three origami cranes to mail to her *obaasan* (grandmother) in Japan. Paper cranes are also central to Allen Say's *Tree of Cranes*, in which the author describes the wonder he felt growing up in Japan when his California-raised mother decorated a small pine tree with paper cranes at Christmas.

Looking for an activity to link with Chinese New Year-themed books such as *The Runaway Wok: A Chinese New Year Tale* by Ying Chang Compestine or Laurence Yep's autobiographical chapter book *The Star Maker*? A Chinese love knot is easy enough for children to make. It's also a fun way to send a secret message to someone, so you can also use it for other programs during the year.

CRAFT: CHINESE LOVE KNOT

Supplies: Long strips of paper, any size; scissors

Directions:
1. Write a secret message on one side of a strip of paper.
2. Fold the strip in half lengthwise, like a hot dog.
3. Next, fold the strip **forward** along dotted line (fig. 1) so the two sides (AB and BC) are perpendicular. It will look like a sideways L.
4. Fold the longer leg **backward** (fig. 2) so BC is parallel and close to AB. The BC leg will be longer than the AB leg.
5. Fold the longer leg DE (fig. 3) backward on the dotted line. It will now be in back of and perpendicular to AB.

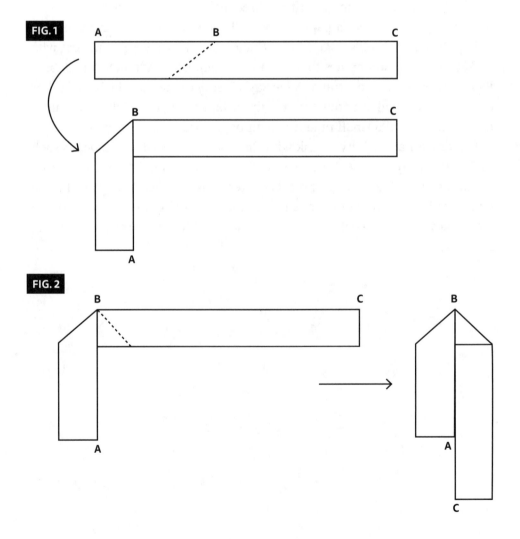

6. Carefully flip leg AB behind leg DE (fig. 4) It will seem to snap into place, forming a little envelope that won't come apart unless/until you undo it.

7. Write the name of the person to whom you are giving your love knot on the front of leg E. Now it's ready to deliver!

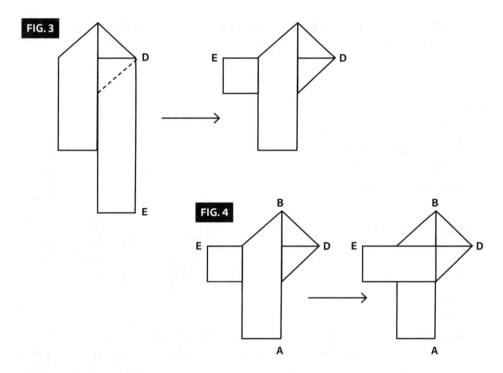

Fold-and-Cut Rhymes

Fold-and-cut nursery rhymes are fun for everyone. Use them as fillers between stories or as a finale to a story-hour program. Each of the paper-cut designs below is created by making accordion folds in a wide sheet of paper and then lightly penciling the illustration as shown. You can begin with colored origami paper, which is thin and easy to cut; as you become more adept, try construction paper. Repeat the rhyme several times, with the children joining you. During the second and third recitation, fold and cut the shape. Use sharp scissors, and cut carefully.

Mary, Mary, Quite Contrary

Mary, Mary, quite contrary.
How does your garden grow?
With silver bells and cockle shells
And pretty maids all in a row.

Shake a Pine Cone

 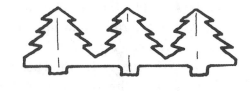

Shake a pine cone,
Plant a tree;
Make a forest
For you and me.

This one is perfect for Earth Day or Arbor Day. The longer your strip of paper and the more folds, the more trees you'll have in your forest.

Henry and Mary

Henry was a worthy king,
Mary was his queen.
He gave to her a lily
Upon a stalk of green.

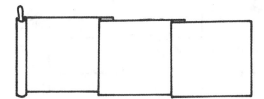 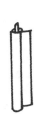 

Make a roll of paper (green shelf or wrapping paper with a green leaf or vine pattern would be great, if you have any). Before you roll it up, though, put a little piece of masking tape at the top of the paper so it sticks up like a little tab. This will help you find the center when you need it later. A rubber band or little piece of tape around the middle will keep it rolled. (If you don't want to invest in fancy paper, simply use three double-spread sheets of newspaper or kraft paper, and, if you're feeling industrious, paint them green.)

Fold down a few inches along the outer left edge of the first sheet and start rolling to the right. When you get near the end of the sheet, place the next sheet on top, overlapping it by several inches, and keep rolling. Do the same with the third sheet. Hold the roll together with a rubber band or tape around the middle. Using heavy-duty shears, a sharp knife, or a single-edged razor blade, make four or five vertical cuts into the roll, several inches long. Fold back the outer "leaves" and pull upward gently at the center of the roll to form the lily stalk. If you used a piece of tape at the top of the fold when you started, the center will be very easy to find. Or just wet your finger, insert it into the center, and pull upward. Of course, the more paper you use, the leafier the stalk.

Old Betty Blue

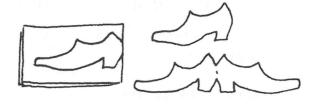

Old Betty Blue
Lost a holiday shoe
What can old Betty do?
Give her another
To match the other,
And then she may swagger in two.

Fold lengthwise. Show single shoe, then open to show the pair of shoes.

Ring Around the Rosie

Ring around the rosie,
Pocket full of posies;
Ashes, ashes,
We all fall down.

Below are two types of paper dolls you can cut.

1. Fold a large sheet of paper, such as a newspaper double-spread, in half.
2. Fold in half again.
3. Fold corner A diagonally to bring folded edges AB and BC together.
4. Turn the paper over and fold it diagonally in half again, bringing edges BE and BAC together.
5. Draw figure on surface AFB and cut to make ring.

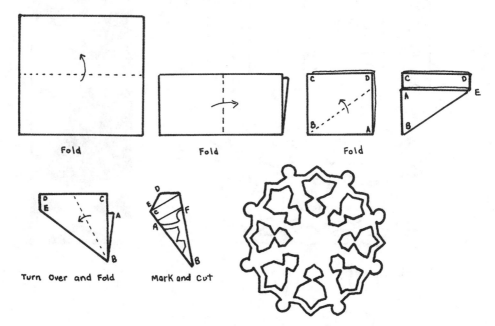

Fold   Fold   Fold

Turn Over and Fold   Mark and Cut

The Three Billy Goats Gruff: A Paper Fold-and-Cut Story

Now that you've had some practice, let's look at how to tell a familiar story using paper props.

PREPARING THE PATTERNS

As you tell the story, you will be snipping away with scissors, so it's a good idea to draw out the characters in advance. Use one sheet of blank newsprint paper for the goats and one for the troll. It's probably a good idea to prepare extra drawings in case your hand slips and you need to start again. Also, you'll want to practice the paper cutting several times before you try it with an audience.

THE GOAT PATTERN

Cut one piece to measure 24 inches wide by 12 inches high. Holding the paper the long way—landscape style—fold it into thirds, first from the left and then from the right. The folds should overlap each other (fig. 1). If you mark these folding lines at 8-inch intervals, you can be sure the widths will all be the same. Now fold the paper in half, from right to left. Your paper is now 4 inches wide and 12 inches high (fig. 2). Making sure the center fold is on the right-hand side, draw out the goat, with the chain-link pattern (fig. 3). The chain link ties the three heads firmly together (fig.4).

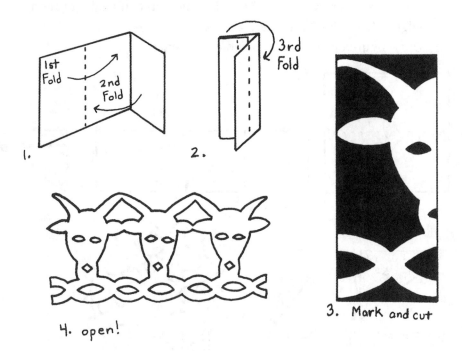

1.

2.

3. Mark and cut

4. open!

THE TROLL PATTERN

Cut the second piece of paper to measure 9 inches wide by 32 inches high. Holding the paper the tall way—portrait style—fold the strip in half (from the bottom up), then up from the bottom in half again. It will now stand 8 inches high, with the fold on the bottom, and 9 inches wide (fig. 1). Now fold it in half again so it's 8 inches high and 4½ inches wide (fig. 2). Finally, fold it in half again so it measures 4 inches high and 4½ inches wide. With the 4½-inch fold on the bottom and the 4-inch fold on the right side (fig. 3) and using the diagram (fig. 4), draw the troll's face. His ears, mouth, nose, and feet are all very simple shapes that can easily be cut out during the telling. The result is a surprisingly intricate design achieved from a minimum amount of cutting (fig. 5).

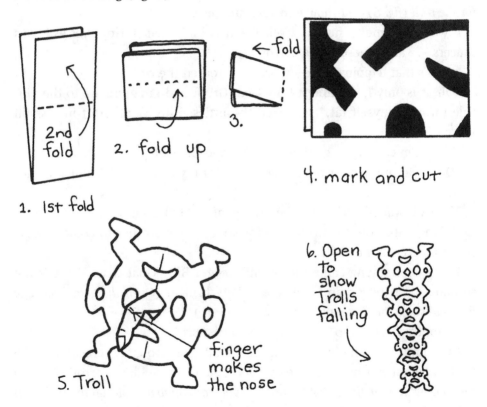

WHAT TO SAY AND DO

As you make this introduction, cut the goats.

One fine day, the three Billy Goats Gruff were feeling very hungry. They decided to go across the river to where the fields were lush and green. The journey was but a short distance . . . just over the narrow river bridge . . . though little did they realize the difficulties they would encounter along the way!

When the cutting is complete, carefully open the center fold and show just one goat as you say:

The littlest Billy Goat Gruff was the first to go over the bridge . . . here he is . . . trip-trapping over the shaky wooden timbers to get to the other side. "Trip, trap, trip, trap!" went the bridge.

But halfway over the rickety bridge, he was stopped by a strange creature. Let me cut this other folded paper packet and show you how the creature looked!

Place the goat figure (still opened to show only one goat) on the table while you cut the troll. Open the troll one fold to show the creature's full face. Hold it up carefully with one hand (you don't want to separate the layers yet). Poke the index finger of your other hand through the central cut-out to form a long nose for the troll (fig. 5) and show it to your audience.

It was a big, mean, hungry troll. The troll had great staring eyes as big as saucers . . . and a nose like a carrot!

"Who's that tripping over my bridge?" roared the troll.

"Oh, it is only I, the tiniest Billy Goat Gruff, and I'm going up to the hillside to make myself fat," squeaked the littlest Billy Goat Gruff in a small voice.

"Now, I'm coming to gobble you up," said the troll.

"Don't eat me. I'm far too skinny. Wait for my brother. He's much bigger than I am."

The troll wanted to eat up the little goat . . . but then he said, "All right. Get along with you, then. I'll wait for your bigger brother to come along." (*Place the troll on the table.*)

Pretty soon, along came the second, bigger Billy Goat Gruff. Here is the second goat trip-trapping over the rickety bridge! (*Open the goat head one fold and show the first and second goats, joined.*)

"Trip, trap, trip, trap, trip, trap!" went the bridge.

Out jumped that a big, mean, hungry troll. You probably remember—the troll had great staring eyes, like saucers . . . and a nose like a carrot! (*Hold up the troll, with your finger for his nose. If you can manage, hold up the troll with one hand and the double goats in the other.*)

"Who's that tripping over my bridge?" roared the troll.

"Oh, it is only I, the second Billy Goat Gruff, and I'm going up to the hillside to make myself fat," bleated the second Billy Goat Gruff in a not-so-small voice.

"Now, I'm coming to gobble you up," said the troll.

"Don't eat me. I'm far too skinny. Wait for my brother. He's much bigger than I am."

The troll wanted to eat up the second goat . . . but then he said, "All right. Get along with you, then. I'll wait for your bigger brother to come along." (*Place the troll on the table.*)

Pretty soon, along came the third and biggest Billy Goat Gruff. Here is the third goat trip-trapping over the rickety bridge! (*Open the goat head another fold and show all three goats.*)

"Trip, trap, trip, trap, trip, trap, trip, trap!" went the bridge, creaking and groaning because the third Billy Goat Gruff was so heavy.

Out jumped that big, mean, hungry troll. You probably remember—the troll had great staring eyes as big as . . . do you remember? Oh, yes, of course. Saucers! And a nose like a . . . what was it? A carrot? That's exactly right. He had a nose like a carrot! (*Hold up the troll, with your finger for his nose.*)

"Who's that tripping over my bridge?" roared the troll.

"It is I, the third Billy Goat Gruff, and I'm going up to the hillside to make myself fat," roared the third Billy Goat Gruff.

"Now, I'm coming to gobble you up," said the troll.

The third goat hollered,

"Well, come along, then! I've got two spears,
And I'll poke your eyeballs out at your ears;
I've got besides two curling-stones,
And I'll crush you to bits, body and bones."

The greedy troll had a great shock when he realized how big that third Billy Goat Gruff was. He had obviously bitten off more than he could chew! The eldest goat put down his head and charged at the troll with his horns and butted that mean troll right into the river . . . and this is how he looked as he tumbled off the bridge and fell into the water with a mighty splash!

Pick up the troll and hold him by his heels. Holding on to one layer of heels, allow the chain of trolls to fall open (fig. 6). Pick up the three attached paper goats and conclude the story:

With the troll vanquished, the biggest Billy Goat Gruff joined his brothers on the hillside, where they all ate their fill of the good green grass. They got so fat they were scarcely able to walk home again. And if the fat hasn't fallen off them, why, they're still fat; and so,

Snip, snap, snout.
This tale's told out.

BOOKLIST: STORIES TO USE WITH PAPER CRAFTS

Angleberger, Tom. *The Strange Case of Origami Yoda.* Illus. by the author. Amulet, 2010. Dwight, the weirdest kid at McQuarrie Middle School, creates an origami finger puppet that offers life-changing advice to anyone who asks. Visit the author's website, www.origamiyoda.com, for instructions on making the Yoda puppet. (Gr. 3–6)

Asbjørnsen, P. C., and J. E. Moe. *The Three Billy Goats Gruff.* Illus. by Marcia Brown. Harcourt, 1957. This is a classic version of the Norwegian folktale. (PreK–Gr. 2)

Coerr, Eleanor. *Sadako.* Illus. by Ed Young. Putnam, 1993. A somber picture-book version of Coerr's *Sadako and the Thousand Paper Cranes* (1977), which is based on the true story of a Japanese girl who died of leukemia following the bombing of Hiroshima. Sadako attempted to fold one thousand origami paper cranes to make herself well; children can make paper cranes in tribute. (Gr. 2–6)

Compestine, Ying Chang. *The Runaway Wok: A Chinese New Year Tale.* Illus. by Sebastia Serra. Dutton, 2011. On Chinese New Year's Eve, Mama Zhang sends her son, Ming, to the market, where he trades his eggs for a magic wok. (PreK–Gr. 4)

Davol, Marguerite W. *The Paper Dragon.* Illus. by Robert Sabuda. Atheneum, 1997. A Chinese dragon asks an artist to bring him fire, wind, and the strongest thing in the world, each of which must be wrapped in paper. (K–Gr. 4)

Freeman, Judy. "The Rainhat" in *Once Upon a Time: Using Storytelling, Creative Drama, and Reader's Theater with Children in Grades PreK–6.* Libraries Unlimited, 2007. In this story, use a large sheet of paper to fold a rain hat, a firefighter's hat, a pirate's hat, a pirate ship, and, finally, a surprise. (Professional)

Galdone, Paul. *The Three Billy Goats Gruff.* Illus. by the author. Clarion, 1973. Compare Galdone's sprightly illustrations for this classic Norwegian folktale with the Asbjørnsen and Moe version illustrated by Marcia Brown, above. (PreK–Gr. 2)

George, Kristine O'Connell. *Fold Me a Poem.* Illus. by Lauren Stringer. Harcourt, 2005. In thirty-one spare, haiku-like poems, a boy chronicles his day folding origami animals. (Gr. 1–4)

Say, Allen. *Tree of Cranes.* Illus. by the author. Houghton Mifflin, 1991. A young boy in Japan learns about Christmas in America from his mother, who grew up in California. (PreK–Gr. 3)

Wells, Rosemary. *Yoko's Paper Cranes.* Illus. by the author. Hyperion, 2001. Having no money to buy her grandmother a birthday present, Yoko makes three origami paper cranes and mails them from her home in California to her grandparents in Japan. (PreK–Gr. 1)

Yep, Laurence. *The Star Maker.* Harper, 2011. Artie looks back at five pivotal months of his childhood in San Francisco's Chinatown, starting in September 1953, the year he was eight. (Gr. 2–5)

BOOKLIST: BOOKS ABOUT PAPER CRAFTS

Bauer, Caroline Feller. *Leading Kids to Books through Crafts.* *Illus. by Richard Laurent. American Library Association, 2000.* Each craft idea comes with patterns, instructions, a story to tell, a poem, and an annotated booklist of related children's books. Just plain nifty. (Professional)

Brodek, Ayako. *The New Encyclopedia of Origami and Papercraft Techniques.* *Running Press, 2011.* The color photos of finished crafts—including origami, pop-ups, paper sculpture, weaving, paper cutting, collage, and more—will inspire projects with your children. (Professional)

De Las Casas, Dianne. *Handmade Tales: Stories to Make and Take.* *Libraries Unlimited, 2008.* A storytelling dynamo shares twenty-seven delightful tales with accompanying crafts to wow your kids. (Professional)

Harbo, Christopher L. *Easy Animal Origami.* *Capstone, 2011.* Fold a dog, cat, butterfly, ladybug, bunny, parakeet, and swan, with colorful layouts of easy-to-follow, step-by-step instructions. Others in the series, all by Harbo, include: *Easy Holiday Origami* (2011), *Easy Magician Origami* (2012), *Easy Ocean Origami* (2011), *Easy Origami Toys* (2011), and *Easy Space Origami* (2012). (Gr. 1–4)

Irvine, Joan. *How to Make Super Pop-Ups.* *Illus. by Linda Hendry. Dover, 2008, c1992.* Children will have fun with these pop-up ideas. See also the author's *Easy-to-Make Pop-Ups*, illustrated by Barbara Reid (Dover, 2005, c1987). (Gr. 3–6)

Jackson, Paul. *Origami Zoo: 25 Fun Paper Animal Creations! Gibbs Smith, 2011.* Instructions for making each animal are clear and easy to follow; included are sixty sheets of origami paper. (Gr. 1–6)

Lewis, Amanda. *The Jumbo Book of Paper Crafts.* *Illus. by Jane Kurisu. Kids Can, 2002.* Full-color, step-by-step instructions for seventy paper projects involving folding, cutting, weaving, gluing, and paper making. (Gr. 3–7)

Meinking, Mary. *Easy Origami.* *Capstone, 2009.* This is the first book in a series, with each book a bit more challenging than the last. Each volume has color photos and includes ten or so projects. Follow up with Meinking's *Not-Quite-So-Easy Origami*, and then Chris Alexander's *Sort-of-Difficult Origami* and *Difficult Origami* (all 2009). (Gr. 2–8)

Van Sicklen, Margaret. *The Joy of Origami.* *Workman, 2005.* Fifty-seven paper-folding projects, from simple (ladybug, newspaper hat) to complex (wiener dog, Tyrannosaurus Rex). The book comes with one hundred sheets of origami paper. (Professional)

Wickings, Ruth. *Pop-up: Everything You Need to Know to Create Your Own Pop-up Book.* *Illus. by Frances Castle. Candlewick, 2010.* Learn the basics of making pop-ups by putting together four pop-up scenes using the components of the book itself. (Gr. 3–8)

Draw-and-Tell Stories and Rhymes

A chalkboard, a dry-erase whiteboard, and a flip chart are familiar features in most classrooms, lecture halls, clubhouses, and libraries. Now also standard are a number of interactive electronic devices including SMART Boards or Promethean boards and document cameras (a high-tech update of an overhead projector and an opaque projector). All of these can be used to illustrate a story as you tell it. Although the same result can be accomplished with magic markers and a large drawing pad on an easel or a simple flip chart—both perfectly terrific low-tech options—the chalkboard and dry-erase board have the advantage of being reusable. An interactive whiteboard or a document camera may seem a bit impersonal for a draw-and-tell story, but everyone will be able to see what you are doing. And it does seem magical when the kids can see your hand up close while you draw.

Illustrated picture books often inspire children to do their own drawings. *Harold and the Purple Crayon* by Crockett Johnson has always amazed kids who wish they could draw their own adventures and have them come to life. More recently, there's the Caldecott Honor book *Journey* by Aaron Becker, about a lonely girl who draws her way into a magical land; and *The Pencil* by Allan Ahlberg, illustrated by Bruce Ingman, about a lonely little pencil that draws a boy, a dog, a cat, and a paintbrush.

In response, children can narrate their own adventure stories, illustrating them as they tell them. Put on music and let them draw what they hear and make up stories about it. Draw along with them and make your own pictures. Many grown-ups tend to be art phobic, having not picked up a crayon since they were in school. Working with children, who can be so creative and innovative as artists, might inspire you to dig out your old sketchbook and start doodling.

Hold on. Why are you shaking your head? A couple of pages ago, we heard you complaining that you were no good at paper folding. Now you're moaning because you think you can't draw? Relax. There are many stories and rhymes that require only simple illustrations. When you do a draw-and-tell story, you can always lightly pencil in the illustrations beforehand until you become confident in your abilities. Your kids won't mind (or even notice).

Our draw-and-tell examples are for people who are not artists, but if you are skilled, the possibilities mushroom. Be aware, however, that your audience will become restless if you painstakingly complete a masterwork. Stand to the side as you draw so everyone can see, and always practice before presenting a story so you feel at ease with the combined drawing/telling activity. The following interactive rhymes and stories will start you on your way. Have children draw along with you when you retell each story.

Rain, Rain, Go Away

Make little circles for rain on your drawing or painting surface as you recite the first two lines. Add colorful petals around the circles plus green stems and leaves as you recite the last two.

> Rain, rain, go away.
> Come again another day.
> April showers
> Bring May flowers.

Oh Where, Oh Where Has My Little Dog Gone?

Ask the children to sing as you draw. This also works well as a paper-cutting activity: draw the image on a piece of folded paper, with the fold on top, to make a two-sided, stand-up dog.

> Oh where, oh where has my little dog gone?
> Oh where, oh where can he be?
> With his ears so short
> And his tail so long,
> Oh where, oh where can he be?

Because the illustration looks a bit like a fox, leave it on the chalkboard or marker board. Ask the children to sing the next song. At the words "We'll catch a fox," draw a box around the animal, erasing it when the children sing the last line.

Oh, A-Hunting We Will Go

> Oh, a-hunting we will go,
> A-hunting we will go.
> We'll catch a fox
> And put him in a box
> And then we'll let him go.

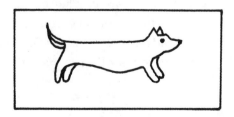

T Is for Tommy

Retold by Caroline Feller Bauer

T

T is for Tommy.

T   C

C stands for Charles.

⊡   C

Tommy builds a house and
puts windows in it.

⊡   C

He adds two chimneys.

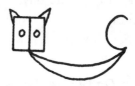

Tommy visits Charles's house.

He comes back by way of
another route.

He's been bewitched, because
he kicks, and kicks, and kicks,
and kicks . . .

And turns into a cat.

Judy Freeman has her own version of the cat story, much extended, originally based on the little picture book *Tale of a Black Cat* by Carl Withers and illustrated by Alan Cober (Holt, Rinehart and Winston, 1966), which is long out of print. You can find her rendition in her *Once Upon a Time: Using Storytelling, Creative Drama, and Reader's Theater with Children in Grades PreK–6*. Paul O. Zelinsky also wrote and illustrated a most charming picture-book version, *The Maid and the Mouse and the Odd-shaped House: A Story in Rhyme* (Dodd, Mead, 1981), that your library may still have.

Where's My Dog?

Retold by Judy Freeman

This story was drawn and told to Judy Freeman by Patrick Shafer, age twelve, and his brother Matthew Shafer, age nine, from North Wales, Pennsylvania, on a packed train going to New York City on the Saturday before Christmas 2007. When they disembarked at Penn Station twenty minutes later, Judy had received the most wonderful Christmas present ever—a new story. She has told it all over the US and always asks if her audience has heard it before. Only a few children have. You can find several versions on the Internet, but none exactly like this one.

Once there was a man
who had no arms.

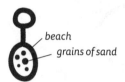

One day his dog got lost. He went looking for his dog, but he couldn't find him anywhere. He went to the beach. But all he found there were grains of sand.

He walked all around in a circle. But his dog was not there. He couldn't find his dog. He couldn't find his dog anywhere. He sat down on the grass to think, but he was attacked by angry ants, so he got up.

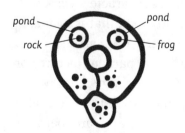

There was a pond nearby, so he went to look there, but all he saw were rocks. There was another pond nearby, so he went there to look, too, but all he saw were frogs. He couldn't find his dog. He couldn't find his dog anywhere.

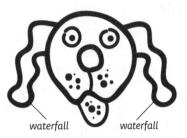

There was a waterfall nearby, so he went to look there. He walked under the waterfall, but his dog wasn't there. There was another waterfall nearby, so he went to look there, too. He walked under the other waterfall, but all he found was water. He couldn't find his dog. He couldn't find his dog anywhere.

By now, the man was hungry, so he decided to eat his lunch. He sat down on a big rock and unpacked his bag. He pulled out a loaf of bread, an apple, an orange, and two biscuits. And for dessert, a Twizzler! And what do you know—as soon as he finished, he looked up and there was his dog!

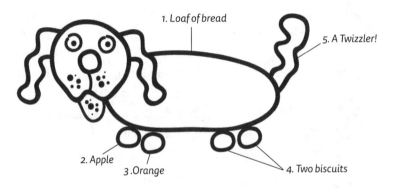

Story Cards and Other Ideas for Using Pictures

STORY CARDS

When one of your popular picture books is falling apart, don't toss it! Cut out the characters or scenes and mount them on poster board with rubber cement. Books that have repetitive action or sequential characters work well for such use. If you're sharing a story from a picture book that is available in paperback, purchase two copies and take one apart. You can also use a color copier to reproduce the illustrations. Zoom in on parts of pictures or scan the entire illustration, save your copies as PDFs, enlarge them before printing them out, and laminate them if you want them to last. You can also enlarge pictures and attach them to big sheets of tagboard, cardboard, or heavy paper. Anything larger than 2 feet by 3 feet will usually be too difficult to handle. You can rest the pictures on an easel or a table, or hold them up, one by one, as your story progresses.

When you use these "story cards" you are paying homage to an old tradition of Japanese storytelling called *kamishibai*. *Kamishibai* (pronounced kah-MEE-she-bye) is part of a long tradition of oral folk literature in Japan. In the 1920s, performers called *kamishibai* men would traverse the streets on their bicycles, stopping along the way to set up small, portable wooden stages and tell stories to children using colorful cards to illustrate each tale. After telling their stories, they would sell candy. In his poignant picture book *Kamishibai Man*, Allen Say tells of a once-popular storyteller, now retired, who mourns the loss of his audience to the spread of television: "How can they like those blurry pictures more than my beautiful paintings?" Say's delicate watercolors and heartfelt story-within-a-story will resonate with older children, who might recall something they loved, took for granted, rejected, or left behind as they grew older.

To buy ready-made *kamishibai* story cards and find background and teaching ideas on the art form, go to www.kamishibai.com, the website for Kamishibai for Kids. There you can buy sets of colorfully illustrated cards to go with an assortment of Japanese folktales, *hyoshigi* (wooden clappers), and even a wooden *kamishibai* stage. You'll find many stories and practical ideas in Dianne de Las Casas's *Kamishibai Story Theater: The Art of Picture Telling*.

If you enjoy drawing, you may want to illustrate your own cards. Flip cards decorated with your own drawings or with children's art make the story more personal and meaningful. Keep your pictures simple and uncluttered so that the sense of each will immediately be clear to your audience. Not every story detail needs to be portrayed; you don't want the cards to distract from the story. For example, to tell "Little Red Riding Hood," draw the girl with her mother as she sets out for Grandma's house; the first encounter with the wolf; the wolf in bed, pretending to be Grandma; and finally the scene when the hunter frees Grandma and Little Red Riding Hood. The story cards can help you to introduce the story—which some children may not know—after which you can present some classic picture-book versions: Trina Schart Hyman's *Little Red Riding Hood* (Holiday, 1982), for which she won a Caldecott Honor; James Marshall's *Red Riding Hood* (Dial, 1987), with broadly comical illustrations; and Jerry Pinkney's *Little Red Riding Hood* (Little, Brown, 2007), which is set in snowy winter.

You can illustrate a chapter from one of your favorite fiction books with flip cards, or even create a picture book of your own for a favorite story that has no suitable illustrations. The most satisfying project is to have the children in your audience write and illustrate their own cards, using folktales they know or creating their own stories, the text of which they can then copy onto the back of the cards.

BIG BOOKS

Big books—oversize paperbacks of picture books—are often used in classrooms. The teacher reads the text aloud and the children repeat it, thus showing the relationship between a word as it sounds and as it is written. Big books are also used for group-thinking skills exercises. The teacher breaks up the story by posing such questions as, "What do you think will happen next?" or "Can you identify words that use the same sound?" The big book can be a treat for an audience just because it offers a new way to hear a story, and everyone can see the pictures.

You can become an instant big-book artist using document camera or the venerable opaque projector, which may be gathering dust in a closet somewhere. Both machines are perfectly functional for projecting pictures or objects onto a wall or screen. Attach poster board or paper onto the wall with masking or painter's tape. Trace around the outlines of the picture you want to show with marker, crayon, or pencil. You can fill in the colors later. You can use fabric, tissue paper, string, and whatever else you can think of to create a three-dimensional effect. The pictures then become tactile, too, so that the children can touch and feel the story after they have seen and heard it.

ROLL STORIES

On a roll of adding machine, newsprint, or wrapping paper, draw your story scene by scene. The larger the scroll, the easier it will be for children to see the story. When the story is unrolled, the scenes and characters appear in sequence. After you finish the story, you can use the long length of paper on your bulletin board or as a wall decoration. The roll can also be installed in a box cut out to look like a television set. In the bottom of the box, cut a square hole the size of the width of the paper. Cut a half-inch slit in the two sides of the box for the paper to pass through the viewing window. The paper roll can be pulled through as the story is told, or you can use a dowel rod, available at the lumberyard or hardware store, to make a neater roll.

This is a good technique for children to try themselves. After you tell a story, have each child draw a picture. Paste all the pictures onto the roll in a sequence. Now each child will be able to say to the group, "That's my picture." To avoid having too many pictures of the same scene (twelve Rapunzels in the tower, for instance, and no witches), go over the story, characters, and scenes with the children beforehand and have each child claim a story element to re-create.

BOOKLIST: BOOKS TO DRAW AND TELL

Ahlberg, Allan. *The Pencil.* *Illus. by Bruce Ingman. Candlewick, 2008.* When a lonely little pencil begins to draw, it creates a boy named Banjo, a dog named Bruce, and a cat named Mildred. (PreK–Gr. 3)

Becker, Aaron. *Journey.* *Illus. by the author. Candlewick, 2013.* A bored girl draws her way to adventure with a magical red marker. (PreK–Gr. 2)

Carle, Eric. *The Mixed-Up Chameleon.* *Illus. by the author. HarperCollins, 1975.* A chameleon changes colors and shapes. (PreK–Gr. 1)

De Las Casas, Dianne. *A Is for Alligator: Draw and Tell Tales from A-Z.* *Illus. by Marita Gentry. Libraries Unlimited, 2011.* Twenty-six original and appealing draw-and-tell stories. (Professional)

De Las Casas, Dianne. *Kamishibai Story Theater: The Art of Picture Telling.* *Illus. by Philip Chow. Teacher Ideas Press, 2006.* Twenty-five Asian folktales for grades 2–6, adapted for story-card presentations, a type of Japanese storytelling. (Professional)

Freeman, Judy. *Once Upon a Time: Using Storytelling, Creative Drama, and Reader's Theater with Children in Grades PreK–6.* *Libraries Unlimited, 2007.* Freeman's version of the draw-and-tell story "T *Is for Tommy*" takes Tommy and his best friend, Sally, on an adventure with a basket of apples. (Professional)

Hutchins, Pat. *The Doorbell Rang.* *Illus. by the author. Greenwillow, 1986.* Draw a plate of cookies on the chalkboard and erase them as they are eaten. (PreK–Gr. 1)

Johnson, Crockett. *Harold and the Purple Crayon.* *Illus. by the author. HarperCollins, 1983, c1958.* A little boy draws pictures to accompany his evening adventure. (PreK–Gr. 2)

Langstaff, John. *Oh, A-Hunting We Will Go.* *Illus. by Nancy Winslow Parker. Atheneum, 1974.* A familiar folk song, with enchanting illustrations and nicely silly rhymes. (PreK–Gr. 2)

Look, Lenore. *Brush of the Gods.* *Illus. by Meilo So. Schwartz & Wade, 2013.* Fictionalized account of China's most famous painter, Wu Daozi (ad 689–759), whose paintings were said to be so realistic, they would come to life. (K–Gr. 4)

Pellowski, Anne. *Drawing Stories from Around the World and a Sampling of European Handkerchief Stories.* *Libraries Unlimited, 2005.* Thirty delightful tales that you draw as you tell, with step-by-step instructions. (Professional)

Pinkwater, Daniel. ***Bear's Picture.*** *Illus. by D. B.* Johnson. Houghton Mifflin, 2008. Two "fine, proper gentlemen" disparage Bear's painting, saying, "Bears can't paint pictures." (PreK–Gr. 2)

Say, Allen. ***Kamishibai Man.*** *Illus. by the author. Houghton Mifflin, 2005.* A retired Japanese storyteller still wants to share his stories with children. (Gr. 1–6)

Silverstein, Shel. ***The Missing Piece.*** *Illus. by the author. HarperCollins, 1976.* A circle searches for a missing part, only to discover that life loses its fascination when everything is too perfect. (PreK–Gr. 2)

Thompson, Richard. ***Frog's Riddle, and Other Draw-and-Tell Stories.*** *Illus. by the author. Annick, 1990.* Twelve clever, original draw-and-tell stories. (Professional)

Wilder, Laura Ingalls. ***On the Banks of Plum Creek.*** *Illus. by Garth Williams. HarperCollins, 1937.* A drawing of a duck is the final picture in the drawing story that Ma tells to Laura and her sisters during a blizzard, in the chapter "The Day of Games." (Gr. 2–5)

Board Stories

If you have never used props in a program, experimenting with a flannel, felt, Velcro, or magnet board is a good way to begin. The idea is to tell a story while illustrating it with cutout figures that are placed on the board.

PREPARATION

Of course you need a good story, but you also need one that is suitable for a storyboard presentation. You don't want a lot of tiny, hard-to-see objects crowding the board, so choose a story with a few simple, large characters or objects. Nor do you want to be constantly changing the pictures, especially if you aren't adept at talking and doing at the same time. A story that begins with one character and builds up to many is particularly successful, especially for beginners. The storyteller simply adds to the cutouts already on the board.

Boards are most effectively used on an easel, although you can also sit on the floor and lean the board against something sturdy, or install one permanently on the wall. You will also need a table or a floor area on which to arrange the cutouts that will go on the board. Number or label these on the back for easy identification. Silhouettes may be all you need; you want to leave room for a child's imagination to work.

Keep all the pieces belonging to one story in a labeled clear plastic envelope or heavy-duty Ziploc bag. Also include a copy of the story in the envelope so you can easily relearn it if necessary. If you have a copy of the book from which the story came, show it to your audience before or after your telling. Or read the story from the book first and use the board pieces with your children while you (or they) retell the tale.

When using a board, be careful not to talk to the board rather than to the audience, and always face the audience after you put an object on the board. If a piece falls off, simply pick it up and put it back. If you don't, the children will laugh and point, which will disrupt the presentation. Choose a story in which the placement of the object on the board is not crucial. Your story should move along smoothly; you don't want to take an excessive amount of time arranging your board.

You might want to use music during your telling. Not only does it make your presentation more professional, it also provides an interlude while you are moving figures around. Once you've told the story, ask for some help in taking down the pictures; you'll find that children who handle the figures may be better at recalling the story. You will also find that children enjoy retelling the story to each other and making their own cutouts.

FLANNEL AND FELT BOARDS

When the first edition of this book came out, way back in 1977, the most popular boards for storytime were flannel and felt boards. While they are being replaced in many libraries and classrooms by Velcro boards and other devices, they are still used in many places. Their popularity stems from the fact that they are inexpensive and easily stored. Felt boards can be purchased commercially or made quite easily at home; you'll find plenty of instruction sites online.

Felt is easy to shape, comes in vibrant colors, and is readily available, already cut into squares, at craft and fabric shops. When cutting shapes, don't make them too large; large ones tend to droop or drop off. Pattern spray, available in fabric stores, can be sprayed on the back of cutouts to adhere them to felt. (If you use pattern spray, place paper between the figures when storing them). Pellon, a material used to stiffen fabrics, easily adheres to both felt and flannel and can be colored with paint or crayon. Any sturdy art paper can also be used to make cutouts. Simply paste sandpaper to the back of the cutout picture and stick it to the board.

VELCRO BOARDS

Here's a fun fact: In 1941, Georges de Mestral, a Swiss engineer, returned from a hunting trip and noticed his trousers were covered with burrs. Looking at them under a microscope, he saw that the tiny hooks on the burdock seeds would hold fast to anything with a loop. This ordinary experience inspired him to develop the two-part nylon fabric closure we know as Velcro. It works on the same principle as the burr: the tiny hooks on one piece of fabric catch the tiny loops on another.

You can hang almost anything on Velcro strips—from a sheet of paper to a heavy book. As you tell a story, each object that you name can be hung on a board or a strip fastened to the wall. The hooked side of Velcro won't hold well on a felt board, but the loop side of a Velcro-covered board can substitute for a felt board, and sandpaper-backed objects will adhere to it well. Caroline had both a storytelling apron and a vest made of Velcro, which allowed her to become a human storyboard.

MAGNETIC BOARDS

A magnetic board utilizes magnets to attach pictures or artifacts to its surface. One of the advantages of the magnetic board is that pictures adhere quickly and securely, almost like magic. The board can be any metal surface to which a magnet will cling. For a small board, a steel cookie sheet will work. The side of a steel filing cabinet also makes a useful board if it happens to be well placed in your classroom or library. A magnetic board also can be cut to size by your local roofing supplier. Sheet-metal shops will sell you pieces of sheet metal that can be framed in plywood. The material comes in different weights; ask for a piece that won't flex too much. Magnetic boards are also available commercially.

To make the board more useful, paint the surface of the board with chalkboard paint; you now have a combination chalkboard and magnetic board to use with an easel. If you glue Velcro or felt on the reverse side of your combination board, you'll have three boards in one.

Several types of magnets are available for use with your board. Your local crafts store or office supply store sells rubberized strip magnets, about ¾ inch wide and 12 inches long, which are easily cut with scissors. They have an adhesive on one side that sticks to fabric, tagboard, or paper.

A STORY TO TELL ON A BOARD

Let's try a good board story, shall we? You pick the type of board. Reproduce and enlarge, as needed, the animals below and place them on your board or apron as you tell the story. Be prepared for laughter as you repeat and mispronounce "ossopit."

The Ossopit Tree

Retold by Caroline Feller Bauer

Compare Caroline's retelling of this story with Celia Barker Lottridge's picture-book version, The Name of the Tree: A Bantu Tale.

One terribly hot summer in the forests of Africa, there was a great shortage of anything to eat. The animals had been hunting around here, there, and everywhere and had finally eaten up the very last twig and root. They were very hungry indeed.

Suddenly they came upon a wonderful-looking tree, hung with the most tempting, juicy-looking fruit. But, of course, they didn't know whether the fruit was safe to eat or not because they had no idea what its name was.

Luckily the hare knew that the tree belonged to an old lady called Jemma. So the animals decided to send the hare, their fastest runner, to ask her what the name of the tree was.

Off went the hare as fast as his legs could carry him, and he found old Jemma in front of her hut.

"Oh, Mrs. Jemma," he said. "We animals are dying of hunger. If you could only tell us the name of that wonderful tree of yours, you could save us all from starving."

"Gladly I will do that," answered Jemma. "It's perfectly safe to eat the fruit. Its name is ossopit."

"Oh," said the hare. "That's a very difficult name. I shall forget it by the time I get back."

"No, it's really quite easy," said Jemma. "Just think of 'opposite' and then sort of say it backwards, like this: opposite—ossopit."

"Oh, thanks very much," said the hare, and off he scampered.

As he ran he kept muttering, "Opposite, ottipis, ossipit" and he got all mixed up. So that when he got back to the other animals all he could say was:

"Well, Jemma did tell me the name but I can't remember whether it's ossipit, ottipis, or ossupit. I do know it's got something to do with 'opposite.'"

"Oh dear," they all sighed. "We had better send someone with a better memory."

"I'll go," said the goat. "I never forget anything." So he headed straight for Jemma's hut, grunting and snorting all the way.

"I'm sorry to bother you again, Mrs. Jemma," he panted, "but that silly hare couldn't remember the name of the tree. Do you mind telling it me once more?"

"Gladly I will," replied the old woman "It's ossopit. Just think of 'opposite' and then sort of say it backwards: opposite—ossopit."

"Righteo," said the goat, "and thank you very much, I'm sure."

And off he galloped, fast as he could, kicking up clouds of dust, and all the way he kept saying:

"Ottopis, oppossit, possitto, otto . . ." until he got back to the other animals.

"I know the name of that tree," he said. "It's oppitis, n—no . . . ossipit, n—no . . . otup . . . oh dear . . . I just can't get it right."

"Well, who can we send this time?" they all asked. They didn't want to bother old Jemma again.

"I'm perfectly willing to have a go," piped up a young sparrow. "I'll be back in no time," and with a whisk of his tail he had flown off before anyone could stop him.

"Good morrow, gentle Jemma," he said. "Could you please tell me the name of that tree just once more? Hare and goat could not get it right."

"Right gladly I will," said old Jemma patiently. "It's ossopit, oss-o-pit. It's a wee bit difficult, but just think of 'opposite' and then sort of say it backwards: opposite—ossopit."

"I'm most grateful, madam," said the sparrow and flew off twittering to himself: "Opposite, ossitup, ottupus, oissopit," until he finally got back to his famishing friends.

"Do tell us, sparrow," they all cried.

"Yes," chirped the sparrow, "It's definitely 'ossitup,' n—no . . . oittuisip, n—no . . . oippisuit . . . Oh dear, I give up. So very sorry."

By now the animals were desperate. Just imagine them all sitting round the gorgeous tree and unable to pick any of its mouth-watering fruits.

Up spoke the tortoise, the oldest animal of all. "I shall go," he said. "I know it will take a bit of time, but I will not forget the name once I've been told. My family has the finest reputation in the world for good memories."

"No," they moaned. "You are too slow. We shall all be dead by the time you get back."

"Why not let me take tortoise on my back?" asked the zebra. "I'm hopeless at remembering things, but my speed is second to none. I'll have him back here in no time at all."

They all thought this was a splendid idea, and so off raced the zebra with the tortoise clinging to his back.

"Good morning, Madam Jemma," said the tortoise. "I'm sorry I have no time to alight. But if we don't get the name of that tree, most of us will be dead by tonight. That's why I've come on zebra's back. He's a bit faster than I am, you know."

"Yes, I rather think he is," smiled old Jemma benignly. "Well, it's ossopit. Just think of 'opposite' and then sort of say it backwards, like this: opposite—oss-o-pit."

"Just let me repeat it three times before I go," said the tortoise, "just to see if I get it right." And then he said it very, very slowly, deliberately and loudly, and nodding his tiny head at each syllable:

"Oss-o-pit, oss-o-pit, oss-o-pit."

"Bravo!" said Jemma. "You'll never forget it now."

And she was right.

The zebra loped back to the tree where the animals were waiting.

The old tortoise was never in any doubt that he had the name right at last. "It's oss-o-pit," he announced to his ravenous friends.

"Ossopit, ossopit, ossopit," they all cried. "It's an ossopit tree, and it's perfectly safe to eat." And they all helped themselves to the wonderful fruit. You just can't imagine how delicious it tasted.

And to show how grateful they were, they appointed the tortoise Chief Adviser on Important Matters (he has C.A.I.M. after his name). And he still is Chief Adviser to this very day.

BOOKLIST: BOOKS TO USE WITH A BOARD

Alborough, Jez. *The Gobble Gobble Moooooo Tractor Book*. *Illus. by the author. Kane/ Miller, 2010.* Sheep, Cat, Turkey, Goose, and Cow take a pretend ride on Farmer Dougal's tractor. (PreK–Gr. 1)

Beaumont, Karen. *Move Over, Rover!* *Illus. by Jane Dyer. Harcourt, 2006.* When the rain begins, Cat, Raccoon, Squirrel, Blue Jay, and Snake all come into lonely Rover's doghouse until Skunk shows up. (PreK–Gr. 1)

Carle, Eric. *The Very Hungry Caterpillar*. *Illus. by the author. Philomel, 1969.* This classic story is perfect for board telling. (PreK–Gr. 1)

De Las Casas, Dianne. *Tangram Tales: Story Theater Using the Ancient Chinese Puzzle*. *Libraries Unlimited, 2009.* Scripts for twenty-five folktales from eighteen countries are paired with art that can be re-created with the eight geometrical pieces of a tangram set. (Professional)

DePaola, Tomie. *Jack*. *Illus. by the author. Penguin/Nancy Paulsen, 2014.* On his way to the city to ask the king to help him find a house, Jack is joined by a chick, a duck, a goose, a dog, and more. Each child can hold a flannel animal and, making the animal's noise, add it to the growing line across your board. (PreK–Gr. 1)

Dodd, Emma. *Meow Said the Cow*. *Illus. by the author. Scholastic/Arthur A. Levine, 2012.* An orange cat casts a magic spell on the barnyard, making the pig cluck and the chickens oink. (PreK–Gr. 1)

Flack, Marjorie. *Ask Mr. Bear*. *Illus. by the author. Macmillan, 1958.* A boy asks the farm animals what to give his mother for her birthday. The gifts make good objects for the board. (PreK–Gr. 1)

Gibbons, Gail. *Tool Book*. *Illus. by the author. Holiday House, 1982.* Attach the tools to the Velcro board. (PreK–Gr. 1)

Harter, Debbie. *Walking through the Jungle*. *Illus. by the author. Orchard, 1997.* A young girl is chased by a variety of animals. (PreK–Gr. 1)

Hoberman, Mary Ann. *It's Simple, Said Simon*. *Illus. by Meilo So. Knopf, 2001.* Simon needs to get away from the tiger that plans to have him for supper. (PreK–Gr. 1)

Hutchins, Pat. *Good-Night, Owl!* *Illus. by the author. Macmillan, 1972.* Keep adding birds to a tree as you tell how noisy birds kept Owl up all day. (PreK–Gr. 1)

Isaacs, Anne. *Pancakes for Supper*. *Illus. by Mark Teague. Scholastic, 2006.* In a New England forest, a little girl offers her clothes to the wild animals so they won't eat her. (PreK–Gr. 2)

Kroll, Steven. *The Biggest Pumpkin Ever.* *Illus. by Jeni Bassett. Holiday House, 1984.* Two mice fall in love and compete for a pumpkin. Felt pumpkins in different sizes can show the pumpkin as it gets bigger. (PreK–Gr. 1)

Lottridge, Celia Barker. *The Name of the Tree: A Bantu Tale.* *Illus. by Ian Wallace. McElderry, 1989.* Hungry animals send a messenger to King Lion to ask the name of a fruit-filled tree. (PreK–Gr. 3)

Murray, Marjorie Dennis. *Don't Wake Up the Bear!* *Illus. by Patricia Wittmann. Marshall Cavendish, 2003.* On a cold winter's night, a hare, a badger, a fox, a squirrel, and a mouse snuggle against a sleeping bear. (PreK–Gr. 2)

Polacco, Patricia. *Oh, Look!* *Illus. by the author. Philomel, 2004.* Three frisky goats go through a gate, across a bridge, up a hill, into a pond, and over to the fair. (PreK–Gr. 1)

Schade, Susan. *The Noisy Counting Book.* *Illus. by Jon Buller. Random House, 2010, c1987.* One frog says, "Ga-dunk!" Use puppets or flannelboard pieces to act out the text. (PreK–Gr. 1)

Seuss, Dr. *And to Think That I Saw It on Mulberry Street.* *Illus. by the author. Vanguard, 1937.* Add different figures until the entire board is a grand parade. (PreK–Gr. 3)

Shaw, Charles G. *It Looked Like Spilt Milk.* *Illus. by the author. HarperCollins, 1947.* A cloud can look like many things. Ask listeners to make their own felt clouds that look like something interesting. (PreK–Gr. 2)

Slobodkina, Esphyr. *Caps for Sale: A Tale of a Peddler, Some Monkeys, and Their Monkey Business.* *Illus. by the author. W. R. Scott, 1947.* Cut out monkeys and colored caps for this classic story of a frustrated peddler. (PreK–Gr. 1)

Smith, Jeff. *Little Mouse Gets Ready.* *Illus. by the author. TOON, 2009.* Little Mouse gets dressed all by himself. Make a mouse and an outfit for him. (PreK–Gr. 1)

Taback, Simms. *There Was an Old Lady Who Swallowed a Fly.* *Illus. by the author. Viking, 1997.* A riotous version of the ubiquitous swallowing song, using die cuts to show the old lady's increasing belly. (PreK–Gr. 2)

Thomas, Jan. *What Will Fat Cat Sit On?* *Illus. by the author. Harcourt, 2007.* A fat cat contemplates sitting on a cow, a pig, a dog, and a chicken, until a mouse devises a better solution. (PreK–Gr. 1)

Thomson, Pat. *Drat That Fat Cat!* *Illus. by Ailie Busby. Scholastic, 2003.* A fat cat in search of food eats a rat, a duck, a dog, an old lady, and finally, a bee. (PreK–K)

Weeks, Sarah. *Mrs. McNosh Hangs Up Her Wash.* *Illus. by Nadine Bernard Westcott. HarperCollins, 1998.* Mrs. McNosh washes everything she sees—even Grandpa McNosh's false teeth—and hangs each item on the clothesline. String a white rope across the top of your board and hang items with clothespins. (PreK–Gr. 1)

Westcott, Nadine Bernard. *I Know an Old Lady Who Swallowed a Fly*. *Illus. by the author. Little, Brown, 1980.* Make a big old lady and add animals to her growing tum as you sing this silly folk song. (PreK–Gr. 1)

Williams, Linda. *The Little Old Lady Who Was Not Afraid of Anything*. *Illus. by Megan Lloyd. HarperCollins, 1986.* An old lady encounters two clomping shoes, a wiggling pair of pants, a shaking shirt, two clapping gloves, a nodding hat, and a scary pumpkin head that says, "Boo!" (PreK–Gr. 1)

Wilson, Karma. *The Cow Loves Cookies*. *Illus. by Marcellus Hall. McElderry, 2010.* Each rhyming description of the grub a farmer feeds his animals ends with, "but the cow loves cookies." (PreK–Gr. 1)

Wood, Audrey. *The Napping House*. *Illus. by Don Wood. Harcourt, 1984.* On a rainy day, snoring granny, a dreaming child, a dozing dog, and other animals sleep, one atop another, on a cozy bed. (PreK–Gr. 1)

WEBSITES: BOARD STORIES

Archie McPhee *www.mcphee.com*
A wonderful resource for an ever-evolving array of weird, wacky, and unusual props, including a jumbo handlebar mustache, an inflatable beard, and a chicken mask, not to mention the original shushing librarian—the action figure modeled after well-known Seattle librarian Nancy Pearl.

Dr. Jean Feldman *www.drjean.org/html/monthly_act/act_2009/02_Feb.*
The effervescent workshop leader shares some of her favorite stories, including flannelboard, tell-and-draw, file-folder, overhead, paper-tear, and participation stories.

Flannel Friday *flannelfridaystorytime.blogspot.com and pinterest.com/flannelfriday*
On this blog, a "weekly online event for sharing flannelboard and other library storytime activity ideas," you'll find so many crafts, patterns, and links, you won't know which one to try first.

Storytime Katie *storytimekatie.com*
Subtitled "One Librarian's Journey into Storytimeland," this librarian's blog is filled with color photos and descriptions of her innovative flannelboards and crafts.

Sunflower Storytime *sunflowerstorytime.com*
In her blog Leah Kulikowski—aka "Ms. Leah," who presents storytimes at a Kansas public library—provides a wide range of crafts and ideas for anyone "who needs a little storytime inspiration."

chapter 2

Puppetry

Life's like a movie, write your own ending. Keep believing, keep pretending.
—KERMIT THE FROG, *THE MUPPET MOVIE*

AND NOW, LADIES AND GENTLEMEN, OUR FEATURED SPEAKER! Heads turn to the back of the room where a black-shrouded figure makes her way down the aisle and steps up on stage. Two puppets pop out from under the shroud and lament the fact that children don't read enough anymore.

This entrance is greeted either with puzzled expressions or applause—depending on the audience. Either way, it's an arresting use of puppets, guaranteed to make an impression. Anyone who has used a puppet to introduce a story, present a booktalk, or put on a puppet show knows that children are fascinated with the way an inanimate object is suddenly imbued with life.

One of Caroline's fondest puppet memories came from a presentation she made to a special education class in a preschool in Alaska. Unfortunately, one of children was having a tantrum. Caroline's first instinct was to let the teacher handle the situation, but since Caroline was holding a cat puppet, she began to meow instead. The child was fascinated and immediately became quiet. Children believe in puppets.

You may not have the skills of a puppet master, but children will long remember each show you put on in your library or classroom. You'll find lots of useful tips, puppet patterns, and puppet-show suggestions in this chapter.

The Puppet Tradition

Puppetry has been performed for education and entertainment for thousands of years. It thrived in the society of ancient Egypt and in the religious rituals of Greece and Rome. Around the globe, puppets are still a major art form and a theatrical institution. In England, the Punch & Judy Fellowship (www.thepjf.com) is devoted to keeping alive the tradition of the comical Punch-and-Judy show. In Salzburg, Austria, a permanent puppet theater offers entire operas performed by marionettes. Turkish shadow shows feature the comic characters Karagöz and Hacivat. Japanese Bunraku puppets perform serious classical drama. In Thailand intricately costumed rod puppets appear in temple courtyards. In India, street performers manipulate a variety of marionettes. You can find out more about puppetry traditions at www.sagecraft.com/puppetry/traditions.

The US has borrowed from many of these traditions, but it has added innovations of its own. *Kukla, Fran and Ollie*, created for television by Burr Tillstrom, ran from 1948 to 1957. It featured doll-like Kukla along with Ollie, a dragon with a single tooth. Fran Allison, the show's human host, mediated the puppets' relationships. Fred Rogers, host of *Mr. Rogers' Neighborhood* (1968–2001), presided over the Neighborhood of Make-Believe, a land populated entirely by hand puppets. Jim Henson's Muppets were an instant hit when *Sesame Street* first appeared on TV in 1969. Read about Henson's life and career in Kathleen Krull's interesting picture-book biography, *Jim Henson: The Guy Who Played with Puppets*. In the Star Wars movies, Yoda's voice and movements were coordinated by puppeteer Frank Oz. And life-size puppets were used to astonishing effect in the Broadway plays *The Lion King* and *War Horse*.

Anthony "Tony" Frederick Sarg (1880–1942) was known as "America's puppet master." Sarg's most momentous achievement was inventing and creating the gargantuan marionettes for the now iconic Macy's Thanksgiving Day Parade, which began in 1924. *Balloons over Broadway*, Melissa Sweet's multiple-award-winning picture book about Sarg, is an exuberant introduction to the man who redefined puppetry. The book has become a Thanksgiving read-aloud staple. Try pairing it with Laurie Halse Anderson's picture-book biography about Sarah Josepha Hale, *Thank You, Sarah: The Woman Who Saved Thanksgiving* (Simon & Schuster, 2002) and Alison Jackson's whimsical *I Know an Old Lady Who Swallowed a Pie* (Dutton, 1997), which ends with the old lady becoming a balloon in Macy's parade.

Types of Puppets

Puppets fall into two major groups: puppets designed to fit on a puppeteer's hand and puppets manipulated by strings or rods, which take more skill to operate. Puppet aficionados who feel marionettes are superior say they have a life of their own because they are separated from the manipulator; those who favor hand puppets feel the puppet becomes part of the body and is therefore more realistic. Hand puppets are best used when there's lots of dialogue, as the audience will be focusing on the puppet's head. String puppets are better suited to plays with a great deal of physical action; the sophisticated ones have jointed arms, legs, and heads so they can dance, pick up objects, and move with ease. If you are a beginning puppeteer, experiment until you find what suits your needs and gives you the most pleasure.

COMMERCIAL HAND PUPPETS

If you aren't fond of crafts or feel you cannot make a puppet good enough to use with kids, visit your local crafts shop or street fair where handmade puppets are often sold. You can also find splendid puppets in toy stores and online. Since the 1970s, Folkmanis (www.folkmanis.com), a family-run company in California, has been producing magnificent plush puppets of animals; when you manipulate them well, children may be convinced you are holding a real, live fox, rooster, or even a shark. There are more than two hundred creatures in their collection, from adorable little finger puppets to an almost three-foot-long American alligator. No matter where you find them, you can't have too many puppets in your story-hour treasure chest.

GLOVE PUPPETS

Most of the puppets that are available commercially or in kits are glove puppets because they are the easiest for beginners to make and manipulate. This type of puppet, which may be created from a variety of materials, is operated either by using your palm and thumb or by putting your index finger into the head, while the thumb operates one hand of the puppet and the remaining fingers operate the other.

If you are handy, take an old glove and embroider a different face on each finger so each one represents a different character. You can also use a lunch-size paper bag as a hand puppet. A sock puppet is great fun. Just attach three buttons (two eyes and a mouth) to an old sock using glue or a needle and thread. You can also split the back of a stuffed animal and remove the stuffing to create a hand puppet. Or stitch together three sides of two pieces of fabric and paint a character's face on it. Or open it a bit at the top so you can use a Styrofoam ball for a head and the fabric as the puppet's costume.

FINGER PUPPETS

Little puppets that fit onto one or more fingers have the advantage of being extremely portable, but since they can't be seen from far away, reserve them for storytelling with small groups. Experiment with anything that fits over your finger: the finger cut off of an old glove makes a good beginning. You will probably want to let the puppets do the talking while you act as narrator, introducing the characters as they appear. You can also use your hand as a puppet; draw right on your fingers with washable felt-tip pens. Or use a dab of rubber cement to glue construction paper or felt to your hand to make a face and a costume. Make little puppets from heavy paper. Color them and stick them to your finger with a loop of tape. Easy.

Finger Puppets Can Ask Riddles

Use the template below to make yourself an elephant finger puppet to perform elephant jokes for your group. Or, better yet, run off copies for the children to color and cut out and have them retell the riddles to each other. Much laughter will ensue.

Elephant Jokes

Why did the elephant stand on the marshmallow?
So he wouldn't fall into the cocoa.

What do elephants have that no other animals have?
Baby elephants.

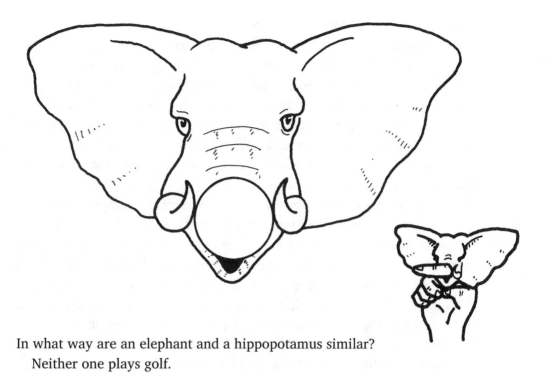

In what way are an elephant and a hippopotamus similar?
  Neither one plays golf.

What's gray and has four legs and a trunk?
  A mouse going on a trip.

How do you know that peanuts are fattening?
  Have you ever seen a skinny elephant?

Why does an elephant have cracks between his toes?
  To carry his library card.

How can you tell if an elephant has been in your refrigerator?
  By his footprints in the butter.

What time is it when an elephant sits on a fence?
  Time to buy a new fence.

What's the difference between an elephant and a jar of peanut butter?
  An elephant doesn't stick to the roof of your mouth.

Why do elephants wear dark glasses?
  If you had all those awful jokes told about you, you wouldn't want
  to be recognized, either.

MARIONETTES OR STRING PUPPETS

Marionettes vary in complexity, but since their strings tangle easily, they are probably not the best starting point for the beginning puppeteer.

The simplest marionette of all is a handkerchief with one corner tied onto a string. Wiggle the knot to make the handkerchief twist, dance, and go to sleep. If you tie two inanimate objects on strings (for example, a comb and a brush), you can have them talk about their owner. Attach two strings to anything pliable, such as a chain or a bead necklace, and make your abstract puppet dance to music. Can you give it a personality? Is it shy? Tired? Happy? Move your puppet to show emotions and temperament.

To help middle-grade children appreciate the skill required to put on a show with marionettes, read Laura Amy Schlitz's Newbery Honor Book *Splendors and Glooms.* Set in Victorian England in 1860, the suspenseful fantasy features a master puppeteer-magician; his assistants, two orphaned children; a poor little rich girl; and an elderly witch. Since marionettes are at the heart of the story, it's the perfect time to introduce them to your audience. And don't forget Carlo Collodi's *The Adventures of Pinocchio.* If you're only familiar with the Disney movie, you will be in for a surprise by Collodi's dark, engrossing tale about the wooden boy whose nose grows with every untruth.

STICK PUPPETS

Stick puppets are the simplest of all for beginners to use. Puppet characters can be cut from cardboard or plywood. Attach a stick or rod, and you have a puppet that is quick to make and easy to use. You can paint or paste a face on a wooden spoon, and you have a simple rod puppet. Or you can cut characters and scenery from plywood or poster board and tape, staple, or glue them on ¼-inch doweling available at the hardware store or lumberyard. A more sophisticated puppet uses several long rods to manipulate the arms, legs, or head of a jointed puppet.

Purchase popsicle sticks or tongue depressors at a drugstore or dollar store. Seat the children around big tables. In the center of each table, put found materials such as cloth scraps, yarn, and sequins, plus scissors and glue for them to share. Then, let them create their own puppets. Or, after telling or reading a story, have children make simple stick puppets of the characters and reenact what they've heard or make up new skits.

Marjorie Weinfeld's first-grade class at James Monroe School in Edison, New Jersey, made Elephant and Piggie stick puppets to go with Mo Willems's beloved easy-reader series, which includes *There Is a Bird on My Head.*

The beauty of these hilarious books is that they are told entirely in balloon dialogue. Each book is its own little play. The children drew on cardstock, and then colored, cut out, and glued them onto popsicle sticks. Puppeteers sat in pairs, side by side with a book on their laps, and, holding their stick puppets, acted out the conversation with great expression and enthusiasm. Willems says he never draws anything a three-year-old can't copy, and children love drawing his characters.

Telling a Story with Stick Puppets

Find reproducible patterns for almost any animal you can name at www .google.com/imghp. Mount them onto poster board. Decorate them with crayons, markers, or poster paint. Using an index card, create a pocket on the back of the puppet by taping three sides with heavy-duty tape, leaving the bottom side open. Insert a paint stirrer—available from any paint or hardware store—into the pocket and secure it with tape.

As each animal appears in your story, hand the appropriate puppet to a child to hold. In this way you involve members of the audience. Choose one of the animal books in the list below, or tell Caroline's story "The Cows," below. Tell or read your story once, then do it again, letting your audience act it out with their new puppets.

The Cows

Retold by Caroline Feller Bauer

Encourage your audience to join in and make the animal sounds. This participation story is particularly appropriate for preschoolers, or for older children who are learning English or wish to tell their own stories to younger children.

One day, a boy named Paul called to the cows in the meadow, "Come home, cows."

The cows continued to graze. They did not come home. Paul sat on a rock in front of the barn and cried, "Boo hoo."

A cat walked up to Paul and asked, "Why are you crying?"

"I'm crying because the cows won't come home."

"I'll help you," said the cat. She ran to the field and cried, "Meoow."

The cows continued to graze. They did not come home.

Paul sat on a rock and cried, "Boo hoo." The cat cried too: "Meoow!"

A dog walked up to Paul and asked, "Why are you crying?"

"I'm crying because the cows will not come home."

"I'll help you," said the dog. He ran to the field and barked, "Bow Wow!"

The cows continued to graze. They did not come home. Paul sat on a rock in front of the barn and cried, "Boo hoo." The cat cried, "Meoow," and the dog cried, "Bow wow!"

A duck waddled up to Paul and asked, "Why are you crying?"

"I'm crying because the cows won't come home."

"I'll help you," said the duck. She ran to the field and quacked, "Quaaack!"

The cows continued to graze. They did not come home.

Paul sat on a rock in front of the barn and cried, "Boo hoo." The cat cried, "Meoow," the dog cried, "Bow wow!" and the duck cried, "Quaaack."

A bee flew up to Paul and asked, "Why are you crying?"

"I'm crying because the cows will not come home."

"I'll help you," said the bee.

She flew to the field where the cows were grazing. She buzzed and buzzed and sat down on the rump of one of the cows. "Buzzzzz. Sting!"

One cow lumbered to the barn. The other two lumbered after her. Paul stopped crying and laughed. "Thank you, Bee," he said. The cat meowed, dog barked, and the duck quacked, "Thank you, Bee," and the cows mooed, "OUCH!"

And then they all went home.

MASKS AND BODY PUPPETS

Most of the puppets mentioned above are manipulated with your hands, but there are also puppets that can be used with other parts of your body. Masks carved from wood, for example, were used by many Native American tribes in the performance of stories and plays. You can make your own masks with large paper bags—or better yet, let your listeners create their own. Plan a show based on books such as Maurice Sendak's *Where the Wild Things Are* and Pat Hutchins's *Good-Night, Owl,* or fairy tales like "Snow White and the Seven Dwarfs." You will also find a wonderful mask story, "Lazy as an Ox," on page 95.

To use a whole-body puppet, a performer sticks his head and hands through openings in an immobile costume. To make your own, draw a figure without a face or arms on a 2-by-3-foot piece of posterboard. Cut a hole for the face and two armholes. Preschoolers can wear costumes like this to act out a play.

SHADOW PUPPETS

Shadowgraphy is an ancient art. Most children have used their hands to create shadow figures on the wall. As a storyteller, you can manipulate your hands to tell an entire story. If you are in a school, use a document camera or an overhead projector for an instant shadow-puppet activity as the bats do in Brian Lies's *Bats at the Library* and a Brooklyn family does in John Rocco's Caldecott Honor Book, *Blackout.* When you watch a shadow show, you see only the silhouette or shadow of the puppet rather than the puppet itself. The performance usually takes place behind a screen, with the light source behind the puppet and with the performer below the level of the screen. You can use hand puppets or cutouts or even human beings to create shadow shows. Any translucent material—such as thin paper or a sheet—can serve as a screen, and a small spot reflector light or flashlight can be used for light.

Experiment with both solid and translucent shapes. On your computer's browser, look up *images for shadow puppets for kids*, and you'll find interesting results that may prove helpful and inspiring. You might also want to watch the performance by Attraction, a shadow theater troupe of dancers, who appeared at a *Britain's Got Talent* audition (www.youtube.com/watch?v = a4Fv98jttYA).

Puppet Stages

If you can't locate a volunteer to construct a puppet theater for you, you'll find a number of different ones at all price points on the Internet. If you're a do-it-yourselfer, however, stage construction can be as easy as stringing a curtain across a corner or as complicated as building a permanent wooden structure. Any number of items can work as a stage. You can use an empty refrigerator box, but since it is bulky to store, use it as a play store or individual reading corner, too. Tables can be instant puppet stages; children can kneel behind one that has been tipped on its side. An empty picture frame can become a stage. You can even cover your head with black cloth and cut two openings for your eyes and one for your mouth and stand or sit behind your puppets. (Actually, it often adds to the puppet performance if the puppeteer is visible. The audience will immediately transfer the performer's voice to the puppet.)

If having a theater is your preference, here are directions for constructing two stages.

PORTABLE-DOORWAY PUPPET THEATER

This puppet theater can be easily stored. It works in most doorways, is portable, and, best of all, can be raised or lowered depending on the height of the puppeteer, child or adult.

Supplies:
- A spring curtain rod, 2½ feet long
- ½-inch wood dowel, 2½ feet long
- 3½ yards of heavyweight fabric, such as denim or duck, cut and hemmed to make a screen approximately 26 by 54 inches

Directions:
1. Sew a 2-inch open hem across one width of the fabric for inserting the spring rod. This is the top of the screen.
2. Cut a 12-by-17-inch opening 12 inches from the top and hem around it to give it body.
3. Sew a 1-inch open hem across the other (bottom) width of the fabric.
4. Insert the dowel in the hem to give the screen weight and keep it hanging evenly.

CHINESE-HAT PUPPET THEATER

Totally contained, one-person puppet theaters have been used for centuries in China. You can make your own by adapting a wide-brimmed Chinese straw hat or even a Mexican sombrero, either of which may be bought at import or gift shops or online. To the hat's brim, attach solid-color fabric, long enough to reach to the floor and wide enough to encircle you and the hat. Sew a zipper or a long strip of Velcro to connect the front seam, leaving a 2-foot semicircular opening at the top for the puppets to perform. You wear the puppet theater on your head. At the end of the performance, the entire production—puppets, puppeteer, and stage—walks off.

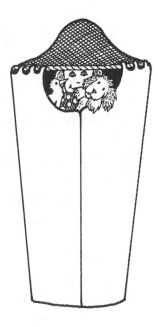

Puppets in Your Program

Puppets may be incidental visitors to your book program or the stars of a whole story-hour puppet show. Begin simply. Don't use elaborate scenery or pick something that requires many scene changes. Exaggerate your puppet's actions, but don't feel compelled to move your puppet without a purpose; make each action meaningful. Here is a list of common emotions to practice with your puppet:

happiness	fright	sleepiness	curiosity
loneliness	sadness	excitement	thankfulness
bravery	anger	repentance	embarrassment

First, practice using actions alone to express emotions. Next, act out the feelings using simple phrases or sentences. Add other feelings that might characterize your puppet. Each movement should be planned and fulfill a purpose, and every action must be both simplified and exaggerated to be easily interpreted by an audience. Puppets are too small for subtleties and yet they can be as graceful as dancers. Puppets perform to each other and to the audience; they shouldn't face the puppeteer or constantly be seen in side view.

Be sure to speak up and out because the stage will muffle your voice. You might experiment with a taped soundtrack so you and other puppeteers can concentrate on moving the puppets. Music between acts or scenes helps the continuity of your performance. Lighting need not be complex, but it must be sufficient to light the action.

Don't try to do everything yourself. Enlist the aid of friends, colleagues, and children. If you decide to perform for an invited audience—which, after all, is the point of puppetry—be sure you have rehearsed your show. If you think you would be proud to have your mother-in-law see your puppet show, then you are ready for an audience!

THE PUPPET AS HOST

When working with a preschool group, a puppet is a great way to greet children and introduce each story. If you use a special puppet just for your preschool story hour (an elephant, say, that your children have named Arnold), children will come to associate it with your books, poems, and stories.

If you have a puppet—a dog, for example—that you feel comfortable with, take a few minutes to think about your dog's personality. Is it a girl or a boy? Is it shy, aggressive, knowledgeable, naive? Introduce the puppet as soon as they are settled. A simple introduction—"Boys and girls, I'd like you to meet my friend, Cleo"—will do. Don't change your voice when the puppet is speaking unless you feel confident that you can remember to use the same voice every time the puppet speaks. Most children understand make-believe better than adults, and they will respond to your puppet just as they talk to a pet or stuffed animal. Here's an example of a dialogue you might have with your puppet to introduce a story:

> *You:* This morning we are going to read a story all about a boy's very first experience in the snow.
>
> *Puppet:* Oh, good. What's it called?
>
> *You: The Snowy Day* by Ezra Jack Keats.
>
> *Puppet:* I love snow. Hurry up and read it!

Now put your puppet out of sight, and read the story. At the end of the story hour use the puppet again to say goodbye, and remind your audience of the date of the next story hour.

Three Plays

One way to begin your work with puppetry is to pick a story or play that you like and then find or make the puppet characters. If you are working alone, find a story with no more than two or three characters. The third character can appear when one of the main characters is offstage, but remember that exchanging one puppet for another may take time while the audience waits.

You may want to have one of your puppets tell the story; or you, acting as narrator, can give the descriptive passages while puppets act the conversational parts. Or you can simply hold up each character while you tell the whole story. In this way, puppets act as a three-dimensional illustration of the story.

Some puppeteers script their plays; each character has a set speech to deliver at a particular time. This has advantages and disadvantages. A script must be read aloud or memorized; if one person loses her place or forgets her lines, the entire play will be affected. Since there are many variables to putting on a play, it is usually best to use something your audience and cast already know. If you have two puppeteers, start with an old favorite like "The Three Bears," with no more than four characters on stage at once. In terms of logistics—manipulating puppets, props, and scenery—the fewer characters the better when selecting a story to dramatize. As you become more proficient, you can graduate to a more intricately plotted story.

After you decide on a story, cast the characters and try performing it without the puppets. Tape the action or write it down. Then read it over and edit your script. If your students are presenting the play, let them outline, write, improvise, and/or adapt their own scripts. Children who read, memorize, and perform scripts they have written are simultaneously developing and practicing multiple reading, writing, and presentation skills.

Improvising dialogue is another possibility. Decide on the story you are going to present. Read it aloud. Discuss the different characters with your performers. Outline the plot so that everyone is sure what happens when. Decide who will take which parts. Rehearse the show, critiquing the dialogue and puppets' movements as you go. Add props, scenery changes, costume accouterments, songs, and wacky sound effects as you deem necessary.

A One- or Two-Person Play

We'll start out with a simple nonsense play that will delight preschoolers, though children through fourth grade will find it amusing as well. You can put this on yourself using cat and dog puppets or have pairs of students make their own simple puppets, practice the script, and perform the play.

The Dog and the Cat Go to Market

By Caroline Feller Bauer

Cast: Cat, Dog

Sets: A meadow and a fair (or a backdrop that says "Village Fair," decorated with fair-like pictures)

Props: A box of doughnut holes (real or made from clay); a miniature bushel basket of tiny potatoes or potato-like stones; a nickel (Note: The doughnuts and potatoes could easily be pretend, since they do not speak. Just display an empty doughnut box and a little basket.)

SCENE 1: THE MEADOW

Dog: Good morning, Cat.

Cat: Good morning, Dog.

Dog: Tomorrow is the Village Fair. Let's sell something. We can make enough money to go on a trip.

Cat: Good idea. I can sell doughnuts.

Dog: I can sell my famous baked potatoes.

Cat: Excellent! I'll see you in the morning.

SCENE 2: THE FAIR

Dog: Good morning, Cat.

Cat: Good morning, Dog.

Dog: Look, I've brought a bushel basket of hot baked potatoes.

Cat: I have this box of fried doughnuts.

Dog: We should make a lot of money. Everything smells delicious.

Cat: Let's set up our stalls next to each other.

WEB This script is available on ALA's Web Extras page at alaeditions.org/webextras.

Dog: Good idea. I want to buy a doughnut from you right now.

Cat: That will be five cents, please.

Dog: Here you are. (*Dog takes a doughnut and eats it.*) Very good, Cat.

Cat: Thank you. Now that I have a nickel, I can buy one of your potatoes. Here's a nickel. (*Cat takes a potato and eats it.*)

Dog: Thank you. Now that I have a nickel, I can buy another doughnut. Here you are. (*Dog takes a doughnut and eats it.*)

Cat: Thank you. Now that I have a nickel, I can buy another potato. Here you are. (*Cat takes a potato and eats it.*)

SCENE 3: THE MEADOW

Cat: What a day. I'm exhausted.

Dog: Me, too. We had so much business.

Cat: Yes. I sold a lot of doughnuts. I have none left.

Dog: I sold a lot of potatoes. I haven't got any left, either.

Cat: I bet we made a lot of money.

Dog: I'm sure we did.

Cat: Let's count it.

Dog: How much do you have?

Cat: I have the nickel you gave me.

Dog: I don't have anything.

Cat: How can that be? We have no food left to sell and business was brisk all day.

Dog: I think we were our only customers.

Cat: Yes. But still, why aren't we rich?

Dog: Oh well, at least we aren't hungry anymore.

Cat: Good night, Dog.

Dog: Good night, Cat.

A Two- or Three-Person Play

Next, we have taken an old joke and turned it into a one-act skit. It works beautifully in tandem with the "The Dog and the Cat Go to Market," as it is also about doughnuts.

If you already have puppets in human shapes, use them in this skit. Dress one in jeans and T-shirt and the other in white with a white hat. If you want children to act out this skit in pairs or trios and you don't have enough puppets to go around, have the kids make their own stick puppet characters. What about props and scenery? You'll need a bakery counter made from a box or folded cardboard. Cut four muffin shapes from piece of bread and place them on a plate made of a folded piece of aluminum foil. Add a platter of Cheerios for doughnuts. That's really all you need; the fewer the props, the easier it is.

An After-School Snack

By Caroline Feller Bauer

Roles: Narrator, Student, Baker (You don't really need a narrator in this play unless you need to provide more parts. The person playing the student can simply expand his or her lines, on the order of, "School was so tiring today. I'm hungry. I'm very hungry. And I could use some extra energy. I know! I'll stop at the bakery on the way home.")

Narrator: A student was walking home from school.

Student: I'm hungry. I'm very hungry.

Narrator: He stopped to count his money.

Student: I haven't got very much money. Maybe I'll buy a doughnut. No, a muffin would be cheaper.

Narrator: The student stopped at a bakery.

Baker: Good afternoon. May I help you?

Student: Yes, please. I would like a muffin.

Narrator: The baker sold the student a muffin.

Baker: Here you are. Enjoy it.

Student: Thank you.

WEB This script is available on ALA's Web Extras page at alaeditions.org/webextras.

Narrator: The student ate the muffin.

Student: (*eating*) This is very good, but I am still hungry. Maybe I'll buy a doughnut. No, a muffin is cheaper.

Baker: Good afternoon. May I help you again?

Student: Yes, please. I would like another muffin.

Baker: Here you are. Enjoy it.

Student: Thank you.

Narrator: The student ate the muffin.

Student: (*eating*) This is very good, but I am still hungry. Maybe I'll buy a doughnut. No, a muffin is cheaper.

Baker: Good afternoon. May I help you, once again?

Student: Yes, please. I would like another muffin.

Narrator: The baker sold the student another muffin.

Baker: Here you are. Enjoy it.

Student: Thank you.

Narrator: The student ate the muffin.

Student: (*eating*) This is very good, but I am still hungry. This time I will buy a doughnut.

Baker: Here again? What would you like this time?

Student: A doughnut, please.

Narrator: The baker sold the student a doughnut.

Baker: Here you are. Enjoy it.

Student: Thank you.

Narrator: The student ate the doughnut.

Student: (*eating*) This doughnut was delicious. I don't feel hungry anymore, either. If I had just eaten the doughnut first, just *think* of all the money I would have saved!

WORKING ON VOICES

When the audience doesn't see your face, dialogue must be delivered with excellent volume and far more expression than you would use when telling a story in person. If you aren't speaking loudly or using a microphone, your voice will be too muffled. You will also need to differentiate your characters' voices clearly so your audience knows who's who. If children are performing this skit, talk with them about the possible voices they might use for the characters. The student might have a high-pitched voice; the baker, a deep one.

In addition to thinking about the volume and enunciation, expression and meaning must be considered. Once everyone is familiar with the script, have them practice delivering and fooling around with the climactic line: "This is very good, but I am still hungry. This time I will buy a doughnut." Have everyone try it aloud, and listen for the differences in each interpretation. Which ones work best? Assure your participants that they can say the line a dozen times and it can be different every time. Talk about what the main character is thinking and feeling at this point in the play. What tone of voice should the character use when the line is spoken? Which words should be emphasized and why? Using the dialogue below, try to capture the three different ways for reading and decide on what works best:

"This is very good (*appreciative, admiring, noncommittal*), but I am still hungry (*frustrated, uncomprehending, puzzled*). This time I will buy a dough-nut (*emphatic, decisive, resigned*)."

A Three-or-More-Person Play

This next play, a noodlehead story from Latin America for grades 2 through 6, works well with hand or finger puppets. You'll find instructions for making foam-ball characters below. You can learn and play all the parts yourself, or have groups of four or five youngsters practice and perform the story with one or two narrators. Since each person will play one part, actors can start out by using a script; once they become familiar with their lines, they can perform without it.

Have the "storyteller" or narrators stand on either side of the puppet stage, like sentinels. If you don't have enough actors, have Pedro assume the lines of the narrators and speak directly to the audience. Instead of the narrator saying, "On Sunday, Pedro went looking for Maria," simply have Pedro say, "On Sunday, I went looking for Maria," and so on. And instead of the repeated line, "Pedro went home," Pedro can say, "I didn't know what to say. So I went home."

Pedro  Mother  Maria

FOAM-BALL PUPPET

Supplies: A Styrofoam ball; one ⅜–inch dowel at least 12 inches long; 2 wooden barbecue skewers; a bandana; 2 shank eyes; fur, yarn, or a boa for hair

Directions:

1. Glue one end of the dowel to the inside center of the bandana.
2. Cut a slit in the ball and glue it firmly in place over center of the dowel.
3. Cut two small eye-socket slits in the ball and glue the eyes in place.
4. Glue on the hair.
5. Knot the bandana in two opposite corners for hands.
6. Carefully insert the barbecue skewers under the knots and glue in place.

To make the puppets more elaborate, detail the features by shaping the foam ball; fingernail scissors work well for this. Or glue on extra foam shaped like a nose, eyebrows, or ears. You can also cut out hands and attach them over the barbecue skewer rod; glue helps hold them in place. Make the puppet's costume as elaborate and detailed as your imagination dictates.

Pedro Courts Maria

By Caroline Feller Bauer

Cast: Storytellers, Pedro, Mother, Maria
Sets: Pedro's house, Maria's garden, the road between the two houses

Storyteller: Pedro's mother was worried about her son.

Mother: Pedro, my son, you need to get married.

Pedro: Oh, Mother, who would marry me?

Mother: How about Maria? She is often sitting at home.

Storyteller: On Sunday Pedro went looking for Maria. She was on her way to church.

Pedro: Maria. Maria. How do you do? Why are you always sitting at home?

Maria: Pedro. Pedro. What are you saying? As you see, I am not sitting at home. I'm on my way to church.

Storyteller: Pedro went home.

Mother: How did you get along with Maria?

Pedro: Badly. Very badly. She was on her way to church and I asked her why she was always sitting at home.

Mother: Oh, Pedro. You should have said, "Would you like to go dancing?"

Storyteller: On Sunday Pedro went looking for Maria. Her father had died and she was sitting by his coffin.

Pedro: Maria, Maria. How do you do? Would you like to go dancing?

Maria: Pedro, Pedro. What are you saying? Can't you see my father has just died?

Storyteller: Pedro went home.

Mother: How did you get along with Maria?

Pedro: Badly. Very badly. She was sitting by her father's coffin and I asked her to go dancing.

WEB This script is available on ALA's Web Extras page at alaeditions.org/webextras.

Mother: Oh, Pedro. You should have said, "May he go to heaven."

Storyteller: On Sunday Pedro went looking for Maria. She had just killed a pig.

Pedro: Maria, Maria. How are you? Ah, you have killed a pig. May he go to heaven.

Maria: Pedro. Pedro. What are you saying? You want my pig to go to heaven?

Storyteller: Pedro went home.

Mother: How did you get along with Maria?

Pedro: Badly. Very badly. She had just killed a pig and I said, "May it go to heaven."

Mother: Oh, Pedro. You should have said, "May you have many more and may they grow fat."

Storyteller: On Sunday Pedro went looking for Maria. She was sitting in the sun touching a pimple on her chin.

Pedro: Maria, Maria. How are you? I see you have a pimple on your chin. May it grow fat and may you have many more.

Maria: Pedro. Pedro. What are you saying? You want me to have more pimples?

Storyteller: Pedro went home.

Mother: How did you get along with Maria?

Pedro: Badly. Very badly. I wished that her pimple would grow big and fat.

Mother: Oh, Pedro, you should have said, "May it dry up and die."

Storyteller: On Sunday Pedro went looking for Maria. She was in the yard watering a rosebush.
Pedro: Maria. Maria. How are you? I see you have a rosebush. May it dry up and die.
Maria: Pedro. Pedro. What are you saying? You want my rosebush to die?
Storyteller: Pedro went home.

Mother: How did you get along with Maria?

Pedro: Badly. Very badly. I wished that her rosebush would dry up and die.

Mother: Oh, Pedro, you should have said, "May it grow roots and live a thousand years."

Storyteller: On Sunday Pedro went to visit Maria. She was in the yard with a thorn stuck in the palm of her hand.

Pedro: Maria. Maria. How are you? I see you have a thorn stuck in your palm. May it grow roots and live a thousand years.

Maria: Pedro. Pedro, what are you saying? You want this thorn to grow roots. You want my rosebush to dry up and die. You want my pimple to grow fat. You want my pig to go to heaven. You want to go dancing when my father has died. You ask me why I am at home when I am on my way to church. What do you really want?

Pedro: Maria. Maria. Will you marry me?

Storyteller: (*to the audience*) What do you think Maria said? You are right. She said yes, of course. Wouldn't you?

At the end of the story, the narrator asks the audience a question. Give them an opportunity to answer. Then you can ask them why Maria said yes or if they think she should have said no. They can weigh in on their opinions and then have the actors give voice to a different ending. (We're rooting for Pedro and Maria.)

BOOKLIST: PICTURE BOOKS TO USE WITH PUPPETS

Folktales often make wonderful puppet shows, but picture books can do quite nicely, too. You need only have the appropriate puppets. Preliterate children can act out the story based on their recollections from your read-aloud. Older children can turn stories into reader's theater scripts to read aloud as a group with their puppets, and then perform as a play. Keep in mind that just because a book is easy to read doesn't mean it will be easy to turn into a play. The booklist below will give you some good suggestions.

Asch, Frank. *Mr. Maxwell's Mouse. Illus. by the author. Kids Can, 2004.* A dignified gray cat decides on a live mouse for lunch, but his intended meal has other ideas. Help the children make stick puppets to perform this story. (Gr. 2–6)

Buzzeo, Toni. *Dawdle Duckling. Illus. by Margaret Spengler. Dial, 2003.* Mama Duck's fourth little duckling says to his patient mama, "NO! Quack! Quack! I won't catch up." Use a glove puppet, with the thumb as Mama and the pinky as Dawdle. (PreK–K)

Dunrea, Olivier. *Ollie. Illus. by the author. Houghton Mifflin, 2003.* Geese friends Gossie and Gertie have been waiting for an egg to hatch. If you use hard-boiled eggs and make popsicle-stick puppets for the geese, everyone can act this out. (PreK–Gr. 1)

Emberley, Rebecca, and Ed Emberley. *Chicken Little. Illus. by the authors. Roaring Brook, 2009.* Not the "brightest chicken in the coop," Chicken Little is doing nothing when an acorn hits him on the head and knocks him senseless. Delightfully zany to act out with puppets. (PreK–Gr. 1)

Emberley, Rebecca, and Ed Emberley. *The Red Hen. Illus. by the authors. Roaring Brook, 2010.* Red Hen finds a wonderful recipe for a "Simply Splendid Cake," but the cat, rat, and frog refuse to help her make it. (PreK–Gr. 1)

Fleming, Denise. *The Cow Who Clucked. Illus. by the author. Henry Holt, 2006.* Cow awakes to find she has lost her moo. The story has lots of good animal parts. (PreK–Gr. 1)

Ginsburg, Mirra. *The Chinese Mirror. Illus. by Margot Zemach. Harcourt, 1988.* When a Korean man brings home a mirror he has bought in China, his family sees unfamiliar faces in the glass. Use a small hand mirror and hand puppets for this tale. (Gr. 1–4)

Haughton, Chris. *Little Owl Lost. Illus. by the author. Candlewick, 2010.* A "where's my mommy?" story with a nice collection of forest animals as characters. (PreK–Gr. 1)

Hutchins, Pat. *Good-Night, Owl! Illus. by the author. Macmillan, 1972.* Owl tries to sleep during the day, but the other animals keep making noise. (PreK–Gr. 1)

Lies, Brian. *Bats at the Library. Illus. by the author. Houghton Mifflin, 2008.* In this narrative poem, bats swoop into an open window at the library and spend a delightful, book-filled night. Turn on the overhead projector and make shadow puppets like the bats do. (PreK–Gr. 2)

McKissack, Patricia C., and Onawumi Jean Moss. *Precious and the Boo Hag. Illus. by Kyrsten Brooker. Atheneum, 2005.* Precious is home alone when Pruella the Boo Hag comes calling. Third graders at Van Holten School in Bridgewater, New Jersey, made large stick puppets of the characters and wrote their own scripts, with each student group responsible for a different scene. (Gr. 1–4)

Pilkey, Dav. *Dragon's Fat Cat*. *Illus. by the author. Orchard, 1992.* Dragon and his cat are the main characters in these five easy-reader stories. Each pair of puppeteers can put on one of the chapters. (PreK–Gr. 2)

Pinkney, Jerry. *The Lion & the Mouse*. *Illus. by the author. Little, Brown, 2009.* For this wordless "retelling" of the Aesop fable, help kids make lion and mouse puppets. They can act out the story in pairs, adding dialogue between the two creatures. (PreK–Gr. 3)

Rash, Andy. *Are You a Horse?* *Illus. by the author. Scholastic, 2009.* Roy may be dressed like a cowboy, but it's only when he gets a saddle that he discovers what a horse is. Make hand or stick puppets for each character. (PreK–Gr. 2)

Rocco, John. *Blackout*. *Illus. by the author. Disney-Hyperion, 2011.* During a power failure in Brooklyn, NY, the kids watch Dad make shadow puppets on the wall. Show kids how to create their own shadow puppets with flashlights or an overhead projector as their light source. (PreK–Gr. 3)

Rosenthal, Amy Krouse. *Duck! Rabbit!* *Illus. by Tom Lichtenheld. Chronicle, 2009.* "That's not a duck. That's a rabbit." Or is it? Make a two-sided stick puppet from heavy felt, based on the white duck and rabbit shapes in the book. Draw the faces with magic marker—the rabbit on one side, the duck on the other. Children can create their own copies from heavy white paper and then act out the story in pairs. (PreK–Gr. 2)

Scieszka, Jon. *Cowboy & Octopus*. *Illus. by Lane Smith. Viking, 2007.* Nine weird and wacky short stories feature two pals: a paper-doll cowboy and a big blue octopus. Make a paper cowboy and a felt octopus stick puppet. Have each pair of children practice a different story and then perform it for the group. (PreK–Gr. 3)

Seeger, Laura Vaccaro. *Dog and Bear: Two Friends, Three Stories*. *Illus. by the author. Roaring Brook, 2007.* Three brief, easy-to-read adventures about a little brown dachshund and his best friend, Bear, a multicolored stuffed teddy. Find commercial puppets for these characters on Amazon.com, or make stick puppets. (PreK–Gr. 1)

Sendak, Maurice. *Where the Wild Things Are*. *Illus. by the author. HarperCollins, 1963.* Make reproducible pictures of the Wild Things for children to color and glue to popsicle sticks, or let them design new "wild things." (PreK–Gr. 1)

Shields, Carol Diggery. *Wombat Walkabout*. *Illus. by Sophie Blackall. Dutton, 2009.* This counting-down rhyme features a hungry dingo and six wooly wombats. Make small felt wombat finger puppets, a larger hand-puppet dingo, and a flannel bag where the dingo can stash his wombat "breakfast." Tip a long table on its side so the wombats appear single file on their walkabout. (PreK–Gr. 1)

Smee, Nicola. *Clip-Clop.* *Illus. by the author. Sterling, 2006.* "Who wants a ride?" asks Mr. Horse, and a variety of animals jump on his back. Hand puppets or stuffed animal puppets will work well with this story. (PreK–Gr. 1)

Thomas, Jan. *Rhyming Dust Bunnies.* *Illus. by the author. Beach Lane, 2009.* "We rhyme . . . all the time!" say Ed, Ned, and Ted—but Bob, the fourth dust bunny, seems befuddled. Use colored tangles of yarn as puppets. Attach them to your fist with a loop of tape. (PreK–Gr. 1)

Thomas, Shelley Moore. *Get Well, Good Knight.* *Illus. by Jennifer Plecas. Dutton, 2002.* The Good Knight's three little dragon friends come down with sneezes, coughs, and fevers. Look for a script for this book at spaldinglae3414.wikis paces.com/Readers + Theater. (PreK–Gr. 1)

Waber, Bernard. *An Anteater Named Arthur.* *Houghton Mifflin, 1967.* Each chapter makes a funny two-character puppet play between Arthur and his mother. (PreK–Gr. 2)

Willems, Mo. *There Is a Bird on My Head.* *Illus. by the author. Hyperion, 2007.* Elephant is not happy when Piggie tells him there are two lovebirds building a nest on his head. Other books in this series make excellent puppet plays, too. (PreK–Gr. 2)

BOOKLIST: BOOKS ABOUT PUPPETRY

Almoznino, Albert. *The Art of Hand Shadows.* *Dover, 2002.* Illustrated instructions for making more than seventy hand shadows on the wall. (Professional)

Bauer, Caroline Feller. *Leading Kids to Books through Puppets.* *Illus. by Richard Laurent. American Library Association, 1997.* A small book packed with directions for making and using all types of puppets, accompanied by poems, stories, plays, and annotated lists of related children's books. (Professional)

Beaton, Mabel, and Les Beaton. *The Complete Book of Marionettes.* *Dover, 2005, c1948.* A full treatment for the marionette aficionado. (Professional)

Bryan, Ashley. *Ashley Bryan's Puppets: Making Something from Everything.* *Photos by Rich Entel. Atheneum, 2014.* Author/artist/storyteller Ashley Bryan presents three dozen of his elegant puppets, crafted from a wealth of found materials, with a poem describing each one. These will inspire children (and you) to make puppets out of unusual scraps. (Gr. 1–6)

Bryant, Jill, and Catherine Heard. *Making Shadow Puppets (Kids Can Do It).* *Illus. by Laura Watson. Kids Can, 2002.* Directions and templates for nine easy-to-make puppets. (Gr. 3–6)

Champlin, Connie. *Storytelling with Puppets.* *Second edition. American Library Association, 1998.* Practical advice on making, using, and staging puppet productions, including puppet patterns, information on puppet theaters, annotated bibliographies of children's books to adapt, and warm-up and follow-up activities. (Professional)

Collodi, Carlo. *The Adventures of Pinocchio.* *Illus. by Roberto Innocenti. Knopf, 1988.* The thrilling and unforgettable classic Italian saga of the wooden-puppet-turned-boy, with masterful, brooding paintings. (Gr. 3–7)

Currell, David. *Shadow Puppets & Shadow Play.* *Crowood Press, 2008.* A puppeteer presents information on everything from the history of shadow puppetry, staging, lighting, sound, and more. Also by the author: *Making and Manipulating Marionettes* (2005) and *Puppets and Puppet Theatre* (1999). (Professional)

Faurot, Kimberley K. *Books in Bloom: Creative Patterns and Props That Bring Stories to Life.* *Illus. with photos. American Library Association, 2003.* Scripts, patterns, instructions, and related activities for presenting stories from six picture books. (Professional)

Frey, Yvonne Amar. *One-Person Puppetry Streamlined & Simplified: With 38 Folktale Scripts.* *American Library Association, 2005.* Following useful tips and techniques, Frey offers puppet show scripts adapted from traditional folklore. (Professional)

Krull, Kathleen. *Jim Henson: The Guy Who Played with Puppets.* *Illus. by Steve Johnson and Lou Fancher. Random House, 2011.* Picture-book biography about the creator of the Muppets. (Gr. 1–6)

Lowe, Joy L., and Kathryn I. Matthew. *Puppet Magic.* *Neal-Schuman, 2008.* How to buy, make, and use simple puppets related to children's books, stories, and songs. (Professional)

Minkel, Walter. *How to Do "The Three Bears" with Two Hands: Performing with Puppets.* *American Library Association, 2000.* Wide-ranging advice, including five comical puppet play scripts. (Professional)

Schlitz, Laura Amy. *Splendors and Glooms.* *Candlewick, 2012.* After marionette master and magician Professor Grissini and his two young assistants perform their show at Clara Wintermute's twelfth birthday party, Clara disappears. This suspenseful and riveting novel, set in Victorian England in 1860, will get readers interested in working with marionettes. (Gr. 5–8)

Sierra, Judy. *Fantastic Theater: Puppets and Plays for Young Performers and Young Audiences.* *H. W. Wilson, 1991.* Sierra offers directions for making and manipulating shadow and rod puppets, as well as scripts for puppet plays adapted from rhymes, folk songs, myths, and folktales. (Professional)

Sierra, Judy, and Robert Kaminski. *Multicultural Folktales: Stories to Tell Young Children.* Oryx, 1991. These twenty-five stories from around the world are accompanied by suggestions for telling and using felt-board figures and puppets. (Professional)

Sweet, Melissa. *Balloons over Broadway: The True Story of the Puppeteer of Macy's Parade.* Illus. by the author. Houghton Mifflin, 2011. This 2012 Sibert Medal picture-book biography for children introduces the marionette master Anthony "Tony" Frederick Sarg, who started the Macy's Thanksgiving Day Parade in New York City in 1924. (K–Gr. 4)

Wisniewski, David, and Donna Wisniewski. *Worlds of Shadow: Teaching with Shadow Puppetry.* Teacher Ideas Press, 1997. A thorough, gorgeously illustrated exploration of how to create shadow puppets and perform plays for and with children. (Professional)

Wright, Denise Anton. *One-Person Puppet Plays.* Illus. by John Wright. Libraries Unlimited, 1990. Short scripts and simple patterns to produce one-person puppet shows. (Professional)

WEBSITES: PUPPETRY

Axtell Expressions *www.axtell.com*
A resource for beautiful professional puppets and props for puppeteers, ventriloquists, and magicians. Even if most of these are beyond your budget, you'll be inspired by the demonstration videos and information on the site.

Center for Puppetry Arts *www.puppet.org*
This hands-on puppetry museum in Atlanta, Georgia, sponsors performances, curriculum-based workshops, distance learning, and outreach programs. Lots of links, educator resource guides, and exhibits.

Dr. Jean Feldman *www.drjean.org/html/monthly_act/act_2009/10_Oct/pg04.html*
The effervescent workshop leader shares favorite puppet-making craft activities.

Folkmanis Puppets *www.folkmanis.com*
More than two hundred beautiful, realistic-looking, plush animal puppets are available along with demos, a handful of downloadable play scripts, and links to puppet organizations and other useful websites.

Puppeteers of America *www.puppeteers.org*
This national nonprofit organization has been dedicated to the art of puppetry since its founding in 1937. The site provides useful links and information about puppetry centers and theaters throughout the US. Members receive *Puppetry Journal.*

Puppetry Home Page *www.sagecraft.com/puppetry*

This free resource contains a wealth of information, articles, and links on everything puppetry: definitions, traditions, construction, uses for puppets, organizations, festivals, and more.

Unima-USA *www.unima-usa.org*

The organization links puppeteers around the world and offers support for puppeteers and works to "stimulate the general public's interest in the art of puppetry; and promote the visibility of American puppeteers all over the world." Its Puppetry Yellow Pages contain a wealth of information.

Creative Drama

Drama is life with the dull parts left out. —ALFRED HITCHCOCK

ARE CHILDREN AS IMAGINATIVE AS THEY USED TO BE? WE CAN'T help but wonder, given the proliferation of television, movies, and personal computers and handheld devices with their endless games and social media. If children are always shown the action, they get less practice in using their mind's eye. We hope this chapter will help spark their imaginations. Let's start with an exercise in visualization that involves the body, the voice, and a whole lot of laughter.

Go Bananas

There are a zillion versions of this call-and-response chant (and many are on YouTube), but if your audience doesn't know it, prompt them by asking, "What kind of fruit has a yellow peel you can't eat, but could make you slip?" Many will call out, "Bananas!" "Bananas?" you cry. "Did somebody say bananas?" Then stand up straight and bellow, "Bananas of the world, unite!" Motion for everyone to stand up and instruct them to repeat every-thing you say and do. Ready? Here we go.

"Bananas of the world, unite!"
  (*clasp hands over your head*)

Form banana, form form banana.
  (*slowly curl one arm over your head*)

Form banana, form form banana.
  (*slowly curl other arm over your head, and make a point with your hands*)

And you peel banana, peel, peel banana.
  (*slowly lower one arm to your side, like you're peeling the banana*)

Peel banana, peel, peel banana.
  (*slowly lower other arm to your side in the same way*)

Then you go bananas, go, go bananas!
  (*wave your arms in air and go a little crazy*)

And you go bananas, go, go bananas!
  (*wave your arms in air and go a little crazy*)

Continue with other verses, and then make up new ones until you are exhausted:

Form the corn . . . shuck the corn . . . pop the corn!
  (*pop up and down*)

Form the apple . . . peel the apple . . . chop the apple!
  (*make chopping motions with hands*)

Form the orange . . . peel the orange . . . squeeze the orange!
  (*hug self or person beside you*)

Form the potato . . . peel the potato . . . mash the potato!
  (*mash with your feet, like the dance "The Mashed Potato"*)

Form the avocado . . . peel the avocado . . . Guacamole,
  gua-gua-camole, guacamole, gua-gua-camole!
  (*lift one leg to side and lower, and then the other one*)

Build the house (*put your arms over your head to form a roof*) . . .
  paint the house (*pretend to paint your neighbor*) . . .
  rock the house! (*dance, arms akimbo*)

Creative Drama

The most active—and in some ways the most satisfying—type of participation program is one in which your audience spontaneously acts out stories or elements of stories. Unlike more formal drama, creative drama is not meant to end in a highly polished performance. In addition to learning to work with others, carry out directions, and express oneself through movement and language, creative drama encourages logical thinking, imagination, and creative play.

If you are a classroom teacher, you can schedule creative drama during your usual read-aloud and storytelling hour—perhaps every afternoon at one o'clock for a week. If you are a public or school librarian, advertise a creative drama program for fixed number of weeks. For the most part, you will be telling stories and reciting poems as inspiration for pantomime and improvisation.

Starting at the End

How best to introduce children to creative dramatics? We suggest working backward: skip the preliminaries and plunge directly into playmaking.

Case in point: While spending a delectable day with three- and four-year-olds in her sister-in-law Ann Guthrie's class at the Antioch School in Yellow Springs, Ohio, Judy was privileged to spend an hour telling and reading them stories. One of the books she read aloud was *The Mitten* by Jim Aylesworth, where a little boy loses one of the red mittens his doting grandmother has knitted for him. Wild animals discover it in the snow and crawl inside the ever-expanding mitten to get warm. Ann's children wasted no time joining in the many repeated refrains.

Afterwards, the class went out to the playground for some R&R. Some children played on the swings; others chased each other. A third group, without any prompting or instructions, started to act out *The Mitten*, taking on the parts of the boy and the animals. In playing, they put on an impromptu play—which is, after all what a play is: exuberant play, creative drama at its most creative.

Let's start our play with *Wake Up, Sun*, a story young children will love to act out once you have told it to them. The story is full of repetition and is easy to learn. Children will be hard pressed not to join right in with the chantable refrains of this quick participation story. If you're talking about voice and reading with expression and characterization, this is an ideal exercise to demonstrate those concepts. Actors get a chance to use a variety of voices and emotions in a very basic way.

Wake Up, Sun!

Retold by Caroline Feller Bauer

I'm sure that you have noticed that the sun comes up every morning and goes to bed each night. This is what *usually* happens, but it doesn't always work like that.

Once, back when your great-grandparents were young, there was a morning when the sun didn't come out. At first, it didn't matter so much. People slept late and, although the children didn't get up for school and breakfast didn't get cooked or eaten, no one really cared.

Soon, though, some people began to worry. It was so dark without the sun. A picnic for the Duchess's birthday was planned for that afternoon. She had pictured a beautiful summer day with the guests playing croquet on the lawn and enjoying birthday cake with pink icing. She was worried. A picnic by candlelight sounded romantic, but she wanted the sun.

The Duchess was a kind and lovely lady who always wore elegant clothes. She was a fine linguist and could speak many languages. She used English to call up the sun.

"Wake up, sun!" she called in a cultured voice.

The sun did not wake up.

The Duke tried to call up the sun. He had spent many years traveling abroad. The sun had always appeared in those foreign lands.

He called first in English, "Wake up, sun!" Then he tried in French: "*Réveillez-vous, soleil!*" And then in Spanish: "*¡Despiertese, Señor Sol!*"

The sun did not wake up.

The police officer thought that he might be able to force the sun to wake up. He was used to being obeyed. He called in a tough voice, "Wake up, sun!"

The sun did not wake up.

The judge thought she might be able to wake the sun up by a threat of jail. She ordered, in a commanding voice, "Wake up, sun!"

The sun did not wake up.

The baker, who had prepared the delicious birthday cake, came out from her kitchen and called sweetly, "Wake up, sun!"

The sun did not wake up.

The schoolteacher, who had taught most of the children and adults in town and stood for no nonsense, thought he could teach the sun to wake up.

He called impatiently, "Wake up, sun!"

The sun did not wake up.

The banker was a very rich and self-important man. He thought that having lots of money meant he could make anyone do anything. He shouted angrily, "Wake up, sun!"

The sun did not wake up.

The Duchess's personal assistant was concerned about the darkness. How could she possibly get the Duchess ready for the picnic in the dark? She called worriedly, "Wake up, sun!"

The sun did not wake up.

The young kitchen maid came up behind the grown-ups. She said, "I think I know who could help." She brought the rooster from the barnyard.

The rooster called, "Cock-a-doodle-doo!"

The sun woke up. Everyone cheered. And the Duchess's birthday picnic was a great success.

Acting Out a Story

Chances are good that your group of children—if left to their own devices with some free playtime after hearing the story—will spontaneously begin to act it out without any encouragement on your part. "Let's play 'Wake Up, Sun,'" one child will suggest, adding, "I want to be the police officer!" Another will say, "I want to be the the Duke!" And the casting and then reenactment will begin, with much merry intensity, as the children approximate the dialogue and action of the tale.

Let your group take as much responsibility as possible for the making and implementing of decisions. If the children are old hands at listening to stories, you can say, "Choose one of the stories that we've shared recently and put on a play." Or simply begin by telling a story. If the story is complicated, encourage children to discuss elements such as the following:

THE CHARACTERS IN THE STORY

- How many characters are there and how many actors do you need?
- What are their physical characteristics
- What are their personalities? (*kind, brave, bossy, mean*)
- How do the characters change in the course of the story?

THE SETTING OF THE STORY—TIME AND PLACE

- How much time elapses?
- When and where does the story take place?
- How many and what kinds of scene changes are there?
- What would each of the settings look like?

THE PLOT OF THE STORY

- What kind of action does the story contain?
- What problem needs to be solved?
- What is the sequence of events in the story?

Keep this preliminary discussion to a minimum at your first session. The play's the thing and you will want to get on with it. Next, cast the play. Let children decide who will play which role, but if that doesn't work, assign parts. Everyone should get a chance to be a player, but not necessarily at the same session; children who have leads one time can have walk-on parts the next. Don't forget that people can play inanimate objects as well as animals or humans. Remember *Stone Soup*? The stones are leading characters. Someone can also be the director, and others can be stagehands, in charge of coming up with costumes and scenery, if the play warrants it, plus setting up for each scene. Those who don't act become the audience, a role just as important as performing.

Next, reread or retell the story. We all think we know "Little Red Riding Hood," for example, until we find ourselves in the middle of the forest and can't remember what happens next. Use the old storyteller's technique of asking the participants to help outline the story into ten brief phrases or bullet points and jot them down on a chart or board.

Now let the players decide how to put on the story. Set a time limit for preparation, and then on with the show. After the play, everyone usually feels triumphant; don't dampen their enthusiasm with criticism, no matter how constructive.

Exploring the Senses through Creative Drama

An awareness of the way our senses work will help children more clearly project these senses to an audience. Most information comes through our eyes and secondarily through our ears. Use the simple tests, games, and experiments below to demonstrate the operation of the five senses. One sense activity each session will probably be plenty.

TASTE

These activities combine drama with science. You'll need enough popsicle sticks for each child to have several, one for each different food. You will also need to check with parents about food allergies and omit any potential problem foods.

Assemble a variety of tasteables (brown sugar, fresh lemons, salt, banana slices, baby carrots, apples, raisins, pickles, and so on) and keep them hidden. Blindfold the children or ask them to close their eyes; then place a dab of each food in turn on each tongue. As the children sample each item, have them use adjectives to describe the taste without naming the food itself. Is it sweet, sour, crunchy, slippery, bitter, mild, sticky, salty, spicy, hot? When the sampling is complete, have children remove their blindfolds and show them what they tasted.

For another activity, have pairs of children reach into a bag and pull out a card with a food name on it. Give them one minute to rehearse a pantomime of preparing and eating the food. The rest of the group can guess what it is. Try watermelon, sushi with chopsticks, spicy chili, wobbly Jell-O, corn on the cob, pizza, a peanut-butter-and-jelly sandwich, a hard-boiled egg. Then plan a pretend menu, and as a group enjoy an imaginary party. Make it a potluck supper, with each child pantomiming the dish and how it tastes.

Have younger children discuss the foods they love and hate. Help them make a chart of these foods, noting how foods on some children's "love" column are on other children's "hate" list. Ask children to name some foods they've never tasted. As a follow-up, read Lauren Child's *I Will Never Not Ever Eat a Tomato*, where Charlie tries to get his fussy little sister, Lola, to taste carrots, peas, and mashed potatoes.

For children in grades 4 to 8, if you want to combine science, drama, and an exquisite read-aloud, dive into the fiction book, *Liar & Spy* by Rebecca Stead (Random House, 2012), where a vital plot point revolves around science teacher Mr. Landau's seventh-grade science unit, "How We Taste."

SMELL

The sense of smell is the least evolved of the human senses, yet in many other animals it is the most highly developed. Discuss with your group the importance of a sense of smell in humans and animals.

Choose a variety of smells for the group to identify. Each item should be in its own container. Use egg cartons with slots cut in the top or small plastic or sturdy glass containers (like baby-food jars) wrapped with a strip of colored duct tape or construction paper so children can't see the contents.

Fresh herbs, cinnamon, orange juice, coffee, a rose, vinegar, shaving lotion, pencil shavings, vanilla, and baby powder are good choices. Have children keep a numbered list, identifying each scent. When you are finished testing, ask them to compare their lists with what's in your containers. Dav Pilkey's comical and pun-filled picture book, *Dog Breath: The Horrible Trouble with Hally Tosis*, about the Tosis family's odiferous dog, Hally, makes a good follow-up.

Often a particular smell will bring back memories of a forgotten occasion. Discuss some of these odors. Some memories could include baking bread, which makes one think of Thanksgiving dinner; the smell of brewing coffee at Sunday breakfast; or the nose-wrinkling stink of rubbing alcohol, which puts you in mind of the time you had to get a shot. Have children write and illustrate a brief essay about their olfactory reminiscences.

TOUCH

Most people relate touch to hands, yet we actually use our whole bodies to touch. Put various objects (such as a marble, paper clip, penny, sandpaper, comb, rubber band, feather, and harmonica) into small paper bags and let the children feel, describe, and name each item.

Collect samples of fabric, such as polyester, lace, wool, fur, corduroy, and so on, and attach them to a large board. Let children feel and discuss the different textures. Is the fabric soft, rough, smooth, stiff, pliable, spongy, silky, rigid? Read Ed Young's *Seven Blind Mice*, a classic book about seven blind mice that spend seven days exploring the various parts of mystery creature. The moral: "Knowing one part may make a fine tale, but wisdom comes from seeing the whole."

With children in grade 3 and up, share with them "The Blind Men and the Elephant," a classic narrative poem of that name by John Godfrey Saxe (1816–1887). You can find the whole poem online at: en.wikisource .org/wiki/The_Blindmen_and_the_Elephant. It starts:

> It was six men of Indostan
> To learning much inclined,
> Who went to see the Elephant
> (Though all of them were blind),
>
> That each by observation
> Might satisfy his mind.
> The first approached the Elephant
> And happening to fall

Against his broad and sturdy side
At once began to bawl:
"Bless me, it seems the Elephant
Is very like a wall."

SOUND

The world is full of sounds that we often ignore. Have your participants sit quietly on the floor, close their eyes, and concentrate on sounds outside the room. Then ask them to listen to the sounds in the room. Finally, ask them to eliminate all external sounds and listen to the sounds their own bodies make. Next, introduce a variety of sounds and ask them to guess what is making them. You can:

- Shake coins in a bowl.
- Shuffle a deck of cards.
- Click a ballpoint pen.
- Open and close a zipper.
- Shift coins from hand to hand.
- Wrinkle paper.
- Sharpen a pencil.
- Crack an egg into a bowl.
- Bite into a crisp apple.

Make a recording of sound effects that students create from found materials, objects, and furniture around the room. They'll discover plenty of good noises. To start, they can:

- Raise or lower the blinds.
- Bang on the radiator or on an overturned trash can as a drum.
- Create other percussion with blocks, pencils, rulers, and boxes.
- Tap pencils or rulers on a table, on a chair leg, or a wooden shelf.
- Open and close a book cover.
- Crumple a piece of paper.
- Bounce a ball on the floor.

San Francisco teacher Edgar Camago (aka DJ Overeasy) and his third-grade class created an original song—"Schoolhouse Remix!"—composed entirely of voice fragments and sounds made from familiar classroom objects. (You can hear it at www.youtube.com/watch?v=7k2HONn7AQw.) For a memorable participatory story with lots of animal noises, read or tell Ann McGovern's

Too Much Noise. See "How to Make a Small House into a Large One," Caroline's grandfather's version of this old Yiddish folktale on page 287.

SIGHT

Sight is the most developed of the senses, but we don't all see things the same way. That becomes clear in Amy Krouse Rosenthal's *Duck! Rabbit!* in which two unseen speakers have an argument over what they see in the optical illusion–ish illustrations. (There's an adorable trailer for the book at www.youtube.com/watch?v=hPCoe-6RRks.)

As for introducing the concept of optical illusions, all will be intrigued by Walter Wick's nonfiction book *Walter Wick's Optical Tricks*, with an intriguing array of full-page color photographs that flummox the eye using light, shadows, mirrors, and odd angles.

See how the eye perceives color with Eric Carle's *Hello, Red Fox*, which introduces Goethe's theory of complementary colors and his color wheel. On each left-hand page is a large illustration of an animal in an unusual hue. When you stare at the green fox for ten seconds and then focus your gaze on the all-white facing page, the fox will magically appear there in its complementary color, red. All ages will be fascinated by the tricks the eyes and the brain can play on your sense of sight.

One way to cultivate the power of observation is to have children look at the world around them through a pinhole poked in a piece of cardboard. Ask them if they see things differently when they look through the hole. How? Encourage them to imagine they are an ant in a cornfield. What would they see? As a giant in the same cornfield, how would they see things differently?

The memory game, an old party game, still works wonderfully in the classroom or library. Bring out a tray with twenty objects on it: a pencil, a stapler, an apple, a shoe . . . anything you have on hand. Give children one minute to look at the objects. Then cover the tray with a cloth or take it away. Hand out pencils and paper and give your players one minute to list as many objects as they can recall. Go over the lists collaboratively to see if the group can come up with all twenty objects. Then bring back the tray and see if they missed any.

This observation test is also fun: Select someone to leave the room. Have the other participants collaboratively list what the absent person was wearing. When the person returns, compare the list with what the child is actually wearing. Next, choose something that everyone in the group has passed so many times they no longer really see it: the statue in front of the school, the motto above the library door, or the like. Have all the participants write down its description. Read some of these descriptions to the group and discuss the need to develop the habit of observing.

BOOKLIST: FIVE SENSES

Aliki. *My Five Senses*. *Illus. by the author. HarperCollins, 1989.* Simple, attractive nonfiction picture book about our senses and how we use them. (PreK–Gr. 1)

Babbitt, Natalie. *The Search for Delicious*. *Illus. by the author. Farrar, 1985.* The king sends twelve-year-old Gaylen to find which food best fits the definition of "delicious." (Gr. 3–6)

Carle, Eric. *Hello, Red Fox*. *Illus. by the author. Simon & Schuster, 1998.* In a study of seven complementary colors, Little Frog invites his friends—Red Fox, Purple Butterfly, Orange Cat—and other colorful animals to his birthday party. (K–Gr. 6)

Chancellor, Deborah. *I Wonder Why Lemons Taste Sour and Other Questions about the Senses*. *Kingfisher, 2008.* Kid-friendly answers to more than thirty interesting questions. (K–Gr. 4)

Child, Lauren. *I Will Never Not Ever Eat a Tomato*. *Illus. by the author. Candlewick, 2000.* Charlie persuades his picky eater little sister, Lola, to try the foods that she insists she does not eat. (PreK–Gr. 2)

Cobb, Vicki. *How to Really Fool Yourself: Illusions for All Your Senses*. *Illus. by Jessica Wolk-Stanley. John Wiley, 1999.* More than seventy very cool science activities to try. (Gr. 4–7)

Cole, Joanna. *The Magic School Bus Explores the Senses*. *Illus. by Bruce Degen. Scholastic, 1999.* Ms. Frizzle's class rides the Magic School Bus into an eye, an ear, and even into their teacher's mouth. (K–Gr. 4)

Cole, Joanna. *You Can't Smell a Flower with Your Ear! All about Your 5 Senses*. *Illus. by Mavis Smith. Grosset & Dunlap, 1994.* Simple explanations of how and why our senses work. (K–Gr. 3)

Cottin, Menena. *The Black Book of Colors*. *Illus. by Rosanna Faria. Groundwood, 2008.* On each black page is a description of a color by Thomas, a blind boy. Blind children can read the Braille; sighted children can feel the pictures to see if they can identify them. Ask children to express how a color tastes, feels, sounds, or smells. (Gr. 1–6)

Ehlert, Lois. *Color Zoo*. *Illus. by the author. HarperCollins, 1989.* Die-cut pages of geometrical shapes reveal different animals. (PreK–Gr. 1)

Gerstein, Mordicai. *Carolinda Clatter*. *Illus. by the author. Roaring Brook, 2005.* Young Carolinda's great love of noise wakens a sleeping giant. (PreK–Gr. 2)

Handford, Martin. *Where's Waldo?* *Illus. by the author. Candlewick, 1987.* Find the guy in the red-and-white-striped cap. Visual discrimination at its best. (All Ages)

Henkes, Kevin. *Old Bear.* *Illus. by the author. Greenwillow, 2009.* While sleeping through the winter, Old Bear dreams about the seasons. (PreK–Gr. 1)

Hoberman, Mary Ann. *The Seven Silly Eaters.* *Illus. by Marla Frazee. Harcourt, 1997.* Patient Mrs. Peters grows weary of catering to her fussy children's tastes in food. (PreK–Gr. 3)

Hopkinson, Deborah. *Annie and Helen.* *Illus. by Raúl Colón. Schwartz & Wade, 2012.* A chronicle of Annie Sullivan and Helen Keller's first five months together in 1887. (Gr. 2–5)

Jenkins, Steve, and Robin Page. *What Do You Do With a Tail Like This?* *Illus. by the authors. Houghton Mifflin, 2003.* Identify the noses, ears, tails, eyes, mouths, and feet of thirty different creatures. (PreK–Gr. 3)

Johnson, David A. *Snow Sounds: An Onomatopoeic Story.* *Houghton Mifflin, 2006.* On a snowy day, a boy gets ready for school, with onomatopoeic words accompanying each blue-and-white illustration. (PreK–Gr. 2)

Jonas, Ann. *Round Trip.* *Illus. by the author. Greenwillow, 1983.* Black-and-white silhouette illustrations chronicle a trip to the city; flip over the book, and the pictures now show the trip back to the country. (PreK–Gr. 4)

Krall, Dan. *The Great Lollipop Caper.* *Illus. by the author. Simon & Schuster, 2013.* Jealous of sweet Lollipop, whom all the children love, tiny pickled sourpuss Mr. Caper devises a dastardly plan. Have children taste lollipops and capers and see which they prefer. (PreK–Gr. 3)

Kunhardt, Dorothy. *Pat the Bunny.* *Illus. by the author. Simon and Schuster, 1940.* All about textures and how they feel, from a bunny's soft tail to Daddy's scratchy beard. (PreK)

Lester, Helen. *Listen, Buddy.* *Illus. by Lynn Munsinger. Houghton Mifflin, 1995.* Because Buddy never listens properly, the long-eared rabbit finds himself a captive in Scruffy Varmint's cave. (PreK–Gr. 2)

Macaulay, David. *Two Bad Ants.* *Illus. by the author. Houghton Mifflin, 1988.* Drawn and described from an ant's perspective, this chronicles two ants' encounters in a kitchen. (K–Gr. 5)

MacDonald, Suse. *Alphabatics.* *Illus. by the author. Simon & Schuster, 1986.* Each letter of the alphabet is transformed into an object beginning with that letter. (PreK–Gr. 2)

Marsalis, Wynton. *Squeak, Rumble, Whomp! Whomp! Whomp! A Sonic Adventure.* *Illus. by Paul Rogers. Candlewick, 2012.* An African American boy in New Orleans revels in the rhythms and the everyday sounds that evoke instruments all around him. (PreK–Gr. 2)

Martin, Bill Jr. *Brown Bear, Brown Bear, What Do You See?* Illus. by Eric Carle. Henry Holt, 1967. A classic call-and-response book of animals, colors, and observations. Continue the fun with *Polar Bear, Polar Bear What Do You Hear?* (1991). (PreK–Gr. 1)

Marzollo, Jean. *I Spy: A Book of Picture Riddles.* Photos by Walter Wick. Scholastic, 1992. First in the beloved I Spy series, featuring photo collages of objects for children to find. (PreK–Gr. 3)

McClements, George. *Night of the Veggie Monster.* Illus. by the author. Bloomsbury, 2008. Harrowing narrative of a young boy forced to eat dreaded PEAS. Ask your listeners to name some foods they thought they hated until they actually tried them. Print out Judy Freeman's reader's theater script at media.bloomsbury.com/rep/files/veggie-monster-theatre.pdf. (PreK–Gr. 2)

McGovern, Ann. *Too Much Noise.* Illus. by Simms Taback. Houghton Mifflin, 1967. A man who can't sleep in his noisy house is advised to bring his animals inside. (PreK–Gr. 2)

Miller, Margaret. *My Five Senses.* Photos by the author. Simon & Schuster, 1994. An appealing photo essay of children exploring the world with their senses. (PreK–K)

Millman, Isaac. *Moses Goes to a Concert.* Illus. by the author. Farrar, 1998. A class of deaf children attend an orchestra conference where they see and "feel" the music. (PreK–Gr. 2)

Palatini, Margie. *Gorgonzola: A Very Stinkysaurus.* Illus. by Tim Bowers. HarperCollins, 2008. A triceratops with serious D.O. (dinosaur odor) gets a hygiene makeover. (PreK–Gr. 2)

Palatini, Margie. *Sweet Tooth.* Illus. by Jack E. Davis. Simon & Schuster, 2004. Stewart's talking molar yells, "I NEED A CANDY BAR. NOW-OW!" (PreK–Gr. 3)

Pilkey, Dav. *Dog Breath: The Horrible Trouble with Hally Tosis.* Illus. by the author. Blue Sky/Scholastic, 1994. The Tosis family owns a dog with such horrible breath, even skunks avoid her. (PreK–Gr. 2)

Rinck, Maranke. *I Feel a Foot!* Illus. by Martijn van der Linden. Lemniscaat/Boyds Mills, 2008. One pitch-black night, Turtle and his friends find a creature in the field and try to identify it by touch. (PreK–Gr. 2)

Rosenthal, Amy Krouse. *Duck! Rabbit!* Illus. by Tom Lichtenheld. Chronicle, 2009. That's not a duck. That's a rabbit. Or is it? An intriguing picture book about not seeing what you think you see. (PreK–Gr. 6)

Rosenthal, Amy Krouse. *Little Pea.* Illus. by Jen Corace. Chronicle, 2005. "If you don't finish your candy, you can't have dessert," says Mama Pea. (PreK–Gr. 2)

Rosoff, Meg. *Wild Boars Cook.* *Illus. by Sophie Blackall. Henry Holt, 2008.* Wild boar Doris finds a recipe for the "biggest, messiest, stickiest, gooiest, chewiest, most delicious pudding in the whole wide world." See Judy Freeman's reader's theater script at: us.macmillan.com/uploadedFiles/custompage contents/ titles/WildBoarsCookRT.pdf. (PreK–Gr. 2)

Seeger, Laura Vaccaro. *Green.* *Illus. by the author. Roaring Brook, 2012.* Die-cut pages and simple, two-word phrases survey the color green in surprising ways. (PreK–Gr. 2)

Shaw, Charles. *It Looked like Spilt Milk.* *Illus. by the author. HarperCollins, 1947.* Children look at clouds that resemble everyday objects. (PreK–Gr. 2)

Showers, Paul. *The Listening Walk.* *Illus. by Aliki. HarperCollins, 1991.* A little girl, her father, and their dog go on a silent "listening walk," where they listen to the sounds around them. (PreK–Gr. 2)

Staake, Bob. *Bob Staake's Look! Another Book! Illus. by the author. Little, Brown, 2012.* This busy seek-and-find book is a companion to Look! A Book! (2011). (PreK–Gr. 2)

Stojic, Manya. *Rain.* *Illus. by the author. Crown, 2000.* On the African savanna, the animals anticipate the rain by using their senses. (PreK–Gr. 1)

Tullet, Hervé. *Mix It Up! Illus. by the author. Chronicle, 2014.* Mix primary colors into secondary ones by pretending to rubbing the daubs of paint on each page. (PreK–Gr. 2)

Underwood, Deborah. *The Quiet Book. Houghton Mifflin, 2010.* Follow a group of animal kids from "first one awake quiet" to "sound asleep quiet." Follow with its companion, The Loud Book (2011). (PreK–Gr. 1)

Wick, Walter. *Walter Wick's Optical Tricks. Scholastic, 1998.* Wick uses color photographs and text to explain fourteen beguiling optical illusions. (Gr. 2–6)

Young, Ed. *Seven Blind Mice.* *Illus. by the author. Philomel, 1992.* Seven differently colored blind mice spend a week discovering the identity of a large creature they can feel but not see. (PreK–Gr. 3)

Pantomime

In pantomime, actors use only body movements and facial expressions to express actions and emotions. The following games and exercises will help participants learn the basics while they have some fun.

PASS AN OBJECT

Sit in a circle. Pass an invisible "hot potato" or a "delicate crystal glass" around the circle. Then pick someone to decide on an imaginary object to pass. The last person tells what it was that was being passed. Let the children enjoy themselves, but caution them to pay attention and try to envision each object, concentrating on how it looks and feels.

ACTION PANTOMIMES

Announce each of these mini scenes and give all the children in your group about thirty seconds to do each one.

- Fly a kite.
- Walk a tightrope.
- Row a boat.
- Pick a delicate blossom.
- Play the piano.
- Drive a car.
- Lift a heavy tray.
- Make a snowman.
- Eat a lemon wedge.
- Melt slowly like an iceberg in the sun.

ACTION EXERCISES

Now stand in a semicircle with room for each child to move around. Try some of these exercises as a group, individually, or with a partner.

- Grow from a seed to a flower.
- Wave goodbye to someone you dislike but are polite to.
- Open a door to your own surprise party.
- Take a shower.
- Look in a mirror (one partner mirrors the other's actions).
- Read a sad book.
- Climb a ladder.
- Blow up a balloon that pops.
- Explore a cave.

These can be little vignettes for groups or pairs to develop:
- Watch a sports event in a crowded stadium.
- Wait at the dentist's office with a painful tooth.
- Eat spaghetti at a fancy restaurant.
- Ride a carousel.

- Be a fish enjoying a frolic in the ocean until a shark swims by.
- Be a cat stalking a bird.
- Catch a fish (one partner wields the rod and the other becomes the fish).
- Change a flat tire on a car.
- Make and eat a pizza.
- Take your dog for a walk (one person is the dog).
- Be a rock 'n' roll band performing a hit song.

ACTIVITY CARDS

Write the following ideas on cards. Let each child pick a card and act out the activity while the group guesses what the performer is doing. Music adds another dimension to pantomime. Download a variety of musical selections—classical, jazz, rock—to your device of choice, or if you are lucky enough to have a piano and a talented accompanist, all the better. Do the exercises both with and without music.

Open a/an:

umbrella	can of soda	can of paint	packet of seeds	letter
suitcase	safe	fortune cookie	bottle of catsup	box of candy

You are:

happy	tired	excited	sad	cold
angry	hungry	hot	worried	thirsty

You are a:

mosquito	mouse	cat	bird	snake
fish	monkey	horse	whale	elephant

You are a:

bus driver	hairdresser	teacher	musician	painter
chef	ballet dancer	lion tamer	carpenter	doctor

ANIMAL BAG

Assemble a variety of small wooden or stuffed animals, an assortment of animal shapes from poster board, or some animal crackers. Place the animals in a bag or box. Each child picks an animal from the bag and acts out in pantomime the animal's movements. To add books to this activity, let each child search the library for a story or poem about his or her animal.

Charades

Divide your group into two teams, with one child selected as captain for each team. Decide in advance if you will use movies, book titles, fairy tales, songs, proverbs, historical events, or (for younger children) just simple words. Each group brainstorms a secret list (one item for each player on the opposite team) and writes each charade on a slip of paper. (Be sure to read each paper in advance to make sure it makes sense, is readable, and is possible to act out.)

One team captain gives an activity slip to a member of the opposing team to act out.

To begin, the actor first indicates how many words are in the phrase by holding up that number of fingers. If there are four words, she can then hold up one finger for the first word, two for the second, and so on. You'll want to do a demonstration round in advance to familiarize players with some of the hand signals associated with the game, or have them work out their own hand signals to indicate common words and phrases. We've given you a few examples below.

> *Sounds like:* Pull your earlobe.
> *Longer word:* Pull your hands apart like you're stretching a rubber band.
> *Shorter word:* Chop one hand against opposite palm.
> *Small word (and, on, a, the, to):* Hold out your thumb and forefinger close together.
> *The whole phrase:* Make a circle with your arms.
> *Syllables:* For a word that you plan to divide into syllables, place the number of fingers on your forearm to relay the number of syllables in the word. Then place one finger on your forearm to show it's the first syllable.

As the pantomime progresses, the actor's teammates must deduce the answer. The actor may work on a whole phrase, single words, or even syllables. To keep the game lively, you may want to limit each player's turn to two or three minutes.

WEBSITE LIST: CHARADES

YourDictionary.com *grammar.yourdictionary.com/games-puzzles-and-worksheets/charades-word-lists-kids.html*
> Bills itself as "The easiest to use on-line dictionary and thesaurus" and includes an excellent list of charades words and phrases for kids, including book titles.

The Game Gal *www.thegamegal.com/2011/10/19/charades-word-list*
> Instructions for playing dozens of games for all ages, with lists of suggested Charades phrases.

Statemaster *www.statemaster.com/encyclopedia/Charades*
> Includes rules of the game and an extensive list of signals to use.

MEET MARCEL MARCEAU

Introduce the greatest pantomimist ever with the gripping picture-book biography *Monsieur Marceau* by Leda Schubert, illustrated by Gerard DuBois. Wanting to be like the silent film star Charlie Chaplin, Marcel Mangel amused his friends with his own pantomiming. At sixteen, as World War II began, Marcel joined the French Resistance and helped lead hundreds of Jewish children from a French orphanage to safety in Switzerland. His father died in a concentration camp, after which Marcel changed his own last name to a non-Jewish one. He stated later, "My name is Mangel. I am Jewish. Perhaps that, unconsciously, contributed towards my choice of silence." At twenty-four, he created the character of Bip, with his stovepipe hat, white face paint, red mouth, and red carnation, which brought him global acclaim. The final page contains advice for getting started in miming from circus director Rob Mermin—who studied with Marceau—and some situations for children to try that will engage their senses. YouTube holds many videos of Marceau in performance, which should fascinate young mimes-in-training.

Improvisation

Improvisation adds speech to creative drama, but it is not scripted speech. Suggest a topic and let the children act it out. Try not to direct the play too much, and if possible let the children choose their parts and set up the action.

Try these exercises in expressing one's thoughts orally. Give the children a chance to collect their thoughts before they begin and don't let them talk for too long. Have them describe what it feels like to:

- Hit a home run
- Fail a spelling test
- Not be asked to a birthday party
- Be an ant on a picnic table

Next, without using their hands or other body parts, have children describe how to

- Make a bed
- Ride a bicycle
- Play pin the tail on the donkey
- Jump rope
- Get into a sleeping bag

Then try more advanced problems in expressing oral thought. Have each child

- Describe a family member, good points and bad
- Give reasons why he or she should be allowed to get a dog or a cat
- Confess to breaking mother's favorite vase
- Give a closing argument to convince a jury that your client is innocent

The following situations are useful for group activities. Actors can turn them into one- to three-minute skits with dialogue and drama.

- *Scene:* Living room
  Characters: Father, mother, children
  Situation: A family holds a meeting to discuss summer vacation.

- *Scene:* Car
  Characters: Father, mother, children
  Situation: On the way to summer vacation, the family is lost.

- *Scene:* Veterinarian's office
  Characters: Various people and their pets (eccentric old lady, young boy, etc.)
  Situation: Each person describes his or her pet's problem to an attendant.

- *Scene:* School auditorium
  Characters: Principal, teachers, parents, students, reporters
  Situation: Choose a problem and have a meeting about it.

- *Scene:* Living room
  Characters: Two friends (at least one female)
  Situation: One friend has come to visit the other. The hostess is newly engaged, with a new ring; she wants her friend to notice the ring without actually telling her about it.

For more improv ideas and games, see

- Matt Buchanan's "Improvs and Warmups," www.childdrama.com/warmups.html
- "Improv Games & Show Ideas," freedrama.net/improv.html#games
- "Improv Games and Exercises" by Barbara Selby, www.kidactivities.net/post/Improv-Games-and-Exercises.aspx

A Performance Exercise

If you are searching for an easy play for children to produce without any advance preparation, as actors or using puppets, divide them into groups of five. Let each group pick three pieces of paper from a box: one indicating a character, one a setting, and one an object. The group must decide on a skit involving the character, setting, and object chosen. Give a time limit for the preparation and performance. Caution your students to speak up and out, so that they can be heard and seen as they perform for the other groups.

Here are some ideas for the big three:

Character	Setting	Object
teacher	jungle	diamond bracelet
musician	New York City	book
explorer	desert island	treasure chest
witch	sailing ship	telephone
librarian	haunted house	magic wand
monster	department store	roast turkey
storekeeper	cave	baby elephant
rock singer	art museum	flashlight
pirate	theater	Uncle Jonathan's will
king or queen	spaceship	secret message
ghost	hotel	new shoes

Character	Setting	Object
baby	school	baseball
president	snowstorm	magnifying glass
artist	limousine	flower
scientist	farm	wooden spoon
prince or princess	mountaintop	laptop computer or tablet
astronaut	school	cell phone
cowboy	hospital	tennis racket
doctor	ranch	frog
wizard	wishing well	hat

Stories to Dramatize

After you have experimented with some of the exercises, try a story or two. To begin, read or tell a story aloud to your group. Then, list the various parts on a chalkboard and let people volunteer for parts. Now read or tell the story again, and outline the order of the action. It's not necessary for children to memorize the lines; the idea is to follow the outline of the plot and act it out.

The story below, "Lazy as an Ox," is perfect for creative drama. The protagonist, who is just plain lazy, is about to learn a lesson or two.

USING MASKS

Masks have been used to tell stories in many cultures. Native Americans, the indigenous people of Sri Lanka, and the tribes of Africa are particularly noted for using them. In creative drama, masks allow characters to change identities instantly. Just be sure, however, that the actors can be heard through their masks. This story works especially well with masks.

Lazy as an Ox: A Korean Tale

Retold by Caroline Feller Bauer

This is a morality tale, leavened by Wan Le's antics as an ox. If you tell this story to children, they will be amused at the storyteller holding a mask to her or his face and bellowing, "Moo!" Adults are never sure whether they should laugh or not. Perhaps they have thought once or twice that life might be easier as an ox.

Long ago, in Korea, a young man named Wan Le became an apprentice to a mask maker. No one was very confident that Wan Le would actually learn enough to fashion masks himself since he was quite lazy. The master often discovered him taking a nap in the courtyard using a half-finished mask as a sunshade.

There was some talk in the village that Wan Le would actually lose his apprenticeship and have no job at all. In such an industrious nation, it was almost unheard of to be chronically lazy.

Wan Le's mother was even more upset than the mask maker. She worried about what would happen to her son if he continued to be so lethargic.

"You don't seem happy in your work. You are always avoiding it," she said one night when Wan Le returned home after another nonproductive day. "Is there some other profession that would please you more?"

Wan Le was almost too lazy to answer. In fact, he felt ready for his nap, his third of the day. How to end his mother's nightly tongue-lashing? He chanced to look outside and saw their ox lying by the door, switching flies with his tail. "I'd like to be an ox," answered Wan Le. "They seem to have the perfect life, lying about in the pastures and on the roadways."

Wan Le's mother was angry. What a foolish boy she had raised. "Go then and be an ox," she said.

The next morning, Wan Le walked slowly to the mask maker's shop. He would be late as usual. He thought, but not very hard, as he shuffled along. "It would be nice to be an ox. They have someone to feed them and a place to live." Arriving at the shop he found that today's task was to finish painting an oxen mask for the spring festival. Wan Le sighed. He would have to work fast and furiously all day. There might not even be time for a nap. "I'd better take my nap now," mused Wan Le. Even though Wan Le had just arrived for work, he lay down on his workbench and laid the unfinished ox mask on his face. Soon he was fast asleep, dreaming of sleeping, no doubt.

When Wan Le awoke, he walked outside for a breath of fresh air. The mask still covered his face. A herd of oxen being driven to market were coming down the road. The ox master saw Wan Le in the doorway. "Here, ox. Get a move on."

Wan Le laughed to be mistaken for an ox, but the mask muffled his voice, so it sounded like "Moo." Soon he found himself being herded along with the oxen. He tried to remove his mask, but it was stuck fast to his face. "Moo," called Wan Le.

Driven with the rest of the herd to the holding pen, Wan Le found that he had gotten his wish. He was treated just like an ox. For supper there was a meager supply of hay, which he had to share with the other oxen. "Moo, moo," bellowed Wan Le. It wasn't so wonderful to be an ox after all. In the next few days, he had to haul heavy wagons loaded with goods for the market. There was no time to rest, and it was hard, monotonous work throughout the day. At night he worked pulling a wagon with travelers from one town to the other. "Moo, moo," complained Wan Le, but no one listened.

And so the weeks passed. Wan Le was so exhausted from his work as an ox that he hardly remembered what it was like to be a man. One day he found himself driven back to his hometown and chanced to see his old master carrying a load of bark, materials for a new line of handcrafted masks. At the time Wan Le was hauling a load of grain to market. He was tired and thirsty. His ox brain began to work and he found himself thinking that he should volunteer to help carry the mask maker's materials. "Moo, moo," bellowed Wan Le as he strained against the wagon load. The ox mask fell to the ground. Wan Le found himself a man again.

"There you are," said the master. "I was wondering where you've been."

"Let me help you carry that bark," volunteered Wan Le.

Wan Le became a respected mask maker. His work was bought by scholars and peasants alike. His specialty was the carving of lifelike representations of the faces of tired oxen.

His mother always wondered why he always kept an early unfinished mask hanging on the wall. But it served as a reminder to Wan Le that an oxen's life is not a lazy one.

"Moo."

––––––––––––––––

Reader's Theater

While children can act out the stories they read, hear, and write, they can also create scripts and act out the same stories as more concrete plays where the dialogue stays the same with each performance. We call that *reader's theater*. If you want children to practice their reading fluency, handing out a script for a story you've just read or told is the most painless, effective, and enjoyable way to achieve that.

Give out parts and have them read aloud the story as a play. With reader's theater, you don't need costumes, props, or scenery unless you want them. Children read and act simultaneously. When putting on puppet plays, children either memorize their parts or read them from a script while manipulating a puppet. In reader's theater, the actors stand or sit in a line and read their parts aloud with expression. They're practicing their reading skills while bringing a story to life.

The first time children read a script aloud, they'll stumble, make lots of mistakes, and still manage to have a marvelous time. Have them present their scripts two or more times and you'll see their performances improve with each reading. Acting out stories in reader's theater builds confidence in your actors, increases their comprehension of a story, and gives them practice in both public speaking and working collaboratively within a group.

Good sources for reader's theater productions include easy readers, picture books, folk and fairy tales, episodes in fiction and nonfiction books, and narrative poems. You'll find several scripts in chapter 2, "Puppetry."

Here's a play just right for a good-sized group. "Down with President Stomach" is adapted from a West African folktale. Each time a character speaks, he or she should perform the same mechanical action described below. There are ten roles listed here. When you have more actors than parts, you can add extra narrators to alternate lines, and also have two actors each for the feet, hands, eyes, and ears, which gives you fifteen or more as needed.

To be able to differentiate each actor, have children make breastplates for their roles—a foot, hand, eye, ear, nose, mouth, throat, and stomach—out of heavystock paper. Punch a hole on either side and attach yarn so that children can easily hang the illustration of their body part over their heads.

Down with President Stomach

By Caroline Feller Bauer

Roles and Actions:

Narrator: Stands to side and narrates action

God: Stands tall, arms folded in front of chest

Feet: Lifts feet up and down

Hands: Waves hands sideways, back and forth

Eyes: Circles eyes with thumb and index finger, opens wide and blinks

Ears: Cup ears with hands

Nose: Wrinkles nose and sniffs

Mouth: Opens and closes mouth, clicking teeth

Throat: Strokes throat and makes loud swallowing noise

Stomach: Sits up straight and pats stomach with both hands

Narrator: God created man with feet, hands, eyes, ears, nose, teeth, throat, and a stomach. God made the heart the secretary and the stomach the president. God was satisfied.

God: (*stands tall, arms folded in front of chest*) This is good. Each part of the body will have a particular job to perform.

Feet: (*lifts feet up and down*) We walk.

Hands: (*waves hands sideways, back and forth*) We hold, cut, and grab.

Eyes: (*circles eyes with thumb and index finger, opens eyes wide and blinks*) We see.

Ears: (*cups ears with hands*) We hear.

Nose: (*wrinkles nose and sniffs*) I smell.

Mouth: (*opens and closes mouth, clicking teeth*) I chew.

Throat: (*strokes throat and makes loud swallowing noise*) I swallow.

Stomach: (*sits up straight and pats stomach with both hands*) I keep all the food that comes into the body. I am the most important one of all!

Narrator: After a day, the parts of the body began to feel jealous. They seemed to be working for Stomach and getting nothing in return.

Throat: Listen, all the food that goes through me is gone in a minute. I think Stomach ties a rope around it and pulls it down for himself. Let's elect a new president and do away with Stomach.

Mouth: You're right. We chew the food, but Stomach is the one who takes it in and enjoys it by himself. You better vote against this president or I will leave and go to live in a different body.

Eyes: You're in a better situation than we are. After all, friend Throat, at least the food does pass through you. All we get to do is look.

Ears: And all we get to do is listen.

Feet: We are also unhappy. We only walk to the food, but never get anything to eat.

Hands: Let's go and talk to God.

Nose: We will tell him that Stomach is greedy and makes a poor president.

Narrator: Stomach heard them complaining about him.

Stomach: I do the best I can. They just don't appreciate me.

All (except Stomach): Yes! Yes! Let's go.

Narrator: The body parts all agreed. They went as a delegation to see God.

All (except Stomach): We are against President Stomach.

Narrator: God asked them if they knew what they were talking about.

God: Do you know what you are talking about?

Nose: Yes, of course we know what we are talking about. We do not want Stomach for president.

Eyes: Look at him over there. He looks like an overstuffed lady's handbag.

God: Say nothing that you will be sorry for in the future. Here's what you must do. Go home and decide who it is you want for president instead of Stomach. But you must not eat anything—not one morsel—lest President Stomach keeps using your work. I will see you back here in two days.

Narrator: They were happy that God was going to help them. On their way home, whom did they see but President Stomach.

Stomach: Hello, my dear subjects. How are you today?

Eyes: Don't look at him.

Ears: Don't listen to him.

Mouth: Stomach thinks he is the only one created by God. We'll show him we don't need him.

Throat: I'm glad God said we shouldn't feed him.

All (except Stomach): (*chanting*) No! No! Down with President Stomach!

Stomach: You'll be sorry, all of you. Don't say I didn't warn you.

Narrator: On the morning of the third day, the opposition had not eaten for two long days. Each part of the body was mighty hungry. They asked Left Eye to be president, but Left Eye said:

Eyes: I cannot see very well today; I cannot be president.

Narrator: Then they asked Left Ear.

Ears: I cannot hear very well today; I cannot be president.

Narrator: Then they asked Left Foot.

Feet: Sorry, I cannot be president. I can hardly stand up today.

Mouth: I couldn't chew anything even if there was something to chew. I cannot be president.

Nose: I haven't smelled anything for at least a day; I cannot be president.

Hands: It is hard for me to hold, cut, or grab. I must decline any suggestion that I be president.

Narrator: At last, they decided they wanted Stomach to be their leader. Now they could see that Stomach had been fair dividing the food equally among them.

Stomach: I tried to tell them, but they just didn't want to listen.

Narrator: They returned to God and explained that they had reconsidered.

Feet: Lord, we have decided. We want Stomach to be our leader.

Mouth: Yes, we would like him for our king.

God: Hands, cook dinner and feed it to the Stomach. He shall be your king.

Hands: I can do that!

Narrator: Hands made supper and the body ate it. A short time later, everyone was feeling better.

Eyes: I can see again.

Ears: I can hear again.

Nose: I can smell again.

Feet: I can walk again.

Throat: I feel better.

Mouth: I feel better.

Mouth: Let us sing to our new leader.

All (except Stomach): Long live King Stomach! Long live King Stomach!

Stomach: (*smiles and pats his stomach*) I knew they'd appreciate me after all. Thank you, my dear subjects. And now, let's have some dessert!

BOOKLIST: BOOKS TO USE FOR CREATIVE DRAMA

Another booklist with excellent titles to consider for creative drama is "Picture Books to Use with Puppets" on page 68.

Aylesworth, Jim. Aunt Pitty Patty's Piggy. *Illus. by Barbara McClintock. Scholastic, 1999.* In this New England version of "The Old Woman and Her Pig," Aunt Pitty Patty's niece enlists everyone and everything she meets to make the stubborn new piggy enter the gate. (PreK–Gr. 1)

Baker, Keith. *LMNO Peas.* Illus. by the author. *Beach Lane, 2010.* In a rhyming jaunt through the alphabet, personified peas demonstrate their jobs and hobbies. Children can become the pea-ple, pantomiming each profession as you read the story. (PreK–Gr. 2)

Beaumont, Karen. *Move Over, Rover!* Illus. by Jane Dyer. *Harcourt, 2006.* When the rain begins, all the other animals want to crowd into Rover's doghouse. (PreK–Gr. 1)

Billingsley, Franny. *Big Bad Bunny.* Illus. by G. Brian Karas. *Atheneum, 2008.* Big Bad Bunny is on a rampage while Mama Mouse's Baby Boo-Boo is missing. Listeners will have fun emoting the repeated refrain. (PreK–Gr. 1)

Brown, Marcia. *Once a Mouse . . . A Fable Cut in Wood.* Illus. by the author. *Atheneum, 1961.* In a story based on an ancient fable from India, a hermit rescues a mouse and transforms it into a cat, a dog, and a tiger. Children can pantomime the transformations. (PreK–Gr. 3)

Bruel, Nick. *Bad Kitty.* Illus. by the author. *Roaring Brook, 2005.* Confronted with an alphabet of dreadful food, a good kitty turns bad. Act out each of the four alphabets that make up the book. The companion book, *Poor Puppy* (Roaring Brook, 2007), is also bouncy for acting out. (PreK–Gr. 2)

Daugherty, James. *Andy and the Lion.* Illus. by the author. *Viking, 1938.* Andy helps a lion remove the thorn embedded in its paw. Try pantomiming in pairs. (PreK–Gr. 3)

Feldman, Eve. *Billy & Milly, Short & Silly.* Illus. by Tuesday Mourning. *Putnam, 2009.* Fourteen little stories told in pictures and four rhyming words. Working in pairs, children can add dialogue as they act out each story for the rest of the group. (PreK–Gr. 2)

Fleming, Denise. *The Cow Who Clucked.* Illus. by the author. *Henry Holt, 2006.* Cow has lost her moo and sets off to find it. Have children act out her interactions with the barnyard creatures she encounters. (PreK–Gr. 1)

Florian, Douglas. *I Love My Hat.* Illus. by the author. *Two Lions, 2014.* Farmer Brown invites clothes-loving animals to hop aboard his tractor as he drives to town. Make up the tune for the rhyming refrain each animal sings, and act this out, setting up chairs to represent the farmer's tractor. (PreK–Gr. 1)

Frazee, Marla. *Walk On! A Guide for Babies of All Ages.* Illus. by the author. *Harcourt, 2006.* A toddler learns to walk. Children can approximate his trials. (PreK–Gr. 2)

Henkes, Kevin. *Old Bear.* Illus. by the author. *Greenwillow, 2008.* Old Bear dreams of the seasons. Performers can pantomime his dreams as you read. (PreK–Gr. 1)

Hughes, Shirley. *Alfie Gets in First.* Illus. by the author. *Red Fox, 2009, c1981.* Alfie accidentally locks himself in the house, and the neighbors try to help. Listeners can act out the drama. (PreK–Gr. 1)

LaRochelle, David. *The End.* Illus. by Richard Egielski. Scholastic/Arthur A. Levine, *2007.* This lively story of a knight falling in love with a clever princess starts at the end and is told backward. Listeners can add sound effects for each character. (PreK–Gr. 3)

Lionni, Leo. *Frederick.* Illus. by the author. Pantheon, *1967.* A mouse teaches his friends the worth of words when they scorn him for not preparing for winter. Kids can act out the story, approximating the dialogue. (PreK–Gr. 2)

Litwin, Eric. *Pete the Cat: I Love My White Shoes.* Illus. by James Dean. HarperCollins, *2010.* Does Pete the Cat cry when he soils his new sneakers? "Goodness, no!" He keeps on singing. Your kids will warm to this interactive story, with a refrain that will become part of their lingo. (PreK–Gr. 1)

Lum, Kate. *What! Cried Granny: An Almost Bedtime Story.* Illus. by Adrian Johnson. *Dial, 1999.* Patrick is having his first sleepover at Granny's, but there's no bed, pillow, blanket, or teddy. Children can act out how Granny creates each of these things. (PreK–Gr. 1)

Mack, Jeff. *Good News, Bad News.* Illus. by the author. Chronicle, *2012.* On a picnic, Rabbit is the optimist, Mouse is the pessimist. Have kids assume the personas of the two friends and invent further dialogue. (PreK–Gr. 2)

Martin, Bill Jr. *Baby Bear, Baby Bear, What Do You See?* Illus. by Eric Carle. Henry Holt, *2007.* With a variety of action verbs, this rousing call-and-response animal book is great for children to act out and join in on the refrain. (PreK–Gr. 1)

McCarthy, Meghan. *Steal Back the Mona Lisa.* Illus. by the author. Harcourt, *2006.* Young Jack sets out to find the culprits who stole the famous painting. If you condense the narrative, kids can pantomime Jack's preparations to capture the crooks. (PreK–Gr. 2)

McCloskey, Robert. *Blueberries for Sal.* Illus. by the author. Viking, *1948.* A little girl and a bear cub lose their respective mothers while picking blueberries. Children can be Sal, the cub, or the mommies. (PreK–Gr. 1)

McClure, Nikki. *How to Be a Cat.* Illus. by the author. Abrams, *2013.* Visually sumptuous black paper cutouts of two cats are accompanied by a single action verb on each page. Read each word aloud and watch your listeners transform themselves into kitties. (PreK–Gr. 2)

Murphy, Jill. *Peace at Last.* Illus. by the author. Dial, *1980.* Mr. Bear can't get any sleep. Kids can imitate sounds that keep him awake and act out the ways he tries to get some shuteye. (PreK–Gr. 2)

O'Malley, Kevin. *Straight to the Pole.* Illus. by the author. Walker, *2003.* A solitary child trudges through a snowstorm on his way to the bus stop. Children can pantomime his movements and act out the story. (PreK–Gr. 2)

Pinkney, Jerry. *Aesop's Fables.* *Illus. by the author. Chronicle, 2000.* This handsome collection is filled with tales perfect for small group performance. (Gr. 2–8)

Pinkney, Jerry. *The Little Red Hen.* *Illus. by the author. Dial, 2006.* Hen's neighbors—a dog, a rat, a goat, and a pig—decline to help her make bread, so she does it herself. A natural for acting out in sequence. (PreK–Gr. 1)

Rathmann, Peggy. *Good Night, Gorilla.* *Illus. by the author. Putnam, 1994.* After stealing the zookeeper's keys, Gorilla lets the other animals out of their cages. Create a line of animals soundlessly following the zookeeper. (PreK–Gr. 1)

Salley, Coleen. *Epossumondas.* *Illus. by Janet Stevens. Harcourt, 2002.* Epossumondas the possum can't seem to follow his mother's directions. There are lots of chantable refrains and animal encounters in this noodlehead story. (PreK–Gr. 2)

Savage, Stephen. *Where's Walrus?* *Illus. by the author. Scholastic, 2011.* In a zany wordless adventure, a walrus escapes from his pool at the city zoo and hides in plain sight from the zookeeper. Your group can pantomime the walrus's many disguises. (PreK–Gr. 1)

Schubert, Leda. *Monsieur Marceau.* *Illus. by Gérard DuBois. Roaring Brook, 2012.* Meet the "superstar of silence, the maestro of mime" in this picture-book biography, which introduces childen to the art of pantomime. (Gr. 2–5)

Seeger, Laura Vaccaro. *Dog and Bear: Two Friends, Three Stories.* *Illus. by the author. Roaring Brook, 2007.* Three mini adventures of a little brown dachshund and a stuffed teddy bear. Have pairs of kids act out each story. (PreK–Gr. 1)

Shea, Bob. *Dinosaur vs. Bedtime.* *Illus. by the author. Hyperion, 2008.* A fierce little red Dinosaur wins every challenge except bedtime. Perfect for pantomime, with actors coming up new "Dinosaur vs." situations to act out. (PreK–Gr. 1)

Shields, Carol Diggery. *Wombat Walkabout.* *Illus. by Sophie Blackall. Dutton, 2009.* "Early one morning when the sun came out, / Six wooly wombats went walkabout." A counting-down rhyme, fun to act out in a line. (PreK–Gr. 1)

Sierra, Judy. *The Sleepy Little Alphabet: A Bedtime Story from Alphabet Town.* *Illus. by Melissa Sweet. Knopf, 2009.* It's "sleepytime in Alphabet Town," but the letters are too busy to go to bed. Read the story a second time, without showing the pictures, and ask your group to recite as many of the words as they can from memory. Then have them stand up and act out the action of the story as you read it yet again. (PreK–Gr. 1)

Smee, Nicola. *Clip-Clop.* *Illus. by the author. Sterling, 2006.* "Who wants a ride?" asks Mr. Horse, and onto his back jump a cat, a dog, a pig, and a goose. Go for a pretend ride on Mr. Horse. (PreK)

Stevens, April. ***Waking Up Wendell.*** *Illus. by Tad Hills. Schwartz & Wade, 2007.* The song of a little yellow bird awakens a pig on Fish Street, leading to other noises that rouse all the other porcine sleepers on the block. Listeners will join in on the sound effects and can then act out the whole cause-and-effect tale. (PreK–Gr. 1)

Thomas, Jan. ***Is Everyone Ready for Fun?*** *Illus. by the author. Beach Lane, 2011.* Three brown cows announce it is time to JUMP! on Chicken's sofa. The first time you act out this wacky story, you play the stressed-out chicken while children are the cows. Then they can act out the story themselves in small groups. (PreK–Gr. 1)

Turkle, Brinton. ***Deep in the Forest.*** *Illus. by the author. Dutton, 1976.* In a wordless turnabout of "The Three Bears," a bear cub makes a mess in a pioneer family's cabin. Children can pantomime the story or add their own dialogue. (PreK–Gr. 2)

Vere, Ed. ***Banana!*** *Illus. by the author. Henry Holt, 2010.* One monkey has a banana; another monkey wants it. Have children act out the many emotions depicted in this expressive, nearly wordless book. (PreK–Gr. 1)

Willems, Mo. ***Don't Let the Pigeon Drive the Bus.*** *Illus. by the author. Hyperion, 2003.* The bus driver makes us promise not to let Pigeon drive the bus, but Pigeon is so persistent! In pairs, one child can play the pigeon, trying to persuade the other to let him do something unwise. (PreK–Gr. 3)

Willems, Mo. ***That Is Not a Good Idea.*** *Illus. by the author. Balzer + Bray, 2013.* A hungry fox asks a sweet lady goose to go for a stroll into the deep, dark woods. At each turn, four yellow baby geese, observing the action between the devious fox and the seemingly clueless goose, announce, "That is REALLY NOT a good idea!" Ridiculously fun to act out. (PreK–Gr. 2)

Williams, Linda. ***The Little Old Lady Who Was Not Afraid of Anything.*** *Illus. by Megan Lloyd. HarperCollins, 1986.* Heading home, an old lady encounters two clomping shoes, a wiggling pair of pants, a shaking shirt, two clapping gloves, a nodding hat, and one scary pumpkin head. Kids can act this out with props and old clothes. (PreK–Gr. 2)

Williams, Sue. ***I Went Walking.*** *Illus. by Julie Vivas. Harcourt, 1989.* "What did you see?" we ask a little boy who goes walking. A great call-and-response story, which you can follow with a walk around the room as kids act out each animal the boy sees. (PreK–Gr. 1)

BOOKLIST: PROFESSIONAL BOOKS FOR CREATIVE DRAMA

Bany-Winters, Lisa. ***On Stage: Theater Games and Activities for Kids.*** *Second edition. Chicago Review Press, 2012.* A kid-centric gold mine of more than 125 warm-up, theater, improv, and creative drama games, plus a handful of monologues and scripts.

Barchers, Suzanne I. *Fifty Fabulous Fables: Beginning Readers Theatre.* Libraries Unlimited, 1997. Fifty easy-to-read scripts retelling mostly well-known Aesop fables, each including a summary, presentation suggestions, props, and other tips on how to use them. Barchers has written so many indispensable books of scripts, including *Multicultural Folktales: Readers Theatre for Elementary Students* (2000) and *From Atalanta to Zeus: Readers Theatre from Greek Mythology* (2001).

Bauer, Caroline Feller. *Presenting Reader's Theater: Plays and Poems to Read Aloud. Illus. by Lynn Gates Bredeson. H. W. Wilson, 1987.* The more than fifty scripts based on children's literature and folklore, most of which are easy to read, got many of us started with reader's theater.

DeMille, Richard. *Put Your Mother on the Ceiling: Children's Imagination Games. Gestault Journal Press, 1997, c1955.* Ways to stimulate creativity through "imagination games."

Elkind, Samuel. *Improvisation, Theater Games and Scene Handbook. Players Press, 2003, c1976.* Theater games and scenes to perform, from the Players Press Performance Workshop series.

Fredericks, Anthony D. *American Folklore, Legends, and Tall Tales for Readers Theatre. Libraries Unlimited, 2008.* Twenty-three lively scripts, plus an excellent first chapter of tips and information on the advantages of doing RT with students. Fredericks has written many similar compilations, including: *African Legends, Myths, and Folktales for Readers Theatre* (2008), *Fairy Tales Readers Theatre* (2009), *Frantic Frogs and Other Frankly Fractured Folktales for Readers Theatre* (1993), *Nonfiction Readers Theatre for Beginning Readers* (2007), and *Songs and Rhymes Readers Theatre for Beginning Readers* (2007).

Lee, Allison. *A Handbook of Creative Dance and Drama: Ideas for Teachers. Heinemann, 1992.* Loads of drama exercises to try with elementary-school children.

MacDonald, Margaret Read. *The Skit Book: 101 Skits from Kids. Illus. by Marie-Louise Scull. August House, 2006, c1990.* Funny, short skits, created by children and submitted by camps, schools, and youth groups, which are ideal for introducing children to creative dramatics.

Shepard, Aaron. *Stories on Stage: Children's Plays for Readers Theater with 15 Play Scripts from 15 Authors. Shepard Publications, 2005.* Plays from the King of Readers' Theater. You'll also want his *Folktales on Stage: Children's Plays for Readers Theater* (2003) and of course *Readers on Stage: Resources for Readers Theater, with Tips, Worksheets, and Reader's Theatre Play Scripts, or How to Do Simple Children's Plays That Build Reading Fluency and Love of Literature* (2004), all worthy and available for next to nothing, price-wise, on Amazon.

Sierra, Judy, and Robert Kaminski. *Multicultural Folktales: Stories to Tell Young Children. Oryx, 1991.* These twenty-five stories from around the world, with suggestions for using felt-board figures and puppets, can be adapted for creative drama and reader's theater.

Sloyer, Shirlee. *From the Page to the Stage: The Complete Educator's Guide to Readers' Theatre.* *Libraries Unlimited, 2003.* This one has it all: benefits of reader's theater, how to select and adapt material, prep and performance, photos and dialogue of kids in action, and a plethora of scripts.

Spolin, Viola. *Theater Games for the Classroom: A Teacher's Handbook.* *Northwestern University Press, 1986.* More than 130 acting games for students in elementary through high school. Max Schaefer has produced *Viola Spolin's Theater Games for the Classroom: A Multimedia Teacher's Guide* (2003), a CD-ROM based on the book, with his fifth-grade students participating in more than fifty games and exercises.

Swados, Elizabeth. *At Play: Teaching Teenagers Theater.* *Faber and Faber, 2006.* In her autobiographical look at theater, playwright and director Swados describes more than four hundred innovative exercises to use with teens, many of which can be adapted for use with middle graders.

West, Sherrie, and Amy Cox. *Literacy Play: Over 300 Dramatic Play Activities That Teach Pre-reading Skills.* *Illus. by Kathy Dobbs. Gryphon House, 2004.* Simple-to-initiate drama activities for young children accompanied by suggestions for art projects.

WEBSITES: CREATIVE DRAMA

Look online to find ideas, techniques, lesson plans, scripts, and guidelines for writing, acting, and staging. Try these for starters.

Aaron Shepard *www.aaronshep.com/rt*
Check out author Aaron Shepard's amazing website where you can download one of his many fine reader's theater scripts, or buy one of his books.

ChildDrama *www.childdrama.com*
Playwright and drama teacher Matt Buchanan offers scripts of his original plays, lesson plans, detailed curriculum outlines, and a bibliography of professional books.

Creative Drama and Theatre Education Resource Site *www.creativedrama.com*
Ideas for reader's theater, classroom activities, and theater games, plus an extensive list of helpful books.

Drama Resource *dramaresource.com*
Splendid site by British drama consultant David Farmer, who has assembled games, strategies, lessons, and resources.

Kid Activities *www.kidactivities.net/category/Literacy-Drama-and-Drama-Games.aspx*
This terrific, idea-filled site—put together by school-age care consultant Barb Shelby—includes an extensive section on dramatic play.

chapter 4

Storytime Fillers

*Fingerplays, Tongue Twisters, Riddles, Jokes,
Rhymes, and Other Nonsense*

A little nonsense now and then / Is relished by the wisest men. —ANONYMOUS

The Chicken in the Library

Retold by Caroline Feller Bauer and Judy Freeman

A chicken walked into the library. She hopped up to the librarian at the circulation desk, flapped her wings, and said, "Bawk, bawk!"

"What, you want a book? All right, I'll get you a book," the librarian said. She handed the chicken a book. The chicken slid the book under her wing and walked out the door.

A couple of minutes later, the chicken walked back into the library, dropped the book on the circulation desk, and said, "Bawk, bawk! Bawk, bawk!"

The librarian said, "What, you want more books? Okay, I'll give you more books." The librarian handed the chicken two books. The chicken slid the books under her wing and walked out the door.

A couple of minutes later, the chicken walked back into the library, dropped the books on the circulation desk and said, "Bawk, bawk! Bawk, bawk! Bawk, bawk!"

The librarian said, "What, you want still more books? No problem, I'll give you more books." The librarian handed the chicken three books—really good ones, too. The chicken slid the books under her wing and walked out the door.

By now, the librarian was curious. "What is going on with this chicken and all those books?" she said. "I'm going to follow her and find out."

She followed the chicken out the door and down to the pond nearby. The chicken walked over to the edge of the pond. In the middle of the pond there was a great big lily pad, and sitting on the lily pad was a great big bullfrog. As the librarian watched, the chicken held up the books, one at a time, and the bullfrog said, "Red-it, red-it, red-it!"

Silly, isn't it? But it may be a perfect bit of transitional material between stories or poems in your story hour. We're always amazed at how successful riddles and jokes are with children. Even adults laugh (as they groan). You will find that the riddles and jokes in children's books are often recycled from your own childhood. They are examples of folklore and wordplay, passed on from generation to generation. In this chapter, we'll explore some engaging forms of folk literature, including tongue twisters, riddles, jokes, underground rhymes, chants, and games children play.

The word *folklore* gives some people the impression that to collect "lore," one has to know peasants or grandmothers. Emphasize that everyone is part of a group, and one need not take a trip to some faraway place, for folklore is all around us. Start collecting for yourself, from your family and friends.

Folk groups are made up of people who have something in common; all of us are members of more than one folk group at any given time. For example, a school is one large folk group. Within a school, there are smaller groups— the sophomore class, the track team, the science club, among others—each of which has its own customs and sayings. Proverbs, riddles, jokes, and tongue twisters are folk sayings; games, crafts, food preparation, and graffiti are folk customs, with groups of their own.

Nursery rhymes—along with jump-rope jingles, nonsense verse, and autograph rhymes—are a widespread oral folklore tradition still alive in our society. Begin your own collection of folklore with older children by reciting a few folk sayings, rhymes, or riddles in a story hour and ask your listeners if these remind them of other sayings that they know. Encourage them to submit some riddles or sayings, writing them down exactly as they've heard them. The person who gives you the material is the "informant" whose name, address, age, background, and education should be included in your compilation. You can also simply put a collection box in the library or classroom. In some ways, this is the best method. You won't necessarily get signed responses, but what you get will be completely authentic. (Sometimes these are downright eyebrow raisers—such as children's underground rhymes that they recite when they think the grown-ups aren't looking.)

Don't be surprised if some examples you receive or read in the following sections seem familiar. It just proves how folklore is transmitted across large geographic areas and generations.

Mother Goose

This is where it all begins—with rhymes repeated day after day until we know them by heart. Most children get their introduction to poetry, rhythm, and rhyme from Mother Goose poems, which their parents recite as they bounce their babies on their knees. Sadly, too many children come to school without any foundation of nursery rhymes, and their teachers and librarians work to fill this hole, reading aloud and reciting selections to their preschool and primary students. We all need to know our nursery rhymes—modern culture alludes to them regularly in movies, books, songs, and the media. And then, sometimes, we fool around with and even subvert these little verses into parodies.

We all need to know the Goose, though not everyone appreciates her. Some folks deem her violent, inappropriate, old fashioned, and politically incorrect, and they are appalled by characters like that dreadful Old Woman Who Lived in a Shoe, "who whipped (her children) soundly and sent them to bed!"

Mother Goose is a good example of how folklore travels across the ages. Mother Goose rhymes have remained with us for a reason: children continue to respond to the rhythm and nonsense of the verses, burnished through the years. What's more, modern culture routinely refers to the Goose's rhymes in movies, books, songs, and electronic media. If you don't fancy a rhyme, simply pick another one or turn the page.

Fortunately, there are many resources to get us (and our children) up to speed with the Goose. We can make it a point to read aloud and recite nursery rhymes in school and at the library. Judy says, "If you don't know your nursery rhymes and fairy tales, you'll never to able to complete *The New York Times* crossword puzzle!"

School librarian Rachel Hinds from Pearland, Texas, wrote on LM_NET, the school librarian's listserv, "I was doing a lesson on the nursery rhyme 'Simple Simon' with my kindergarten classes this week. While trying to help them understand what a 'pieman' is, I asked, 'What do we call a person who bakes pies, cakes, and cookies?' A little voice enthusiastically shouted out 'Grandma!' The teacher and I both roared with laughter. I love kindergarten classes!"

Although you probably remember a number of Mother Goose rhymes, you will still want to have a book on hand, not only to refresh your memory but also to show children how various artists interpret them. There are many beautiful editions currently in print. Some books contain collections of rhymes (e.g., *Tomie dePaola's Mother Goose*), while in others a single rhyme is profusely illustrated (e.g., Gennady Spirin's version of *A Apple Pie*). There is, in addition, a wide choice in style of illustration ranging from the traditional (the handsome watercolors in *Sylvia Long's Mother Goose*) to the ultramodern (the urban color photographs of Nina Crews in *The Neighborhood Mother Goose*). It is only a matter of exploring various editions to discover which version will please you and your charges. Once a child hears the music of Mother Goose, he or she will be open to hearing other poetry too. Nonsense verse is popular with small children, who love to repeat the sounds.

Mother Goose is still with us because children respond to the rhythmic and sensible nonsense of the verses, burnished from years of telling. As Iona Opie says in her introduction to *My Very First Mother Goose*,

> Mother Goose will show newcomers to this world how astonishing, beautiful, capricious, dancy, eccentric, funny, goluptious, haphazard, intertwingled, joyous, kindly, living, melodious, naughty, outrageous, pomsidillious, querimonious, romantic, silly, tremendous, unexpected, vertiginous, wonderful, exciting, yo-heave-ho-ish, and zany it is. And when we come to be grandmothers, it is just as well to be reminded of these twenty-six attributes.

Fingerplays and Action Rhymes

Mother Goose and other nursery rhymes are often recited with pat-a-cake and other hand motions, many invented by parents on the spot, ending with a tickle or a squeeze. There are endless numbers of fingerplays, action rhymes, and counting rhymes that you can use in your programming. The activities are primarily meant to be fun, but they also help children with articulation in speech and reading readiness skills, plus they give children a chance to stretch a bit between stories. In any case, it will take only a minute or so to learn a couple for your lapsit, preschool, or primary-grade story-hour sessions. Repeat each fingerplay several times so that the children can copy your actions. There's no need to stop and explain. Those who can't follow you the first or second time will catch on soon.

I'm a Little Bunny

I'm a little bunny (*make a fist*)

With a nose so funny. (*wiggle your thumb*)

This is my home in the ground.
    (*put your other hand on your hip*)

When a noise I hear, I perk up my ears,
    (*wiggle your fist; hold up your index and middle fingers for ears*)

And jump into the ground. (*put "bunny" into "hole" of your arm*)

Ten Little Penguins

Ten little penguins stand up straight (*raise both hands, fingers rigid*)

Ten little penguins make a gate (*interlace the fingers of both hands*)

Ten little penguins make a ring
    (*make one big circle with both thumbs and forefingers*)

Ten little penguins bow to the king
    (*extend fingers of both hands upwards and bend them downward*)

Ten little penguins waddle all day
    (*bend your wrists; wiggle your fingers downward*)

Ten little penguins run away (*put both hands behind your back*)

Five Little Ducks

Raffi's picture-book version, Five Little Ducks, *with sweet illustrations by Jose Aruego and Ariane Dewey, can be sung as well as read. If you don't know the tune, listen to Raffi's heartrending version on YouTube.com.*

Five little ducks went out one day
 (*hold up five fingers on your right hand*)

Over the hills and far away; (*your head is the hill they go over*)

Mother duck said, (*make the mother duck's bill with your left hand*)

"Quack, quack, quack, quack."

But only four little ducks came back. (*make one duck disappear*)

Repeat the rhyme with four little ducks, and then count down each time until the mother duck is all alone, ending with:

Sad mother duck went out one day
 (*hold up five fingers on your right hand*)

Over the hills and far away; (*your head is the hill they go over*)

Mother duck said, (*make the mother duck's bill with your left hand.*)

"Quack, quack, quack, quack." (*quack loudly*)

And all of the five little ducks came back!
 (*show all five fingers of your right hand*)

The Farm

Start the rhyme with closed fists facing toward you. Raise the thumb of one hand first and then raise each finger, ending with the opposite thumb. On the last line, put your hands under your arms and move your elbows up and down to create flapping wings.

One is a cat that says meow!

Two is a dog that says bow-wow!

Three is a crow that says caw-caw!

Four is a donkey that says hee-haw!

Five is a lamb that says baa-baa!

Six is a sheep that says maa-maa!

Seven is a chick that says chuck-chuck!

Eight is a hen that says cluck-cluck!

Nine is a cow that says moo-moo!

Ten is a rooster crowing COCK-A-DOODLE DOO!

My Garden

This is my garden; (*extend one hand forward, palm up*)

I'll rake it with care, (*make raking motion on your palm with three
    fingers of your other hand*)

And then some flower seeds (*hold up seeds*)

I'll plant right there. (*make a planting motion with two fingers*)

The sun will shine (*make a circle with your hands*)

And the rain will fall, (*let your fingers flutter down to your lap*)

And my garden will blossom
    (*cup your hands together, and extend the upward slowly*)

And grow straight and tall. (*hold your arms above your head*)

Grandma and Grandpa

*Say Grandma's part in a high voice and Grandpa's in a low, gruff one. Suit your
actions to the words.*

Here are Grandma's glasses;

Here is Grandma's hat.

Grandma claps her hands like this,

And folds them in her lap.

Here are Grandpa's glasses;

Here is Grandpa's hat.

This is the way he folds his arms

And takes a little nap.

The Lady

Here are the lady's knives and forks.
   (*with your palms up, intertwine your fingers*)

Here is the lady's table. (*turn your hands over to make a table*)

Here is the lady's looking glass,
   (*cup your hands and hold them up to your face*)

And here is the baby's cradle. (*clasp hands and rock arm*)

Touch Your Nose

Suit your actions to the words.

Touch your nose,

Touch your chin,

That's the way this game begins.

Touch your eyes,

Touch your knees,

Now pretend you're going to sneeze.

Touch your hair,

Touch one ear,

Touch your two red lips right here.

Touch your elbows

Where they bend—

That's the way this touch game ends.

Japanese Rhyme

Point to the corresponding part of your face each time you say a word. The last line leads you back to the beginning. Do it slowly at first; once children learn the words, increase the speed each time.

Hana, hana, hana, kuchi (*nose, nose, nose, mouth*)

Kuchi, kuchi, kuchi, mimi (*mouth, mouth, mouth, ear*)

Mimi, mimi, mimi, me (*ear, ear, ear, eye*)

Me, me, me, hana (*eye, eye, eye, nose*)

Pronunciation:

hana: hah-nah

kuchi: kuh-CHEE

mimi: mee-mee

me: may

Draw a Little Circle in the Air
Suit your actions to the words.

Draw a little circle in the air, in the air,

Draw a little circle in the air.

Draw with all your might,

Keep it up all night.

Draw a little circle in the air.

Draw a bigger circle in the air, in the air,

Draw a bigger circle in the air.

Going 'round in the breeze,

Keep it going, if you please!

Draw a bigger circle in the air.

Draw a great big circle in the air, in the air,

Draw a great big circle in the air.

Draw it higher, draw it lower,

Draw it slower, slower, slower . . .

And now there's no more circle in the air!

BOOKLIST: NURSERY RHYMES AND FINGERPLAYS

Let's start with a look at some of the easiest poems for babies, toddlers, and up through first grade, though you can certainly feel free to use them with older children as well.

Ada, Alma Flor, and F. Isabel Campoy, eds. ¡*Muu, Moo! Rimas de Animales / Animal Nursery Rhymes. English versions by Rosalma Zubizarreta*. Illus. by Viví Escrivá. *HarperCollins/Rayo, 2010*. Sixteen nursery rhymes, in Spanish, accompanied by English translations that preserve the rhyming patterns. Find more in the companion book, *Pío Peep: Traditional Spanish Nursery Rhymes* (2003). (PreK–Gr. 1)

Brown, Marc. Hand Rhymes. *Illus. by the author. Dutton, 1985.* Fourteen finger-plays, with diagrams showing how to do them. *Playtime Rhymes: A Treasury for Families to Learn and Play Together* (Little, Brown, 2013) is also splendid. (PreK–Gr. 1)

Cole, Joanna, and Stephanie Calmenson. *The Eentsy, Weentsy Spider: Fingerplays and Action Rhymes.* *Illus. by Alan Tiegreen. Morrow, 1991.* Black-and-white cartoons illustrate the activities. (PreK–Gr. 1)

Crews, Nina, comp. *The Neighborhood Mother Goose.* *Photos by the author. Greenwillow, 2004.* Color photos show a multicultural cast of kids in Brooklyn acting out forty-one Mother Goose rhymes. (PreK–Gr. 1)

DePaola, Tomie, comp. *Tomie dePaola's Mother Goose.* *Illus. by Tomie dePaola. Putnam, 1985.* An essential collection. (PreK–Gr. 1)

Dominguez, Angela. *Maria Had a Little Llama / María tenía una llamita.* *Illus. by the author. Henry Holt, 2013.* In English and Spanish, this charming version is set in a mountain village in Peru. (PreK–Gr. 2)

Duffy, Chris, ed. *Nursery Rhyme Comics: 50 Timeless Rhymes from 50 Celebrated Cartoonists.* *Illus. by Patrick McDonnell et al. First Second, 2011.* Fifty well-known cartoonists each picked a favorite Mother Goose rhyme and illustrated it, graphic-novel style. (PreK–Gr. 8)

Engelbreit, Mary. *Mary Engelbreit's Mother Goose: One Hundred Best-Loved Verses.* *Illus. by the author. HarperCollins, 2005.* Old-fashioned illustrations depict a multiracial cast of well-clad children. (PreK–Gr. 1)

Foreman, Michael, comp. *Michael Foreman's Playtime Rhymes.* *Illus. by the author. Candlewick, 2002.* Seventy-four nursery rhymes, chants, fingerplays, and songs, illustrated with lovely watercolors. (PreK–Gr. 1)

Galdone, Paul. *Three Little Kittens.* *Illus. by the author. Clarion, 1986.* A charming, complete version of the nursery song. (PreK–Gr. 1)

Hale, Sarah Josepha Bell. *Mary Had a Little Lamb.* *Illus. by Tomie dePaola. Holiday House, 1984.* This has all of the verses to sing. (PreK–Gr. 1)

Hammill, Elizabeth, comp. *Over the Hills and Far Away: A Treasury of Nursery Rhymes.* *Illus. by more than seventy celebrated artists. Candlewick, 2015.* Breathtakingly illustrated collection of 150 rhymes, many familiar, but with others from around the globe. (PreK–Gr. 1)

Hillenbrand, Will. *Mother Goose Picture Puzzles. Illus. by the author. Marshall Cavendish, 2011.* Twenty mostly well-known nursery rhymes with rebus pictures in place of some of the nouns. (PreK–Gr. 1)

Long, Sylvia, ed. *Sylvia Long's Mother Goose. Illus. by Sylvia Long. Chronicle, 1999.* Version abounds with graceful, elegant watercolors. (PreK–Gr. 1)

Marshall, James, comp. *James Marshall's Mother Goose. Illus. by James Marshall. Farrar, 1979.* Thirty-four rhymes, accompanied by Marshall's goofy animal pictures. (PreK–Gr. 1)

Martin, Sarah Catherine. *The Comic Adventures of Old Mother Hubbard and Her Dog. Illus. by Tomie dePaola. Harcourt, 1981.* The nineteenth-century rhyme, with all the original verses. (PreK–Gr. 1)

Mathers, Petra. *The McElderry Book of Mother Goose: Revered and Rare Rhymes. McElderry, 2012.* Full-page watercolors illustrate fifty-seven rhymes—some familiar, others little known, and all full of charm. (PreK–Gr. 1)

Mavor, Sally. *Pocketful of Posies: A Treasury of Nursery Rhymes. Illus. by the author. Houghton Mifflin, 2010.* Sixty-four mostly familiar rhymes, illustrated by amazing "hand-sewn fabric relief collages." (PreK–Gr. 1)

Moses, Will. *Mary and Her Little Lamb: The True Story of the Nursery Rhyme. Illus. by the author. Philomel, 2011.* A somewhat fictionalized account of how this indelible American poem came to be. (PreK–Gr. 3)

Moses, Will, comp. *Will Moses Mother Goose. Illus. by Will Moses. Philomel, 2003.* Delicate folk-art paintings accompany seventy mostly familiar nursery rhymes. (PreK–Gr. 1)

Opie, Iona, comp. *My Very First Mother Goose. Illus. by Rosemary Wells. Candlewick, 1996.* An oversize collection of sixty-eight well-chosen verses, illustrated with Wells's personable entourage of bunnies, pigs, and cats. Other splendid collaborations between Opie and Wells include *Here Comes Mother Goose* (1999), *Mother Goose's Little Treasures* (2007), and *Tail Feathers from Mother Goose: The Opie Rhyme Book* (1988). (PreK–Gr. 1)

Prelutsky, Jack, comp. *Read-Aloud Rhymes for the Very Young. Illus. by Marc Brown. Knopf, 1986.* Lovely colored-pencil illustrations decorate a feast of more than two hundred brief poems by time-honored poets. (PreK–Gr. 1)

Sanderson, Ruth. *Mother Goose and Friends. Illus. by the author. Little, Brown, 2008.* More than five dozen richly illustrated, traditional nursery rhymes. (PreK–Gr. 1)

Scheffler, Alex. *Mother Goose's Storytime Nursery Rhymes. Illus. by the author. Scholastic, 2007.* One hundred rhymes told by Mother Goose to her goslings. (PreK–Gr. 1)

Spirin, Gennady. *A Apple Pie.* *Illus. by the author. Philomel, 2005.* English nursery rhymes, dating back to the seventeenth century, about children cutting and eating an apple pie. (A facsimile of Kate Greenaway's classic version, first published in 1886, is available online.) (PreK–Gr. 1)

Taback, Simms. *This Is the House That Jack Built.* *Illus. by the author. Putnam, 2002.* A colorfully illustrated version of the children's chant, first published in 1755. (PreK–Gr. 1)

Wright, Blanche Fisher. *The Real Mother Goose.* *Illus. by Blanche Fisher Wright. Scholastic, 1994, c1916.* A vintage collection of three hundred nursery rhymes, which can also be accessed online at bygosh.com/mothergoose/index.htm. (PreK–Gr. 1)

Yolen, Jane, ed. *Switching on the Moon: A Very First Book of Bedtime Poems.* *Illus. by G. Brian Karas. Candlewick, 2010.* Sixty sweet, simple bedtime poems, paired with gorgeous full-page paintings. Also beautiful is *Wee Rhymes: Baby's First Poetry Book*, illustrated by Jane Dyer (Simon & Schuster, 2013), with a collection of seventy-five new and classic rhymes. (PreK–Gr. 1)

Yolen, Jane, ed. *This Little Piggy: Lap Songs, Finger Plays, Clapping Games, and Pantomime Rhymes.* *Illus. by Will Hillenbrand. Musical arrangements by Adam Stemple. Candlewick, 2005.* Sixty essential little fingerplay ditties, acted out by pig characters, with an accompanying CD. (PreK–Gr. 1)

Yolen, Jane, and Andrew Fusek Peters, eds. *Here's a Little Poem: A Very First Book of Poetry.* *Illus. by Polly Dunbar. Candlewick, 2007.* A luscious anthology of sixty poems from the US, Great Britain, the Caribbean, and Australia. (PreK–Gr. 1)

BOOKLIST: PROFESSIONAL BOOKS FOR NURSERY RHYMES AND FINGERPLAYS

Diamant-Cohen, Betsy. *Mother Goose on the Loose: A Handbook and CD-ROM Kit with Scripts, Rhymes, Songs, Flannel-board Patterns, and Activities for Promoting Early Childhood Development.* *Neal-Schuman, 2006.* This practical resource includes ten teaching sessions and an audio CD. Also based on this book, but for Spanish-speaking children, is the companion book and CD *Early Literacy Planning in Español: Mother Goose on the Loose: Programs for Bilingual Learners* (2010).

Low, Elizabeth Cothen. *Big Book of Animal Rhymes, Fingerplays, and Songs.* *Libraries Unlimited, 2009.* More than 650 A to Z animal rhymes (some in Spanish with translations), plus musical scores.

Poulsson, Emilie. *Finger Plays for Nursery and Kindergarten.* *Illus. by L. J. Bridgman. Music by Cornelia C. Roeske. Dover, 1971.* This book was first published in 1893, and the fingerplays are still relevant.

Scott, Barbara A. *1,000 Fingerplays & Action Rhymes: A Sourcebook & DVD. Neal-Schuman, 2010.* In forty-two chapters arranged alphabetically by theme, find a magnificent roundup of poems, songs, and notes. The DVD shows Scott interacting with preschoolers.

Silberg, Jackie, and Pam Schiller. *The Complete Book of Rhymes, Songs, Poems, Finger-plays, and Chants. Illus. by Deborah C. Wright. Gryphon House, 2002.* Arranged alphabetically by title, the seven hundred selections in this anthology cover everything from nursery rhymes and folksongs to jump-rope rhymes.

WEBSITES FOR NURSERY RHYME AND FINGERPLAYS

When you Google *Mother Goose* or *nursery rhymes* or *fingerplays*, the number of hits is staggering. Below you'll find several sites we think are stellar.

Dr. Jean *www.drjean.org*
Includes links to five great YouTube videos of fingerplays performed by Dr. Jean Feldman, the well-known preschool workshop goddess.

Kids and Bibs *rhymes.kidsandbibs.com*
An alphabetically arranged list of hundreds of traditional nursery rhymes, with vintage illustrations.

Leading to Reading *www.rif.org/kids/leadingtoreading*
Reading Is Fundamental's excellent website features nursery rhymes, fingerplays, lullabies, songs, and stories—all of which you can listen to and/or watch as well as read.

Mother Goose: A Scholarly Exploration *eclipse.rutgers.edu/goose*
Professor Kay Vandergrift delves into Mother Goose, providing extensive commentary, resources, and bibliographies.

Natural Learning *www.naturallearning.com/fingerplays.html*
Dozens of cute fingerplays with motions.

Songs for Teaching *www.songsforteaching.com/fingerplays*
A solid collection of songs and fingerplays, with photographs of actions and musical excerpts.

YouTube *www.youtube.com*
Look up *fingerplays*, *Mother Goose*, or *nursery rhymes* and you'll find a rich assortment of videos appropriate for your programs.

Fooling Around with Mother Goose

Humpty Dumpty?

> Humpty Dumpty sat on a wall,
>
> Humpty Dumpty had a great fall;
>
> All the King's horses and all the King's men
>
> Had omelets.

Since nursery rhymes loom so large in our culture, they are natural targets for parody or humorous retellings. Have fun with them. After you recite the Goose's "Humpty Dumpty," for instance, read Bob Graham's irreverent *Dimity Dumpty: The Story of Humpty's Little Sister*. Humpty, a plump white egg, and his parents are trapeze artists—the Tumbling Dumpties—with a traveling circus. A bit of a budding juvenile delinquent, Humpty slips and falls from a factory wall while spraying graffiti ("Humpty Rules," he tags). Lucky for him, his shy little sister, Dimity, a good egg, saves the day.

Humpty Dumpty stars in two other nursery-rhyme-themed picture books: *Detective Blue* by Steve Metzger and Jeanie Franz Ransom's *What Really Happened to Humpty? (From the Files of a Hard-Boiled Detective)*. Kids of any age can write, draw, and ponder the circumstances of other nursery rhyme characters: What's up with that Jack-Be-Nimble guy? And why was Old Mother Hubbard's cupboard bare? Creating backstories like these will give children a foundation of Mother Goose that they'll eventually pass along to their own kids.

BOOKLIST: FOOLING AROUND WITH MOTHER GOOSE

Edwards, Pamela Duncan. *The Neat Line: Scribbling Through Mother Goose.* *Illus. by Diann Cain Blumenthal. HarperCollins, 2005.* After much practice, a scribble grows up to be a Neat Line, and heads off into the first page of a book of Mother Goose's Nursery Rhymes. (PreK–Gr. 2)

Graham, Bob. *Dimity Dumpty: The Story of Humpty's Little Sister.* *Illus. by the author. Candlewick, 2007.* Now the true story can be told about the role Humpty's little sister, Dimity, played after his big fall. (PreK–Gr. 2)

Grey, Mini. *The Adventures of the Dish and the Spoon.* *Illus. by the author. Knopf, 2006.* Dish and Spoon run away to New York City, where they become a famous vaudeville act. (K–Gr. 3)

Metzger, Steve. *Detective Blue.* *Illus. by Tedd Arnold. Orchard, 2011.* Detective Blue, aka Little Boy Blue, used to look after cows and sheep, but now he solves mysteries. (K–Gr. 3)

Palatini, Margie. *The Cheese. Illus. by Steve Johnson and Lou Fancher. HarperCollins, 2007.* Rat decides to eat that big hunk of cheddar standing alone in the farmer's dell. (PreK–Gr. 2)

Ransom, Jeanie Franz. *What Really Happened to Humpty? (From the Files of a Hard-Boiled Detective). Illus. by Stephen Axelsen. Charlesbridge, 2009.* Narrator and detective Joe Dumpty thinks his brother, Humpty, was pushed off that wall. (K–Gr. 3)

Stevens, Janet, and Susan Stevens Crummel. *And the Dish Ran Away with the Spoon. Illus. by Janet Stevens. Harcourt, 2001.* When Dish and Spoon don't return after their performance of "Hey diddle diddle," Cat, Dog, and Cow set off to find them. (K–Gr. 3)

Tongue Twisters

The tongue twister is a verbal game in which an individual pronounces a combination of alliterative words quickly and clearly. Speech teachers often use tongue twisters to help students articulate more clearly, but the verbal challenges really exist for the simple purpose of playing with words. As with any other folk material, most tongue twisters are passed along orally among children or adults. The most popular have been collected and can be found in books. A tongue twister contest can be great fun. Announce the contest in advance to give contestants time to practice. Tongue twisters also make a good ending for a program. The audience leaves the room practicing loudly and reciting as fast as they can such phrases, sentences, and rhymes as:

- The big black bug bled black blood.
- Double bubble gum gives double bubble trouble.
- Fruit float, fruit float, fruit float
- Good blood, bad blood
- Lame lambs limp.
- Lemon liniment
- Six, slick, slim saplings
- Shallow sallow Sally
- Shadows shade the sheltered swallows.
- The sixth sick sheik's sixth sheep is sick.
- Strange strategic statistics
- Three new blue beans in a new blown bladder

TONGUE-TWISTER POEMS

Now that you're warmed up, give these tongue-twister poems a go.

I Saw Esau

I saw Esau kissing Kate.

I saw Esau, he saw me,

And she saw I saw Esau.

A Fly

A fly and a flea flew up a flue.

Said the flea, "What shall we do?"

Said the fly, "Let us flee!"

Said the flea, "Let us fly!"

So they flew through a flaw in the flue.

A Canner

A canner, exceedingly canny,

One morning remarked to his granny,

"A canner can can

Anything that he can;

But a canner can't can a can, can he?"

Theophilus Twistle

On two thousand acres too tangled for tilling,

Where thousands of thorn trees grew thrifty and thrilling,

Theophilus Twistle, less thrifty than some,

Thrust three thousands thistles through the thick of his thumb.

She Was a Thistle-Sifter

If you saw the Academy Award–winning movie The King's Speech, *you might recall actor Geoffrey Rush reciting a version of this tongue twister.*

She was a thistle sifter

And she sifted thistles.

She had a sieveful of sifted thistles,

And a sieveful of unsifted thistles.

The sieveful of unsifted thistles

She had to sift because

She was a thistle sifter.

She Sells Seashells

This familiar tongue twister was composed in 1908 by Terry Sullivan in reference to Mary Anning (1799–1847), a self-taught fossil collector and paleontologist from Lyme Regis, England. Try using it to introduce fossils or remarkable women in science, or pair it with excellent picture-book biographies such as: Don Brown's Rare Treasure: Mary Anning and Her Remarkable Discoveries *(Houghton Mifflin, 1999) and Jeannine Atkins's* Mary Anning and the Sea Dragon *(Farrar, 1999).*

She sells seashells on the seashore.

The shells she sells are seashells, I'm sure.

For if she sells shells on the seashore,

Then I'm sure she sells seashore shells.

Did You Ever

Try this as a call-and-response: you say the first line, your group responds with the second. They can act it out as well, walking like each of the crazy-legged sailors and their wives.

Call: Did you ever, ever, ever in your long-legged life, see a long-legged sailor with a long-legged wife?

Response: No, I never, never, never in my long-legged life, saw a long-legged sailor with a long-legged wife.

Other possible verses: short-legged, bow-legged, pigeon-toed, bull-legged, hairy-legged. *You can also ask kids to think of more.*

Trickiest Tongue Twister

And, finally, before you're finished twisting your tongue, don't forget the shortest but trickiest tongue twister of all:

Toy boat

BOOKLIST: TONGUE TWISTERS

Agee, Jon. *Orangutan Tongs: Poems to Tangle Your Tongue.* *Illus. by the author. Disney-Hyperion, 2009.* Thirty-four comical tongue twister poems, "inspired by classic English language tongue twisters," illustrated with zany full-page watercolors. (Gr. 1–5)

Artell, Mike, and Joseph Rosenbloom. *Tongue Twisters.* *Illus. by Mike Artell and Dennis Kendrick. Sterling, 2005.* Hundreds of funny tongue twisters, arranged alphabetically. Also see Artell's Ten-Second Tongue Twisters (2006). (Gr. 2–6)

Bauer, Caroline Feller. *Read for the Fun of It.* *Illus. by Lynn Bredesen. H. W. Wilson, 1992.* The book includes "The Tongue Twister," a reader's theater script with a tongue twister. (Professional)

Chmielewski, Gary. *The Classroom Zone: Jokes, Riddles, Tongue Twisters & "Daffynitions."* *Illus. by Jim Caputo. Norwood House, 2008.* A collection of good groaners; *The Animal Zone, The Computer Zone, The Fright Zone,* and *Let's Eat in the Funny Zone* are some of the companion volumes. (Gr. 2–5)

Cleary, Brian P. *Six Sheep Sip Thick Shakes, and Other Tricky Tongue Twisters.* *Illus. by Steve Mack. Millbrook, 2011.* Twenty-four slippery, silly tongue twister sentences. (K–Gr. 5)

Cole, Joanna, and Stephanie Calmenson. *Six Sick Sheep: 101 Tongue Twisters.* *Morrow, 1993.* A good, kid-friendly collection. (Gr. 1–4)

Freeman, Judy. *Once Upon a Time: Using Storytelling, Creative Drama, and Reader's Theater with Children in Grades K–6.* *Libraries Unlimited, 2007.* Stories, chants, songs, annotated booklists, ideas, and more to share with children, including "The Tongue Twister Song." (Professional)

Just Joking: 300 Hilarious Jokes, Tricky Tongue Twisters, and Ridiculous Riddles. *Illus. with photos. National Geographic, 2012.* A rich assortment, illustrated on every page with glossy color photos. (Gr. 2–6)

Schwartz, Alvin, comp. *A Twister of Twists, A Tangler of Tongues.* *Illus. by Glen Rounds. Lippincott, 1972.* An excellent collection arranged by subject; now out of print but well worth finding. (Gr. 2–6)

WEBSITES: TONGUE TWISTERS

Complete A to Z Tongue Twister for Kids Online *www.tonguetwisters.in/complete-a-to-z-tongue-twister-for-kids.html*
Hundreds of them, in alphabetical order.

Thinks.com *thinks.com/words/tonguetwisters.htm*
A huge collection of "family-friendly" puzzles and games, including a very good section on tongue twisters.

Tongue Twisters for Kids *tonguetwistersforkids.com*
A goodly assortment.

Twister King *www.twisterking.com*
Thousands of tongue twisters, arranged alphabetically.

Riddles and Jokes

What's the difference between a riddle and a joke? The lines blur, but basically, a riddle is a brief, often ridiculous question that often starts with the word *what, why, when,* or *how.* "What do you call a fish with two knees?" The listener is expected to come up with a solution or say, "I don't know. What?" The riddler provides the answer, triumphantly exclaiming, "A two-knee fish!" A joke is a short story or anecdote that ends with a punch line that the listener is not expected to provide.

Because wordplay can be located in a number of sections in the library, kids may have trouble finding the books they crave. Some librarians select one number for jokes and riddles and re-catalog them in, say, 793.7 to make them more accessible. Most kids don't need to see the distinction between folklore-based riddles (398.6), recreational riddles (793.7), and literary riddles (808 and 818). They just want to laugh.

RIDDLES

Riddles are, by turns, ridiculous, insidious, incongruous, mind-bending, daffy, and ingenious. A *riddle* is a question with an unexpected answer that is supposed to demonstrate the brilliance of the questioner and test the wit and intelligence of the respondent. A *conundrum* is a riddle based on punning, a double entendre, or a play on words. Riddles are often used as tests of cleverness for characters in literature and folk stories, but they are generally considered fun word games—which can also be used to introduce readers, especially reluctant ones, to the world of books.

Children will already know some riddles you use in your story hours and impulsively shout out the answer. But they won't necessarily understand the wordplay. They laugh because they know it's supposed to be funny. It's okay—even better than okay—to explain the answer or ask one of the kids to do so. Riddles help us puzzle out the wonderful complexity and weirdness of the English language: "Two-knee fish. Get it? Two-knee—tuna fish!"

When you use a riddle, you might want to identify the country of origin or mention that a particular riddle was "recorded in the Tennessee mountains in 1911," for example. Nowadays, of course, riddles can travel the world instantaneously online.

Ask that each member of your group find a riddle and bring it in to share with everyone. There may be many duplicates, but you'll also have a lively session. Children participating in extemporaneous storytelling sometimes tend to wander away from the subject, but a riddle gives them a chance to "perform" briefly before a group.

Try some of the following riddles on kids, then ask them to tell you some of their favorites. If you can't figure out the answers, go ask a ten-year-old.

> What do you put on a pig with an itchy itchy rash?
>   Oinkment.

> Why couldn't the pony sing?
>   He was just a little horse.

> When is a turkey like a ghost?
>   When he's a-gobblin'.

> What is a bird's favorite cookie?
>   Chocolate chirp.

> What's a cat's favorite color?
>   Purrrple.

> How do bears jump out of airplanes?
>   With bearachutes.

> What is black and white and red all over?
>   A blushing zebra. (Or a hot fudge sundae with catsup on it.
>   (*New variations on an oldie.*)

> Why do sharks swim in saltwater?
>   Because pepper water makes them sneeze.

> What is a shark's favorite game?
>   Swallow the leader.

> What does a mother buffalo say to her child every morning when he
>   heads out for school?
>   Bi-son.

What do you call a deer with no eyes?
  No-eye deer.

What do you call a deer with no eyes and no legs?
  Still no-eye deer.

What is the Easter Bunny's favorite type of music?
  Hip-hop.

What would you call a country where all the cars are pink?
  A pink car nation.

What did the mama ghost say to the baby ghost when they got in the car?
  "Fasten your sheet belt."

What does a tuba call his father?
  Oom-pa-pa.

What gets wetter and wetter the more it dries?
  A towel.

Where was the Declaration of Independence signed?
  At the bottom.

What nut is like a sneeze?
  A cashew (*ca-shoo*).

Why do cucumbers laugh when you touch them?
  Because they're picklish.

Who is bigger, Mrs. Bigger or Mrs. Bigger's baby?
  The baby is just a little Bigger.

What do you get when you cross a monster with a genius?
  Frank Einstein.

What did the computer do at lunchtime?
  Had a byte.

What does a baby computer call his father?
  Data! *(Pronounced DAH-da instead of DAY-da.)*

What kinds of grades does a pirate get in school?
  High C's.

How much does it cost a pirate to get his ears pierced?
>A buccaneer.

What did one math book say to another?
>"I don't know about you, but I have a lot of problems!"

Why did the librarian slip and fall down?
>Because she was in the non-friction section.

Why was Cinderella bad at sports?
>Because she ran away from the ball.

And here's the oldest riddle we know, the one the Sphinx asked Oedipus:

What walks on four legs in the morning, two legs in the afternoon,
and three legs at night?

>Man—
>As a baby, he crawls on all fours.
>As a young man, he walks on two legs.
>As an old man, he walks with a cane.

JOKES

Of course, children's jokes differ from adult ones. While grown-ups' jokes are often political, ethnic, or off-color, children's jokes are usually quite simple and involve plays on words. Adults may consider these jokes silly and inconsequential. Perhaps they are, but a sophisticated sense of humor develops over time, and nonsense humor is a good place to begin. Think of these as a gateway to Shakespeare.

Jokes and riddles should be used sparingly in story hours. They are most effective for relaxing a tense group or lightening the mood after you have told a sad or touching story. Some of the stories you will tell are really extended jokes—as in the Turkish Hodja stories, for example. Some jokes are, in effect, short, two-person plays. Children like the repartee they have with a partner as they practice their delivery to make the joke funny for an audience. Talk with them about what makes a joke work—including timing, voices, and delivery. Here are some sample jokes for them to try in pairs.

SHORT JOKES

My sister and I together know everything in the whole world.

Really? What's the capital of France?

That's one my sister knows.

Get up, I heard a mouse squeak.

What do you want me to do? Oil it?

Watch out! There's a henweigh on your neck!

What's a henweigh?

Oh, about three pounds.

I can tell the score of this football game before it even begins.

Really? What is it?

Nothing to nothing.

My cat is lost.

Why don't you put an ad in the newspaper?

She can't read.

I'm glad that I'm not a bird.

Why?

I can't fly.

They used to call the Middle Ages the Dark Ages.

Why is that?

Because there were so many knights.

A friend was amazed at a dog's obvious attention at a drive-in theater's showing of *The Little Prince*.

"I'm amazed, too," said the owner. "He didn't enjoy the book at all."

Shopper: I'd like some alligator shoes, please.

Shoe Salesman: What size is your alligator?

What kind of dog is that?

A police dog.

He doesn't look like one.

Of course not. He's in the Secret Service.

Student: Do you punish people for things they didn't do?

Teacher: No, of course not!

Student: Good, because I didn't do my homework last night.

Shirley: I sure hope we get our keys out of our locked convertible soon.

Laverne: Me too. I've been trying to get the window open with this coat hanger for the past hour.

Shirley: Well, hurry up. It looks like it's going to rain and the top is down.

LONGER JOKES

Longer jokes are usually little stories with a punch line or a funny ending. Here are a few we've heard lately that you can pass along to your kids.

A man was standing on the street corner, stamping his left foot up and down, up and down. A policeman came over. "Are you all right, sir? Is there a problem? Why are you stamping your foot like that?"

The man said, "I'm stomping my foot to keep the elephants away."

The policeman said, "You know, sir, there aren't any elephants for five thousand miles around here."

"That's right," said the man. "It's working."

———

A man phones the town librarian at home in the middle of the night. The librarian picks up the phone. "Hello. Who is this? What is it?" she asks.

"When will the library open?" asks the man.

"Nine a.m. tomorrow," says librarian, quite annoyed.

"Not any sooner?" he asks.

"No," she says. "What's your hurry to get in, anyways?"

He says, "Who's talking about getting in? I want to get *out*!"

———

A duck walks into a Starbucks, steps up to the counter, and says to the barista, "Hey, man, you got any corn?"

The barista looks down, sees the duck, and says, "No, duck. This is a coffeehouse. We brew coffee and tea. We don't sell corn."

So the duck leaves. The next day he comes back and says, "Hey, man, you got any corn?"

The barista looks down, sees the duck again, and says, "I told you, duck. This is a coffeehouse. We don't have any corn. Get lost!"

So the duck leaves. The next day he comes back again and says, "Hey, man, you got any corn?"

The barista looks down, sees the duck again, and says, "I told you, duck. No corn. Get out!"

So the duck leaves. The next day he comes back again and says, "Hey, man, you got any corn?"

The barista says, "For the last time, we don't have corn! If you ever come back, I'm going to nail those little webbed feet of yours to the floor!"

So the duck leaves. The next day the duck pokes his head in the door and says, "Hey, man, you got any nails?"

The bartender says, "No, of course not. Why would a Starbucks have nails?"

The duck says, "Good. You got any corn?"

A man went to visit a friend and was amazed to find him on the porch, playing chess with his dog. He watched the game in astonishment for a while. "I can hardly believe my eyes!" he exclaimed. "That's the smartest dog I've ever seen."

"He's not so smart," the friend replied, "I've just beaten him three games out of five."

A boy was crossing a road one day when a frog called out to him and said, "If you kiss me, I'll turn into a beautiful princess." The boy picked up the frog and put it in his pocket.

The frog said, "Hey, if you kiss me and turn me back into a beautiful princess, I'll love you forever." The boy took the frog out of his pocket, smiled at it, and put it back in his pocket.

The frog yelled, "If you kiss me and turn me back into a princess, I'll clean your house, cook for you, and love you forever." The boy took the frog out, smiled at it, and put it back.

Finally the frog asked, "What is it with you? I've told you I'm a beautiful princess, that I'll cook and clean for you, and love you forever. Why won't you kiss me?"

The boy said, "Look, I'm a kid. I don't have time for girlfriends, but a talking frog is really cool."

KNOCK-KNOCK JOKES

A knock-knock joke is a wacky cross between a riddle and a joke, even if kids don't always quite get the punch line. There's nothing funnier than watching little ones make up knock-knocks: "Knock-knock." "Who's there?" "Piano." "Piano who?" "There's a piano on your head." Oh. The wordplay is beyond them, but they know the answer should be something absurd. Sharing knock-knocks with kids will help them become more experienced wordsmiths and, in the short run, get everyone laughing together.

Knock, knock.
   Who's there?
Cargo.
   Cargo who?
Cargo BEEP BEEP!

Knock, knock.
   Who's there?
Cow.
   Cow who?
Cows don't hoo. Owls hoo. Cows moo!

Knock, knock.
   Who's there?
Honeydew and cantaloupe.

Honeydew and cantaloupe who?
Honeydew you love me? We cantaloupe now.

Knock, knock.
    Who's there?
Panther.
    Panther who?
Panther nopanth, I'm going thwimming!

Knock, knock.
    Who's there?
Boo.
    Boo who?
Well, you don't have to cry about it.

Knock, knock.
    Who's there?
Impatient cow.
    Impatient cow—
MOOOO!
(*Also can be done as "interrupting cow."*)

Best Knock-Knock Joke Ever
You say, "Want to hear my favorite knock-knock joke?" and your friend will say, "Sure." Then you say, "Okay, you start." And your friend will say, "Knock, knock," and you say, "Who's there?" and your friend will stop short and say, "Hey! Wait a minute . . ." And you say, "Gotcha!"

BOOKLIST: RIDDLE AND JOKE COLLECTIONS

One can never have too many joke and riddle books. Collections for children are often recycled over the years, so the riddles that you asked your best friend in second grade may well be the same ones your students are asking each other today. To give old riddles a new look, publishers often package them thematically.

Adler, David A. *Calculator Riddles.* *Illus. by Cynthia Fisher. Holiday House, 1995.* Kids can grab their calculator to solve the math problem that goes with each of these riddles. The answer is spelled out when they turn their calculators upside down. (Gr. 2–4)

Anderson, Dee. *Reading Is Funny! Motivating Kids to Read with Riddles.* *American Library Association, 2009.* Ways to share riddles with children, plus a compendium of riddles about children's books, stories, and popular subjects. (Professional)

Blank, Eva, Alison Benjamin, Rosanne Green, and Ilana Weitzman. *Jokelopedia: The Biggest, Best, Silliest, Dumbest Joke Book Ever.* *Workman, 2006.* "What kind of books do skunks read? Best-smellers." You'll find 1,700 other jokes and funnies in this treasury. (Gr. 2–8)

Brewer, Paul. *You Must Be Joking! Lots of Cool Jokes.* *Illus. by the author. Cricket, 2003.* A meaty, truly funny collection. Graduate to *You Must Be Joking, Two! Even Cooler Jokes, Plus 11½ Tips for Laughing Yourself into Your Own Stand-Up Comedy Routine* (2007). (Gr. 3–6)

Chmielewski, Gary. *The Classroom Zone: Jokes, Riddles, Tongue Twisters & "Daffy-nitions."* *Illus. by Jim Caputo. Norwood House, 2008.* A varied assortment of good funnies. Continue with *The Computer Zone, The Ghost Zone, The Fright Zone, The History Zone,* and *Let's Eat in the Funny Zone.* (Gr. 2–5)

Cole, Joanna, and Stephanie Calmenson. *Why Did the Chicken Cross the Road? And Other Riddles Old and New.* *Illus. by Alan Tiegreen. Morrow, 1994.* Two hundred easy-to-understand riddles, arranged by theme. (Gr. 2–5)

Eisenberg, Lisa. *Creepy Riddles.* *Illus. by S. D. Schindler. Dial, 1998.* An easy-reader riddle book, with your basic cast of Halloween creatures spewing forth some grand groaners: "What do werewolves say when they meet? Howl do you do." (K–Gr. 4)

Eisenberg, Lisa. *Silly School Riddles.* *Illus. by Elwood H. Smith. Dial, 2008.* A cute collection of school-based wordplay, such as, "Which state is the best place to buy school supplies? Pencil-vania." (K–Gr. 4)

Hall, Katy, and Lisa Eisenberg. *Simms Taback's Great Big Book of Spacey Snakey Buggy Riddles.* *Illus. by Simms Taback. Viking, 2008.* Three easy-to-read books in one—*Buggy Riddles* (1986), *Snakey Riddles* (1990), and *Spacey Riddles* (1992), illustrated with cheerful illustrations. (K–Gr. 4)

Johnstone, Michael. *1,000 Crazy Jokes for Kids.* *Ballantine, 1987.* Patient: "Doctor, people always ignore me. What can I do about it?" Doctor: "Next." (Gr. 4–8)

Just Joking: 300 Hilarious Jokes, Tricky Tongue Twisters, and Ridiculous Riddles. Illus. with photos. National Geographic, 2012. A rich assortment, illustrated on every page with glossy color photos. (Gr. 2–6)

***Knock, Knock!** Illus. by Saxton Freymann and others. Dial, 2007.* Fourteen favorite knock-knock jokes, each illustrated by a well-known children's book artist. (PreK–Gr. 5)

Leedy, Loreen. *My Teacher Is a Dinosaur, and Other Prehistoric Poems, Jokes, Riddles, & Amazing Facts. Marshall Cavendish, 2010.* A little of everything; just right for a program on dinosaurs in fact and fiction. (Gr. 2–5)

Lewis, J. Patrick. *Scien-Trickery: Riddles in Science. Illus. by Frank Remkiewicz. Harcourt, 2004.* Sixteen snappy riddle poems that challenge readers to identify scientific subjects, from Albert Einstein to the number zero. Readers can practice math with the similarly formatted *Arithme-Tickle: An Even Number of Odd Riddle-Rhymes* (Harcourt, 2002). (Gr. 2–5)

Maestro, Marco, and Giulio Maestro. *What Do You Hear When the Cows Sing? And Other Silly Riddles. Illus. by Giulio Maestro. HarperCollins, 1996.* Twenty-one easy-to-read riddles. (K–Gr. 3)

O'Malley, Kevin. *Animal Crackers Fly the Coop. Illus. by the author. Walker, 2010.* Aspiring comedians Hen, Dog, Cat, and Cow run away from the farm and open a comedy club in a riddle-filled story based on the Grimm Brothers' "The Bremen-Town Musicians." (Gr. 1–4)

Rosenbloom, Joseph. *The Biggest Riddle Book in the World. Illus. by Joyce Behr. Sterling, 1976.* More than enough, but if not, continue with *Giggles, Gags & Groaners* (2005, c1987). (Gr. 3–6)

Rosenbloom, Joseph. *696 Silly School Jokes & Riddles. Illus. by Dennis Kendrick. Sterling, 1986.* Who knew there could be this much funny material about school? (Gr. 1–5)

Tang, Greg. *The Grapes of Math: Mind-Stretching Math Riddles. Illus. by Harry Briggs. Scholastic, 2001.* Rhyming riddles involving counting, addition, and looking for patterns. (Gr. 2–5)

Terban, Marvin. *Funny You Should Ask: How to Make Up Jokes and Riddles with Wordplay. Illus. by John O'Brien. Clarion, 1992.* Using homonyms, near homonyms, homographs, and idioms, riddle master Terban shows how wordplay works, step by step. (Gr. 3–6)

Terban, Marvin. *Too Hot to Hoot: Funny Palindrome Riddles. Illus. by Giulio Maestro. Clarion, 1985.* The answer to each riddle or question is a palindrome, a word spelled the same forward and backward. (Gr. 2–6)

Weitzman, Ilana, Eva Blank, and Roseanne Green. *Jokelopedia: The Biggest, Best, Silliest, Dumbest Joke Book Ever.* *Illus. by Mike Wright. Workman, 2000.* Dip into this compendium for jokes, riddles, practical jokes, and advice on becoming a comedian. (Gr. 2–8)

Why Did the Chicken Cross the Road? *Illus. by Jon Agee et al. Dial, 2006.* Fourteen well-known children's book illustrators created art for the title riddle. (Gr. 2–5)

WEBSITES: RIDDLES AND JOKES

A lot of joke websites are too off-color for children. Not to worry—all of these are fine.

Aha! Jokes *www.ahajokes.com/kids_jokes.html*
Bills itself as "The leader in clean jokes and funny pictures!" Posts a new kids' joke every day, along with its vast array of jokes sorted by themes.

Ducksters *ducksters.com/jokesforkids*
Scores of riddles, arranged by topic.

Jokes by Kids *jokesbykids.com*
Hundreds of jokes and riddles, all submitted by kids, arranged by subject.

My Fun Teacher *myfunteacher.com/jokes.htm*
An activity-based website, created by Las Vegas teacher Karen Powell, featuring five hundred riddles and sixty "plexers," which are picture puzzles of words and phrases.

NIEHS Kids' Pages *kids.niehs.nih.gov/games/riddles*
The National Institute of Environmental Health Sciences' site offers a healthy section of humorous wordplay in its "Riddles & Brainteasers" section.

Squigly's Playhouse *www.squiglysplayhouse.com/JokesAndRiddles*
Hundreds of jokes, riddles, and knock-knocks submitted by children.

Thinks.com Tongue Twisters *thinks.com/words/tonguetwisters.htm*
"Family-friendly" puzzles and games.

Underground Rhymes, Chants, and Nonsense Verse

Children have always recited subversive—sometimes gory—little rhymes and chants ("The worms crawl in, the worms crawl out, the worms play pinochle on my snout . . ."). They memorize their favorites and have a repertoire that they keep secret from their parents. That's pretty funny, because often parents chanted the same rhymes when they were young, which they tried to keep secret from *their* parents.

Tiny Tim

I had a little brother;
His name was Tiny Tim.
I put him in the bathtub
To teach him how to swim.

He drank up all the water,
He ate up all the soap;
He died last night
With a bubble in his throat.

In came the doctor,
In came the nurse,
In came the lady
With the alligator purse.

"Dead," said the doctor.
"Dead," said the nurse.
"Dead," said the lady
With the alligator purse.

Out went the doctor,
Out went the nurse;
Out went the lady
With the alligator purse.

Remember that one? This was the way children recited the rhyme in Philadelphia in the 1950s where Judy grew up, and maybe in your hometown, too. These days the rhyme has been sanitized, although many children can recite the original by heart. In Nadine Bernard Westcott's popular picture-book version, *The Lady with the Alligator Purse*, instead of "He died last night with a bubble in his throat," the text reads, "He tried to eat the bathtub but it wouldn't go down his throat." Instead of "Dead," the doctor, nurse, and lady say, "Pizza!" By changing the language, are we being too protective of our children? You decide.

Here's another dark and disastrous bathtub poem gleeful children recite and enjoy:

Gladys, Where Are You Going?

Gladys, where are you going?

"Upstairs to take a bath."

Gladys, with legs like toothpicks,

And a neck like a giraffe;

Upstairs into the bathtub,

Pull out the plug and then—

Oh my goodness, oh my soul,

There goes Gladys down that hole—

GLUB GLUB GLUB

During Judy's visit with her sister Sharron Freeman and her brother-in-law, Steve Alloy, the conversation turned to childhood chants and how they are a form of children's underground folklore. The sisters began to reminisce about the ones they knew from way back when, including these "spelling" rhymes:

Chicken in the car, the car can't go.

That's the way you spell *Chicago*.

Knife and a fork, a bottle and a cork

That's the way you spell *New York*.

Judy subsequently looked up those rhymes online and discovered another one:

A woman and a man, sitting in a pan

And that's the way you spell *Japan*.

Judy then recalled a favorite she had learned from a school librarian in Chicago:

Cinderella, dressed in yella

Went downtown to meet her fella;

On her way, her girdle busted—

How many people were disgusted?

Steve was sitting there, listening and shaking his head. "I don't remember anything like that from my childhood."

"Sure you do," Judy told him, and started singing:

Miss Lucy Had a Steamboat

Miss Lucy had a steamboat; the steamboat had a bell;

Miss Lucy went to heaven and the steamboat went to . . .

Hello, operator, please give me number 9,

And if you disconnect me, I'll kick you in the . . .

Behind the refrigerator, there was a piece of glass;

Miss Lucy sat upon it, and it broke her little . . .

Ask me no more questions, I'll tell you no more lies;

The boys are in the bathroom, zipping up their . . .

Flies are in the meadow, the bees are in the park;

Miss Lucy and her boyfriend are sitting in the

D-A-R-K, D-A-R-K, DARK DARK DARK!

He knew that one, all right—most boys do—and joined right in. Then he said, "Wait a minute. I *do* remember one!"

He started to sing:

Shaving Cream

My Bonnie fell out of a window

I feared that her head would be split;

But my Bonnie was lucky,

She fell in a bucket of shhhhh—

Chorus:

Shaving cream, be nice and clean.

Shave everyday and you'll always look keen.

Which he proceeded to sing about forty times after that, emphasizing the words *shaving cream* to make sure they got the joke, so happy to have redis-covered his profligate youth. Judy later Googled it to see if she could find it and discovered more than thirty verses—no fooling—all ridiculously juvenile, puerile, and funny. Go ask your friends and relatives about the chants of childhood, and you'll have a pretty good collection when you're done; not that you can use ones like "Shaving Cream" with your kids (until they're adolescents, maybe).

The folksong "My Bonnie Lies Over the Ocean" seems to be a rich source for parody. Here's a variant one Judy heard from a librarian in Las Vegas:

My Bonnie?

My Bonnie climbed up on a gas tank,

The height of its contents to see;

She lighted a match to see clearly,

Oh, bring back my Bonnie to me.

Then there's this one:

Last night as I lay on my pillow,

Last night as I lay all alone,

I dreamt that I ate a marshmallow;

Next morning, my pillow was gone.

Bring back, bring back, bring back my pillow to me, to me.

Bring back, bring back, bring back my pillow to me.

Last night as I lay on my pillow,

Last night as I lay on my bed,

I stuck my feet out of the window,

Next morning my neighbors were dead.

Bring back, bring back, bring back my neighbors to me, to me.

Bring back, bring back, bring back my neighbors to me.

MARY HAD A LITTLE LAMB

Mary and her little lamb also appear to be targets for wacky rewrites, starting with the simple "Mary had a little lamb; the doctors were amazed."

Mary Had a Little Lamb: Three Alternate Versions

I

Mary had a little lamb,

A lobster, and some prunes,

A little pie, a little Coke,

And some macaroons.

It made the naughty waiters grin

To see her order so,

And when they carried Mary out,

Her face was white as snow.

II

Mary had a little lamb, a little pork, a little jam;

Some ice cream soda topped with fizz,

And oh how sick our Mary is.

III

Mary had a little lamb and then a little beef;

She then consumed some coleslaw with some chilis underneath,

And then some bread and butter and some pork chops served with
thyme;

How strange to find such a greedy girl in an English nursery rhyme!

Did you notice the factual error in the last line? The poem is really an early nineteenth-century American rhyme, not an English one. How would one know this? Read Will Moses's fact-based *Mary and Her Little Lamb: The True Story of the Nursery Rhyme,* and you'll learn about young Mary Elizabeth Sawyer, who in 1810 nursed a sickly newborn lamb on her family's Massachusetts farm. On the first day of class, the lamb followed Mary to school and settled under her desk. A visitor to the classroom that day, Mr. John Roulstone, was so tickled by the sight that he wrote the first four lines of the rhyme we now know so well. Sarah Josepha Hale, who usually gets full credit for the poem, added another verse and published the longer version in 1830. Lowell Mason, a well-known composer of hymns, set it to music. In 1877 Thomas Edison recited the rhyme into the speaker of his newly invented phonograph; it was the first recording of the human voice.

The pastel-colored full-page oil paintings in folk-art style are reminiscent of Grandma Moses, and no wonder as she was great grandmother to Will Moses, who himself began painting at age four. Have children examine the illustrations closely to come up with a list of ways life at home and at school was different and the same two hundred years ago.

Here are the original verses by John Roulstone and expanded by Sarah Josepha Hale:

> Mary had a little lamb, its fleece was white as snow;
>
> And everywhere that Mary went, the lamb was sure to go.
>
> It followed her to school one day, which was against the rule;
>
> It made the children laugh and play, to see a lamb at school.
>
> And so the teacher turned it out, but still it lingered near,
>
> And waited patiently about till Mary did appear.
>
> "Why does the lamb love Mary so?" the eager children cry;
>
> "Why, Mary loves the lamb, you know," the teacher did reply.

And here's a rewrite, in ramped-up vocabulary. Before mentioning any of the above versions, original or snarky, read it aloud and see if your listeners can identify and recite the actual verse.

Mary's Ovine

Mary was the proprietress of a diminutive incipient ovine, whose outer covering was as devoid of colours as congealed atmospheric vapour, and to all localities to which Mary perambulated, her young South-down was morally sure to follow. It tagged her to the dispensary of learning one diurnal section of time, which was contrary to all precedent and excited cachinnation to the seminary attendants when they perceived the presence of a young mutton at the establishment of instruction. Consequently, the preceptor expelled it from the interior, but he continued to circumnavigate in the immediate vicinity, without fretfulness, until Mary once more became visible.

"What caused this specimen of the genus ovis to bestow so much affection on Mary?" the impetuous progeny vociferated.

"Because Mary reciprocated the wool-producer's esteem, you understand," the teacher responded.

Once you've read "Mary's Ovine" aloud, the original "Row, Row, your Boat" might be too simple for your listeners. Why not try singing this more "sophisticated" version:

Propel Your Craft

Propel, propel, propel your craft

Gently down the liquid solution,

Ecstatically, ecstatically, ecstatically, ecstatically,

Life is but an illusion.

Have children sit in pairs, facing each other at arms' length, knees bent, feet against feet. As they sing the verse, they rock back and forth in a push-me-pull-you fashion to make a human teeter-totter-like rowboat. Too fun!

THOITY POIPLE BOIDS

Yes, there's some erudite language in those examples above, but now get acquainted with the patois of "Joisey." As in New Jersey. Jersey girl Judy Freeman thinks this selection sounds more like Brooklyn than Jersey, but that's up for debate. Pair the poem with the story "Hoimie the Woim," in

Judy's *Once Upon a Time: Using Storytelling, Creative Drama, and Reader's Theater with Children in Grades K–6.*

> Thoity poiple boids sittin' on a coib,
>
> Choipin' and boipin' and eatin' doity woims.
>
> Along came Boit with a squoit named Goit,
>
> Who woiked in a shoit factory in Joisey.
>
> They saw thoity poiple boids sittin' on the coib,
>
> Choipin' and boipin' and eatin' doity woims.
>
> Boy, was they pertoibed!
>
> Boy, was they distoibed!

Nonsense Verse

Next we give you some fine nonsense that will have your listeners scratching their heads and saying, "Huh? That makes no sense." Exactly! Rhymes like the two below can help children recognize nonsense whenever they hear it, whether in folklore, in the news of the day, or in everyday life.

Ladies and Jellybeans

> Ladies and jellybeans and dogs without fleas;
>
> Cover your ears and listen up, please!
>
> I come here before you to stand here behind you,
>
> To tell a story I know nothing about.
>
> There's a meeting this evening, right before breakfast
>
> To decide what color to whitewash the church.
>
> The admission is free, so pay at the door,
>
> Pull up a chair and sit on the floor.

One Bright Day

> One bright day in the middle of the night,
>
> Two dead men decided to fight.
>
> Back to back and facing each other,

They pulled out their swords and shot one another.

A deaf policeman heard the noise

And came to arrest the two dead boys.

If you don't believe this lie is true,

Ask the blind man—he saw it, too.

Call-and-Response Chants

It's fun to do call-and-response chants that allow your audience to copy you in both word and motion. To start you off, we give you two traditional ones. Folksinger Ella Jenkins made the first one famous. You can hear her singing a good snippet of it at www.folkways.si.edu/TrackDetails.aspx?itemid=28363.

Did You Feed My Cow?

Did you feed my cow? *(Yes, ma'am.)*

Could you tell me how? *(Yes, ma'am.)*

What did you feed her? *(Corn and hay.)*

What did you feed her? *(Corn and hay.)*

Did you milk her good? *(Yes, ma'am.)*

Now did you milk her like you should? *(Yes, ma'am.)*

How did you milk her? *(Squish, squish, squish.)*

How did you milk her? *(Squish, squish, squish.)*

Did my cow get sick? *(Yes, ma'am.)*

Was she covered with tick? *(Yes, ma'am.)*

How did she die? *(Uh, uh, uh.)*

How did she die? *(Uh, uh, uh.)*

Did the buzzards come? *(Yes, ma'am.)*

Did the buzzards come? *(Yes, ma'am.)*

How did they come? *(Flop, flop, flop.)*

How did they come? *(Flop, flop, flop.)*

If you feel badly about that cow dying, go to YouTube and look up "Did You Feed My Cow?" where you'll find a slightly altered version by Eric Litwin, sung by kids. (Litwin is the author of the call-and-response hit picture book, *Pete the Cat: I Love My White Shoes.*) Then go to www.youtube.com/watch?v=rfmUFe9O5Zg to see a spirited kindergarten class act out the song with motions (and a cute new ending where the vet gives the cow a healing shot).

Miss Mary Mack

This is a well-known call-and-response chant, which can be sung on its own or as a jump-rope rhyme.

> Miss Mary Mack, Mack, Mack
>
> All dressed in black, black, black
>
> With silver buttons, buttons, buttons
>
> All down her back, back, back
>
> She asked her mother, mother, mother
>
> For fifty cents, cents, cents
>
> To see the elephants, elephants, elephants
>
> Jump the fence, fence, fence.
>
> They jumped so high, high, high
>
> They reached the sky, sky, sky
>
> And they never came back, back, back
>
> Till the Fourth of July, lie, lie
>
> (*Spoken*) It's not good to lie!

Next are examples of call-and-response chants that require children to follow you line for line. Recite slowly and then faster each time through until your audience gets exhausted. Set up a rhythm by slapping one thigh and then the other, or slap your thighs once and then clap once, or slap your thighs twice and then clap twice. Change the motions each time you start over, which will be a fun challenge for the kids. Add motions; have kids jump or scratch or swat.

Froggie!

Dog.

Dog, cat.

Dog, cat, mouse.

Froggie!

Itsy bitsy, teeny weeny little bitty froggie.

Jump, jump, jump, jump, jump little froggie.

Spiders and flies are scrum-deli-icious.

Ribbit, ribbit, ribbit, ribbit, ribbit, ribbit, CROAK.
   (*jump up on the word "CROAK"*)

Flea, Fly

Flea.

Flea, fly.

Flea, fly, mosquito.

Swat 'em!

Calamine, calamine, calamine lotion.

Oh, no more calamine lotion.

Itchy, itchy, scratchy, scratchy, got one on my backy, backy.

Ohy, ohy, owwy, owwy, wish he'd go away.

Quick get the bug spray, I think he went that-away—**shhhhhh!**
   (*pretend to use spray can*)

Jump-Rope Rhymes

Skipping rope and the accompanying jingles are a part of folklore, too. School-age children will have no trouble telling you—or showing you—their favorite jump-rope rhymes. And the rhythms you jumped to a child are the same children are skipping to today, no matter where they live. Many children may have forgotten how to jump rope, but you can reintroduce the traditional playground sport. To refresh your memory, we've collected a few perennial rhymes here. When you try these with an actual jump rope, you'll be getting back in shape as well. For instructions and other information, visit the "World's Rope Skipping Experts" at www.jumprope.com.

House for rent,

Inquire within;

When I move out,

Let Hilary move in. (*the jumper moves out and next in line moves in*)

When you fall down

And hurt your knee,

Just jump up quick

And think of me.

Fudge, fudge tell the judge

Mama's going to have a baby.

Wrap it up in tissue paper;

Send it on the elevator.

How many floors did it go?

1, 2, 3 (*the jumper jumps fast with no skips–what we used to call pepper or chili pepper–until he or she misses*)

Sheep in the meadow,

Cows in the corn;

Tell me the month that you were born.

January, February, March . . .
(*the jumper jumps out on the mention of his or her birthday*)

Late last night and the night before

Twenty-four robbers came to my door.

I got up, let 'em in,

Hit 'em on the head with a rolling pin.

One, two, three, four . . . (*pepper jump until the jumper misses*)

Salt, Mustard

Salt, mustard, vinegar, pepper,

French almond rock,

Bread and butter for your supper,

That's all Mother's got.

Fish and chips and Coca-Cola,

Put them in a pan,

Irish stew and ice cream soda,

We'll eat all we can.

Salt, mustard, vinegar, pepper,

French almond rock,

Bread and butter for your supper,

That's all Mother's got.

Eggs and bacon, salted herring,

Put them in a pot,

Pickled onions, apple pudding,

We will eat the lot.

Salt, mustard, vinegar, pepper,

Pig's head and trout,

Bread and butter for your supper,

O-U-T spells *out*.

Dutch Girl

Caroline heard this from someone who learned it growing up in Jamestown, New York.

I'm a pretty little Dutch girl.

As pretty as I can be.

And all the boys in my hometown

Go rickety-rack for me.

My boyfriend gave me peaches.

My boyfriend gave me pears.

My boyfriend gave me fifty cents

To kiss him on the stairs.

I gave him back his peaches.

I gave him back his pears.

I gave him back his fifty cents
And kicked him down the stairs.

The peaches, they were rotten.
The pears, they were stale.
The fifty cents was counterfeit
So I kicked him down the stairs.

My mother was born in England.
My father was born in France.
But I was born in diapers
Because I had no pants!

Autograph Rhymes and Mottos

Autograph books, yearbooks, and autograph dolls begin to appear as summer vacations shine on the horizon. The sayings written in memory books today are often the same ones your grandmother wrote in her best friend's book way back in the old days. You may enjoy using the following in a story hour, especially if you are discussing different types of folk sayings.

Yours till banana splits
Yours till ice screams
Yours till dogwood barks
Yours till the sun beams

U R 2 young and 2 pretty 4 boys
U R 2 good 2 B 4 gotten
I C U R 2 Ys for me
O G I feel 2 sad N rotten

When you're in the kitchen
Learning how to cook,
Remember it was Joni
Who wrote this in your book.

Roses are red,
Violets are blue,

The sidewalk is cracked,
And so are you.

I saw you on the mountain,
I saw you in the sea,
I saw you in the bathtub—
Oops! Pardon me!

The Oral Tradition in the Age of the Internet

Finally, here is Judy's favorite chant, which she learned from Mary Ellen Smith, a teacher from Salt Lake City.

Hey, Cousin Jenny

Hey, Cousin Jenny (*cup your hands to your mouth*)

Look at Uncle Benny (*make eyeglasses with your fingers*)

Down by the seashore
  (*point over your shoulder with your thumb, twice*)

Learning how to swim (*stroke, stroke*)

First he does the sidestroke (*pantomime the sidestroke*)

Then he does the backstroke (*pantomime the backstroke*)

Then he goes and beats against the tide, 1, 2.
  (*slap twice on your thighs; clap twice; slap twice on your thighs; clap once on the last word*)

For more than a year Judy searched for the origin of the rhyme. Then Allison Peters, a librarian in Denver, came up to her at a conference and said, "I heard something like that called "Hey, Aunt Jackie," from a fabulous storyteller named Gary Dulabaum." Judy looked up Dulabaum and found him at www.garydulabaum.com. Here's his version, as printed on his website.

Hey, Aunt Jackie

Hey, Aunt Jackie, look at your Uncle Jim.

He's standin' in the duck pond

Learnin' how to swim.

First, he does the backstroke.

Then he does the crawl.

Now he's under water doin' nothin' at all.

Then, using the keywords *duck pond* and *swim*, Judy went back online and discovered the following version on the website of the King's Road Primary School in Manchester, England:

Oh, Jemima

Oh Jemima, oh Jemima,

Look at your uncle Jim!

He's down in the duck pond

Learning how to swim.

First he's on his left leg,

Then he's on his right—

Now he's on a bar of soap,

Skidding out of sight!

She kept searching and hit pay dirt at the Mudcat Café, a wonderful database and forum containing more than nine thousand folksongs and other information, and found an entire thread on the Jemima poem (www.mudcat .org/thread.cfm?threadid = 35057). Apparently it originated in England and was often sung to the tune of the "Deposons les armes" ("Soldier's Chorus") in Charles Gounod's opera *Faust*. Here are two of the many funny versions posted on Mudcat.

I

Oh Jemima, look at your Uncle Jim.

He's in the bathtub learning how to swim.

First he does the backstroke, them he does the side;

Now he's under the water swimming against the tide.

II

Oh Jemima, look at your Uncle Jim;

He's in the duck pond learning how to swim.

First he tries the breaststroke, then he tries the crawl;

Now he's disappeared from sight and may never come back at all.

That's the oral tradition at work, with the Internet making the world so much more accessible. And yet, Judy still hasn't found a single reference to the original rhyme she learned, "Hey, Cousin Jenny."

Ask family, friends, and others to search their memory for chants and rhymes, and have children ask parents, grandparents, and siblings for material. Write down these little ditties and compile them into a school/camp/scouts/library book. Run off copies with a few blank pages at the end so everyone can have one and can continue adding to it. Here are some books to jog your memory and get you started.

BOOKLIST: UNDERGROUND RHYMES AND CHANTS

Booth, David, comp. *Doctor Knickerbocker and Other Rhymes. Illus. by Maryann Kovalski. Ticknor & Fields, 1993.* Each page is packed with children's rhymes and nonsense verses—some well-known, some not—and witty, Victorian-flavored pen-and-inks. (Gr. 2–5)

Bronner, Simon J. *American Children's Folklore. August House, 1988.* Part of the American Folklore series, this is a dandy compendium of children's sometimes indecorous song parodies, nonsense rhymes, riddles, and more. (Professional)

Cole, Joanna. *Anna Banana: 101 Jump-Rope Rhymes. Illus. by Alan Tiegreen. Morrow, 1991.* Rhymes are accompanied by directions for jumping. (Gr. 2–6)

Cole, Joanna, and Stephanie Calmenson, comps. *Miss Mary Mack and Other Children's Street Rhymes. Illus. by Alan Tiegreen. HarperCollins, 1990.* One hundred traditional ball-bouncing, hand-clapping, and counting rhymes. (K–Gr. 4)

Delamar, Gloria T., comp. *Children's Counting-Out Rhymes, Fingerplays, Jump-Rope and Bounce-Ball Chants and Other Rhythms: A Comprehensive English Language Reference. McFarland, 1983.* A rich compendium for adults to use with children. (Professional)

Farjeon, Eleanor. *Elsie Piddock Skips in Her Sleep. Illus. by Charlotte Voake. Candlewick, 2008.* Tell (or read) this delightful story during the skip-rope season. It's long but well worth learning. (K–Gr. 3)

Gourley, Robbin. *Bring Me Some Apples and I'll Make You a Pie: A Story about Edna Lewis. Illus. by the author. Clarion, 2009.* In this picture-book tribute to the late African American chef and cookbook author, you'll find many old rhymes and sayings incorporated into the story. (Gr. 1–4)

Hoberman, Mary Ann. *Miss Mary Mack: A Handclapping Rhyme.* *Illus. by Nadine Bernard Westcott. Little, Brown, 1998.* Ten wild new verses to read, recite, or sing about that fence-jumping elephant. (PreK–Gr. 2)

Lass, Bonnie, and Philemon Sturges. *Who Took the Cookies from the Cookie Jar?* *Illus. by Ashley Wolff. Little, Brown, 2000.* Based on the classic name-game chant, Skunk seeks the cookie-stealing culprit through the southwestern desert. (PreK–Gr. 1)

O'Neill, Alexis. *The Recess Queen.* *Illus. by Laura Huliska-Beith. Scholastic, 2002.* That bully, Mean Jean, pushes and smooshes everyone on the playground until a new girl, teeny tiny Katy Sue, asks her to jump rope. (K–Gr. 2)

Opie, Iona, and Peter Opie, eds. *I Saw Esau: The Schoolchild's Pocket Book.* *Illus. by Maurice Sendak. Candlewick, 1992.* A collection of children's chants, rhymes, riddles, tongue twisters, and insults that children recite when they think there are no grown-ups nearby. (Gr. 1–5)

Rosen, Michael, comp. *Walking the Bridge of Your Nose.* *Illus. by Chloë Cheese. Kingfisher, 1995.* More than ninety nonsense wordplay poems. (Gr. 1–5)

Schwartz, Alvin, comp. *And the Green Grass Grew All Around: Folk Poetry from Everyone.* *Illus. by Sue Truesdale. HarperCollins, 1992.* A meaty and essential collection of more than three hundred children's poems, autograph rhymes, songs, riddles, and chants. (Gr. 2–6)

Schwartz, Alvin, comp. *I Saw You in the Bathtub, and Other Folk Rhymes.* *Illus. by Syd Hoff. HarperCollins, 1989.* Three dozen funny kid rhymes and chants, delivered easy-reader style. (K–Gr. 3)

Sierra, Judy, comp. *Schoolyard Rhymes: Kids' Own Rhymes for Rope Skipping, Hand Clapping, Ball Bouncing, and Just Plain Fun.* *Illus. by Melissa Sweet. Knopf, 2005.* Chant along with almost four dozen wacky children's rhymes. (Gr. 1–5)

Westcott, Nadine Bernard. *The Lady with the Alligator Purse.* *Illus. by the author. Little, Brown, 1988.* Tiny Tim survives in this picture-book version of a traditional chant. Wescott's *Peanut Butter and Jelly: A Play Rhyme* (Dutton, 1987) is another good choice. (PreK–Gr. 2)

WEBSITES: UNDERGROUND RHYMES AND CHANTS

Mudcat Café *www.mudcat.org/jumprope/jumprope_display_all.cfm*
Literally thousands of jump-rope rhymes, clapping games, a folksong database, and a forum for questions and answers.

NIEHS Kids' Pages: Riddles & Brainteasers
kids.niehs.nih.gov/games/riddles
Part of the National Institute of Environmental Health Sciences's site, this section includes a large selection of doublespeak proverbs rewritten with "big words"—in the vein of "Mary's Ovine," above—for your listeners to figure out.

chapter 5

Music

If I were not a physicist, I would probably be a musician. I often think in music. I live my daydreams in music. I see my life in terms of music. —ALBERT EINSTEIN

ADDING MUSIC TO A STORY HOUR CAN HELP MAKE YOUR PREsentation lively and colorful while encouraging your audience to join in. There are lots of different ways to include music in your programs. Use a musical theme to begin and end the program. Tell a story that includes singing or use a song to encourage audience participation. Even if you are not particularly musical, don't skip this chapter! There are ideas for you here, too.

Why Use Music with Children?

In days gone by, kindergarten teachers were mandated to learn the piano as part of their educational training. They used those pianos, stationed in their classrooms, during the school day, singing activity songs and playing chords to get the kids' attention. Now it's rare to find a piano in a kindergarten room. In fact, many districts have dispensed with music teachers and music altogether. Why waste time with something as frivolous as a music class when children aren't tested in music? Here are ten reasons why this cavalier attitude toward music is both foolish and shortsighted.

1. MUSIC IS A LIFE-AFFIRMING STATEMENT OF WHO WE ARE.

Humans are innately musical. Judy Freeman's junior high school music teacher once asked his class, "What is the most important, perfect, and oldest instrument in the world?" The students guessed piano, violin, guitar, and drums, but the teacher only said, "No, no, no, and no." The students were baffled. What could be more important than those? The teacher then smiled and said, "The most important and perfect and oldest instrument in the world is the human voice. You don't even have to buy or make an instrument—you already have your own."

Music is one of our languages. Even tone-deaf individuals are teachable. We get better at music the same way we get better at reading, writing, and thinking, by learning its skills.

2. IT HELPS DEVELOP RHYTHM AND COORDINATION.

When children sing and dance, they are learning how to use their bodies in different ways. Take a walk tonight after work and try this little experiment: Set out from point A and, timing yourself, walk briskly for five minutes, with no music playing in your earbuds. Now turn around and turn on the music—something lively and fast paced—and, keeping track of your starting time, walk back to your starting place. Did you get there faster than five minutes? Bet you did. Music gets our bodies moving in a syncopated, free-flowing way. Children who have trouble with coordination and sequencing—kids who can't bounce or catch a ball or follow a simple set of instructions—will improve when they perform these actions to music. Clapping out the rhythm of a song or dancing a choreographed dance routine will improve both fine and gross motor skills.

Though humans are the only primates who move to the beat in music, check out www.wimp.com/birddances and watch a cocky cockatoo dancing to the song "Gangnam Style" (mega hit and video of 2012, recorded by the South Korean musician Psy) to see we're not the only animals with built-in rhythm.

3. IT STRENGTHENS READING, WRITING, MEMORIZATION, AND LEARNING.

How many songs do you know? Make a list; include pop songs, show tunes, and TV jingles. The number will astonish you. Your brain has been storing these ditties for a long time; you remember them because music strengthens the capacity to recall. Songs make excellent mnemonic devices, like the ABC song that helps every child learn the alphabet. Kids can absorb mnemonically the days of the week, colors, numbers, the fifty states, and other primary concepts through songs they quickly learn by heart. Our brains hold information more effectively when we add music and rhythm.

You get a double bonus if you hand out the lyrics to the song you sing, even ones children already know. We call this *singers' theater*. One can't sing a song one word at a time; as their eyes flow across each line, children develop fluency and comprehension. Of course they won't realize they're working on reading skills; they just think they're having a ball.

4. IT BUILDS ORAL LANGUAGE SKILLS.

Studies have shown that the more words a child hears before age five, the better that child will do in school and life. In addition to helping children increase their vocabulary, songs demonstrate sentence structure and introduce poetry and the verbal hijinks of language. Singing can also improve enunciation, which will strengthen public-speaking skills and help children develop confidence and poise. Want kids to learn a foreign language without sounding like a mealy-mouthed English speaker? Encourage them to listen to and sing the songs of that country.

5. IT NURTURES DISCRIMINATING TASTE.

Play background music in your classroom or library to calm children and help them concentrate. Children don't necessarily hear a variety of music at home. Expand their knowledge by introducing different musical genres—opera, rock, country, swing, jazz, blues, and hip-hop, if it's age appropriate. Listening to trained singers and instrumentalists will help children learn to appreciate talented voices and proficient playing that will inspire, transfix, and move them.

6. IT'S FUN.

Children's songs are a blast to sing. This chapter is filled with numbers that will crack kids up and get them singing with oomph. Look for artists who specialize in children's songs: Laurie Berkner, Tom Chapin, Dr. Jean, Arlo Guthrie, Ella Jenkins, The Learning Station, Lisa Loeb, Elizabeth Mitchell, Hap Palmer, Raffi, and Dan Zanes, for starters. Alert kids to KPR, Kids Public Radio (www.kidspublicradio.org), a free station sponsored by National Public Radio, where they can tune in 24/7 to wonderful songs and stories.

7. IT BUILDS RELATIONSHIPS.

Whether singing in unison or playing in a band, children are learning to be part of a team, part of a larger community. They will soon realize that to make good music, they must not only be disciplined but also share the spotlight and cooperate with others for the good of the group. They will be partaking in an enjoyable experience with other people, joined by a shared love and appreciation of sound.

8. IT TAKES US BACK TO OUR ROOTS AND KEEPS US IN TUNE WITH NATURE, HISTORY, AND THE FOUR CORNERS OF THE EARTH.

Children hear the music of nature all around them, from the breeze in the trees to the chirping of the crickets. Music can magically transport them to other countries and into the past, and it can introduce them to some of the cultural icons of civilization, such as the three Bs: Bach, Beethoven, and the Beatles. Hear an old song on the radio and chances are, you'll be transported back to the first time you heard it, in a reconnection to your youth.

9. IT'S SOOTHING TO BOTH BODY AND SPIRIT.

When children get upset and have meltdowns, one thing that helps them soothe themselves is music. That's why parents sing lullabies to their babies, to gentle them into sleep. Singing employs the kind of breathing that floods our brains with endorphins, calms us down, relaxes our muscles, or even makes us euphoric. Music allows all of us to forget our worries for a bit, to tune out bad thoughts and noises, and listen to the world with new ears. Have you ever observed a child transfixed by a good song, belting it out spontaneously with obvious delight? (We're talking about you, "Frozen.") Music can bring on good karma.

10. IT GIVES US A LIFETIME OF ENJOYMENT, PEACE, HARMONY, AND JOY.

Canadian neuroscientists Robert J. Zatorre and Valorie N. Salimpoor found that "music that people described as highly emotional engaged the reward system deep in their brains—activating subcortical nuclei known to be important in reward, motivation and emotion."[1] When we know the crescendo is coming, we feel extreme joy. Music: it's just as effective as chocolate and with none of the calories. Whether it becomes a passion, a pleasurable pastime, or a career, we are lucky to have music in our lives.

Using Music and Dance in Programs

Play recorded music as the children enter the room, find their seats, remove their coats, and place their toys and books aside. If you are passionate about music, you could choose different types for every story session. Use circus music for a circus program, quiet music with thoughtful books, folk songs from the country you are reading about.

When you open the first book, turn the music down. You can turn it up again at the end of the story hour when the children are leaving. Some librarians sing the same song to start each session and have the children join in. Sing songs as transitional devices between stories or activities and to get kids ready to pay attention after recess, lunch, or a break.

Music is also effective when you are showing a book without words, either by hand, on your document camera or SMART Board, or as a PowerPoint presentation. Again, choose your music carefully to suit the mood of your story. You may want to record your own music and sound effects, although this may be more time consuming than you think.

Take songs you already know and put new words to them:

> Put your libros away and sit here on the floor
>
> It's time to practice our Español, so join me, por favor.

Did you hear the tune as you read that? It's just "Row, Row, Row Your Boat." It's simple, to the point, recognizable, and a friendly way to transition to a new activity, such as your weekly Spanish lesson.

Encourage children to make up songs about their daily life in school or at home. They may sing off key, but it's a delight to hear a preschooler singing happily about getting up or going to bed. And don't hesitate to make singing the focal point of your whole story hour.

Music is everywhere on the Internet now; you've probably downloaded some of your favorite songs. The great thing is that you can listen to an excerpt of the song or album online before you buy it.

Laurel Sharp, librarian at the Liverpool (New York) Public Library, says,

> I've been using podcasts of my songs and rhymes for "Sing-A-Long Story Time" for a couple of years. I use folk songs, or get permission from composers whose songs I use. I wanted families to share the things they learned in story time during the week.

To record myself and my guitar, I used Audacity, an easy-to-use open-source audio editing platform for recording sound. I cut and paste whatever songs/stories/rhymes I'm using that week. The library keeps the past year's podcasts on the website. Go to lpl.org, then click on "Kids' World," then "Kids' Programs," and then "Sing Along Storytime" for samples of my podcasts. Under "For Storytime Parents," I include the lyrics of the songs and fingerplays we'll be doing so parents can reinforce what we've been doing (personal communication).

You don't have to be a professional singer or musician to share music with children. If a song is meant to be sung in a sweet, lilting voice and you croak like a frog, just plunge in and do it your way. If you're someone who simply would rather not sing, though, don't worry. You've still got the poetry—recite the song instead of singing it. You can even play a CD or a YouTube version and lip-synch.

Many adults have never attended an opera, ballet, or concert. To give your charges an opportunity to see such a musical event, plan a field trip to a dance festival or musical performance in your town. If the nearest event is some miles away, enlist parents or a local business to provide funds and volunteers to chaperone. Children who cannot afford such a trip can be subsidized with donations or a grant, or put the field trip idea into your next budget. Children will remember the event for a long time to come.

Pinky Panky Pang

By Leroy F. Jackson, from The Peter Patter Book of Nursery Rhymes, ©1918

A tortoise sat on a slippery limb

And played his pinky pang

For a dog-fish friend that called on him,

And this is what he sang:

"Oh, the skies are blue, and I wait for you

To come where the willows hang,

And dance all night by the white moonlight

To my pinky, pinky, pang!"

When you read a poem like that aloud, it makes you want to sing and dance. Put on music of your choice and have a dance party. When you stop the music, children must freeze in their position.

Of course, you don't need to turn your story hour into a dance class, but you can still encourage children to respond to the mood of a story or record. Let them tap out the rhythm of a tongue twister or the repeated rhyme in a story. If your community has a ballet or modern dance studio, invite the older students to perform at your story hour. To ensure success, be sure to ask beforehand about floor-space requirements and what sort of audio or other equipment will be needed.

Here's a story that will have everyone dancing, especially if you play some African music with drums.

The Goat Well

By Harold Courlander

The great folklorist Harold Courlander collected many tellable tales. This one, from Ethiopia, contains lots of action. The teller gets a chance to call into the well, "Goats, are you there? Are you there, goats?" and, to the rhythmic clapping of the audience, can dance at the end of the story.

A man named Woharia was once traveling across the plateau when he came to an abandoned house. He was tired and hungry, so he rested in the house and ate some of his bread, called *injera*. When he was about to leave he heard the baa-ing of a goat. He looked in all directions, but he saw nothing except the dry brown landscape. He heard the goat again, and finally he went to the old well and looked down into it. There, standing on the dry bottom, was the animal, which had somehow fallen in while searching for water to drink.

"What luck!" Woharia said. He climbed down and tied a rope around the goat, and then he came up and began to pull her out of the well.

Just at this moment a Cunama trader, with three camels loaded with sacks of grain, approached him. He greeted Woharia and asked if he might have water there for his thirsty camels.

"Naturally, if there were water here, you would be welcome to it," Woharia said. "But unfortunately, this is only a goat well."

"What is a goat well?" the Cunama asked.

"What do you think? It's a well that produces goats," Woharia said, and he pulled on his rope again until he got the goat to the top.

"This is really extraordinary!" the Cunama said. "I've never before heard of a goat well!"

"Why, I suppose you're right," Woharia said. "They aren't very common."

"How does it work?" the Cunama trader asked.

"Oh, it's simple enough," Woharia said. "Every night you throw a pair of goat's horns into the well, and in the morning you find a goat. Then all you have to do is draw her out."

"Unbelievable!" the Cunama said. "Man, how I'd like to own such a well!"

"So would everyone else," Woharia said, untying the goat and letting her run loose. "But few people can afford to buy such an unusual thing."

"Well, I'll tell you," the Cunama said, thinking very hard. "I'm not a rich man, but I'll pay you six bags of durra grain for it."

Woharia laughed. "That wouldn't pay for many goats," he said.

"I'll give you twelve bags of durra, all that my camels are carrying!" the Cunama said anxiously.

Woharia smiled and shook his head.

"Seven goats a week," he said as though he were talking to himself. "Thirty goats a month. Three hundred sixty-five goats a year . . ." But the Cunama had set his heart on owning the well.

"Look at my young sleek camels! I have just bought them in Keren! Where will you ever find better camels than these? I'll give you my twelve bags of grain and my three camels also. I'd give you more, but I own nothing else in the whole world, I swear it to you!"

Woharia thought silently for a moment.

"Since you want it so much, I'll sell it to you," he said finally. The Cunama leaped down from his camel and embraced Woharia. "For this goodness, may you live long!" he said. "May Allah bring you many good things to give you joy!"

"Ah," Woharia said, looking at camels, "he has already done so." He took the three camels loaded with grain, his goat, and his few other possessions, and prepared to leave.

"Before you go, tell me your name?" the Cunama asked.

"People call me Where-I-Shall-Dance," Woharia replied. And then he went away to the south, leaving the Cunama with the well.

The Cunama was very impatient to begin getting goats from the well. When evening came, he dropped two goat's horns into it and lay down in the house to sleep. The next morning, when it was barely light, he rushed out again to draw up his first goat, but when he peered into the well, he saw nothing except the old horns he had thrown in.

He became very anxious.

"There must be some mistake!" he said to himself.

That evening he threw down two more horns, and again in the morning he rushed out to get his first goat, but once more he saw only the old goat's horns there. This time he was very worried. He scoured the country to find old goat's horns, and he threw armful after armful into the well. And all night long he sat by the well, shouting into it:

"Goats, are you there? Goats, are you there?"

But nothing at all happened. When morning came at last, the Cunama was angry and unhappy. He realized that he had been duped by his own anxiousness to get the well. There was nothing left to do but to go out and find the man who had taken his camels and his precious grain.

The trader traveled southward, as Woharia had done. At last, when night had fallen, he came to a village. When he arrived in the village square, where many people were gathered, he went up to them and asked:

"Do you know Where-I-Shall-Dance?"

"Why, it doesn't matter, dance anywhere you like," the people answered. "Dance right here if you wish!" And they began to sing and make music for him.

"No, no, you don't understand," he said. "What I want to know is, do you know Where-I-Shall-Dance?"

"Yes, dance here!" they said again.

The Cunama was very angry because he thought the people were making fun of him, so he went out of the village and continued his journey southward, stopping only to sleep at the edge of the road.

The next day, he came to another village, and he went to the marketplace and said in a loud voice:

"Does anybody know Where-I-Shall-Dance?"

The people gathered around him instantly and shouted: "Dance here! Dance here!" They clapped their hands and a drummer came and beat his drum, and everyone waited for the Cunama to dance.

He turned and fled from the village, believing that the people were ridiculing him. Again, he came to a village, and again he asked:

"Do you know Where-I-Shall-Dance?"

And once more the people began clapping their hands and answered: "Yes, dance here!"

The same thing happened in every village the man entered. He began to feel very hopeless, and sometimes thought he might even be losing his mind. He began to be afraid to ask his question. Finally, one day, he came to the village of the chief of the district. When he asked his question here and the people gave him the usual answer, the news was carried to the chief, who immediately sent for him.

"Now, what sort of nonsense is this?" the chief asked. "You ask the people where you should dance and then you refuse to dance."

The unhappy man told how he had bought the dry well in exchange for his three young camels and his grain. The chief listened sympathetically. He remembered that a man named Woharia had recently settled in a nearby village, and that he had come with three camels and twelve bags of grain.

"Sit down and rest," the chief said. "I will handle this matter now." He sent a messenger to Woharia, and when the messenger found him, he said, as he had been instructed:

"There is a man waiting to see you at the house of the chief. His name is What-I-Shall-Do. The chief wishes you to come at once."

Woharia went immediately to the house of the chief, and the servants let him in.

"What can I do for you?" the chief asked.

"Why, do you know What-I-Shall-Do?" Woharia asked.

"Yes, I know what you shall do," the chief said. "You shall give back the Cunama trader his three camels and his twelve bags of grain." Woharia was crestfallen and ashamed. He gave the Cunama back the camels and the grain. The Cunama took them and went out. As he passed through the market place the people shouted:

"Dance here! Dance here!"

And the trader was so happy that this time he danced in the marketplace.

BOOKLIST: DANCE

Ackerman, Karen. *Song and Dance Man*. *Illus. by Stephen Gammell. Knopf, 1988.* Grandpa sings and dances for his grandchildren, remembering his vaudeville days. (K–Gr. 4)

Barasch, Lynne. *Knockin' on Wood: Starring Peg Leg Bates*. *Illus. by the author. Lee & Low, 2004.* A picture-book biography of African American tap dancer Clayton Bates, who lost half his leg at age twelve in 1919 in an accident and went on to become a vaudeville sensation. (Gr. 1–4)

Bird, Betsy. *Giant Dance Party.* *Illus. by Brandon Dorman. Greenwillow, 2013.* Five-year-old Lexi tries to teach five furry blue giants to dance. (PreK–Gr. 1)

Dempsey, Kristy. *A Dance Like Starlight: One Ballerina's Dream.* *Illus. by Floyd Cooper. Philomel, 2014.* In 1951, a young African American girl who yearns to be a dancer goes to see Janet Collins, the "first colored prima ballerina," at the Metropolitan Opera House in New York City. (Gr. 1–4)

DePaola, Tomie. *Oliver Button Is a Sissy.* *Illus. by the author. Harcourt, 1979.* In spite of being mocked, Oliver tap-dances at the local talent show. (K–Gr. 2)

Edwards, Pamela Duncan. *Honk! The Story of a Prima Swanerina.* *Illus. by Henry Cole. Hyperion, 1998.* Mimi, a ballet-loving swan, becomes a star at the Paris Opera House. (K–Gr. 2)

Feiffer, Jules. *Rupert Can Dance.* *Illus. by the author. Farrar/Michael di Capua, 2014.* Inspired by his little girl, Mandy, who dances all day, Rupert the cat slips on her dancing shoes and dances the night away. (PreK–Gr. 1)

Greenberg, Jan, and Sandra Jordan. *Ballet for Martha: Making Appalachian Spring.* *Illus. by Brian Floca. Roaring Brook/Flash Point, 2010.* Learn how the classic ballet "Appalachian Spring" was created in 1944. (Gr. 2–6)

Harter, Debbie. *The Animal Boogie.* *Illus. by the author. Barefoot, 2000.* Animals and children go "shake, shake, boogie, woogie, oogie" through the jungle. The book comes with a CD of the song performed by Fred Penner. (PreK–Gr. 1)

Holabird, Katharine. *Angelina on Stage.* *Illus. by Helen Craig. Crown, 1986.* The beloved ballet-loving mouse is jealous of her younger cousin, Henry, when they both are chosen to dance in a ballet. Also read *Angelina Ballerina* (1983). (PreK–Gr. 2)

Idle, Molly. *Flora and the Flamingo.* *Illus. by the author. Chronicle, 2013.* In a gorgeous wordless book with flaps that lift up and down, a girl in a pink bathing suit and brown flippers dances a pas de deux with a graceful pink flamingo. (PreK–Gr. 2)

Isadora, Rachel. *Lili at Ballet.* *Illus. by the author. Putnam, 1993.* Ballet steps and a performance are seen through the eyes of a young ballet student. (PreK–Gr. 2)

Isadora, Rachel. *Max.* *Illus. by the author. Macmillan, 1976.* When Max takes a ballet class, his baseball skills improve. (PreK–Gr. 2)

Isadora, Rachel. *The Twelve Dancing Princesses.* *Illus. by the author. Putnam, 2007.* The traditional Grimm Brothers' tale reset in Africa. Compare it to two classically illustrated versions: one retold and illustrated by Ruth Sanderson (Little, Brown, 1990) and the other by Marianna Mayer, illustrated by K. Y. Craft (Morrow, 1989). (K–Gr. 5)

Kinerk, Robert. *Clorinda.* *Illus. by Steven Kellogg. Simon & Schuster, 2002.* Clorinda the cow moves to New York City to become a ballerina. (PreK–Gr. 3)

Lobel, Arnold. *Ming Lo Moves the Mountain.* *Illus. by the author. Greenwillow, 1982.* In a literary folktale set in China, an old man and his wife attempt to move the mountain overshadowing their house by dancing it away. (PreK–Gr. 2)

Marshall, James. *Swine Lake.* *Illus. by Maurice Sendak. HarperCollins, 1999.* A hungry wolf is entranced by the Boarshoi Ballet's pig-filled production of Swine Lake. (Gr. 1–4)

Martin, Bill Jr., and John Archambault. *Barn Dance. Illus. by Ted Rand. Henry Holt, 1986.* A little boy joins the farm animals and a scarecrow in a nighttime dance. (PreK–Gr. 2)

McKissack, Patricia C. *Mirandy and Brother Wind.* *Illus. by Jerry Pinkney. Knopf, 1988.* Mirandy wants the wind to be her partner for the cakewalk contest. (Gr. 1–4)

Powell, Patricia Hruby. *Josephine: The Dazzling Life of Josephine Baker.* *Illus. by Christian Robinson. Chronicle, 2014.* A sumptuous ninety-page picture-book biography, filled with free-verse text and theatrical acrylic cartoon-like illustrations about the life of Josephine Baker (1906–1975), who grew up poor in East St. Louis and became a singing and dancing sensation in Paris starting in the 1930s. (Gr. 3–6)

Ray, Mary Lyn. *Deer Dancer.* *Illus. by Lauren Stringer. Beach Lane, 2014.* A young girl, practicing her ballet moves in a grassy field, encounters and dances with a young deer. (PreK–Gr. 1)

Reich, Susanna. *José! Born to Dance.* *Illus. by Raúl Colón. Simon & Schuster, 2005.* The story of Mexican-born José Limón (1908–1972), who emigrated as a boy to the US and rose to fame in the dance world. (Gr. 1–4)

Shannon, George. *Dance Away.* *Illus. by Jose Aruego and Ariane Dewey. Greenwillow, 1982.* Rabbit's love of dance saves his friends from a hungry fox. (PreK–Gr. 2)

Smith, Cynthia Leitich. *Jingle Dancer.* *Illus. by Cornelius Van Wright and Ying-Hwa Hu. Morrow, 2000.* Jenna, of the Muscogee (Creek) Nation, needs to add more jingles to her dress to do the jingle dance at the upcoming powwow. (K–Gr. 4)

Thompson, Lauren. *Ballerina Dreams: A True Story. Photos by James Estrin. Feiwel and Friends, 2007.* An inspiring photo essay in which four young girls with muscular disorders prepare for an upcoming ballet recital. (K–Gr. 4)

Wallace, Ian. *Chin Chiang and the Dragon's Dance. Illus. by the author. Groundwood, 1992, c1984.* A young boy participating in a Chinese New Year's parade worries that his clumsiness will bring bad fortune. (PreK–Gr. 2)

Wheeler, Lisa. *Boogie Knights. Illus. by Mark Siegel. Atheneum, 2008.* In rollicking rhyme, a little prince watches rascals at the castle dance at the Madcap Monster Ball. (PreK–Gr. 3)

Willems, Mo. *Elephants Cannot Dance. Illus. by the author. Hyperion, 2009.* Piggie tries to teach Gerald to dance—but it's not easy. (PreK–Gr. 2)

Wilson, Karma. *Hilda Must Be Dancing. Illus. by Suzanne Watts. McElderry, 2004.* Hilda Hippo's jungle friends suggest she take up knitting, but her passion is dancing. (PreK–Gr. 1)

Musical Instruments in Programs

Do you play an instrument? If you haven't picked it up since you were a kid, dust it off and start practicing. You don't need to be a virtuoso; simple chords are enough to enthrall your audience. Maybe you have a friend who plays an instrument? Invite him or her to perform as a guest. After the performance, the musician may enjoy showing the instrument to the children and explaining a little about it.

Bring out a variety of musical instruments to demonstrate or to let the children try. You don't need a baby grand to introduce children to a piano; an inexpensive portable electric keyboard will do—or even a flexible, roll-up keyboard, if you need to travel light.

Teach your kids to play this little ditty that helps them become familiar with the black keys on the piano. (Look it up on YouTube to hear the whole thing.)

I Dropped My Dolly

I dropped my dolly in the dirt,

I asked my dolly if it hurt,

And all my dolly said to me was

Whaa whaa whaa!

Here's the score, in its simplest form:

First three lines: F# A# F# G# F# D# F# C#

Last line: lower A# F# lower G#

 WEB

This score is available on ALA's Web Extras page at alaeditions.org/webextras.

I Dropped My Dolly in the Dirt

Anonymous

I dropped my dol - ly in - the dirt, I asked my dol - ly if it hurt;

and all my dol - ly said to me was, "Wah wah, wah."

One of Judy's missions as a school librarian was to help children become enthusiastic about songs and music. One year, as she pulled out her guitar, a new fifth-grade boy looked at it with barely concealed horror: "Do we have to sing? This isn't music class."

"We do all kinds of crazy things in the library," Judy responded. "Sometimes we draw—and this isn't the art room. Sometimes we do science experiments or magic tricks, and this isn't the science lab. Sometimes we write, or act out plays, and this isn't a theater. Our library represents the whole universe and everything in it. Today, I'm in the mood for a good song. Let me introduce my best friend to you new kids. His name is . . . the Beast."

It never took long for new kids to join in the rest of the class in cheering, "Yay! It's the Beast!" Each spring when the dreaded testing season arrived, the children would get exhausted from reading dull little paragraphs and bubbling in little circles for days on end. Judy would schedule a "library sing" with three classes at a time for R&R. She compiled a little songbook for each student to take home, filled with wacky songs, some familiar, some not. For thirty brain-restoring minutes, the groups would laugh and sing with great gusto. As the children sang, they read the song lyrics for a bit of singers' theater. By the time they headed back to class, you could feel the change in their mood from deflated to elated. Singing does that.

Even though Judy is no longer a school librarian, she still loves presenting story, song, poetry, and book-filled assemblies at elementary schools each year. She always brings her trusty traveling Martin Backpacker guitar, which a first grader named Bigfoot. She tells them Bigfoot is a music lover who loves to hear children sing out in their most beautiful voices. In response, that's just what they do. Amazingly, when she returns to a school, there are always children who shout, "I know you! You came here last year. Did you bring Bigfoot?" They might not recall Judy's name, but they sure do remember her little guitar.

If you want to learn to play the guitar, the Backpacker, made by C.F. Martin & Co., is resilient, lightweight (a bit over two pounds), and portable; it will withstand lots of bumps and bruises. Backpackers, widely available at music stores and online, cost around $200. Get the classical nylon-string, not the steel-string, especially if you are a new player with tender fingertips or don't play enough to keep your callouses intact.

HOMEMADE RHYTHM INSTRUMENTS
Hold a separate musical-crafts workshop in the public library—or collaborate with the art teacher in your school—and have children construct their own musical instruments out of found or recycled materials. Here are a few easy ideas:

- Fill small plastic containers, small boxes, and matchboxes with buttons, rice, macaroni, marbles, pebbles, or anything else that will rattle. Close them with thick rubber bands or sturdy tape.
- Put a piece of heavy tape over the tip of a large nail, and let kids use it to thump a rhythm on a cake rack, pot top, or tin can.
- Empty oatmeal boxes and cylindrical coffee containers make great small drums.
- Put rubber bands across an open box, sugar scoop, or plastic container to make a stringed instrument you or a child can strum.
- Use two of a kind to bump together: large bolts, jar lids, pot tops, tin cans.
- Opened tin cans make good percussion instruments. If the edges are sharp, tape them with duct tape. Drill a hole in the center of the bottom and poke a long knotted string through it. The string should be long enough so you can hold the can in the air or hang it around your neck, leaving your hands free to tap, pound, or hit it with a metal spoon or ruler.
- Make more percussion instruments, such as paper-plate shakers— fold a paper plate in in half, put some dried popcorn in it, and staple the edges. Or castanets: Take old library book pockets and glue

flat buttons on front. Put your thumb into one, and your fingers into other, with the buttons facing each other, and tap away.

- Make a glass piano by filling several water glasses to different levels; tap them with a spoon to produce a melody.
- Make a kazoo out of a wax paper-covered comb; hum a tune through the paper.
- Construct a flute (which will sound like a kazoo) out of a paper or plastic straw. Flatten one end of the straw, cut a V into it, and blow through that end. You can cut tiny notches along the straw and play it like a recorder flute, changing the pitch. You can even make a paper-straw trombone by inserting another straw into the end of the first one. As you blow into the first straw, slide the second one up or down.
- For clear tutorials on making a xylophone, a rainstick, an oboe out of a straw, and many other instruments, go to YouTube and search *how to make musical instruments for kids.*

Children can use these instruments to participate in your story hour. They can tap out a rhythm while singing and "play" their instruments in time to it.

SONGS TO USE WITH MOTIONS
We can make rhythm instruments with our bodies simply by snapping our fingers, clapping our hands, and stamping our feet in time to a song. Folk-songs with familiar choruses make good material for body-based rhythm instruments and noise-making. Try "Clementine," "Oh, Susannah," "The Erie Canal," and "Yankee Doodle," or begin with this well-known song every kid knows (or should):

If You're Happy
Sing this as a group or divide your group so that some are singing and some are playing their instruments. Many verses can be sung by adding actions such as: stamp your feet, turn around, touch the ground, raise your hands, blink your eyes, cluck your tongue—or whatever you and your children can think up.

> If you're happy and you know it, clap your hands;
>
> If you're happy and you know it, clap your hands;
>
> If you're happy and you know it, and you really want to show it;
>
> If you're happy and you know it, clap your hands.

BOOKLIST: STORIES WITH RHYTHMIC PHRASES

Here are some stories with refrains that inspire rhythm activities. Slap your hands on your thighs, snap your fingers, clap your hands, or stamp your feet in time with the repeated words.

Birdseye, Tom. *Soap! Soap! Don't Forget the Soap! An Appalachian Folktale.* *Illus. by Andrew Glass. Holiday House, 1993.* This sprightly picture-book version of a story—also found in Richard Chase's Grandfather Tales (Houghton Mifflin, 1948) as "Soap, Soap, Soap!"—offers several repeating phrases to chant. (K–Gr. 4)

Gravett, Emily. *Monkey and Me.* *Illus. by the author. Simon & Schuster, 2008.* "Monkey and me, Monkey and me, Monkey and me, we went to see . . ." penguins, bats, elephants, and more. (PreK–Gr. 1)

Hoberman, Mary Ann. *Miss Mary Mack: A Handclapping Rhyme.* *Illus. by Nadine Bernard Westcott. Little, Brown, 1998.* Ten wild verses about a fence-jumping elephant to read, recite, or sing. (PreK–Gr. 2)

Perkins, Al. *Hand, Hand, Fingers, Thumb.* *Illus. by Eric Gurney. Random House, 1969.* In this lively emergent reader, monkeys bang on drums and chant, "Dum ditty dum ditty dum dum dum." (PreK–Gr. 1)

Stutson, Caroline. *By the Light of the Halloween Moon.* *Illus. by Kevin Hawkes. Lothrop, 1993.* A girl "smacks the sprite who bites the ghost who trips the ghoul who swats at the bat . . ." as she taps a tune "by the silvery light of the Halloween moon!" (PreK–Gr. 2)

Westcott, Nadine Bernard. *The Lady with the Alligator Purse.* *Illus. by the author. Little, Brown, 1988.* In this picture-book version of the old nonsense chant, Tiny Tim survives! (PreK–Gr. 2)

Westcott, Nadine Bernard. *Peanut Butter and Jelly: A Play Rhyme.* *Illus. by the author. Dutton, 1987.* This well-loved chant explains how to make a peanut-butter-and-jelly sandwich. (PreK–Gr. 2)

Silly Songs Children Love

Here are a bunch of songs kids will revel in, even if they already know them. The wordplay will help kids develop their command of the English language and, equally important, their sense of humor. Songs like these are the folklore of children, passed down from generation to generation. Make a collaborative book of these songs and chants with your students.

We've assembled a short selection of some of our favorite funny folksongs to introduce to your groups. Some of them are scored; all of them include simple guitar chords. If you don't know the tune or read music or know how to play the guitar, you can find the songs on YouTube. Look for more poems, chants, and songs in chapter 4, under "Underground Rhymes, Chants, and Nonsense Verse" on page 139.

Judy has added simple chord changes to give you a good starting point for the guitar, piano, or piano, and, when the music might be unfamiliar, the score as well.

SILLY SONGS ABOUT MACHINERY

Tin Ford

Collected by Robert Rubenstein

The tune for this song is based on "Skip to My Lou," but you can find may other versions, each one different. Feel free to add your own motions and write new verses. That's the folk process in action. You can sing this song slowly until everyone knows it, and then speed up the chorus each time you repeat it, using actions for each word, until you're zooming through it.

C
I've got a little pile of tin.

G
Nobody knows what shape it's in.

C
It's got four wheels and a running board.

G   **C**
It's a Ford. Oh! It's a Ford.

Chorus:

Honk, honk (*pull ear lobe twice*)

Rattle, rattle, rattle (*shake head*)

CRASH (*tap chin with heel of hand*)

Beep, beep. (*tap nose with pads of fingers*)

Honk, honk (*pull ear lobe twice*)

Rattle, rattle, rattle (*shake head*)

CRASH (*tap chin with heel of hand*)

Beep, beep. (*tap nose with pads of fingers*)

Got no bottom, got no top;

Throw out the anchor when you want to stop.

Got no windows, got no brakes;

All I've got are small earthquakes. (*chorus*)

Additional verses:

Romeo and Juliet,

On a balcony they set.

Scram, you guys, I got a date.

Shakespeare's comin' at a half-past eight. (*chorus*)

    (*Alternate line:* Shakespeare's comin' in a '48)

Called myself on the telephone

Just to see if I was home.

Asked my self out on a date.

Picked me up at a half past eight. (*chorus*)

I love myself, I think I'm grand.

I go to the movies and I hold my hand.

Wrapped my arms around my waist;

Got so fresh, I slapped my face. (*chorus*)

Dunderbeck's Machine

Traditional text; to the tune of "A Rambling Wreck from Georgia Tech";
collected by Edmund F. Soule

C   **G7**   **C**
There was a little butcher, and his name was Dunder-beck;

            G
He kept cold meat and sauerkraut and sausage by the peck.

 F   **C**   **F**   **G7**
He had a little butcher shop, the finest ever seen

  C   **G**   **C**
And one day he invented a sausage-meat ma-chine.

Chorus:

O Dunderbeck, O Dunderbeck, how could you be so mean;

For ever having invented that terrible old machine;

The longtailed rats and kittycats will never more be seen,

For they'll all be ground to sausage-meat in Dunderbeck's machine!

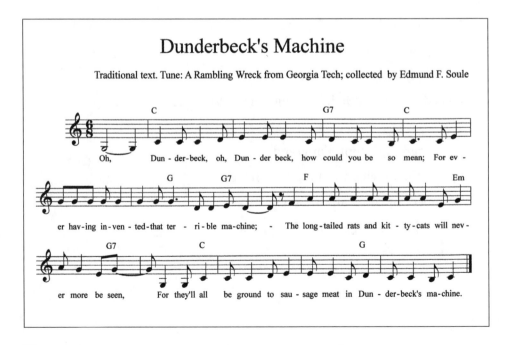

Dunderbeck's Machine

Traditional text. Tune: A Rambling Wreck from Georgia Tech; collected by Edmund F. Soule

WEB This score is available on ALA's Web Extras page at alaeditions.org/webextras.

One day a very little boy came walking into the store;

He wanted to buy a sausage that was lying on the floor.

While he waited for it, it whistled a merry tune

And all the sausages got up and danced around the room. (*chorus*)

Now something was the matter, the machine it would not go,

And Dunderbeck he crawled inside the trouble for to know.

His wife was having nightmares and waking in her sleep;

She gave the crank a terrible yank and Dunderbeck was meat! (*chorus*)

SILLY SONGS ABOUT PEOPLE

Johnny Has a Head Like a Ping-Pong Ball

To the tune of "The William Tell Overture"

D
Johnny has a head like a ping-pong ball,

              A7
Johnny has a head like a ping-pong ball,

D
Johnny has a head like a ping-pong ball,

A7   **D**
Just like a ping-pong ball.

Bm
Johnny has a head like a ping-pong, ping-pong, ping-pong, ping-
pong, ping-pong ball.

Johnny has a head like a ping-pong, ping-pong,

         E7   **A**
ping-pong, ping-pong ball.

Em   **G**   **D**   **A**
Ping, ping, ping, ping, ping, ping, ping, ping, ping.

Em   **G**   **D**   **A**
Pong, pong, pong, pong, pong, pong, pong, pong, pong.

Hey!

You can find an alternate, energetic, full-body version (not to mention your aerobic workout for the day) at www.youtube.com/watch?v = plu70as-2dI. Add the following motions when you sing. Repeat, a little faster each time, until you're exhausted.

> If I (*point to your chest with your thumbs*) had a head (*point to sides of your head with your index fingers*) like a ping-pong ball, (*hold your arms in an arc over your head*)
>
> If I (*point to your chest with your thumbs*) had a head (*point to the sides of your head with your index fingers*) like a ping-pong ball, (*hold your arms in an arc over your head*)
>
> If I (*point to your chest with your thumbs*) had a head (*point to the sides of head with your index fingers*) like a ping-pong ball, (*hold your arms in an arc over your head*)
>
> I (*point to your chest with your thumbs*) would surely float. (*hold your arms to you sides as if you're floating away*)
>
> Like a ping, like a ping, like a ping-pong, ping-pong, ping-pong ping-pong ping-pong ball. (*bounce on toes every time you sing the word "ping"*)
>
> Like a ping, like a ping, like a ping-pong, ping-pong, ping-pong ping-pong ping-pong ball. (*bounce on toes every time you sing the word "ping"*)

We Do Nothing

To the tune of "Reuben, Reuben, I've Been Thinking"

Sing this first verse over and over until you're good and sick of it (which could take quite some time). Then move on to the second part. When you sing the second verse, put one elbow on the table, with your head resting on your hand. Each time you sing the word "SWITCH," switch to the other elbow and lean on that hand. Start singing slowly; each time around, sing it a bit faster, until you're singing it and switching elbows at top speed.

A
We do nothing, nothing, nothing,

E
We do nothing all day long;

A   D   A
We do abso-lutely nothing.

                   E   A
How do you like our nothing song?

(*Spoken*) Second verse, same as the first, a little bit louder and a
    little bit worse.

A
I don't care if I go crazy,

          E
1–2–3–4–5–6 SWITCH!

A   D   A
Crazy go I if care don't I,

       E   A
6–5–4–3–2–1 SWITCH!

SILLY SONGS ABOUT CLOTHING

Pink Pajamas

To the tune of "Battle Hymn of the Republic"

G
I wear my pink pajamas in the summer when it's hot.

C   G
I wear my flannel nighties in the winter when it's not.
And sometime in the springtime and sometimes in the fall.

Am   D7   G
I jump right in between the sheets with nothing on at all.

G
Glory, glory, hallelujah;

C   G
Glory, glory, what's it to ya?
Balmy breezes blowing through ya,

      Am   D7   G
With nothing on at all.

Bye-Bye, Long Johns

To the tune of "Bye-Bye, Blackbird"

| A | | E | A |

I just lost my underwear; I don't care, I'll go bare.

E

Bye-bye, long johns.

Bm   F#   E

They were very close to me. Tickled me, hee, hee, hee.

A

Bye-bye, long johns.

G   F#

How I miss that old trap door be-hind me.

Bm   E

When you see them you'll know where to find me.

A   G   F#

I just lost my underwear; I'll go bare, I don't care.

Bm   E   A

Long johns, bye-bye.

God Bless My Underwear

To the tune of "God Bless America"

E   B7   E   E7

God bless my underwear, my only pair.

A   E

Stand be-side them, and guide them,

B7   E

Through the rips, through the holes, through the tears.

B7   E   B7   E   E7

From the washer, to the dryer, to the clothesline in the air.

A   E   B7 E   E7

God bless my underwear, my only pair.

A   E   B7 E

God bless my underwear, my only pair.

Black Socks

You can sing this as a round and add motions, too.

G   C   G
Black socks, they never get dirty;

    C   G   D7   G
The longer you wear them the blacker they get.

         C   G
Sometimes I think I should wash them,

    C   G   D7   G
But something in-side me keeps saying not yet.

Not yet, not yet, not yet, not yet.

WEB This score is available on ALA's Web Extras page at alaeditions.org/webextras.

SILLY SONGS ABOUT FOOD

Thanksgiving Song

Collected by Nell Givler; second verse by Judy Freeman, 2012;
to the tune of "Frère Jacques"

This song will get your group in the mood for a celebration. It works beautifully as a round. It is the easiest song on earth to play on the guitar because you can pick a starting chord, like D, and just strum it all the way through. If you want to get a tad fancier, play two alternating chords.

D   A7 D   A7   D
Tur-key dinner, tur-key dinner.

D   A7 D   A7   D
Ga-ther round, ga-ther round.

D   A7   D
Who will get the drumstick?

          A7   D
Yummy, yummy drumstick.

   A7 D   A7 D
All sit down, all sit down.

Sweet potatoes, mashed potatoes.

Gravy, too, toodle-oo.

Plates are overflowing, appetites are growing,

Chew and chew, chew and chew.

Cornbread muffins, chestnut stuffing,

Pumpkin pie, one foot high.

All of us were thinner

Until we came to dinner

Me-o-my, me-o-my.

Bananas, Coconuts, and Grapes

To the tune of "The Battle Hymn of the Republic"

Sing this three or four times: the first time as loud as you can; the second time a little softer; the third time whisper all but the "Tarzan" part, which you yell each time. The fourth time, just mouth the words until everybody shouts in unison, "TARZAN OF THE APES!"

G   **G7**
I like bananas, coconuts, and grapes.

C **Am** **G**   **D7**
I like bananas, coconuts, and grapes.

G   **B7**   **Em**
I like bananas, coconuts, and grapes.

Am   **D7**   **G**
That's why they call me: (*yelling*) TARZAN OF THE APES!

SILLY SONGS ABOUT SCHOOL

You can sing these three as a medley, one after another. Your children will cheer.

It's Off to School We Go

To the tune of "Hi Ho, Hi Ho, It's Off to Work We Go"

D   **G** **E7**   **A7**
Hi ho, hi ho, it's off to school we go;

  G **D**   **G**   **D**
The water tastes like turpen-tine,

  G   **D** **G**   **D**   **A7**
The teachers look like Franken-stein, hi ho, hi ho, hi ho,

  D **G** **E7**   **A7**
Hi ho, hi ho, I bit the teacher's toe;

  G   **D**   **G** **E7**   **D** **A** **D**
The dirty rat, she bit me back, hi ho, hi ho.

I've Been Working on My Schoolbooks

To the tune of "I've Been Working on the Railroad"

D
I've been working on my schoolbooks,

G   **D** **A7**
All the livelong day;

D
I've been working on my schoolbooks

Just to pass.

And, no, we didn't leave off the last line. Though you'll end abruptly with "Just to pass," often people, continue with "the time away . . ." That's when you say, "No, that's not right. Let's try that ending again." Once the kids get it, they will find it hilarious.

Joy to the World?

To the tune of "Joy to the World"

Judy heard this one from a third-grade girl, who sang it for her, with obvious glee and gusto, at International School Manila in 1998.

G **D7** **G** **C** **G** **D7** **G**
Joy to the world, my tea-cher's dead;

   C **D7** **G**
They barbe-cued her head.

     C **G**
What happened to her body?

     C **G**
They flushed it down the potty.

Oh, hear that flushing sound . . .

   D   **D7**
Oh, hear that flushing sound . . .

   G **C** **G** **D7** **G**
Oh, he—ee—ear that flushing sound.

SILLY SONGS ABOUT ANIMALS

Bill Grogan's Goat

Sing this as a call-and-response or as an echo song; you sing one line, the audience sings it back. Some folks sing it to the tune of "How Dry I Am," but the tune we reprinted below is better known, since it's a melody that children commonly prepare for their first two-hand piano recital. After your children learn the lyrics of the regular version below, continue with the following wackier version.

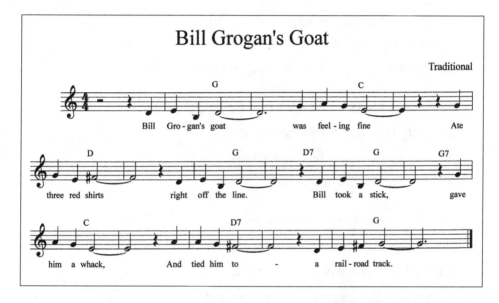

Bill Grogan's Goat — Traditional

| G   C |
Bill Grogan's goat was feeling fine,

| D   G   D7 |
Ate three red shirts right off the line.

| G   G7   C |
Bill took a stick, (*rest*) gave him a whack,

| D7   G |
And tied him to a railroad track.

WEB This score is available on ALA's Web Extras page at alaeditions.org/webextras.

The whistle blew, the train grew nigh,

Bill Grogan's goat was doomed to die.

He gave a shriek of mortal pain,

Coughed up those shirts, and flagged the train.

Then try this loony version of the song.

> Bill Grogan's goaty-oaty-oaty-oaty-oat
> Was doing finey-iney-iney-iney-ine,
> Ate six red shirty-irty-irty-irty-irts
> From off the liney-iney-iney-iney-ine.
>
> I took a sticky-icky-icky-icky-ick
> And gave a whacky-acky-acky-acky-ack,
> And tied him tooy-ooy-ooy-ooy-oo
> The railroad tracky-acky-acky-acky-ack.
>
> The whistle blewy ewy ewy ewy ew
> The train drew nighy-ighy-ighy-ighy-igh,
> Bill Grogan's goaty-oaty-oaty-oaty-oat
> Was sure to diey-iey-iey-iey-ie.
>
> But with a groany-oany-oany-oany-oan
> Of mortal painy-ainy-ainy-ainy-ain,
> Coughed up the shirty-irty-irty-irty-irts
> And flagged the trainy-ainy-ainy-ainy-ain.

Mules

To the tune of "Auld Lang Syne"

This seems like a nonsensical song, but if you know that mules are prone to kicking, it makes sense. Sing it formally. Definitely hand out the words so your listeners can figure it out as they sing.

```
    D             A           D    D7    G
On mules we find two legs behind, and two we find be-fore;

    D           A7                    Bm    G     D
We stand behind be-fore we find, what the two be-hind be for.
```

<pre>
A   D   A7   D   D7   G
</pre>
When we're behind the two behind, we find what these be for;

<pre>
D   A7   Bm   G   D
</pre>
So stand before the two be-hind, and behind the two be-fore.

Señor Don Gato

When you sing this wry song with adults in the audience, you will see several people sit up and grin in recognition and delight. A lot of elementary school music teachers taught this song to their students way back when, and those who sang it never quite forgot it. "I learned that in third grade!" grown-ups will exclaim, and many still recall all the lyrics.

After Judy sang it with an audience of adults during a workshop, one teacher said, "When I was a kid, we always clapped three times after the first, second, and last lines of each verse. We put our arms up to the right the first time—*clap, clap clap*—and then to the left the next time—*clap, clap clap*—alternating each time, like we were playing castanets."

Try it that way with your kids. It sounds great.

Based on an original Spanish song, this English version does not share a tune with the original; instead it uses the score of an altogether different Spanish folk song, "*Ahora que vamos despacio.*" The lyrics in Spanish are quite different from the English ones as well.

You can hear the whole song below, with sing-along subtitles, at www.you tube.com/watch?v = Gqpvy8p-WzQ.

<pre>
      Am   G   Am
</pre>
Oh, Se-ñor Don Gato was a cat; (*clap, clap, clap*)

<pre>
           G   Am
</pre>
On a high red roof Don Gato sat. (*clap, clap, clap*)

<pre>
                 A   Dm
</pre>
He went there to read a letter, meow, meow, meow,

<pre>
                      E   Am
</pre>
Where the reading light was better, meow, meow, meow;

<pre>
     E7   Am
</pre>
'Twas a love note for Don Gato. (*clap, clap, clap*)

WEB This score is available on ALA's Web Extras page at alaeditions.org/webextras.

"I adore you," wrote the lady cat,

Who was fluffy, white, and nice and fat.

There was not a sweeter kitty, meow, meow, meow

In the country or the city, meow, meow, meow,

And she said she'd wed Don Gato.

Oh, Don Gato jumped so happily,

He fell off the roof and broke his knee;

Broke his ribs and all his whiskers, meow, meow, meow

And his little solar plexus, meow, meow, meow;

"Ay Caramba," cried Don Gato.

Then the doctors all came on the run,

Just to see if something could be done.

And they held a consultation, meow, meow, meow

About how to save their patient, meow, meow, meow,

How to save Señor Don Gato.

But in spite of everything they tried,

Poor Señor Don Gato up and died.

And it wasn't very merry, meow, meow, meow

Going to the cemetery, meow, meow, meow,

For the ending of Don Gato.

When the funeral passed the market square,

Such a smell of fish was in the air.

Though his burial was slated, meow, meow, meow

He became reanimated, meow, meow, meow;

He came back to life, Don Gato!

Making Up Your Own Songs

When you can't find a song to go with your program, think of a simple one you already know and write new lyrics. (Or, if music is more your thing, find a poem you love and set it to a tune you know or compose a new one.)

I'm Bringing Home a Scary Vampire Bat

By Judy Freeman; to the tune of "I'm Bringing Home a Baby Bumblebee"

Your boys and ghouls might want to compose new verses about other characters and creatures for this one.

      E   **A**   **E**
I'm bringing home a scary vampire bat;

B7   **A**   **B7**
Won't my mommy be a 'fraidy cat,

            E   **A**   **E**
'Cause I'm bringing home a baby vampire bat.
(*Spoken in creature's voice*) CHOMP!

      B7
(*Spoken*) Ooh, it bit me!

I'm bringing home a scary big white ghost;

Won't my mommy think he is the most,

'Cause I'm bringing home a scary big white ghost.

(*Spoken in creature's voice*) BOO!

(*Spoken*) Ooh, he scared me!

I'm bringing home a scary Frankenstein;

Won't my mommy think he is divine,

'Cause I'm bringing home a scary Frankenstein.

(*Spoken in creature's voice*) ARRRGGHH!

(*Spoken*) Ooh, he stepped on me!

I'm bringing home a scary skeleton;

Won't my mommy have a lot of fun,

'Cause I'm bringing home a scary skeleton.

(*Spoken in creature's voice*) CREAK, CRACK!

(*Spoken*) Ooh, it rattled my bones!

I'm bringing home a scary mean old witch;

Won't my mommy tremble and twitch,

'Cause I'm bringing home a scary mean old witch.

(*Spoken in creature's voice*) HEH HEH HEH!

(*Spoken*) Oh nooooo, she turned me into a frog . . .
    Ribbit, ribbit, ribbit.

Going to the Beach

By Judy Freeman, ©1989; to the tune of Tom Paxton's "Going to the Zoo"

When Judy needed a beach-themed song to go with Gene Zion's picture book Harry by the Sea *(HarperCollins, 1965) and James Stevenson's easy reader,* Clams Can't Sing *(Greenwillow, 1980), she thought of folksinger Tom Paxton's classic "Going to the Zoo," and rewrote it to suit the new locale. She has been singing this "down the shore" version ever since. Best of all, children can compose new verses on the spot. If you don't know Paxton's classic tune, you can hear it on YouTube, including this 1964 version covered by a very young Paul Simon: www.youtube.com/watch?v = xPtqGt9aP7I.*

D
Papa's taking us to the beach tomorrow,

A
Beach tomorrow, beach tomorrow,

D
Papa's taking us to the beach tomorrow.

A   **D**
We can stay all day.

Chorus:

D7   **G**
We're going to the beach, what fun,

         D
Playing in the blazing sun,

            A7
Swimming 'til the day is done;

           D   **G**   **D**
We're going to the beach, what fun.

Look at the crab, climbing in the sand,
Climbing all around in the wet wet sand,
Burying himself in the wet wet sand.
We can stay all day. (*chorus*)

Jumping in the waves, they're knocking us over,
Crashing on our heads, just knocking us over;
Water up my nose, just knocking us over.
We can stay all day. (*chorus*)

It's time for lunch, our bellies grumbling,
Tuna fish and sand, our bellies grumbling;
We need another cookie, our bellies grumbling.
We can stay all day. (*chorus*)

Piling up the seashells, wash 'em in the water,
All shapes and sizes, wash 'em in the water;
Take 'em all home and wash 'em in the water.
We can stay all day. (*chorus*)

We've been to the beach; we're droopy and drowsy,
Cruising in the van all droopy and drowsy;
Sunburned and sandy and droopy and drowsy.
We have stayed all day.

Sing slowly and pretend to fall asleep:

> We've been to the beach, what fun;
>
> We played in the blazing sun.
>
> We swam 'til the day was done.
>
> We've been to the beach what fun.

Wake up, singing brightly, with renewed energy:

> Papa's taking us to the beach tomorrow,
>
> Beach tomorrow, beach tomorrow,
>
> Papa's taking us to the beach tomorrow.
>
> We can stay all day. (*chorus*)

The Presidents Song

To the tune of "Yankee Doodle"

And sometimes you can add on to an existing song. We haven't been able to find who wrote this clever ditty, which appeared in a video produced by Nebraska Public Television around 1980. We think it may have originally been written during President Coolidge's term, 1923–1929. If you have information on the song, please contact us. We found it at www.livinghistoryfarm.org/farmingin the30s/lrRead04.html.

D　　　　　　　　　　　　　A7
Washington was first, and then came

D　　　　　　　A7
Adams and Tom Jefferson,

D　　　　　G　　　E
Madison, Monroe, and Adams,

A　　　　　　　　D
Jackson, and Van Buren.

G　　　　　　Em
Harrison, Tyler, Polk, and Taylor,

D
Fillmore, Pierce, Buchanan,

```
G                    E          E7
```
Lincoln, Johnson, Grant, and Hayes, and

```
D       A7      D
```
Garfield ruled the land then.

Arthur was the 21st and

22 was Cleveland,

Harrison was 23 and

Back came President Cleveland.

McKinley and then Roosevelt,

Taft, and Woodrow Wilson,

Harding, and then Coolidge, and then

Maybe, someday you can.

At a New Jersey conference, Judy sang this song and suggested librarians give their kids a list of all the subsequent presidents and have them write new verses. At the end of the program, Suzanne Ng, a school librarian from South Orange, New Jersey, handed her a piece of paper. "Here you go," she said. This is what she wrote:

Hoover and then FDR,

Truman, Eisenhower,

JFK and LBJ,

Nixon, Ford, and Carter

Ronald Reagan and Bush Senior,

Clinton, oh, the drama;

Then it was Bush Junior's turn,

And now, Barack Obama.

By the time you read this, there will be another president or more to add.

Stories to Tell with Music

Some stories from folklore include a song to sing. If not, you may want to integrate songs into the stories you tell and the books you read aloud. When you integrate music in your programs, you increase the chances that children will grow up to appreciate music and pass that love to their own children.

The following circular story includes two refrains that children can sing. You can use a guitar, autoharp, keyboard, or fiddle to accompany the song—or simply do each chorus a cappella.

Happy-Go-Lucky

By Judy Freeman

Long before your great-grandmother wore pigtails and your great-grandfather wore knickers, a cheerful young man moved into a small cottage just this side of town. He planned to earn his living as a painter, painting houses for money and pictures for himself. He called himself Happy-Go-Lucky. Times were tough and he hadn't had any luck finding folks who needed his services. His larder was nearly empty, and while he was content making his own paintings, he was, truth be told, a wee bit lonely.

"If I want to make my way in this world, I need to go and find some work to do," he said to himself one cool, sunny, mid-autumn morning. Happy-Go-Lucky headed for town to see what good fortune might greet him.

As he ambled along, he sang this song:

 G   G7   C
Happy-Go-Lucky, that's my name,

    G7   C
Living and laughing, that's my game;

    C7   F
I go a-long, singing a song,

 G   G7   C
Happy-Go-Lucky, that's me.

He hadn't gone far when he spied a fine young orange cat, perched high up in a maple tree, meowing piteously.

Happy-Go-Lucky

Judy Freeman

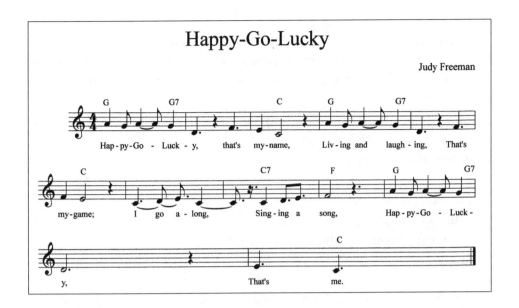

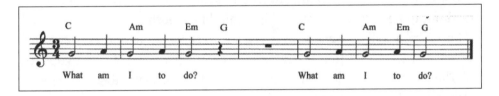

Happy-Go-Lucky greeted the cat.

"Good day to you, puss, but what is the mat-ter?

Is there something I can do to soothe your misery?"

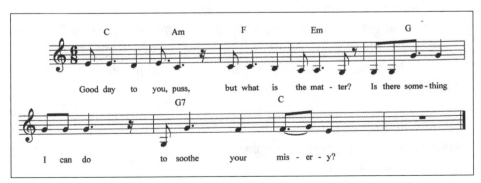

And with that, Happy-Go-Lucky climbed the tree and scooped the cat into his arms. He rubbed it under the chin and tickled it behind the ears. The cat climbed up onto the young man's shoulders, settled down for a snooze, and commenced to purr.

"Lucky I am with a cat to keep my neck warm," he said as he continued down the road to seek his good fortune.

As he walked, he sang:

"Happy-Go-Lucky, that's my name,
Living and laughing, that's my game;
I go along, singing a song,
Happy-Go-Lucky, that's me."

So it was that he walked along until he came to a wooden house with a yard full of tall hollyhocks. In the vegetable garden, there crouched an old woman, wailing and clutching her head in her hands.

"What am I to do?" she moaned. "What am I to do?"

"Good day to you, ma'am, but what is the matter?" Happy-Go-Lucky called out to her. "Is there something I can do to soothe your misery?"

"Misery you well may call it," she replied. "I came out to harvest some vegetables, and what do I find but mole hills everywhere. Rabbits and gophers, too. They'll tunnel and chew through my crops till there's nothing left to pick."

Happy-Go-Lucky bowed to the old woman and said,

"I'll make you a trade, if you will but barter;
A cat for some greens, swap me one for the other."

The old woman said, "Of what use is a cat to me?"

Happy-Go-Lucky smiled and placed the orange cat on the ground. The cat pounced on a tunnel and caught a gray mole.

"Lucky I am with a bushel of vegetables to fill my empty larder," he said as he hoisted a basket of carrots, string beans, summer squash, and new potatoes to his shoulder and bade the old woman and her new cat goodbye.

He continued down the road, singing:

"Happy-Go-Lucky, that's my name,
Living and laughing, that's my game;
I go along, singing a song,
Happy-Go-Lucky, that's me."

So it was that he walked along until he came to a stone house with a front yard filled with tubs of orange begonias. The door sprang open, and out ran a young woman holding a squalling baby in one arm, and two smoking, blackened loaves of bread wrapped in a towel in the other.

"What am I to do?" she wailed. "What am I to do?"

"Good day to you, mistress, but what is the matter?" Happy-Go-Lucky called out to her. "Is there something I can do to soothe your misery?"

"Misery you well may call it," she replied. "My husband has gone off to fetch my mother-in-law, and my grandmother-in-law, and my great-grandmother-in-law, too. And what am I to feed them? The cheese is moldy, the milk spilled, and now I have burnt my new-baked bread to a crisp."

Happy-Go-Lucky bowed to the woman and said,

"I'll make you a trade, if you will but barter;
My basket for bread, swap me one for the other."

The woman said, "Of what use is a basket to me?"

Happy-Go-Lucky smiled and placed the basket at her feet.

"Vegetables!" she cried thankfully. "I'll make soup."

The woman handed him the long, thin loaves of bread, as hard as branches.

"You're welcome to these," she said. "Though what you want with my sorry baking is more than I can fathom."

"Lucky I am with crumbs to feed the birds," he said as he tucked the bread under his arm and continued down the road to seek his good fortune, singing:

"Happy-Go-Lucky, that's my name,
Living and laughing, that's my game;
I go along, singing a song,
Happy-Go-Lucky, that's me."

So it was that he walked along until he came to a field filled with yellow dandelions, and a woods nearby. There he saw two young ruffians with a large brown sack at their feet, and a puppy cowering between them. They were laughing and shouting curses at the hapless dog and kicking it with their scuffed brown boots.

Happy-Go-Lucky stopped in his tracks. "Why should two grown boys be tormenting a poor, defenseless pup?"

The dog whimpered piteously as if to say, "What am I to do? What am I to do?"

"Good day, stout young fellows, but what is the matter?" Happy-Go-Lucky called out. "Is there something I can do to soothe your misery?"

"Misery you well may call it," sneered one ruffian, and shook his fist threateningly. "If you won't mind your own affairs, we'll give you a taste of misery."

Happy-Go-Lucky bowed to the hooligans and said,

"I'll make you a trade, if you will but barter;
My bread loaves for the dog, swap me one for the other."

The two scoundrels laughed raucously. "Fool! Of what use are two miserable burnt loaves of bread to us?"

Happy-Go-Lucky smiled and stepped closer to the rapscallions. "Allow me to show you," he said.

And with that, he began to beat the two bullies with the hard, stick-like loaves. He thrashed them soundly while they fell over themselves trying to get away. They ran for the woods, leaving both the dog and the brown sack behind.

Happy-Go-Lucky picked up the pup, who licked his face gratefully. Then he lifted the sack and shook it. It jingled. In the sack were silver coins, and silver spoons, and a dainty gold ring with a ruby in the center.

"Lucky I am with a dog to keep me company and a bag of treasures, too," he said as he tucked the puppy into his jacket and continued down the road to seek his good fortune, singing:

"Happy-Go-Lucky, that's my name,
Living and laughing, that's my game;
I go along, singing a song,
Happy-Go-Lucky, that's me."

So it was that he walked along until he came to a brick house with a front yard filled with red roses. There, sitting in the doorway, was a young woman, crying as if her heart were broken.

"What am I to do?" she sobbed. "What am I to do?"

"Good day to you, miss, but what is the matter?" Happy-Go-Lucky called out to her. "Is there something I can do to soothe your misery?"

"Misery you well may call it," she replied, wiping her eyes with her handkerchief but never looking up. "Not an hour past, robbers broke into the house while I was out and made off with the life savings of my parents and me. They stole the ruby ring that my grandmother left me. From that I could recover, but they even took my sweet young dog, and I'll never find another I love so well."

Holding tight to the pup, who wiggled and squirmed at the sight and sound of his mistress, Happy-Go-Lucky bowed to the young woman and said,

"I'll make you a trade, if you will but barter;
A smile for your treasures, swap me one for the other."

He placed the dog on the ground. With a joyous whimper and bark, it bounded over and licked the face of its mistress. Happy-Go-Lucky placed the brown sack at her feet. He reached inside and lifted out the ruby ring, which he placed on her finger.

"How can I ever repay you?" she cried.
"A smile is all I require," he replied.

And wasn't she glad to make that trade. As for Happy-Go-Lucky, he was so taken by her smile that he smiled right back.

Folks say the two of them fell in love right then and there, and not so long after that, they were married. They settled down in Happy-Go-Lucky's house, where they lived a long and luck-filled life, painting houses to pay the bills and portraits of each other to fill the walls.

Never underestimate the power of a smile when you're off to seek your good fortune.

Children's Books about Music

Even if you don't sing or play a musical instrument, you can introduce children to music through picture books, fiction, and nonfiction. There are many fine books that use as their subject a folk song, a composer, a musician, or an instrument. We've selected read-aloud and sing-aloud ones that we think every music lover should know.

BOOKLIST: PICTURE-BOOK VERSIONS OF SONGS

Arnold, Tedd. *Catalina Magdalena Hoopensteiner Wallendiner Hogan Logan Bogan Was Her Name*. *Illus. by the author. Scholastic, 2004*. A wacky picture-book version of the old camp song. (K–Gr. 4)

Aylesworth, Jim. *Our Abe Lincoln: An Old Tune with New Lyrics*. *Illus. by Barbara McClintock. Scholastic, 2009*. A catchy song version of Lincoln's life, to the tune of "The Old Gray Mare." (PreK–Gr. 2)

Bates, Katharine Lee. *America the Beautiful: Together We Stand*. *Illus. by Bryan Collier et al. Orchard, 2013*. Each line of the song is elucidated in a color double-page illustration by one of ten top children's book illustrators. A feast to pore over and sing. (PreK–Gr. 6)

Beaumont, Karen. *I Ain't Gonna Paint No More*. *Illus. by David Catrow. Harcourt, 2005*. An unrepentant little boy paints pictures on the floor, ceiling, and walls. Sing to the tune of "It Ain't Gonna Rain No More." (PreK–Gr. 2)

Brett, Jan. *The Twelve Days of Christmas*. *Illus. by the author. Putnam, 1989*. Gorgeous watercolors will have children gazing with awe as you sing the old song. (All Ages)

Bryan, Ashley. *Let It Shine: Three Favorite Spirituals*. *Illus. by the author. Atheneum, 2007*. Wildly colorful illustrations accompany the lyrics to "This Little Light of Mine," "Oh, When the Saints Go Marching In," and "He's Got the Whole World in His Hands." (PreK–Gr. 5)

Cabrera, Jane. *If You're Happy and You Know It*. *Illus. by the author. Holiday House, 2005*. Clap, stomp, and roar with animals while singing the familiar interactive song for optimists. (PreK–Gr. 1)

Cabrera, Jane. *Old MacDonald Had a Farm*. *Illus. by the author. Holiday House, 2008*. A colorful version of an essential song for kids. (PreK–Gr. 1)

Carle, Eric. *Today Is Monday*. *Illus. by the author. Philomel, 1993*. A jaunty, colorful version of a song about food and the days of the week. (PreK–Gr. 1)

Child, Maria L. *Over the River and through the Wood: The New England Boy's Song about Thanksgiving Day.* *Illus. by Matt Tavares. Candlewick, 2011.* A picture-book version of that old-timey trip by sleigh to Grandfather's house. (PreK–Gr. 3)

Coots, J. Fred, and Haven Gillespie. *Santa Claus Is Comin' to Town.* *Illus. by Steven Kellogg. HarperCollins, 2004.* Sing along with this cheerful version of the famous Christmas song. (PreK–Gr. 2)

Emberley, Rebecca. *If You're a Monster and You Know It.* *Illus. by Rebecca Emberley and Ed Emberley. Orchard, 2010.* A monster version of "If You're Happy and You Know It." (PreK–Gr. 1)

Frazee, Marla. *Hush, Little Baby: A Folk Song with Pictures.* *Harcourt, 1999.* An eighteenth-century pioneer family brings presents to the baby in the cradle to stop his crying. (PreK–Gr. 1)

Galdone, Paul. *Cat Goes Fiddle-I-Fee.* *Illus. by the author. Clarion, 1985.* A cumulative folk song about farm animals and the sounds they make. (PreK–Gr. 2)

Guthrie, Woody. *This Land Is Your Land.* *Illus. by Kathy Jakobsen. Little, Brown, 1998.* A picture-book rendition of Woody Guthrie's folk anthem. (Gr. 1–6)

Hort, Lenny. *The Seals on the Bus.* *Illus. by G. Brian Karas. Henry Holt, 2001.* A riotous animal-filled rewrite of "The Wheels on the Bus." (PreK–K)

Jackson, Alison. *I Know an Old Lady Who Swallowed a Pie.* *Illus. by Judith Byron Schachner. Dutton, 1997.* A ravenous guest eats everything in sight in a raucous Thanksgiving rewrite of "I Know an Old Lady Who Swallowed a Fly." (PreK–Gr. 2)

Jones, Carol. *Old MacDonald Had a Farm.* *Illus. by the author. Houghton Mifflin, 1989.* Die-cut peepholes let readers and singers guess what the next animal will be. (PreK–Gr. 1)

Katz, Alan. *I'm Still Here in the Bathtub: Brand New Silly Dilly Songs.* *Illus. by David Catrow. Simon & Schuster, 2003.* Fourteen seriously silly songs, each one a parody of a well-known folksong. Other crazy collections by Katz include: *Going, Going, Gone! And Other Silly Dilly Sports Songs* (2009), *Mosquitoes Are Ruining My Summer! And Other Silly Dilly Camp Songs* (2011), *On Top of the Potty and Other Get-Up-and-Go Songs* (2008), *Smelly Locker: Silly Dilly School Songs* (2010), *Take Me Out of the Bathtub and Other Silly Dilly Songs* (2001), *Too Much Kissing! And Other Silly Dilly Songs about Parents* (2009), and *Where Did They Hide My Presents? Silly Dilly Christmas Songs* (2005). (PreK–Gr. 3)

Keats, Ezra Jack. *The Little Drummer Boy.* *Words and music by Katherine Davis, Henry Sonority, and Harry Simeone. Macmillan, 1968.* The classic Christmas song. (PreK–Gr. 3)

Keats, Ezra Jack. *Over in the Meadow.* *Illus. by the author. Four Winds, 1971.* A classic counting rhyme, with text based on the original version by Olive A. Wadsworth. (PreK–Gr. 2)

Laínez, René Colato. *Señor Pancho Had a Rancho.* *Illus. by Elwood Smith. Holiday House, 2013.* On facing pages, the song of "Old MacDonald Had a Farm" and the jaunty Hispanic equivalent, which starts, "Señor Pancho had a rancho, cha-cha-cha-cha-cha. ¡Hola!" (PreK–Gr. 2)

Langstaff, John M. *Frog Went A-Courtin'.* *Illus. by Feodor Rojankovsky. Harcourt, 1955.* A Caldecott Medal–winning picture-book version of the song about Miss Mousie's disastrous wedding. (PreK–Gr. 2)

Long, Sylvia. *Hush Little Baby.* *Illus. by the author. Chronicle, 1997.* New lyrics for a familiar lullaby, sung by a mama rabbit to her young'un. (PreK–Gr. 1)

Mora, Pat. *A Piñata in a Pine Tree: A Latino Twelve Days of Christmas.* *Illus. by Magaly Morales. Clarion, 2009.* In an exuberant version of the classic Christmas song, with all-new lyrics in Spanish, a little girl receives a new gift each day from her "Secret Amiga." (K–Gr. 4)

Nelson, Kadir. *He's Got the Whole World in His Hands.* *Illus. by the author. Dial, 2005.* Glorious illustrations picturing an African American boy and his multiethnic family accompany the lyrics to this well-known spiritual. (PreK–Gr. 3)

Norworth, Jack. *Take Me Out to the Ballgame.* *Illus. by Alec Gillman. Four Winds, 1993.* The classic 1908 baseball anthem, set against a background of Game 5 of the 1947 World Series, with Jackie Robinson up at bat. (K–Gr. 6)

O'Brien, John. *The Farmer in the Dell.* *Illus. by the author. Boyd Mills Press, 2000.* Comical version of the song features the farmer being rescued from the dell by a cumulative cast of characters. (PreK–Gr. 1)

Paxton, Tom. *Going to the Zoo.* *Illus. by Karen Lee Schmidt. Morrow, 1996.* Sing along with Tom Paxton's classic zoo animal song. (PreK–Gr. 1)

Peek, Merle. *Mary Wore Her Red Dress and Henry Wore His Green Sneakers.* *Illus. by the author. Clarion, 1985.* Adapted from an old folk song; you can go through the color wheel and make up new verses "all day long." (PreK–Gr. 1)

Raffi. *Down by the Bay.* *Illus. by Nadine Bernard Westcott. Crown, 1987.* Animals are having fun "where the watermelons grow." Great fun to sing, inspiring children to write new rhyming verses. (PreK–Gr. 2)

Raffi. *Five Little Ducks.* *Illus. by Jose Aruego and Ariane Dewey. Crown, 1988.* In a song you can sing, Mother Duck's brood leaves her, one by one. (PreK–Gr. 1)

Raffi. *Spider on the Floor.* *Words and music by Bill Russell. Illus. by True Kelley. Crown, 1993.* This song about a spider climbing up an old lady's leg is deliciously singable, but just right for squeamish kids to make up spidery new verses. (PreK–Gr. 3)

Spier, Peter. *The Fox Went Out on a Chilly Night: An Old Song.* *Illus. by the author. Doubleday, 1961.* Folk song about a fox raiding a henhouse. (PreK–Gr. 4)

Spier, Peter. *The Star-Spangled Banner.* *Illus. by the author. Doubleday, 1973.* Three verses of the National Anthem by Francis Scott Key and heroic illustrations depict the 1812 bombardment of Fort McHenry. (All Ages)

Sturges, Philemon. *She'll Be Comin' 'Round the Mountain.* *Illus. by Ashley Wolff. Little, Brown, 2004.* In this picture-book version of the old folk song, the animal residents of Reederville await their traveling librarian, a javelina who drives a bookmobile called "Six White Horses." (PreK–Gr. 1)

Taback, Simms. *There Was an Old Lady Who Swallowed a Fly.* *Illus.by the author. Viking, 1997.* Die-cut holes reveal the fly, spider, and other creatures the old woman devours. (PreK–Gr. 2)

Trapani, Iza. *The Itsy Bitsy Spider.* *Illus. by the author. Whispering Coyote, 1993.* The verse you know, plus five new ones by the author that extend the story of the adventurous spider. Trapani's colorful songbooks include *Row, Row, Row Your Boat* (Charlesbridge, 1989) and *The Bear Went over the Mountain* (Sky Pony, 2012). (PreK–Gr. 1)

Westcott, Nadine Bernard. *I Know an Old Lady Who Swallowed a Fly.* *Illus. by the author. Little, Brown, 1980.* A frantically fun illustrated version of the cumulative folksong. Westcott's *I've Been Working on the Railroad: An American Classic* (Hyperion, 1996) is a rousing version of another old folksong. (PreK–Gr. 2)

Zelinsky, Paul O. *The Wheels on the Bus.* *Illus. by the author. Dutton, 1990.* An interactive version of the song, with movable parts that pop up, pull out, and roll. (PreK–Gr. 1)

BOOKLIST: PICTURE BOOKS ABOUT MUSIC AND MUSICIANS

Ackerman, Karen. *Song and Dance Man.* *Illus. by Stephen Gammell. Knopf, 1988.* Remembering his vaudeville days, Grandpa sings and dances for his grandchildren. (K–Gr. 4)

Brett, Jan. *Berlioz the Bear.* *Illus. by the author. Putnam, 1991.* Berlioz and his fellow bear musicians are on their way to give a concert when their wagon gets stuck. (PreK–Gr. 3)

Corey, Shana. *Players in Pigtails.* Illus. *by Rebecca Gibbon. Scholastic Press, 2003.* In 1943 Katie Casey signs up to play with All-American Girls Professional Baseball League. Katie is a fictional character, but her name comes from Jack Norworth's 1908 song, "Take Me Out to the Ballgame," which begins, "Katie Casey was baseball mad, had the fever and had it bad." You can get all the lyrics online. (Gr. 1–5)

Cox, Judy. *My Family Plays Music.* Illus. *by Elbrite Brown. Holiday House, 2003.* A young African American girl introduces each member of her musical family. (K–Gr. 3)

Cronin, Doreen. *Dooby Dooby Moo.* Illus. *by Betsy Lewin. Atheneum, 2006.* To win first prize at the county fair talent show, Duck and the other animals rehearse renditions of "Twinkle, Twinkle, Little Star," "Home on the Range," and "Born to Be Wild." (PreK–Gr. 2)

Curtis, Gavin. *The Bat Boy and His Violin.* Illus. *by E. B. Lewis. Simon & Schuster, 1998.* Reginald loves playing the violin; his father, manager of a Negro League team, would rather he played baseball. (Gr. 1–4)

Falconer, Ian. *Olivia Forms a Band.* Illus. *by the author. Atheneum, 2006.* Piglet Olivia plans to be a one-girl band at the town picnic. (PreK–Gr. 2)

Gordon, Gus. *Herman and Rosie.* Illus. *by the author. Roaring Brook, 2013.* In the big city, two aspiring musicians—Herman, an oboe-playing alligator, and Rosie, a jazz-singing goat—would be a great team, if only their paths would cross. (PreK–Gr. 3)

Helquist, Brett. *Roger, the Jolly Pirate.* Illus. *by the author. HarperCollins, 2004.* Roger, an incompetent pirate, tries to get other pirates to like him by baking a cake. Sing the appended song, "The Ballad of Jolly Roger." (PreK–Gr. 3)

Hopkinson, Deborah. *Stagecoach Sal: Inspired by a True Tale.* Illus. *by Carson Ellis. Hyperion, 2009.* While driving her Pa's stagecoach, Sal encounters the high-wayman, Poetic Pete, and sings him to sleep. (K–Gr. 3)

Howe, James. *Horace and Morris Join the Chorus (But What about Dolores?).* Illus. *by Amy Walrod. Atheneum, 2002.* Moustro Provolone accepts two mice pals into the school chorus, but he tells their friend Dolores that she doesn't have an ear for music. (PreK–Gr. 2)

Huling, Jan. *Ol' Bloo's Boogie-Woogie Band and Blues Ensemble.* Illus. *by Henri Sorensen. Peachtree, 2010.* On their way to sing in a New Orleans honky-tonk, four animals stop off at a cabin to sing for their supper. A down-home version of "The Bremen-Town Musicians." (Gr. 1–5)

Hurd, Thatcher. *Mama Don't Allow.* Illus. *by the author. HarperCollins, 1984.* Possum Miles and his swamp band learn that alligators don't make a good audience. (PreK–Gr. 2)

Isadora, Rachel. *Ben's Trumpet.* *Illus. by the author. Greenwillow, 1979.* In awe of the jazz musicians at the Zig Zag Jazz Club, a young boy plays his pretend trumpet. (PreK–Gr. 2)

Johnson, Paul Brett. *On Top of Spaghetti.* *Lyrics by Tom Glazer. Illus. by the author. Scholastic, 2006.* Yodeler Jones, a hound dog who serves only meatballs and spaghetti at his restaurant, describes what happens when, "On top of spaghetti, / All covered with cheese, / I lost my poor meatball, / When somebody SNEEZED." (PreK–Gr. 2)

Kovalski, Maryann. *Jingle Bells.* *Illus. by the author. Fitzhenry & Whiteside, 1989.* Grandma and two little girls sing their way through Central Park. (PreK–Gr. 2)

Krosoczka, Jarrett J. *Punk Farm.* *Illus. by the author. Knopf, 2005.* After Farmer Joe heads for bed, his animals begin rehearsing for the evening's rock 'n' roll concert. (PreK–Gr. 1)

Lies, Brian. *Bats in the Band.* *Illus. by the author. Houghton Mifflin Harcourt, 2014.* Bats gather in a theater late one night to put on a magnificent concert. (PreK–Gr. 2)

Lionni, Leo. *Geraldine, the Music Mouse.* *Illus. by the author. Knopf, 1979.* Geraldine's carving of a flute-playing mouse from cheese seems to play beautiful music for her every night. (PreK–Gr. 2)

Lithgow, John. *The Remarkable Farkle McBride.* *Illus. by C. F. Payne. Simon & Schuster, 2002.* Young Farkle masters every instrument until finding his true musical calling—as a conductor. (Gr. 1–4)

Litwin, Eric. *Pete the Cat: I Love My White Shoes.* *Illus. by James Dean. HarperCollins, 2010.* Singing as he saunters down the street in his new white sneakers, does Pete the Cat cry when he steps in strawberries, blueberries, and mud? "Goodness, no!" He just keeps on singing. Groovy! (PreK–Gr. 2)

McCloskey, Robert. *Lentil.* *Illus. by the author. Viking, 1940.* Lentil saves the day with his harmonica. Have the kids suck on lemon wedges as you play the harmonica. (Gr. 1–4)

Mitchell, Stephen. *The Nightingale.* *Illus. by Bagram Ibatoulline. Candlewick, 2002.* In a sumptuously illustrated version of the Hans Christian Andersen tale, the shortsighted emperor banishes a real nightingale in favor of a mechanical one. (K–Gr. 5)

Moss, Lloyd. *Zin! Zin! Zin! A Violin.* *Illus. by Marjorie Priceman. Simon & Schuster, 1995.* Introducing, in rhyme, the sights and sounds of ten different instruments in the orchestra. (K–Gr. 5)

Myers, Walter Dean. *The Blues of Flats Brown.* *Illus. by Nina Laden. Holiday House, 2000.* A guitar-pickin' blues-singin' mutt and his best friend head for Memphis and New York to make music. (K–Gr. 3)

Price, Leontyne. *Aida*. *Illus. by Leo and Diane Dillon. Harcourt, 1990.* A sumptuously illustrated story of the Verdi opera. (Gr. 4–6)

Raschka, Chris. *Charlie Parker Played Be Bop*. *Illus. by the author. Orchard, 1992.* While reading this, play jazz great Parker's "A Night in Tunisia," on which this onomatopoeic book is based. (Gr. 1–6)

Seeger, Pete. *Abiyoyo*. *Illus. by Michael Hays. Simon & Schuster, 1986.* A story-song, based on a South African lullaby, about a fearsome giant and the boy who conquers him with music. (K–Gr. 2)

Sendak, Maurice. *Maurice Sendak's Really Rosie: Starring the Nutshell Kids*. *Lyrics and illus. by the author. Music by Carole King. HarperCollins, 1975.* This large-format paperback contains the script, music, and illustrations from the TV special, still available in audio and video formats, and accessible on YouTube. (Gr. 1–5)

Steig, William. *Zeke Pippin*. *Illus. by the author. HarperCollins, 1997.* Upset when his family falls asleep every time he plays his newfound harmonica, Zeke, a young pig, runs away. (K–Gr. 3)

Uegaki, Chieri. *Hana Hashimoto, Sixth Violin*. *Illus. by Qin Leng. Kids Can, 2014.* Though she's only taken three lessons, young Hana signs up to play her violin for the school talent show. (PreK–Gr. 3)

Weaver, Tess. *Opera Cat*. *Illus. by Andrea Wesson. Clarion, 2002.* Madame Soso's singing cat comes to the rescue when the diva comes down with laryngitis. (K–Gr. 3)

Wheeler, Lisa. *Jazz Baby*. *Illus. by R. Gregory Christie. Harcourt, 2007.* Baby bounces and boogies with his African American family to a record on the record player. (PreK–Gr. 1)

Williams, Vera B. *Something Special for Me*. *Illus. by the author. Greenwillow, 1983.* In a sequel to A Chair for My Mother (1982), Rosa chooses an accordion for her birthday present. Follow with Music, Music for Everyone (1984), in which Rosa and her girlfriends form a band to play in the neighborhood. (K–Gr. 4)

Winter, Jeannette. *Follow the Drinking Gourd*. *Illus. by the author. Knopf, 1989.* Five slaves escape on the Underground Railroad to Canada, inspired by a song, which is appended. (Gr. 1–4)

BOOKLIST: FICTION BOOKS ABOUT MUSIC AND MUSICIANS

Blume, Lesley M. M. *The Rising Star of Rusty Nail*. *Knopf, 2007.* In the sleepy town of Rusty Nail, Minnesota, in 1953, Franny—who loves playing piano—is determined to outdo spoiled brat Nancy in a school piano competition. (Gr. 4–7)

Curtis, Christopher Paul. *Bud, Not Buddy*. *Delacorte, 1999*. During the Depression, ten-year-old Bud Caldwell sets off in search of his real father, whom he thinks is the well-known jazz musician Herman E. Calloway. (Gr. 4–7)

King-Smith, Dick. *A Mouse Called Wolf*. *Illus. by Jon Goodell. Crown, 1997*. Wolfgang Amadeus Mouse, who has perfect pitch, is tutored in singing by a human concert pianist, Mrs. Honeybee. (Gr. 1–4)

Namioka, Lensey. *Yang the Youngest and His Terrible Ear*. *Joy Street, 1992*. Nonmusical, baseball-loving Yingtao and violin-loving, baseball-hating Matthew create an ingenious plan for Yingtao's upcoming music recital. (Gr. 3–5)

Streatfeild, Noel. *Ballet Shoes*. *Illus. by Diane Goode. Random House, 1991, c1937*. A classic English ballet story about three orphaned sisters who attend a performing arts school. (Gr. 4–7)

Urban, Linda. *A Crooked Kind of Perfect*. *Harcourt, 2007*. Zoe dreams of playing the piano, but her father buys her "a wood grained, vinyl-seated, wheeze-bag organ instead." (Gr. 4–6)

BOOKLIST: NONFICTION BOOKS ABOUT MUSIC AND MUSICIANS

Aliki. *Ah, Music*. *Illus. by the author. HarperCollins, 2003*. In a charming overview, a music-loving group of children explore music and what makes it compelling. (Gr. 1–4)

Anderson, M. T. *Handel, Who Knew What He Liked*. *Illus. by Kevin Hawkes*. Candlewick, *2001*. A high-spirited picture-book biography about Handel, from his childhood through his composition of *Messiah*. (Gr. 2–6)

Bertholf, Bret. *The Long Gone Lonesome History of Country Music*. *Illus. by the author. Little, Brown, 2007*. A rip-roaring overview of the stars and history of country music. (Gr. 3–6)

Christensen, Bonnie. *Django*. *Illus. by the author. Roaring Brook/Flash Point, 2009*. A picture-book biography of one of the world's greatest jazz guitarists. (Gr. 2–6)

Christensen, Bonnie. *Woody Guthrie: Poet of the People*. *Illus. by the author. Knopf, 2001*. Woodcut-style illustrations accompany a picture-book biography of the folksinger who wrote "This Land Is Your Land." (Gr. 3–6)

Dunleavy, Deborah. *The Kids Can Press Jumbo Book of Music*. *Illus. by Louise Phillips. Kids Can, 2001*. Directions for making and using more than fifty musical instruments created from household stuff. (Gr. 2–6)

Freedman, Russell. *The Voice That Challenged a Nation: Marian Anderson and the Struggle for Equal Rights*. *Illus. with photos. Clarion, 2004*. This compelling biography of African American opera star Marian Anderson culminates with her groundbreaking Easter Sunday concert on the steps of the Lincoln Memorial in 1939. (Gr. 5–12)

Gerstein, Mordicai. *What Charlie Heard: The Story of the Composer Charles Ives.* Illus. by the author. *Farrar, 2002.* American composer Ives is profiled in an affectionate picture-book biography of his sound-filled life and music. (Gr. 2–6)

Gourley, Robbin. *Talkin' Guitar: A Story of the Young Doc Watson.* Illus. by the author. *Clarion, 2015.* How young Arthel "Doc" Watson (1923–2012), blind since birth, learned to listen to and make music growing up on his family's farm in North Carolina. (PreK–Gr. 3)

Greenberg, Jan, and Sandra Jordan. *Ballet for Martha: Making Appalachian Spring.* Illus. by Brian Floca. *Roaring Brook/Flash Point, 2010.* How Martha Graham's classic ballet "Appalachian Spring" came together. (Gr. 2–6)

Hayes, Ann. *Meet the Orchestra.* Illus. by Karmen Thompson. *Harcourt, 1991.* An introduction to the instruments of an orchestra, as played by formally dressed animal musicians. (K–Gr. 3)

Hopkinson, Deborah. *A Band of Angels: A Story Inspired by the Jubilee Singers.* Illus. by Raúl Colón. *Atheneum, 1999.* Aunt Beth tells her niece the story of her great-great-grandmother, who helped found the Jubilee Singers, the famous African American gospel choir. (Gr. 2–5)

Hopkinson, Deborah. *Home on the Range: John A. Lomax and His Cowboy Songs.* Illus. by S. D. Schindler. *Putnam, 2009.* A fictionalized picture-book biography about the ethnomusicologist who collected folk songs of the American people. (Gr. 2–5)

Igus, Toyomi, comp. *I See the Rhythm.* Illus. by Michele Wood. *Children's Book Press, 1998.* Trace the roots of African American music in a poetic exploration of slave songs, blues, ragtime, jazz, gospel, soul, rock 'n' roll, funk, and hip-hop. (Gr. 4–8)

Krull, Kathleen. *M Is for Music.* Illus. by Stacy Innerst. *Harcourt, 2003.* From classical to pop to jazz, dozens of music-related words are introduced in this alphabet book. (K–Gr. 6)

Krull, Kathleen, and Paul Brewer. *The Beatles Were Fab (and They Were Funny).* Illus. by Stacy Innerst. *Harcourt, 2013.* A lively (and funny) picture-book introduction to the Fab Four. (Gr. 1–5)

Kuskin, Karla. *The Philharmonic Gets Dressed.* Illus. by Marc Simont. *HarperCollins, 1982.* The members of the orchestra are shown getting ready for a stage appearance. (K–Gr. 4)

Moses, Will. *Mary and Her Little Lamb: The True Story of the Nursery Rhyme.* Illus. by the author. *Philomel, 2011.* A fictionalized but fact-based account of how the American poem (and song) came to be. See p. 143 for more background on the original rhyme. (PreK–Gr. 3)

Neri, G. *Hello, I'm Johnny Cash.* *Illus. by A. G. Ford. Candlewick, 2014.* Poetic picture-book bio of J. R. Cash, who grew up poor and became a country music legend. (Gr. 3–6)

Parker, Robert Andrew. *Piano Starts Here: The Young Art Tatum.* *Illus. by the author. Schwartz & Wade, 2008.* The life and times of the African American jazz great who started playing piano as a young boy in spite of being nearly blind. (Gr. 1–5)

Pinkney, Andrea Davis. *Duke Ellington: The Piano Prince and His Orchestra.* *Illus. by Brian Pinkney. Hyperion, 1998.* A jazzy picture-book biography of the pianist and composer known as the King of the Keys. In Pinkney's *Ella Fitzgerald: The Tale of a Vocal Virtuosa* (2002), hip alley cat Scat Cat Monroe recounts the life and rise to fame of the jazz singer. (Gr. 2–6)

Powell, Patricia Hruby. *Josephine: The Dazzling Life of Josephine Baker.* *Illus. by Christian Robinson. Chronicle, 2014.* A sumptuous ninety-page picture-book biography, filled with free-verse text and theatrical acrylic cartoon-like illustrations about the life of Josephine Baker (1906–1975), who grew up poor in East St. Louis and became a singing and dancing sensation in Paris starting in the 1920s. (Gr. 3–6)

Raschka, Chris. *The Cosmo-Biography of Sun Ra: The Sound of Joy Is Enlightening.* *Illus. by the author. Candlewick, 2014.* Whimsical, radiant, and out-of-sight picture-book bio of jazz pianist Sun Ra (1914–1993), who said, "You may think that it is gravity that holds us all together, but it is not—it is music." (Gr. 2–6)

Richards, Keith, with Barnaby Harris and Bill Shapiro. *Gus & Me: The Story of My Granddad and My First Guitar.* *Illus. by Theodora Richards. Little, Brown, 2014.* A heartfelt picture-book memoir and tribute by Rolling Stones guitarist Keith Richards about his beloved grandfather, Theodore Augustus "Gus" Dupree, and how he helped to jump-start Keith's life as a musician. (Gr. 1–5)

Russell-Brown, Katheryn. *Little Melba and Her Big Trombone.* *Illus. by Frank Morrison. Lee & Low, 2014.* In a picture-book biography that thrums with music, meet Melba Liston, a little girl who took up the trombone at age seven and grew up to become a well-respected jazz virtuoso. (The first two minutes of the *Women in Jazz* documentary features Melba Liston playing her trombone. Play the segment at www.youtube.com/watch?v = XLCcQvboXig.) (Gr. 2–5)

Ryan, Pam Muñoz. *When Marian Sang.* *Illus. by Brian Selznick. Scholastic, 2002.* A picture-book account of African American opera sensation Marian Anderson's triumphant concert on the steps of the Lincoln Memorial in 1939. (Gr. 2–6)

Stamaty, Mark Alan. *Shake, Rattle & Turn That Noise Down! How Elvis Changed Music, Me and Mom.* *Illus. by the author. Knopf, 2010.* With comic book style illustrations, this autobiographical picture book recalls 1955, the year the author got a radio for his birthday, leading to a lifelong passion for Elvis Presley's music. (Gr. 2–6)

Weatherford, Carole Boston. *Leontyne Price: Voice of a Century.* *Illus. by Raúl Colón. Knopf, 2014.* How a poor African American girl, born in Mississippi in 1927, became a world-famous opera singer. (Gr. 1–5)

Winter, Jonah. *Dizzy.* *Illus. by Sean Qualls. Scholastic, 2006.* A swinging picture-book biography of famed jazz trumpeter Dizzy Gillespie. (Gr. 3–8)

Winter, Jonah. *The Fabulous Feud of Gilbert & Sullivan.* *Illus. by Richard Egielski. Scholastic/Arthur A. Levine, 2009.* A fictionalized but fact-based picture-book account of how the team of Gilbert and Sullivan came to compose and stage *The Mikado* in 1885. (Gr. 2–5)

BOOKLIST: COLLECTIONS OF CHILDREN'S SONGS

Some of these songbooks are out of print, but they're so outstanding and there are so few books of this sort published in the past decade, we listed them anyway, hoping you could locate them in your library or for sale online.

Boynton, Sandra. *Frog Trouble, and Eleven Other Pretty Serious Songs.* *Lyrics and illus. by the author. Music by Sandra Boynton and Michael Ford. Workman, 2013.* Another gorgeously designed book of hilarious, original country songs for kids, with lyrics, music, and a CD with songs sung by top-notch performers. Other brilliant collaborations include *Blue Moo: 17 Jukebox Hits From Way Back Never* (2007), *Dog Train: A Wild Ride on the Rock-and-Roll Side* (2005), *Philadelphia Chickens: A Too-Illogical Zoological Musical Revue* (2002), and *Rhinoceros Tap: 15 Seriously Silly Songs* (2004). (PreK–Adult)

Crews, Nina, comp. *The Neighborhood Sing-Along.* *Photos by the author. Greenwillow, 2011.* This amiable collection of thirty-four mostly familiar folk songs is illustrated with photos of a multicultural cast of kids from Crews's Brooklyn neighborhood. (PreK–Gr. 3)

Delacre, Lulu, ed. *Arroz con leche: Popular Songs and Rhymes from Latin America.* *English lyrics by Elena Paz. Musical arr. by Ana-Maria Rosado. Illus. by Lulu Delacre. Scholastic, 1989.* Illustrated collection of folk songs accompanied by lyrics in both Spanish and English. (PreK–Gr. 3)

Fox, Dan, ed. *Go In and Out the Window: An Illustrated Songbook for Young People.* *Metropolitan Museum of Art/Henry Holt, 1987.* Sixty childhood songs, illustrated with paintings from the Metropolitan Museum of Art in New York City. (PreK–Gr. 6)

Fox, Dan, and Dick Weissman. *The Great Family Songbook: A Treasury of Favorite Show Tunes, Sing Alongs, Popular Songs, Jazz & Blues, Children's Melodies, International Ballads, Folk Songs, Hymns, Holiday Jingles, and More for Piano and Guitar.* *Illus. by Sarah Wilkins. Black Dog and Leventhal, 2010.* A spiffy spiral-bound compendium of one hundred songs, including music for piano and chords for guitar. (All Ages)

Glazer, Tom. *Tom Glazer's Treasury of Songs for Children.* *Illus. by John O'Brien. Doubleday, 1988.* More than one hundred western, nursery, and folk songs arranged for piano and guitar. (PreK–Gr. 6)

Hart, Jane. *Singing Bee! A Collection of Favorite Children's Songs.* *Illus. by Anita Lobel. Lothrop, 1982.* More than one hundred traditional children's nursery songs. (PreK–Gr. 2)

Krull, Kathleen. *I Hear America Singing! Folk Songs for American Families.* *Illus. by Allen Garns. Knopf, 2003.* A friendly collection of sixty tunes all kids should know, with piano and guitar arrangements. First published in 1992 under the title Gonna Sing My Head Off! American Folk Songs for Children. (K–Gr. 6)

Loeb, Lisa. *Lisa Loeb's Silly Sing-Along: The Disappointing Pancake, and Other Zany Songs.* *Illus. by Ryan O'Rourke. Sterling, 2011.* Ten fun songs accompanied by a CD of the author singing each wacky number. Kids will also have a ball with *Lisa Loeb's Songs for Movin' & Shakin': The Air Band Song and Other Toe-Tapping Tunes* (2013). (PreK–Gr. 5)

MacDonald, Margaret Read, and Winifred Jaeger. *The Round Book: Rounds Kids Love to Sing.* *Illus. by Yvonne LeBrun Davis. August House, 2006.* A great collection of eighty songs to sing as rounds. (Gr. 3–6)

Ralph, Theodore. *The American Song Treasury: 100 Favorites.* *Dover, 1986.* Music, lyrics, and background for a load of folk songs. (All Ages)

Seeger, Ruth Crawford, comp. *American Folk Songs for Children in Home, School and Nursery School: A Book for Children, Parents and Teachers.* *Illus. by Barbara Cooney. Doubleday, 1948.* More than 90 folk songs and games, compiled by Pete Seeger's mom. (PreK–Gr. 4)

Thomas, Marlo. *Free to Be . . . You and Me.* *Thirty-fifth anniversary edition. Developed and edited by Carole Hart and others; original volume, ed. by Francine Klagsbrun. Redesigned and illus. by Peter H. Reynolds. Running Press Kids, 2008, c1974.* Newly illustrated anthology of songs, poems, and stories aimed at freeing children from sexism. Watch the 1974 TV special online at www.dailymotion.com/video. (K–Gr. 6)

BOOKLIST: PROFESSIONAL BOOKS ABOUT MUSIC

Carlow, Regina. *Exploring the Connection between Children's Literature and Music.* *Libraries Unlimited, 2008.* Twenty lesson plans using songs, chants, "found" instruments, poetry, and movement activities correlated with children's books for kindergarten through grade 5.

Cohen, Arlene. *Stories on the Move: Integrating Literature and Movement with Children, from Infants to Age 14.* *Illus. by Andrea Fitcha McAllister. Libraries Unlimited, 2007.* Creative movement activities to use with children's books and songs as part of fourteen extensive story programs for librarians, teachers, parents, and caregivers.

Reid, Rob. *Shake & Shout: 16 Noisy, Lively Story Programs.* *Upstart Books, 2008.* A series of lessons and activities for library programs (preschool to grade two), incorporating movement, music, and picture books.

Reid, Rob. *Something Musical Happened at the Library: Adding Song and Dance to Children's Story Programs.* *American Library Association, 2007.* All things musical for the picture-book crowd, featuring eight lesson plans, each containing song lyrics and recording suggestions, dance ideas, and picture-book tie-ins. A companion to Reid's *Children's Jukebox: The Select Subject Guide to Children's Musical Recordings,* second edition. (2007).

Silberg, Jackie, and Pam Schiller. *The Complete Book of Rhymes, Songs, Poems, Fingerplays, and Chants.* *Illus. by Deborah C. Wright. Gryphon House, 2002.* Alphabetical by title, this anthology features more than seven hundred folk songs, funny songs, action rhymes, jump-rope rhymes, and more.

WEBSITES: ABOUT MUSIC

BusSongs *www.bussongs.com*
"Created to help parents, teachers and children remember the words of their favorite children songs," this site features lyrics, music, and videos for more than two thousand songs.

Daria *www.dariamusic.com*
Folksinger Daria's site bursts with videos, songs, instruments to listen to online, music related activities, and ideas for parents, homeschoolers, and teachers.

Kid Songs *kidsongs.wordpress.com*
Lyrics (and sometimes music) to hundreds of children's songs, listed by topic or alphabetically by title, and searchable by keyword.

KIDiddles *www.kididdles.com*
More than two thousand children's songs (some downloadable), printable song lyrics, sheet music, and activity sheets.

KPR *www.kidspublicradio.org*
An offshoot of National Public Radio, this commercial-free, web-based radio network is just right for kids. Offerings include music to put kids to sleep, storytelling, comedy programs, and "Cosquillas," which airs Spanish songs and stories. Listening makes you want to be a kid again.

Mama Lisa's World *www.mamalisa.com*
Lisa Yannucci's site features thousands of traditional songs from more than a hundred countries as well as a major collection of English Mother Goose rhymes. Choose songs by continent, country, or language, and find the lyrics and background for songs, games, chants, and rhymes, plus many MP3 or MIDI recordings and/or live videos.

Nancy Stewart *www.nancymusic.com*
Folksinger Stewart offers more than 150 free audio file recordings of her delightful, often interactive, children's songs, along with printable activity sheets and sheet music with guitar chords.

SFS Kids *www.sfskids.org*
On the San Francisco Symphony's interactive site, children can learn about the orchestra and its instruments and listen to classical pieces.

Songs for Teaching *www.songsforteaching.com/fingerplays*
This site has dozens of songs and fingerplays, including photographs of actions and recordings.

The Teacher's Guide: Children's Songs *www.theteachersguide.com/kidsongs*
Lyrics to three hundred children's songs, each of which can be downloaded as a PDF and printed out for kids to read as they sing.

NOTE

1. Robert J. Zatorre and Valorie N. Salimpoor, "Why Music Makes Our Brain Sing," *New York Times*, June 7, 2013, www.nytimes.com/2013/06/09/opinion/sunday/why-music-makes-our-brain-sing.html.

Magic

What the eyes see and the ears hear, the mind believes.
—HARRY HOUDINI

WHILE HELPING A FRIEND MOVE BACK IN THE 1970s, Caroline came upon a box labeled "magic." "What's this?" she asked her friend. "Those are my magic tricks," he answered. His interest in magic was sparked when he was a child; as his skills improved, he performed at parties and other places in his hometown. Although he was no longer actively involved in magic, Carolyn persuaded him to entertain her—a fair trade for her efforts in helping him move. As a result, she joined several magic clubs and became a member of the Magic Castle in Los Angeles, which is now a private club and the home of the Academy of Magical Arts, a nonprofit social order devoted to the advancement of the ancient art of magic (www .magiccastle.com).

Caroline's interest in magic carried over into her storytelling programs. Magic, after all, has universal appeal; tricks are a natural addition to any book program. You can use them to introduce a story, or as transitional material. Many traditional tales deal with magic or magicians, and the art of conjuring is as old as the tales themselves. Conjuring—the performing of magic tricks for entertainment—may have originated in Greece. In the second century, the Greek author Alciphron described a still-popular sleight-of-hand trick known as the "cups and balls." Conjuring as performed by a magician (which has nothing to do with witches, sorcerers, or demons) was a major form of entertainment around the world. Today, even with the magic of computers, the Internet, and other modern-day marvels, magicians entertain and delight audiences using tricks that may have been invented centuries ago.

Children are particularly fascinated with magic tricks. Just like their parents, they want to figure out how the trick was done. Interestingly, very young children do not always make good audiences for conjurers. Perhaps they simply take miraculous events for granted. And some magical tricks depend on misdirection. For example, the conjurer hides a ball in one hand while the other hand is moving in an eye-catching manner. The adult eye usually follows the larger action automatically and misses the smaller, more important action. Young children, however, are more likely to follow the smaller action, frustrating the magician. Children in the middle and upper grades, however, react in the same way as most adults and are excited by the simplest of tricks.

Harry Houdini (1874–1926), David Copperfield, and Penn & Teller are familiar names to audiences all over the world. Chances are good that any great magician you've ever heard of has a huge video presence on You-Tube—even Houdini, with a terrific documentary done about him by Bio at www.biography.com/people/harry-houdini-40056.

Okay, in this chapter, we're not going to tell you how to make the Statue of Liberty disappear, as illusionist David Copperfield did in 2006 (though you can find quite a few sites online that reveal how it was done). We're just not that good as magicians. We will, however, explore some simple, basic, and sometimes silly conjuring tricks. The mixture of awe and excitement that accompanies the performance of magic will make learning the tricks well worth the effort.

Types of Conjuring

There are three general types of magic: close-up magic, table or platform magic, and stage magic. Close-up magic requires the audience to be close enough to see small objects such as coins or cards being manipulated. For table magic, the audience tends to be a little farther away from the magician. Stage magic generally uses big apparatuses, such as water tanks for spectacular escapes or cages in which people disappear and animals appear in their place. It is usually performed by professional magicians onstage before hundreds of people. Card and coin magic performed in a close-up situation is the specialty most suitable for teachers and librarians.

Magic effects usually come under one of seven categories. The more successful tricks include two or more:

- *A production or creation.* Something comes from nothing—a rabbit from a seemingly empty hat.
- *A disappearance.* The opposite of production—the rabbit seems to vanish.
- *A transformation.* An object changes from one thing to another—a rabbit seems to become a duck.
- *A transposition.* Two objects exchange places—a red handkerchief seems to change places with a blue handkerchief in another location.
- *Defiance of natural laws.* A trick seems physically impossible—cutting off someone's head or climbing an unsupported rope.
- *Secret motive power.* Inanimate objects appear to move under their own power—a rising pencil (see our Rising Pencil trick on pages 233–234).
- *Mental tricks.* The performer reads the thoughts of those in his audience (see our Book Telepathy trick on pages 230–231).

Sleight of Hand

If you are more than just casually interested in conjuring, why not try some sleight of hand, a magical effect that relies mainly on manual dexterity? In a typical maneuver, the conjurer shows a single ball to an audience and with a series of hand maneuvers seemingly makes the ball disappear or multiply. There are books to teach you the basics of sleight of hand, but even after you know the moves, you will need to spend many hours practicing to become proficient.

For a glimpse of what magicians go through to master seemingly effortless tricks, look at New York City magician Steve Cohen's blog, which describes, in detail, how he prepared for an appearance on *The Late Show with David Letterman* (www.chambermagic.com/letterman-show-behind-scenes). He designed a routine, based on a century-old trick, "Borrowed Ring in Walnut," that concluded with a borrowed ring appearing inside a walnut which was inside an egg which was inside a lemon. After you read Cohen's description of his intensive training, you can simply watch the segment online at www.chambermagic.com/letterman-video. Even if you watch his hands closely, you still won't figure out how he managed it. Neither did Letterman.

Magic Supplies for Novices

We've finally arrived at our kind of magic: a trick whose secret you can buy. Google *magic for kids*, and you'll get 1.5 million hits. At Amazon, under "Toys and Games," type *magic tricks for kids* in the search bar to find hundreds of items. Though many are for children to try themselves (like the Melissa & Doug Deluxe Magic Set, which is pretty spiffy), you'll find a plethora to use in your programs. You can buy capes, top hats, and, of course, magic wands galore.

You'll have a blast looking through props and gags on various online magic sites, the best of which we have listed on pages 249–250. Even eBay has an extensive collection.

What can you buy? Magic bubbles that won't pop and multiplying sponge bananas (both from the Magic Warehouse, www.themagicwarehouse.com); a cane that appears from thin air (the Fantasio Appearing Cane from www.penguinmagic.com); a magic teakettle that pours a variety of colored liquids and a milk pitcher that never empties (both from Stoner's FunStore, www.funnygoofycrap.com); and a Beach Bucket Lota, which looks like a metal bucket, from which you can pour a seemingly endless supply of water (from Tannen's Magic, www.tannens.com). You can find an endless variety of magic pans that produce endless silks or even a rabbit, silks that change colors, seemingly empty dove pans (also called candy pans) from which you can make small items or even pop-up cakes appear, and a multitude of change bags that help you switch items or make them seem to disappear.

Plan how you can use a magic trick in your book programs. There's a 3D Rainbow in Your Hand Flipbook for sale at Tannen's Magic. It looks like a little book, but when you flip the pages, a rainbow appears to rise from it. When you're talking with children about the magic that can be found in books, watch their amazed faces when they see the rainbow.

Novelty shops and magic stores have plenty to offer. In many cases, the clerks are aspiring magicians themselves. They will be happy to demonstrate the secret of a trick after you purchase it. To find a store near you, go to MagicGizmo's store locator (magicgizmo.com/home/Magic-Shop-Locator).

Learning about Magic

In the old days, no magician would willingly give away a secret. (Though Penn & Teller made a career doing just that—revealing step-by-step exactly how some of their tricks are done. It's fascinating to see. Look on YouTube, natch.) These days, the Internet has revealed the inner workings of many a magic trick. Look up *magic tricks for kids* on YouTube and you will find a plethora of instructional videos. It is easier than ever to learn magic tricks and to develop good patter.

If you become a serious magic student, you may want to spend big bucks (around $200) for what is still considered the gold standard in magic books: the illustrated, eight-volume *Tarbell Course in Magic*, which you can find at www.penguinmagic.com and www.tannens.com. Compiled in 1928 by Dr. Harlan Tarbell as a correspondence course for aspiring magicians, it weighs in at 3,300 pages, and features one hundred lessons.

Practice, Patter, and Presentation

Like storytelling, magic is not a skill that you just pick up on the fly. Some tricks and illusions are certainly quick to learn, but finding ones you find personally appealing requires research, patience, and perseverance. Comb magic books written for children as well as those written for adults, research writings and videos on the Internet, keep your eyes peeled for ideas you can borrow from other magic-loving folks, and seek out live magic shows so you can watch the experts do it.

For each new bit you want to perform, you must rehearse until everything is smooth and perfect. No coins fumbled, no cards dropped, no water spilled in error, no ropes knotted the wrong way. Every magician occasionally goofs, but it is embarrassing—so practice diligently. Something else to keep in mind: never repeat a trick in the same show. If your viewers know what to expect, they will be much more alert the second time. And never reveal the secret of a trick—no matter how charming the request!

Some magicians perform wordlessly to music, but many have a patter to go with their tricks. *Patter* refers to what a magician says while performing. It is not enough to simply follow the directions for a trick; what you say during presentation is often as important as what you do. Your words misdirect the audience in much the same way as your actions, and they can help make the trick believable. Many books talk about how to develop patter and can help you figure out what lines will work best, what humorous or mysterious mood to set, and what your audience needs or doesn't need to hear and know. Each time you perform a trick anew, you will refine your monologue and timing, just as you do when you're telling a story.

As you become more proficient, you will develop your own signature style and presentation skills that will serve you well even in book programs that do not include magic. The trick is to develop a good performer-audience relationship—whatever the subject of your presentation—to continue to hone your public-speaking and storytelling skills, and to have fun.

Magic Tricks

Magic can tie in well with any book presentation. Use it when you are reading aloud, telling stories, giving a booktalk, getting ready for a science lesson, or presenting a poem. Lots of story-and-magic-trick pairs are included in this chapter, but if you become as intrigued by matching magic with books as we are, you'll come up with plenty of your own combinations.

Although most beginners don't have a wide enough repertoire to sustain forty minutes of magic, you may eventually feel confident enough to do a whole program. On the other hand, you can simply do one trick this week and another next week. There are many stories with magical elements that lead nicely into a trick or two. It's probably best to perform your tricks after you tell a story rather than before. No matter how well you tell a story, a magic trick can be hard to follow.

The tricks that we describe below are easy to learn and require only a minimum of preparation—perfect for busy teachers and librarians. They are classic or comical effects that have been specially adapted to fit into book or storytelling programs. For more of magic tricks and book tie-ins, you'll also want to consult Caroline's book *Leading Kids to Books through Magic*.

For some tricks, you will need to buy commercial supplies or equipment such as change bags, dove pans, spring flowers, or magic wands. Others rely on simpler materials you probably have on hand.

The Change Bag

One essential commercial prop that has multiple uses is the change bag. You can make an object seem to disappear or you can change it into something else. Small objects—such as a ring, a watch, cards, or a handkerchief—work well. Some change bags have a zipper on the bottom. You can make quite a show of unzipping the bag and putting your hand in and then out the bottom. Turn it inside out and put your hand through. (Of course, you never mention that there's a secret compartment in the bag.) You can get a wide variety of change bags for under $30 on Amazon.com and at the online magic stores listed on pages 249–250.

Use a change bag when presenting a story featuring American history or heroes. *Flight* by Robert Burleigh, the harrowing story of Charles Lindberg's historic 1927 flight across the Atlantic, is a dramatic choice. After reading the picture book aloud or telling your own version of the event, show the change bag empty. Then, with a flourish, hold up a white silk, a red silk, and a blue silk, and insert each one in the bag. Next, reach in, pull out an American flag (or a French flag, since the colors are the same), and wave it. Finally, hold out the bag so the audience can see it is empty once again.

When sharing the nonfiction picture book *Just a Second: A Different Way to Look at Time* by Steve Jenkins, talk about watches as personal keepers of time. Explain that the problem with watches is that they are sometimes misplaced or simply disappear. Then use your own watch in a change bag to demonstrate.

Books in which characters misplace something are perfect lead-ins for change-bag tricks. In the picture book *Adèle & Simon* by Barbara McClintock, Simon keeps losing his possessions, including his scarf; make a silk scarf magically appear from your empty change bag. Make a ring disappear in the bag when you read Tomie dePaola's *Big Anthony and the Magic Ring* or book-talk Bruce Coville's chapter book, *The Monster's Ring*. Find and lose a toy tooth after reading Penda Diakité's *I Lost My Tooth in Africa*, Bob Graham's *April and Esme, Tooth Fairies*, or Margie Palatini's *Sweet Tooth*.

The Dove Pan

Caroline's favorite magic trick for a book program uses a dove pan, a round aluminum or black plastic pan with a dome lid named for the live doves magicians pull out of them. You can purchase a variety of them online, starting at about $20 for the plastic ones.

First, find a miniature children's book that fits into your pan. Many dove pans are only five inches around inside, so a Beatrix Potter book or a book from Maurice Sendak's Nutshell Library, such as *Chicken Soup with Rice*, will work best. If you buy a bigger pan, you can choose a bigger book.

Show the empty aluminum pan to your audience. Ask the children, "What makes a book a book?" When they say, "Paper! Words! Pictures!" you respond, "What a coincidence! I have all those ingredients right here."

Then pull out a page of a newspaper, tear it into pieces, and pour the bits into the pan—all the while explaining that making a good book is just like making a cake. Next, hold up a color photocopy of a book illustration, and repeat the actions. Then say, "Now I need fire to bake my pages into a book. I'm not allowed to play with matches, so I'll just add a picture of a flaming match. That should do the trick." Add a small (untorn) picture of a match to the mix.

When you remove the pan's lid, the shredded paper has magically been replaced with that tiny book—which you proceed to read aloud. This is a spectacular trick that you can use over and over again.

If you were a magician, you would use flash paper in your pan and light it for a spectacular flame that you would quickly cover with the lid. While flash paper burns out immediately and leaves no ash, it is still fire, and you shouldn't use it with children unless you're a pro. It looks great, though, in a dove pan. There are flaming dove pans that produce their own flames at the touch of a button, but unless you have conjured up a stray hundred-dollar bill, you probably don't need one.

Use your magic pan to produce endless silks, popcorn or candy to share, or even a stuffed rabbit. (Magicians use real ones, of course.) Want something smaller? That would be the chick pan. Bigger? Look for a duck pan. These are all lightweight but sturdy, with quick-action releases. With a double-load dove pan, you can put in an egg, a cup of flour, and a stick of butter. When you remove the cover—voilà, a birthday cake! You can buy sponge cakes, created from highly compressible foam, that are made to fit inside a pan. Delicious picture books to share before doing this trick include *A Birthday for Bear* by Bonnie Becker, *The Bake Shop Ghost* by Jacqueline K. Ogburn, and, of course, *Clever Jack Takes the Cake* by Candace Fleming. For older children, read or booktalk *The Great Cake Mystery: Precious Ramotswe's Very First Case* by Alexander McCall Smith or the already magical *11 Birthdays* by Wendy Mass.

Spring Flowers and the Botania

You might also consider purchasing "spring" flowers (the synthetic kind that fold flat and spring into a large bouquet when released) or botania (a more expensive, more advanced version of feather flowers) hidden inside a seemingly empty tube. Spring flowers can be put into a dove pan or a change bag, or even placed inside a book. When triggered, they expand into a bouquet of colorful blooms. You can find nice ones, including the Cloth Flower Botania, at Silk Magic Tricks (stores.silkmagictricks.com).

Any good story or poem about flowers, gardening, or spring works perfectly with a flower trick. Pull out your magic after you read *Grandpa Green* by Lane Smith, *Old Bear* by Kevin Henkes, or even Robert Kraus's classic, *Leo the Late Bloomer,* in which Leo, a hapless young tiger, finally matures, or "blooms," in his own good time.

Use your flowers after reading or telling the Greek myth "Persephone." Sally Clayton's picture book, *Persephone,* is particularly dark, dramatic, and mysterious. The flowers will certainly lighten the mood, along with a real pomegranate, which you can cut up and share with your listeners. Each child should eat six seeds to bring on winter; the flowers are to remind them that spring will come.

BOOKLIST: BOOKS TO USE WITH COMMERCIAL MAGIC TRICKS

Burleigh, Robert. *Flight: The Journey of Charles Lindbergh. Illus. by Mike Wimmer. Philomel, 1991.* A thrilling picture book about Lindbergh's historic flight from New York to Paris in 1927. (Gr. 3–6)

Clayton, Sally. *Persephone. Illus. by Virginia Lee. Eerdmans, 2009.* After Hades abducts Persephone and brings her to the Underworld, her mother, Demeter, curses the land and refuses to allow anything to grow. (Gr. 4–8)

Coville, Bruce. *The Monster's Ring. Illus. by Katherine Coville. Pantheon, 1982.* A magic ring turns Russell into a monster that scares the meanness out of bully Eddy. (Gr. 3–5)

DePaola, Tomie. *Big Anthony and the Magic Ring. Illus. by the author. Harcourt, 1979.* When Big Anthony borrows Strega Nona's magical ring and sings her magic song to it, he becomes handsome. (K–Gr. 4)

Diakité, Penda. *I Lost My Tooth in Africa. Illus. by Baba Wagué Diakité. Scholastic, 2006.* On a trip to Mali with her family, Amina loses a tooth and gets a chicken from the African tooth fairy. (PreK–Gr. 3)

Graham, Bob. *April and Esme, Tooth Fairies. Illus. by the author. Candlewick, 2010.* Two young fairy sisters fly out for the first time to gather a tooth from a human boy. (PreK–Gr. 2)

Henkes, Kevin. *Chrysanthemum. Illus. by the author. Greenwillow, 1991.* Chrysanthemum loves her name—until she starts school and her mouse classmates make fun of it. (PreK–Gr. 2)

Henkes, Kevin. *Old Bear. Illus. by the author. Greenwillow, 2008.* While sleeping through the long, snowy winter, Old Bear dreams that spring has arrived. (PreK–Gr. 1)

Jenkins, Steve. *Just a Second: A Different Way to Look at Time.* *Illus. by the author. Houghton Mifflin, 2011.* Amazing time-based facts and illustrations about animals, people, and the world. (K–Gr. 4)

Kraus, Robert. *Leo the Late Bloomer.* *Illus. by Jose Aruego. Windmill, 1971.* Leo, a young tiger, can't do anything well, but his mother knows to just be patient. (PreK–Gr. 2)

Mass, Wendy. *11 Birthdays.* *Scholastic, 2009.* When Amanda awakens the morning after her awful eleventh birthday, she is appalled to realize that, somehow, it's her birthday all over again. (Gr. 4–6)

McClintock, Barbara. *Adèle & Simon.* *Illus. by the author. Farrar, 2006.* "Simon, please try not to lose anything today," says Adèle, Simon's older sister, as they head home from school through the streets of Paris. (PreK–Gr. 2)

Palatini, Margie. *Sweet Tooth.* *Illus. by Jack E. Davis. Simon & Schuster, 2004.* Stewart's talking molar yells, "I NEED A CANDY BAR. NOW-OW!" (PreK–Gr. 3)

Smith, Alexander McCall. *The Great Cake Mystery: Precious Ramotswe's Very First Case.* *Illus. by Iain McIntosh. Random House/Anchor Books, 2012.* Precious, a schoolgirl from Botswana, Africa, solves her first mystery when a thief steals a piece of cake that a classmate has brought for a snack. (Gr. 3–5)

Smith, Lane. *Grandpa Green.* *Illus. by the author. Roaring Brook, 2011.* Tour the garden of a boy's great-grandfather, whose elaborate topiaries depict the highlights of his interesting life. (PreK–Gr. 2)

Mixing Colors

This activity can be used anytime you are reading a book that involves color. These would include Leo Lionni's *Little Blue and Little Yellow,* Laura Vaccaro Seeger's *Green,* and Lois Ehlert's *Color Farm* and *Color Zoo.* Ann Jonas's *Color Dance* is another good choice; children dance through the pages with colored scarves, illustrating the magic of color mixing.

The Trick

Plain, clear water turns red, then yellow, then blue, and finally, by combining the yellow and blue, the water becomes green.

You Will Need

Three small glasses and one large glass (plastic so you don't have to worry about breakage); box of food coloring (red, yellow, green, and blue)

Preparation

Put a drop of red food coloring in the bottom of one of the small glasses, a drop of blue in another glass, and a drop of yellow in the remaining one. Fill the large glass with water.

Patter and Presentation

As you probably know, the three primary colors are red, yellow, and blue. (*Sweep your hand over the empty glasses.*) I have some glasses here that I will fill with green water. First I will fill this glass with green water. (*Pick up the glass with the red color in it, holding it by the base so the drop of food coloring doesn't show, and pour some water from the large glass into it. The water will turn red.*) Whoops. Sorry. This is red. I'll try it with this glass. (*Pick up the glass with the color blue.*) Ladies and gentlemen, the color green! (*Pour some water into the glass.*) Oh, no! Sorry again. This is blue. I'm sure this one will work. (*Pick up the glass with yellow color and add the remainder of the water.*) Dear me, it appears to be yellow. Wait a minute! What do yellow and blue make? Right. Let's try the two together. (*Pour the yellow water and the blue water into the larger glass.*) I did it! (*Triumphantly display the green water.*) Ladies and gentlemen, GREEN WATER!

Hint: If you want to share the water with your audience, use ginger ale or 7 Up. If you don't want to give kids sugary soda, use seltzer water. Children will love it!

BOOKLIST: BOOKS ABOUT COLORS

Barton, Chris. *The Day-Glo Brothers: The True Story of Bob and Joe Switzer's Bright Ideas and Brand-New Colors.* *Illus. by Tony Persiani. Charlesbridge, 2009.* In a high-spirited picture-book biography, meet the brothers who invented Day-Glo paint in 1935. (Gr. 3–6)

Carle, Eric. *The Artist Who Painted a Blue Horse.* *Illus. by the author. Philomel, 2011.* A young artist paints nine unconventionally colored animals. (PreK–Gr. 1)

Carle, Eric. *Hello, Red Fox.* *Illus. by the author. Simon & Schuster, 1998.* In a study of seven complementary colors, Little Frog invites Red Fox, Purple Butterfly, Orange Cat, and other colorful animals to his party, but when they arrive, they all seem to be the wrong hue. (K–Gr. 6)

Daywalt, Drew. *The Day the Crayons Quit.* *Illus. by Oliver Jeffers. Philomel, 2013.* One color at a time, a boy's crayons write him letters—mostly complaints—about the way he's been treating them. (K–Gr. 3)

Ehlert, Lois. *Color Zoo.* *Illus. by the author. HarperCollins, 1989.* On die-cut pages with clear colors, common shapes transform into animals with each page turn. Pair this with *Color Farm* (1990). (PreK–Gr. 2)

Frame, Jeron Ashford. *Yesterday I Had the Blues.* *Illus. by R. Gregory Christie. Tricycle, 2003.* A young African American boy explains how the colors all around him make him feel. (Gr. 1–4)

Jonas, Ann. *Color Dance.* *Illus. by the author. Greenwillow, 1989.* Three children dancing with primary-colored scarves show how colors can blend to form new ones. (PreK–Gr. 2)

Lionni, Leo. *Little Blue and Little Yellow.* *Illus. by the author. McDowell, Obolensky, 1959.* Two best friends—made of hand-torn scrap-paper circles—hug each other and turn green. (PreK–Gr. 2)

Litwin, Eric. *Pete the Cat: I Love My White Shoes.* *Illus. by James Dean. HarperCollins, 2010.* Pete the Cat steps in strawberries, blueberries, and mud, each of which turns his new white sneakers a different color. (PreK–Gr. 2)

Seeger, Laura Vaccaro. *Green.* *Illus. by the author. Roaring Brook, 2012.* Die-cut pages and simple, two-word phrases survey the color green in surprising ways. (PreK–Gr. 2)

Sidman, Joyce. *Red Sings from Treetops: A Year in Colors.* *Illus. by Pamela Zagarenski. Houghton Mifflin, 2009.* A celebration in verse of colors and how they look and feel in each season. (Gr. 1–4)

Read to Your Dog

Try this trick when you're sharing one or more of your favorite dog stories, like "The Poor Old Dog" from Arnold Lobel's *Fables*. The original fable below should be read or told just as it is written. It's only one page long, so it isn't difficult to memorize. We have suggested a few crackerjack titles below to help start you brainstorming about other dog books you love.

The Trick

The magician shows an empty envelope, representing a doghouse. She puts a picture of a barking dog into the house. When the house is opened, out comes a picture of a sleeping dog.

You Will Need

Two 9-by-12-inch manila envelopes; a picture of a barking dog; a picture of the same dog (or the same type of dog) sleeping. (Print out color photos from Google Images or draw your own pictures.)

Preparation

Mount the two dog pictures on heavystock paper if you want them to stay in good shape. Carefully apply rubber cement to the front of the two envelopes—including the flaps—and stick them together, making sure the edges are well adhered. Very lightly, mark a number 1 at the top right of one side of the envelope, and a number 2 on the other side, just so you'll remember which side is which. Insert the picture of the sleeping dog in side 2.

Patter and Presentation

My dog couldn't sleep. (*Hold up the picture of the barking dog for all to see.*) He was barking and keeping my Mom and Dad awake. "Shhh," I whispered, but he kept on barking. "Go back to bed," I said, but he kept on barking. "Here, boy, I'll put you into your doghouse." (*Holding open the number 1 side of the envelope to show that there is nothing else inside, slip the picture inside.*) I sat outside his doghouse and read him my favorite story about a dog. (*Mention and hold up your favorite dog title. Without being obvious, turn the envelope to the number 2 side while you are holding up the book.*) He liked it so much, he stopped barking. Now it seemed very quiet in the house. I looked inside his doghouse. At last he was fast asleep. (*Reach inside the number 2 side of the envelope and take out the picture of the sleeping dog.*) Oh, good, he's still asleep. I better let the "sleeping dog lie."

   Hint: On another occasion, you can use the two-sided envelope to exchange one card for another, or you can show one side empty and magically make something appear.

BOOKLIST: DOG BOOKS

Calmenson, Stephanie. *May I Pet Your Dog? The How-to Guide for Kids Meeting Dogs (and Dogs Meeting Kids).* *Illus. by Jan Ormerod. Clarion, 2007.* Harry, a dachshund, gives a boy practical instructions on how to be friends with a dog. (K–Gr. 2)

Cleary, Beverly. *Strider*. *Illus. by Paul O. Zelinsky. Morrow, 1991.* Leigh finds a dog on the beach and coaxes him home. (Gr. 5–7)

DiCamillo, Kate. *Because of Winn-Dixie*. *Candlewick, 2000.* Ten-year-old India Opal Buloni brings home the mutt she finds at the supermarket to the trailer she shares with her preacher father. (Gr. 4–6)

Feiffer, Jules. *Bark, George*. *Illus. by the author. HarperCollins, 1999.* George's mother tells him to bark, but instead he meows, quacks, oinks, or moos. (PreK–Gr. 1)

Gormley, Greg. *Dog in Boots*. *Illus. by Roberta Angaramo. Holiday House, 2011.* "Bow WOW!" Dog exclaims when he buys a splendid set of boots, just like the ones he saw in the book Puss in Boots. Bring in different types of shoes to show. (PreK–Gr. 2)

Lobel, Arnold. *Fables*. *Illus. by the author. HarperCollins, 1980.* From this Caldecott Medal–winning collection of original fables, read aloud or tell "The Poor Old Dog," a one-page story about a dog who gets his wish. (Gr. 2–6)

MacDonald, Margaret Read. *The Great Smelly, Slobbery, Small-Tooth Dog: A Folktale from Great Britain*. *Illus. by Julie Paschkis. August House/Little Folk, 2007.* A dog saves a man's life and wants the hand of the man's beautiful daughter as a reward. (PreK–Gr. 4)

Meddaugh, Susan. *Martha Speaks*. *Illus. by the author. Houghton Mifflin, 1992.* When the alphabet soup Martha has eaten goes to her brain instead of her stomach, the lovable mutt can't stop talking. (PreK–Gr. 3)

Pilkey, Dav. *Dog Breath: The Horrible Trouble with Hally Tosis*. *Illus. by the author. Scholastic/Blue Sky, 1994.* The Tosis family owns a good dog with one big problem: she has such horrible breath, even skunks avoid her. (PreK–Gr. 2)

Shannon, David. *Good Boy, Fergus!* *Illus. by the author. Scholastic/Blue Sky, 2006.* A mischievous little Westie chases cats, begs for table scraps, and eats his dog food only when his owner tops it with whipped cream. (PreK–Gr. 2)

Vande Velde, Vivian. *Smart Dog*. *Harcourt, 1998.* Fifth-grader Amy aids an ultra-intelligent talking dog that has escaped from a college research lab. (Gr. 3–6)

Book Telepathy

The Trick
By pretending to read a volunteer's mind, you will make reading irresistible.

You Will Need
Three books you've planned to use in your book program or booktalk; a bookmark; two pieces of paper; and an envelope. Suppose, for example, you are giving a booktalk on school stories and you choose *The Strange Case of*

Origami Yoda by Tom Angleberger, *No Talking* by Andrew Clements, and *Wonder* by R. J. Palacio.

Preparation

On a piece of paper, write, "You will choose *The Strange Case of Origami Yoda.*" Put the paper into an envelope. On the back side of the bookmark, print, "You will choose *No Talking.*" On the back cover of *No Talking*, attach a small sign that says, "You will choose *Wonder.*"

Patter and Presentation

After your booktalk, announce, "I am a book magician and I can read your mind. I know that someone in this room can't wait to read one of these wonderful books. If you fit that description, let me read your mind!"

Select a volunteer. Stand up the three books in a row. Say to the child, "You may have first choice of one of these books. Don't tell me the title or say anything out loud. I want you to think of the book you most want to read. Think hard, but remember, don't say a word . . . Do you have the title in your head? Good. Don't tell me. I have already read your mind. Now, take this bookmark and place it in the book that is your number one choice."

If *The Strange Case of Origami Yoda* is chosen, have the volunteer look inside the envelope and read what is written there.

If *No Talking* is chosen, have the volunteer turn over the bookmark and read it aloud.

If *Wonder* is chosen, tell your volunteer to turn over *No Talking* and read aloud what is written there.

Now you can hand out the other two books. Don't repeat this trick with the same group.

Television versus Books

The Trick

This is a fun way to illustrate the benefits of reading over watching television.

You Will Need

Three 8-by-10-inch pieces of cardboard; a manila envelope just large enough to hold (and easily permit the removal of) the cards.

Preparation

- On the envelope, draw different TV call letters on each side (say, *CBS* on one side, *NBC* on the other). Draw them in portrait, not landscape mode and make them large enough so that your audience can easily see them.

- Carefully trim ¼ inch from three sides of one of the cards.
- With a ruler and a pencil, lightly draw a ¼-inch black border around the card so that it looks like an old-fashioned TV screen.
- Color in the border with a black marker. Draw wavy lines on the "screen" (in landscape, not portrait mode).
- On the other side of the same card, draw and color in an identical border, but draw stars and stripes on the "screen."
- Make a "sheath card":

    1. Using ½-inch invisible tape, tape the other untrimmed two cards together, leaving one short side open.
    2. On one side, carefully redraw an identical border and screen with the wavy lines.
    3. On the other side, draw the border, but on the "screen" write the words, in large, easy-to-read, and colorful letters: NEXT TIME, READ A BOOK!

Patter and Presentation

Tell your audience, "I have to tell you that reading books is better than watching television. Every time I sit down to look at television, I get terrible reception, even with my brand-new, high-def, smart high-tech TV." (*Show the envelope, open it, and take out the single card with the wavy lines on it. Show it to your group, making sure you don't show the other side.*)

"So, I usually switch to another channel." (*Place the card inside the envelope. Turn the envelope around and pull out the same card, but this time showing the side painted with stars and stripes.*)

"But, I am here to tell you, the reception is just as bad on that channel as it is on the first one! So, I switch to another channel." (*Put the card inside the envelope again and take out the card with the wavy lines on it. The audience assumes that you are just showing the other side of the card again.*)

"That one is terrible, too! What's a person to do?" (*Place the card inside the envelope. Turn the envelope around. The audience expects to see the stars and stripes again, but instead, when you pull out the card and hold it up, a notice is printed on the other side that says, "NEXT TIME, READ A BOOK!"*)

"Isn't that the truth? 'Next time, read a book!'" (*Now open the manila envelope and hold it so that the audience can see there is nothing inside. Then throw the envelope behind you in disgust.*)

The trick is that the second time you place the card inside the envelope, you carefully slide the first card into the "sheath" card that is already in there. Then pull out the sheath card and hold it up. The audience will never notice that the sheath card is slightly larger. Just be sure they don't see the opening on the side.

Prediction Pencil

The Trick
A magic pencil answers a series of yes-and-no questions about books, such as "Did J. K. Rowling write *Diary of a Wimpy Kid?*" or "Was Hans Christian Andersen from Denmark?"

You Will Need
A pencil with an eraser; a piece of black thread about 18 inches long; a thin sewing needle or glue; a dark-colored glass bottle

Preparation
- Put a slit in the pencil's eraser. Slip the black thread into the slit on the eraser and fasten it with a dab of clear glue, or use a thin sewing needle, threaded and inserted at the base of the eraser.
- Fasten the other end of the thread to a bottom button on your black jacket, shirt, or belt loop.
- Drop the pencil, eraser side down, into an empty dark-colored glass bottle. As you slowly draw the bottle away from you, the pencil will rise in the glass in a most mysterious way.
- If you make the pencil rise, the answer to the magician's question is yes; if you let it drop back into the bottle, the answer is no. Practice a bit to get good at manipulating the string.

Patter and Presentation
"I have here a magic pencil that knows all about books; I am going to ask it some yes-or-no questions. If the pencil rises out of the bottle when I ask it a book question, the answer is yes. If it stays in the bottle, the answer is no. Let's try an easy question to make sure the pencil is awake."

"Magic Pencil, did the monsters make Max the King of All Wild Things when he sailed to the land of *Where the Wild Things Are*?" (*The pencil rises.*) "I believe you are correct, Magic Pencil. Let me ask you another question. Is Dr. Seuss still alive?" (*The pencil starts to rise but falls back into the bottle.*) "Very good, Magic Pencil. Dr. Seuss died a long time ago, in 1991, but we still have all his many wonderful books. Now let's try some harder questions."

You can have your children brainstorm some book-related questions to ask. (First, announce that you need to put the pencil and bottle away in another room so it can't hear you discussing possible book questions), and then bring it out to have the children read their queries.

A Word from Smokey the Bear

This trick can be used after telling stories with forest settings.

The Trick
A broken match magically repairs itself.

You Will Need
Two wooden matches; a scarf.

Preparation
Sew one match inside the hem of a scarf.

Patter and Presentation
Show the group a wooden match that you then place under a scarf. Ask a child to break the match—with the scarf still wrapped around it—in two. When you take hold of the scarf, the match drops out unharmed. "You can never be too careful," you exclaim. When the child breaks the match, he is really breaking the one sewn into the scarf. Meanwhile, take the match that you displayed into your hand. When you open the scarf, let the match in your hand fall out. Tell your listeners that they must be careful to always put out fires and be careful never to play with matches. Remind them that matches should be broken in two and dipped in water to make sure that they are out.

A Proverb Trick

The Trick
An egg yields a rain of confetti instead of a chick.

You Will Need
A raw egg; a needle; a bowl; clear tape or glue; confetti

Preparation
- Put a small pinhole in one end of an egg and a larger hole in the other end.
- Holding the egg over a bowl, with the smaller hole to your mouth, carefully blow the egg contents into the bowl. (Scrambled eggs for breakfast!)
- Let the eggshell dry for a few days, or dry it in a warm oven.
- Using the end of the pin, fill the shell with confetti through the larger hole.
- Seal the egg with tape or a dab of clear glue.

Patter and Presentation

For middle graders, first tell the "Milkmaid and Her Pail," below, and then read aloud the chapter that mirrors it, "The Spelling Goddess" from Candace Fleming's updated tribute to Aesop's fables, *The Fabulous Fourth Graders of Aesop Elementary School.* After you've finished, say, "Speaking of eggs . . ." and then recite the nursery rhyme "Humpty Dumpty." Say, "Is it possible to put an egg back together again?" Crack the egg, scatter the confetti, and say, "Nope. I don't think it is."

Make sure you have a broom and dustpan handy. This is a spectacular trick, but very messy.

The Milkmaid and Her Pail

Retold by Judy Freeman

While many people assume that this is an Aesop fable, it actually dates back only to the fourteenth century in Europe and was retold in rhyme by Jean de La Fontaine in his book Fables, *published in France in 1668.*

One fine day, a milkmaid was carrying a pail of milk on her head as she headed to the dairy. As she walked along, she thought to herself, "With the money that I shall get from this milk, I will buy dozens of eggs. When the eggs hatch, I'll have some fine chicks to raise. Soon they will grow into plump chickens and I'll take them to the market to sell them. Surely I'll get a generous price for them. With all the money I make, I'll buy myself a beautiful green gown to wear to the dance on May Day. All the young man will think me so comely, they'll come a-courtin'. I will dance with them and listen to their flattering words, but they shan't turn my head."

Envisioning those prospective suitors and their flattering words, the milk-maid tossed her head scornfully. The pail flew from her head and clattered onto the ground, and the fine fresh milk splashed into the dirt. There went the milkmaid's dreams, her eggs, her chicks, her money, her beautiful new dress, and all the admiring young men.

Moral: Don't count your chickens before they hatch.

The Four Thieves

The Trick
Do this card trick after have told or read a version of "The Musicians of Bre-men," a tale retold by the Brothers Grimm. (You can find the original Grimm tale online at www.pitt.edu/~dash/grimm027.html.) The four Jacks will represent the robbers; the rest of the deck is the house. Tell your audience you are going to put the robbers into different rooms in the house but that, in the end, they will all end up at the door, ready to run away.

You Will Need
A deck of playing cards

Preparation
Place any three cards behind the four Jacks. When you fan out the cards, show only the Jacks, keeping the three extra cards hidden behind the last Jack.

Patter and Presentation
"Here are the four robbers ready to enter the house. The deck of cards can represent the house." (*Fan out and show the Jacks, being careful not to show the three cards on top of the final Jack, then place them facedown on top of the deck. The three extra cards are now on the top of the deck.*)

"The first robber went in and made himself comfortable in the basement." (*Pick up the deck and place one of the extra cards on the bottom of the deck.*)

"The second robber went into the house and sat in the kitchen." (*Place the second card anywhere in the deck.*)

"The third robber went into the bedroom and lay down." (*Place the third extra card anywhere in the deck.*)

"The fourth robber stood guard at the door." (*You can show this last card, the first Jack on the top of the pile.*)

"The cock, the cat, the dog and the donkey began their concert. The rob-bers all ran out the door" (*show all the Jacks—one, two, three, four, which seem to have risen to the surface*) "and were never seen again!"

BOOKLIST: VERSIONS OF "THE BREMEN-TOWN MUSICIANS"

Grimm, Jacob, and Wilhelm Grimm. *The Bremen Town Musicians: A Tale. Illus. by Bernadette Watts. Trans. by Anthea Bell. North-South, 1992.* A classic version with handsome paintings. (PreK–Gr. 4)

Huling, Jan. *Ol' Bloo's Boogie-Woogie Band and Blues Ensemble. Illus. by Henri Sorensen. Peachtree, 2010.* In this down-home retelling, Ol' Bloo Donkey, Gnarly Dog, One-Eyed Lemony Cat, and Rusty Red Rooster—on their way to New Orleans to sing in a honky-tonk—stop at a cabin to sing for their supper. (Gr. 1–5)

O'Malley, Kevin. *Animal Crackers Fly the Coop. Illus. by the author. Walker, 2010.* A modern-day take on the classic tale. Aspiring comedians Hen, Dog, Cat, and Cow set off to open a comedy club. (Gr. 1–4)

Plume, Ilse. *The Bremen-Town Musicians. Illus. by the author. Doubleday, 1980.* With soft, sweet illustrations, this is a gentle retelling just right for younger children. (PreK–Gr. 2)

Mathemagic Mind Reading

The Trick
Use this amusing mind-reading trick with children able to multiply single-digit numbers.

You Will Need
Scratch paper and a pencil for each child; a SMART Board, PowerPoint presentation, document camera, or flipchart.

Patter and Presentation
Tell your audience—whether it's one person or more—"Did you know I am a world-famous mind reader? Let's see if I can read your mind. I'm going to ask you a series of questions. Don't say any of your answers out loud; just write them down on your scratch paper." As you read aloud each step below, show it printed on your SMART Board, PowerPoint, document camera, or flipchart.

1. Pick a number between 1 and 9. Remember, don't say any of your answers out loud.
2. Now multiply that number by 9.
3. Add those two numbers together.
4. Subtract 5. (*Note: Their answer will always be 4.*)

5. Pick the letter of the alphabet that corresponds with your number. A is 1, B is 2, and so on. Do not tell me your answer. (*Note: Their answer will always be* D.)

6. Think of country starting with that letter.

7. Now, take the second letter of that country and think of an animal starting with that letter. Do not tell me what it is, but picture that animal in your mind's eye.

8. Now envision the color of that animal. Can you see it in your mind?

9. And how is that gray elephant in Denmark anyhow? (*Take a bow when they gasp.*)

Okay, they won't all think of a gray elephant from Denmark, but most will, and they will be astonished that you read their minds! If they didn't come up with an elephant, they might have come up with *eagle, earthworm, earwig, echidna, eel, egret, elk,* or *emu,* but *elephant* is usually the first thing that comes to mind. Why will they end up with *Denmark*? Because only four countries in the world start with the letter *D,* and most children (and adults) won't think of *Djibouti, Dominica,* or *Dominican Republic.* Children who come up with a completely different color, animal, or country probably counted, multiplied, or subtracted wrong. Whoops.

I Can Guess Your Birthday

The Trick
You will be able to tell each player the month and day of his or her birthday. Reserve this for students old enough to multiply three numbers by two numbers (or able to use a calculator with some facility).

You Will Need
Paper and pencils for each student; a SMART Board, white board, or flipchart

Patter and Presentation
Put the instructions—one step at a time as you go—on your SMART Board or flipchart. Ask your students to number their papers from one to nine. Using their own birthdays, they will need to do the following calculations and write down each equation and answer on their paper. Take your time and repeat the instructions so the students don't get lost. You might want to use your own birthday as an example. Here's Judy's:

1. Enter the number 7. (7)

2. Multiply by the month of your birth. ($7 \times 1 = 7$)

3. Subtract 1. $(7-1=6)$
4. Multiply by 13. $(6\times13=78)$
5. Add the day of your birth. $(78+23=101)$
6. Add 3. $(101+3=104)$
7. Multiply by 11. $(104\times11=1144)$
8. Subtract the month of your birth. $(1144-1=1143)$
9. Subtract the day of your birth. $(1143-23=1120)$

One at a time, have students tell you their final number. Here's the tricky part. In your head, you must calculate the following:

1. Take the final number and divide by 10. $(1120\div10=112)$
2. Add 11. $(112+11=123)$
3. Add a decimal point. $(123 \rightarrow 1.23)$

Then announce, with authority, "Your birthday is . . . January 23!"

They will be dumbfounded! Have them break into groups and, pooling their own calculations, try to figure out the mathematical tricks. Write up the directions and give each student a copy so they can try it out on their parents, grandparents, older siblings, and friends.

Riddle Trick

The Trick

Use this at the end of a story hour featuring stories about riddles. (See chapter 4 for some good riddles, plus suggestions of laugh-aloud riddle books for kids.)

You Will Need

A brightly colored little bag; a decorated box that will fit inside the bag; an unshelled walnut; a nutcracker

Preparation

Put the walnut in the box and the box in the bag.

Patter and Presentation
With great intensity, tell the group, "I am about to show you something that I have never seen before, that you have never seen before, and that no one on earth has ever seen before. And after you see it, no living person will ever see it again!" After declaring this, pull out a brightly colored little bag and open it. From the bag, pull out the decorated little box. Open that box and lift out . . . an unshelled walnut! Crack it open with a nutcracker, and eat the nut inside. "Mmmmm. Delicious!" you say as you chew.

Biography Prediction

The Trick
You will "magically" show a picture that you have drawn of the subject of a biography that a volunteer has secretly selected.

You Will Need
A pad of drawing paper; a pencil; a selection of biographies

Patter and Presentation
Booktalk several of your favorite biographies. Select a volunteer and tell him that you will draw a picture of the person in the biography of his choice. Take out your drawing pad and draw a picture while the volunteer chooses a biography. The volunteer then holds up the biography. Show your picture, saying, "That's exactly the picture I drew—a picture of Abraham Lincoln . . . as a baby!" Or simply draw a baby crib and say, "This is the crib where he (or she) slept every day. Shhh. He's in there right now. Don't wake him up!"

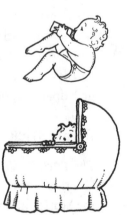

Hint: You can sketch in faint pencil lines of your drawing ahead of time if you feel that you can't draw a baby or a crib freehand. Use a marker or crayon to fill in quickly a finished picture.

Using Books about Magic and Magicians

One obvious opportunity to use magic tricks is when reading aloud or booktalking books about magic and magicians. Folklore and fantasy are filled with tales of enchanters, magician's apprentices, witches, conjurers, and characters magically transformed. Adding a magic trick at the end of a magic-themed story hour will make kids even more eager to read the books you have showcased. In the booklists below, you'll find picture books, fiction, biographies, and, of course, nonfiction on the art of magic, so aspiring conjurers can learn their own tricks and investigate more magic books on the 793.8 shelves.

"Books Are Magic"

Children in grades 2 through 5 are a wonderful audience for story hours with a magical component. Kick off a two- or three-part program using the theme "Books Are Magical." First, take children on a walk-and-talk around the library, showing the many places books relating to magic can be found—from nonfiction to biography, to fiction to picture books. Because the life of Harry Houdini still holds us all in thrall, gather your group in your story corner and introduce the great magician. Read aloud several descriptions of his astonishing feats and show photographs from one or more biographies. Brian Selnick's *The Houdini Box* is a great read-aloud choice to keep the excitement going. Next, show them live footage of Houdini's great rope trick (www.youtube.com/watch?v = EbvZZsYZmEY) or footage of him wriggling out of a straitjacket (easily found at Google.com when you search and click on "videos"). Let kids hear his voice online in a recording he made in 1914 at Internet Archive (archive.org/details/EdisonMachineRehearsalByHarry Houdini1914).

"Kids Do Magic"

This next part can be a one- or two-part session, depending on your time frame. Tell children that they are going to be the magicians. Divide your participants into four or five groups, with two to four in a group.

Preparation

Look through your library's magic books on the 793.8 shelf and select four or five tricks that are easy to read, comprehend, and perform. Be sure the props or supplies required are readily accessible. To make sure each trick works, try it yourself. If you have trouble, find a different trick. Photocopy a set of trick instructions for each group member. Prepare a "Box of Magic" for each group, filling a small box with necessary supplies, props and instructions sheets.

Procedure

Go over what you want the children to do in their groups:

1. Read the directions together and examine the props and/or supplies in the box.
2. Figure out how the trick is done.
3. Assign a job to each person in the group. Everyone must participate, collaborate, and cooperate. It's up to the group to make sure no one is left out.
4. Have the children practice the trick at least three times, with each person having something to do as part of the presentation.
5. Ask the group to develop a patter as they practice to make the trick more entertaining and mysterious.

Last, have each group put on a mini-magic show, presenting its trick to the other children. If you have only three groups, the children will probably have time to complete their performances in this session. If you have four or five groups, save the performances for next time so the children won't be too rushed. You might want to tape their shows so they can watch themselves. The presentations will make an entertaining feature on a school news show . . . and you won't have a single magic book on your shelves for the rest of the year.

BOOKLIST: PICTURE BOOKS ABOUT MAGIC

Agee, Jon. *Milo's Hat Trick.* *Illus. by the author. Hyperion, 2001.* Milo, a not-so-competent conjurer, needs a rabbit to pull out of his hat—but he gets a bear instead. (K–Gr. 3)

Baker, Keith. *The Magic Fan.* *Illus. by the author. Harcourt, 1989.* Yoshi finds a magic fan, but discovers that there is magic in himself. (K–Gr. 3)

Cate, Annette LeBlanc. *The Magic Rabbit.* *Illus. by the author. Candlewick, 2007.* The Amazing Ray, a young magician, and his loyal rabbit assistant, Bunny, are separated when Bunny is chased by a dog. (PreK–Gr. 2)

Egan, Tim. *Burnt Toast on Davenport Street.* *Houghton Mifflin, 1997.* A buzzing fly offers Arthur, a skeptical dog, three wishes if Arthur spares his life. (K–Gr. 3)

Lin, Grace. *Ling & Ting: Not Exactly the Same! Little, Brown, 2010.* Meet Chinese American twins Ling and Ting in six short chapters, including one where

Ling attempts a magic card trick. (PreK–Gr. 2)

Meddaugh, Susan. *The Witch's Walking Stick.* Illus. by the author. *Houghton Mifflin, 2005.* A stray dog grabs a witch's magic walking stick and runs off with it. (PreK–Gr. 3)

Paul, Ruth. *Hedgehog's Magic Tricks.* Illus. by the author. *Candlewick, 2013.* Hedgehog holds a magic show for his friends, but he can't make anyone disappear. (PreK–Gr. 1)

Seuss, Dr. *Bartholomew and the Oobleck.* *Random House, 1949.* King Derwin orders his magicians to make a new kind of weather fall from the sky. (Gr. 1–4)

Thurber, James. *Many Moons.* Illus. by Louis Slobodkin. *Harcourt, 1943.* The king asks the Lord High Chamberlain, the Royal Wizard, and the Royal Mathematician to get the moon for his daughter, but they all say it's impossible. (See also the 1998 edition, newly illustrated by Marc Simont.) (Gr. 2–4)

Van Allsburg, Chris. *The Garden of Abdul Gasazi.* Illus. by the author. *Houghton Mifflin, 1979.* Venturing into a magician's garden to retrieve Fritz, the dog he is minding, Alan is aghast to discover the man has turned the dog into a duck. (K–Gr. 5)

Van Allsburg, Chris. *Jumanji.* Illus. by the author. *Houghton Mifflin, 1981.* Judy and Peter play a magical board game that comes to life in dramatic and dangerous ways. Follow with the companion book *Zathura* (2002). (K–Gr. 5)

Van Allsburg, Chris. *Probuditi!* Illus. by the author. *Houghton Mifflin, 2006.* After attending a magic show, Calvin constructs a hypnotizing machine that causes his little sister, Trudy, to act like a dog. (K–Gr. 5)

BOOKLIST: FICTION BOOKS ABOUT MAGIC

See how children use magic spells, sorcery, and other trickery in fiction books. As J. K. Rowling has famously said, "I don't believe in the kind of magic in my books. But I do believe something very magical can happen when you read a good book."

Beaty, Andrea. *Dorko the Magnificent.* *Amulet, 2013.* Fifth-grader Robbie thinks he has suffered enough disasters as an aspiring magician, but then Grandma Melvyn moves in. (Gr. 4–6)

Blackwood, Sage. *Jinx.* *Harper, 2013.* Abandoned in the forest by his cruel step-father, young Jinx is taken in as a servant by a wizard. (Gr. 4–7)

DeKeyser, Stacy. *The Brixen Witch.* *McElderry, 2012.* After twelve-year-old Rudy brings home a witch's gold coin, he starts having fearsome nightmares and his village is overrun with rats. (Gr. 5–8)

DiCamillo, Kate. *The Magician's Elephant.* Illus. by Yoko Tanaka. Candlewick, 2009. When a ten-year-old orphan asks a fortune teller if his younger sister is alive, he's told to "follow the elephant. She will lead you there." (Gr. 3–6)

Epstein, Adam Jay, and Andrew Jacobson. *The Familiars.* Illus. by Bobby Chiu. Harper-Collins, 2010. Aldwyn—a mangy but personable black-and-white alley cat—is chosen as a companion by Jack, a wizard-in-training, who is celebrating his eleventh birthday. (Gr. 4–7)

Hurwitz, Johanna. *Magical Monty.* Illus. by Anik McGrory. Candlewick, 2012. First-grader Monty, who has a new baby sister, is learning the tricks in the magic set his grandmother gave him. (K–Gr. 2)

Ibbotson, Eva. *The Ogre of Oglefort.* Illus. by Lisa K. Weber. Dutton, 2011. The Hag of the Dribble and her young orphan friend are charged with rescuing a princess and killing a hideous ogre. (Gr. 3–6)

Jones, Diana Wynne. *Earwig and the Witch.* Illus. by Paul O. Zelinsky. Greenwillow, 2012. Adopted by a witch named Bella Yaga who needs an extra pair of hands, Earwig—a girl with a "very strong personality"—decides it's time to learn some spells. (Gr. 2–4)

Knudsen, Michelle. *The Dragon of Trelian.* Candlewick, 2009. Calen, slacker apprentice to the castle's mage, is befriended by Princess Meglynne, who reveals she's been hiding a young dragon in a cave deep in the forest. (Gr. 4–7)

Lalicki, Tom. *Danger in the Dark: A Houdini & Nate Mystery.* Illus. by Carlyn Cerniglia. Farrar, 2006. After Nate's wealthy great-aunt falls prey to a crooked medium, Harry Houdini helps the boy get justice. The first in a series. (Gr. 4–7)

Landy, Derek. *Skulduggery Pleasant.* HarperCollins, 2007. Twelve-year-old Stephanie teams up with Skulduggery Pleasant—a walking, talking skeleton and detective—to solve her uncle's murder and save the world from rogue magicians. (Gr. 5–8)

Oliver, Lauren. *Liesl & Po.* Illus. by Kei Acedera. HarperCollins, 2011. Three days after Liesl's father dies, two ghosts from the Other Side appear in her attic bedroom: a child named Po and pet named Bundle. (Gr. 4–7)

Prineas, Sarah. *The Magic Thief: Book One.* Illus. by Antavier Caparo. HarperCollins, 2008. After Connwaer, an orphan boy and expert pickpocket, nicks a magic stone from an old wizard, he is taken on as the wizard's apprentice. (Gr. 3–6)

Riordan, Rick. *The Red Pyramid.* Disney-Hyperion, 2010. Fourteen-year-old Carter and twelve-year-old Sadie Kane are with their Egyptologist dad on Christmas

Eve when he unwittingly unleashes an ancient god and destroys the British Museum. (Gr. 5–9)

Rowling, J. K. *Harry Potter and the Sorcerer's Stone. Illus. by Mary GrandPré. Scholastic, 1998.* Inexplicable things always happen to Harry in this first of seven magical books that changed the world. (Gr. 3–8)

Schlitz, Laura Amy. *Splendors and Glooms. Candlewick, 2012.* After marionette master and magician Professor Grissini and his two young assistants perform their show at Clara Wintermute's twelfth birthday party, Clara disappears. (Gr. 4–8)

Selznick, Brian. *The Houdini Box. Illus. by the author. Knopf, 1991.* Ten-year-old Victor, an aspiring magician, meets the great Houdini, who promises to reveal his secrets to the boy. (Gr. 2–5)

Stanley, Diane. *The Silver Bowl. Harper, 2011.* Seven-year-old Molly, who can see visions of the future, is sent away by her father to work as a scullery maid at Dethemere Castle. (Gr. 5–8)

Stroud, Jonathan. *The Amulet of Samarkand. Hyperion, 2003.* Nathaniel, a twelve-year-old magician's apprentice, summons Bartimaeus, a jinn, to steal an ancient artifact from another magician. (Gr. 5–9)

Ursu, Anne. *Breadcrumbs. Illus. by Erin McGuire. HarperCollins/Walden Pond, 2011.* Hazel heads into the snowy Minnesota woods to rescue her best friend, Jack, who has gone off with the White Witch on her sleigh drawn by wolves. (Gr. 4–7)

Ursu, Anne. *The Real Boy. Illus. by Erin McGuire. HarperCollins/Walden Pond, 2013.* Working as a hand for the first true magician in Asteri in a generation, eleven-year-old Oscar must figure out what to do when the town's magic begins to go awry. (Gr. 4–7)

BOOKLIST: NONFICTION BOOKS ABOUT MAGIC

Adler, David A., and Michael S. Adler. *A Picture Book of Harry Houdini. Illus. by Matt Collins. Holiday House, 2009.* An excellent introduction to Houdini's magic-filled life. (Gr. 1–3)

Barnhart, Norm. *Amazing Magic Tricks. Illus. with photos. Capstone, 2009.* Four books in one big paperback, with tricks at four different levels of difficulty. (Gr. 4–8)

Becker, Helaine. *Magic Up Your Sleeve: Amazing Illusions, Tricks, and Science Facts You'll Never Believe. Illus. by Claudia Davila. Maple Tree Press, 2010.* Thirty tricks integrate math, chemistry, physics, and other sciences. (Gr. 4–7)

Bertrand, Isabelle. *It's All Fun and Games. Illus. by Joelle Dreidemy, Aurelien Debat, and Roland Garrigue. OwlKids, 2008.* A spiral-bound collection of 230 activities, arranged in categories such as crafts, logic and strategy games, experiments, magic tricks, all kinds of games, songs and rhymes, and shadow puppets. (Gr. 3–6)

Carlson, Laurie. *Harry Houdini for Kids: His Life and Adventures with 21 Magic Tricks and Illusions.* Illus. with photos. *Chicago Review Press, 2009.* A breezy account of Houdini's life and career, with period photographs and instructions for twenty-one tricks. (Gr. 4–8)

Charney, Steve. *Amazing Tricks with Everyday Stuff.* Illus. with photos. *Capstone, 2011.* A professional magician describes eight easy-to-read-and-follow tricks, illustrated with photos of kids performing them. The other books in the Easy Magic Trick series (all 2011) are: *Awesome Coin Tricks, Cool Card Tricks,* and *Incredible Tricks at the Dinner Table.* (Gr. 1–4)

Charney, Steve. *The Kids' Guide to Magic Tricks.* Illus. with photos. *Capstone, 2013.* Ten entertaining tricks that make use of easy-to-find props and have easy-to-follow instructions. (Gr. 4–6)

Cobb, Vicki. *Harry Houdini: A Photographic Story of a Life.* Illus. with photos. *DK, 2005.* An informative, photo-filled biography, with descriptions (and sometimes explanations) of Houdini's tricks and escapes. (Gr. 5–8)

Colgan, Lynda. *Mathemagic! Number Tricks.* Illus. by Jane Kurisu. *Kids Can, 2011.* Ten cool math magic tricks using calculators, dice, finger multiplication, playing cards, and more. (Gr. 3–6)

Einhorn, Nicholas. *Stunts, Puzzles, and Stage Illusions.* Rosen, 2011. Color photos and clear directions explain how to perform fifty tricks. Part of the Inside Magic series, along with *Close-Up Magic* and *Stand-Up Magic and Optical Illusions* (all 2011). (Gr. 5–8)

Fleischman, Sid. *Escape: The Story of the Great Houdini.* Illus. with photos. *Harper-Collins, 2006.* An ebullient biography of Houdini, Fleischman's lifelong hero, including information on the magician's untimely death. Go to www.sidfleischman.com/magic.html to find instructions for a "wondrous magic trick" with playing cards. (Gr. 4–8)

Jarrow, Gail. *The Amazing Harry Kellar: Great American Magician.* Illus. with photos and reprods. *Calkins Creek, 2012.* A swanky biography of Kellar (1849–1922), whom Houdini regarded as a mentor. One of his famous illusions was self-decapitation. Loaded with old photos and posters. (Gr. 4–8)

King, Mac. *Mac King's Campfire Magic: 50 Amazing, Easy-to-Learn Tricks and Mind-Blowing Stunts Using Cards, String, Pencils, and Other Stuff from Your Knapsack.* Illus. by Bill King. Foreword by Penn & Teller. *Black Dog & Leventhal, 2010.* As Las Vegas magician Mac King says in his breezy intro, "There are tricks here that range from the ridiculously simple to the somewhat difficult, but thankfully none that are ridiculously difficult." (Gr. 4–8)

Kronzek, Allan Zola. *A Book of Magic for Young Magicians: The Secrets of Alkazar.* *Illus. by Joseph K. Schmidt. Dover, 1992.* An oldie but goodie, with information on how to do thirteen tricks and advice on patter and misdirection. (Gr. 5–8)

Krull, Kathleen. *Houdini: World's Greatest Mystery Man and Escape King.* *Illus. by Eric Velasquez. Walker, 2005.* Five of Houdini's greatest tricks, including the milk-can escape, are highlighted in this dramatic picture-book biography. (Gr. 2–5)

Lane, Mike. *Card Magic.* *Illus. by David Mostyn. Windmill, 2012.* Ten simple tricks with good-natured cartoon illustrations. This is the first in a six-volume set, Miraculous Magic Tricks, which also includes *Close-Up Magic, Coin Magic, Mind Magic, Paper Magic*, and *Performing Magic* (all 2012). (Gr. 3–7)

Leeming, Joseph. *Easy Magic Tricks.* *Dover, 2008.* Originally published in 1951 as The Real Book of Magic, this no-frills collection includes 127 clearly explained tricks that children can do with coins, handkerchiefs, cards, strings, and dice. (Gr. 5–8)

MacLeod, Elizabeth. *Harry Houdini.* *Illus. by John Mantha. Kids Can, 2009.* A good beginner's biography, with colorful illustrations on each page. MacLeod's *Harry Houdini: A Magical Life* (2005), for children in grades 4–6, is a more complex (and not always admiring) account. (Gr. 2–3)

Martineau, Susan. *Marvelous Magic.* *Illus. by Martin Ursell. Windmill, 2012.* A dozen simple tricks, illustrated with cheerful artwork. (Gr. 3–6)

Robinson, Tom. *The Everything Kids' Magical Science Experiments Book.* *Puzzles by Beth L. Blair. Adams Media, 2007.* A consumable workbook of fifty nifty chemistry, physics, and other science-based tricks and experiments, plus thirty puzzles. (Gr. 3–6)

Schafer, Albert D. *Illusionology: The Secret Science of Magic.* *Illus. by David Wyatt and Levi Pinfold. Candlewick, 2012.* A gorgeously illustrated cornucopia of tricks, magic secrets revealed, pop-ups, manipulatives, and more. (Gr. 4–Adult)

Tarr, Bill. *Now You See It, Now You Don't! Lessons in Sleight of Hand.* *Illus. by Barry Ross. Vintage, 1976.* More than one hundred tricks, graded for difficulty, and 1,500 line drawings, including close-ups of hands illustrating the meticulous moves for sleight of hand with cards, coins, balls, thimbles, and more. (Gr. 6–Adult)

Weaver, Janice. *Harry Houdini: The Legend of the World's Greatest Escape Artist.* *Illus. by Chris Lane. Abrams, 2011.* A well-researched biography, filled with photos, posters, playbills, primary-source quotes, and descriptions of Houdini's feats. (Gr. 4–7)

Wiese, Jim. *Magic Science: 50 Jaw-Dropping, Mind-Boggling, Head-Scratching Activities for Kids.* *Jossey-Bass, 1998.* Each entertaining, instructive trick is broken into sections: Materials, The Setup, Magic Science, Time, Effect, and Explanation. (Gr. 3–6)

Wyler, Rose, and Gerald Ames. *Magic Secrets*. *Revised edition. Illus. by Arthur Dorros. Harper, 1990*. A colorfully illustrated easy reader, featuring simple-to-do magic tricks. (K–Gr. 3)

BOOKLIST: PROFESSIONAL BOOKS ABOUT MAGIC

Bauer, Caroline Feller. *Leading Kids to Books through Magic*. *Illus. by Richard Laurent. American Library Association, 1996*. More than two dozen easy tricks and annotated lists of books, stories, and poems to use with them.

Card & Magic Tricks Handbook. *Illus. with photos. Chartwell, 2009*. More than one hundred card tricks, conjuring tricks, and other magical doings, with color photos illustrating each step.

Einhorn, Nicholas. *The Art of Magic and Sleight of Hand: How to Perform Amazing Close-Up Tricks, Baffling Optical Illusions and Incredible Mental Magic*. *Photos by John Freeman. Southwater, 2011*. One hundred–plus magic tricks accompanied by clear photos showing each one.

Einhorn, Nicholas. *The Illustrated Compendium of Magic Tricks: The Complete Step-by-Step Guide to Magic, with More than 375 Fun and Simple-to-Learn Tricks*. *Photos by Paul Bricknell. Lorenz Books, 2008*. Lots to digest for those new to magic (including older children) and other magic lovers who will carefully examine the many photographs to see how each trick works.

Fajuri, Gabe. *Mysterio's Encyclopedia of Magic and Conjuring*. *Illus. by Tony Dunn. Quirk, 2008*. Tricks and illusions based on the performances of the Amazing Mr. Mysterio, a well-known magician who died (onstage!) in 1936. Each trick is broken down into sections—Effect, Required, Preparation, and Performance—and illustrated with black-and-white drawings.

Jay, Joshua. *Joshua Jay's Amazing Book of Cards: Tricks, Shuffles, Stunts & Hustles Plus Bets You Can't Lose*. *Illus. with photos. Workman, 2010*. Fifty-eight card tricks—one for every card in the deck and then some—plus photos and a DVD to show how they are done.

Jay, Joshua. *Magic: The Complete Course*. *Illus. with photos. Workman, 2008*. More than one hundred tricks, five hundred color photos, and a DVD.

Kaufman, Richard. *Knack Magic Tricks: A Step-by-Step Guide to Illusions, Sleights of Hand, and Amazing Feats*. *Foreword by David Copperfield. Photos by Elizabeth Kaufman. Knack, 2010*. Plenty of photos showing card, coin, string, rope, napkin, fruit, and cup tricks, along with some mental magic and a chapter on getting kids to perform magic.

Pogue, David. *Magic for Dummies*. *Illus. with photos. IDG Books Worldwide, 1998*. Not as flashy as some books, but incredibly meaty, with more than ninety tricks and contributions by more than thirty working magicians. You'll love the "Ten Things to Say When Things Go Wrong" list.

Schindler, George. *Magic with Everyday Objects: Over 150 Tricks Anyone Can Do at the Dinner Table. Illus. by Ed Tricomi. Scarborough House, 2000, c1976.* Crazily funny tricks using silverware, salt, pepper, bread, napkins, and plates all accompanied by breezy patter. Supper will never be the same.

WEBSITES: MAGIC AND MAGICIANS

We can't even begin to list all the magic shops online, not to mention the gazillions of "how-to-do magic" websites and videos, but here are a few with interesting and varied inventories and information to get you started along with sites for some of the best-known magician's associations.

Classic Magic *www.classicmagic.net*
Hundreds of tricks, broken into categories. More practical for finding out how a trick is done than doing it yourself.

Clown Antics *www.clownantics.com*
"Your one stop clown shop" has it all, including clown gear and extensive supplies for magic tricks.

David Ginn Magic Catalog *www.ginnmagic.com*
Ginn, who does three hundred magic shows at schools each year, writes a monthly newsletter; his site features his books and a wonderful array of props for sale.

International Brotherhood of Magicians *www.magician.org*
The website of the world's largest organization dedicated to magic.

Kidzone: Magic Tricks! *www.kidzone.ws/magic*
A score of magic tricks kids can do, described in great detail, including card tricks, coin tricks, and "magic" objects tricks.

Magic Café *www.themagiccafe.com*
This message board forum displays posts from both aspiring and experienced magicians.

Magic Dove Magic Shop *shop.magicdove.com*
The online presence of a Florida magic store, the site has a huge inventory of tricks and props.

Magic Geek *www.magicgeek.com*
New content is added frequently to this hip site, which has a video demo for every trick they have in stock, with many originals including the 'Fraid Knot and the Tiny Plunger. You can consult the staff of professional-level magicians by phone or e-mail and peruse their video-filled blog.

Magic Gizmo *magicgizmo.com*
Site for magicians and magic collectors; includes a discussion forum, articles, a magic-shop locator, videos of performers, and an online newsletter.

Magic Warehouse *www.themagicwarehouse.com*
Hundreds of tricks to buy, from inexpensive to yowie!

Penguin Magic *www.penguinmagic.com*
Based in Las Vegas, Penguin Magic sells tricks, DVDs, and supplies to magicians of all skill levels. Many of the props come with brief demonstration videos.

Silk Magic Tricks *stores.silkmagictricks.com*
A huge selection of silk magic tricks, props, accessories, and devices.

Society of American Magicians *magicsam.com*
A membership organization for collectors, historians, enthusiasts, and professional performers. You need to become a member to access most of the website.

Society of Young Magicians *magicsam.com/s-y-m-youth-program*
This offshoot of the Society of American Magicians runs nearly a hundred local chapters (called Assemblies) around the world for magic lovers ages seven through seventeen. Yearly membership is inexpensive and includes a monthly newsletter.

Stoners FunStore *www.stoners.com*
When you browse this website for Dick Stoners's store in Fort Wayne, Indiana, you'll find an extensive collection of tricks, supplies, and books.

Tannen's Magic *www.tannens.com*
A New York City institution since 1925, Tannen's Magic Shop hosts lectures, classes, a magic camp, a blog, and carries thousands of magic-related items in its online store.

Teach by Magic *www.teachbymagic.com/SearchVideos.aspx*
Watch scores of excellent videos of down-to-earth magicians who show a trick and then, in a follow-up video, demonstrate how it was done. Subscribe for full access to the site.

Trends Times *www.trendtimes.com/magic-tricks.html#top*
Along with all kinds of novelties, you'll find a wide range of magic tricks here. Their motto: "Because fun has no age."

part 2

PROGRAMS

THE TWO CHAPTERS IN THIS SECTION EACH ADDRESS A RANGE OF ages. Chapter 7, "Programs for Preschool and Primary School Children, From Birth to Age 7," deals with books, stories, and ideas to use with young children, from babies through second grade, though you'll find materials there that your third graders will enjoy as well. Chapter 8, "Programs for Upper Elementary and Middle School Children, Ages 8 to 14," targets tweens—children in grades three through eight.

Once upon a time, children had to wait until they reached the ripe old age of three or four to attend storytime. Over the years, the age has crept downward, and now, in addition to weekly storytimes for ages three to five, librarians conduct toddler storytimes and lapsit programs, with stories, rhymes, fingerplays, and songs. They have also stepped up to help parents and caregivers see the importance—and fun—of these activities. and to inform them about the wonderful resources they'll find in nursery schools, day-care centers, and especially, libraries.

For the littlest children, you're working each time to increase their attention spans and interest levels. By age four, children will be more engaged in your program and feel like old hands. Four- and five-year-olds can sit through longer, more complex stories and will have a veritable repertoire of songs they can sing by heart (especially if the adults in their lives—parents, teachers, librarians—have been singing with them all along). They love to pretend, too, and have fun with simple creative drama activities you initiate during or after a story.

Slightly older children—kindergarten through second graders (what we generally call the primary grades)—are overtly enthusiastic and appreciative; their enjoyment will make you feel that all your preparation was worthwhile. If a story has a repeating phrase, these children will join in immediately. At this age, it's always easy to see who has been read to and exposed to stories, poems, and songs by how they respond to you. If the adults in their lives have parked them in front of the TV or a device instead of reading to them, you will see the difference in their attention span. If their teachers have felt more compelled to complete worksheets than hold read-alouds, then it will be your job to model the obvious advantages of developing listening skills over testing skills.

Primary-grade children who have not heard a lot of stories can quickly be drawn into the storytelling environment. They love it when the storyteller makes exaggerated movements or uses a variety of different voices. Their imaginations run rampant at this age, and they can readily see or live each story in their mind's eye. They will appreciate longer programs, perhaps half an hour to forty-five minutes in length. A funny story or two followed by a set of riddles, a picture book, and a poem or song to finish makes the perfect combination.

Primary-grade children also enjoy picture books intended for preschoolers, in addition to more sophisticated material. In addition, those books you introduced at toddler storytimes with simple one-sentence-per-page texts then enjoy a second life, just right as emergent readers for kindergarten through second graders learning to read. As Pete the Cat would say, "It's all good."

As frequent presenters and storytellers, we can predict fairly accurately how preschoolers through second graders will respond to a story. For instance, as soon as a repetitive pattern appears in a story, young children realize they are expected to join in. If you are used to such enthusiastic responses, you may find telling stories to older kids a bit disconcerting.

Tween, a blend of the words *between* and *teen*, is a new-ish word to describe youths between childhood and the teenage years, ages eight to twelve. These kids aren't quite grown up yet, so they'll still do something fun and silly, if you play your cards right. They can be very receptive listeners, their interests are varied, and their curiosity is boundless. There's probably not a single idea in this book these kids won't appreciate, even though they are old enough to listen to more sophisticated selections and have the stamina and concentration to sit attentively for up to an hour.

Somewhere in middle school, though, some unseen presence convinces children that it's not cool to call out or laugh in response to a funny or sad part in a story. This learned reserve is reflected in young adult audiences, too. Sometimes kids will roll their eyes and act bored, which can be downright unnerving. Don't think you aren't reaching your audience just because they don't respond enthusiastically. They *are* listening. These kids want you to like them, and they want to like you—but they need to display a bit of ennui in front of their friends. Peer pressure dictates that they don't want to let you know that they want to like you.

One way to get beyond this is to give your group permission to react. Try Caroline's crazy little warm-up before you introduce your first story to older listeners. Come to think of it, this will work just as well with younger children. And since these next two chapters are full of programming ideas, it should work with all you grown-up readers, too. Here goes:

"My part is to tell you a story. Your part is to listen. If it's a funny story go ahead and laugh. Now practice your part and laugh." (*Pause for laughter.*)

"Very good. If it's a sad story, you may feel like crying. Now practice crying." (*Pause for crying.*)

"Excellent. If you're bored, you may want to sleep. How about a little snoring." (*Pause for snoring. At this point, they'll be wondering who this nutty person is, up at the front of the room.*)

"If you enjoy the story, you may want to applaud. Practice that now." (*Pause for applause.*)

"What a sweet sound. If you really love the story, you can cheer and whistle." (*Pause for cheers and whistles.*)

"And if you hate it, you may want to throw tomatoes. I'll give you a chance to go buy some tomatoes in a few minutes, but first, I'm going to tell you a story."

chapter 7

Programs for Preschool and Primary School Children
from Birth to Age 7

I am enough of an artist to draw freely upon my imagination. Imagination is more important than knowledge. Knowledge is limited. Imagination encircles the world.
—ALBERT EINSTEIN

IN COME THE CHILDREN FOR STORYTIME. THIS IS THE SETTLING-DOWN period, a time for everyone to get acquainted. Consider using a puppet or an interesting artifact to introduce yourself and the stories you are going to tell. Children believe in puppets. They may not notice or engage with you (until they get to know you better), but they will love chatting up your puppet. This preliminary period should be kept brief; otherwise children may get more involved in socializing than in anticipating your stories.

Start and end with a bang—a song or a lively story will galvanize everyone's attention. Between stories, invite children to participate in a group activity such as a fingerplay, a song, or a movement activity. This makes for a good intermission and a physical stretch to activate their fine-motor or gross-motor skills. If one story isn't working, wrap it up quickly and go on to the next thing. Over-planning is your best strategy.

During the actual telling of stories or books, you'll often need to ignore or deflect comments or questions by the children. Storytime is a group activity; you don't want one chatty child to monopolize the conversation. You can say, "Let's talk about that afterwards. Right now, I can't wait to tell you my newest story," and plunge right in. In between, try to keep rambling discussion to a minimum. There's only so much time children will listen to each other without zoning out.

In the public library, the children usually adjourn to tables for a make-and-take craft activity related to the theme of the day or one of the stories you shared. For some children, this is their first exposure to art, and they will revel in the profusion of crayons, paint, markers, clay, and glue. School librarians and classroom teachers are always looking for interesting follow-up ideas as well, though the activities are more likely to be curriculum-based, with children writing and drawing stories modeled on or inspired by the book they just heard.

Here are a few other things to think about:

- Whatever the age of your group, select appealing, punchy stories and books with large, clear illustrations and a straightforward story line or narrative so it's easy for your audience to follow along. Whether you are presenting to children sitting on parents' laps or to older children with grown-ups sitting alongside or at the back of the room, make sure that everyone can see the pictures. This may sound obvious, but it's frustrating and disruptive when children begin complaining, "I can't see, I can't see!"

- Decide where your audience will sit: on the floor, on cushions, on chairs? If children sit on the floor and you are standing, you may seem too far away for them. On the other hand, it's easier for a larger group to see you if you are standing or sitting above them. If you are a beginning storyteller, try different arrangements to see what works for you.

- If the children are unfamiliar with listening to stories in a group, begin with shorter, simpler books. After they have attended several sessions, they will be ready for longer or more complicated stories.

- After the program, when kids hit the stacks, watch out for the dreaded "library mind lock" where kids (and their caregivers) don't know where to look or what to pick. Always make sure you have a plethora of enticing titles on display everywhere to help them make good choices. An enthusiastic librarian working the crowd is always invaluable and appreciated.

Participation Stories

We'll start with a few of our favorite participation stories that are sure to be a hit with all ages, capped off with a list of action-based books to try with your kids. Not every story lends itself to interaction, of course, but when you tell one with a refrain that can be repeated, a call-and-response motif, or an action that can be imitated, you'll find that your whole group will want to join in. For the storyteller, such participation offers visual proof that the story is being enthusiastically received.

Participation stories are most often told to preschool and primary-age children, but other age groups will enjoy them, too. Adults are sometimes reluctant to join in, but they are among the most enthusiastic participants once their reserve is broken. Even older elementary and junior-high students—who are usually reticent about calling out when there are strangers present—can be convinced to "help" tell the story.

Lion Hunt

By Caroline Feller Bauer

Stand in front and have the children stand, too—for a little aerobic work-out. Children should repeat each line and join in on all the sound effects and actions. An oversize picture-book version of this action story is Michael Rosen's now classic *We're Going on a Bear Hunt,* illustrated by Helen Oxenbury. You'll find Judy Freeman's rhyming version ("We're Going on a Lion Hunt") in her book *Once Upon a Time: Using Storytelling, Creative Drama, and Reader's Theater with Children in Grades PreK–6* (Libraries Unlimited, 2007).

Everyone get ready.

Stand up straight. (*motion to have everyone stand up*)

We're going on a lion hunt.

Ready?

Ready!

Get set, go.

I see, I see, I see a road.

Let's walk down the road. (*tap your hands on your thighs*)

Tramp, tramp, tramp,

I see, I see, I see a field.

Let's walk through the field.
   (make wide swinging motions with your arms)
Swish, swish, swish.

I see, I see, I see a swamp.
Let's walk through the muck. *(lift your legs up high)*
Squish, squish, squish.

I see, I see, I see a tree.
Let's climb up it. *(climb hand over hand)*
Climb, climb, climb.

I see, I see, I see a bridge.
Let's run over the bridge. *(pretend to run in place;*
   click your tongue on the roof of your mouth)
Tap, tap, tap.

I see, I see, I see a cave.
Let's go into the cave. *(drag your feet slowly)*
Slowly, slowly, slowly

I see . . .
I see . . .
I see . . . a lion!

ROAR!!!

RUN! *(pretend to run in place)*

Over the bridge, *(click your tongue on the roof of mouth)*
Tap, tap, tap,

Up the tree, *(climb hand over hand)*
Climb, climb, climb,

Through the muck, *(lift your legs up high)*
Squish, squish, squish,

Through the field, *(make wide swinging motions with your arms)*
Swish, swish, swish,

Down the road, *(tap your hands on your thighs)*

Tramp, tramp, tramp—

Wow, we made it! *(collapse into a chair)*

Let's Go on a Space Trip

Now that you have faced a ferocious lion and lived to retell the tale, it's time for another heart-stopping adventure. This time, however, you and your audience will be blasting into space. In addition, your group will learn a mnemonic device they'll use for the rest of their lives: My Very Educated Mother Just Served Us Nachos! *(Mercury, Venus, Earth, Mars, Jupiter, Saturn, Uranus, and Neptune)*

Found unattributed and anonymous on the Internet, this story was adapted and expanded by Judy Freeman. (If anyone has any more information on the genesis of this tale, let Judy know.) To tell this story, you'll want to seat the children in a circle or in rows as though they are in a space shuttle. Have them repeat each line and do all motions as a call-and-response.

Hey, astronauts!

Let's go on a space trip.

Don't forget your toothbrush.

Time to suit up.

Put on your space suit.

Put on your helmet.

Climb aboard the spaceship.

Strap yourself in.

Ready to launch?

Count down time.

10, 9, 8, 7, 6, 5, 4, 3, 2, 1 , 0, LIFT OFF!

Now we're going faster!

Hold on tight! *(shake as though you are moving fast)*

Through Earth's atmosphere.

Now we're in space and gravity-free.
    (wave your arms as though you are floating)

WEB This script is available on ALA's Web Extras page at alaeditions.org/webextras.

Wow, we're weightless!

Oh, look.

There's the moon! (*peer out a window*)

It's a big, big moon. (*make a big circle with your arms*)

Can't go over it.

Can't go under it.

Can't go through it.

Let's orbit around it.

Oh, look. There's the sun! (*peer out a window*)

It's so bright it hurts my eyes. (*squint and shade your eyes*)

Nope, we can't go there.

Better turn around.

Oh, look.

There are the eight planets! (*peer out a window*)

Mercury, Venus, Earth, Mars, Jupiter, Saturn, Uranus, Neptune.

Let's try that again.

Mercury, Venus, Earth, Mars, Jupiter, Saturn, Uranus, Neptune.

My Very Educated Mother Just Served Us Nachos!

Can't go over them.

Can't go under them.

Can't go through them.

Let's orbit around them.

Mercury, zoom.

Venus, zoom.

Earth? Never mind. We know that one already.

Mars, zoom.

Jupiter, zoom.

Saturn, zoom.

Uranus, zoom.

Neptune, zoom.

That's a lot of zooming.

I miss my home sweet home: Earth!

Time to orbit back.

Look, there's Earth.

What a beautiful blue ball.

Now it's getting closer.

We're reentering Earth's atmosphere.

Hold tight! (*shake as though you are moving fast*)

The space capsule's parachute is open.

We're floating down.

SPLASH DOWN!

Earth! Home sweet home!

The Wonderful Shrinking Shirt

By Leone Castell Anderson

Use a bit of pantomime when you tell this. Show Sarah sousing and dousing the shirt, and hanging it up on an imaginary clothesline. Use different voices and inflections for the many people who say, "That is a fine shirt!" And pantomime how the shirt looks, with the shirtsleeves up to your elbows and the collar choking you. It's a story that your children will intuitively join in on once they catch on to all the refrains.

The first time Judy read the picture book The Wonderful Shrinking Shirt *back in 1983, she knew she had to tell it. Deciding the story needed a surprise finish, she cut, glued, and hand-stitched together a doll-sized yellow flannel shirt with purple stripes. Every time she gets to the last line of the story, she takes a box out of her pocket, lifts out the little shirt, and holds it up. The children never fail to gasp. What they assumed was just a story now seems quite real to them. She tells them that baby Wilbur is all grown up now and he loaned the shirt to her so she could tell everyone his amazing story. Often they believe her.*

One day Elbert said, "I could use a new shirt to wear to church."

Sarah, his wife, said, "You surely could, Elbert."

Janie, their daughter, said, "You surely could, Paw."

Baby Wilbur didn't say anything. He was too little.

When Elbert went to the general store, he saw a yellow flannel shirt with purple stripes. "That is just what I want," he said. He bought the shirt and took it home.

He wore the shirt to church on Sunday. And the deacon said, "My, Elbert, that is a fine shirt."

So Elbert wore the shirt to the fireman's ball on Friday. And all the ladies said, "My, Elbert, that is a fine shirt."

He liked the shirt so much, he wore it when he sat with his friends in the courthouse square on Saturday morning. And all his friends said, "My, Elbert, that is a fine shirt."

But then his wife said, "Elbert, that shirt needs a washing." So she soused it and doused it and rinsed it clean and hung it in the sun to dry.

Sunday Elbert put on his yellow flannel shirt with the purple stripes to wear to church. "Sarah!" he called. "Whatever did you do to my shirt?"

"I soused it and doused it and rinsed it clean and hung it in the sun to dry."

She looked at Elbert. The shirtsleeves came to his elbows. The shirttails came to his waist. The collar choked him.

"Land-a-mighty!" said Sarah. "It shrunk!"

Elbert couldn't bear to throw it out. "Looks like it might fit you, wife," he said. He gave the shirt to Sarah to wear.

She wore it to the ladies' club tea on Wednesday. And all her friends said, "My, Sarah, that is a fine shirt."

So she wore the shirt to choir practice on Thursday. And the choir director said, "My, Sarah, that is a fine shirt."

She liked it so much she wore it to the chicken supper on Friday. And all the men said, "My, Sarah, that is a fine shirt."

But then Sarah said to herself, "This shirt needs a washing." So she soused it and doused it and rinsed it clean and hung it in the sun to dry.

Sunday, Sarah put on her yellow flannel shirt with the purple stripes to wear to church. "Sarah," she asked herself, "whatever did you do to this shirt?"

The shirtsleeves came to her elbows. The shirttails came to her waist. The collar choked her.

"Land-a-mighty," said Sarah. "It shrunk again!"

She couldn't bear to throw it out. "Looks like it might fit you, Janie," she said. She gave the shirt to her daughter to wear.

Janie wore the shirt to Sunday school. And the Sunday school teacher said, "My, Janie, that is a fine shirt."

So Janie wore the shirt to the square dance Tuesday night. And Georgie Green said, "My, Janie, that is a fine shirt."

Janie liked the shirt so much that she wore it to school three days in a row, until everyone in the class had said, "My, Janie, that is a fine shirt."

But then her maw said, "Janie, that shirt needs a washing."

So Sarah soused it and doused it and rinsed it clean and hung it in the sun to dry.

Sunday, Janie put on her yellow flannel shirt with the purple stripes to wear to church. "Maw!" she yelled. "Whatever did you do to this shirt?"

The shirtsleeves came to her elbows. The shirttails came to her waist. The collar choked her.

"Land-a-mighty," said her maw. "It shrunk again! But it's just the right size for Baby Wilbur. It will make him a fine christening dress."

So Baby Wilbur wore the shirt to church, and the parson baptized him. And everyone said, "My, what a fine christening dress."

But before the day was over, Baby Wilbur had wet clear through that yellow flannel shirt with the purple stripes.

So Sarah soused it and doused it and rinsed it clean and hung it in the sun to dry.

When she held up the shirt next to Baby Wilbur, she said, "Land-a-mighty. I just knew it would shrink again." Sarah shook her head.

"Looks like it won't fit anyone anymore, Wilbur," she said. "Into the rag-bag with it."

Baby Wilbur didn't say anything. He was too little. But he liked that shirt so much he couldn't bear to have his maw throw it out. He cried. And he cried. He cried through Monday and on through Tuesday.

So Wilbur's maw let Wilbur keep that wonderful shrinking shirt!

BOOKLIST: PARTICIPATION STORIES

Look for stories like these, with refrains or motions to involve listeners physically and verbally in the story.

Aardema, Verna. *Why Mosquitoes Buzz in People's Ears*. *Illus. by Leo Dillon and Diane Dillon. Dial, 1975.* This classic cumulative African pourquoi tale starts when a mosquito tells a lie to an iguana. Children join in on the sound effects and the repeated, ever-growing explanation of the terrible repercussions of mosquito's thoughtless action. (PreK–Gr. 2)

Asch, Frank. *Just Like Daddy.* *Illus. by the author. Simon & Schuster, 1981.* Children will wake up with a yawn and a stretch and get ready to go fishing with Daddy, just like Little Bear. (PreK–K)

Beaumont, Karen. *I Ain't Gonna Paint No More.* *Illus. by David Catrow. Harcourt, 2005.* Sing this to the tune of "It Ain't Gonna Rain No More" and have kids anticipate the body part the unrepentant boy will paint next: "Aw, what the heck! Gonna paint my . . ." (K–Gr. 2)

Brett, Jan. *Honey, Honey—Lion! A Story from Africa.* *Illus. by the author. Putnam, 2005.* A honey-finding bird leads Badger across the African landscape to what Badger thinks will be a beehive. The call-and-response format is similar to "I'm Going on a Bear Hunt." (PreK–Gr. 2)

Cordell, Matthew. *Hello! Hello!* *Illus. by the author. Disney-Hyperion, 2012.* When a leaf blows in through the front door, a little girl leaves her computer and other devices to go outside. Have children join in on her dialogue with increasing delight. This is a marvelous stop-and-smell-the-roses book for our techno-obsessed kids. (K–Gr. 4)

Cronin, Doreen. *Click, Clack, Peep!* *Illus. by Betsy Lewin. Atheneum, 2015.* The new baby duck keeps up all the other animals with his peep-peep-peeping. Act out all of the animals' solutions. (PreK–Gr. 1)

Cuyler, Margery. *We're Going on a Lion Hunt.* *Illus. by Joe Mathieu. Marshall Cavendish, 2008.* A teacher leads her young children on a classic call-and-response lion hunt. A good companion to our Lion Hunt story on page 257. (PreK–Gr. 2)

DePaola, Tomie. *Jack.* *Illus. by the author. Penguin/Nancy Paulsen, 2014.* On his way to the city to ask the king to help him find a house, Jack meets a profusion of animals, all of whom ask to join him. Lots of repetition and animal noises make this a peppy tale for kids to enact. (PreK–Gr. 1)

Donaldson, Julia. *The Gruffalo.* *Illus. by Axel Scheffler. Dial, 1999.* A mouse taking a stroll through the wood encounters a hungry fox, an owl, and a snake, but scares them off by describing the fearsome creature he is awaiting. This beloved story has many refrains for all to join in. (PreK–Gr. 2)

Feiffer, Jules. *Bark, George.* *Illus. by the author. HarperCollins, 1999.* In one of the best picture books ever, George's mother tells him to bark, but the floppy brown pup meows, quacks, and moos instead. Children delight in making the many animal noises and pretending to be the vet who pulls the noisy animals from deep, deep, deep within George. (PreK–Gr. 6)

Fleming, Denise. *In the Tall, Tall Grass.* *Illus. by the author. Henry Holt, 1992.* A boy watches many creatures as they crunch, munch, dart, and dip through the tall green grass. Children will have great fun echoing the spare rhymed text. (PreK–Gr. 1)

Florian, Douglas. *I Love My Hat.* *Illus. by the author. Two Lions, 2014.* Farmer Brown invites clothes-loving animals to hop aboard his tractor as he drives to town. "Nice hat, calico cat," says the farmer, and the cat sings, "I love my hat." Make up the tune for the rhyming refrain each animal sings. (PreK–Gr. 1)

Gormley, Greg. *Dog in Boots.* *Illus. by Roberta Angaramo. Holiday House, 2011.* Dog is so inspired by the story of Puss in Boots that he visits the local shoe shop to find a splendid pair of boots for himself. As you read, ask children to pretend they are Dog and describe what's wrong with each new pair of shoes he buys. (PreK–Gr. 2)

Kennedy, Anne Vittur. *The Farmer's Away! Baa! Neigh!* *Illus. by the author. Candlewick, 2014.* In a rhyming text comprised solely of animal noises, the animals on a farm have themselves a field day. (PreK–Gr. 1)

London, Jonathan. *Froggy Gets Dressed.* *Illus. by Frank Remkiewicz. Viking, 1992.* Froggy gets dressed to play outside in the snow, but forgets a few important items of clothing. Have children pantomime getting dressed along with Froggy, making zippy sound effects for each item of clothing: zoop! zup! zat! zwit! zum! (PreK–Gr. 1)

MacDonald, Margaret Read. *Mabela the Clever.* *Illus. by Tim Coffey. Albert Whitman, 2001.* Mabela is the only mouse who pays attention when a cat entreats the mice to follow her into the forest. Children can recite (or, if you put a tune to it, sing) this wonderful refrain as they march like the mice: "When we are marching, / we NEVER look back! / The cat is at the end, / Fo Feng! / FO FENG!" (PreK–Gr. 2)

Mack, Jeff. *Ah Ha!* *Illus. by the author. Chronicle, 2013.* Using only two letters of the alphabet, A and H, to make the words in the text, Mack unfurls the saga of a frog who is captured in a glass jar (AAHH!) and escapes (AH HA!), only to go in and out of danger all over again. Even the youngest children can follow the dialogue as you read each word with expression. (PreK–Gr. 2)

Massie, Diane Redfield. *The Baby Beebee Bird.* *Illus. by Steven Kellogg. HarperCollins, 2000, c1963.* Children can echo the call of the little bird who keeps the zoo animals awake with its incessant but joyous cry, "Beebeebobbibobbi beebeebobbibobbi." (PreK–Gr. 1)

Perkins, Al. *Hand, Hand, Fingers, Thumb.* *Illus. by Eric Gurney. Random House, 1969.* (PreK–Gr. 1) In this rhyming easy reader, monkeys drum on drums, with the infectious refrain, "Dum ditty dum ditty dum dum dum." Get out the drums and let kids beat out the rhythm. (PreK–Gr. 1)

Raschka, Chris. *A Ball for Daisy.* *Illus. by the author. Schwartz & Wade, 2011.* In this wordless Caldecott, Daisy the dog is bereft when her beloved ball is ruined. Ask children to add dialogue and sound effects to the story and come up with adjectives to describe the emotions Daisy expresses in her body language. (PreK–Gr. 1)

Rash, Andy. *Are You a Horse? Illus. by the author. Scholastic, 2009.* Roy's friends give him a saddle for his birthday, but now he needs to find a horse. Have each child pantomime an animal for the others to guess. When the group asks, "Are you a horse?" the child can say something like, "No, I'm a robin. Robins eat worms and fly. A horse eats grass and gallops." (PreK–Gr. 3)

Root, Phyllis. *Rattletrap Car. Illus. by Jill Barton. Candlewick, 2001.* Poppa doesn't know if he and his kids will make it to the lake in his old jalopy. Great fun, with wonderful sound effects. Sit kids in rows so they can pretend they are bouncing along in the car. (PreK–Gr. 2)

Rosen, Michael. *We're Going on a Bear Hunt. Illus. by Helen Oxenbury. McElderry, 1989.* A grand adventure with three little kids and a dad: "We're going on a bear hunt. / We're going to catch a big one. / What a beautiful day! / We're not scared." (PreK–Gr. 2)

Rosenthal, Amy Krouse. *Duck! Rabbit! Illus. by Tom Lichtenheld. Chronicle, 2009.* The story is told in dialogue between two unseen narrators who begin, "Hey, look! A duck!" "That's not a duck. That's a rabbit." It all depends on your perspective in looking at these optical-illusion illustrations. Divide your group in half to pair-read this clever book. (PreK–Gr. 6)

Sattler, Jennifer Gordon. *Pig Kahuna. Illus. by the author. Bloomsbury, 2011.* At the beach, piglet Fergus and his baby brother, Dink, befriend a big surfboard that washes onto the sand, naming it Dave. If you can, bring in a surfboard (or simply cut out paper surfboards from white kraft paper) and let kids hang ten on dry land. (PreK–Gr. 2)

Seeger, Laura Vaccaro. *Bully. Illus. by the author. Roaring Brook, 2013.* Rejected by a big bull, a small bull takes out his frustration on his animal friends. Children will read aloud the simple balloon dialogue in character. To see an excerpt, narrated by children, go to www.youtube.com/watch?v = Mz7X3WGMGRk. (PreK–Gr. 6)

Silverman, Erica. *Big Pumpkin. Illus. by S. D. Schindler. Macmillan, 1992.* A witch needs help from her ghoulish friends to pull a pumpkin off the vine. Listeners will want to do some pulling themselves as they repeat the chantable refrains, including "Drat!" which will soon become part of their vocabulary. (PreK–Gr. 2)

Tullet, Hervé. *Press Here. Illus. by the author. Handprint, 2011.* Here's an antidote to too much high-tech: a nifty picture book that puts you to work. Follow its simple commands to press, rub, tilt, and clap. "It's magic," delighted readers will say, and you'll agree, "Yup. Books are magic, all right." (PreK–Adult)

Wood, Audrey. *King Bidgood's in the Bathtub. Illus. by Don Wood. Harcourt, 1985.* Chant or sing the page's lament: "King Bidgood's in the bathtub and he won't get out! Oh, who knows what to do." (PreK–Gr. 3)

Programs for Babies and Toddlers

The trick to a successful baby or toddler program is to use short, varied activities, going, say, from fingerplay to told story to picture book to movement activity to keep kids surprised and involved. Action rhymes, simple songs, big books, short picture books, a board story, the introduction of a puppet, and short traditional stories comprise perfect literature interludes for ages one to three. Look for stories and songs that have animal noises you can make, name body parts you can point to, or contain other interactive features. Tell simple stories that lend themselves to flannel- or felt- board telling. Bring in rhythm instruments for small hands—such as rhythm sticks or bells—to shake along with a song.

Don't zoom through your story or your activities. Little ones get lost if you speak too fast. Repetition is good. If you do a new fingerplay, repeat it two or more times, and then do it again the next week so children will remember it. Read a story twice, so they can focus on it and anticipate what's coming next. If you sing "The Wheels on the Bus" this week, prepare to sing it next week, too, and maybe the week after.

Encourage caregivers to join in on your songs and stories along with their children. Duplicate the words to songs and action rhymes and give them to parents to take home and use with their children. Some librarians display the words on a poster, put them online, or project them on a screen. Parents will be grateful for any help you can provide.

Don't expect all the children to stay still and watch quietly at this age. As Jenn Fisher children's librarian at the Matawan (New Jersey) Public Library, says, when recalling the toddler storytimes she has done, "Sitting down—not mandatory!" There will be crawling, roaming, and parents taking children out for diaper changes. Be flexible and good natured, and don't take it personally. A twenty-minute program may be all they can handle. Frequent breaks with action and movement are the way to get the wiggles out. Use a bubble gun to shoot bubbles in the air, or toss handkerchiefs up high for them to catch. Don't feel you've done something wrong if they get antsy. "Now let's stand up for a little marching game," you say cheerfully, ditching those last two activities you had planned. If crying starts, break into song. "You Are My Sunshine" will placate many agitated children, especially if the grown-ups join in.

Want to see a crackerjack librarian in action? Go to www.youtube.com/watch?v = j3oMQsWQxlk and watch how Kristy Raffensberger (a former student in Judy Freeman's storytelling class at Pratt Institute in NYC) puts it all together for her toddler storytime at one of the branches of the New York Public Library. In the eight-minute video with kids and their caretakers, she does fingerplays, action songs, and a story for toddlers who are actively involved and delighted. Be sure to watch the video to the end to learn the best action rhyme ever, which she learned from her dad at the dinner table. She's turned it into a train rhyme, as follows. She says she tells the kids, "Get your train arms ready." Start slowly, and speed it up with each line.

Train!

Choo choo choo choo, choo choo choo choo
    (*alternate your arms at your sides in a circle, like a train;*
    or for extra oomph, add your legs, too, stepping in time)

Mushroom, mushroom, mushroom, mushroom
    (*same arms, a little faster*)

Cheese and crackers, cheese and crackers, cheese and crackers,
    cheese and crackers (*still faster*)

Chicken fricassee, chicken fricassee, chicken fricassee, chicken fricas-
    see (*very fast*)

SOUP, SOUP, SOUP, SOUP (*use a high voice, like a train whistle, and
    pull on an imaginary cord each time you say the word "SOUP"*)

Best Books for Baby and Toddler Storytimes

Below is a list of our top one hundred essential titles—treasures all—for your baby or toddler book programs. Books that are appropriate for this age group usually have a very simple text and pictures. They are often cumulative or rhythmic so that children can start to imitate sounds. Experiment with books that might be appealing to your particular group.

Next time you see a toddler carrying a picture book, look carefully at how he treasures it. Look at how huge it is proportionate to the size of the child. Not that toddlers mind, mind you. Once they get to know and love their own books, they carry them around like stuffed animals—beloved and a bit battered, best friends for life.

BOOKLIST: BEST PICTURE BOOKS FOR BABIES AND TODDLERS

Allen, Pamela. *Who Sank the Boat?* *Illus. by the author. Coward-McCann, 1983.* Many animals pile into the boat, but who sank it?

Ashman, Linda. *Rub-a-Dub Sub.* *Illus. by Jeff Mack. Harcourt, 2003.* Boy has ocean adventures in his bathtub sub.

Baker, Keith. *Big Fat Hen.* *Illus. by the author. Harcourt, 1994.* Colorful version of "One, Two, Buckle My Shoe."

Barton, Byron. *My Car.* *Illus. by the author. Candlewick, 2001.* Sam describes how he keeps his car in shape and drives safely.

Bee, William. *And the Train Goes . . .* *Illus. by the author. Candlewick, 2007.* Lots of lovely passengers and train noises, "clickerty-click, clickerty-clack."

Bornstein, Ruth Lercher. *Little Gorilla.* *Illus. by the author. Clarion, 1976.* Everyone loves Little Gorilla, who grows and grows.

Boynton, Sandra. *Moo, Baa, La La La!* *Illus. by the author. Little Simon, 1982.* Blithe rhyming description of what animals say.

Brown, Margaret Wise. *Goodnight Moon.* *Illus. by Clement Hurd. HarperCollins, 1947.* The very best goodnight book of all time.

Browne, Anthony. *One Gorilla: A Counting Book.* *Illus. by the author. Candlewick, 2013.* Gorgeous watercolors of ten different primates as we count them from one to ten.

Bunting, Eve. *Have You Seen My New Blue Socks?* *Illus. by Sergio Ruzzier. Clarion, 2013.* In rhyme, Duck seeks lost socks.

Bunting, Eve. *Hurry! Hurry!* *Illus. by Jeff Mack. Harcourt, 2007.* Farm animals rush to the barn to greet a hatching chick.

Burningham, John. *Mr. Gumpy's Outing.* *Illus. by the author. Henry Holt, 1970.* An old man and many animals take a boat ride.

Campbell, Rod. *Dear Zoo: A Lift-the-Flap Book.* *Illus. by the author. Four Winds, 1982.* "I wrote to the zoo to send me a pet." They send an elephant, a giraffe, a camel, and more in this classic lift-the-flap board book.

Carle, Eric. *From Head to Toe.* *Illus. by the author. HarperCollins, 1997.* Animals show kids how to move.

Carle, Eric. *The Very Hungry Caterpillar.* *Illus. by the author. Philomel, 1969.* A caterpillar eats his way through the week.

Christelow, Eileen. *Five Little Monkeys Jumping on the Bed.* *Illus. by the author. Clarion, 1989.* Jaunty version of the traditional rhyme.

Cousins, Lucy. *Peck, Peck, Peck.* *Illus. by the author. Candlewick, 2013.* A baby wood-pecker is learning to peck, peck, peck everything, even the cover of this book.

Crews, Donald. *Freight Train.* *Illus. by the author. Greenwillow, 1978.* See the colors moving by in a freight train.

Cronin, Doreen. *Click, Clack, Peep!* *Illus. by Betsy Lewin. Atheneum, 2015.* The new baby duck keeps up all the other animals with his peep-peep-peeping.

Davis, Katie. *Who Hops?* *Illus. by the author. Harcourt, 1998.* See which animals hop, fly, slither, swim, and crawl.

De Moüy, Iris. *Naptime.* *Groundwood, 2014.* "I DON'T WANT TO HAVE A NAP," says the zebra, and the other wild animals quite agree.

Degen, Bruce. *Jamberry.* *Illus. by the author. HarperCollins, 1983.* It's the berries in this rhyming tale of a boy and bear in their search for berries.

Dewdney, Anna. *Llama Llama Red Pajama.* *Illus. by the author. Viking, 2005.* At bedtime, Baby Llama wants Mama Llama—now!

Dunrea, Olivier. *Gossie.* *Illus. by the author. Houghton Mifflin, 2002.* A little yellow gosling can't find her red boots. First in a series. See also *Ollie* (2003), about a gosling that refuses to hatch.

Ehlert, Lois. *Color Zoo.* *Illus. by the author. HarperCollins, 1989.* Die cuts in bright bold colors and shapes depict wild animals.

Emberley, Ed. *Go Away, Big Green Monster!* *Illus. by the author. Little Brown, 1992.* Each die-cut page reveals a bit more of the monster's face.

Falwell, Cathryn. *Feast for 10.* *Illus. by the author. Clarion Books, 1993.* An African American family prepares dinner in a rhyming counting book.

Feiffer, Jules. *Bark, George.* *Illus. by the author. HarperCollins, 1999.* Every time the dog tries to bark, he meows, quacks, oinks, or moos instead.

Flack, Marjorie. *Angus and the Cat.* *Illus. by the author. Doubleday, 1931.* Angus, a curious Scottie dog, chases the new cat around the house. Continue with *Angus and the Ducks* (1930) and *Angus Lost* (1932).

Fleming, Denise. *The Cow Who Clucked.* *Illus. by the author. Henry Holt, 2006.* Cow awakes to find she has lost her moo. You'll also love the farm-based *Barnyard Banter* (1994).

Fox, Mem. *Hattie and the Fox.* *Illus. by Patricia Mullins. Bradbury, 1987.* A hen sees a fox, but the other animals ignore her warning.

Fox, Mem. *Hello Baby!* *Illus. by Steve Jenkins. Beach Lane, 2009.* A rhyming look at baby animals.

Fox, Mem. *Ten Little Fingers and Ten Little Toes.* *Illus. by Helen Oxenbury. Harcourt, 2008.* A nursery rhyme–like tribute to babies everywhere.

Fox, Mem. *Where Is the Green Sheep?* *Illus. by Judy Horacek. Harcourt, 2004.* Rhyming text and lots of sheep for little ones to identify.

Freeman, Don. *Corduroy.* *Illus. by the author. Viking, 1968.* A stuffed bear searches for his missing button.

Gibbs, Edward. *I Spy with My Little Eye.* *Illus. by the author. Candlewick/Templar, 2011.* Die cuts and a clue let viewers identify one animal per page.

Gravett, Emily. *Monkey and Me.* *Illus. by the author. Simon & Schuster, 2008.* A little girl and her stuffed monkey pretend to visit other animals.

Guarino, Deborah. *Is Your Mama a Llama?* *Illus. by Stephen Kellogg. Scholastic, 1989.* Lloyd the llama meets other baby animals as he looks for his mama.

Hacohen, Dean. *Tuck Me In.* *Illus. by the author. Candlewick, 2010.* "'It's time for bed. Who needs to be tucked in?'/ 'I do!'" say seven baby animals, whom the reader tucks in with a turn of a blanket/flap.

Harrington, Janice N. *Busy-Busy Little Chick.* *Illus. by Brian Pinkney. Farrar, 2013.* While Mama Nsoso and her three chicks munch cricky-cracky crickets, Little Chick works to build them a new *ilombe*, or house.

Henkes, Kevin. *A Good Day.* *Illus. by the author. Greenwillow, 2007.* A bad day turns into a good one for a little yellow bird, a white dog, an orange fox, and a brown squirrel.

Henkes, Kevin. *Kitten's First Full Moon.* *Illus. by the author. Greenwillow, 2004.* Kitten thinks the full moon is a little bowl of milk in the sky, and she wants it.

Hill, Eric. *Where's Spot?* *Illus. by the author. Putnam, 1980.* Lift the flaps to help Sally find her lost puppy, Spot.

Hills, Tad. *What's Up, Duck? A Book of Opposites.* *Illus. by the author. Schwartz & Wade, 2008.* Duck, Goose, and their bluebird friend, Thistle, demonstrate opposites in this sweet board book.

Hort, Lenny. *The Seals on the Bus.* *Illus. by G. Brian Karas. Henry Holt, 2000.* Fun-to-sing animal takeoff on "The Wheels on the Bus."

Hutchins, Pat. *Good-Night Owl!* *Illus. by the author. Macmillan, 1972.* The noisy animals around Owl keep him awake.

Jones, Carol. *Old MacDonald Had a Farm.* *Illus. by the author. Houghton Mifflin, 1989.* A die-cut circle reveals the next animal or character in a colorful version of this easy-to-sing song.

Kalan, Robert. *Jump, Frog, Jump!* Illus. *by Byron Barton. Greenwillow, 1981.* In a cumulative story, a frog jumps to escape getting eaten by bigger animals in the pond.

Klausmeier, Jesse. *Open This Little Book.* Illus. *by Suzy Lee. Chronicle, 2013.* Open a little red book to read about Ladybug who opens a little green book . . .

Krauss, Ruth. *The Carrot Seed.* Illus. *by Crockett Johnson. HarperCollins, 1945.* A little boy plants a carrot seed and waits for it to grow.

Kunhardt, Dorothy. *Pat the Bunny.* Illus. *by the author. Golden Books, 1968.* In a baby's first interactive book, pat the bunny, feel Daddy's beard, and wave goodbye.

LaRochelle, David. *It's a Tiger!* Illus. *by Jeremy Tankard. Chronicle, 2012.* "That's not a monkey. It's a TIGER!" says the child exploring the jungle.

Lewin, Betsy. *Thumpy Feet.* Illus. *by the author. Holiday House, 2013.* Big orange cat eats his foodie food and plays with his toy mousie mouse.

Litwin, Eric. *Pete the Cat: I Love My White Shoes.* Illus. *by James Dean. HarperCollins, 2010.* Does Pete cry when his new white sneakers are stained red, blue, and brown? "Goodness, no!"

Lurie, Susan. *Swim, Duck, Swim!* Photos *by Murray Head. Feiwel and Friends, 2014.* Accompanied with color close-up photos, a duckling explains, in rhyme, why he does not want to go in the water.

Mack, Jeff. *Ah Ha!* Illus. *by the author. Chronicle, 2013.* "AH HA," "AAHH," and "HA HA" are the only words used in showing the story of a frog's capture and many escapes.

Martin, Bill Jr. *Brown Bear, Brown Bear, What Do You See?* Illus. *by Eric Carle. Henry Holt, 1967.* In a perfect call-and-response book, we see animals in all colors, looking back at us. View ten North American animal babies in *Baby Bear, Baby Bear, What Do You See?* (2007).

Moore, Eva. *Lucky Ducklings.* Illus. *by Nancy Carpenter. Orchard, 2013.* Firemen come to the rescue when Mama Duck's ducklings fall through the grate of a storm drain.

Murray, Alison. *Apple Pie ABC.* Illus. *by the author. Disney-Hyperion, 2011.* Alphabetically, a little black-and-white dog covets the apple pie that his little girl has just put into the oven. *One Two That's My Shoe!* (2012) is the companion counting story, where the dog takes off with one of the girl's shoes.

Patricelli, Leslie. *The Birthday Box.* Illus. *by the author. Candlewick, 2007.* Diaper-clad toddler and new stuffed dog play with the box the dog came in.

Patricelli, Leslie. *Higher! Higher!* *Illus. by the author. Candlewick, 2009.* Little girl's father pushes her swing so high, she ends up in space. Follow with *Faster! Faster!* (2012), in which he gives her a high-speed horsey ride on his back. All of Patricelli's board books rock!

Pinkney, Jerry. *Three Little Kittens.* *Illus. by the author. Dial, 2010.* Classic nursery rhyme, depicted in charming watercolors, of lost mittens and a reward of pie.

Raschka, Chris. *A Ball for Daisy.* *Illus. by the author. Schwartz & Wade, 2012.* In this wordless Caldecott Medal book, Daisy, a little gray-and-white dog, is bereft when her beloved red ball is broken.

Rathmann, Peggy. *Good Night, Gorilla.* *Illus. by the author. Putnam, 1994.* After lifting the zookeeper's ring of keys, Gorilla lets all the other animals out of their cages, and they follow the zookeeper home to bed.

Rinker, Sherri Duskey. *Goodnight, Goodnight, Construction Site.* *Illus. by Tom Lichtenheld. Chronicle, 2011.* After a hard day's work, Crane Truck, Cement Mixer, Dump Truck, Bulldozer, and Excavator get ready for bed. Snooze-resistant kids will also adore the companion, *Steam Train, Dream Train* (2013).

Robbins, Maria Polushkin. *Mother, Mother I Want Another.* *Illus. by Jon Goodell. Knopf, 2005, c1978.* Mother thinks that Little Mouse wants a new mother when all he really wants is another goodnight kiss.

Rohmann, Eric. *A Kitten Tale.* *Illus. by the author. Knopf, 2008.* Three kittens, scared of being cold, watch from inside a warm house while their brother cavorts in the snow.

Savage, Stephen. *Supertruck.* *Illus. by the author. Roaring Brook, 2015.* Meet the brave truck that digs out the whole city after a blizzard.

Savage, Stephen. *Where's Walrus?* *Illus. by the author. Scholastic, 2011.* In a zany wordless adventure, a big gray walrus escapes from his pool at the zoo and hides in plain sight throughout the city.

Schertle, Alice. *Little Blue Truck.* *Illus. by Jill McElmurry. Harcourt, 2008.* Blue gets stuck trying to help Dump Truck out of the mud, but his farm animal friends come to help.

Seeger, Laura Vaccaro. *Dog and Bear: Two Friends, Three Stories.* *Illus. by the author. Roaring Brook, 2007.* Three small adventures with a little brown dachshund and his best friend, Bear, a multicolored stuffed teddy.

Shea, Bob. *Dinosaur vs. Bedtime.* *Illus. by the author. Disney-Hyperion, 2010.* A little red dinosaur wins every contest until he faces his biggest challenge—bedtime. Revisit the same fella in *Dinosaur vs. the Potty* (2012).

Singer, Marilyn. *I'm Your Bus.* Illus. *by Evan Polenghi. Scholastic, 2009.* A friendly, smiling school bus says, "Howdy, you can count on us. / Morning, evening, I'm your bus."

Slobodkina, Esphyr. *Caps for Sale.* Illus. *by the author. HarperCollins, 1947.* A favorite for storytime. Children can imitate the monkeys, who imitate a peddler.

Smee, Nicola. *Clip-Clop.* Illus. *by the author. Henry Holt, 2006.* "Who wants a ride?" asks Mr. Horse, and upon his back jump a cat, a dog, a pig, and a goose.

Stein, David Ezra. *Pouch!* Illus. *by the author. Putnam, 2009.* Ready to explore, Joey hops out (and back into) Mama Kangaroo's pouch.

Stickland, Paul, and Henrietta Stickland. *Dinosaur Roar!* Illus. *by the authors. Dutton, 1997.* "Dinosaur roar, / dinosaur squeak, / dinosaur fierce, / dinosaur meek," begins a rhyming book of dinosaur opposites.

Taback, Simms. *Simms Taback's City Animals.* Illus. *by the author. Blue Apple, 2009.* Six "Who am I?" animal riddles fold out into an impressive 18-by-18-inch, four-paneled spreads of animals.

Tafuri, Nancy. *Have You Seen My Duckling?* Illus. *by the author. Greenwillow, 1984.* Children will spot the duckling in each picture as the mama duck looks for her.

Thomas, Jan. *What Will Fat Cat Sit On?* Illus. *by the author. Harcourt, 2007.* A fat cat contemplates sitting on a cow, a pig, a dog, and a chicken, until the mouse comes up with a better solution.

Vere, Ed. *Banana!* Illus. *by the author. Henry Holt, 2010.* One monkey has a banana; the other monkey wants it.

Waddell, Martin. *Owl Babies.* Illus. *by Patrick Benson. Candlewick, 1992.* Three owls awaken in their nest in the night, worried about their mama, who isn't there.

Walsh, Ellen Stoll. *Mouse Count.* Illus. *by the author. Harcourt, 1991.* Ten sleepy mice are caught by a hungry snake and put in a jar, but one by one, they get away. See how the mice learn about colors in *Mouse Paint* (1989).

Warhola, James. *If You're Happy and You Know It!* Illus. *by the author. Orchard, 2007.* Exuberant kids and zoo animals act out this beloved song on the playground. Join right in.

Willems, Mo. *Cat the Cat, Who Is That?* Illus. *by the author. Balzer + Bray, 2010.* Cat the Cat introduces us to Mouse the Mouse, Duck the Duck, and Fish the Fish, but who is that monster-like creature? Follow up with other funny books in the Cat the Cat series (all 2010): *Let's Say Hi to Friends Who Fly! Time to Sleep, Sheep the Sheep!* and *What's Your Sound, Hound the Hound?*

Willems, Mo. *Don't Let the Pigeon Drive the Bus.* Illus. *by the author. Hyperion, 2003.* Children will cry "NO!" each time Pigeon tries to persuade us to let him drive that bus.

Williams, Sue. *I Went Walking.* Illus. by Julie Vivas. Harcourt, 1989. "I went walking / What did I see? / I saw a brown horse / Looking at me," says a child who encounters six such animals.

Wilson, Karma. *Bear Snores On.* Illus. by Jane Chapman. McElderry, 2002. Mouse, hare, badger, gopher, mole, wren, and raven spend a snow-stormy night in a sleeping bear's cave.

Wolff, Ashley. *Baby Bear Sees Blue.* Illus. by the author. Beach Lane, 2012. After waking in spring, Baby Bear spends the day exploring the meadow and asking his mama about the colors he sees. The companion winter story is *Baby Bear Counts One* (2013).

Wood, Audrey. *The Napping House.* Illus. by Don Wood. Harcourt, 1984. A cumulative tale shows animals and a granny trying to take a nap until a flea starts a chain reaction and they all wake up.

Yolen, Jane. *How Do Dinosaurs Say Good Night?* Illus. by Mark Teague. Scholastic/Blue Sky, 2000. Description, told in rhyme, of how ten oversize dinosaur children balk (or don't balk) at going to bed.

Zelinsky, Paul O. *The Wheels on the Bus.* Illus. by the author. Dutton, 1990. Glorious pop-up interactive version to sing.

Pulling Together Themed Programs

In this section, we want to give you concrete ideas for putting together a cohesive program. To that end, we've gathered together many books, fingerplays, songs, and poems, and a wide assortment of follow-up activities on many topics. We'll begin with two full-length thematic programs on two broad topics: bedtime and food. For both "Time for Bed" and "I'm Hungry" you can get started with ease, selecting and learning your favorites of the simple stories to tell that we've included, gathering some of the books that are recommended, and pulling together the supplies needed for one or more of the follow-up crafts or activities. Because we recognize you need far more than two programs to use with your kids, we've compiled a "Quicklist of Thematic Program Starters for Young Children, Birth to Age 7," with more than 130 topics to peruse. We hope you'll find these elemental "mini-programs" so easy to build on, you'll wonder how you ever managed without them.

A theme or activity program is the perfect way to extend your book program beyond the stories themselves. The majority of time spent in preschool and primary sessions in school and public libraries and classrooms is usually devoted to reading and showing picture books. Picture books with a strong story can be told orally without the book, including folktales with simple plots and repetitive action. You may also enjoy introducing songs, short poems, fingerplays, and action rhymes, as well as puppets, creative drama, and games, all of which make good transitional material. Language development is vital if we want our kids to succeed as readers, writers, and learners.

SELECTING MATERIALS FOR A STORYTIME PROGRAM

Since picture books are one of the focal points of your program—along with told stories—you will naturally want to choose books of the highest literary and artistic quality for reading aloud. You may already have your own favorites, but there are also many lists online and in books to help you select books to read. The Association for Library Service to Children (www .ala.org/alsc), a division of the American Library Association, gives annual awards—the Caldecott Medal for most distinguished contribution to American illustration for children, the Sibert Medal for informational books, the Theodor Seuss Geisel Medal for best early reader, and more—and puts out a Notable Children's Books list each January. Reviews of books and annual Best Books lists in professional journals (including *Booklist*, *Horn Book*, *Kirkus*, *Publishers Weekly*, and *School Library Journal*) help keep you up-to-date and aware of the year's latest and greatest titles. Nothing, however, can take the place of your own reading to determine which books will best suit your purposes and the needs and interests of your particular group.

Throughout this book, we've given you reading lists galore. These are not chosen frivolously to be shoehorned into a given subject or activity. Rather, they are the best of the best, books we've unearthed out of the many tens of thousands we've read over the past many decades. Our ratio of books selected to books read is about one in thirty. There are a lot of mediocre books published every year, and we wanted—in this book and in the companion volume, *The Handbook for Storytellers*—to include only the ones that rose to the top, like cream. No skim milk here.

That said, there is absolutely no guarantee that you will or should agree with all our choices. Rather, you need to pick and choose the books that speak to you and your children. If you are not enamored with a particular title we rave about, there are an awful lot of children's books out there. Your never-ending quest is to find the ones that best suit your curriculum, your goals and objectives, and your tastes. It is a thrill to find that perfect book, however, and to weave it into your program, gathering together other like-minded materials to make a gorgeous package for your children.

Putting together a story program is like baking a cake or making a stew. You gather together some read-aloud titles and stories to tell as your main ingredients, and spice it all up with surprises—a magic trick here, an inter-active song there—and finish it off by setting the table with an interesting craft or activity that will further the pleasure and get kids thinking about the delicious storytime they just experienced.

It is not necessary to have the two or three books you use in each story hour relate to each other. However, books that complement each other do make a more cohesive session. School librarians and teachers tend to tie their storytimes to the school curriculum. If the children are doing a unit on weather or mammals in science, a study of the Pilgrims around Thanksgiv-ing, or a session on rhyming words for language arts, you can tie books and stories to those basic themes. Afterwards, they are likely to follow up with a writing or drawing prompt, a related craft, or a science experiment.

Many public librarians have the freedom to decide what themes or topics they want to cover with their audiences, looking to give children a literary overview, expose them to the sounds and power of language, and get them comfortable around books. Such librarians don't need to stay within the con-fines of the academic when they plan an after-story craft. Children are freer to create an art project for the sake of making something fun and creative.

Which strategy is best? Thankfully, they're both valuable and interesting for children. The best way to approach literature is with balance—some fic-tion, some nonfiction; some songs or poems, some facts; some stories read aloud, others told. Children don't have the same monolithic interests any more than you do, and benefit from being stretched by books.

You will probably want to present the new and unusual, but don't feel that you have to present something different at each session. Remember that to children, all the books are new—even those published when Mommy was a little girl. Moreover, it doesn't bore a child to hear a story again and again. Each telling is slightly different, and children seem to learn something new each time.

MAKING CONNECTIONS

In selecting multiple stories to tell or read during your programs, look for a common thread that winds between them. Each story you select has multi-ple hooks. Your job is to decide which connections to make; it's impractical and impossible to do everything.

For example, take a picture book like Ann Whitford Paul's *Tortuga in Trouble,* illustrated by Ethan Long (Holiday House, 2009). Tortuga (Turtle) is planning to bring a basket of goodies—tamales, *ensalada,* and flan—to his *abuela* (grandmother), and he doesn't want his friends Conejo (rabbit),

Iguana, and Culebra (snake) to tag along. Lucky for him, they trail him and save him from Coyote, who, dressed like Abuela, awaits him at her home.

Here's how Judy's thoughts progressed after choosing *Tortuga in Trouble* to use with a group of children leading to a basketful of program possibilities.

First off, the story is one of a series of comical picture books about the four friends: *Mañana, Iguana* (2004), *Fiesta Fiasco* (2007), and *Count on Culebra: Go from 1 to 10 in Spanish* (2008). Certainly, we'll want to have these on hand to hold up and give to children.

Perhaps we should branch off into folktales or stories about the same animals: rabbits with *Tops & Bottoms* by Janet Stevens (Harcourt, 1995); iguanas with *Why Mosquitoes Buzz in People's Ears* by Verna Aardema, illustrated by Leo and Diane Dillon (Dial, 1975); snakes with *Verdi* by Janell Cannon (Harcourt, 1997); and of course, turtles or tortoises with *Anansi Goes Fishing* by Eric A. Kimmel, illustrated by Janet Stevens (Holiday House, 1992). Or maybe we should focus on that bad boy, Coyote, and introduce trickster tales like *Coyote: A Trickster Tale from the American Southwest* by Gerald McDermott (Harcourt, 1994) or *Coyote Steals the Blanket* by Janet Stevens (Holiday House, 1993).

Because Spanish words are integrated into the text, we could look at other bilingual books. Then there's the *abuela* thread, which would lead to books about Spanish grandmothers—such as *Mice and Beans* by Pam Muñoz Ryan, illustrated by Joe Cepeda (Scholastic, 2001) or *Abuela* by Arthur Dorros, illustrated by Elisa Kleven (Dutton, 1991)—or to books about grandmothers in general.

Really, Tortuga should be grateful to his friends for saving his life, which could open the way to Pat Mora's *Gracias / Thanks,* illustrated by John Parra (Lee & Low, 2009), in which a young boy expresses thanks, in English and Spanish, for the big and little things in his life. This could get kids to think about what they appreciate in their own lives.

Then again, it's plain that Tortuga's three friends covet the food in his basket. How about pulling in stories about food, especially the Spanish-laced, folktale-based *Too Many Tamales* by Gary Soto, illustrated by Ed Martinez (Putnam, 1993); *The Three Little Tamales* by Eric A. Kimmel, illustrated by Valeria Docampo (Marshall Cavendish, 2009); and Helen Ketteman's *Armadilly Chili,* illustrated by Will Terry (Albert Whitman, 2004). And, what do you know! Kimmel and Ketterman's books are set in the Sonoran desert, as is *Tortuga in Trouble*. Maybe another book about the desert would work here, too. Jerry Pinkney's Caldecott winner, *The Tortoise & the Hare: An Aesop Fable* (Little, Brown, 2013) fits that bill, but it would also be smart to give the kids concrete information about that particular habitat. Pat Mora's nonfiction picture book *Listen to the Desert / Oye al desierto*, illustrated by Francisco X. Mora (Clarion, 1994), would be just the ticket.

And since *Tortuga in Trouble* is first and foremost a humorous retelling of "Little Red Riding Hood," why not pull out other versions for comparison: James Marshall's hilarious *Red Riding Hood* (Dial, 1987); Niki Daly's *Pretty Salma: A Little Red Riding Hood Story from Africa* (Clarion, 2007); Lisa Campbell Ernst's parody, *Little Red Riding Hood: A Newfangled Prairie Tale* (Simon & Schuster, 1995); and even one in rhyme that incorporates Spanish words, *Little Roja Riding Hood* by Susan Middleton Elya, illustrated by Susan Guevara ((Putnam, 2014). Since one can't assume the children will know the original story, Trina Schart Hyman's faithful retelling of the Brothers Grimm, *Little Red Riding Hood* (Holiday House, 1983), would be appropriate as well.

Which reminds me—in my collection of toys and props, I have the most wonderful set of wooden nesting dolls of "Little Red Riding Hood" (or were they from "The Three Little Pigs"?). No matter; I know the largest one is a wolf, and we can talk about how the wolf in the original story has been replaced in this tale by a coyote and why that is.

Tortuga packs a basket to take to Abuela's house. Wouldn't it be fun to pack a basket of books and props? The kids would love that. Hmmm. Picnics. Maybe we could put a colorful sheet on the floor for the kids to sit on, as if we were at a picnic. There's that cute site with ideas and books for a picnic-themed story hour (stepbystepcc.com/picnic.html).

Wait, that brings to mind Raffi's picnic song! I'll check for the lyrics online. I'm not sure I remember the tune. Let me play a snippet of Raffi's version on Amazon.com. Maybe I'll just download the song for 99 cents, put it on my iPod, and play it for the kids. We could make up new verses, based on the food in Tortuga's picnic basket. We could even make up other verses using Spanish words for the foods . . .

Wow. Talk about going overboard! And that's not even taking into account that *Tortuga in Trouble* would make a great board story, a puppet show, and/or a creative drama or reader's theater activity. While marvelous possibilities abound, your job as Story Maestro is to figure out what two or three ideas will fit best into the time you have and the goals you set up for your program. You can't do everything, so pick the thread you most want to follow and build your program from there.

At the end of the session, there's that dash to the shelves, where children delve into books, delighted by the freedom they have to choose books to take home. Assist them in their choices by having on hand stories related to the ones you just shared—on the same theme, subject, or by the same authors.

Last but not least, here is one invaluable reference book for the story planner: *A to Zoo: Subject Access to Children's Picture Books* by Carolyn W. Lima and Rebecca L. Thomas (9th ed., Libraries Unlimited, 2014, updated every four years or so), which lists 23,000 picture books by subject.

TWO THEMED PROGRAMS FOR AGES 1–7

To whet your whistle, we've assembled a range of enticing materials for sample programs on two familiar topics—bedtime and food—with stories to tell, books, fingerplays, songs, and poems, and a wide assortment of follow-up activities.

Themed Program: Time for Bed

One cousin with kids complained to Judy, "What's with all the bedtime stories about kids who don't want to go to bed? That's the last thing I want to read to my kids at night! It gets them all riled up." Good point. If you've ever read Bob Shea's *Dinosaur vs. Bedtime* at bedtime, know that there will be no sleeping afterwards, just kids yelling, "Dinosaur wins!" when you pull up the covers and they throw them off again.

So here is a unit to do with children who are not actually planning on going to bed. You can do it during the day, or at a bedtime story hour you hold in the library in the early evening—with kids in pj's, maybe—but not necessarily on the cusp of bedtime. When you do want them to go to sleep, read books that are quiet, soothing, repetitive, and calm (though the person those stories knock out may well be you).

NURSERY RHYMES AND FINGERPLAYS

Wee Willie Winkie

> Wee Willie Winkie runs through the town,
> Upstairs and downstairs in his nightgown;
> Knocking at the window and crying through the lock,
> "Are all the children in their beds, it's past eight o'clock?"

Diddle Diddle Dumpling

Diddle, diddle, dumpling, my son John
Went to bed with his stockings on;
One shoe off, one shoe on,
Diddle, diddle, dumpling, my son John.

Hey Diddle Diddle

Hey diddle diddle,
The cat and the fiddle,
The cow jumped over the moon;
The little dog laughed to see such sport,
And the dish ran away with the spoon.

Ten in the Bed

This classic is also great as a flannelboard or finger-puppet activity. For very young children, count down from five instead of ten. You'll find an adorable video of preschoolers acting out the story at www.squidoo.com/bedtime -storytime-ideas.

There were ten in the bed and the little one said, (*hold up ten fingers*)
"Roll over, roll over." (*roll your arms*)
So they all rolled over and one fell out.
    (*hold up one finger*)
There were nine in the bed and the little
    one said,
"Roll over, roll over." (*roll your arms*)
So they all rolled over and one fell out . . .

(*Continue counting down in the same way until you get to the number one.*)

There was one in the bed and the little one
    said,
"Good night!"

Teddy Bear

This works as a jump-rope, ball-bounce, or act-it-out rhyme; it's just right for getting children up and moving. Add new verses as needed.

Teddy bear, teddy bear, turn around;
Teddy bear, teddy bear, touch the ground.
Teddy bear, teddy bear, jump up high;
Teddy bear, teddy bear, touch the sky.

Teddy bear, teddy bear, touch your knees;
Teddy bear, teddy bear, sit down please.
Teddy bear, teddy bear, bend down low;
Teddy bear, teddy bear, touch your toe.

Teddy bear, teddy bear, read the news;
Teddy bear, teddy bear, shine your shoes.
Teddy bear, teddy bear, go upstairs;
Teddy bear, teddy bear, say your prayers.

Teddy bear, teddy bear, turn out the light;
Teddy bear, teddy bear, say goodnight.

SONGS

Rockabye Baby

First verse traditional; second verse unknown; third verse by Judy

Rockabye baby, on the treetop;
When the bough bends, the cradle will rock;
When the bough breaks, the cradle will fall,
And down will come baby, cradle and all.

Rockabye baby, up on the moon,
Eating her cornflakes with a big spoon;
When the wind blows, the moon it will break,
And down will come baby on a cornflake.

Rockabye baby, up in the stars,
Waving to Earth and waving to Mars;

When the stars shine, the sky will be bright,
And down will come baby with a night light.

Frère Jacques

Frères Jacques, Frères Jacques,

Dormez-vous? Dormez-vous?

Sonnez les matines, sonnez les matines,

Din dan don, din dan don.

Are you sleeping, are you sleeping,

Brother John, Brother John?

Morning bells are ringing, morning bells are ringing,

Ding dang dong, ding dang dong.

Goodnight, Ladies

Alternate "ladies" with "gentlemen" so the boys don't feel left out.

Goodnight, ladies! Goodnight, ladies! Goodnight, ladies!
We're going to leave you now.
Chorus:
Merrily we roll along, roll along, roll along,
Merrily we roll along, o'er the dark blue sea.

Farewell, ladies! Farewell, ladies! Farewell, ladies!
We're going to leave you now. (*chorus*)

Sweet dreams, ladies! Sweet dreams, ladies! Sweet dreams, ladies!
We're going to leave you now. (*chorus*)

Day Is Done (aka "Taps")

Day is done,
Gone the sun,
From the lake, from the hills, from the sky.
All is well, safely rest,
God is nigh.

Moon Moon Moon

By the wonderful Laurie Berkner Band, in three-part harmony. To play this charmer of a goodnight song for your group, mosey on over to www.youtube .com/watch?v = B-jo_d1jKk.

When the Red, Red Robin Comes Bob-Bob-Bobbin' Along

By Harry M. Woods, 1926. Wake everyone up after your bedtime program with this irresistible old number, which will have them dancing in the aisles. You'll find many jaunty renditions on YouTube.

> When the red, red robin comes bob-bob-bobbin' along, along,
> There'll be no more sobbin' when he starts throbbin' his own sweet song.
> Wake up, wake up, you sleepyhead,
> Get up, get up, get out of bed,
> Cheer up, cheer up; the sun is red,
> Live, love, laugh, and be happy.
>
> What if I've been blue; now I'm walking through fields of flowers,
> Rain may glisten, but still I listen for hours and hours.
> I'm just a kid again, doing what I did again, singing a song,
> When the red, red robin comes bob-bob-bobbin' along.

Reveille

In the US military, "Reveille" is the bugle call that wakes everyone in the morning. There are no official lyrics, but here are three verses that folks often sing. The second and third verses are from the bugler's point of view.

> You've got to get up, you've got to get up,
>   you've got to get up this morning;
> You've got to get up, you've got to get up,
>   get up with the bugler's call.
> The major told the captain, the captain told the sergeant,
> The sergeant told the bugler, the bugler told them all.
>
> I can't get 'em up, I can't get 'em up, I can't get 'em up this morning;
> I can't get 'em up, I can't get 'em up, I can't get 'em up at all!
> The corporal's worse than the privates,
>   the sergeant's worse than the corporals,
> Lieutenant's worse than the sergeants, and the captain's worst of all!

I can't get 'em up, I can't get 'em up, I can't get 'em up this morning;

I can't get 'em up, I can't get 'em up, I can't get 'em up at all!

And tho' the sun starts peeping, and dawn has started creeping,

Those lazy bums keep sleeping, they never hear my call!

POEMS

Bed in Summer

By Robert Louis Stevenson, from A Child's Garden of Verses, *1885*

In winter I get up at night

And dress by yellow candle-light.

In summer, quite the other way,

I have to go to bed by day.

I have to go to bed and see

The birds still hopping on the tree,

Or hear the grown-up people's feet

Still going past me in the street.

And does it not seem hard to you,

When all the sky is clear and blue,

And I should like so much to play,

To have to go to bed by day?

Wynken, Blynken, and Nod

By Eugene Field, 1889. You may recall that this classic poem is often sung to a very pretty tune originally sung by Carly Simon and her sister, Lucy Simon. It was Lucy who wrote the music when she was a teen in the 1960s. On YouTube you can listen to it performed by any number of singers.

Wynken, Blynken, and Nod one night

Sailed off in a wooden shoe—

Sailed on a river of crystal light,

Into a sea of dew.

"Where are you going, and what do you wish?"

The old moon asked the three.

(continued)

"We have come to fish for the herring fish
That live in this beautiful sea;

Nets of silver and gold have we!"
Said Wynken, Blynken, and Nod.

The old moon laughed and sang a song,
As they rocked in the wooden shoe,
And the wind that sped them all night long
Ruffled the waves of dew.

The little stars were the herring fish
That lived in that beautiful sea—
"Now cast your nets wherever you wish—
Never afeard are we."

So cried the stars to the fishermen three:
Wynken, Blynken, and Nod.

All night long their nets they threw
To the stars in the twinkling foam—
Then down from the skies came the wooden shoe,
Bringing the fishermen home;

'Twas all so pretty a sail it seemed
As if it could not be,
And some folks thought 'twas a dream they'd dreamed
Of sailing that beautiful sea—

But I shall name you the fishermen three:
Wynken, Blynken, and Nod.

Wynken and Blynken are two little eyes,
And Nod is a little head,
And the wooden shoe that sailed the skies
Is a wee one's trundle-bed.

So shut your eyes while Mother sings
Of wonderful sights that be,
And you shall see the beautiful things
As you rock in the misty sea,

Where the old shoe rocked the fishermen three:
Wynken, Blynken, and Nod.

STORIES TO TELL ABOUT BEDTIME

Here are two of our very favorite stories to tell about noisy or interrupted bedtimes.

How to Make a Small House into a Large One

Retold by Caroline Feller Bauer

The following is a story that Caroline's grandpa used to tell when she was a child. You can find variants in several collections, as well as two excellent picture-book versions: It Could Always Be Worse: A Yiddish Folk Tale *by Margot Zemach and* Too Much Noise *by Ann McGovern. Of course, Caroline liked the way her grandpa told it best. Use plenty of animal sounds, add as many animals to the house as you wish for as long as you have the children's attention. You can have everyone make every noise, or divide the audience into small groups and assign each an animal. Because this is an old Jewish tale, don't let a pig move in; that wouldn't be kosher.*

WEB This script is available on ALA's Web Extras page at alaeditions.org/webextras.

There was once an old man and an old woman who lived in a one-room cottage. It was very tiny. A table, some chairs, a bed, and a stove were the only furniture. One day the man received a letter from his daughter. She and her husband and their baby wished to come and live with their parents. The man was outraged. How could two more people and a baby possibly fit into their small house? The old woman suggested that her husband visit the Rabbi, the wisest man in town, and ask his advice.

The man explained his problem to the Rabbi. Instead of agreeing with the man, the Rabbi said, "That's wonderful! Of course you must write immediately and tell your daughter's family to come. Your house may not be as small as you think."

What could the old man do? No one argued with the Rabbi, the wisest man in town. He went home and wrote a letter to his daughter. In no time at all the daughter, her husband, and the baby arrived. Now the house was very crowded. The baby woke up every morning at six o'clock and cried, "Wah, wah, wah."

The man returned to the Rabbi and asked his help.

"Ah, ha. I see you do have a problem. Indeed, I'm sure that I can help. Do you own a cow?"

Yes, of course, the man owned a cow. Her name was Yasha.

"Go home. Bring Yasha the cow into the house to live with you."

The man was astonished, but no one argued with the Rabbi. He went home and put Yasha the cow into the house. The baby cried, "Wah wah," the cow mooed, "Moo, moo," and, indeed, it was very crowded in the house. Yasha kept swishing her tail back and forth into the man's face. The baby crawled between the cow's legs.

The man returned once more to the Rabbi and pleaded for his help. The Rabbi said, "Here's a thought. Do you own any chickens?"

Yes, of course, the man owned chickens. In fact, he had one rooster, five hens, and twelve baby chicks. The Rabbi said, "Go home. Bring the rooster, the five hens, and the twelve baby chicks into the house to live with you."

The man couldn't believe his ears, but no one argued with the Rabbi. When he got home, he brought the rooster, the five hens, and the twelve baby chicks into the house. What a ruckus!

The baby cried, "Wah, wah, wah."

The cow lowed, "Moo, moo, moo."

The rooster woke up at four o'clock every morning: "Cock-a-doodle-doo."

The hens screeched, "Cluck, cluck."

The hens had no place to lay their eggs. One laid an egg right on top of the man's head. The chicks darted in and out of the woman's path. "Here, chick, chick, chick," called the woman.

In desperation, the man called on the Rabbi again. The Rabbi stroked his long white beard and asked, "I wonder. What other animals do you own?"

The old man said, "We have sheep, ducks, geese, and a horse."

"Bring them all inside," the Rabbi commanded.

What could the man do but obey. No one argued with the Rabbi. He brought the sheep, the ducks, the geese, and the horse into the house. The house was unbearably cramped and noisy. All the animals he owned were now living in the house with him and his wife, their daughter, her husband, and their baby.

"Wah, wah, wah."

"Moo, moo, moo."

"Cock-a-doodle-doo."

"Cluck, cluck."

"Here, chick, chick, chick."

And now the sheep baaed, "Baa, baa."

The ducks quacked, "Quack, quack."

The geese honked, "Honk, honk."

The horse whinnied, "Neigh, neigh."

There was no place for anyone to sleep, work, play or eat. All night long there was nothing but noise.

"Wah, wah, wah."

"Moo, moo."

"Cock-a-doodle-doo."

"Cluck, cluck."

"Here, chick, chick, chick."

"Baa, baa."

"Quack, quack."

"Honk, honk."

"Neigh, neigh."

Haggard with lack of sleep, the man trudged back to the Rabbi's house. "Help us, Rabbi. Our house is bursting and the noise is unbearable."

"Go home," said the Rabbi, "and take all the animals out of the house. Take Yasha the cow, the rooster, the five hens, the twelve chicks, the sheep, the ducks, the geese, and even the horse out of the house."

The old man was relieved. He went home and took all the animals out of the house. It looked enormous without the animals. With only four people and one small baby, the house felt empty. The only noise was the baby making a satisfying crying sound.

So, if you want to make a small house into a big house, now you know just what to do.

The Squeaky Door

Retold by Laura Simms

Once there was a little boy who was afraid of the sound of a squeaky door. He lived with his grandma in a house on a hill near a forest in Puerto Rico. Every single night, the little boy got in his bed, pulled the covers up tight, and nestled his head on the pillow.

Then his grandma would come into the room and say, "Tonight, when I turn off the light and it's dark and I close the squeaky door to your room, are you going to get scared and jump under the bed and start to cry?"

The little boy always said, "No, not me."

And the grandma would answer, "Good. I am so old and so tired. I need my sleep."

But every single night, when the room grew dark and she closed the squeaky door, the little boy got scared and jumped under the bed and started to cry. Night after night, his old grandma had to take him into her room to sleep.

One night, the grandma said, "Are you going to be scared tonight?"

The little boy answered proudly, "No, not me."

She said, "Good. Because tonight you are staying in *your* bed."

So she turned off the light. The room grew very dark, and she closed the squeaky door. *Squeeeeeak!* The little boy got scared and jumped under the bed and started to cry—*waaa waaa waaa!*

The grandma came back into the room and she said, "You're driving me crazy. I can't get any sleep."

Then she got an idea. "I know. I'll put a cat in the bed so you won't be scared."

So the little boy got in the bed, and a cat got in the bed.

"Now," said the grandmother, "are you going to be scared?"

He snuggled up against the cat and said happily, "No, not me."

"Good," she said. She turned off the light, and the room grew very dark. Then she closed the squeaky door. *Squeeeeeak!*

The little boy jumped under the bed and started to cry—*waaa waaa waaa!* And the cat jumped under the bed—*meow meow meow!*

The grandma came back into the room and sighed. "You are driving me crazy. I'm getting mad. What am I going to do? I know. I'll put a dog in the bed."

So the boy got in the bed. The cat got in the bed. And the dog got in the bed.

"Are you going to be scared now?" asked the grandma.

"No, not me," said the boy as he curled up beside the dog.

"Good," she said. "I need to get some sleep." She turned off the light, and the room grew very dark. Then she slowly closed the squeaky door. *Squeeeeeak!*

The little boy got scared and jumped under the bed—*waaa waaa waaa!* The cat jumped under the bed—*meow meow meow!* And the dog jumped under the bed—*woof woof woof!*

The grandma came back into the room. "You're driving me crazy. I'm mad, mad, mad. I know. I'll put a pig in the bed."

The boy got in the bed. The cat got in the bed. The dog got in the bed. And the pig got in the bed.

The little boy pulled the covers up tight and put his arms around the pig.

The grandma yawned and asked, "Are you going to be scared tonight?"

"No, not me," he said, and he closed his eyes.

She turned off the light, and as soon as it was dark, she closed the squeaky door. *Squeeeeeak!*

But the boy jumped under the bed and began to cry—*waaa waaa waaa!*

The cat jumped under the bed—*meow meow meow!* The dog jumped under the bed—*woof woof woof!*

And the pig jumped under the bed—*oink oink oink!*

The old grandma came into the room and said, "I'm going to pull out every hair in my head. You're driving me crazy. I'm mad, mad, mad." Then she smiled and said, "I'll try a snake in the bed."

The boy got in the bed. The cat got in the bed. The dog got in the bed. And the snake got in the bed.

"Are you going to be scared tonight?" she asked.

"No, not me," said the boy as the snake curled up beside him.

Then the grandma kissed him goodnight and turned off the light. The room grew very dark, and she closed the squeaky door. *Squeeeeeak!*

The boy jumped under the bed and started to cry—*waaa waaa waaa!* The cat jumped under the bed—*meow meow meow!* The dog jumped under the bed—*woof woof woof!* The pig jumped under the bed—*oink oink oink!* And the snake slithered under the bed—*hiss ssss ssss!*

The old grandma came back into the room. She switched on the light and sighed. "What am I going to do?" She down on the edge of his bed and whispered, "You are driving me crazy. I'm mad, mad, mad. We need to go to sleep."

Then all of a sudden she stood up and said, "Why didn't I think of this in the first place? I'll put a horse in the bed."

The boy got in the bed. The cat got in the bed. The dog got in the bed. The pig got in the bed. The snake got in the bed. And the horse got in the bed.

"Now, are you going to be scared tonight?"

"No, not me," the little boy said. And before he finished speaking, his eyes were closed.

So the grandma turned off the light, and the room grew very dark. Then she carefully closed the squeaky door. *Squeeeeeak!*

But the boy opened his eyes and jumped under the bed and started to cry—*waaa waaa waaa!* The cat jumped under the bed—*meow meow meow!* The dog jumped under the bed—*woof woof woof!* The pig jumped under the bed—*oink oink oink!* The snake slithered under the bed—*hiss ssss ssss!* And the horse jumped under the bed—*neigh neigh neigh!*

And, with that, the bed collapsed!

The cat leaped out the window. The dog ran out the door. The pig broke down a wall. The snake slid under the floor. And the horse leaped and galloped and stamped until the whole house fell down.

So the boy and his grandma, the dog and the cat, the, snake, the pig, and the horse had to move to a new house.

The new house had no squeaky door. And there they lived happily, and quietly, ever after.

Activities and Crafts about Bedtime

- **Pajama-day storytime.** Children come to school or to the library in pajamas and slippers and bring their pillows, blankets, and teddy bears. After storytime, have them lie down on their blankets and pretend to go to sleep for a minute or two. Wake them up with an alarm clock, a song, or a trumpet rendition of "Reveille" from YouTube.
- **Bedtime rituals.** Pantomime getting ready for bed. Children can brush their teeth, put on their pajamas, get under the covers, and give a little snore.

- **Worry dolls.** Make a bed for a tiny worry doll. You can find these dear little dolls, handcrafted in Guatemala, online in inexpensive bags of a hundred. Children can use matchboxes for beds, leftover fabric for sheets and blankets, and cotton balls for pillows, and then put their dolls to sleep. According to Guatemalan legend, before going to bed, children can tell one worry to each doll and then place it beneath their pillow. While the children sleep, the dolls will take their worries away! It's worth a try.

- **Musical Beds game.** Put large sheets of brown kraft paper or cardboard on the floor for beds. As peppy music plays, the children walk around. When music stops, they must find a bed and pretend to sleep. Remove a bed for the next round, and so on, until there's only one bed left. Afterwards, children can work together to draw or paint murals of their favorite bedtime stories on the paper, which can be displayed on the walls.

- **Creative drama.** After reading Karen Rostoker-Gruber's noisy picture book *Rooster Can't Cock-a-Doodle-Doo*, children can act it out together.

- **New constellations.** Show how constellations like the Big Dipper and Orion's Belt got their names. Using black paper and white chalk or crayons, ask children to draw stars, connect them to make a constellation, and then give their constellation a name.

- **Big teddies.** Cut out one or more oversize teddy shapes from corduroy or other sturdy fabric. Have children sew the pieces together, inside out, using large needles and heavy-duty thread. Make sure they leave several inches unsewn for stuffing. Turn the bear right side out. Add button eyes and a felt nose, and stitch a mouth. Children can stuff the bears with cut-up foam or other stuffing material, after which you can finish the stitching. Place the bears on small chairs so children snuggle with and read to their teddies.

- **Stuffed-animal sleepover.** Ask each child to bring one animal to spend the night in the classroom or the library. Take pictures of the animals doing funny things, or make a PowerPoint or video showing what went on in the room overnight to present to the children the next day. See how active the stuffies were during their overnight Stuffed Animal Sleepover 2010 at the Olathe Public Library in Kansas at www.youtube.com/watch/?v=vZxwAI00bug. Look up "Stuffed Animal Sleepover" on YouTube for other videos of toys-filled overnights. So creative!

- **Magic trick.** Do the "Read to Your Dog" magic trick in chapter 6 on page 228.
- **Discussion points / writing-and-illustrating prompts.** After you've read books and told stories about kids who didn't want to go to bed or couldn't fall asleep when they did, start a conversation, asking: What time is bedtime for you? What do you do when your parents tell you it's time for bed? What are your bedtime rituals? How do you fall asleep at night? What advice do you have for a friend who can't fall asleep at night?

BOOKLIST: TIME FOR BED

Allen, Elanna. *Itsy Mitsy Runs Away.* Illus. by the author. Atheneum, 2011. "No more bedtime. I'm gone," says the little girl to her dad. (PreK–K)

Appelt, Kathi. *Bubba and Beau Go Night-Night.* Illus. by Arthur Howard. Harcourt, 2003. Baby Bubba and his dog companion love to go bye-bye, but not night-night. (PreK–K)

Becker, Bonny. *Bedtime for Bear.* Illus. by Kady MacDonald Denton. Candlewick, 2010. Mouse comes to spend the night at Bear's house. (PreK–Gr. 2)

Billingsley, Franny. *Big Bad Bunny.* Illus. by G. Brian Karas. Atheneum, 2008. At naptime, Mama's mouse, Baby Boo-Boo, is missing, and there's a Big Bad Bunny on the loose. (PreK–Gr. 1)

Black, Michael Ian. *Naked!* Illus. by Debbie Ridpath Ohi. Simon & Schuster, 2014. An ebullient little boy races through the house first naked, then caped, as he delays getting into bed. (PreK–Gr. 2)

Blechman, Nicholas. *Night Light.* Illus. by the author. Orchard, 2013. Die cuts and lift-the-flaps make this a fun guessing and counting game about ten vehicles at night. (PreK–Gr. 1)

Boynton, Sandra. *The Going to Bed Book.* Illus. by the author. Little Simon, 1982. Big, goofy animals prepare for bed. (PreK)

Brown, Margaret Wise. *Goodnight Moon.* Illus. by Clement Hurd. HarperCollins, 1947. The best baby bedtime story ever, with a young rabbit bidding goodnight to all the items in his room. (PreK)

Christelow, Eileen. *Five Little Monkeys Reading in Bed.* Illus. by the author. Clarion, 2011. When Mama's too tired to read more bedtime stories, her five rambunctious monkeys read aloud to each other instead of going to sleep. (PreK–Gr. 2)

Cronin, Doreen. *Click, Clack, Peep!* Illus. by Betsy Lewin. Atheneum, 2015. The new baby duck keeps up all the other animals with his peep peep peep-ing. (PreK–Gr. 1)

DaCosta, Barbara. *Nighttime Ninja.* *Illus. by Ed Young. Little, Brown, 2012.* At midnight, a stealthy ninja makes his way to the kitchen for a snack. (PreK–Gr. 2)

Dewdney, Anna. *Llama Llama Red Pajama.* *Illus. by the author. Viking, 2005.* Feeling alone without his mama at bedtime, Baby Llama gets upset. (PreK–K)

Docherty, Helen. *The Snatchabook.* *Illus. by Thomas Docherty. Sourcebooks, 2013.* When all the bedtime storybooks disappear, Eliza Brown, a brown bunny, finds the culprit: a furry little creature who has no one to read to him. (PreK–Gr. 2)

Durand, Hallie. *Mitchell's License.* *Illus. by Tony Fucile. Candlewick, 2011.* Mitchell "drives" to bed at night with his own special "car"—aka Dad's shoulders. (PreK–Gr. 1)

Fox, Mem. *Time for Bed.* *Illus. by Jane Dyer. Harcourt, 1997.* Parents of a mouse, goose, sheep, cat, snake, and fish lure their young ones to sleep in the wild with a rhyming lullaby. (PreK–K)

Frazee, Marla. *Hush, Little Baby: A Folk Song with Pictures.* *Illus. by the author. Harcourt, 1999.* A nineteenth-century frontier family tries to get the baby to stop crying. (PreK–Gr. 1)

Gal, Susan. *Night Lights.* *Illus. by the author. Knopf, 2009.* A little girl and her dog look at all the lights illuminating their city apartment and neighborhood at night. (PreK–Gr. 1)

Gerstein, Mordicai. *The Night World.* *Illus. by the author. Little, Brown, 2015.* A boy is woken in the middle of the night by his cat, Sylvie, who leads him outside into the dark to watch for what's coming. (PreK–Gr. 2)

Hartland, Jessie. *Night Shift.* *Illus. by the author. Bloomsbury, 2007.* Meet fourteen people who work at night while you sleep, from the doughnut baker to the zookeeper. (PreK–Gr. 2)

Ho, Minfong. *Hush! A Thai Lullaby.* *Illus. by Holly Meade. Orchard, 1996.* In Thailand, a mother admonishes the wild animals nearby—lizard, water buffalo, elephant, monkey, frog—to be quiet so her baby can sleep. (PreK–K)

Hoban, Russell. *Bedtime for Frances.* *Illus. by Lillian Hoban. HarperCollins, 1960.* It's late, but Frances the badger isn't tired yet. (PreK–Gr. 2)

Hort, Lenny. *How Many Stars in the Sky?* *Illus. by the author. HarperCollins, 1991.* At night, when a boy and his father can't sleep, they set out to count the stars. (PreK–Gr. 2)

John, Jory. *Goodnight Already!* *Illus. by Benji Davies. Harper, 2015.* Finally in bed for the winter, exhausted Bear is awakened by his neighbor, Duck, who is bored and wants to hang out. (PreK–Gr. 2)

Katz, Alan. *Stalling.* *Illus. by Elwood H. Smith. McElderry, 2010.* Dan's too busy catching armadillos, taming a crocodile, and climbing up Mount Clothes to go to bed. (PreK–Gr. 2)

Lamb, Albert. *Tell Me the Day Backwards.* *Illus. by David McPhail. Candlewick, 2011.* On their first day awake after a long winter's hibernation, Timmy Bear and Mama recall everything they did all day in reverse order. (PreK–K)

Lobel, Arnold. *Mouse Tales.* *Illus. by the author. HarperCollins, 1972.* Papa Mouse tells seven brief bedtime stories, one for each mouse. (PreK–Gr. 1)

Logue, Mary. *Sleep Like a Tiger.* *Illus. by Pamela Zagarenski. Houghton Mifflin, 2012.* A little girl who insists she is still wide awake climbs into bed and listens to her parents describe some of the many sleeping animals in the world. (PreK–Gr. 2)

Long, Sylvia. *Hush Little Baby.* *Illus. by the author. Chronicle, 1997.* "Hush little baby, don't say a word, Mama's going to show you a hummingbird," sings Mama Rabbit to her pajama-clad bunny. (PreK–K)

Lum, Kate. *What! Cried Granny: An Almost Bedtime Story.* *Illus. by Adrian Johnson. Dial, 1999.* At bedtime, Patrick's Granny plucks chickens to stuff his pillow, shears sheep to weave him a blanket, and sews him a giant teddy. (PreK–Gr. 2)

Mack, Jeff. *Duck in the Fridge.* *Illus. by the author. Two Lions, 2014.* Daddy tells his little one why he always reads her Mother Goose before bed, and it's a wild story. (PreK–Gr. 1)

Markes, Julie. *Shhhhh! Everybody's Sleeping.* *Illus. by David Parkins. HarperCollins, 2005.* This gently rhyming poem looks in on the town's community helpers—librarian, police officer, zookeeper, teacher, and doctor—while they sleep. (PreK–Gr. 1)

McGovern, Ann. *Too Much Noise.* *Illus. by Simms Taback. Houghton Mifflin, 1967.* A man who can't sleep is advised to bring all his animals into the house. (PreK–Gr. 2)

Pinkney, Andrea. *Sleeping Cutie.* *Illus. by Brian Pinkney. Harcourt, 2004.* Night Owl takes little Cutie LaRue to the Dreamland Nightclub, where she can party all night long. (PreK–Gr. 2)

Rathmann, Peggy. *The Day the Babies Crawled Away.* *Illus. by the author. Putnam, 2003.* An enterprising boy follows runaway babies and brings them home in time for bed. (PreK–Gr. 2)

Rathmann, Peggy. *Good Night, Gorilla.* *Illus. by the author. Putnam, 1994.* Unbeknownst to the zookeeper, the gorilla lets all the other animals out of their cages. (PreK–Gr. 1)

Rathmann, Peggy. *10 Minutes Till Bedtime*. *Illus. by the author. Putnam, 1998.* With his father counting down the minutes, a boy is getting ready for bed when a family of hamsters arrives to take the "10-Minute Bedtime Tour." (PreK–Gr. 2)

Rinker, Sherri Duskey. *Goodnight, Goodnight, Construction Site*. *Illus. by Tom Lichtenheld. Chronicle, 2011.* After a hard day's work, trucks get ready for bed. Snooze-resistant kids will also adore the companion, *Steam Train, Dream Train* (2013). (PreK–Gr. 2)

Robbins, Maria Polushkin. *Mother, Mother, I Want Another*. *Illus. by Jon Goodell. Knopf, 2005, c1978.* Mother thinks that Little Mouse wants a new mother, when all he really wants is another goodnight kiss. (PreK–K)

Rohmann, Eric. *Clara and Asha*. *Illus. by the author. Roaring Brook, 2005.* Late at night, young Clara frolics in the sky with her friend, Asha, a huge blue fish. (PreK–Gr. 2)

Rosenthal, Amy Krouse. *Little Hoot*. *Illus. by Jen Corace. Chronicle, 2008.* A little owl would love to go to bed early, but his parents insist he stay up for another hour. (PreK–Gr. 1)

Rylant, Cynthia. *Night in the Country*. *Illus. by Mary Szilagyi. Atheneum, 1986.* The sights and sounds of the country at night. (PreK–Gr. 2)

Saltzberg, Barney. *Chengdu Could Not, Would Not, Fall Asleep*. *Illus. by the author. Disney-Hyperion, 2014.* While everyone else in the bamboo grove is sound asleep, Chengdu, a young panda, is wide awake. (PreK–Gr. 1)

Shea, Bob. *Dinosaur vs. Bedtime.* *Illus. by the author. Disney-Hyperion, 2008.* A bedtime-fighting little dinosaur roars, jumps, slurps spaghetti, runs and, at last, falls asleep. (PreK–Gr. 1)

Sierra, Judy. *Sleepy Little Alphabet: A Bedtime Story from Alphabet Town.* *Illus. by Melissa Sweet. Knopf, 2009.* It's "sleepytime in Alphabet Town" in this merry, rhyming, alliterative story. (PreK–Gr. 1)

Singer, Marilyn. *Nine o'Clock Lullaby.* *Illus. by Frané Lessac. HarperCollins, 1991.* When it's bedtime in Brooklyn, see what people are doing in other time zones all around the world. (PreK–Gr. 2)

Stein, David Ezra. *Interrupting Chicken.* *Illus. by the author. Candlewick, 2010.* Little Red Chicken interrupts Papa's bedtime fairy tales to give life-saving advice to Hansel and Gretel, Little Red Riding Hood, and Chicken Little. (PreK–Gr. 2)

Swanson, Susan Marie. *The House in the Night.* *Illus. by Beth Krommes. Houghton Mifflin, 2008.* Told in cumulative verse, take a fantastical trip through the night with a girl getting ready for bed. (PreK–Gr. 2)

Thomas, Shelley Moore. *Good Night, Good Knight.* *Illus. by Jennifer Plecas. Dutton, 2000.* The Good Knight helps three lonely little dragons get ready for bed in their deep, dark cave. (PreK–Gr. 2)

Viorst, Judith. *My Mama Says There Aren't Any Zombies, Ghosts, Vampires, Creatures, Demons, Monsters, Fiends, Goblins, or Things.* *Illus. by Kay Chorao. Atheneum, 1987.* Nick is afraid of nighttime monsters, and he doesn't quite believe his mother's assurances to the contrary. After all, "Sometimes even mamas make mistakes." (PreK–Gr. 2)

Waber, Bernard. *Bearsie Bear and the Surprise Sleepover Party.* *Illus. by the author. Houghton Mifflin, 1997.* It's snowing, and Bearsie Bear's friends all want to spend the night. (PreK–Gr. 1)

Waber, Bernard. *Ira Sleeps Over.* *Illus. by the author. Houghton Mifflin, 1973.* Heading to Reggie's house for a sleepover, Ira faces a dilemma—to bring his teddy bear or not. (PreK–Gr. 2)

Waddell, Martin. *Can't You Sleep, Little Bear?* *Illus. by Barbara Firth. Candlewick, 1992.* Little Bear is afraid of his dark cave until Big Bear takes him outside to see the moon and stars. (PreK–Gr. 1)

Walton, Rick. *So Many Bunnies: A Bedtime ABC and Counting Book.* *Illus. by Paige Miglio. HarperCollins, 1998.* A rhyming bedtime romp with Old Mother Rabbit and her twenty-six rabbit children. (PreK–Gr. 1)

Wells, Rosemary. *Max and Ruby's Bedtime Book.* *Illus. by the author. Viking, 2010.* Grandma tells the rabbit siblings three bedtime stories. (PreK–Gr. 1)

Willems, Mo. *Don't Let the Pigeon Stay Up Late.* *Illus. by the author. Hyperion, 2006.* Pigeon does his best to persuade us he's not a bit tired, but he can't stop yawning. Your audience will also like Mo Willems's Cat the Cat book Time to Sleep, Sheep the Sheep! (2010). (PreK–Gr. 2)

Yolen, Jane. *How Do Dinosaurs Say Good Night?* *Illus. by Mark Teague. Scholastic/ Blue Sky, 2000.* Rhymes describe how ten oversize dinosaur children face bedtime. (PreK–Gr. 1)

Zemach, Margot. *It Could Always Be Worse: A Yiddish Folk Tale.* *Illus. by the author. Farrar, 1976.* Chaos in his overcrowded hut drives a poor Russian man to the Rabbi for advice. (PreK–Gr. 3)

Themed Program: I'm Hungry

The previous edition of this book contained a delicious chapter called "Book Parties," with recipes and ideas for programs that ended with a snack. In the past twenty-five years, so many children have been diagnosed with food allergies that many schools have nixed most classroom treats. Fresh fruits and vegetables are usually okay, but before distributing any food, check with parents, teachers, or the school nurse who will have a list of children with allergy concerns.

We may not be able to feed children in our story hours now, but we can still read about, sing about, salivate over, and celebrate food through our programs. Just think of the calories we'll save.

NURSERY RHYMES AND FINGERPLAYS

Pat-a-Cake

> Pat-a-cake, pat-a-cake, baker's man,
> Bake me a cake as fast as you can;
> Prick it and pat it and mark it with a *B*,
> And put it in the oven for Baby and me.

Pease Porridge Hot

> Pease porridge hot,
> Pease porridge cold,
> Pease porridge in the pot
> Nine days old.

(continued)

Some like it hot,
Some like it cold,
Some like it in the pot
Nine days old.

Five Little Sausages

Five little sausages sizzling in a pan. (*waggle five fingers*)
All of a sudden, one went BAM! (*clap your hands on "BAM!"*)

Four little sausages sizzling in a pan. (*waggle four fingers*)
All of a sudden, one went BAM! (*clap your hands on "BAM!"*)

Three little sausages sizzling in a pan. (*waggle three fingers*)
All of a sudden, one went BAM! (*clap your hands on "BAM!"*)

Two little sausages sizzling in a pan. (*waggle two fingers*)
All of a sudden, one went BAM! (*clap your hands on "BAM!"*)

One little sausage sizzling in a pan. (*waggle your index finger*)
And he sang:
> (*while you wiggle your index finger in time, sing the following, in a plaintive but triumphant voice, to the tune of "He's Got the Whole World in His Hands"*)

I've got the whole pan to myself,
I've got the whole pan to myself,
I've got the whole pan to myself,
I've got the whole pan to myself—
YAY!

The Chocolate Cake

Start with your hands facing you. Each time you blow, "Wh! Wh!" put down a finger. This can also be done as a poster rhyme. Using Velcro, attach candles to a picture of a cake. Remove them as the children chant.

Ten little candles on a chocolate cake. Wh! Wh! Now there are eight.
Eight little candles on candlesticks. Wh! Wh! Now there are six.
Six little candles and not one more. Wh! Wh! Now there are four.
Four little candles, red, white and blue. Wh! Wh! Now there are two.
Two little candles standing in the sun. Wh! Wh! Now there are none.

Who Took the Cookies from the Cookie Jar?

Bonnie Lass and Philemon Sturges wrote a peppy rhyming picture book, Who Took the Cookies from the Cookie Jar?, *based on this rhyme. You might also want to share the charming book* Cookies: Bite-Size Life Lessons *by Amy Krouse Rosenthal, which uses baking and eating cookies as a metaphor for how to live an ethical life. Play this name game with your audience sitting in a circle. Then find out how people contribute to cookie making in George Shannon's* Who Put the Cookies in the Cookie Jar?

> *Group:* Who took the cookies from the cookie jar?
>
> *Leader:* Sharron took the cookies from the cookie jar.
>
> *Sharron:* Who, me?
>
> *Group:* Yes, you!
>
> *Sharron:* Couldn't be.
>
> *Group:* Then who?
>
> *Sharron:* Judy took the cookies from the cookie jar. (*continue around the circle with the next child's name*)

SONGS

Ravioli

Sing this to the tune of "Alouette." Repeat the items mentioned in reverse order, pointing to each body part or item of clothing, ending with "Everywhere" as you sing each verse.

> *All:* Ravioli, I like ravioli; ravioli, it's so good for me.
>
> *Leader:* Do I have it in my hair?
>
> *Response:* Yes, you have it in your hair.
>
> *Leader:* In my hair?
>
> *Response:* In your hair.
>
> *Leader:* Everywhere?
>
> *Response:* Everywhere.
>
> *All:* OHHHH . . .
>
> Ravioli, I like ravioli; ravioli, it's so good for me.
>
> *Other verses: On my chin, shirt, jeans, shoes, etc.*

If You're Hungry and You Know It

Sing this to tune of "If You're Happy and You Know It"; new lyrics by Judy Freeman, ©2012

If you're hungry and you know it, pat your belly,

If you're hungry and you know it, pat your belly.

Would you like some cheese that's smelly, and some tuna fish with jelly?

If you're hungry and you know it, pat your belly.

If you're hungry and you know it, wink your eye,

If you're hungry and you know it, wink your eye.

Would you like a pizza pie, topped with bee and dragonfly?

If you're hungry and you know it, wink your eye.

If you're hungry and you know it, nod your heady,

If you're hungry and you know it, nod your heady.

Would you like some hot spaghetti, made with worms and old confetti?

If you're hungry and you know it, nod your heady.

If you're hungry and you know it, moan and groan,

If you're hungry and you know it, moan and groan.

Would you like an ice cream cone flavored with a doggy bone?

If you're hungry and you know it, moan and groan.

As you think of the other foods you love, write new verses to sing and lose your appetite a little.

The Doughnut Song

To the tune of "Turkey in the Straw"

Well, I went to Cincinnati and I walked around the block,

And I walked right in to a bakery shop;

I picked three doughnuts out of the grease,

And handed the lady a five-cent piece.

Well, she looked at the nickel and she looked at me.

She said, "This nickel's no good to me;

There's a hole in the middle and it's all the way through."
Said I, "There's a hole in the doughnuts, too.

Thanks for the doughnuts,
Goodbye!"

You'll find two more silly songs about food in chapter 5, "Music," on pages 184–185.

POEMS

Potato Chips

A potato chip is something never ceasing to amuse
I love its funny wrinkles
and the crunchy way it chews.

—*Anthony E. Gallagher*

Bananas and Cream

Bananas and cream,
Bananas and cream,
All we could say was
Bananas and cream.

We couldn't say fruit,
We wouldn't say cow,
We didn't say sugar—
We don't say it now.

Bananas and cream,
Bananas and cream,
All we could shout was
Bananas and cream.

We didn't say why,
We didn't say how;
We forgot it was fruit,
We forgot the old cow;

We never said sugar,
We only said WOW!

*Bananas and cream,
Bananas and cream;
All that we want is
Bananas and cream!*

We didn't say dish,
We didn't say spoon;
We said not tomorrow,
But NOW and HOW SOON.

Bananas and cream,
Bananas and cream?
We yelled for bananas,
Bananas and scream!

—*David McCord*

STORIES

Pepper Stew

Retold by Caroline Feller Bauer

This story is easy to dramatize. There is lots of action to mime, and children can make up their own dialogue to embellish the story.

Elizabeth and Eric were in charge of the three younger children while Mom and Dad were working. "What shall we make for dinner?" asked Eric. It was a special day because it was their parents' wedding anniversary.

"Dad loves beef stew. Let's try making it."

"I'll get the pot."

"I'll cut up the beef."

"I'll slice the carrots."

"I'll dice the celery."

"I'll find the bay leaves."

"I'll peel the potatoes."

"I'll chop the potatoes."

"I'll mince the parsley."

"I'll slice the onions. I'm crying already."

"Put the beef in the pot. Put the carrots in the pot. Put the celery in the pot. Put the bay leaves and parsley in the pot. Put the potatoes in the pot. Put the onions in the pot. Add water to cover. Turn on the stove. Now, stir the stew and put in a pinch of salt."

"Let's go finish our chores while it simmers."

Eric went into the garden. Elizabeth went into the laundry room. Kim went to the bedroom. Randy went into the living room. Lou went to the barn.

Then Eric suddenly remembered the stew. He called to the other children:

"We forgot to put fresh ground pepper in the stew. I'm busy weeding the garden. I can't do it."

"I haven't got the time," said Elizabeth. "I'm just doing the wash."

"I'm upstairs," said Kim, "making my bed."

"Sorry," said Randy. "I'm washing the windows."

"I'm milking the cow," called Lou.

Eric stopped working. "I'd better put the pepper in the stew." Eric went into the kitchen and put some pepper in the pot and returned to the garden.

WEB This script is available on ALA's Web Extras page at alaeditions.org/webextras.

Elizabeth dried her hands. "I better put some pepper in the stew." Elizabeth went into the kitchen and put some pepper in the pot and returned to the laundry room.

Kim smoothed the bed. "I better put some pepper in the stew." Kim went into the kitchen and put some pepper in the pot and returned to the bedroom.

Randy wrung out the window cloth. "I better put some pepper in the stew." Randy went into the kitchen and put some pepper in the pot and returned to the living room.

Lou stopped milking the cow. "I better put some pepper in the stew." Lou went into the kitchen and put some pepper in the pot and returned to the barn.

Three hours later, Eric and Elizabeth called, "The stew is ready. Let's set the table." The children came into the dining room and set the table. They used a pretty tablecloth and the good china. They put flowers from the garden into a vase. The table looked beautiful.

"Just in time. Here come Mom and Dad."

"Surprise! We've made your favorite stew for your anniversary."

Eric carried the stew to the table and served it to the family.

Mom tasted the stew and coughed. Dad tasted the stew and sputtered. Eric tasted the stew and laughed. Elizabeth, Kim, Randy and Lou all tasted the stew. "Yuck." "Fire!" "Hot." "Wow!" "Help!" they said while fanning themselves.

"I think we all found the time to put pepper in the stew," said Eric. "It's no longer beef stew. It's pepper stew!"

"Thank you for all your effort," said Mom.

"Yes, thanks," said Dad. "Let's go out to dinner. After all, it's our anniversary."

Everyone cheered, "Hurray for pepper stew!"

ACTIVITIES AND/OR CRAFTS

- **Play the food-alphabet game.** "A, my name is Amy and I like applesauce," etc. Go around the room giving the children a chance to match their name with a food they like. If kids are stumped, they can use their middle or last names.

- **Fruits-and-vegetables activity.** Bring in a variety of fruits and vegetables: an unpeeled banana, an apple, a whole lemon, a string bean, and a carrot. Ask the kids to close their eyes (or use a blindfold) and feel each object to see if they can identify it. Next, have them smell a jar of pickles, a just-peeled orange, a lemon, and a piece of ripe tomato. Then, have them taste a chunk of apple, a grape, a banana, a baby carrot, and a piece of cucumber. Finally, ask them to look at and try to identify some less familiar fruits and vegetables: an avocado, a lime, a radish, a tangerine, or a mango, which you can then peel or slice and cut into tiny pieces for tasting.

- **Lollipops.** Make huge, swirly, rainbow-colored lollipops from heavy-stock paper, using markers and glitter glue pens to make the swirls. Use a paint stirrer or roll brown paper into a thin cylinder and tape it on the back of the lollipop as the stick.

- **Vegetable prints.** Use carrot halves (cut on the diameter and lengthwise), potato halves, broccoli, peapods. Dip them in different colors of poster paints and press onto construction paper.

- **Favorite dinner.** Give children white paper plates and have them draw their very favorite dinner on it. Hand out plastic forks and knives so they can then pretend to eat and savor each thing on the plate. Give them smaller plates for dessert. Or have them construct their dinner out of paper. You'll find an instructional video for this activity at www.simplekidscrafts.com/video/easy-paper-crafts-food. You can also use Model Magic to make peas, string beans, and other simple foods.

- **Place mats.** Make place mats out of construction paper. Laminate them so they can be used for a while at home.

- **Place cards.** Children can create place cards by decorating an index card with a crayon portrait for each family member. When children go home, have them surreptitiously put out the cards in their proper places before supper.

- **Chef hats.** Talk about what a chef does. Make chef hats for children to wear by gluing the edges of one sheet of tissue paper to the edges of a headband made of heavy paper. Have the children cook a pretend meal, or use the hats when playing the restaurant game, described below.

- **The restaurant game.** Set up a pretend restaurant in your room.

  Supplies: Multiple menus collected from restaurants, or mock up and duplicate a menu so each child can have the same one; order pad and pencil; aprons (optional); paper plates, plastic flatware, napkins, and paper cups; play money

  Cast: Diners and a restaurant staff

  Directions: Customers are greeted at the door by the maître d', who seats them at a table. The server comes over and gives out the menus. Diners decide what they're having. The server takes the order on an order pad and brings it to the kitchen. The chefs cook and serve the pretend food. The diners eat and enjoy. At the end of the meal, the server delivers the bill, and the diners pay.

  Note: If the children in your group are older, they can write their own menus (a creative writing project), set the table with a paper tablecloth or placemats, and figure out the price per person, including a 20 percent tip.

- **Reader's theater.** Act out reader's theater scripts of "The Dog and the Cat Go to Market" on page 60 and "An After-School Snack" on page 62.

BOOKLIST: FOOD

(*See also* Apples; Flowers and Plants; Fruits and Vegetables; *and* Gardens; *alphabetically listed in the* "Quicklist of Thematic Program Starters for Young Children, Birth to Age 7" *on page 312.*)

Snacks

DePaola, Tomie. *The Popcorn Book. Illus. by the author. Holiday House, 1978.* Learn facts about popcorn as twins Tiny and Tony make some. (K–Gr. 2)

Ehlert, Lois. *Growing Vegetable Soup. Illus. by the author. Harcourt, 1987.* Growing veggies, from seed to soup. (PreK–Gr. 1)

Hoban, Russell. *Bread and Jam for Frances. Illus. by Lillian Hoban. HarperCollins, 1964.* Frances, a young badger, would like to eat bread and jam at every meal. (PreK–Gr. 1)

Rattigan, Jama Kim. *Dumpling Soup. Illus. by Lillian Hsu-Flanders. Little, Brown, 1993.* A Hawaiian girl makes dumplings for New Year's. (PreK–Gr. 2)

Sendak, Maurice. *Chicken Soup with Rice: A Book of Months*. *Illus. by the author.* *HarperCollins, 1962.* Revel in a rhyming year of chicken soup, month by month. (PreK–Gr. 2)

Sheth, Kashmira. *Tiger in My Soup*. *Illus. by Jeffrey Ebbeler. Peachtree, 2013.* A tiger pops out of a boy's soup bowl and chases him around the kitchen. (PreK–Gr. 2)

Sturges, Philemon. *The Little Red Hen (Makes a Pizza)*. *Illus. by Amy Walrod. Dutton, 1999.* Duck, Dog, and Cat refuse to help Hen make pizza, but they still want to eat some. (PreK–Gr. 2)

Titus, Eve. *Anatole*. *Illus. by Paul Galdone. McGraw-Hill, 1956.* A French mouse helps a cheese factory thrive with his anonymous critiques of their cheeses. (K–Gr. 2)

Westcott, Nadine Bernard. *Peanut Butter and Jelly: A Play Rhyme*. *Illus. by the author. Dutton, 1987.* An interactive rhyme on how to make a PB&J sandwich. (PreK–Gr. 2)

Main Courses

Barrett, Judi. *Cloudy with a Chance of Meatballs*. *Illus. by Ron Barrett. Atheneum, 1978.* Food falls from the sky in the town of ChewandSwallow. (K–Gr. 4)

Bruel, Nick. *Bad Kitty*. *Illus. by the author. Roaring Brook, 2005.* She was a good kitty till her people started feeding her an alphabet of bad food. (PreK–Gr. 2)

Calmenson, Stephanie. *Dinner at the Panda Palace*. *Illus. by Nadine Bernard West-cott. HarperCollins, 1991.* From one to ten, the animals flock to Mr. Panda's restaurant. (PreK–Gr. 2)

Compestine, Ying Chang. *The Story of Chopsticks*. *Illus. by YongSheng Xuan. Holiday House, 2001.* Kùai, the youngest of three boys in the Kang family, invents chopsticks. (K–Gr. 3)

DePaola, Tomie. *Strega Nona: An Original Version of an Old Tale*. *Illus. by the author. Prentice-Hall, 1975.* Italian tale about Big Anthony and lotsa pasta. (PreK–Gr. 4)

Dooley, Norah. *Everybody Bakes Bread*. *Illus. by Peter J. Thornton. Carolrhoda, 1996.* Carrie visits seven neighbors and tastes seven types of bread. (K–Gr. 2)

Fleming, Denise. *Lunch*. *Illus. by the author. Henry Holt, 1992.* A hungry mouse feasts on fruits and vegetables, each a different color. (PreK–Gr. 1)

Freymann, Saxton, and Joost Elffers. *Food for Thought: The Complete Book of Concepts for Growing Minds*. *Illus. by Saxton Freymann. Scholastic, 2005.* Food creatures made from real fruits and vegetables demonstrate shapes, colors, numbers, letters, and opposites. (PreK–Gr. 1)

Friedman, Ina R. *How My Parents Learned to Eat.* Illus. by Allen Say. Houghton Mifflin, 1984. A girl explains how her Japanese mother and American father fell in love and learned to eat with silverware and chopsticks, respectively. (K–Gr. 4)

Hoberman, Mary Ann. *Seven Silly Eaters.* Illus. by Marla Frazee. Harcourt, 1997. Mrs. Peters's seven children have different tastes in food. (PreK–Gr. 2)

Hong, Lily Toy. *How the Ox Star Fell from Heaven.* Illus. by the author. Albert Whitman, 1991. This Chinese pourquoi tale explains why we eat three times a day and why oxen are now beasts of burden. (K–Gr. 3)

Hopkinson, Deborah. *Fannie in the Kitchen: The Whole Story from Soup to Nuts of How Fannie Farmer Invented Recipes with Precise Measurements.* Illus. by Nancy Carpenter. Atheneum, 2001. A fictionalized story based on cookbook author Fannie Farmer's experiences as a mother's helper. (K–Gr. 3)

Ketteman, Helen. *Armadilly Chili.* Illus. by Will Terry. Albert Whitman, 2004. Miss Billie Armadilly, an armadillo, needs help making armadilly chili, but all her animal pals say they are too busy. (PreK–Gr. 2)

Kimmel, Eric A. *The Three Little Tamales.* Illus. by Valeria Docampo. Marshall Cavendish, 2009. Three enterprising tamales build themselves little casitas and try to fend off hungry Señor Lobo, the wolf. (PreK–Gr. 2)

Manushkin, Fran. *The Shivers in the Fridge.* Illus. by Paul O. Zelinsky. Dutton, 2006. Papa Shivers and his family live in a little box in the refrigerator. (PreK–Gr. 2)

Paul, Ann Whitford. *Mañana, Iguana.* Illus. by Ethan Long. Holiday House, 2004. Iguana needs help planning a fiesta, but his friends Conejo, Tortuga, and Culebra won't cooperate. (PreK–Gr. 2)

Paul, Ann Whitford. *Tortuga in Trouble.* Illus. by Ethan Long. Holiday House, 2009. When Tortuga (tortoise) heads for Abuela's house with a basket of supper, drooling Coyote follows. (PreK–Gr. 2)

Reich, Susanna. *Minette's Feast.* Illus. by Amy Bates. Abrams, 2012. A story about how Julia Child learned to cook in Paris and found herself a cat. (Gr. 1–4)

Rosenthal, Amy Krouse. *Spoon.* Illus. by Scott Magoon. Disney-Hyperion, 2009. Spoon thinks the other utensils have it better than he does. (PreK–Gr. 2)

Schneider, Josh. *Tales for Very Picky Eaters.* Illus. by the author. Clarion, 2011. Josh's dad tells him wacky stories to get him to eat foods he hates. (K–Gr. 2)

Seuss, Dr. *Green Eggs and Ham.* Illus. by the author. Random House, 1960. Sam-I-Am tries everything to persuade his friend to eat green eggs and ham. (PreK–Gr. 2)

Soto, Gary. *Too Many Tamales.* Illus. by Ed Martinez. Putnam, 1993. Maria thinks she's lost her mother's diamond ring in the Christmas tamales she made, so she asks her cousins to help her eat them to find it. (PreK–Gr. 3)

**Stevens, Janet, and Susan Stevens Crummel. *Cook-a-Doodle-Doo!* Illus. *by Janet Stevens. Harcourt, 1999.* Big Brown Rooster asks friends to help him make the recipe for strawberry shortcake that he found in the cookbook belonging to his great-grandmother, the Little Red Hen. (PreK–Gr. 3)

**Wood, Audrey. *Heckedy Peg.* Illus. *by Don Wood. Harcourt, 1987.* An old witch turns seven children into seven types of food. (K–Gr. 3)

**Yolen, Jane. *How Do Dinosaurs Eat Their Food?* Illus. *by Mark Teague. Scholastic/ Blue Sky, 2005.* Ten dinosaur picky eaters learn some manners. (PreK–Gr. 2)

Fruits, Vegetables, and Side Dishes

**Child, Lauren. *I Will Never Not Ever Eat a Tomato.* Illus. *by the author. Candlewick, 2000.* Charlie gets his picky eater little sister, Lola, to eat carrots and mashed potatoes. (PreK–Gr. 1)

**Ehlert, Lois. *Eating the Alphabet: Fruits and Vegetables from A to Z.* Illus. *by the author. Harcourt, 1989.* An alluring alphabet of seventy-five fruits and vegetables. (PreK–Gr. 1)

**Gourley, Robbin. *Bring Me Some Apples and I'll Make You a Pie: A Story about Edna Lewis.* Illus. *by the author. Clarion, 2009.* A tribute to African American chef and cookbook author Edna Lewis, depicting her as a girl on her family's farm. (K–Gr. 3)

**LaRochelle, David. *How Martha Saved Her Parents from Green Beans.* Illus. *by Mark Fearing. Dial, 2013.* Martha refuses to eat green beans until a gang of mean green beans swaggers into town and kidnaps her parents. (PreK–Gr. 2)

**Lipson, Eden Ross. *Applesauce Season.* Illus. *by Mordicai Gerstein. Roaring Brook, 2009.* A boy and his grandma make applesauce together. (PreK–Gr. 2)

**McClements, George. *Night of the Veggie Monster.* Illus. *by the author. Bloomsbury, 2008.* A young boy is forced to eat three whole peas at dinnertime. (PreK–Gr. 1)

**Reynolds, Aaron. *Creepy Carrots!* Illus. *by Peter Brown. Simon & Schuster, 2012.* Jasper Rabbit eats the carrots growing in Crackenhopper Field until the carrots start following him. (PreK–Gr. 2)

**Sayre, April Pulley. *Rah, Rah, Radishes! A Vegetable Chant.* Photos *by the author. Beach Lane, 2011.* A gung-ho rhyming cheer for fresh vegetables, with color photos of a farm stand and its produce. Also introduce *Go, Go, Grapes! A Fruit Chant* (2012) and *Let's Go Nuts! Seeds We Eat* (2013). (PreK–Gr. 2)

**Stevens, Janet. *Tops & Bottoms.* Illus. *by the author. Harcourt, 1995.* Hare offers to plant and harvest crops for Bear and split the veggies down the middle, which seems like a good idea. (PreK–Gr. 3)

Vere, Ed. *Banana!* *Illus. by the author. Henry Holt, 2010.* One monkey has a banana; the other monkey wants it. (PreK–Gr. 1)

Williams, Vera B. *Cherries and Cherry Pits.* *Illus. by the author. Greenwillow, 1986.* Bidemmi draws and tells three stories about cherries. (K–Gr. 2)

Desserts

Aylesworth, Jim. *The Gingerbread Man.* *Illus. by Barbara McClintock. Scholastic, 1998.* Cookie runs away. (PreK–Gr. 1)

Balian, Lorna. *The Sweet Touch.* *Illus. by the author. Abingdon, 1976.* Peggy's wish comes true: everything she touches turns to candy. (PreK–Gr. 1)

Fleming, Candace. *Clever Jack Takes the Cake.* *Illus. by G. Brian Karas. Schwartz & Wade, 2010.* Jack, a poor boy, makes the princess a cake for her birthday present, but his trip to the castle to give it to her isn't easy. (PreK–Gr. 3)

Hutchins, Pat. *When the Doorbell Rang.* *Illus. by the author. HarperCollins, 1989.* Ma's dozen home-baked cookies must be shared with visitors. (PreK–Gr. 1)

Khan, Rukhsana. *Big Red Lollipop.* *Illus. by Sophie Blackall. Viking, 2010.* Invited to her first birthday party, Rubina is mortified when her mother insists she take along her pesky little sister, Sana. (PreK–Gr. 3)

Kraft, Erik. *Chocolatina.* *Illus. by Denise Brunkus. Scholastic, 1998.* "You are what you eat" becomes true when Tina becomes chocolate. (PreK–Gr. 2)

Krall, Dan. *The Great Lollipop Caper.* *Illus. by the author. Simon & Schuster, 2013.* Sour Mr. Caper is jealous when all of the children prefer sweet Lollipop. (PreK–Gr. 3)

Lass, Bonnie, and Philemon Sturges. *Who Took the Cookies from the Cookie Jar?* *Illus. by Ashley Wolff. Little, Brown, 2000.* In a story based on the classic chant, Skunk travels the Southwestern desert seeking a cookie-stealing culprit. (PreK–Gr. 1)

Muir, Leslie. *The Little Bitty Bakery.* *Illus. by Betsy Lewin. Disney-Hyperion, 2011.* When an elephant pastry chef is too busy to make herself a birthday cake, her mouse friends take charge. (PreK–Gr. 1)

Murray, Alison. *Apple Pie ABC.* *Illus. by the author. Disney-Hyperion, 2011.* A little black-and-white dog covets the apple pie that a little girl just put into the oven. (PreK–Gr. 1)

Numeroff, Laura. *If You Give a Mouse a Cookie.* *Illus. by Felicia Bond. HarperCollins, 1985.* In a classic cause-and-effect story, a mouse gets his cookie but wants more. (PreK–Gr. 2)

Ogburn, Jacqueline K. *The Bake Shop Ghost.* *Illus. by Marjorie Priceman. Houghton Mifflin, 2005.* After master baker Cora Lee Merriweather dies, she haunts her bake shop to run off the new owner. (K–Gr. 3)

Palatini, Margie. *Sweet Tooth.* *Illus. by Jack E. Davis. Simon & Schuster, 2004.* Stuart's nagging sweet tooth demands more candy bars. (PreK–Gr. 2)

Polacco, Patricia. *Thunder Cake.* *Illus. by the author. Philomel, 1990.* As a thunderstorm approaches the farm, Grandma and her little girl bake a cake. (PreK–Gr. 1)

Priceman, Marjorie. *How to Make a Cherry Pie and See the U.S.A.* *Illus. by the author. Knopf, 2008.* The girl from *How to Make an Apple Pie and See the World* (1994) now scours the country to gather the ingredients she needs for pie. (PreK–Gr. 3)

Rosenthal, Amy Krouse. *Cookies: Bite-Size Life Lessons.* *Illus. by Jane Dyer. HarperCollins, 2006.* Two dozen sensible definitions for words like *patient, proud, respect,* and *honest,* all tie into making a batch of cookies. Rosenthal's *Little Pea* (2005) is another delightful food-based tale. (PreK–Gr. 2)

Shannon, George. *Who Put the Cookies in the Cookie Jar?* *Illus. by Julie Paschkis. Henry Holt, 2013.* Folk art illustrations show the global mix of people who make, grow, and supply what a girl and her mother need to make a simple batch of cookies. (PreK–Gr. 1)

Vamos, Samantha R. *The Cazuela That the Farm Maiden Stirred.* *Illus. by Rafael López. Charlesbridge, 2011.* In a Spanish-infused cumulative story, told in the style of "This Is the House That Jack Built," a farm maiden makes a delicious pot of *arroz con leche,* aka rice pudding. (PreK–Gr. 3)

Wheeler, Lisa. *Ugly Pie.* *Illus. by Heather Solomon. Harcourt, 2010.* Ol' Bear gathers ingredients from friends for a delicious—but unattractive—sour apple and raisin pie. (PreK–Gr. 2)

Quicklist of Thematic Program Starters for Young Children, Birth to Age 7

The following quicklist offers a multitude of program themes from which you can assemble storytimes. You'll find more than 130 topics to peruse, with an A to Z of high-interest areas—animals, the natural world, families, vehicles, oceans, siblings, trucks, Halloween, and shapes—as well as topics that cross the curriculum.

Each entry consists of three parts. The first, "Read-Alouds," is a list of our top choices of picture books (fiction as well as informational books) you can use successfully in preschool and primary story hours. Whether you read these books aloud or choose to tell them as stories, as we discuss in *The Handbook for Storytellers* (2014), they are all selections that will make kids holler for more. We promise. All told, the read-aloud lists provide more than 1,400 carefully selected titles we've read, used with kids, and loved.

The second part of each entry, "Verse," features a selection to get your creative juices flowing: a song, a chant, a fingerplay, an action rhyme, and/ or a poem. If a selection is one we're pretty sure you already know, we just listed its title; otherwise, we added the words. If you don't know the tune or want to see someone else perform it, you can usually find it online.

In the third part, "Activity," we suggest easy, doable ideas for a follow-up project—a make-and-take craft, a discussion possibility, a writing and/or illustrating prompt, a game, and more—to help you turn the day's theme into story-hour gold.

Of course, the Internet is a fabulous resource, with lesson plans, songs, chants, stories, activities and more, posted by teachers, librarians, and parents. And if you need visuals, Pinterest (www.pinterest.com) has more ideas than you could use in a lifetime. Chose what works best for you and your children, tweaking each activity to fit your objective, your talents, and your personality.

Our thanks to the talented teachers, librarians, and crafty family members who helped us brainstorm and come up with some of the titles, songs, poems, and activities below—among them Maren Vitali, Jenn Fisher, Margaret Feldman, and Ann Guthrie.

AFRICAN AMERICANS

Read-Alouds

Evans, Shane W. *Underground: Finding the Light to Freedom.* *Illus. by the author. Roaring Brook/Neal Porter, 2011.* (Gr. 1–3)

Hamilton, Virginia. *The People Could Fly: The Picture Book.* *Illus. by Leo Dillon and Diane Dillon. Knopf, 2004.* (Gr. 1–6)

Howard, Elizabeth Fitzgerald. *Virgie Goes to School with Us Boys.* *Illus. by E. B. Lewis. Simon & Schuster, 2000.* (Gr. 1–4)

Johnson, Angela. *All Different Now: Juneteenth, the First Day of Freedom.* *Illus. by E. B. Lewis. Simon & Schuster, 2014.* (Gr. 1–5)

McKissack, Patricia C. *Goin' Someplace Special.* *Illus. by Jerry Pinkney. Atheneum, 2001.* (Gr. 1–4)

Medearis, Angela Shelf. *Seven Spools of Thread: A Kwanzaa Story.* Illus. by Daniel Minter. Albert Whitman, 2000. (K–Gr. 4)

Newton-Chocolate, Deborah M. *My First Kwanzaa Book.* Illus. by Cal Massey. Scholastic, 1992. (PreK–Gr. 2)

Rappaport, Doreen. *Martin's Big Words: The Life of Dr. Martin Luther King, Jr.* Illus. by Bryan Collier. Disney-Hyperion, 2001. (K–Gr. 4)

Ringgold, Faith. *Aunt Harriet's Underground Railroad in the Sky.* Illus. by the author. Crown, 1992. (Gr. 1–4)

Woodson, Jacqueline. *The Other Side.* Illus. by E. B. Lewis. Putnam, 2001. (K–Gr. 4)

Woodson, Jacqueline. *Show Way.* Illus. by Hudson Talbott. Putnam, 2005. (K–Gr. 6)

Verse

Sing "Follow the Drinking Gourd," which you can find at www.songsfor teaching.com/folk/followthedrinkinggourd.php.

Activity

Introduce children to Martin Luther King Jr. by reading Doreen Rappaport's glorious *Martin's Big Words: The Life of Dr. Martin Luther King, Jr.*

AIRPLANES (*See also* Bicycles; Boats and Ships; Cars and Buses; Trains; Trucks)

Read-Alouds

Floca, Brian. *Five Trucks.* Illus. by the author. Atheneum/Richard Jackson, 2014. (PreK–Gr. 1)

Kuhlmann, Torben. *Lindbergh: The Tale of a Flying Mouse.* Illus. by the author. North-South, 2014. (Gr. 1–6)

Light, Steve. *Planes Go.* Illus. by the author. Chronicle, 2014. (PreK–K)

Lyon, George Ella. *Planes Fly.* Illus. by Mick Wiggins. Atheneum, 2013. (PreK–Gr. 1)

Provensen, Alice, and Martin Provensen. *The Glorious Flight: Across the Channel with Louis Blériot, July 25, 1909.* Illus. by the author. Viking, 1983. (K–Gr. 4)

Rohmann, Eric. *My Friend, Rabbit.* Illus. by the author. Roaring Brook, 2002. (PreK–Gr. 1)

Van Lieshout, Maria. *Flight 1-2-3.* Illus. by the author. Chronicle, 2013. (PreK–Gr. 1)

Willems, Mo. *Knuffle Bunny Free: An Unexpected Diversion.* Illus. by the author. Balzer + Bray, 2010. (PreK–Gr. 2)

Verse

Sing "Down at the Airport" (to the tune of "Down by the Station"):

> Down at the airport, early in the morning,
> See the little aeroplanes all in a row.
> Watch when the pilot pulls on the joystick—
> Swoosh, swoosh, zoom, zoom—off you go!

Activity

Have kids decorate 9-by-12-inch construction paper with crayons or paint. Fold the paper into paper airplanes and have a flying contest to see how far the planes can go. (Find great paper airplane tutorials on YouTube.)

ALLIGATORS AND CROCODILES   (*See also* Reptiles and Amphibians)

Read-Alouds

Chen, Chih-Yuan. *Guji Guji.* *Illus. by the author. Kane/Miller, 2004.* (PreK–Gr. 1)

Dahl, Roald. *The Enormous Crocodile.* *Illus. by Quentin Blake. Knopf, 1978.* (K–Gr. 3)

Marcellino, Fred. *I, Crocodile.* *Illus. by the author. HarperCollins, 1999.* (Gr. 1–4)

Sendak, Maurice. *Alligators All Around.* *Illus. by the author. HarperCollins, 1962.* (PreK–Gr. 1)

Waber, Bernard. *Lyle, Lyle, Crocodile.* *Illus. by the author. Houghton Mifflin, 1965.* (PreK–Gr. 3)

Willems, Mo. *Hooray for Amanda and Her Alligator.* *Illus. by the author. Balzer + Bray, 2011.* (PreK–Gr. 1)

Verse

Recite the title poem in Alligator Pie by Dennis Lee (Harper Collins, 2012, or find on YouTube).

Activity

Give everyone a green clothespin (paint them in advance). Have children paste on googly eyes and draw on teeth with magic marker, and voilà!—they have a puppet to play with. You can also put magnetic tape on one side of the clothespin to create a refrigerator magnet.

ALPHABET BOOKS

Read-Alouds

Baker, Keith. *LMNO Peas*. Illus. by the author. Beach Lane, 2010. (PreK–Gr. 1)

Bataille, Marion. *ABC3D*. Illus. by the author. Roaring Brook, 2008. (PreK–Gr. 3)

Bayer, Jane. *A My Name Is Alice*. Illus. by Steven Kellogg. Dial, 1984. (PreK–Gr. 2)

Bingham, Kelly. *Z Is for Moose*. Illus. by Paul O. Zelinsky. Greenwillow, 2012. (PreK–Gr. 2)

Bruel, Nick. *Bad Kitty*. Illus. by the author. Roaring Brook, 2005. (PreK–Gr. 2)

Escoffier, Michaël. *Take Away the A*. Illus. by Kris Di Giacomo. Enchanted Lion, 2014. (Gr. 1–4)

Fleming, Denise. *Alphabet Under Construction*. Illus. by the author. Henry Holt, 2002. (PreK–Gr. 1)

Jeffers, Oliver. *Once Upon an Alphabet*. Illus. by the author. Philomel, 2014. (K–Gr. 4)

Johnson, Stephen T. *Alphabet City*. Illus. by the author. Viking, 1995. (PreK–Gr. 1)

Kalman, Maira. *What Pete Ate from A–Z*. Illus. by the author. Putnam, 2001. (PreK–Gr. 2)

Lobel, Arnold. *On Market Street*. Illus. by Anita Lobel. Greenwillow, 1981. (PreK–Gr. 1)

MacDonald, Suse. *Alphabatics*. Illus. by the author. Simon & Schuster, 1986. (PreK–Gr. 1)

Martin, Bill Jr., and John Archambault. *Chicka Chicka Boom Boom*. Illus. by Lois Ehlert. Simon & Schuster, 1989. (PreK–Gr. 1)

McLeod, Bob. *SuperHero ABC*. Illus. by the author. HarperCollins, 2006. (PreK–Gr. 2)

Seeger, Laura Vaccaro. *The Hidden Alphabet*. Illus. by the author. Roaring Brook, 2003. (PreK–Gr. 1)

Sierra, Judy. *The Sleepy Little Alphabet: A Bedtime Story from Alphabet Town*. Illus. by Melissa Sweet. Knopf, 2009. (PreK–Gr. 1)

Walton, Rick. *So Many Bunnies: A Bedtime ABC and Counting Book*. Illus. by Paige Miglio. HarperCollins, 1998. (PreK–Gr. 1)

Verse

Sing the alphabet song, of course.

Activity

Go on an Alphabet Hunt around the room or outside where children look for items starting with letters you call out.

AMERICA	(*See* United States)

AMPHIBIANS	(*See* Reptiles and Amphibians)

ANIMALS

Read-Alouds

Bayer, Jane. *A My Name Is Alice.* Illus. by Steven Kellogg. Dial, 1984. (PreK–Gr. 1)

Beaumont, Karen. *Move Over, Rover!* Illus. by Jane Dyer. Harcourt, 2006. (PreK–Gr. 1)

Brett, Jan. *The Umbrella.* Illus. by the author. Putnam, 2004. (PreK–Gr. 2)

Calmenson, Stephanie. *Dinner at the Panda Palace.* Illus. by Nadine Bernard Westcott. HarperCollins, 1991. (PreK–Gr. 2)

Cannon, Janell. *Stellaluna.* Illus. by the author. Harcourt, 1993. (PreK–Gr. 2)

Carle, Eric. *"Slowly, Slowly, Slowly," Said the Sloth.* Illus. by the author. Philomel, 2002. (PreK–Gr. 1)

Collard, Sneed B. III. *Animal Dads.* Illus. by Steve Jenkins. Houghton Mifflin, 1997. (PreK–Gr. 3)

Cox, Lynne. *Elizabeth, Queen of the Seas.* Illus. by Brian Floca. Schwartz & Wade, 2014. (PreK–Gr. 4)

Cronin, Doreen. *Diary of a Worm.* Illus. by Harry Bliss. HarperCollins/Joanna Cotler, 2003. (K–Gr. 3)

Davis, Katie. *Who Hops?* Illus. by the author. Harcourt, 1998. (PreK–K)

De Regniers, Beatrice Schenk. *May I Bring a Friend?* Illus. by Beni Montressor. Atheneum, 1964. (PreK–Gr. 1)

Donaldson, Julia. *Superworm.* Illus. by Axel Scheffler. Scholastic/Arthur A. Levine, 2014. (PreK–Gr. 1)

Ehlert, Lois. *Color Zoo.* Illus. by the author. HarperCollins, 1989. (PreK–Gr. 1)

Elliott, David. *In the Wild.* Illus. by Holly Meade. Candlewick, 2010. (PreK–Gr. 3)

French, Jackie. *Diary of a Wombat.* Illus. by Bruce Whatley. Clarion, 2003. (PreK–Gr. 2)

Gibbs, Edward. *I Spy with My Little Eye.* Illus. by the author. Candlewick/Templar, 2011. (PreK–Gr. 1)

Guarino, Deborah. *Is Your Mama a Llama?* Illus. by Stephen Kellogg. Scholastic, 1989. (PreK–Gr. 1)

Jenkins, Steve. *Actual Size.* Illus. by the author. Houghton Mifflin, 2004. (PreK–Gr. 4)

Jenkins, Steve, and Robin Page. *What Do You Do with a Tail Like This?* Illus. by Steve Jenkins. Houghton Mifflin, 2003. (PreK–Gr. 2)

Kurtz, Jane, and Christopher Kurtz. *Water Hole Waiting.* Illus. *by Lee Christiansen. Greenwillow, 2002.* (PreK–Gr. 1)

Logue, Mary. *Sleep Like a Tiger.* Illus. *by Pamela Zagarenski. Houghton Mifflin, 2012.* (PreK–Gr. 1)

Martin, Bill Jr. *Brown Bear, Brown Bear What Do You See?* Illus. *by Eric Carle. Henry Holt, 1967.* (PreK–Gr. 1)

McCall, Francis, and Patricia Keeler. *A Huge Hog Is a Big Pig: A Rhyming Word Game. Greenwillow, 2002.* (K–Gr. 2)

Murray, Marjorie Dennis. *Don't Wake Up the Bear!* Illus. *by Patricia Wittmann. Marshall Cavendish, 2003.* (PreK–Gr. 1)

Raffi. *Down by the Bay.* Illus. *by Nadine Bernard Westcott. Crown, 1987.* (PreK–Gr. 2)

Shapiro, Arnold L. *Mice Squeak, We Speak: A Poem.* Illus. *by Tomie dePaola. Putnam, 1997.* (PreK–Gr. 1)

Shea, Susan A. *Do You Know Which Ones Will Grow?* Illus. *by Tom Slaughter. Blue Apple, 2011.* (PreK–Gr. 2)

Verse

Sing "Animal Crackers" (to the tune of "99 Bottles of Beer on the Wall"):

> Oh, once I ate a lion, and then a tall giraffe.
>
> But when I ate the elephant, he really made me laugh.
>
> Now, you might think I'm fooling, but I will tell you true
>
> That they were ANIMAL CRACKERS, and you can eat them, too!

Activity

Using Play-Doh or Model Magic, have children make little animal cracker–size animals (not for eating, of course), and have an animal parade.

ANTS

(*See also* Insects)

Read-Alouds

Allinson, Beverly. *Effie.* Illus. *by Barbara Reid. Scholastic, 1990.* (PreK–Gr. 2)

Dorros, Arthur. *Ant Cities.* Illus. *by the author. HarperCollins, 1987.* (PreK–Gr. 2)

Hoose, Philip, and Hannah Hoose. *Hey, Little Ant.* Illus. *by Debbie Tilley. Tricycle, 1998.* (PreK–Gr. 2)

Peet, Bill. *The Ant and the Elephant.* Illus. by the author. Houghton Mifflin, 1972. (PreK–Gr. 2)

Pinczes, Elinor J. *One Hundred Hungry Ants.* Illus. by Bonnie MacKain. Houghton Mifflin, 1993. (PreK–Gr. 2)

Van Allsburg, Chris. *Two Bad Ants.* Illus. by the author. Houghton Mifflin, 1988. (K–Gr. 3)

Verse

Sing "The Ants Go Marching One by One," which you can find at www .kididdles.com/lyrics/allsongs.html; or use the fingerplay "The Ant Hill":

Here's the ant hill, with no ants about; (*make a fist*)

And I say, "Little ants, won't you please come out?" (*look at your fist*)

Out they come trooping in answer to my call (*lift each finger from your fist to represent the ants*)

One, two, three, four, five, and that's all. (*have the ants crawl about*)

Activity

Kids can make pipe-cleaner ants and have them march around the room.

APOLOGIES, FORGIVENESS, AND MANNERS

Read-Alouds

Havill Juanita. *Jamaica's Blue Marker.* Illus. by Anne Sibley O'Brien. Houghton Mifflin, 1995. (PreK–Gr. 2)

Henkes, Kevin. *Lilly's Purple Plastic Purse.* Illus. by the author. Greenwillow, 1996. (PreK–Gr. 2)

Joslin, Sesyle. *What Do You Say, Dear?* Illus. by Maurice Sendak. HarperCollins, 1958. (PreK–Gr. 2)

Muth, Jon J. *Zen Shorts.* Illus. by the author. Scholastic, 2005. (K–Gr. 3)

Seeger, Laura Vaccaro. *Bully.* Illus. by the author. Roaring Brook, 2013. (PreK–Gr. 6)

Seeger, Pete. *Abiyoyo.* Illus. by Michael Hays. Simon & Schuster, 1986. (PreK–Gr. 2)

Soto, Gary. *Too Many Tamales.* Illus. by Ed Martinez. Putnam, 1993. (PreK–Gr. 3)

Willems, Mo. *I Love My New Toy.* Illus. by the author. Hyperion, 2008. (PreK–Gr. 2)

Verse

Recite "Table Manners" by Gelett Burgess, ©1900:

> The Goops they lick their fingers,
>
> And the Goops they lick their knives;
>
> They spill their broth on the tablecloth,
>
> Oh, they lead disgusting lives!
>
> The Goops they talk while eating,
>
> And loud and fast they chew;
>
> And that is why I'm glad that I
>
> Am not a Goop—are you?

Activity

Have children practice making apologies and using their manners in different silly situations, such as, "I'm so sorry my cat ate your goldfish," or "Thank you for this delicious lima-bean-Brussels-sprouts-and-broccoli stew." This activity was inspired by Sesyle Joslin's book on manners and apologies, *What Do You Say, Dear?*

APPLES   (*See also* Fruits and Vegetables)

Read-Alouds

Codell, Esmé Raji. *Seed by Seed: The Legend and Legacy of John "Appleseed" Chapman.* *Illus. by Lynne Rae Perkins. Greenwillow, 2012.* (Gr. 1–4)

Hall, Zoe. *The Apple Pie Tree.* *Illus. by Shari Halpern. Scholastic/Blue Sky, 1996.* (PreK–Gr. 1)

Kleven, Elisa. *The Apple Doll.* *Illus. by the author. Farrar, 2007.* (PreK–Gr. 1)

Lipson, Eden Ross. *Applesauce Season.* *Illus. by Mordicai Gerstein. Roaring Brook, 2009.* (PreK–Gr. 2)

Maestro, Betsy. *How Do Apples Grow?* Illus. by Giulio Maestro. HarperCollins, 1992. (PreK–Gr. 2)

Murray, Alison. *Apple Pie ABC.* *Illus. by the author. Disney-Hyperion, 2011.* (PreK–Gr. 1)

Verse

Sing "I Like to Eat Apples and Bananas," which you can find at www.kididdles .com/lyrics/allsongs.html.

Activity

Make homemade applesauce. Quarter apples and place them in a large saucepan. Add ½ to one cup of water for every four apples; cover and simmer till very soft, about twenty minutes. Run apples through a food mill or Foley grinder to remove the seeds and skin. Stir in sugar to taste (two to four tablespoons per four apples), cinnamon, and, if you like, a small pat of butter. Yum.

APRIL FOOL'S DAY

Read-Alouds

Bateman, Teresa. *April Foolishness.* Illus. by Nadine Bernard Westcott. Albert Whitman, 2004. (PreK–Gr. 2)

Egan, Tim. *Serious Farm.* Illus. by the author. Houghton Mifflin, 2003. (PreK–Gr. 2)

LeSieg, Theo. *Wacky Wednesday.* Illus. by the author. Beginner Books, 1974. (PreK–Gr. 2)

McMullan, Kate. *Pearl and Wagner: One Funny Day.* Illus. by R. W. Alley. Dial, 2009. (PreK–Gr. 2)

Verse

Sing "April Fool." You'll find the lyrics, sheet music, and MIDI file kids can sing along to at www.msu.edu/~eulenber/John/Songs/AprilFool.html.

Activity

For a snack, make individual plastic cups of Jell-O. Place a straw in each cup (and maybe a tiny plastic bag) so when the Jell-O hardens, it looks like a cup of juice. (Be sure to check with caregivers about allergies first.)

ARITHMETIC   (*See* Counting; Mathematics)

ART AND ARTISTS

Read-Alouds

Carle, Eric. *The Artist Who Painted a Blue Horse.* Illus. by the author. Philomel, 2011. (PreK–Gr. 3)

Colón, Raul. *Draw!* Illus. by the author. Simon & Schuster, 2014. (PreK–Gr. 2)

Degen, Bruce. *I Gotta Draw.* Illus. by the author. HarperCollins, 2012. (PreK–Gr. 3)

DePaola, Tomie. *The Art Lesson.* Illus. by the author. Putnam, 1989. (PreK–Gr. 3)

Gerstein, Mordicai. *The First Drawing.* Illus. by the author. Little, Brown, 2013. (PreK–Gr. 2)

Hurd, Thacher. *Art Dog.* Illus. by the author. HarperCollins, 1996. (PreK–Gr. 2)

Johnson, Crockett. *Harold and the Purple Crayon.* HarperCollins, 1955. (PreK–Gr. 2)

LaMarche, Jim. *The Raft.* Illus. by the author. HarperCollins, 2000. (PreK–Gr. 2)

Lichtenheld, Tom. *Bridget's Beret.* Illus. by the author. Henry Holt/Christy Ottaviano, 2010. (K–Gr. 2)

Light, Kelly. *Louise Loves Art.* Illus. by the author. Balzer + Bray, 2014. (PreK–Gr. 2)

McCarthy, Meghan. *Steal Back the Mona Lisa.* Illus. by the author. Harcourt, 2006. (PreK–Gr. 2)

Reynolds, Peter H. *The Dot.* Illus. by the author. Candlewick, 2003. (K–Gr. 4)

Wiesner, David. *Art & Max.* Illus. by the author. Clarion, 2010. (PreK–Gr. 3)

Verse

To the tune of "Frères Jacques," sing "Cezanne's Apples" as you take an online tour of the Metropolitan Museum of Art in New York City (www .metmuseum.org/metmedia/kids-zone/start-with-art/sing-along).

Activity

Children pair off and draw portraits of each other. Show the portraits to the whole group and see if they can guess who is who.

ASTRONAUTS	(*See* Space)
ASTRONOMY	(*See* Space)
AUTHORS	(*See* Books and Reading; Libraries and Librarians)
AUTOMOBILES	(*See* Cars and Buses; Trucks)
AUTUMN	(*See* Seasons; Weather; Winter)

BABIES

Read-Alouds

Bertrand, Lynne. *Granite Baby.* Illus. by Kevin Hawkes. Farrar, 2005. (PreK–Gr. 3)

Fox, Mem. *Ten Little Fingers and Ten Little Toes.* Illus. by the author. Harcourt, 2008. (PreK)

Frazee, Marla. *The Boss Baby*. Illus. by the author. Beach Lane, 2010. (PreK–Gr. 3)

Frazee, Marla. *Walk On! A Guide for Babies of All Ages*. Illus. by the author. Harcourt, 2006. (PreK–Gr. 2)

Harris, Robie H. *Mail Harry to the Moon!* Illus. by Michael Emberley. Little, Brown, 2008. (PreK–Gr. 2)

Henkes, Kevin. *Julius, the Baby of the World*. Illus. by the author. Greenwillow, 1990. (PreK–Gr. 2)

Hoban, Russell. *A Baby Sister for Frances*. Illus. by Lillian Hoban. HarperCollins, 1964. (PreK–Gr. 2)

James, Simon. *Baby Brains*. Illus. by the author. Candlewick, 2004. (PreK–Gr. 1)

Keats, Ezra Jack. *Peter's Chair*. Illus. by the author. HarperCollins, 1967. (PreK–Gr. 1)

Schaefer, Lola M. *One Special Day (A Story for Big Brothers and Sisters)*. Illus. by Jessica Meserve. Disney-Hyperion, 2012. (PreK–Gr. 1)

Sturges, Philemon. *How Do You Make a Baby Smile?* Illus. by the author. HarperCollins, 2007. (PreK–Gr. 1)

Williams, Vera B. *"More More More" Said the Baby: 3 Love Stories*. Illus. by the author. Greenwillow, 1990. (PreK–Gr. 1)

Verse
Recite or sing "Hush Little Baby, Don't Say a Word," which you can find at www.kididdles.com/lyrics/allsongs.html, and "Rockabye Baby" on page 282.

Activity
Make rattles out of empty salad-dressing bottles by filling them with colored beads, sealing them with glue, and covering the labels with decorated drawings.

BABYSITTERS AND BABYSITTING

Read-Alouds
Child, Lauren. *Clarice Bean, Guess Who's Babysitting?* Illus. by the author. Candlewick, 2001. (K–Gr. 2)

Hughes, Shirley. *An Evening at Alfie's*. Illus. by the author. Lothrop, 1984. (PreK–Gr. 1)

Long, Melinda. *Pirates Don't Change Diapers*. Illus. by David Shannon. Harcourt, 2007. (PreK–Gr. 1)

Schwartz, Amy. *Willie and Uncle Bill*. Illus. by the author. Holiday House, 2012. (PreK–Gr. 2)

Verse

Read the poem "The Sitter" from *A Light in the Attic* by Shel Silverstein.

Activity

Ask children what makes a great babysitter and ask them to make a list of the fun things they do with their favorite sitters.

BAKERS AND BAKING　　　(*See* Themed Program: I'm Hungry on page 299)

BALLET　　　(*See* Booklist: Dance on page 168)

BASEBALL　　　(*See* Sports)

BATHS

Read-Alouds

Andreasen, Dan. *The Treasure Bath*. *Illus. by the author. Henry Holt, 2009.* (PreK–Gr. 1)

Arnold, Tedd. *No More Water in the Tub!* *Illus. by the author. Dial, 1995.* (PreK–Gr. 1)

Conrad, Pam. *The Tub People*. *Illus. by Richard Egielski. HarperCollins, 1989.* (PreK–Gr. 1)

Goodman, Joan Elizabeth. *Bernard's Bath*. *Illus. by Dominic Catalano. Boyds Mills, 1996.* (PreK–Gr. 1)

Pomerantz, Charlotte. *The Piggy in the Puddle*. *Illus. by James Marshall. Macmillan, 1974.* (PreK–Gr. 2)

Willems, Mo. *The Pigeon Needs a Bath*. *Illus. by the author. Hyperion, 2014.* (PreK–Gr. 5)

Wood, Audrey. *King Bidgood's in the Bathtub*. *Illus. by Don Wood. Harcourt, 1985.* (PreK–Gr. 3)

Zion, Gene. *Harry the Dirty Dog*. *Illus. by Margaret Bloy Graham. HarperCollins, 1956.* (PreK–Gr. 2)

Verse

Sing or recite "Gladys, Where Are You Going?" on page 140.

Activity

Children can take a pretend bubble bath with bubbles you shoot from a bubble gun. They can use a pretend hose to rinse off and a pretend towel to dry themselves.

BEACHES (*See* Ocean and Seashore)

BEARS (*See also* Stuffed Animals and Toys)

Read-Alouds

Becker, Bonny. *A Visitor for Bear.* Illus. by Kady MacDonald Denton. Candlewick, 2008. (PreK–Gr. 2) (And others in the Bear series.)

Beer, Hans de. *Little Polar Bear.* Illus. by the author. North-South, 1987. (PreK–Gr. 1)

Brett, Jan. *Goldilocks and the Three Bears.* Illus. by the author. Putnam, 1987. (PreK–Gr. 2)

Brett, Jan. *Three Snow Bears.* Illus. by the author. Putnam, 2007. (PreK–Gr. 2)

Elya, Susan Middleton. *Rubia and the Three Osos.* Illus. by Melissa Sweet. Disney-Hyperion, 2010. (PreK–Gr. 2)

Henkes, Kevin. *Old Bear.* Illus. by the author. Greenwillow, 2008. (PreK–Gr. 1)

John, Jory. *Goodnight Already!* Illus. by Benji Davies. Harper, 2015. (PreK–Gr. 2)

Kinsey-Warnock, Natalie. *The Bear That Heard Crying.* Illus. by Ted Rand. Dutton, 1993. (PreK–Gr. 2)

Lamb, Albert. *Tell Me the Day Backwards.* Illus. by David McPhail. Candlewick, 2011. (PreK–Gr. 1)

McCloskey, Robert. *Blueberries for Sal.* Illus. by the author. Viking, 1948. (PreK–Gr. 1)

Murray, Marjorie Dennis. *Don't Wake Up the Bear!* Illus. by Patricia Wittmann. Marshall Cavendish, 2003. (PreK–Gr. 1)

Pinkwater, Daniel. *Irving and Muktuk: Two Bad Bears.* Illus. by Jill Pinkwater. Houghton Mifflin, 2003. (PreK–Gr. 2)

Rosen, Michael. *We're Going on a Bear Hunt.* Illus. by Helen Oxenbury. McElderry, 1989. (PreK–Gr. 2)

Soman, David. *Three Bears in a Boat.* Illus. by the author. Dial, 2014. (PreK–Gr. 2)

Stevens, Janet. *Tops & Bottoms.* Illus. by the author. Harcourt, 1995. (PreK–Gr. 3)

Stower, Adam. *Silly Doggy!* Illus. by the author. Orchard, 2012. (PreK–Gr. 1)

Turkle, Brinton. *Deep in the Forest.* Illus. by the author. Dutton, 1976. (PreK–Gr. 1)

Ward, Lynd. *The Biggest Bear.* Illus. by the author. Houghton Mifflin, 1952. (PreK–Gr. 2)

Verse

Sing "The Bear Went Over the Mountain," which you can find at www
.kididdles.com/lyrics/allsongs.html.

Activity

Encourage children to bring in their teddies and have a teddy-bear party.

BEDTIME (*See* Themed Program: Time for Bed on page 280)

BEHAVIOR (*See* also Bullies; Compassion and Kindness; Emotions)

Read-Alouds

Allard, Harry. *Miss Nelson Is Missing*. *Illus. by James Marshall. Houghton Mifflin,*
1985. (K–Gr. 3)

Ashman, Linda. *M Is for Mischief: An A to Z of Naughty Children*. *Illus. by Nancy Car-*
penter. Dutton, 2008. (K–Gr. 2)

Beaumont, Karen. *I Ain't Gonna Paint No More*. *Illus. by David Catrow. Harcourt,*
2005. (K–Gr. 2)

Becker, Bonny. *Bedtime for Bear*. *Illus. by Kady MacDonald Denton. Candlewick,*
2010. (PreK–Gr. 2)

Bottner, Barbara. *Bootsie Barker Bites*. *Illus. by Peggy Rathmann. Putnam, 1992.*
(PreK–Gr. 1)

Brown, Peter. *My Teacher Is a Monster! (No, I Am Not.) Illus. by the author. Little,*
Brown, 2014. (PreK–Gr. 2)

Cooper, Ilene. *Jake's Best Thumb*. *Illus. by Claudio Munoz. Dutton, 2008.* (PreK–Gr. 1)

Cordell, Matthew. *Trouble Gum*. *Illus. by the author. Feiwel and Friends, 2009.*
(PreK–Gr. 2)

Dewdney, Anna. *Llama Llama Mad at Mama*. *Illus. by the author. Viking, 2007.*
(PreK–K)

Elliott, David. *Finn Throws a Fit*. *Illus. by Timothy Basil Ering. Candlewick, 2009.*
(PreK–Gr. 2)

Gall, Chris. *Substitute Creacher*. *Illus. by the author. Little, Brown, 2011.* (K–Gr. 2)

Knudsen, Michelle. *Big Mean Mike*. *Illus. by Scott Magoon. Candlewick, 2012.*
(PreK–Gr. 2)

O'Neill, Alexis. *The Recess Queen*. *Illus. by Laura Huliska-Beith. Scholastic, 2002.*
(PreK–Gr. 2)

Rosenthal, Amy Krouse. *Cookies: Bite-Size Life Lessons.* Illus. by Jane Dyer. Harper-Collins, 2006. (PreK–Gr. 2)

Salley, Coleen. *Epossumondas.* Illus. by Janet Stevens. Harcourt, 2002. (PreK–Gr. 2)

Shannon, David. *David Gets in Trouble.* Illus. by the author. Scholastic, 2002. (PreK–Gr. 1)

Viorst, Judith. *Alexander, Who's Trying His Best to Be the Best Boy Ever.* Illus. by Isidre Monés. Atheneum, 2014. (PreK–Gr. 2)

Willems, Mo. *Leonardo the Terrible Monster.* Illus. by the author. Hyperion, 2005. (PreK–Gr. 2)

Woodson, Jacqueline. *Each Kindness.* Illus. by E. B. Lewis. Penguin/Nancy Paulsen, 2012. (K–Gr. 4)

Verse

Tell and sing "Little Bunny Foo Foo." You can find our version in volume 1, *The Handbook for Storytellers,* or online at bussongs.com/songs/little-bunny-foo-foo.php.

Activity

Act out the "Little Bunny Foo Foo" story in groups of four (with one Foo Foo, one Fairy Godmother, and two field mice who say, "Ouch!").

BICYCLES

(*See also* Airplanes; Boats and Ships; Cars and Buses; Trains; Trucks)

Read-Alouds

Gerstein, Mordicai. *How to Bicycle to the Moon to Plant Sunflowers: A Simple but Brilliant Plan in 24 Easy Steps.* Illus. by the author. Roaring Brook, 2013. (PreK–Gr. 2)

Hobbie, Holly. *Everything But the Horse.* Illus. by the author. Little, Brown, 2010. (K–Gr. 3)

McLeod, Emilie Warren. *The Bear's Bicycle.* Illus. by David McPhail. Little Brown, 1975. (PreK–Gr. 1)

Mollel, Tololwa M. *My Rows and Piles of Coins.* Illus. by E. B. Lewis. Clarion, 1999. (PreK–Gr. 3)

Raschka, Chris. *Everyone Can Learn to Ride a Bicycle.* Illus. by the author. Schwartz & Wade, 2013. (PreK–Gr. 2)

Rey, H. A. *Curious George Rides a Bike.* Illus. by the author. Houghton Mifflin, 1952. (PreK–Gr. 2)

Shannon, David. *Duck on a Bike.* Illus. by the author. Scholastic, 2002. (PreK–Gr. 1)

Verse
Recite "My Bicycle" (be seated when you do it):

> One wheel, two wheels on the ground.
>
> My feet make the pedals go round and round. (*pedal with feet*)
>
> Handlebars help me steer so straight
> > (*hold hands on bars and pretend to steer*)
>
> Down the sidewalk and through the gate!
> > (*hold handlebars while pedaling with feet*)

Activity
Make bicycle streamers with rubber bands (to go around handlebars or wrists), tied with ribbons.

BIRDS   (*See also* Chickens; Ducks and Geese; Owls; Penguins)

Read-Alouds
Brett, Jan. *Honey, Honey—Lion!* Illus. by the author. Putnam, 2005. (PreK–Gr. 2)

Ehlert, Lois. *Feathers for Lunch.* Illus. by the author. Harcourt, 1990. (PreK–Gr. 1)

Elliott, David. *On the Wing.* Illus. by Becca Stadlander. Candlewick, 2014. (K–Gr. 4)

Graham, Bob. *How to Heal a Broken Wing.* Illus. by the author. Candlewick, 2008. (PreK–Gr. 3)

Henkes, Kevin. *Birds.* Illus. by Laura Dronzek. Greenwillow, 2009. (PreK–Gr. 1)

Hutchins, Pat. *Good-Night, Owl!* Illus. by the author. Macmillan, 1972. (PreK–Gr. 1)

James, Simon. *George Flies South.* Illus. by the author. Candlewick, 2011. (PreK–Gr. 1)

Kirby, Pamela F. *What Bluebirds Do.* Photos by the author. Boyds Mills, 2009. (PreK–Gr. 2)

Ruddel, Deborah. *Today at the Bluebird Café: A Branchful of Birds.* Illus. by Joan Rankin. McElderry, 2007. (PreK–Gr. 3)

Sayre, April Pulley. *If You Should Hear a Honey Guide.* Illus. by S. D. Schindler. Houghton Mifflin, 1995. (PreK–Gr. 2)

Soltis, Sue. *Nothing Like a Puffin.* Illus. by Bob Kolar. Candlewick, 2011. (PreK–Gr. 2)

Stewart, Melissa. *Feathers: Not Just for Flying*. *Illus. by Sarah S. Brannen. Charlesbridge, 2014.* (Gr. 1–4)

Ward, Jennifer. *Mama Built a Little Nest*. *Illus. by Steve Jenkins. Beach Lane, 2014.* (PreK–Gr. 3)

Willems, Mo. *Don't Let the Pigeon Drive the Bus*. *Illus. by the author. Hyperion, 2003.* (PreK–Gr. 6) (And others in the Pigeon series.)

Willems, Mo. *There Is a Bird on Your Head*. *Illus. by the author. Hyperion, 2007.* (PreK–Gr. 2)

Young, Ed. *Hook*. *Illus. by the author. Roaring Brook, 2009.* (PreK–Gr. 3)

Verse

Recite the fingerplay "Two Little Blackbirds":

> Two little black birds, sitting on the hill.
> > (*hold up one finger of each hand*)
>
> One named Jack, the other named Jill.
>
> Fly away, Jack! (*put one hand behind your back*)
>
> Fly away, Jill! (*put the other hand behind you back*)
>
> Come back, Jack! (*bring the first hand from behind your back*)
>
> Come back, Jill! (*bring the second hand from behind your back*)

Activity

Make handprint peacocks and other birds with paint and paper.

BIRTHDAYS   (*See also* Gifts)

Read-Alouds

Becker, Bonny. *A Birthday for Bear*. *Illus. by Kady MacDonald Denton. Candlewick, 2009.* (PreK–Gr. 2)

Carle, Eric. *The Secret Birthday Message*. *Illus. by the author. Crowell, 1972.* (PreK–Gr. 1)

Flack, Marjorie. *Ask Mr. Bear*. *Illus. by the author. Macmillan, 1932.* (PreK–K)

Howe, James. *Houndsley and Catina and the Birthday Surprise*. *Illus. by Marie-Louise Gay. Candlewick Press, 2006.* (PreK–Gr. 1)

Keats, Ezra Jack. *A Letter to Amy*. *Illus. by the author. HarperCollins, 1968.* (PreK–Gr. 1)

Khan, Rukhsana. *Big Red Lollipop.* Illus. by Sophie Blackall. Viking, 2010. (PreK–Gr. 3)

Kleven, Elisa. *Hooray! A Piñata!* Illus. by the author. Dutton, 1996. (PreK–Gr. 2)

Kulka, Joe. *Wolf's Coming!* Illus. by the author. Carolrhoda, 2007. (PreK–Gr. 1)

Patricelli, Leslie. *The Birthday Box.* Illus. by the author. Candlewick Press, 2007. (PreK)

Ryan, Pam Muñoz. *Mice and Beans.* Illus. by Joe Cepeda. Scholastic, 2001. (PreK–Gr. 2)

Soto, Gary. *Chato and the Party Animals.* Illus. by Susan Guevara. Putnam, 2000. (PreK–Gr. 2)

Zolotow, Charlotte. *Mr. Rabbit and the Lovely Present.* Illus. by Maurice Sendak. HarperCollins, 1962. (PreK–Gr. 1)

Verse
Sing "Happy Birthday to You."

Activity
Hold an un-birthday party with balloons, candles to blow out, a game of "Pin the Tail on the Donkey," and maybe even a piñata.

BLACK HISTORY MONTH   (*See* African Americans)

BLIZZARDS   (*See* Weather; Winter)

BOATS AND SHIPS
(*See also* Airplanes; Bicycles, Cars and Buses; Trains; Trucks)

Read-Alouds

Burningham, John. *Mr. Gumpy's Outing.* Illus. by the author. Henry Holt, 1970. (PreK–Gr. 1)

Crews, Donald. *Sail Away.* Illus. by the author. Greenwillow, 1995. (PreK–Gr. 1)

De Sève, Randall. *Toy Boat.* Illus. by Loren Long. Philomel, 2007. (PreK–Gr. 1)

Floca, Brian. *Lightship.* Illus. by the author. Atheneum, 2007. (PreK–Gr. 1)

Gramatky, Hardie. *Little Toot.* Illus. by the author. Putnam, 1939. (PreK–Gr. 1)

McMullan, Kate. *I'm Mighty.* Illus. by Jim McMullan. HarperCollins, 2003. (PreK–Gr. 1)

Verse

Sing "Sailing, Sailing, Over the Bounding Main" (Lyrics and tune at www
.kididdles.com/lyrics/i075.html), and "A Sailor Went to Sea," an action
rhyme with lots of fun verses (kidsongs.wordpress.com/2008/04/09/sailor
-went-to-sea).

Activity

Make floating boats with found materials like aluminum foil, little Styrofoam trays, corks, and popsicle sticks for masts. Float them in a puddle or a
wading pool.

BOOKS AND READING   (*See also* Libraries and Librarians)

Read-Alouds

Barnett, Mac. *Chloe and the Lion.* *Illus. by Adam Rex. Disney-Hyperion Books, 2012.*
(K–Gr. 4)

Becker, Bonny. *A Library Book for Bear.* *Illus. by Kady MacDonald Denton. Candlewick, 2014.* (PreK–Gr. 2)

Bottner, Barbara. *Miss Brooks Loves Books! (And I Don't).* *Illus. by Michael Emberley.
Knopf/Borzoi, 2010.* (PreK–Gr. 2)

Christelow, Eileen. *Five Little Monkeys Reading in Bed.* *Illus. by the author. Clarion,
2011.* (PreK–Gr. 1)

Donaldson, Julia. *Charlie Cook's Favorite Book.* *Illus. by Axel Scheffler. Dial, 2006.*
(PreK–Gr. 2)

Ernst, Lisa Campbell. *Stella Louella's Runaway Book.* *Illus. by the author. Simon &
Schuster, 1998.* (PreK–Gr. 2)

Freedman, Deborah. *The Story of Fish and Snail.* *Illus. by the author. Viking, 2013.*
(PreK–Gr. 1)

Joyce, William. *The Fantastic Flying Books of Mr. Morris Lessmore.* *Illus. by the author
and Joe Bluhm. Atheneum, 2012.* (K–Gr. 4)

Kirk, David. *Library Mouse.* *Illus. by the author. Abrams, 2007.* (PreK–Gr. 2)

Klausmeier, Jesse. *Open This Little Book.* *Illus. by Suzy Lee. Chronicle, 2013.*
(PreK–Gr. 2)

Kohara, Kazuno. *The Midnight Library.* *Illus. by the author. Roaring Brook, 2014.*
(PreK–Gr. 1)

McDonnell, Patrick. *A Perfectly Messed-Up Story.* Illus. by the author. Little, Brown, 2014. (PreK–Gr. 2)

McPhail, David. *Fix-It.* Illus. by the author. Dutton, 1984. (PreK–Gr. 1)

Rylant, Cynthia. *Mr. Putter and Tabby Write the Book.* Illus. by Arthur Howard. Harcourt, 2004. (PreK–Gr. 2)

Sierra, Judy. *Wild about Books.* Illus. by Marc Brown. Knopf, 2004. (PreK–Gr. 3)

Willems, Mo. *We Are in a Book!* Illus. by the author. Hyperion, 2010. (PreK–Gr. 2)

Verse

Sing "Hi Ho Librario" by Jane Scherer, ©1980 (to the tune of the "The Farmer in the Dell"):

The author writes the book, the author writes the book;
> (*pantomime writing or typing*)

Hi ho librario, the author writes the book.

The illustrator draws, the illustrator draws; (*pantomime painting*)

Hi ho librario, the illustrator draws.

The publisher puts it together, the publisher puts it together; (*hold hands out as if you are holding a book, and then slap them closed*)

Hi ho librario, the publisher puts it together.

The copyright tells us when they made the book, and then,
> (*draw a great big letter C in the air and a circle around it, like the sign for copyright: ©*)

Hi ho librario, let's sing it once again.

Activity

Make a book out of one piece of paper, folded in quarters. Staple the middle fold, slice through the top where the paper is folded, and you have an eight-page book for kids to use to write and illustrate a little story.

BOOTS AND SHOES   (*See also* Clothing and Dress; Hats)

Read-Alouds

Daly, Niki. *Not So Fast, Songololo.* Illus. by the author. Frances Lincoln, 2001, c1986. (PreK–Gr. 2)

Dunrea, Olivier. *Gossie.* Illus. by the author. Houghton Mifflin, 2002. (PreK–K)

Gormley, Greg. **Dog in Boots**. *Illus. by Roberta Angaramo. Holiday House, 2011.* (PreK–Gr. 2)

Hughes, Shirley. **Alfie's Feet**. *Lothrop, 1982.* (PreK–Gr. 1)

Hurwitz, Johanna. **New Shoes for Silvia**. *Illus. by Jerry Pinkney. Morrow, 1993.* (PreK–Gr. 1)

Litwin, Eric. **Pete the Cat: I Love My White Shoes**. *Illus. by James Dean. HarperCollins, 2010.* (PreK–Gr. 1)

Murray, Alison. **One Two That's My Shoe!** *Illus. by the author. Disney-Hyperion Books, 2012.* (PreK–Gr. 1)

Swinburne, Stephen R. **Whose Shoes? A Shoe for Every Job**. *Photos by the author. Boyds Mills, 2010.* (PreK–Gr. 1)

Winthrop, Elizabeth. **Shoes**. *Illus. by William Joyce. HarperCollins, 1986.* (PreK–Gr. 1)

Verse
Recite the nursery rhyme "There Was an Old Woman Who Lived in a Shoe."

Activity
Play the Pass the Shoe Game, described in Chapter 1 on page 8.

BROTHERS   (*See* Siblings)

BULLIES

Read-Alouds
Buehner, Caralyn. **Dex: The Heart of a Hero**. *HarperCollins, 2004.* (PreK–Gr. 2)

Cannon, Janell. **Crickwing**. *Illus. by the author. Harcourt, 2000.* (PreK–Gr. 2)

Caseley, Judith. **Bully**. *Illus. by the author. Greenwillow, 2001.* (PreK–Gr. 6)

Hoose, Philip, and Hannah Hoose. **Hey, Little Ant**. *Illus. by Debbie Tilley. Tricycle, 1998.* (PreK–Gr. 2)

Lester, Helen. **Hooway for Wodney Wat**. *Illus. by Lynn Munsinger. Houghton Mifflin, 1999.* (PreK–Gr. 2)

Meddaugh, Susan. **Martha Walks the Dog**. *Illus. by the author. Houghton Mifflin, 1998.* (PreK–Gr. 2)

Otoshi, Kathryn. **One**. *Illus. by the author. KO Kids, 2008.* (PreK–Gr. 2)

Pinkney, Brian. *The Adventures of Sparrowboy.* *Illus. by the author. Simon & Schuster, 1997.* (PreK–Gr. 2)

Rostoker-Gruber, Karen. *Ferret Fun.* *Illus. by Paul Rátz de Tagyos. Marshall Cavendish, 2011.* (PreK–Gr. 1)

Seeger, Laura Vaccaro. *Bully.* *Illus. by the author. Roaring Brook, 2013.* (PreK–Gr. 6)

Swope, Sam. *The Araboolies of Liberty Street.* *Illus. by Barry Root. Crown, 1989.* (PreK–Gr. 3)

Verse

Recite "Terrible Tim" by Leroy F. Jackson, from *The Peter Patter Book of Nursery Rhymes*, ©1918:

> Haven't you heard of Terrible Tim!
> Well, don't you get in the way of him.
> He eats lions for breakfast and leopards for lunch,
> And gobbles them down with one terrible crunch.
> He could mix a whole city all up in a mess,
> He could drink up a sea or an ocean, I guess.
> You'd better be watching for Terrible Tim,
> And run when you first get your peepers on him.

Activity

Brainstorm with children some words to say to stop a bully in his or her tracks. On one set of sentence strips, have children write kind and polite words; on another, write words bullies use. Kids can sort them and use the kind words to start a dialogue. At the close of the activity, dramatically throw the mean words in a trash can.

BUTTERFLIES

Read-Alouds

Aston, Dianna Hutts. *A Butterfly Is Patient.* *Illus. by Sylvia Long. Chronicle, 2011.* (PreK–Gr. 3)

Bishop, Nic. *Nic Bishop Butterflies and Moths.* *Photos by Nic Bishop. Scholastic, 2009.* (PreK–Gr. 3)

Carle, Eric. *The Very Hungry Caterpillar.* *Illus. by the author. Philomel, 1969.* (PreK–Gr. 1)

Edwards, Pamela Duncan. *Clara Caterpillar.* *Illus. by Henry Cole. HarperCollins, 2001.* (PreK–Gr. 1)

Ehlert, Lois. *Waiting for Wings.* *Illus. by the author. Harcourt, 2001.* (PreK–Gr. 1)

Heiligman, Deborah. *From Caterpillar to Butterfly.* *Illus. by Bari Weissman. Harper-Collins, 1996.* (PreK–Gr. 2)

Swope, Sam. *Gotta Go! Gotta Go!* *Illus. by Sue Riddle. Farrar, 2000.* (PreK–Gr. 2)

Verse

Recite "A Rabble of Butterflies" by R. Wayne Freeman:

> Once as I wandered, lonely as a cloud,
>
> I heard loud shouts from a far away crowd:
>
> "It's a bird, it's a plane, look up in the skies!"
>
> It was only a rabble of butterflies.

Activity

Make butterflies out of tissue paper and pipe cleaners.

CANDY   (*See* Themed Program: I'm Hungry on page 299)

CARS AND BUSES

(*See also* Airplanes; Bicycles, Boats and Ships; Trains; Trucks)

Read-Alouds

Barton, Byron. *My Car.* *Illus. by the author. Greenwillow, 2001.* (PreK–K)

Bee, William. *And the Cars Go. . . . Illus. by the author. Candlewick, 2013.* (PreK–Gr. 1)

DiCamillo, Kate. *Mercy Watson Goes for a Ride.* *Illus. by Chris Van Dusen. Candlewick, 2006.* (K–Gr. 2)

Floca, Brian. *The Racecar Alphabet.* *Illus. by the author. Atheneum, 2003.* (PreK–Gr. 1)

Hort, Lenny. *The Seals on the Bus.* *Illus. by G. Brian Karas. Henry Holt, 2000.* (PreK–Gr. 1)

Medina, Meg. *Tía Isa Wants a Car.* *Illus. by Claudio Muñoz. Candlewick, 2011.* (PreK–Gr. 3)

Root, Phyllis. *Rattletrap Car.* *Illus. by Jill Barton. Candlewick, 2001.* (PreK–Gr. 1)

Singer, Marilyn. *I'm Your Bus.* *Illus. by Evan Polenghi. Scholastic, 2009.* (PreK–Gr. 1)

Steen, Sandra, and Susan Steen. *Car Wash.* *Illus. by G. Brian Karas. Putnam, 2001.* (PreK–Gr. 1)

Van Lieshout, Maria. *Backseat ABC.* Illus. by the author. Chronicle, 2012. (PreK–Gr. 1)

Willems, Mo. *Don't Let the Pigeon Drive the Bus.* Illus. by the author. Hyperion, 2003. (PreK–Gr. 6)

Willems, Mo. *Let's Go for a Drive.* Illus. by the author. Hyperion, 2012. (PreK–Gr. 2)

Zelinsky, Paul O. *The Wheels on the Bus.* Illus. by the author. Dutton, 1990. (PreK–Gr. 1)

Verse
Sing "The Wheels on the Bus."

Activity
Set up chairs—with a big one up front for the bus driver—and act out the song "The Wheels on the Bus" as you sing it. Hand out old CDs or records as your steering wheels, and have children drive around the room, obeying traffic rules (e.g., yield, slow, red light).

CATS

Read-Alouds

Bruel, Nick. *Bad Kitty.* Illus. by the author. Roaring Brook, 2005. (PreK–Gr. 2)

Burningham, John. *It's a Secret!* Illus. by the author. Candlewick, 2009. (PreK–Gr. 1)

Calhoun, Mary. *Cross-Country Cat.* Illus. by Erick Ingraham. Morrow, 1979. (PreK–Gr. 2)

Gág, Wanda. *Millions of Cats.* Illus. by the author. Coward-McCann, 1928. (PreK–Gr. 1)

Gantos, Jack. *Rotten Ralph.* Illus. by Nicole Rubel. Houghton Mifflin, 1976. (PreK–Gr. 1)

Henkes, Kevin. *Kitten's First Full Moon.* Illus. by the author. Greenwillow, 2004. (PreK–Gr. 1)

Litwin, Eric. *Pete the Cat: I Love My White Shoes.* Illus. by James Dean. HarperCollins, 2010. (PreK–Gr. 1)

McClure, Nikki. *How to Be a Cat.* Illus. by the author. Abrams Appleseed, 2013. (PreK–Gr. 1)

Pinkney, Jerry. *Three Little Kittens.* Illus. by the author. Dial, 2010. (PreK–Gr. 1)

Rohmann, Eric. *A Kitten Tale.* Illus. by the author. Knopf, 2008. (PreK–Gr. 1)

Rostoker-Gruber, Karen. *Bandit.* Illus. by Paul Rátz de Tagyos. Marshall Cavendish, 2008. (PreK–Gr. 1)

Schachner, Judith Byron. *The Grannyman.* Illus. by the author. Dutton, 1999. (PreK–Gr. 2)

Schwartz, Viviane. *There Are Cats in This Book.* Illus. by the author. Candlewick, 2008. (PreK–Gr. 1)

Verse

Sing the complete "The Three Little Kittens," found at www.songsforteaching .com/nurseryrhymes/threelittlekittens.php.

Activity

Try out the draw-and-tell story "*T* Is for Tommy" on page 30. Afterwards, make black-cat masks with white-yarn whiskers and attach them to popsicle sticks.

CAUSE AND EFFECT

Read-Alouds

Aardema, Verna. *Why Mosquitoes Buzz in People's Ears.* Illus. by Leo and Diane Dillon. Dial, 1975. (PreK–Gr. 2)

Barton, Byron. *Buzz, Buzz, Buzz.* Illus. by the author. Macmillan, 1973. (PreK–Gr. 1)

Charlip, Remy. *Fortunately.* Illus. by the author. Four Winds, 1964. (PreK–Gr. 2)

Crummel, Susan Stevens. *All in One Hour.* Illus. by Dorothy Donohue. Marshall Cavendish, 2003. (PreK–Gr. 1)

Cuyler, Margery. *That's Good! That's Bad!* Illus. by David Catrow. Henry Holt, 1991. (PreK–Gr. 1)

LaRochelle, David. *The End.* Illus. by Richard Egielski. Scholastic/Arthur A. Levine, 2007. (PreK–Gr. 2)

Mack, Jeff. *Good News Bad News.* Illus. by the author. Chronicle, 2012. (PreK–Gr. 1)

Noble, Trinka Hakes. *The Day Jimmy's Boa Ate the Wash.* Illus. by Steven Kellogg. Dial, 1980. (PreK–Gr. 2)

Numeroff, Laura. *If You Give a Mouse a Cookie.* Illus. by Felicia Bond. HarperCollins, 1985. (PreK–Gr. 2)

Seeger, Laura Vaccaro. *First the Egg.* Roaring Brook, 2007. (PreK–Gr. 1)

Stein, David Ezra. *Because Amelia Smiled.* Illus. by the author. Chronicle, 2012. (PreK–Gr. 2)

Stevens, April. *Waking Up Wendell.* Illus. by Tad Hills. Schwartz & Wade, 2007. (PreK–Gr. 1)

Zolotow, Charlotte. ***The Quarreling Book.*** *Illus. by Arnold Lobel. HarperCollins, 1963.* (PreK–Gr. 1)

Verse

Sing "There's a Hole in the Bucket"; lyrics and audio at www.songsfor teaching.com/folk/theresaholeinthebucket.php.

Activity

Working in pairs, children can brainstorm a cause-and-effect situation (rain and a flower blooming; putting gas in the car so the car will go) and draw two separate pictures, one of cause and the other of effect. When they are done, put all the pictures out on the floor, mixed up, and see if each pair of children can find another matching set.

CHARACTER EDUCATION, ETHICS, AND VALUES

(*See* Apologies, Forgiveness, and Manners; Compassion and Kindness; Cooperation; Courage; Friendship; Generosity; Honesty; Perseverance; Resourcefulness; Responsibility)

CHICKENS
(*See also* Birds; Ducks and Geese; Owls; Penguins)

Read-Alouds

Baker, Keith. ***Big Fat Hen.*** *Illus. by the author. Harcourt, 1994.* (PreK–K)

Byrd, Robert. ***Brave Chicken Little.*** *Illus. by the author. Viking, 2014.* (PreK–Gr. 2)

Cronin, Doreen. ***Click, Clack, Peep!*** *Illus. by Betsy Lewin. Atheneum 2015.* (PreK–Gr. 1)

DiCamillo, Kate. ***Louise, The Adventures of a Chicken.*** *Illus. by Harry Bliss. HarperCollins/Joanna Cotler, 2008.* (PreK–Gr. 3)

Ernst, Lisa Campbell. ***Zinnia and Dot.*** *Illus. by the author. Viking, 1992.* (PreK–Gr. 1)

Harrington, Janice N. ***The Chicken-Chasing Queen of Lamar County.*** *Illus. by Shelley Jackson. Farrar/Melanie Kroupa, 2007.* (PreK–Gr. 2)

Himmelman, John. ***Chickens to the Rescue.*** *Illus. by the author. Henry Holt, 2006.* (PreK–Gr. 1)

Marshall, James. ***Wings: A Tale of Two Chickens.*** *Illus. by the author. Viking Kestrel, 1986.* (PreK–Gr. 2)

Verse

Do "The Chicken Dance"; you'll find music and instructions on YouTube.

Activity

Make pipe-cleaner chicken feet. Children can dip them in different colors of poster paint and create chicken-track pictures.

CHILDREN AND CHILDHOOD   (*See also* Friendship)

Read-Alouds

Agee, Jon. *The Retired Kid.* *Illus. by the author. Disney-Hyperion, 2008.* (K–Gr. 2)

Barnett, Mac. *Sam & Dave Dig a Hole.* *Illus. by Jon Klassen. Candlewick, 2014.* (PreK–Gr. 4)

Black, Michael Ian. *I'm Bored.* *Illus. by Debbie Ridpath Ohi. Simon & Schuster, 2012.* (PreK–Gr. 2)

Bruel, Nick. *Who Is Melvin Bubble?* *Illus. by the author. Roaring Brook, 2006.* (PreK–Gr. 2)

Frazee, Marla. *A Couple of Boys Have the Best Week Ever.* *Illus. by the author. Harcourt, 2008.* (PreK–Gr. 2)

Fucile, Tony. *Let's Do Nothing!* *Illus. by the author. Candlewick, 2009.* (PreK–Gr. 2)

Greenfield. Eloise. *Honey, I Love.* *Illus. by Jan Spivey Gilchrist. HarperCollins, 2003.* (PreK–Gr. 2)

Mack, Jeff. *The Things I Can Do.* *Illus. by the author. Roaring Brook, 2013.* (PreK–Gr. 1)

Rosenthal, Amy Krouse. *Cookies: Bite-Size Life Lessons.* *Illus. by Jane Dyer. Harper-Collins, 2006.* (PreK–Gr. 2)

Viorst, Judith. *Alexander and the Terrible, Horrible, No Good, Very Bad Day.* *Illus. by Ray Cruz. Atheneum, 1972.* (PreK–Gr. 2)

Verse

Do the "Touch Your Nose" fingerplay on page 116.

Activity

Ask kids to divide themselves into groups—by hair color, eye color, gender, hair length, and so on—to demonstrate that although they can be grouped in many ways, they are all still children.

CHINESE NEW YEAR

Read-Alouds

Compestine, Ying Chang. D Is for Dragon Dance. *Illus. by YongSheng Xuan. Holiday House, 2006.* (PreK–Gr. 1)

Compestine, Ying Chang. The Runaway Rice Cake. *Illus. by Tungwai Chau. Simon & Schuster, 2001.* (PreK–Gr. 2)

Compestine, Ying Chang. The Runaway Wok: A Chinese New Year Tale. *Illus. by Sebastia Serra. Dutton, 2011.* (PreK–Gr. 2)

Niemann, Christoph. The Pet Dragon. *Illus. by the author. Greenwillow, 2008.* (PreK–Gr. 2)

Schaefer, Carole Lexa. Dragon Dancing. *Illus. by Pierr Morgan. Viking, 2007.* (PreK–Gr. 1)

Wallace, Ian. Chin Chiang and the Dragon's Dance. *Illus. by the author. Groundwood, 1998.* (PreK–Gr. 2)

Verse

Sing the "Chinese Hello Song" (to the tune of "The Farmer in the Dell"):

> Let's wave and say "Ni hao, (pronounced nee how)"
>
> Let's wave and say "Ni hao."
>
> Let's say hello to all our friends,
>
> Let's wave and say "Ni hao."

Activity

Buy a sack of Chinese red good-luck envelopes at an Asian grocery store or online and hand out one, along with a lucky penny, to each child. Make a long dragon out of a series of paper grocery bags, one per child. (In each bag, cut armholes on the sides. Cut a seam up the front and, from the bottom of the bag, cut out a large circle for the head, turning it into a vest of sorts.) Children can decorate their vests with colorful dragon scales. Wearing their dragon costumes, they then walk in a long, undulating line and do a dragon dance.

CHRISTMAS   (*See also* Gifts)

Read-Alouds

Bunting, Eve. Night Tree. *Illus. by Ted Rand. Harcourt, 1991.* (PreK–Gr. 1)

Coots, J. Fred, and Haven Gillespie. *Santa Claus Is Comin' to Town. Illus. by Steven Kellogg. HarperCollins, 2004.* (PreK–Gr. 2)

Hoban, Lillian. *Arthur's Christmas Cookies. Illus. by the author. HarperCollins, 1972.* (PreK–Gr. 1)

Houston, Gloria. *The Year of the Perfect Christmas Tree: An Appalachian Story. Illus. by Barbara Cooney. Dial, 1988.* (PreK–Gr. 4)

Joyce, William. *Santa Calls. Illus. by the author. HarperCollins/Laura Geringer, 1993.* (PreK–Gr. 2)

Klise, Kate. *Shall I Knit You a Hat?: A Christmas Yarn. Illus. by M. Sarah Klise. Henry Holt, 2004.* (PreK–Gr. 1)

McKissack, Patricia C. *The All-I'll-Ever-Want Christmas Doll. Illus. by Jerry Pinkney. Schwartz & Wade, 2007.* (PreK–Gr. 3)

Mora, Pat. *A Piñata in a Pine Tree: A Latino Twelve Days of Christmas. Illus. by Magaly Morales. Clarion, 2009.* (PreK–Gr. 2)

Polacco, Patricia. *An Orange for Frankie. Illus. by the author. Philomel Books, 2004.* (K–Gr. 4)

Primavera, Elise. *Auntie Claus. Illus. by the author. Harcourt, 1999.* (PreK–Gr. 2)

Rubel, David. *The Carpenter's Gift: A Christmas Tale about the Rockefeller Center Tree. Illus. by Jim LaMarche. Random House, 2011.* (PreK–Gr. 3)

Say, Allen. *Tree of Cranes. Illus. by the author. Houghton Mifflin, 1991.* (K–Gr. 3)

Seuss, Dr. *How the Grinch Stole Christmas. Illus. by the author. Random House, 1957.* (PreK–Gr. 3)

Soto, Gary. *Too Many Tamales. Illus. by Ed Martinez. Putnam, 1993.* (PreK–Gr. 3)

Van Allsburg, Chris. *The Polar Express. Illus. by the author. Houghton Mifflin, 1985.* (PreK–Gr. 3)

Wells, Rosemary. *Max's Christmas. Illus. by the author. Dial, 1986.* (PreK–Gr. 1)

Verse

Sing "Santa Claus Is Coming to Town."

Activity

Make a book tree by decorating a small artificial tree with little book covers of children's favorite books. Scan book covers in color, save as jpegs, print them out in a 2-by-3-inch size, and laminate them.

CIRCUS

Read-Alouds

Dodds, Dayle Ann. *Where's Pup?* Illus. by *Pierre Pratt. Dial, 2003.* (PreK–Gr. 1)

Ehlert, Lois. *Circus.* Illus. by the author. *HarperCollins, 1992.* (PreK–Gr. 1)

Falconer, Ian. *Olivia Saves the Circus.* Illus. by the author. *Atheneum, 2001.* (PreK–Gr. 1)

Frazee, Marla. *The Farmer and the Clown.* Illus. by the author. *Beach Lane, 2014.* (PreK–Gr. 2)

Graham, Bob. *Dimity Dumpty: The Story of Humpty's Little Sister.* Illus. by the author. *Candlewick, 2007.* (PreK–Gr. 2)

Harrison, Hannah E. *Extraordinary Jane.* Illus. by the author. *Dial, 2014.* (PreK–Gr. 1)

Spier, Peter. *Peter Spier's Circus!* Illus. by the author. *Doubleday, 1992.* (PreK–Gr. 1)

Verse
Sing "The Circus Is Coming to Town" (to the tune of "The Caissons Go Rolling Along"). You'll find lyrics and music at www.kidsongs.com/lyrics/the-circus-is-coming-to-town.html.

Activity
Stretch a rope across the floor and have children walk the "high wire" to the music of "The Daring Young Man on the Flying Trapeze" or other circus music.

CITIES AND TOWNS

Read-Alouds

Barracca, Debra, and Sal Barracca. *The Adventures of Taxi Dog.* Illus. by *Mark Buehner. Dial, 1990.* (PreK–Gr. 2)

Burton, Virginia Lee. *The Little House.* Illus. by the author. *Houghton Mifflin, 1942.* (PreK–Gr. 1)

Gordon, Gus. *Herman and Rosie.* Illus. by the author. *Roaring Brook Press, 2013.* (PreK–Gr. 3)

Grimes, Nikki. *C Is for City.* Illus. by *Pat Cummings. Wordsong/Boyds Mills Press, 2002.* (PreK–Gr. 1)

Johnson, Stephen T. *Alphabet City.* Illus. by the author. *Viking, 1995.* (PreK–Gr. 1)

Jonas, Ann. *Round Trip.* Illus. by the author. *Greenwillow, 1983.* (PreK–Gr. 2)

Ringgold, Faith. *Tar Beach.* *Illus. by the author. Crown, 1991.* (PreK–Gr. 3)

Rocco, John. *Blackout.* *Illus. by the author. Disney-Hyperion, 2011.* (PreK–Gr. 2)

Verse

Recite (and explain) the poem "Romulus" by Leroy F. Jackson, ©1918:

> Romulus, Romulus, father of Rome,
>
> Ran off with a wolf and he wouldn't come home.
>
> When he grew up, he founded a city
>
> With an eagle, a bear, and a tortoise-shell kitty.

Activity

Mount a large sheet of kraft paper on a wall and have children make a mural of their town by drawing, coloring, and cutting and pasting people, buildings, parks, and other parts of town.

CLOCKS   (*See* Time)

CLOTHING AND DRESS   (*See also* Boots and Shoes; Hats)

Read-Alouds

Aylesworth, Jim. *The Mitten.* *Illus. by Barbara McClintock. Scholastic, 2009.* (PreK–Gr. 1)

Aylesworth, Jim. *My Grandfather's Coat.* *Illus. by Barbara McClintock. Scholastic, 2014.* (PreK–Gr. 2)

Barrett, Judi. *Animals Should Definitely Not Wear Clothing.* *Illus. by Ron Barrett. Atheneum, 1970.* (PreK–Gr. 1)

DePaola, Tomie. *Charlie Needs a Cloak.* *Illus. by the author. Simon & Schuster, 1973.* (PreK–Gr. 1)

Florian, Douglas. *I Love My Hat.* *Illus. by the author. Two Lions, 2014.* (PreK–Gr. 1)

Hest, Amy. *The Purple Coat.* *Illus. by Amy Schwartz. Macmillan, 1986.* (PreK–Gr. 2)

Isaacs, Anne. *Pancakes for Supper.* *Illus. by Mark Teague. Scholastic, 2006.* (PreK–Gr. 1)

Kellogg, Steven. *The Missing Mitten Mystery.* *Illus. by the author. Dial, 2000.* (PreK–Gr. 1)

Kimmel, Eric A. *Little Britches and the Rattlers.* *Illus. by Vincent Nguyen. Marshall Cavendish, 2008.* (PreK–Gr. 2)

Lester, Julius. *Sam and the Tigers.* Illus. by the author. Dial, 1996. (PreK–Gr. 2)

London, Jonathan. *Froggy Gets Dressed.* Illus. by Frank Remkiewicz. Viking, 1992. (PreK–Gr. 1)

Neitzel, Shirley. *The Jacket I Wear in the Snow.* Illus. by Nancy Winslow Parker. Greenwillow, 1989. (PreK–Gr. 1)

Schertle, Alice. *Button Up! Wrinkled Rhymes.* Illus. by Petra Mathers. Harcourt, 2009. (PreK–Gr. 1)

Smith, Jeff. *Little Mouse Gets Ready.* Illus. by the author. TOON, 2009. (PreK–K)

Taback, Simms. *Joseph Had a Little Overcoat.* Illus. by the author. Viking, 1999. (PreK–Gr. 2)

Weeks, Sarah. *Mrs. McNosh Hangs Up Her Wash.* Illus. by Nadine Bernard Westcott. HarperCollins, 1998. (PreK–Gr. 1)

Willems, Mo. *Naked Mole Rat Gets Dressed.* Illus. by the author. Hyperion, 2009. (PreK–Gr. 2)

Ziefert, Harriet. *A New Coat for Anna.* Illus. by Anita Lobel. Knopf, 1986. (PreK–Gr. 2)

Zion, Gene. *No Roses for Harry!* Illus. by Margaret Bloy Graham. HarperCollins, 1958. (PreK–Gr. 2)

Verse

Recite "The Snowkey Pokey" (to the tune of the "Hokey-Pokey"):

> You put your right mitten in, you take your right mitten out,
> You put your right mitten in, and you shake it all about;
> You do the snowkey pokey and you turn yourself around,
> That's what it's all about.

Other verses: left mitten; right boot, left boot, scarf, hat, your snowself

Activity

Cut felt-paper dolls for a felt board and have kids make various outfits from scraps of cloth to dress their dolls. Tell the story "The Wonderful Shrinking Shirt" by Leone Castell Anderson on page 261.

COLOR

Read-Alouds

Carle, Eric. *The Artist Who Painted a Blue Horse.* Illus. by the author. Philomel, 2011. (PreK–Gr. 3)

Daywalt, Drew. *The Day the Crayons Quit.* Illus. by Oliver Jeffers. Philomel, 2013. (PreK–Gr. 4)

Ehlert, Lois. *Color Zoo.* Illus. by the author. HarperCollins, 1989. (PreK–Gr. 1)

Ehlert, Lois. *Growing Vegetable Soup.* Illus. by the author. Harcourt, 1987. (PreK–Gr. 1)

Ehlert, Lois. *Planting a Rainbow.* Illus. by the author. Harcourt, 1988. (PreK–Gr. 1)

Hoban, Tana. *Is It Red? Is It Yellow? Is It Blue? An Adventure in Color.* Photos by author. Greenwillow, 1978. (PreK–K)

Jonas, Ann. *Color Dance.* Illus. by the author. Greenwillow, 1989. (PreK–Gr. 1)

Lionni, Leo. *Little Blue and Little Yellow.* Illus. by the author. McDowell, Obolensky, 1959. (PreK–Gr. 1)

Litwin, Eric. *Pete the Cat: I Love My White Shoes.* Illus. by James Dean. HarperCollins, 2010. (PreK–Gr. 1)

Martin, Bill Jr. *Brown Bear, Brown Bear What Do You See?* Illus. by Eric Carle. Henry Holt, 1967. (PreK–Gr. 1)

McMillan, Bruce. *Growing Colors.* Photos by the author. Lothrop, 1988. (PreK–Gr. 1)

Otoshi, Kathryn. *One.* Illus. by the author. KO Kids, 2008. (PreK–Gr. 2)

Peek, Merle. *Mary Wore Her Red Dress and Henry Wore His Green Sneakers.* Illus. by the author. Clarion, 1985. (PreK–Gr. 1)

Seeger, Laura Vaccaro. *Green.* Illus. by the author. Roaring Brook, 2012. (PreK–Gr. 3)

Seeger, Laura Vaccaro. *Lemons Are Not Red.* Illus. by the author. Roaring Brook, 2004. (PreK–Gr. 2)

Tullet, Hervé. *Mix It Up!* Illus. by the author. Chronicle, 2014. (PreK–Gr. 2)

Wolff, Ashley. *Baby Bear Sees Blue.* Illus. by the author. Beach Lane, 2012. (PreK–Gr. 1)

Verse

Sing "I Can Sing a Rainbow" by Arthur Hamilton. You'll find many versions of this song on YouTube.

Activity

Use watercolors to mix new colors from primary colors, inspired by Hervé Tullet's interactive book, *Mix It Up!*

COMPASSION AND KINDNESS

Read-Alouds

Beaumont, Karen. *Wild About Us!* Illus. by Janet Stevens. Houghton Mifflin Harcourt, 2015. (PreK–Gr. 2)

Cannon, Janell. *Stellaluna.* Illus. by the author. Harcourt, 1993. (PreK–Gr. 2)

Daugherty, James. *Andy and the Lion.* Illus. by the author. Viking, 1938. (PreK–Gr. 2)

Graham, Bob. *How to Heal a Broken Wing.* Illus. by the author. Candlewick, 2008. (PreK–Gr. 3)

Pinkney, Jerry. *The Lion & the Mouse.* Illus. by the author. Little, Brown, 2009. (PreK–Gr. 2)

Stanley, Diane. *Saving Sweetness.* Illus. by G. Brian Karas. Putnam, 1996. (PreK–Gr. 2)

Stead, Philip C. *A Sick Day for Amos McGee.* Illus. by Erin E. Stead. Roaring Brook, 2010. (PreK–Gr. 1)

Willems, Mo. *Can I Play, Too?* Illus. by the author. Hyperion, 2010. (PreK–Gr. 2)

Willems, Mo. *Leonardo the Terrible Monster.* Illus. by the author. Hyperion, 2005. (PreK–Gr. 2)

Willems, Mo. *My Friend Is Sad.* Illus. by the author. Hyperion, 2007. (PreK–Gr. 2)

Woodson, Jacqueline. *Each Kindness.* Illus. by E. B. Lewis. Penguin/Nancy Paulsen, 2012. (K–Gr. 4)

Verse

Sing "For He's (or She's) a Jolly Good Fellow."

Activity

Ask children to pick a friend or family member and think of a random act of kindness they can do for that person. As the teacher did in Jacqueline Woodson's *Each Kindness*, have children drop a pebble in a bowl of water to see how each kind act they perform goes out like a ripple into the world.

COMPUTERS AND TECHNOLOGY

Read-Alouds

Collins, Suzanne. *When Charlie McButton Lost Power.* Illus. by Mike Lester. Putnam, 2005. (PreK–Gr. 2)

Cordell, Matthew. *Hello! Hello!* Illus. by the author. Disney-Hyperion, 2012. (K–Gr. 4)

McPhail, David. *Fix-It.* Illus. by the author. Dutton, 1984. (PreK–Gr. 1)

Say, Allen. *Kamishibai Man*. Illus. by the author. Houghton Mifflin, 2005. (K–Gr. 4)

Zuckerberg, Randi. *Dot*. Illus. by Joe Berger. Candlewick, 2013. (K–Gr. 2)

Verse

Recite "Gone High Tech" by Douglas Evans, c2014, author of *Apple Island, or, The Truth about Teachers* (Front Street, 1998):

> You may have noticed, teacher,
> I am not in school today,
> But the voice recorder on my desk,
> Will pick up each word you say.
>
> Switch on my laptop's Web cam,
> When you have something to show,
> And if you pass out homework,
> Find my fax number below.
>
> I've e-mail and a smart phone,
> So I won't be hard to reach.
> Since I don't need to be in class,
> I'll do lessons at the beach.

Activity

To help children to learn their addresses, have them type it into Google Maps and find a map of where they live and a photo of the building.

COOKIES (*See* Themed Program: I'm Hungry on page 299)

COOKS AND COOKING (*See* Themed Program: I'm Hungry on page 299)

COOPERATION

Read-Alouds

Edwards, Pamela Duncan. *The Neat Line: Scribbling through Mother Goose*. Illus. by Diann Cain Blumenthal. HarperCollins, 2005. (PreK–Gr. 1)

Ernst, Lisa Campbell. *Zinnia and Dot*. Illus. by the author. Viking, 1992. (PreK–Gr. 1)

Fleming, Candace. *Oh, No!* Illus. by Eric Rohmann. Schwartz & Wade, 2012. (PreK–Gr. 1)

Hills, Tad. *Duck and Goose*. Illus. by the author. Schwartz & Wade, 2006. (PreK–Gr. 1)

Ketteman, Helen. *Armadilly Chili.* *Illus. by Will Terry. Albert Whitman, 2004.* (PreK–Gr. 2)

Kornell, Max. *Me First.* *Illus. by the author. Penguin/Nancy Paulsen, 2014.* (PreK–Gr. 2)

Lionni, Leo. *Swimmy.* *Illus. by the author. Pantheon, 1963.* (PreK–Gr. 1)

Paul, Ann Whitford. *Mañana, Iguana.* *Illus. by Ethan Long. Holiday House, 2004.* (PreK–Gr. 1)

Stevens, Janet, and Susan Stevens Crummel. *The Great Fuzz Frenzy.* *Illus. by Janet Stevens. Harcourt, 2005.* (PreK–Gr. 3)

Sturges, Philemon. *The Little Red Hen (Makes a Pizza).* *Illus. by Amy Walrod. Dutton, 1999.* (PreK–Gr. 2)

Vamos, Samantha R. *The Cazuela That the Farm Maiden Stirred.* *Illus. by Rafael López. Charlesbridge, 2011.* (PreK–Gr. 3)

Waddell, Martin. *Farmer Duck.* *Illus. by Helen Oxenbury. Candlewick, 1991.* (PreK–Gr. 1)

Verse

Recite "Hello, My Name Is Joe" on page 2.

Activity

Play "Follow the Leader" or "Simon Says."

COUNTING   (*See also* Alphabet Books; Mathematics)

Read-Alouds

Baker, Keith. *1-2-3 Peas.* *Illus. by the author. Beach Lane, 2010.* (PreK–Gr. 1)

Blechman, Nicholas. *Night Light.* *Illus. by the author. Orchard, 2013.* (PreK–Gr. 1)

Bruel, Nick. *Poor Puppy and Bad Kitty.* *Illus. by the author. Roaring Brook, 2012.* Originally published as Poor Puppy in 2007. (PreK–Gr. 1)

Catalanotto, Peter. *Daisy 1 2 3.* *Illus. by the author. Atheneum, 2003.* (PreK–Gr. 1)

Christelow, Eileen. *Five Little Monkeys Jumping on the Bed.* *Illus. by the author. Clarion, 1989.* (PreK–Gr. 1)

Crews, Donald. *Ten Black Dots.* *Illus. by the author. Greenwillow, 1986.* (PreK–Gr. 1)

Ehlert, Lois. *Fish Eyes: A Book You Can Count On.* *Illus. by the author. Harcourt, 1990.* (PreK–Gr. 1)

Falwell, Cathryn. *Feast for 10.* *Illus. by the author. Clarion Books, 1993.* (PreK–K)

Gorbachev, Valeri. *Christopher Counting*. *Illus. by the author. Philomel, 2008.* (PreK–Gr. 1)

Litwin, Eric. *Pete the Cat and His Four Groovy Buttons*. *Illus. by James Dean. Harper, 2012.* (PreK–Gr. 1)

Menotti, Andrea. *How Many Jelly Beans? A Giant Book of Giant Numbers*. *Illus. by Yancey Labat. Chronicle, 2012.* (PreK–Gr. 3)

Murray, Alison. *One Two That's My Shoe!* *Illus. by the author. Disney-Hyperion, 2012.* (PreK–Gr. 1)

Walsh, Ellen Stoll. *Mouse Count*. *Illus. by the author. Harcourt, 1991.* (PreK–Gr. 1)

Walton, Rick. *So Many Bunnies: A Bedtime ABC and Counting Book*. *Illus. by Paige Miglio. HarperCollins, 1998.* (PreK–Gr. 1)

Zelinsky, Paul O. *Knick Knack Paddywhack*. *Illus. by the author. Dutton, 2002* *(PreK–Gr. 1)*

Verse
Sing "This Old Man"; lyrics at www.kidsongs.com/lyrics/this-old-man.html.

Activity
Use dried peas or buttons to make sets of ten and one hundred, and then have kids practice counting by tens and by hundreds.

COUNTRY LIFE   (*See* Farm and Country Life)

COURAGE

Read-Alouds
Bryan, Ashley. *Can't Scare Me!* *Illus. by the author. Atheneum, 2013.* (K–Gr. 2)

Gackenbach, Dick. *Harry and the Terrible Whatzit*. *Illus. by the author. Clarion, 1977.* (PreK–Gr. 1)

Henkes, Kevin. *Sheila Rae, the Brave*. *Illus. by the author. Greenwillow, 1987.* (PreK–Gr. 1)

McCully, Emily Arnold. *Mirette on the High Wire*. *Illus. by the author. Putnam, 1992.* (PreK–Gr. 2)

Nash, Ogden. *The Tale of Custard the Dragon*. *Illus. by Lynn Munsinger. Little, Brown, 1995, c1936.* (PreK–Gr. 3)

Sacre, Antonio. *The Barking Mouse*. *Illus. by Alfredo Aguirre. Albert Whitman, 2003.* (PreK–Gr. 2)

Steig, William. *Brave Irene*. *Illus. by the author. Farrar, 1986.* (PreK–Gr. 3)

Verse

Recite "Courage," the Cowardly Lion's speech from the film *The Wizard of Oz*, which you can find with ease on YouTube.

Activity

The military awards medals for courageous acts, such as the Bronze Star and the Purple Heart. Make Courage Medals out of gold foil. From their own experiences, children can write and draw, "I was courageous when . . ." and affix the medals to their papers.

COWBOYS AND COWGIRLS

Read-Alouds

Fleming, Denise. *Buster Goes to Cowboy Camp.* Illus. by the author. Henry Holt, 2008. (PreK–Gr. 1)

Frank, John. *The Toughest Cowboy, or, How the Wild West Was Tamed.* Illus. by Zachary Pullen. Simon & Schuster, 2004. (PreK–Gr. 3)

Icenoggle, Jodi. *'Til the Cows Come Home.* Illus. by Normand Chartier. Boyds Mills, 2010. (PreK–Gr. 1)

Isaacs, Anne. *Meanwhile, Back at the Ranch.* Illus. by Kevin Hawkes. Schwartz & Wade, 2014. (K–Gr. 4)

Johnston, Tony. *The Cowboy and the Black-Eyed Pea.* Illus. by Warren Ludwig. Putnam, 1996. (PreK–Gr. 2)

Silverman, Erica. *Cowgirl Kate and Cocoa.* Illus. by Betsy Lewin. Harcourt, 2005. (PreK–Gr. 2)

Teague, Mark. *How I Spent My Summer Vacation.* Illus. by the author. Crown, 1995. (PreK–Gr. 2)

Verse

Sing "Home on the Range."

Activity

Make lassos out of rope for children to twirl.

COWS

Read-Alouds

Cronin, Doreen. *Click, Clack, Moo: Cows That Type*. *Illus. by Betsy Lewin. Simon & Schuster, 2000.* (PreK–Gr. 3)

Egan, Tim. *Metropolitan Cow*. *Illus. by the author. Houghton Mifflin, 1996.* (PreK–Gr. 2)

Kinerk, Robert. *Clorinda*. *Illus. by Steven Kellogg. Simon & Schuster, 2002.* (PreK–Gr. 1)

LaRochelle, David. *Moo!* *Illus. by Mike Wohnoutka. Walker, 2013.* (PreK–Gr. 2)

Leaf, Munro. *The Story of Ferdinand*. *Illus. by Robert Lawson. Viking, 1936.* (PreK–Gr. 1)

Thomas, Jan. *Is Everyone Ready for Fun?* *Illus. by the author. Beach Lane, 2011.* (PreK–Gr. 1)

Verse

Do the call-and-response chant "Did You Feed My Cow" on page 147.

Activity

Play the moo game: have children act out a feeling or condition (happy, quiet, excited, angry, far away, close, etc.) to act expressively, using only the word *moo*, just as the cow does in David LaRochelle's *Moo!*

DANCE   (*See* Booklist: Dance on page 168)

DESERTS

Read-Alouds

Cowley, Joy. *Big Moon Tortilla*. *Illus. by Dyanne Strongbow. Boyds Mills Press, 1998.* (PreK–Gr. 1)

Lass, Bonnie, and Philemon Sturges. *Who Took the Cookies from the Cookie Jar?* *Illus. by Ashley Wolff. Little, Brown, 2000.* (PreK–Gr. 1)

McLerran, Alice. *Roxaboxen*. *Illus. by Barbara Cooney. Lothrop, 1991.* (PreK–Gr. 2)

Mora, Pat. *Listen to the Desert / Oye al desierto*. *Illus. by Francisco X. Mora. Clarion, 1994.* (PreK–Gr. 1)

Pinkney, Jerry. *The Tortoise & the Hare: An Aesop Fable*. *Illus. by the author. Little, Brown, 2013.* (PreK–Gr. 2)

Verse

Play the sound-effect filled song "Cactus Jackson Had a Ranch," written and recorded in 1948 by Tex Ritter as a companion to that song about that old MacDonald guy and his farm. You can listen to the original record at vintagevinylrevival.com/78/ritter-tex_songs-for-children.

Activity

Make desert-inspired sand paintings with colored sand in Styrofoam trays, or make sand cross-sections in baby-food jars.

DINOSAURS

Read-Alouds

Broach, Elise. *When Dinosaurs Came with Everything*. *Illus. by David Small. Atheneum, 2007.* (PreK–Gr. 2)

Carrick, Carol. *Patrick's Dinosaurs*. *Illus. by Donald Carrick. Clarion, 1983.* (PreK–Gr. 1)

Jenkins, Steve. *Prehistoric Actual Size*. *Illus. by the author. Houghton Mifflin, 2005.* (PreK–Gr. 4)

Judge, Lita. *How Big Were Dinosaurs?* *Illus. by the author. Roaring Brook, 2013.* (PreK–Gr. 2)

McMullan, Kate. *I'm Bad!* *Illus. by Jim McMullan. HarperCollins, 2008.* (PreK–Gr. 2)

Munro, Roxie. *Inside-Outside Dinosaurs*. *Illus. by the author. Marshall Cavendish, 2009.* (PreK–Gr. 1)

Nolan, Dennis. *Dinosaur Dream*. *Illus. by the author. Simon & Schuster, 1990.* (PreK–Gr. 1)

Rosenberg, Liz. *Tyrannosaurus Dad*. *Illus. by Matthew Myers. Roaring Brook, 2011.* (PreK–Gr. 1)

Shea, Bob. *Dinosaur vs. Bedtime*. *Illus. by the author. Disney-Hyperion, 2008.* (PreK–Gr. 1)

Thomson, Bill. *Chalk*. *Illus. by the author. Amazon, 2010.* (PreK–Gr. 3)

Willems, Mo. *Edwina, the Dinosaur Who Didn't Know She Was Extinct*. *Illus. by the author. Hyperion, 2006.* (PreK–Gr. 2)

Willems, Mo. *Goldilocks and the Three Dinosaurs*. *Illus. by the author. Balzer + Bray, 2012.* (PreK–Gr. 2)

Verse

Sing "Dinosaurs" (to the tune of: "Alouette"):

> Allosaurus, Pachycephalosaurus,
>
> Allosaurus, Tyrannosaurus rex.
>
> Stegosaurus, Trachodon,
>
> Triceratops, Pteranodon,
>
> Dinosaurs, dinosaurs, dinosaurs, dinosaurs,
>
> Ooooohhhh—
>
> Allosaurus, Pachycephalosaurus,
>
> Allosaurus, Tyrannosaurus rex.

Activity

Make dinosaur skeletons out of pipe cleaners, and T-rex teeth (actual size 6 to 8 inches) out of Model Magic or clay. Poke a hole in the center of each tooth and string them on yarn to make necklaces to wear.

DOGS

Read-Alouds

Bemelmans, Ludwig. *Madeline's Rescue.* Illus. by the author. Viking, 1953. (PreK–Gr. 2)

Blake, Robert J. *Togo.* Illus. by the author. Philomel, 2002. (PreK–Gr. 2)

Bruel, Nick. *Poor Puppy and Bad Kitty.* Illus. by the author. Roaring Brook, 2012. Originally published as Poor Puppy in 2007. (PreK–Gr. 1)

Calmenson, Stephanie. *May I Pet Your Dog? The How-to Guide for Kids Meeting Dogs (and Dogs Meeting Kids).* Illus. by Jan Ormerod. Clarion, 2007. (PreK–Gr. 2)

Eastman, P. D. *Go, Dog. Go!* Illus. by the author. Beginner Books, 1961. (PreK–Gr. 1)

Feiffer, Jules. *Bark, George.* Illus. by the author. HarperCollins, 1999. (PreK–Gr. 2)

Flack, Marjorie. *Angus Lost.* Illus. by the author. Doubleday, 1931. (PreK–Gr. 1)

Fleming, Denise. *Buster Goes to Cowboy Camp.* Illus. by the author. Henry Holt, 2008. (PreK–Gr. 1)

Frazee, Marla. *Boot & Shoe.* Illus. by the author. Beach Lane, 2012. (PreK–Gr. 1)

George, Kristine O'Connell. *Little Dog Poems.* Illus. by June Otani. Clarion, 1999. (PreK–Gr. 2)

Gravett, Emily. *Dogs.* Illus. by the author. Simon & Schuster, 2010. (PreK–Gr. 1)

Harrison, Hannah E. *Extraordinary Jane.* Illus. by the author. Dial, 2014. (PreK–Gr. 1)

Hest, Amy. *The Dog Who Belonged to No One.* Illus. by Amy Bates. Abrams, 2008. (PreK–Gr. 1)

Kalman, Maira. *What Pete Ate from A–Z.* Illus. by the author. Putnam, 2001. (PreK–Gr. 2)

Keats, Ezra Jack. *Whistle for Willie.* Illus. by the author. Viking, 1964. (PreK–Gr. 1)

Kellogg, Steven. *Pinkerton, Behave.* Illus. by the author. Dial, 1979. (PreK–Gr. 1)

Laden, Nina. *The Night I Followed the Dog.* Illus. by the author. Chronicle, 1994. (PreK–Gr. 2)

MacLachlan, Patricia, and Emily MacLachlan. *Once I Ate a Pie.* Illus. by Katy Schneider. HarperCollins/Joanna Cotler, 2006. (PreK–Gr. 2)

Meddaugh, Susan. *Martha Speaks.* Illus. by the author. Houghton Mifflin, 1992. (PreK–Gr. 3)

Murray, Alison. *Apple Pie ABC.* Illus. by the author. Disney-Hyperion, 2011. (PreK–Gr. 1)

Newgarden, Mark, and Megan Montague Cash. *Bow-Wow's Nightmare Neighbors.* Illus. by the authors. Roaring Brook, 2014. (PreK–Gr. 1)

Pilkey, Dav. *Dog Breath: The Horrible Trouble with Hally Tosis.* Illus. by the author. Scholastic/Blue Sky, 1994. (PreK–Gr. 2)

Pilkey, Dav. *Dogzilla.* Illus. by the author. Harcourt, 1993. (PreK–Gr. 3)

Pitzer, Susanna. *Not Afraid of Dogs.* Illus. by Larry Day. Walker, 2006. (PreK–Gr. 2)

Raschka, Chris. *A Ball for Daisy.* Illus. by the author. Schwartz & Wade, 2011. (PreK–Gr. 1)

Rathmann, Peggy. *Officer Buckle and Gloria.* Illus. by the author. Putnam, 1995. (PreK–Gr. 3)

Rohmann, Eric. *Bone Dog.* Illus. by the author. Roaring Brook, 2012. (K–Gr. 2)

Schwartz, Viviane. *Is There a Dog in This Book?* Illus. by the author. Candlewick, 2014. (PreK–Gr. 1)

Shannon, David. *Good Boy, Fergus!* Illus. by the author. Scholastic/Blue Sky, 2006. (PreK–Gr. 1)

Simont, Marc. *The Stray Dog.* Illus. by the author. HarperCollins, 2001. (PreK–Gr. 1)

Sullivan, Mary. *Ball.* Illus. by the author. Houghton Mifflin, 2013. (PreK–Gr. 1)

Van Allsburg, Chris. *The Garden of Abdul Gasazi.* Illus. by the author. Houghton Mifflin, 1979. (K–Gr. 4)

Willems, Mo. *City Dog, Country Frog.* Illus. by the author. Hyperion, 2010. (PreK–Gr. 3)

Zion, Gene. *Harry the Dirty Dog.* Illus. by Margaret Bloy Graham. *HarperCollins, 1956.* (PreK–Gr. 2)

Verse

Sing "Oh Where, Oh Where Has My Little Dog Gone?" Go to www.kid songs.com/lyrics/where-oh-where-has-my-little-dog-gone.html for the words and the music.

Activity

Do the draw-and-tell story "Where's My Dog?" on page 31.

DOLLS   (*See also* Stuffed Animals and Toys)

Read-Alouds

Grey, Mini. *Traction Man Is Here!* Illus. by the author. Knopf, 2005. (PreK–Gr. 1)

Henkes, Kevin. *Penny and Her Doll.* Illus. by the author. *Greenwillow, 2012.* (PreK–Gr. 1)

Kleven, Elisa. *The Apple Doll.* Illus. by the author. Farrar, 2007. (PreK–Gr. 1)

McKissack, Patricia C. *The All-I'll-Ever-Want Christmas Doll.* Illus. by Jerry Pinkney. *Schwartz & Wade, 2007.* (PreK–Gr. 3)

Miller, Pat Zietlow. *Sophie's Squash.* Illus. by Anne Wilsdorf. *Schwartz & Wade, 2013.* (PreK–Gr. 1)

Polacco, Patricia. *Babushka's Doll.* Illus. by the author. *Simon & Schuster, 1990.* (PreK–Gr. 2)

Stuve-Bodeen, Stephanie. *Elizabeti's Doll.* Illus. by Christy Hale. *Lee & Low, 1998.* (PreK–Gr. 2)

Zolotow, Charlotte. *William's Doll.* Illus. by William Pène du Bois. *HarperCollins, 1972.* (PreK–Gr. 1)

Verse

Teach children to play "I Dropped My Dolly" on the piano, on pages 171–172.

Activity

Using fabrics, buttons, and cotton stuffing, have children design and sew their own dolls.

DRAGONS

Read-Alouds

Carrick, Carol. *Patrick's Dinosaurs*. Illus. by Donald Carrick. Clarion, 1983. (PreK–Gr. 1)

Davol, Marguerite W. *The Paper Dragon*. Illus. by Robert Sabuda. Atheneum, 1997. (K–Gr. 3)

Gág, Wanda. *The Funny Thing*. Coward-McCann, 1929. (PreK–Gr. 1)

LaRochelle, David. *The Best Pet of All*. Illus. by Hanako Wakiyama. Dutton, 2004. (PreK–Gr. 1)

Nash, Ogden. *The Tale of Custard the Dragon*. Illus. by Lynn Munsinger. Little, Brown, 1995, c1936. (PreK–Gr. 2)

Niemann, Christoph. *The Pet Dragon*. Illus. by the author. Greenwillow, 2008. (PreK–Gr. 2)

Nolen, Jerdine. *Raising Dragons*. Illus. by Elise Primavera. Harcourt, 1997. (PreK–Gr. 1)

Rohmann, Eric. *Time Flies*. Illus. by the author. Crown, 1994. (PreK–Gr. 1)

Thomas, Shelley Moore. *Good Night, Good Knight*. Illus. by Jennifer Plecas. Dutton, 2000. (PreK–Gr. 1)

Tucker, Kathy. *The Seven Chinese Sisters*. Illus. by Grace Lin. Albert Whitman, 2003. (PreK–Gr. 2)

Verse

Sing "Puff the Magic Dragon" written by Leonard Lipton and Peter Yarrow in 1961. Find the lyrics and melody at folksongcollector.com/puff.html.

Activity

Let children create their own pet dragon pictures, using sequins, feathers, dazzly plastic jewels, and glitter pens.

DRAWING   (*See* Art and Artists)

DUCKS AND GEESE   (*See also* Birds; Chickens; Owls; Penguins)

Read-Alouds

Andersen, Hans Christian. *The Ugly Duckling*. Adapted and illus. by Jerry Pinkney. Morrow, 1999. (PreK–Gr. 3)

Braun, Trudi. *My Goose Betsy.* Illus. by John Bendall-Brunello. Candlewick, 1998. (PreK–Gr. 1)

Dunrea, Olivier. *Gossie.* Illus. by the author. Houghton Mifflin, 2002. (PreK–Gr. 1)

Duvoisin, Roger. *Petunia.* Knopf, 1950. (PreK–Gr. 1)

Gerstein, Mordicai. *Arnold of the Ducks.* Illus. by the author. HarperCollins, 1983. (PreK–Gr. 1)

Ginsburg, Mirra. *The Chick and the Duckling.* Illus. by Jose Aruego and Ariane Dewey. Macmillan, 1972. (PreK–K)

Hest, Amy. *In the Rain with Baby Duck.* Illus. by Jill Barton. Candlewick, 1995. (PreK–Gr. 1)

Hills, Tad. *Duck and Goose.* Illus. by the author. Schwartz & Wade, 2006. (PreK–Gr. 1)

Hindley, Judy. *Do Like a Duck Does!* Illus. by Ivan Bates. Candlewick, 2002. (PreK–Gr. 1)

Lurie, Susan. *Swim, Duck, Swim!* Photos by Murray Head. Feiwel and Friends, 2014. *(PreK–Gr. 2)*

McCloskey, Robert. *Make Way for Ducklings.* Illus. by the author. Viking, 1941. (PreK–Gr. 2)

Moore, Eva. *Lucky Ducklings.* Illus. by Nancy Carpenter. Orchard, 2013. (PreK–Gr. 2)

Peters, Lisa Westberg. *Cold Little Duck, Duck, Duck.* Illus. by Sam Williams. Greenwillow, 2000. (PreK–Gr. 1)

Raffi. *Five Little Ducks.* Illus. by Jose Aruego and Ariane Dewey. Crown, 1989. (PreK–Gr. 1)

Rosenthal, Amy Krouse. *Duck! Rabbit!* Illus. by Tom Lichtenheld. Chronicle, 2009. (PreK–Gr. 6)

Silverman, Erica. *Don't Fidget a Feather!* Illus. by S. D. Schindler. Macmillan, 1994. (PreK–Gr. 2)

Van Allsburg, Chris. *The Garden of Abdul Gasazi.* Illus. by the author. Houghton Mifflin, 1979. (K–Gr. 4)

Waddell, Martin. *Farmer Duck.* Illus. by Helen Oxenbury. Candlewick, 1991. (PreK–Gr. 1)

Willems, Mo. *That Is Not a Good Idea.* Illus. by the author. Balzer + Bray, 2013. (PreK–Gr. 2)

Verse

Recite or sing "Five Little Ducks" on page 114.

Activity

Purchase some itty bitty rubber ducks (such as the Mini Glow-in-the-Dark Rubber Duckies from www.orientaltrading.com), paper bowls, and plastic green grass. Have kids make wee eggs out of Play-Doh and decorate their bowls with markers to make nests for their ducklings.

EARTH (*See also* United States)

Read-Alouds

Baer, Edith. *This Is the Way We Go to School: A Book about Children around the World.* *Illus.* by Steve Björkman. *Scholastic, 1992.* (PreK–Gr. 2)

Cherry, Lynne. *The Armadillo from Amarillo.* *Illus.* by the author. *Harcourt, 1994.* (PreK–Gr. 2)

Ehlert, Lois. *In My World.* *Illus.* by the author. *Harcourt, 2002.* (PreK–Gr. 1)

Jenkins, Steve. *Hottest, Coldest, Highest, Deepest.* *Illus.* by the author. *Houghton Mifflin, 1998.* (PreK–Gr. 2)

Karas, G. Brian. *On Earth.* *Illus.* by the author. *Putnam, 2005.* (PreK–Gr. 2)

Kerley, Barbara. *One World, One Day.* *Illus.* with photos. *National Geographic, 2009.* (PreK–Gr. 2)

McNulty, Faith. *How to Dig a Hole to the Other Side of the World.* *Illus.* by Marc Simont. *HarperCollins, 1979.* (PreK–Gr. 2)

Priceman, Marjorie. *How to Make an Apple Pie and See the World.* *Illus.* by the author. *Knopf, 1994.* (PreK–Gr. 2)

Singer, Marilyn. *Nine o'Clock Lullaby.* *Illus.* by Frané Lessac. *HarperCollins, 1991* (PreK–Gr. 2)

Verse

Sing "Oh, My Aunt Came Back" to the tune of "How Dry I Am." The revised words by Judy Freeman cover all seven continents. Have kids sing each line back to you.

> Oh, my aunt came back (Oh, my aunt came back)
> From old Japan (From old Japan)
> And brought with her (And brought with her)
> A hand-held fan (A hand-held fan). (*fan your face with your hand*)
>
> From the Sidney fair . . . a rocking chair. (*rock back and forth*)

From the London piers . . . a pinking shears. (*make a scissor motion
with two fingers*)

From the South Pole loop . . . a hula hoop. (*sway your hips in a circle*)

From darkest Peru . . . a golden shoe. (*wag your foot back and forth*)

From a Cairo shed . . . a mummy's head. (*roll your head*)

The New York Zoo . . . a nut like YOU! (*stop all motions and point to
your audience*)

Activity

Children can sing each line after you and do all the cumulative motions of
"Oh, My Aunt Came Back." By the end of the song, they'll be simultaneously rocking, scissoring fingers, swaying hips, wagging a foot, and rolling
a head, which is pretty funny to watch but even funnier to do. Look up all
the places mentioned on a map or globe.

EGGS

Read-Alouds

Aston, Dianna. *An Egg Is Quiet.* Illus. by Sylvia Long. Chronicle, 2006. (PreK–Gr. 3)

Baker, Keith. *Big Fat Hen.* Illus. by the author. Harcourt, 1994. (PreK–K)

Dunrea, Olivier. *Ollie.* Illus. by the author. Houghton Mifflin, 2003. (PreK–K)

Graham, Bob. *Dimity Dumpty: The Story of Humpty's Little Sister.* Illus. by the author. Candlewick, 2007. (PreK–Gr. 2)

Gravett, Emily. *The Odd Egg.* Illus. by the author. Simon & Schuster, 2009. (PreK–Gr. 1)

Guiberson, Brenda Z. *The Emperor Lays an Egg.* Illus. by Joan Paley. Henry Holt, 2001. (PreK–Gr. 2)

Heller, Ruth. *Chickens Aren't the Only Ones.* Illus. by the author. Grosset & Dunlap, 1981. (PreK–Gr. 2)

Hills, Tad. *Duck and Goose.* Illus. by the author. Schwartz & Wade, 2006. (PreK–Gr. 1)

Seeger, Laura Vaccaro. *First the Egg.* Illus. by the author. Roaring Brook, 2007. (PreK–Gr. 1)

Seuss, Dr. *Green Eggs and Ham.* Illus. by the author. Random House, 1960. (PreK–Gr. 1)

Seuss, Dr. *Horton Hatches the Egg.* Illus. by the author. Random House, 1940. (PreK–Gr. 3)

Verse

Recite "Humpty Dumpty" and "Hickety, Pickety, My Black Hen":

Hickety, pickety, my black hen,

She lays eggs for gentlemen.

Sometimes nine and sometimes ten,

Hickety, pickety, my black hen.

Activity

Serve green scrambled eggs by adding a drop of green food coloring to eggs kids have cracked and beaten. Reassure children that the eggs they are using are unfertilized eggs that would never hatch.

ELEPHANTS

Read-Alouds

Arnold, Katya. *Elephants Can Paint, Too!* Illus. by the author. Atheneum, 2005. (PreK–Gr. 2)

Daly, Niki. *Next Stop—Zanzibar Road!* Illus. by the author. Clarion, 2012. (PreK–Gr. 2)

Hoberman, Mary Ann. *Miss Mary Mack.* Illus. by Nadine Bernard Westcott. Little, Brown, 1998. (PreK–Gr. 1)

Howard, Arthur. *The Hubbub Above.* Illus. by the author. Harcourt, 2005. (PreK–Gr. 1)

Knapman, Timothy. *Soon.* Illus. by Patrick Benson. Candlewick, 2015. (PreK–2)

Lobel, Arnold. *Uncle Elephant.* Illus. by the author. HarperCollins, 1981. (PreK–Gr. 1)

Peet, Bill. *The Ant and the Elephant.* Illus. by the author. Houghton Mifflin, 1972. (PreK–Gr. 2)

Seuss, Dr. *Horton Hatches the Egg.* Illus. by the author. Random House, 1940. (PreK–Gr. 3)

Thomas, Patricia. *"Stand Back," Said the Elephant, "I'm Going to Sneeze!"* Illus. by Wallace Tripp. Lothrop, 1971. (PreK–Gr. 2)

Willems, Mo. *There Is a Bird on Your Head.* Illus. by the author. Hyperion, 2007. (And all others in the Elephant and Piggie series) (PreK–Gr. 2)

Young, Ed. *Seven Blind Mice.* Illus. by the author. Philomel, 1992. (PreK–Gr. 3)

Verse

Sing "Miss Mary Mack" on page 148 and "The Elephant":

> An elephant goes like this and that. (*stamp your feet one at a time*)
>
> He's terrible big, (*raise your arms*)
>
> And he's terrible fat. (*spread your arms*)
>
> He has no fingers, (*wiggle your fingers*)
>
> He has no toes, (*touch your toes*)
>
> But goodness gracious, what a nose!
> >   (*draw your hands out indicating a long curly trunk*)

Activity

Make elephant finger puppets, and tell some of the elephant jokes from chapter 2, "Puppetry," on pages 50–51.

EMOTIONS

Read-Alouds

Bang, Molly. *When Sophie Gets Angry—Really, Really Angry*. *Illus. by the author. Scholastic/Blue Sky, 1999.* (PreK–Gr. 1)

Curtis, Jamie Lee. *Today I Feel Silly & Other Moods That Make My Day*. *Illus. by Laura Cornell. HarperCollins/Joanna Cotler, 1998.* (PreK–Gr. 1)

Everitt, Betsy. *Mean Soup*. *Illus. by the author. Harcourt, 1992.* (PreK–Gr. 1)

Frame, Jeron Ashford. *Yesterday I Had the Blues*. *Illus. by R. Gregory Christie. Tricycle, 2003.* (PreK–Gr. 2)

Freymann Saxton, and Joost Elffers. *How Are You Peeling? Foods with Moods*. *Illus. by the authors. Scholastic, 1999.* (PreK–Gr. 1)

Kachenmeister, Cherryl. *On Monday When It Rained*. *Photos by Tom Berthiaume. Houghton Mifflin, 1989.* (PreK–Gr. 1)

Klise, Kate. *Why Do You Cry? Not a Sob Story*. *Illus. by M. Sarah Klise. Henry Holt, 2006.* (PreK–Gr. 1)

Patricelli, Leslie. *Baby Happy, Baby Sad*. *Illus. by the author. Candlewick, 2008.* (PreK)

Raschka, Chris. *A Ball for Daisy*. *Illus. by the author. Schwartz & Wade, 2012.* (PreK–Gr. 1)

Seeger, Laura Vaccaro. *Walter Was Worried*. *Illus. by the author. Roaring Brook, 2005.* (PreK–Gr. 2)

Tankard, Jeremy. *Grumpy Bird.* *Illus. by the author. Scholastic, 2007.* (PreK–Gr. 1)

Vail, Rachel. *Sometimes I'm Bombaloo.* *Illus. by Yumi Heo. Scholastic, 2002.* (PreK–Gr. 1)

Viorst, Judith. *Alexander & the Terrible, Horrible, No Good, Very Bad Day.* *Illus. by Ray Cruz. Atheneum, 1972.* (PreK–Gr. 3)

Willems, Mo. *My Friend Is Sad.* *Illus. by the author. Hyperion, 2007.* (PreK–Gr. 2)

Verse
Sing "If You're Happy and You Know It."

Activity
Photograph children's faces showing different emotions. Print out the photos actual size, mount them on heavystock paper, and add a stick on the back so children can use them as stick puppets.

ETHICS, VALUES, AND CHARACTER EDUCATION
(*See* Apologies, Forgiveness, and Manners; Compassion and Kindness; Cooperation; Courage; Friendship; Generosity; Honesty; Perseverance; Resourcefulness; Responsibility)

ETIQUETTE   (*See* Apologies, Forgiveness, and Manners)

EXTRATERRESTRIAL BEINGS   (*See also* Space)

Read-Alouds
Marshall, Edward. *Space Case.* *Illus. by James Marshall. Dial, 1980.* (PreK–Gr. 1)

O'Malley, Kevin. *Captain Raptor and the Moon Mystery.* *Illus. by the author. Walker, 2005.* (PreK–Gr. 2)

Scieszka, Jon. *Baloney (Henry P.).* *Illus. by Lane Smith. Viking, 2001.* (K–Gr. 3)

Yolen, Jane. *Commander Toad in Space.* *Illus. by Bruce Degen. Coward, 1980.* (PreK–Gr. 2)

Verse
Recite "Five Little Astronauts"

> Five little astronauts playing near the stars. (*hold up five fingers*)
> The first one said, "Let's soar to Mars!" (*hold up one finger*)

The second one said, "There are rockets in the air."
   (*hold up two fingers*)

The third one said, "But we don't care." (*hold up three fingers*)

The fourth one said, "Let's zoom up in the sky." (*hold up four fingers*)

The fifth one said, "It's time to fly!"

Then SWISH went the ship and out went the light (*zoom both hands out from body in an S; clap hands on the word "light"*)

And the five little astronauts flew out of sight! (*zoom both hands in a snake-like path, upward*)

Activity

Pass out modeling clay, feathers, googly eyes, and other materials and let children create their own out-of-this-world creatures from space.

FAMILY LIFE

Read-Alouds

Diakité, Penda. *I Lost My Tooth in Africa.* Illus. by Baba Wagué Diakité. Scholastic, 2006. (PreK–Gr. 3)

Friedman, Ina R. *How My Parents Learned to Eat.* Illus. by Allen Say. Houghton Mifflin, 1984. (PreK–Gr. 3)

Greenfield. Eloise. *Honey, I Love.* Illus. by Jan Spivey Gilchrist. HarperCollins, 2003. (PreK–Gr. 2)

Kroll, Virginia. *Masai and I.* Illus. by Nancy Carpenter. Four Winds, 1992. (PreK–Gr. 2)

Lipson, Eden Ross. *Applesauce Season.* Illus. by Mordicai Gerstein. Roaring Brook, 2009. (PreK–Gr. 2)

Medina, Meg. *Tía Isa Wants a Car.* Illus. by Claudio Muñoz. Candlewick, 2011. (PreK–Gr. 2)

Perkins, Lynne Rae. *The Broken Cat.* Illus. by the author. Greenwillow, 2002. (K–Gr. 3)

Piven, Hanoch. *My Dog Is as Smelly as Dirty Socks: And Other Funny Family Portraits.* Illus. by the author. Schwartz & Wade, 2007. (PreK–Gr. 2)

Rylant, Cynthia. *The Relatives Came.* Illus. by Stephen Gammell. Atheneum, 1985. (PreK–Gr. 2)

Schertle, Alice. *Down the Road.* Illus. by E. B. Lewis. Harcourt/Browndeer, 1995. (PreK–Gr. 2)

Viorst, Judith. *Alexander & the Terrible, Horrible, No Good, Very Bad Day*. *Illus. by Ray Cruz. Atheneum, 1972.* (PreK–Gr. 2)

Willems, Mo. *Knuffle Bunny: A Cautionary Tale*. *Illus. by the author. Hyperion, 2005.* (PreK–Gr. 2)

Verse

Recite "The Family":

> This is Mama, kind and dear. (*point to your thumb*)
>
> This is Papa, standing near. (*point to your index finger*)
>
> This is brother, see how tall! (*point to your middle finger*)
>
> This is sister, not so tall. (*point to your ring finger*)
>
> This is baby, sweet and small. (*point to your pinky*)
>
> These are the family one and all! (*wiggle all your fingers*)

Activity

Cut out leaves of different shapes and give several to each child. Make a leafless tree template and run off copies for everyone. Ask kids to color their trees, put their names on the trunk, write the names or make drawings of their family members on the leaves, and glue the leaves on their trees.

FARM AND COUNTRY LIFE

Read-Alouds

Bateman, Teresa. *Farm Flu*. *Illus. by Nadine Bernard Westcott. Albert Whitman, 2001.* (PreK–Gr. 2)

Buehner, Caralyn. *Fanny's Dream*. *Illus. by Mark Buehner. Dial, 1996.* (K–Gr. 4)

**Cronin, Doreen. *Click, Clack, Peep!* ** *Illus. by Betsy Lewin. Atheneum, 2015.* (PreK–Gr. 1)

**Crum, Shutta. *Thunder-Boomer!* ** *Illus. by Carol Thompson. Clarion, 2009.* (PreK–Gr. 2)

Egan, Tim. *Serious Farm*. *Illus. by the author. Houghton Mifflin, 2003.* (PreK–Gr. 2)

Ehlert, Lois. *Color Farm*. *Illus. by the author. HarperCollins, 1990.* (PreK–Gr. 1)

Elliot, David. *Henry's Map*. *Illus. by the author. Philomel, 2013.* (PreK–Gr. 1)

Elliott, David. *On the Farm*. *Illus. by Holly Meade. Candlewick, 2008.* (PreK–Gr. 2)

Fleming, Denise. *Barnyard Banter*. *Illus. by the author. Henry Holt, 1994.* (PreK–Gr. 1)

Fleming, Denise. *The Cow Who Clucked*. *Illus. by the author. Henry Holt, 2006.* (PreK–Gr. 1)

Gourley, Robbin. *Bring Me Some Apples and I'll Make You a Pie: A Story about Edna Lewis*. *Illus. by the author. Clarion, 2009.* (K–Gr. 3)

Jonas, Ann. *Round Trip*. *Illus. by the author. Greenwillow, 1983.* (PreK–Gr. 2)

Krosoczka, Jarrett J. *Punk Farm*. *Illus. by the author. Knopf, 2005.* (PreK–Gr. 1)

Lindbergh, Reeve. *The Day the Goose Got Loose*. *Illus. by Steven Kellogg. Dial, 1990.* (PreK–Gr. 1)

Long, Loren. *Otis*. *Illus. by the author. Philomel, 2009.* (PreK–Gr. 1)

McCall, Francis, and Patricia Keeler. *A Huge Hog Is a Big Pig: A Rhyming Word Game*. *Illus. by the author. Greenwillow, 2002.* (PreK–Gr. 2)

Palatini, Margie. *The Cheese*. *Illus. by Steve Johnson and Lou Fancher. HarperCollins, 2007.* (PreK–Gr. 1)

Rostoker-Gruber, Karen. *Rooster Can't Cock-a-Doodle-Doo*. *Illus. by Paul Rátz de Tagyos. Dial, 2004.* (PreK–Gr. 1)

Vamos, Samantha R. *The Cazuela That the Farm Maiden Stirred*. *Illus. by Rafael López. Charlesbridge, 2011.* (PreK–Gr. 3)

Verse

Sing "Old MacDonald Had a Farm" and use the fingerplay "The Farm" on page 114.

Activity

Act out "Old MacDonald" with children dressed as the characters

---

FATHERS   (*See* Parents)

FEELINGS   (*See* Emotions)

FISH

Read-Alouds

Bania, Michael. *Kumak's Fish: A Tall Tale from the Far North*. *Illus. by the author. Alaska Northwest, 2004.* (PreK–Gr. 2)

Cousins, Lucy. *Hooray for Fish!* *Illus. by the author. Candlewick, 2005.* (PreK–Gr. 1)

Ehlert, Lois. *Fish Eyes: A Book You Can Count On*. *Illus. by the author. Harcourt, 1990.* (PreK–Gr. 1)

Lionni, Leo. *Fish Is Fish*. *Illus. by the author. Knopf, 1970.* (PreK–Gr. 2)

Lionni, Leo. *Swimmy*. *Illus. by the author. Pantheon, 1963.* (PreK–Gr. 1)

Lloyd-Jones, Sally. *Poor Doreen: A Fishy Tale.* Illus. by Alexandra Boiger. Schwartz & Wade, 2014. (PreK–Gr. 2)

Palmer, Helen. *A Fish Out of Water.* Illus. by P. D. Eastman. Random House, 1961. (PreK–Gr. 2)

Pfister, Marcus. *The Rainbow Fish.* Trans. by J. Alison James. Illus. by the author. North-South, 1992. (PreK–Gr. 1)

Rohmann, Eric. *Clara and Asha.* Illus. by the author. Roaring Brook, 2005. (PreK–Gr. 1)

Roy, Katherine. *Neighborhood Sharks: Hunting with the Great Whites of California's Farallon Islands.* Illus. by the author. Roaring Brook/David Macaulay Studios, 2014. (Gr. 2–5)

Wiesner, David. *Flotsam.* Illus. by the author. Clarion, 2006. (PreK–Gr. 2)

Wise, William. *Ten Sly Piranhas: A Counting Story in Reverse (A Tale of Wickedness—and Worse!).* Illus. by Victoria Chess. Dial, 1993. (K–Gr. 2)

Verse

Don't miss the ebullient John Lithgow singing "At the Codfish Ball," which you can find on his "Singin' in the Bathtub" CD and hear at www.youtube .com/watch?v = iUxQ4Pcx7G4. Or you can sing "Did You Ever See a Fishy" to the tune of "Turkey in the Straw."

> Have you ever seen a fishy on a hot summer's day?
> Have you ever seen a fishy a-swimming in the bay
> With his hands in his pockets (*slide your hands into pretend pockets*)
> And his pockets in his pants? (*slap the sides of your thighs*)
> Have you have ever seen a fishy do the hoochy-koochy dance?
>   (*using alternate index fingers, point in the air while you turn in a circle*)
> You never have! (*clap, clap*) You never will! (*clap*)
>
> Have you ever seen a fishy on a cold winter's day?
> Have you ever seen a fishy a-frozen in the bay?
> With his hands in his pockets and his pockets in his pants?
> Have you have ever seen a fishy do the hoochy-koochy dance?
> You never have! (*clap, clap*) You never will! (*clap*)

Activity

Set up an aquarium in your room for children to observe.

FLOWERS AND PLANTS   (*See also* Fruits and Vegetables; Gardens; Trees)

Read-Alouds

Aston, Dianna Hutts. *A Seed Is Sleepy*. *Illus. by Sylvia Long. Chronicle, 2007.* (PreK–Gr. 3)

Cooney, Barbara. *Miss Rumphius*. *Illus. by the author. Viking, 1982.* (K–Gr. 5)

Fleming, Denise. *Underground*. *Illus. by the author. Beach Lane, 2012.* (PreK–Gr. 1)

Gibbons, Gail. *From Seed to Plant*. *Illus. by the author. Holiday House, 1991.* (PreK–Gr. 2)

Heller, Ruth. *The Reason for a Flower*. *Illus. by the author. Grosset & Dunlap, 1983.* (PreK–Gr. 2)

Lobel, Anita. *Alison's Zinnia*. *Illus. by the author. Greenwillow, 1990.* (PreK–Gr. 1)

Lobel, Arnold. *The Rose in My Garden*. *Illus. by Anita Lobel. Greenwillow, 1984.* (PreK–Gr. 1)

Schaefer, Lola M. *Pick, Pull, Snap! Where Once a Flower Bloomed*. *Illus. by Lindsay Barrett George. Greenwillow, 2003.* (PreK–Gr. 2)

Verse

"Pretty Things" by Leroy F. Jackson, from *The Peter Patter Book of Nursery Rhymes,* ©1918:

> Pretty poppies, pretty trees, pretty little lettuce-leaves,
>
> Pretty pebbles, red and brown, pretty floating thistle-down.
>
> Pretty baby, curly head, standing in a pansy-bed,
>
> Pretty clouds, all white and curled—O the great, big pretty world!

Activity

Start a flower garden or planter outside your school or library.

FOOD   (*See* Themed Program: I'm Hungry on page 299)

FORGIVENESS   (*See* Apologies, Forgiveness, and Manners)

FOXES

Read-Alouds

Edwards, Pamela Duncan. *Four Famished Foxes and Fosdyke*. *Illus. by Henry Cole. HarperCollins, 1995.* (PreK–Gr. 2)

Lowry, Amy. *Fox Tails: Four Fables from Aesop.* *Illus. by the author. Holiday House,* 2012. (PreK–Gr. 2)

Marshall, James. *Wings: A Tale of Two Chickens.* *Illus. by the author. Viking Kestrel,* 1986. (PreK–Gr. 2)

McKissack, Patricia C. *Flossie & the Fox.* *Illus. by Rachel Isadora. Dial, 1986.* (K–Gr. 3)

Palatini, Margie. *Lousy Rotten Stinkin' Grapes.* *Illus. by Barry Moser. Simon & Schuster, 2009.* (K–Gr. 2)

Spier, Peter. *The Fox Went Out on a Chilly Night: An Old Song.* *Illus. by the author. Doubleday, 1961.* (PreK–Gr. 2)

Steig, William. *Doctor De Soto.* *Illus. by the author. Farrar, 1982.* (K–Gr. 2)

Willems, Mo. *That Is Not a Good Idea.* *Illus. by the author. Balzer + Bray, 2013.* (PreK–Gr. 2)

Verse
Sing "The Fox Went Out on a Chilly Night"; lyrics and music can be found at www.kididdles.com/lyrics/f032.html.

Activity
After singing "The Fox Went Out on a Chilly Night," have children act out the story.

FRIENDSHIP   (*See also* Children and Childhood)

Read-Alouds

Bloom, Suzanne. *A Splendid Friend, Indeed.* *Illus. by the author. Boyds Mills, 2005.* (PreK–Gr. 1)

Dubuc, Marianne. *The Lion and the Bird.* *Illus. by the author. Enchanted Lion, 2014.* (PreK–Gr. 2)

Ferry, Beth. *Stick and Stone.* *Illus. by Tom Lichtenheld. Houghton Mifflin Harcourt,* 2015. (PreK–Gr. 2)

Frazee, Marla. *A Couple of Boys Have the Best Week Ever.* *Illus. by the author. Harcourt,* 2008. (PreK–Gr. 12)

Howe, James. *Horace and Morris but Mostly Dolores.* *Illus. by Amy Walrod. Atheneum,* 1999. (PreK–Gr. 2)

Juster, Norton. *Neville.* *Illus. by G. Brian Karas. Schwartz & Wade, 2011.* (PreK–Gr. 3)

Marshall, James. *George and Martha: The Complete Stories of Two Best Friends.* Illus. by the author. Houghton Mifflin, 1997, c1974. (PreK–Gr. 1)

McDonnell, Patrick. *The Gift of Nothing.* Illus. by the author. Little, Brown, 2005. (PreK–Gr. 2)

Raschka, Chris. *Yo! Yes?* Illus. by the author. Orchard, 1993. (PreK–Gr. 3)

Rodman, Mary. *My Best Friend.* Illus. by E. B. Lewis. Viking, 2005. (PreK–Gr. 1)

Rosenthal, Amy Krouse. *Cookies: Bite-Size Life Lessons.* Illus. by Jane Dyer. Harper-Collins, 2006. (PreK–Gr. 2)

Seeger, Laura Vaccaro. *Dog and Bear: Two Friends, Three Stories.* Illus. by the author. Roaring Brook, 2007. (PreK–Gr. 1)

Waber, Bernard. *Evie & Margie.* Illus. by the author. Houghton Mifflin, 2003. (PreK–Gr. 2)

Waber, Bernard. *Ira Sleeps Over.* Illus. by the author. Houghton Mifflin, 1973. (PreK–Gr. 2)

Watt, Mélanie. *Scaredy Squirrel Makes a Friend.* Illus. by the author. Kids Can, 2007. (PreK–Gr. 2)

Willems, Mo. *I Will Surprise My Friend!* Illus. by the author. Hyperion, 2008. (PreK–Gr. 2)

Woodson, Jacqueline. *The Other Side.* Illus. by E. B. Lewis. Putnam, 2001. (K–Gr. 4)

Verse

Sing "The More We Get Together" (to the tune of "Did You Ever See a Lassie"):

> The more we get together, together, together,
>
> The more we get together, the happier we'll be.
>
> For your friends are my friends,
>
> And my friends are your friends.
>
> The more we get together, the happier we'll be.

Activity

Make a friendship chain. Have each child decorate a paper link with his or her name on it, then glue or staple the links together to make one long chain.

FROGS AND TOADS

Read-Alouds

Bishop, Nic. Nic Bishop Frogs. *Photos by the author. Scholastic, 2008.* (PreK–Gr. 3)

Cowley, Joy. Red-Eyed Tree Frog. *Photos by Nic Bishop. Scholastic, 1999.* (PreK–Gr. 1)

Kalan, Robert. Jump, Frog, Jump! *Illus. by Byron Barton. Greenwillow, 1981.* (PreK–Gr. 1)

Lionni, Leo. Fish Is Fish. *Illus. by the author. Knopf, 1970.* (PreK–Gr. 2)

Lobel, Arnold. Frog and Toad Are Friends. *Illus. by the author. HarperCollins, 1970.* (PreK–Gr. 1)

London, Jonathan. Froggy Gets Dressed. *Illus. by Frank Remkiewicz. Viking, 1992.* (PreK–Gr. 1)

Pfeffer, Wendy. From Tadpole to Frog. *Illus. by Holly Keller. HarperCollins, 1994.* (PreK–Gr. 2)

Walton, Rick. Once There Was a Bull . . . (Frog): An Adventure in Compound Words. *Illus. by Greg Hally. Gibbs Smith, 1995.* (PreK–Gr. 2)

Wiesner, David. Tuesday. *Illus. by the author. Clarion, 1991.* (PreK–Gr. 2)

Willems, Mo. City Dog, Country Frog. *Illus. by the author. Hyperion, 2010.* (PreK–Gr. 3)

Wilson, Karma. A Frog in the Bog. *Illus. by Joan Rankin. McElderry, 2003.* (PreK–Gr. 1)

Verse

Recite "Five Little Froggies":

> Five little froggies sitting on a well (*cup hands*)
>
> One peeped in and down he fell (*raise one finger*)
>
> Froggies jumped high (*raise hands and wave above head*)
>
> Froggies jumped low (*lower hands to the floor*)
>
> Froggies jumped everywhere to and fro (*wave arms in all directions*)
>
> (*Continue the counting-down rhyme*) Four little froggies, (*etc.*)

Activity

Help children make origami frog heads. Begin by folding green construction paper, held in landscape mode, into thirds. Glue the open edge. If your paper is 9-by-12 inches folded, it will now be a 9-by-4-inch strip. Fold the strip in half so it now measures 4½ by 4 inches and then accordion fold it in half again, with the two halves folded to the right and left so the paper will stand up like the letter M. Put four fingers into one open slot and your thumb in the other. What does it look like? An open frog mouth! Kids can draw or glue on eyes, and you've got yourself the start of a frog chorus.

FRUITS AND VEGETABLES

(*See also* Apples; Flowers and Plants; Gardens; Trees; and Thematic Unit: I'm Hungry: Books, Stories, and Fun with Food on page 299)

Read-Alouds

Bell, Ceci. *I Yam a Donkey! Illus. by the author. Clarion, 2015.* (PreK–Gr. 3)

Coy, John. *Two Old Potatoes and Me. Illus. by Carolyn Fisher. Knopf, 2003.* (PreK–Gr. 2)

Ehlert, Lois. *Eating the Alphabet: Fruits and Vegetables from A to Z. Illus. by the author. Harcourt, 1989.* (PreK–Gr. 1)

Ehlert, Lois. *Growing Vegetable Soup. Illus. by the author. Harcourt, 1987.* (PreK–Gr. 1)

Falwell, Cathryn. *Mystery Vine: A Pumpkin Surprise. Illus. by the author. Greenwillow, 2009.* (PreK–Gr. 1)

Krauss, Ruth. *The Carrot Seed. Illus. by Crockett Johnson. HarperCollins, 1945.* (PreK–Gr. 1)

McClements, George. *Night of the Veggie Monster.* *Illus. by the author. Bloomsbury, 2008.* (PreK–Gr. 1)

McNamara, Margaret. *How Many Seeds in a Pumpkin?* *Illus. by G. Brian Karas. Schwartz & Wade, 2007.* (PreK–Gr. 2)

Miller, Pat Zietlow. *Sophie's Squash.* *Illus. by Anne Wilsdorf. Schwartz & Wade, 2013.* (PreK–Gr. 1)

Pfeffer, Wendy. *From Seed to Pumpkin.* *Illus. by James Graham Hale. HarperCollins, 2004.* (PreK–Gr. 2)

Reynolds, Aaron. *Creepy Carrots!* *Illus. by Peter Brown. Simon & Schuster, 2012.* (PreK–Gr. 2)

Sayre, April Pulley. *Rah, Rah, Radishes! A Vegetable Chant.* *Photos by the author. Beach Lane, 2011.* (PreK–Gr. 2) Also see **Go, Go, Grapes! A Fruit Chant** (2012) and **Let's Go Nuts! Seeds We Eat** (2013).

Verse

Sing "Eating Goober Peas." If you can't recall the tune, which dates back to the Civil War, listen to the MIDI at www.kididdles.com/lyrics/g114.html. What are goober peas? Peanuts.

> Sitting by the roadside on a summers day,
>
> Chatting with my mess-mates, passing time away,
>
> Lying in the shadow underneath the trees,
>
> Goodness, how delicious eating goober peas.
>
> Peas, peas, peas, peas, eating goober peas,
>
> Goodness, how delicious, eating goober peas.

Activity

Place apple seeds between damp paper towels and refrigerate them for six weeks. Let children plant the sprouted seeds in garden soil. You can also use fast-sprouting seeds, such as radish, bean, or peas.

FUNNIEST PICTURE BOOKS EVER

Read-Alouds

Allard, Harry. *Miss Nelson Is Missing.* *Illus. by James Marshall. Houghton Mifflin, 1977.* (PreK–Gr. 2)

Allard, Harry. *The Stupids Have a Ball.* *Illus. by James Marshall. Houghton Mifflin, 1978.* (PreK–Gr. 1)

Arnold, Tedd. *Parts.* *Illus. by the author. Dial, 1997.* (PreK–Gr. 2)

Barrett, Judi. *Cloudy with a Chance of Meatballs.* *Illus. by Ron Barrett. Atheneum, 1978.* (PreK–Gr. 4)

Beaumont, Karen. *I Ain't Gonna Paint No More.* *Illus. by David Catrow. Harcourt, 2005.* (K–Gr. 2)

Black, Michael Ian. *Naked!* *Illus. by Debbie Ridpath Ohi. Simon & Schuster, 2014.* (PreK–Gr. 2)

Bruel, Nick. *Bad Kitty.* *Illus. by the author. Roaring Brook, 2005.* (PreK–Gr. 1)

Buzzeo, Toni. *One Cool Friend.* *Illus. by David Small. Dial, 2012.* (PreK–Gr. 3)

Cronin, Doreen. *Click, Clack, Moo: Cows That Type.* *Illus. by Betsy Lewin. Simon & Schuster, 2000.* (PreK–Gr. 3)

Cronin, Doreen. *Diary of a Worm.* *Illus. by Harry Bliss. HarperCollins/Joanna Cotler, 2003.* (K–Gr. 3)

DePaola, Tomie. *Strega Nona.* *Illus. by the author. Prentice-Hall, 1975.* (PreK–Gr. 4)

Feiffer, Jules. *Bark, George.* *Illus. by the author. HarperCollins, 1999.* (PreK–Gr. 1)

Isaacs, Anne. *Meanwhile, Back at the Ranch.* *Illus. by Kevin Hawkes. Schwartz & Wade, 2014.* (K–Gr. 4)

Krall, Dan. *The Great Lollipop Caper.* *Illus. by the author. Simon & Schuster, 2013.* (PreK–Gr. 3)

Lester, Helen. *Hooway for Wodney Wat.* *Illus. by Lynn Munsinger. Houghton Mifflin, 1999.* (PreK–Gr. 2)

Long, Melinda. *How I Became a Pirate.* *Illus. by David Shannon. Harcourt, 2003.* (PreK–Gr. 1)

Mack, Jeff. *Duck in the Fridge.* *Illus. by the author. Two Lions, 2014.* (PreK–Gr. 1)

Marshall, James. *George and Martha: The Complete Stories of Two Best Friends.* *Illus. by the author. Houghton Mifflin, 1997, c1974.* (PreK–Gr. 1)

McMullan, Kate. *I Stink.* *Illus. by Jim McMullan. HarperCollins, 2002.* (PreK–Gr. 1)

Meddaugh, Susan. *Martha Speaks.* *Illus. by the author. Houghton Mifflin, 1992.* (PreK–Gr. 3)

Novak, B. J. *The Book with No Pictures.* *Dial, 2014.* (PreK–Gr. 4)

O'Malley, Kevin. *Once Upon a Cool Motorcycle Dude.* *Illus. by Kevin O'Malley, Carol Heyer, and Scott Goto. Walker, 2005.* (K–Gr. 3)

Palatini, Margie. *Piggie Pie.* *Illus. by Howard Fine. Clarion, 1995.* (PreK–Gr. 1)

Pilkey, Dav. *Dog Breath: The Horrible Trouble with Hally Tosis.* *Illus. by the author. Scholastic/Blue Sky, 1994.* (PreK–Gr. 2)

Pilkey, Dav. *Dogzilla.* *Illus. by the author. Harcourt, 1993.* Equally riotous is Kat Kong (1993). (PreK–Gr. 3)

Pomerantz, Charlotte. *The Piggy in the Puddle.* *Illus. by James Marshall. Simon & Schuster, 1974.* (PreK–Gr. 2)

Rash, Andy. *Are You a Horse?* *Illus. by the author. Scholastic, 2009.* (PreK–Gr. 3)

Rathmann, Peggy. *Officer Buckle and Gloria.* *Illus. by the author. Putnam, 1995.* (PreK–Gr. 3)

Reynolds, Aaron. *Creepy Carrots!* *Illus. by Peter Brown. Simon & Schuster, 2012.* (PreK–Gr. 2)

Scieszka, Jon. *The Stinky Cheese Man and Other Fairly Stupid Tales.* *Illus. by Lane Smith. Viking, 1992.* (PreK–Gr. 6)

Scieszka, Jon. *The True Story of the 3 Little Pigs!* *Illus. by Lane Smith. Viking, 1989.* (PreK–Gr. 3)

Shannon, David. *No, David!* *Illus. by the author. Scholastic, 1998.* (PreK–Gr. 1)

Stein, David Ezra. *Interrupting Chicken.* *Illus. by the author. Candlewick, 2010.* (PreK–Gr. 2)

Stevens, Janet, and Susan Stevens Crummel. *And the Dish Ran Away with the Spoon.* *Illus. by Janet Stevens. Harcourt, 2001.* (PreK–Gr. 1)

Teague, Mark. *Dear Mrs. LaRue: Letters from Obedience School.* *Illus. by the author. Scholastic, 2002.* (K–Gr. 4)

Thomas, Jan. *Is Everyone Ready for Fun?* *Illus. by the author. Beach Lane, 2011.* (PreK–Gr. 1)

Thomas, Jan. *Rhyming Dust Bunnies.* *Illus. by the author. Atheneum, 2009.* (PreK–Gr. 1)

Willems, Mo. *Don't Let the Pigeon Drive the Bus.* *Illus. by the author. Hyperion, 2003.* (PreK–Gr. 6)

Willems, Mo. *Knuffle Bunny: A Cautionary Tale.* *Illus. by the author. Hyperion, 2005.* (PreK–Gr. 2)

Willems, Mo. *Watch Me Throw the Ball!* *Illus. by the author. Hyperion, 2009.* (PreK–Gr. 2)

Verse
Sing "We Do Nothing" on pages 180–181.

Activity
Have kids show and tell the funniest books they ever read.

GARDENS   (*See also* Flowers and Plants; Fruits and Vegetables; Trees)

Read-Alouds

Cherry, Lynne. *How Groundhog's Garden Grew*. *Illus. by the author. Scholastic/Blue Sky, 2003.* (PreK–Gr. 1)

Fleming, Candace. *Muncha! Muncha! Muncha!* *Illus. by G. Brian Karas. Atheneum, 2002.* (PreK–Gr. 1)

Fogliano, Julie. *And Then It's Spring*. *Illus. by Erin E. Stead. Roaring Brook, 2012.* (PreK–Gr. 1)

Gourley, Robbin. *Bring Me Some Apples and I'll Make You a Pie: A Story about Edna Lewis*. *Illus. by the author. Clarion Books, 2009.* (K–Gr. 3)

Henkes, Kevin. *My Garden*. *Illus. by the author. Greenwillow, 2010.* (PreK–Gr. 1)

Smith, Lane. *Grandpa Green*. *Illus. by the author. Roaring Brook, 2011.* (PreK–Gr. 2)

Stevens, Janet. *Tops & Bottoms*. *Illus. by the author. Harcourt, 1995.* (PreK–Gr. 3)

Verse

Recite "Mary, Mary, Quite Contrary" and do the fingerplay "My Garden" on page 115.

Activity

Make "fairy garden" terrariums out of plastic roasted-chicken containers. Add two inches of dirt, a little water, small decorative toys and pebbles, and tiny rooted plants, such as baby's breath or ferns, and cover with the clear plastic dome. Children can watch as their gardens grow.

GENEROSITY

Read-Alouds

Lionni, Leo. *Tico and the Golden Wings*. *Illus. by the author. Pantheon, 1964.* (PreK–Gr. 2)

Pfister, Marcus. *The Rainbow Fish*. *Trans. by J. Alison James. Illus. by the author. North-South Books, 1992.* (PreK–Gr. 2)

Vere, Ed. *Banana!* *Illus. by the author. Henry Holt, 2010.* (PreK–Gr. 1)

Willems, Mo. *The Pigeon Finds a Hot Dog*. *Illus. by the author. Hyperion, 2004.* (PreK–Gr. 1)

Willems, Mo. *Should I Share My Ice Cream?* *Illus. by the author. Hyperion, 2011.* (PreK–Gr. 2)

Verse

Sing "This Little Light of Mine." Find lyrics and music at www.songsfor
teaching.com/religious/thislittlelightofmine.htm.

Activity

Children can string bead friendship necklaces and give their creations to
someone else in the group. The kids won't get to keep the one they made,
but they'll get one in return.

GEOGRAPHY   (*See* Earth; United States)

GHOSTS   (*See also* Halloween; Monsters; Witches)

Read-Alouds

LaRochelle, David. *The Haunted Hamburger and Other Ghostly Stories*. Illus. by Paul
Meisel. Dutton, 2011. (K–Gr. 2)

Morales, Yuyi. *Just in Case: A Trickster Tale and Spanish Alphabet Book*. Illus. by the
author. Roaring Brook, 2008. (K–Gr. 2)

Newgarden, Mark, and Megan Montague Cash. *Bow-Wow's Nightmare Neighbors*.
Illus. by the authors. Roaring Brook, 2014. (PreK–Gr. 1)

Pearson, Susan. *We're Going on a Ghost Hunt*. Illus. by S. D. Schindler. Amazon,
2012. (PreK–Gr. 1)

Winters, Kay. *The Teeny Tiny Ghost*. Illus. by Lynn Munsinger. HarperCollins, 1997.
(PreK–Gr. 1)

Verse

Sing "Have You Seen the Ghost of John?" Go to www.music-for-music
-teachers.com/have-you-seen-the-ghost-of-john.html for a recording and
printable sheet music.

> Have you seen the ghost of John?
>
> All white bones with the skin all gone—
>
> Oooh, oooooh,
>
> Wouldn't it be chilly with no skin on?

Activity

Make ghost windsocks. In the center of white construction paper, children
draw round black eyes and a black open mouth. They then roll the paper

into a fat cylinder, with the face on the outside, and glue the seam shut. Glue white crepe paper streams on the inside so they flow outside. Punch holes at top of the cylinder, one on either side, and attach string. Children can take their ghostly creations home to hang in a breezy spot.

GIANTS

Read-Alouds

Bertrand, Lynne. *Granite Baby.* Illus. by Kevin Hawkes. Farrar, 2005. (PreK–Gr. 3)

Briggs, Raymond. *Jim and the Beanstalk.* Illus. by the author. Coward-McCann, 1970. (PreK–Gr. 2)

Bryan, Ashley. *Can't Scare Me!* Illus. by the author. Atheneum, 2013. (K–Gr. 2)

DePaola, Tomie. *Fin M'Coul: the Giant of Knockmany Hill.* Illus. by the author. Holiday House, 1981. (PreK–Gr. 3)

Galdone, Paul. *Jack and the Beanstalk.* Illus. by the author. Clarion, 1974. (K–Gr. 2)

Gerstein, Mordicai. *Carolinda Clatter.* Illus. by the author. Roaring Brook, 2005. (PreK–Gr. 2)

Isaacs, Anne. *Swamp Angel.* Illus. by Paul O. Zelinsky. Dutton, 1994. (K–Gr. 4)

Kellogg, Steven. *Jack and the Beanstalk.* Illus. by the author. Morrow, 1991. (K–Gr. 2)

Mora, Pat. *Doña Flor: A Tall Tale about a Giant Woman with a Great Big Heart.* Illus. by Raúl Colón. Knopf, 2005. (PreK–Gr. 2)

Wood, Audrey. *The Bunyans.* Illus. by David Shannon. Scholastic/Blue Sky, 1996. (K–Gr. 2)

Verse

Recite "Fee Fi Fo Fum" from the English fairy tale, "Jack and the Beanstalk":

Fee-fi-fo-fum,

I smell the blood of an Englishman,

Be he live, or be he dead

I'll grind his bones to make my bread.

Activity

Make a friendly giant for your room out of two huge pieces of kraft paper (seven or eight feet) cut into a human shape. Children can draw clothing (or cut cloth and glue it on) and add facial features. Stuff the giant with crumpled newspaper and use a hot glue gun or staple the edges. Add a tie, a scarf, and other accoutrements. Then sit your friendly giant in a chair to listen to stories with the group.

GIFTS *(See also* Birthdays; Christmas)

Read-Alouds

Bunting, Eve. *The Mother's Day Mice.* *Illus. by Jan Brett. Clarion, 1986.* (PreK–Gr. 1)

Carle, Eric. *The Secret Birthday Message.* *Illus. by the author. HarperCollins, 1972.* (PreK–Gr. 1)

Fleming, Candace. *Clever Jack Takes the Cake.* *Illus. by G. Brian Karas. Schwartz & Wade, 2010.* (PreK–Gr. 3)

McDonnell, Patrick. *The Gift of Nothing.* *Illus. by the author. Little, Brown, 2005.* (PreK–Gr. 2)

McKissack, Patricia C. *The All-I'll-Ever-Want Christmas Doll.* *Illus. by Jerry Pinkney. Schwartz & Wade, 2007.* (PreK–Gr. 3)

Polacco, Patricia. *An Orange for Frankie.* *Illus. by the author. Philomel, 2004.* (K–Gr. 4)

Zolotow, Charlotte. *Mr. Rabbit and the Lovely Present.* *Illus. by Maurice Sendak. HarperCollins, 1962.* (PreK–Gr. 1)

Verse

Sing "I Gave My Love a Cherry" (aka "The Riddle Song"). You'll find the score and lyrics at folksongcollector.com/riddle.html. Most people sing this song slowly and soulfully, but feel free to sing it up tempo to make it more child-friendly.

> I gave my love a cherry that had no stone.
> I gave my love a chicken that had no bone.
> I gave my love a ring that had no end.
> I gave my love a baby with no cryin.'
>
> How can there be a cherry that has no stone?
> How can there be a chicken that has no bone?
> How can there be a ring that has no end?
> How can there be a baby with no cryin'?

A cherry when it's bloomin' it has no stone,

A chicken when it's pippin' (*in the shell*), it has no bone,

A ring, when it's rollin,' it has no end.

A baby when it's sleepin,' there's no cryin'.

Activity

Bring out wrapping paper, tape, and ribbons. Ask children to wrap small crafts they have made and give them as presents to each other to open. You can also have kids draw or print their own wrapping paper.

GORILLAS   (*See* Primates)

GRANDPARENTS

Read-Alouds

Ackerman, Karen. *Song and Dance Man.* Illus. by Stephen Gammell. Knopf, 1988. (PreK–Gr. 2)

Caseley, Judith. *Dear Annie.* Illus. by the author. Greenwillow, 1991. (PreK–Gr. 1)

Daly, Niki. *Not So Fast, Songololo.* Illus. by the author. Frances Lincoln, 2001, c1986. (PreK–Gr. 2)

DePaola, Tomie. *Tom.* Illus. by the author. Putnam, 1993. (PreK–Gr. 2)

Dorros, Arthur. *Abuela.* Illus. by Elisa Kleven. Dutton, 1991. Also see *Abuelo* (2014). (PreK–Gr. 2)

Greenfield, Eloise. *Grandpa's Face.* Illus. by Floyd Cooper. Putnam, 1988. (K–Gr. 2)

Juster, Norton. *The Hello, Goodbye Window.* Illus. by Chris Raschka. Disney-Hyperion, 2005. (PreK–Gr. 1)

Lipson, Eden Ross. *Applesauce Season.* Illus. by Mordicai Gerstein. Roaring Brook, 2009. (PreK–Gr. 2)

Lum, Kate. *What! Cried Granny: An Almost Bedtime Story.* Illus. by Adrian Johnson. Dial, 1999. (PreK–Gr. 2)

Rylant, Cynthia. *Henry and Mudge and the Great Grandpas.* Illus. by Suçie Stevenson. Simon & Schuster, 2005. (PreK–Gr. 1)

Say, Allen. *Grandfather's Journey.* Illus. by the author. Houghton Mifflin, 1993. (K–Gr. 3)

Smith, Lane. *Grandpa Green.* *Illus. by the author. Roaring Brook, 2011.* (PreK–Gr. 2)

Stein, David Ezra. *Love, Mouserella.* *Illus. by the author. Penguin/Nancy Paulsen, 2011.* (PreK–Gr. 2)

Stevenson, James. *Could Be Worse!* *Illus. by the author. Greenwillow, 1977.* (PreK–Gr. 1)

Wells, Rosemary. *Yoko's Paper Cranes.* *Illus. by the author. Disney-Hyperion, 2001.* (PreK–Gr. 1)

Verse

Use the fingerplay "Grandma and Grandpa" on page 115.

Activity

Make paper cranes like Yoko does in Rosemary Wells's *Yoko's Paper Cranes.* After children decorate the paper, help them fold it into cranes, which they can give as gifts to their grandparents. Google *origami cranes* to find multiple sites with instructions, including step-by-step videos if you consider yourself "paper impaired."

HALLOWEEN   (*See also* Ghosts; Monsters; Witches)

Read-Alouds

Cuyler, Margery. *Skeleton Hiccups.* *Illus. by S. D. Schindler. Simon & Schuster, 2002.* (PreK–Gr. 1)

Krosoczka, Jarrett J. *Annie Was Warned.* *Illus. by the author. Knopf, 2003.* (PreK–Gr. 1)

LaRochelle, David. *The Haunted Hamburger and Other Ghostly Stories.* *Illus. by Paul Meisel. Dutton, 2011.* (K–Gr. 2)

Leuck, Laura. *One Witch.* *Illus. by S. D. Schindler. Walker, 2003.* (PreK–Gr. 1)

Marshall, Edward. *Space Case.* *Illus. by the author. Dial, 1980.* (PreK–Gr. 1)

McGhee, Alison. *A Very Brave Witch.* *Illus. by Harry Bliss. Simon & Schuster, 2006.* (PreK–Gr. 1)

McNamara, Margaret. *How Many Seeds in a Pumpkin?* *Illus. by G. Brian Karas. Schwartz & Wade, 2007.* (PreK–Gr. 2)

Meddaugh, Susan. *The Witches' Supermarket.* *Illus. by the author. Houghton Mifflin, 1991.* (PreK–Gr. 2)

Montes, Marisa. *Los Gatos Black on Halloween.* *Illus. by Yuyi Morales. Henry Holt, 2006.* (PreK–Gr. 1)

Paquette, Ammi-Joan. *Ghost in the House.* *Illus. by Adam Record. Candlewick, 2013.* (PreK–Gr. 1)

Pilkey, Dav. *The Hallo-Wiener.* *Illus. by the author. Scholastic/Blue Sky, 1995.* (PreK–Gr. 2)

Rohmann, Eric. *Bone Dog.* *Illus. by the author. Roaring Brook, 2012.* (PreK–Gr. 1)

Savage, Stephen. *Ten Orange Pumpkins.* *Illus. by the author. Dial, 2013.* (PreK–Gr. 1)

Silverman, Erica. *Big Pumpkin.* *Illus. by S. D. Schindler. Macmillan, 1992.* (PreK–Gr. 1)

Wheeler, Lisa. *Boogie Knights.* *Illus. by Mark Siegel. Atheneum, 2008.* (PreK–Gr. 1)

Willems, Mo. *Leonardo the Terrible Monster.* *Illus. by the author. Hyperion, 2005.* (PreK–Gr. 2)

Williams, Linda. *The Little Old Lady Who Was Not Afraid of Anything.* *Illus. by Megan Lloyd. HarperCollins, 1986.* (PreK–Gr. 1)

Winters, Kay. *The Teeny Tiny Ghost.* *Illus. by Lynn Munsinger. HarperCollins, 1997.* (PreK–Gr. 1)

Verse

Sing Judy Freeman's version of the popular bumblebee song, "I'm Bringing Home a Scary Vampire Bat," in chapter 5, "Music," on page 191.

Activity

Decorate pumpkins and small gourds with markers; carve one pumpkin to have children estimate, and then count, the number of seeds it has.

HANUKKAH

Read-Alouds

Howland, Naomi. *Latkes, Latkes Good to Eat: A Chanukah Story.* *Illus. by the author. Clarion, 1999.* (PreK–Gr. 1)

Kimmel, Eric A. *Hanukkah Bear.* *Illus. by Mike Wohnoutka. Holiday House, 2013.* (PreK–Gr. 1)

Kimmel, Eric. *Hershel and the Hanukkah Goblins.* *Illus. by Trina Schart Hyman. Holiday House, 1989.* (K–Gr. 3)

Newman, Lesléa. *Runaway Dreidel!* *Illus. by Kyrsten Brooker. Henry Holt, 2002.* (PreK–Gr. 1)

Verse

Sing "I Had a Little Dreidel"; you'll find lyrics and music at bussongs.com/songs/dreidel-dreidel-dreidel.php.

Activity

Spin dreidels with children. The Hebrew letters on the four sides of the dreidel are: nun, gimmel, hay, and shin, which stand for "A great miracle happened there." Go to www.kidzworld.com/article/27693-how-to-play -dreidel to find the rules and a clear explanation of Hanukkah.

HATS (*See also* Boots and Shoes; Clothing and Dress)

Read-Alouds

Brett, Jan. *The Hat*. *Illus. by the author. Putnam, 1997*. (PreK–Gr. 1)

Geringer, Laura. *A Three Hat Day*. *Illus. by Arnold Lobel. HarperCollins, 1985.* (PreK–Gr. 1)

Keats, Ezra Jack. *Jennie's Hat*. *Illus. by the author. HarperCollins, 1966.* (PreK–Gr. 1)

Kimmel, Eric A. *Stormy's Hat: Just Right for a Railroad Man*. *Illus. by Andrea U'Ren. Farrar, 2008.* (PreK–Gr. 2)

Klassen, Jon. *I Want My Hat Back*. *Illus. by the author. Candlewick, 2011.* (PreK–Gr. 2)

Klassen, Jon. *This Is Not My Hat*. *Illus. by the author. Candlewick, 2012.* (PreK–Gr. 1)

Nodset, Joan L. *Who Took the Farmer's Hat?* *Illus. by Fritz Siebel. HarperCollins, 1963.* (PreK–Gr. 1)

Slobodkina, Esphyr. *Caps for Sale*. *Illus. by the author. HarperCollins, 1947.* (PreK–Gr. 1)

Verse

To the tune of "Turkey in the Straw," sing "Pancake Hat" by Sarah Pirtle, from her album, "The Wind Is Telling Secrets" on the label A Gentle Wind. Find and share more of her music at sarahpirtle.com. She says on the website, "I hope these songs will roost on your shoulder and you'll take them in to live in your heart."

> I went to a party and I brought my hat,
> I put it on a bed and along came a cat;
> Cat sat down and squashed it flat,
> Now I call it my pancake hat.
> Pancake hat, pancake hat, pancake hat, pancake hat,
> Used to be fine with a feather and that,
> Now I call it my pancake hat.

I put on my hat and I went out to play,

Along came the wind and blew it away;

Into a pasture and under a cow;

Cow took a bite—it's a doughnut now.

Doughnut hat, doughnut hat, doughnut hat, doughnut hat,

Used to be fine with a feather and that,

Now I call it my doughnut hat.

Was hot one day so I went for a swim,

I put on my hat and I jumped right in;

My hat swelled up and I said, "DRAT!"

Now I call it my muffin hat.

Muffin hat, muffin hat, muffin hat, muffin hat,

Used to be fine with a feather and that,

Now I call it my muffin hat.

Activity
Children can make hats out of folded newspaper or sheets of kraft paper which they can decorate.

HONESTY

Read-Alouds

Brisson, Pat. *The Summer My Father Was Ten.* Illus. by Andrea Shine. Boyds Mills, 1998. (K–Gr. 3)

Havill, Juanita. *Jamaica and the Substitute Teacher.* Illus. by Anne Sibley O'Brien. Houghton Mifflin, 1999. (K–Gr. 2)

McKissack, Patricia C. *The Honest-to-Goodness Truth.* Illus. by Giselle Potter. Atheneum, 2000. (PreK–Gr. 2)

Sharmat, Marjorie Weinman. *A Big Fat Enormous Lie.* Illus. by David McPhail. Dutton, 1978. (PreK–Gr. 1)

Smothers, Ethel Footman. *The Hard-Times Jar.* Illus. by John Holyfield. Farrar, 2003. (K–Gr. 2)

Soto, Gary. *Too Many Tamales.* Illus. by Ed Martinez. Putnam, 1993. (PreK–Gr. 3)

Verse

Sing "Found a Nickel" (to the tune of "Found a Peanut"). Talk about giving back things you find that aren't yours.

> Found a nickel, found a nickel
> Found a nickel on the ground;
> It wasn't mine, so I returned it.
> It was lost but now it's found.

> *Other verses:* found a: mitten, toy truck, pencil, *etc. Children can think of more.*

Activity

Play "Fact versus Fib." Ask children to come up with one true fact and one lie about themselves, their families, pets, interests, and so on. When they read or tell their two statements aloud, others in the group must guess which is true and which is the fib.

HORSES

Read-Alouds

Angleberger, Tom. Crankee Doodle. *Illus. by Cece Bell. Clarion, 2013.* (K–Gr. 1)

Armstrong, Jennifer. Magnus at the Fire. *Illus. by Owen Smith. Simon & Schuster 2005.* (PreK–Gr. 1)

Hobbie, Holly. Everything But the Horse. *Illus. by the author. Little, Brown, 2010.* (K–Gr. 3)

Isaacs, Anne. Dust Devil. *Illus. by Paul O. Zelinsky. Schwartz & Wade, 2010.* (K–Gr. 3)

McCarthy, Meghan. Seabiscuit the Wonder Horse. *Illus. by the author. Simon & Schuster, 2008.* (K–Gr. 2)

Rash, Andy. Are You a Horse? *Illus. by the author. Scholastic, 2009.* (PreK–Gr. 1)

Silverman, Erica. Cowgirl Kate and Cocoa. *Illus. by Betsy Lewin. Harcourt, 2005.* (PreK–Gr. 1)

Smee, Nicola. Clip-Clop. *Illus. by the author. Henry Holt, 2006.* (PreK–K)

Ward, Lynd. The Silver Pony: A Story in Pictures. *Illus. by the author. Houghton Mifflin, 1973.* (K–Gr. 2)

Verse

Sing "All the Pretty Little Horses." You'll find numerous versions of the tune on YouTube, including a lovely one sung by Joan Baez.

> Hush-a-bye, don't you cry, go to sleepy little baby.
>
> When you wake you shall have all the pretty little horses.
>
> Black and bays, dapples, grays, all the pretty little horses.
>
> Hush-a-bye, don't you cry, go to sleepy little baby.

Activity

Make horse heads from brown paper lunch bags. Draw a face on the bag, glue on ears cut from construction paper, attach yarn for a mane, stuff the bag with crumpled newspaper, and attach it to a dowel rod with rope or duct tape. Giddyup!

HOUSES

Read-Alouds

Bania, Michael. *Kumak's House: A Tale of the Far North*. *Illus. by the author. Alaska Northwest, 2002.* (PreK–Gr. 2)

Barton, Byron. *Building a House*. *Illus. by the author. Greenwillow, 1981.* (PreK–K)

Bean, Jonathan. *Building Our House*. *Illus. by the author. Farrar, 2013.* (PreK–Gr. 2)

Burton, Virginia Lee. *The Little House*. *Illus. by the author. Houghton Mifflin, 1942.* (PreK–Gr. 1)

Hoberman, Mary Ann. *A House Is a House for Me*. *Illus. by Betty Fraser. Viking, 1978.* (PreK–Gr. 1)

McGovern, Ann. *Too Much Noise*. *Illus. by Simms Taback. Houghton Mifflin, 1967.* (PreK–Gr. 1)

Stock, Catherine. *Gugu's House*. *Illus. by the author. Clarion, 2001.* (PreK–Gr. 1)

Taback, Simms. *This Is the House That Jack Built*. *Illus. by the author. Putnam, 2002.* (PreK–Gr. 1)

Verse

Try this fingerplay, "Houses":

> Here is a nest for a robin, (*cup your hands*)
> Here is a hive for a bee.
> > (*make a fist and wrap your other hand around it*)

Here is a hole for a bunny,
   (*make a circle with your thumb and forefinger*)
And here is a house for me.
   (*put your arms above head to make a roof*)

Activity

Tell "How to Make a Small House into a Large One" on page 287.

HUMOROUS STORIES   (*See* Funniest Picture Books Ever)

IMAGINATION AND PLAY

Read-Alouds

Barton, Chris. *Shark vs. Train*. *Illus. by Tom Lichtenheld. Little, Brown, 2010.* (PreK–Gr. 2)

Billingsley, Franny. *Big Bad Bunny*. *Illus. by G. Brian Karas. Atheneum, 2008.* (PreK–Gr. 1)

Chabon, Michael. *The Astonishing Secret of Awesome Man*. *Illus. by Jake Parker. Balzer + Bray, 2011.* (PreK–Gr. 1)

Colón, Raúl. *Draw!* Illus. *by the author. Simon & Schuster, 2014.* (PreK–Gr. 2)

Crews, Nina. *Below*. *Photos by the author. Henry Holt, 2006.* (PreK–Gr. 1)

Fucile, Tony. *Let's Do Nothing!* Illus. *by the author. Candlewick, 2009.* (PreK–Gr. 2)

Grey, Mini. *Traction Man Is Here!* Illus. *by the author. Knopf, 2005.* (PreK–Gr. 1)

Harris, Robie H. *Mail Harry to the Moon!* Illus. *by Michael Emberley. Little, Brown, 2008.* (PreK–Gr. 1)

Henkes, Kevin. *Jessica*. *Illus. by the author. Greenwillow, 1989.* (PreK–Gr. 1)

Lionni, Leo. *Fish Is Fish*. *Illus. by the author. Knopf, 1970.* (PreK–Gr. 2)

O'Malley, Kevin. *Straight to the Pole*. *Illus. by the author. Walker, 2003.* (PreK–Gr. 1)

Rohmann, Eric. *Clara and Asha*. *Illus. by the author. Roaring Brook, 2005.* (PreK–Gr. 1)

Shaw, Charles G. *It Looked Like Spilt Milk*. *Illus. by the author. HarperCollins, 1947.* (PreK–Gr. 1)

Sheth, Kashmira. *Tiger in My Soup*. *Illus. by Jeffrey Ebbeler. Peachtree, 2013.* (PreK–Gr. 2)

Steig, William. *Pete's a Pizza*. *Illus. by the author. HarperCollins, 1998.* (PreK–Gr. 1)

Thomson, Bill. *Chalk*. *Illus. by the author. Amazon, 2010.* (PreK–Gr. 3)

Tullet, Hervé. *Press Here*. *Illus. by the author. Handprint, 2011.* (PreK–Adult)

Van Allsburg, Chris. *Jumanji*. *Illus. by the author. Houghton Mifflin, 1982.* (K–Gr. 2)

Willems, Mo. *Can I Play, Too?* *Illus. by the author. Hyperion, 2010.* (PreK–Gr. 2)

Willems, Mo. *I'm a Frog!* *Illus. by the author. Hyperion, 2013.* (PreK–Gr. 2)

Verse

Sing "Swimming, Swimming" (to the tune of "Sailing, Sailing")

> Swimming, swimming (*pretend to do the swimmer's crawl*)
> In my swimming pool,
>> (*draw a big rectangle in the air with your index fingers*)
> When days are hot (*fan your face with your hands*)
> When days are cold (*hug yourself*)
> In my swimming pool. (*draw a big rectangle with your index fingers*)
>
> Sidestroke, (*do the side stroke with your arms*)
> Breaststroke, (*do the breaststroke with your arms*)
> Fancy diving, too. (*with hands together, pantomime diving up and down*)
> Don't you wish that you had (*wag your index finger*)
> Nothing else to do? (*hold your palms open*)
> But . . .

Note: The first time, sing the whole song with the motions. The second time, leave off the first line ("Swimming, swimming") and just do the motion. Each time you repeat the song, leave off a line, while pantomiming the action. By the tenth time, you will be pantomiming the entire song silently, and ending with just one spoken word: "BUT."

Activity

Play "Out of the Box." Have one child crouch down in a big cardboard box. When you say, "Out of the box!" the child stands up in the box pretending to be an animal. The rest of the group must guess the animal from the sounds and movements the child makes. When you say, "Back in the box!" the child crouches down, stands up as him or herself, and emerges so the next person can have a turn.

INSECTS (*See also* Ants; Butterflies)

Read-Alouds

Aardema, Verna. *Why Mosquitoes Buzz in People's Ears.* *Illus. by Leo and Diane Dillon. Dial, 1975.* (PreK–Gr. 2)

Arnold, Tedd. *Hi! Fly Guy.* *Illus. by the author. Scholastic/Cartwheel, 2005.* (PreK–Gr. 1)

Aylesworth, Jim. *Old Black Fly.* *Illus. by Stephen Gammell. Henry Holt, 1992.* (PreK–Gr. 1)

Bloom, C. P. *The Monkey and the Bee.* *Illus. by Peter Raymundo. Abrams, 2015.* (PreK–Gr. 1)

Cannon, Janell. *Crickwing.* *Illus. by the author. Harcourt, 2000.* (PreK–Gr. 1)

Carle, Eric. *The Grouchy Ladybug.* *Illus. by the author. HarperCollins, 1977.* (PreK–Gr. 1)

DiTerlizzi, Angela. *Some Bugs.* *Illus. by Brendan Wenzel. Beach Lane, 2014.* (PreK–Gr. 2)

Dorros, Arthur. *Ant Cities.* *Illus. by the author. HarperCollins, 1987.* (PreK–Gr. 2)

Fleming, Denise. *Beetle Bop.* *Illus. by the author. Harcourt, 2007.* (PreK–Gr. 1)

Howe, James. *I Wish I Were a Butterfly.* *Illus. by Ed Young. Harcourt, 1987.* (PreK–Gr. 1)

Laden, Nina. *Roberto, the Insect Architect.* *Illus. by the author. Chronicle, 2000.* (PreK–Gr. 2)

Pallotta, Jerry. *The Beetle Alphabet Book.* *Illus. by David Biedrzycki. Charlesbridge, 2004.* (PreK–Gr. 1)

Wheeler, Lisa. *Old Cricket.* *Illus. by Ponder Goembel. Atheneum, 2006.* (PreK–Gr. 1)

Verse

Recite "Here Is the Beehive":

> Here is the beehive, where are the bees?
> (*clench your thumb in your fist*)
> Hidden away where nobody sees.
> Watch and you will see them come out of their hive:
> One, two, three, four, five.
> (*pull out your thumb and then straighten each finger as you count*)
> Buzzzzzzzz! (*tickle someone, or just wave your fingers*)

Activity

Tell the flannelboard story "The Cows" on page 53.

JOKES

(*See* Riddles and Jokes section in Chapter 4, "Storytime Fillers," on page 127 for books, ideas, and jokes to tell)

KINDERGARTEN   (*See* Schools; Teachers)

KINDNESS   (*See* Compassion and Kindness)

KWANZAA   (*See* African Americans)

KNIGHTS AND KNIGHTHOOD

Read-Alouds

Kraegel, Kenneth. *King Arthur's Very Great Grandson.* *Illus. by the author. Candlewick,* *2012.* (PreK–Gr. 1)

Peet, Bill. *Cowardly Clyde.* *Illus. by the author. Houghton Mifflin, 1979.* (K–Gr. 3)

Thomas, Shelley Moore. *Good Night, Good Knight.* *Illus. by Jennifer Plecas. Dutton,* *2000.* (PreK–Gr. 1)

Wheeler, Lisa. *Boogie Knights.* *Illus. by Mark Siegel. Atheneum, 2008.* (PreK–Gr. 1)

Verse

Sing "The Noble Duke of York" (to the tune of "A-Hunting We Will Go").
In this participation song, have children stand on the word "up," sit on the word "down," and crouch halfway up on the last line.

> The noble Duke of York, he had ten thousand men;
>
> He marched them up to the top of the hill,
>
> And he marched them down again.
>
> And when they were up, they were up,
>
> And when they were down, they were down,
>
> And when they were only halfway up,
>
> They were neither up nor down.

Activity

Children can cover poster board, cut into disks, with foil to make shields, attaching duct tape on the back for handles.

LEPRECHAUNS (*See* St. Patrick's Day)

LIBRARIES AND LIBRARIANS (*See also* Books and Reading.)

Read-Alouds

Becker, Bonny. *A Library Book for Bear.* Illus. by Kady MacDonald Denton. Candlewick, 2014. (PreK–Gr. 2)

Bottner, Barbara. *Miss Brooks Loves Books! (And I Don't).* Illus. by Michael Emberley. Knopf/Borzoi, 2010. (PreK–Gr. 2)

Deedy, Carmen Agra. *The Library Dragon.* Illus. by Michael P. White. Peachtree, 1994. (K–Gr. 2)

Ernst, Lisa Campbell. *Stella Louella's Runaway Book.* Illus. by the author. Simon & Schuster, 1998. (PreK–Gr. 1)

Gonzalez, Lucia. *The Storyteller's Candle / La velita de los cuentos.* Illus. by Lulu Delacre. Children's Book Press, 2008. (K–Gr. 3)

Houston, Gloria. *Miss Dorothy and Her Bookmobile.* Illus. by Susan Condie Lamb. Harper, 2011. (K–Gr. 2)

Joyce, William. *The Fantastic Flying Books of Mr. Morris Lessmore.* Illus. by William Joyce and Joe Bluhm. Atheneum, 2012. (K–Gr. 4)

Knudsen, Michelle. *Library Lion.* Illus. by Kevin Hawkes. Candlewick, 2006. (PreK–Gr. 2)

Kohara, Kazuno. *The Midnight Library.* Illus. by the author. Roaring Brook, 2014. (PreK–Gr. 1)

Lies, Brian. *Bats at the Library.* Illus. by the author. Houghton Mifflin, 2008. (PreK–Gr. 2)

Mora, Pat. *Tomás and the Library Lady.* Illus. by Raúl Colón. Knopf, 1997. (K–Gr. 2)

Sierra, Judy. *Wild about Books.* Illus. by Marc Brown. Knopf, 2004. (PreK–Gr. 3)

Williams, Suzanne. *Library Lil.* Illus. by Steven Kellogg. Dial, 1997. (PreK–Gr. 3)

Winter, Jeanette. *Biblioburro: A True Story from Columbia.* Illus. by the author. Beach Lane, 2010. (K–Gr. 3)

Verse

Play or sing "The Library Song" by Michael Mark and Tom Chapin, on Chapin's *Family Tree* album. The Stockton-San Joaquin County Public

Library produced a delightful video of the song, performed by Two of a Kind (www.twoofakind.com)—the husband-and-wife duo David and Jenny Heitler-Klevans—and featuring library staff and customers. Find it at www .youtube.com/watch?v = V-Y60IN2vw0.

Activity
Take children on a walking tour of your library, showing all the different areas and features.

LIONS

Read-Alouds

Brett, Jan. *Honey, Honey—Lion!* *Illus. by the author. Putnam, 2005.* (PreK–Gr. 2)

Cuyler, Margery. *We're Going on a Lion Hunt.* *Illus. by Joe Mathieu. Marshall Cavendish, 2008.* (PreK–Gr. 1)

Daugherty, James. *Andy and the Lion.* *Illus. by the author. Viking, 1938.* (PreK–Gr. 2)

Fatio, Louise. *The Happy Lion.* *Illus. by Roger Duvoisin. McGraw-Hill, 1954.* (PreK–Gr. 2)

Freeman, Don. *Dandelion.* *Illus. by the author. Viking, 1964.* (PreK–Gr. 1)

Knudsen, Michelle. *Library Lion.* *Illus. by Kevin Hawkes. Candlewick, 2006.* (PreK–Gr. 2)

Pinkney, Jerry. *The Lion & the Mouse.* *Illus. by the author. Little, Brown, 2009.* (PreK–Gr. 2)

Sendak, Maurice. *Pierre.* *Illus. by the author. HarperCollins, 1962.* (PreK–Gr. 1)

Verse
Tell the interactive story "Lion Hunt" on page 257.

Activity
Download a beautiful lion's cub mask from kids.nationalgeo graphic.com/kids/activities/ crafts/lion-cub-mask, and make copies for kids to cut out and wear.

LIZARDS (*See* Reptiles and Amphibians)

LOST AND FOUND

Read-Alouds

Bunting, Eve. *Have You Seen My New Blue Socks?* *Illus. by Sergio Ruzzier. Clarion, 2013.* (PreK–Gr. 1)

Ernst, Lisa Campbell. *Stella Louella's Runaway Book.* *Illus. by the author. Simon & Schuster, 1998.* (PreK–Gr. 1)

Falconer, Ian. *Olivia . . . and the Missing Toy.* *Illus. by the author. Atheneum, 2003.* (PreK–Gr. 1)

Feiffer, Jules. *I Lost My Bear.* *Illus. by the author. HarperCollins, 1998.* (K–Gr. 2)

Flack, Marjorie. *Angus Lost.* *Illus. by the author. Doubleday, 1931.* (PreK–Gr. 1)

Haughton, Chris. *Little Owl Lost.* *Illus. by the author. Candlewick, 2010.* (PreK–Gr. 1)

Henkes, Kevin. *Sheila Rae, the Brave.* *Illus. by the author. Greenwillow, 1987.* (PreK–Gr. 1)

Kellogg, Steven. *The Missing Mitten Mystery.* *Illus. by the author. Dial, 2000.* (PreK–Gr. 1)

Kinsey-Warnock, Natalie. *The Bear That Heard Crying.* *Illus. by Ted Rand. Dutton, 1993.* (K–Gr. 2)

McCully, Emily Arnold. *Picnic.* *Illus. by the author. HarperCollins, 2003.* (PreK–Gr. 1)

McPhail, David. *Lost!* *Illus. by the author. Little, Brown, 1990.* (PreK–Gr. 1)

Willems, Mo. *Knuffle Bunny: A Cautionary Tale.* *Illus. by the author. Hyperion, 2005.* (PreK–Gr. 2)

Zion, Gene. *Harry by the Sea.* *Illus. by Margaret Bloy Graham. HarperCollins, 1965.* (PreK–Gr. 1)

Verse

Sing "On Top of Spaghetti." Lyrics and music are at www.kidsongs.com/lyrics/on-top-of-spaghetti.html.

Activity

Ask children to make "Missing" posters for something they have lost.

MAGIC AND MAGICIANS
(*See* Booklist: Picture Books about Magic on page 242.)

MANNERS   (*See* Apologies, Forgiveness, and Manners)

MATHEMATICS   (*See also* Counting)

Read-Alouds

Jenkins, Emily. *Lemonade in Winter: A Book about Two Kids Counting Money*. *Illus. by G. Brian Karas. Schwartz & Wade, 2012.* (K–Gr. 2)

Leedy, Loreen. *Follow the Money!* *Illus. by the author. Holiday House, 2002.* (Gr. 1–4)

Pinczes, Elinor J. *One Hundred Hungry Ants*. *Illus. by Bonnie MacKain. Houghton Mifflin, 1993.* (PreK–Gr. 1)

Rosenthal, Amy Krouse. *This Plus That: Life's Little Equations*. *Illus. by Jen Corace. Harper, 2011.* (K–Gr. 3)

Schwartz, David M. *How Much Is a Million?* *Illus. by Steven Kellogg. Lothrop, 1985.* (PreK–Gr. 3)

Verse

Recite "Five Little Sausages" on page 300.

Activity

Make a grid on cardstock, using three rows of one- to two-inch blocks, four blocks per row. Number the grid from 1 to 12 with black marker. Duplicate and laminate one card for each person. Given two dice, children roll in turn. The child rolling gets to cross off, in erasable marker, either the sum of the dice (as in 7 if he rolls a 3 and a 4), or the numbers that add up to 7 (such as 4, 2, and 1), or the face value of each individual die (3 and 4). The first to cross off all of his or her numbers wins. Kids then wipe cards clean with a damp paper towel and play again.

MICE AND RATS

Read-Alouds

Becker, Bonny. *A Visitor for Bear*. *Illus. by Kady MacDonald Denton. Candlewick, 2008.* (PreK–Gr. 1) (And others in the Bear series.)

Billingsley, Franny. *Big Bad Bunny*. *Illus. by G. Brian Karas.* Atheneum, 2008. (PreK–Gr. 1)

Donaldson, Julia. *The Gruffalo*. *Illus. by Axel Scheffler. Dial, 1999.* (PreK–Gr. 1)

Edwards, Pamela Duncan. *Livingstone Mouse*. *Illus. by Henry Cole. HarperCollins, 1996.* (PreK–Gr. 1)

Fleming, Denise. *Lunch.* Illus. by the author. Henry Holt, 1992. (PreK–Gr. 1)

Henkes, Kevin. *Chrysanthemum.* Illus. by the author. Greenwillow, 1991. (PreK–Gr. 1)

Henkes, Kevin. *Lilly's Purple Plastic Purse.* Illus. by the author. Greenwillow, 1996. (PreK–Gr. 2)

Howe, James. *Horace and Morris but Mostly Dolores.* Illus. by Amy Walrod. Atheneum, 1999. (PreK–Gr. 12)

Kraus, Robert. *Whose Mouse Are You?* Illus. by Jose Aruego. Simon & Schuster, 2000. (PreK–Gr. 1)

Kuhlmann, Torben. *Lindbergh: The Tale of a Flying Mouse.* Illus. by the author. North-South, 2014. (Gr. 1–6)

Lionni, Leo. *Alexander and the Wind-up Mouse.* Illus. by the author. Pantheon, 1969. (PreK–Gr. 1)

Lionni, Leo. *Frederick.* Illus. by the author. Pantheon, 1967. (PreK–Gr. 1)

Lobel, Arnold. *Mouse Tales.* Illus. by the author. HarperCollins, 1972. (PreK–Gr. 1)

MacDonald, Margaret Read. *Mabela the Clever.* Illus. by Tim Coffey. Albert Whitman, 2001. (PreK–Gr. 2)

Numeroff, Laura. *If You Give a Mouse a Cookie.* Illus. by Felicia Bond. HarperCollins, 1985. (PreK–Gr. 2)

Pilkey, Dav. *Dogzilla.* Illus. by the author. Harcourt, 1993. (PreK–Gr. 3)

Pinkney, Jerry. *The Lion & the Mouse.* Illus. by the author. Little, Brown, 2009. (PreK–Gr. 2)

Rohmann, Eric. *My Friend Rabbit.* Illus. by the author. Roaring Brook, 2002. (PreK–Gr. 1)

Ryan, Pam Muñoz. *Mice and Beans.* Illus. by Joe Cepeda. Scholastic, 2001. (PreK–Gr. 1)

Sacre, Antonio. *The Barking Mouse.* Illus. by Alfredo Aguirre. Albert Whitman, 2003. (PreK–Gr. 2)

Smith, Jeff. *Little Mouse Gets Ready.* Illus. by the author. TOON, 2009. (PreK–Gr. 1)

Steig, William. *Doctor De Soto.* Illus. by the author. Farrar, 1982. (K–Gr. 2)

Stein, David Ezra. *Love, Mouserella.* Illus. by the author. Penguin/Nancy Paulsen, 2011. (K–Gr. 2)

Waber, Bernard. *Do You See a Mouse?* Illus. by the author. Houghton Mifflin, 1995. (PreK–Gr. 1)

Walsh, Ellen Stoll. *Mouse Count.* Illus. by the author. Harcourt, 1991. (PreK–Gr. 1)

Wood, Don, and Audrey Wood. *The Little Mouse, the Red Ripe Strawberry, and the Big Hungry Bear.* Illus. by Don Wood. *Child's Play, 1984.* (PreK–Gr. 1)

Young, Ed. *Seven Blind Mice.* Illus. by the author. *Philomel, 1992.* (PreK–Gr. 3)

Verse
Recite "Three Blind Mice" and "The Mouse":

> There is such a little tiny mouse
> > (*show how small it is with your thumb and forefinger*)
>
> Living safely in my house.
>
> Out at night he'll quietly creep (*walk your fingers across a table*)
>
> When everyone is fast asleep. (*fold your hands next to your head*)
>
> But always by the light of day (*open your arms wide*)
>
> He'll quietly, quietly creep away. (*walk your fingers across a table*)

Activity
Show kids the adorable pictures of Mouseland families by artist Maggie Rudy at mouseshouses.blogspot.com. Then let them make their own miniature mouse houses out of shoeboxes, which they can decorate with found materials.

MONEY   (*See* Mathematics)

MONKEYS   (*See* Primates)

MONSTERS   (*See also* Ghosts; Halloween; Witches)

Read-Alouds
Bryan, Ashley. *Can't Scare Me!* Illus. by the author. *Atheneum, 2013.* (K–Gr. 2)

Emberley, Ed. *Go Away, Big Green Monster!* Illus. by the author. *Little, Brown, 1993.* (PreK–Gr. 1)

Emberley, Rebecca, and Ed Emberley. *If You're a Monster and You Know It.* Illus. by the authors. *Orchard, 2010.* (PreK–Gr. 1)

Gackenbach, Dick. *Harry and the Terrible Whatzit.* Illus. by the author. *Clarion, 1977.* (PreK–Gr. 1)

Hutchins, Pat. *The Very Worst Monster.* Illus. by the author. *Greenwillow, 1985.* (PreK–Gr. 1)

Kraegel, Kenneth. *King Arthur's Very Great Grandson.* Illus. by the author. Candlewick, 2012. (PreK–Gr. 1)

Manushkin, Fran. *The Shivers in the Fridge.* Illus. by Paul O. Zelinsky. Dutton, 2006. (PreK–Gr. 2)

Mayer, Mercer. *Liza Lou and the Yeller Belly Swamp.* Illus. by the author. Parents Magazine Press, 1976. (PreK–Gr. 2)

Mayer, Mercer. *There's a Nightmare in My Closet.* Illus. by the author. Dial, 1968. (PreK–Gr. 1)

McElligott, Matthew. *Even Monsters Need Haircuts.* Illus. by the author. Walker, 2010. (PreK–Gr. 2)

Mosel, Arlene. *The Funny Little Woman.* Illus. by Blair Lent. Dutton, 1972. (PreK–Gr. 2)

O'Keefe, Susan Heyboer. *One Hungry Monster: A Counting Book in Rhyme.* Illus. by Lynn Munsinger. Little, Brown, 1989. (PreK–Gr. 1)

Parish, Peggy. *No More Monsters for Me!* Illus. by Marc Simont. HarperCollins, 1981. (PreK–Gr. 1)

Seeger, Pete. *Abiyoyo.* Illus. by Michael Hays. Simon & Schuster, 1986. (PreK–Gr. 2)

Sendak, Maurice. *Where the Wild Things Are.* Illus. by the author. HarperCollins, 1963. (PreK–Gr. 1)

Viorst, Judith. *My Mama Says There Aren't Any Zombies, Ghosts, Vampires, Creatures, Demons, Monsters, Fiends, Goblins, or Things.* Illus. by Kay Chorao. Atheneum, 1973. (PreK–Gr. 2)

Wheeler, Lisa. *Boogie Knights.* Illus. by Mark Siegel. Atheneum, 2008. (PreK–Gr. 2)

Willems, Mo. *Leonardo the Terrible Monster.* Illus. by the author. Hyperion, 2005. (PreK–Gr. 2)

Verse

Sing "Ten Little Monsters" (to the tune of "Ten Little Indians"):

> One little, two little, three little monsters,
> Four little, five little, six little monsters,
> Seven little, eight little, nine little monsters,
> Ten of them can't scare me!

> Ten little, nine little, eight little monsters,
> Seven little, six little, five little monsters,
> Four little, three little, two little monsters,
> One of them can't scare me!
> No, none of them can scare me!

Activity

Let children draw their own pet monsters and describe them, or make monster masks using multiple googly eyes.

MOON   (*See also* Earth, Space)

Read-Alouds

Aston, Dianna Hutts. *The Moon Over Star.* Illus. by Jerry Pinkney. Dial, 2008. (K–Gr. 2)

Brown, Margaret Wise. *Goodnight Moon.* Illus. by Clement Hurd. HarperCollins, 1947. (PreK)

Carle, Eric. *Papa, Please Get the Moon for Me.* Illus. by the author. Picture Book Studio, 1986. (PreK–Gr. 1)

Gerstein, Mordicai. *How to Bicycle to the Moon to Plant Sunflowers: A Simple but Brilliant Plan in 24 Easy Steps.* Illus. by the author. Roaring Brook, 2013. (PreK–Gr. 2)

Henkes, Kevin. *Kitten's First Full Moon.* Illus. by the author. Greenwillow, 2004. (PreK–Gr. 1)

McNulty, Faith. *If You Decide to Go to the Moon.* Illus. by Steven Kellogg. Scholastic, 2005. (PreK–Gr. 3)

O'Malley, Kevin. *Captain Raptor and the Moon Mystery.* Illus. by the author. Walker, 2005. (PreK–Gr. 2)

Verse

Recite "The Man in the Moon" by Anonymous:

> The man in the moon as he sails the sky,
>
> Is a very remarkable skipper,
>
> But he made a mistake when he first tried to take
>
> A drink of milk from the Dipper.
>
> He dipped right out of the Milky Way
>
> And slowly and carefully filled it;
>
> The Big Bear growled and the Little Bear howled,
>
> And scared him so much that he spilled it.

Activity

Play "Hit the Moon with Asteroids." Suspend a large ball (the moon) from the ceiling and have children try to hit it with crumpled tin foil "asteroids."

MOOSE

Read-Alouds

Bingham, Kelly. *Z Is for Moose.* *Illus. by Paul O. Zelinsky. Greenwillow, 2012.* (PreK–Gr. 1)

Jeffers, Oliver. *This Moose Belongs to Me.* *Illus. by the author. Philomel, 2012.* (PreK–Gr. 1)

Numeroff, Laura Joffe. *If You Give a Moose a Muffin.* *Illus. by Felicia Bond. HarperCollins/ Laura Geringer, 1991.* (PreK–Gr. 2)

Rayner, Catherine. *Ernest, the Moose Who Doesn't Fit.* *Illus. by the author. Farrar, 2010.* (PreK–Gr. 1)

Seuss, Dr. *Thidwick the Big-Hearted Moose.* *Illus. by the author. Random House, 1948.* (PreK–Gr. 3)

Verse

Try "The Moose Song" as a call-and-response activity. You sing one line; the children echo you. Find the tune ("Fred the Moose") and a peppy video by the Learning Station, with motions, at www.youtube.com/watch?v = I3 suXTYy2aw/:

> There was a great big moose
> > (*thumbs on temples, fingers outstretched, for antlers*)
> Who liked to drink a lot of juice. (*pantomime drinking a glass of juice*)
> There was a great big moose
> Who liked to drink a lot of juice.
>
> Chorus:
> Singing whoa-oh-oh! (*arms in air, wave left and right*)
> We-oh we-oh we-oh we-oh (*wave arms as you crouch down and up*)
> Whoa-oh-oh!
> We-oh we-oh we-oh we-oh!
>
> The moose's name was Fred.
> He liked to drink his juice in bed.
> The moose's name was Fred.
> He liked to drink his juice in bed. (*chorus*)
>
> He drank his juice with care,
> But he spilt it in his hair.

He drank his juice with care,
But he spilt it in his hair. (*chorus*)

Now there's a sticky moose (*slowly*)
Full of juice (*slowly*)
On the loose! (*slowly*)
(*chorus*)

Activity
Give children patterns of moose antlers to trace (or have them trace their hands on heavy brown paper). Cut out the shapes and glue them onto headbands.

MOTHERS   (*See* Parents)

MUSIC
(*See* Chapter 5: "Music" on page 175 for multiple booklists, songs, ideas, and activities.)

MYSTERY AND DETECTIVE STORIES

Read-Alouds

Biedrzycki, David. *Ace Lacewing: Bug Detective.* Illus. by the author. Charlesbridge, 2008. (K–Gr. 2)

Clement, Rod. *Grandpa's Teeth.* Illus. by the author. HarperCollins, 1998. (PreK–Gr. 1)

Cushman, Doug. *Mystery at the Club Sandwich.* Illus. by the author. Clarion, 2004. (PreK–Gr. 2)

Falconer, Ian. *Olivia . . . and the Missing Toy.* Illus. by the author. Atheneum, 2003. (PreK–Gr. 1)

Hurd, Thacher. *Mystery on the Docks.* Illus. by the author. HarperCollins, 1983. (PreK–Gr. 1)

Laden, Nina. *Private I. Guana: The Case of the Missing Chameleon.* Illus. by the author. Chronicle, 1995. (PreK–Gr. 2)

McCarthy, Meghan. *Steal Back the Mona Lisa.* Illus. by the author. Harcourt, 2006. (PreK–Gr. 1)

Metzger, Steve. *Detective Blue.* Illus. by Tedd Arnold. Orchard, 2011. (PreK–Gr. 2)

Platt, Kin. *Big Max.* Illus. by Robert Lopshire. HarperCollins, 1965. (PreK–Gr. 1)

Ransom, Jeanie Franz. *What Really Happened to Humpty? (From the Files of a Hard-Boiled Detective).* Illus. by Stephen Axelsen. Charlesbridge, 2009. (PreK–Gr. 2)

Sharmat, Marjorie Weinman. *Nate the Great.* Illus. by Marc Simont. Coward, 1972. (K–Gr. 2)

Teague, Mark. *Detective LaRue: Letters from the Investigation.* Illus. by the author. Scholastic, 2004. (PreK–Gr. 4)

Verse
Recite "Who Took the Cookies from the Cookie Jar" on page 301.

Activity
Hide rhyming clues around the room that lead to a trunk filled with miniature magnifying glasses (which you can find very reasonably at www.orientaltrading. Use the magnifying glasses as prizes to help kids solve their next mystery.

NAMES

Read-Alouds

Ahlberg, Allan. *The Pencil.* Illus. by Bruce Ingman. Candlewick, 2008. (PreK–Gr. 1)

Arnold, Tedd. *Catalina Magdalena Hoopensteiner Wallendiner Hogan Logan Bogan Was Her Name.* Illus. by the author. Scholastic, 2004. (PreK–Gr. 2)

Henkes, Kevin. *Chrysanthemum.* Illus. by the author. Greenwillow, 1991. (PreK–Gr. 1)

Juster, Norton. *Neville.* Illus. by G. Brian Karas. Schwartz & Wade, 2011. (PreK–Gr. 3)

Lester, Helen. *A Porcupine Named Fluffy.* Illus. by Lynn Munsinger. Houghton Mifflin, 1986. (PreK–Gr. 1)

Lobel, Anita. *Alison's Zinnia.* Illus. by the author. Greenwillow, 1990. (PreK–Gr. 1)

Mosel, Arlene. *Tikki Tikki Tembo.* Illus. by Blair Lent. Henry Holt, 1968. (PreK–Gr. 2)

Slate, Joseph. *Miss Bindergarten Gets Ready for Kindergarten.* Illus. by Ashley Wolff. Dutton, 1996. (PreK–Gr. 1)

Verse
Sing "The Name-Game Song,"(aka "The Banana Song"). You can see a video on YouTube and get the both words and music at www.kidsongs.com/lyrics/the-name-game.html.

Activity

Play the "The Name-Game Song," with each of the children's names, in the style of: "Shirley / Shirley, Shirley, bo birley, banana fana fo firley, fee fie mo mirley . . . Shirley." Hold Name Day once a week, giving each child a day on which he or she can decide what the group will do for the day.

NIGHT   (*See* Themed Program: Time for Bed on page 280)

NOISES

Read-Alouds

Bee, William. *And the Cars Go . . .* Illus. *by the author. Candlewick, 2013.* (PreK–Gr. 1)

Gerstein, Mordicai. *Carolinda Clatter.* Illus. *by the author. Roaring Brook, 2005.* (PreK–Gr. 2)

Howard, Arthur. *The Hubbub Above.* Illus. *by the author. Harcourt, 2005.* (PreK–Gr. 1)

Johnson, David. *Snow Sounds: An Onomatopoeic Story.* Illus. *by the author. Houghton Mifflin, 2006.* (PreK–Gr. 1)

Light, Steve. *Planes Go.* Illus. *by the author. Chronicle, 2014.* (PreK–K)

MacDonald, Ross. *Achoo! Bang! Crash! The Noisy Alphabet. Disney-Hyperion, 2001.* (PreK–Gr. 1)

Martin, Bill Jr. *Polar Bear, Polar Bear, What Do You Hear?* Illus. *by Eric Carle. Henry Holt, 2004.* (PreK–Gr. 1)

McGovern, Ann. *Too Much Noise.* Illus. *by Simms Taback. Houghton Mifflin, 1967.* (PreK–Gr. 1)

Murphy, Jill. *Peace at Last.* Illus. *by the author. Dial, 1980.* (PreK–Gr. 1)

Shapiro, Arnold L. *Mice Squeak, We Speak: A Poem.* Illus. *by Tomie dePaola. Putnam, 1997.* (PreK–Gr. 1)

Showers, Paul. *The Listening Walk.* Illus. *by Aliki. HarperCollins, 1991.* (PreK–Gr. 1)

Underwood, Deborah. *The Quiet Book.* Illus. *by Renata Liwska. Houghton Mifflin, 2010.* And the companion book, *The Loud Book! (2011).* (PreK–Gr. 1)

Verse

Sing "She'll Be Comin' Round the Mountain." Find lyrics and music at www.kidsongs.com/lyrics/she-ll-be-comin-round-the-mountain.html.

Activity

Go on a listening walk around the school or library or outside. See how many sounds children can list and identify and then ask each child to vocalize one of the sounds for the others to guess.

OCEAN AND SEASHORE   (*See also* Water)

Read-Alouds

Cowan, Catherine. *My Life with the Wave*. *Illus. by Mark Buehner. Lothrop, 1997.* (K–Gr. 2)

Elliott, David. *In the Sea*. *Illus. by Holly Meade. Candlewick, 2012.* (PreK–Gr. 2)

Karas, G. Brian. *Atlantic*. *Illus. by the author. Putnam, 2002.* (PreK–Gr. 2)

Lee, Suzy. *Wave*. *Illus. by the author. Chronicle, 2008.* (PreK–Gr. 1)

Long, Melinda. *How I Became a Pirate*. *Illus. by David Shannon. Harcourt, 2003.* (PreK–Gr. 1)

McLimans, David. *Gone Fishing: Ocean Life by the Numbers*. *Illus. by the author. Walker, 2008.* (PreK–Gr. 2)

Neubecker, Robert. *Wow! Ocean!* *Illus. by the author. Disney-Hyperion, 2011.* (PreK–Gr. 1)

Sattler, Jennifer Gordon. *Pig Kahuna*. *Illus. by the author. Bloomsbury, 2011.* (PreK–Gr. 1)

Sherry, Kevin. *I'm the Biggest Thing in the Ocean*. *Illus. by the author. Dial, 2007.* (PreK–Gr. 1)

Soman, David. *Three Bears in a Boat*. *Illus. by the author. Dial, 2014.* (PreK–Gr. 2)

Wiesner, David. *Flotsam*. *Illus. by the author. Clarion, 2006.* (PreK–Gr. 2)

Verse

Sing "Going to the Beach" in chapter 5, "Music," on page 192.

Activity

Make salt crystals out of un-iodized salt and distilled water. Pour a small pot of boiling water into a glass bowl so everyone can watch. Have the children take turns stirring salt into the water, a teaspoon at a time, until no more will dissolve and you see crystals at the bottom of the bowl. Soak small cardboard squares in the salt solution until they become soggy. Place the cardboard on foil, and let it dry in a warm, sunny location. New salt crystals will form on the cardboard as it dries.

OWLS   (*See also* Birds; Chickens; Ducks and Geese; Penguins)

Read-Alouds

Haughton, Chris. *Little Owl Lost.* Illus. by the author. Candlewick , 2010. (PreK–Gr. 1)

Hutchins, Pat. *Good-Night, Owl!* Illus. by the author. Macmillan, 1972. (PreK–Gr. 1)

Lear, Edward. *The Owl and the Pussycat.* Illus. by Jan Brett. Putnam, 1991. (PreK–Gr. 2)

Lobel, Arnold. *Owl at Home.* Illus. by the author. HarperCollins, 1975. (PreK–Gr. 1)

Rosenthal, Amy Krouse. *Little Hoot.* Illus. by Jen Corace. Chronicle, 2008. (PreK–Gr. 1)

Waddell, Martin. *Owl Babies.* Illus. by Patrick Benson. Candlewick, 1992. (PreK–Gr. 1)

Yolen, Jane. *Owl Moon.* Illus. by John Schoenherr. Philomel, 1987. (PreK–Gr. 2)

Verse

Recite the action rhyme "The Owl":

> There's a wide-eyed owl
>   (*make circles around your eyes with your thumbs and index fingers*)
> With a pointed nose, (*make a nose with your index fingers*)
> Two pointed ears, (*make ears with your index fingers*)
> And claws for toes. (*wiggle two finger "claws" on each hand*)
> He lives high in a tree (*point up high*)
> And he looks at you. (*point to the children*)
> He flaps his wings
>   (*fold your hands into your armpits and flap your arms like wings*)
> And says, "Whoo! Whoo!"

Activity

You can download instructions for a really cute and simple owl paper bag puppet at www.dltk-kids.com/animals/mbagowl.htm.

PARENTS

Read-Alouds

Asch, Frank. *Just Like Daddy.* Illus. by the author. Prentice-Hall, 1981. (PreK–Gr. 1)

Brown, Margaret Wise. *The Runaway Bunny.* Illus. by Clement Hurd. HarperCollins, 1942. (PreK–Gr. 1)

Browne, Anthony. *My Dad.* Illus. by the author. Farrar, 2001. (PreK–Gr. 1)

Buzzeo, Toni. *One Cool Friend.* Illus. by David Small. Dial, 2012. (PreK–Gr. 3)

Collard, Sneed B., III. *Animal Dads.* *Illus. by Steve Jenkins.* Houghton Mifflin, 1997. (PreK–Gr. 3)

Durand, Hallie. *Mitchell's License.* *Illus. by Tony Fucile. Candlewick, 2011.* (PreK–Gr. 2)

Feiffer, Jules. *The Daddy Mountain.* *Illus. by the author. Disney-Hyperion, 2004.* (PreK–Gr. 2)

Feiffer, Kate. *My Side of the Car.* *Illus. by Jules Feiffer. Candlewick, 2011.* (PreK–Gr. 2)

Fox, Mem. *Koala Lou.* *Illus. by Pamela Lofts. Harcourt Brace, 1989.* (PreK–Gr. 2)

Kasza, Keiko. *A Mother for Choco.* *Illus. by the author. Putnam, 1992.* (PreK–Gr. 1)

MacLean, Christine Kole. *Even Firefighters Hug Their Moms.* *Illus. by Mike Reed. Dutton, 2002.* (PreK–Gr. 1)

Robbins, Maria Polushkin. *Mother, Mother, I Want Another.* *Illus. by Jon Goodell. Knopf, 2005, c1978.* (PreK–Gr. 1)

Rosenberg, Liz. *Tyrannosaurus Dad.* *Illus. by Matthew Myers. Roaring Brook, 2011.* (PreK–Gr. 2)

Say, Allen. *The Favorite Daughter.* *Scholastic/Arthur A. Levine, 2013.* (K–Gr. 3)

Scott, Ann Herbert. *On Mother's Lap.* *Illus. by Glo Coalson. Clarion, 1992.* (PreK–Gr. 1)

Tarpley, Natasha Anastasia. *Bippity Bop Barbershop.* *Illus. by E. B. Lewis. Little, Brown, 2002.* (PreK–Gr. 1)

Wells, Rosemary. *Hazel's Amazing Mother.* *Illus. by the author. Dial, 1985.* (PreK–Gr. 2)

Zolotow, Charlotte. *This Quiet Lady.* *Illus. by Anita Lobel. Greenwillow, 1992.* (K–Gr. 3)

Verse

Recite "When Daddy Comes Home" (substitute "Mommy" for "Daddy" the second time you recite this):

> When Daddy comes home, I run to see
> Just what Daddy has brought for me.
> I give him a kiss and hug him too;
> I think daddies are nice, don't you?

Activity

To help kids with their coordination skills and give them practice in following directions, play "Mother, May I" (or "Father, May I"). They can use baby steps, scissor steps, giant steps, jumping jack steps, and so on. Wikipedia has a good description of the rules.

PENGUINS   (*See also* Birds; Chickens; Ducks and Geese; Owls)

Read-Alouds

Buzzeo, Toni. *One Cool Friend*. *Illus. by David Small. Dial, 2012.* (PreK–Gr. 3)

Fromental, Jean-Luc. *365 Penguins*. *Illus. by Joelle Jolivet. Abrams, 2006.* (PreK–Gr. 1)

Gorbachev, Valeri. *Turtle's Penguin Day*. *Illus. by the author. Knopf, 2008.* (PreK–Gr. 1)

Guiberson, Brenda Z. *The Emperor Lays an Egg*. *Illus. by Joan Paley. Henry Holt, 2001.* (PreK–Gr. 2)

Kimmel, Elizabeth Cody. *My Penguin Osbert*. *Illus. by H. B. Lewis. Candlewick, 2004.* (PreK–Gr. 1)

Lester, Helen. *Tacky the Penguin*. *Illus. by Lynn Munsinger. Houghton Mifflin, 1988.* (PreK–Gr. 1)

Richardson, Justin, and Peter Parnell. *And Tango Makes Three*. *Illus. by Henry Cole. Simon & Schuster, 2005.* (PreK–Gr. 2)

Verse

Recite "Ten Little Penguins" on page 113 and sing (to the tune of "I'm a Little Teapot") "I'm a Little Penguin," below, to which you can have children stand up and add movements:

> I'm a little penguin, black and white,
>
> I waddle to the left and I waddle to the right.
>
> I cannot fly, but I can swim,
>
> So I waddle to the water and jump right in!

Activity

Buy a variety of penguin figures (Amazon has adorable little Toob penguins from Safari Ltd. that come a dozen to a tube). Freeze water in various containers so children can play with their penguins on ice.

PERSEVERANCE

Read-Alouds

Becker, Bonny. *A Birthday for Bear*. *Illus. by Kady MacDonald Denton. Candlewick, 2009.* (PreK–Gr. 1)

Blake, Robert J. *Togo. Illus. by the author. Philomel, 2002.* (PreK–Gr. 2)

Davies, Stephen. *Don't Spill the Milk. Illus. by Christopher Corr. Andersen, 2013.* (PreK–Gr. 2)

Fleming, Candace. *Imogene's Last Stand. Illus. by Nancy Carpenter. Schwartz & Wade, 2009.* (K–Gr. 2)

Frazee, Marla. *Walk On! A Guide for Babies of All Ages. Illus. by the author. Harcourt, 2006.* (PreK–Gr. 2)

Hamm, Mia. *Winners Never Quit! Illus. by Carol Thompson. HarperCollins, 2004.* (PreK–Gr. 2)

Hills, Tad. *How Rocket Learned to Read. Illus. by the author. Schwartz & Wade, 2010.* (PreK–Gr. 1)

O'Connor, Jane. *Ready, Set, Skip! Illus. by Ann James. Viking, 2007.* (PreK–Gr. 1)

Willems, Mo. *Elephants Cannot Dance! Illus. by the author. Hyperion, 2010.* (PreK–Gr. 2)

Young, Ed. *Hook. Illus. by the author. Roaring Brook, 2009.* (PreK–Gr. 2)

Verse

Sing "You Gotta Have Heart," with music and lyrics by Richard Adler and Jerry Ross, from the musical *Damn Yankees*, and recite "Perseverance" by Gelett Burgess, ©1900:

> Tony started bright and early, clearing up his room,
> Soon he found he had to stop and make a little broom;
> So then he went into the yard to get a little stick,
> But the garden needed weeding, so he set about it, quick.
>
> Then he found his wagon he intended to repair,
> So he went into the cellar for the hammer that was there;
> He'd just begun to build a box, when it was time for dinner;
> And that's why Tony's father called his son a good beginner.

Activity

Practice skills that require perseverance: juggling handkerchiefs (just toss them up in the air and catch them with one hand), catching bouncing balls, hopping on one foot, whistling, and snapping fingers.

PETS   (*See also* Cats; Dogs; Birds)

Read-Alouds

Arnold, Tedd. *Hi! Fly Guy.* Illus. by the author. *Scholastic/Cartwheel, 2005.* (PreK–Gr. 1)

Baylor, Byrd. *Amigo.* Illus. by Garth Williams. *Macmillan, 1963.* (PreK–Gr. 2)

Buzzeo, Toni. *One Cool Friend.* Illus. by David Small. *Dial, 2012.* (PreK–Gr. 3)

Eaton, Jason Carter. *How to Train a Train.* Illus. by John Rocco. *Candlewick, 2013.* (PreK–Gr. 3)

Keats, Ezra Jack. *Pet Show!* Illus. by the author. *Macmillan, 1972.* (PreK–Gr. 1)

Kellogg, Steven. *The Mysterious Tadpole.* Illus. by the author. *Dial, 1977.* (PreK–Gr. 2)

Kimmel, Elizabeth Cody. *My Penguin Osbert.* Illus. by H. B. Lewis. *Candlewick, 2004.* (PreK–Gr. 1)

Kimmel, Eric A. *The Great Texas Hamster Drive.* Illus. by Bruce Whatley. *Marshall Cavendish, 2007.* (PreK–Gr. 2)

LaRochelle, David. *The Best Pet of All.* Illus. by Hanako Wakiyama. *Dutton, 2004.* (PreK–Gr. 1)

Niemann, Christoph. *The Pet Dragon.* Illus. by the author. *Greenwillow, 2008.* (PreK–Gr. 2)

Noble, Trinka Hakes. *The Day Jimmy's Boa Ate the Wash.* Illus. by Steven Kellogg. *Dial, 1980.* (PreK–Gr. 2)

Pinkney, Jerry. *The Tortoise & the Hare: An Aesop Fable.* Illus. by the author. *Little, Brown, 2013.* (PreK–Gr. 2)

Rostoker-Gruber, Karen. *Ferret Fun.* Illus. by Paul Rátz de Tagyos. *Marshall Cavendish, 2011.* (PreK–Gr. 1)

Rudy, Maggie. *I Wish I Had a Pet.* Illus. by the author. *Beach Lane, 2014.* (PreK–Gr. 1)

Verse

Sing "I'm Bringing Home a Baby Bumblebee." See Judy Freeman's version in her book *Once Upon a Time: Using Storytelling, Creative Drama, and Reader's Theater with Children in Grades PreK–6* (Libraries Unlimited, 2007).

Activity

Have children draw a picture of the pet they wish they had, name it, and describe what's so wonderful about it.

PIGS

Read-Alouds

Aylesworth, Jim. *Aunt Pitty Patty's Piggy*. *Illus. by Barbara McClintock. Scholastic, 1999*. (PreK–Gr. 1)

Cordell, Matthew. *Trouble Gum*. *Illus. by the author. Feiwel and Friends, 2009*. (PreK–Gr. 2)

David, Elliot. *Henry's Map*. *Illus. by the author. Philomel, 2013*. (PreK–Gr. 1)

DiCamillo, Kate. *Mercy Watson to the Rescue*. *Illus. by Chris Van Dusen. Candlewick, 2005*. (PreK–Gr. 2)

Emmett, Jonathan. *The Princess and the Pig*. *Illus. by Poly Bernatene. Walker, 2011*. (PreK–Gr. 3)

Falconer, Ian. *Olivia*. *Illus. by the author. Atheneum, 2003*. (PreK–Gr. 1)

Hobbie, Holly. *Toot & Puddle*. *Illus. by the author. Little, Brown, 1997*. (PreK–Gr. 1)

Marshall, James. *Portly McSwine*. *Illus. by the author. Houghton Mifflin, 1979*. (PreK–Gr. 1)

Palatini, Margie. *Oink? Illus. by Henry Cole. Simon & Schuster, 2006*. (PreK–Gr. 2)

Palatini, Margie. *Piggie Pie*. *Illus. by Howard Fine. Clarion, 1995*. (PreK–Gr. 1)

Peet, Bill. *Chester, the Worldly Pig*. *Illus. by the author. Houghton Mifflin, 1993*. (PreK–Gr. 2)

Pomerantz, Charlotte. *The Piggy in the Puddle*. *Illus. by James Marshall. Simon & Schuster, 1974*. (PreK–Gr. 2)

Rylant, Cynthia. *Poppleton*. *Illus. by Mark Teague. Scholastic/Blue Sky, 1997*. (PreK–Gr. 1)

Sattler, Jennifer Gordon. *Pig Kahuna*. *Illus. by the author. Bloomsbury, 2011*. (PreK–Gr. 1)

Schwartz, Corey Rosen. *The Three Ninja Pigs*. *Illus. by Dan Santat. Putnam, 2012*. (PreK–Gr. 2)

Scieszka, Jon. *The True Story of the 3 Little Pigs! Illus. by Lane Smith. Viking, 1989*. (K–Gr. 3)

Teague, Mark. *Pigsty*. *Illus. by the author. Scholastic, 1994*. (PreK–Gr. 1)

Trivizas, Eugene. *The Three Little Wolves and the Big Bad Pig*. *Illus. by Helen Oxenbury. McElderry, 1993*. (PreK–Gr. 2)

Wiesner, David. *The Three Pigs*. *Illus. by the author. Clarion, 2001*. (PreK–Gr. 1)

Willems, Mo. *Pigs Make Me Sneeze.* *Illus. by the author. Hyperion, 2009.* (PreK–Gr. 2)

Wood, Don, and Audrey Wood. *Piggies.* *Illus. by Don Wood. Harcourt, 1991.* (PreK–Gr. 1)

Verse

Recite the frolicsome rhyming picture book, *The Piggy in the Puddle* by Charlotte Pomerantz listed above.

Activity

Mark off a puddle with a large circle of brown yarn. Hand out small rectangles of "soap" cut from sponges. Have children act out *The Piggy in the Puddle,* with some of them playing the admonishing family members and others playing the piggy cavorting in the "puddle" who says, "Nope!"

PIRATES

Read-Alouds

Florian, Douglas. *Shiver Me Timbers!: Pirate Poems & Paintings.* *Illus. by the author. Beach Lane, 2012.* (PreK–Gr. 3)

Helquist, Brett. *Roger, the Jolly Pirate.* *Illus. by the author. HarperCollins, 2004.* (PreK–Gr. 2)

Long, Melinda. *How I Became a Pirate.* *Illus. by David Shannon. Harcourt, 2003.* (PreK–Gr. 2)

McPhail, David. *Edward and the Pirates.* *Illus. by the author. Little, Brown, 1997.* (PreK–Gr. 1)

Preller, James. *A Pirate's Guide to First Grade.* *Illus. by Greg Ruth. Feiwel and Friends, 2010.* (PreK–Gr. 1)

Verse

Sing "A Pirate's Life" to the tune of "The Sailor's Hornpipe." If you don't remember the tune, you can hear it at www.kidsongs.com/lyrics/a-pirate-s-life.html.

Ohhhh, a pirate's life is the life for me,
I love to sail the deep blue sea;
The whole Spanish Main won't ever be the same,
I'll be the best of the pirate kings!
Ohhhh, a jolly roger is what I need;

My crew will follow where I lead.

We are rough, we are tough and we really know our stuff,

A pirate's life is the life for me.

Ohhhh, the plank is walked most every day;

A pirate needs his time to play.

We huff and we puff and won't ever have enough,

A pirate's life is the life for me.

We're searchin' for a treasure chest;

The gold and silver we like best.

Doubloons everywhere; there's danger in the air,

A pirate's life is the life for me.

Activity

After reading *Roger, the Jolly Pirate,* sing the appended song, "The Ballad of Jolly Roger" for a Shiver-Me-Timbers Story Hour.

PLANES   (*See* Airplanes)

PLANTS   (*See* Flowers and Plants; Fruits and Vegetables; Gardens; Trees)

PLAY   (*See* Imagination and Play)

POLICE AND FIREFIGHTERS

Read-Alouds

Armstrong, Jennifer. *Magnus at the Fire.* Illus. by Owen Smith. Simon & Schuster, 2005. (K–Gr. 2)

DiCamillo, Kate. *Mercy Watson to the Rescue.* Illus. by Chris Van Dusen. Candlewick, 2005. (PreK–Gr. 2)

Ochiltree, Dianne. *Molly, by Golly!: The Legend of Molly Williams, America's First Female Firefighter.* Illus. by Kathleen Kemly. Calkins Creek, 2012. (K–Gr. 3)

Osborne, Mary Pope. *New York's Bravest.* Illus. by Steve Johnson and Lou Fancher. Knopf, 2002. (K–Gr. 3)

Rathmann, Peggy. *Officer Buckle and Gloria.* Illus. by the author. Putnam, 1995. (PreK–Gr. 3)

Teague, Mark. *Detective LaRue: Letters from the Investigation.* Illus. by the author. Scholastic, 2004. (K–Gr. 4)

Verse

Recite "Ten Little Firefighters":

Ten little firefighters, sleeping in a row, (*hold out ten fingers together*)
Ding, ding goes the bell, (*pull a pretend rope*)
And down the pole they go. (*pretend to slide down pole*)
Turn on the engine, oh, oh, oh, (*make a noise like a siren*)
Using the big hose, so, so so. (*hold a pretend hose*)
When all the fire's out, home so slow.

Activity

Take kids on a trip to the firehouse or schedule a visit from your local fire truck.

PRESENTS   (*See* Gifts)

PRIMATES

Read-Alouds

Anholt, Catherine, and Laurence Anholt. *Chimp and Zee.* Illus. by the author. Putnam, 2001. (PreK–Gr. 1)

Applegate, Katherine. *Ivan: The Remarkable True Story of the Shopping Mall Gorilla.* Illus. by G. Brian Karas. Clarion Books, 2014. (K–Gr. 3)

Bloom, C. P. *The Monkey and the Bee.* Illus. by Peter Raymundo. Abrams, 2015. (PreK–Gr. 1)

Browne, Anthony. *One Gorilla: A Counting Book.* Illus. by the author. Candlewick, 2013. (PreK–Gr. 1)

Christelow, Eileen. *Five Little Monkeys Jumping on the Bed.* Illus. by the author. Clarion, 1989. (PreK–Gr. 1)

Howe, James. *The Day the Teacher Went Bananas.* Illus. by Lillian Hoban. Dutton, 1984. (PreK–Gr. 1)

Kurtz, Jane, and Christopher Kurtz. *Water Hole Waiting.* Illus. by Lee Christiansen. Greenwillow, 2002. (PreK–Gr. 1)

McDermott, Gerald. *Monkey: A Trickster Tale from India.* Illus. by the author. Harcourt, 2011. (PreK–Gr. 1)

McDonnell, Patrick. *Me…Jane.* Illus. by the author. Little, Brown, 2011. (PreK–Gr. 2)

Perkins, Al. *Hand, Hand, Fingers, Thumb.* Illus. by Eric Gurney. Random House, 1969. (PreK–Gr. 1)

Rathmann, Peggy. *Good Night, Gorilla.* *Illus. by the author. Putnam, 1994.* (PreK–Gr. 1)

Rey, H. A. *Curious George.* *Illus. by the author.* Houghton Mifflin, 1941. (PreK–Gr. 2)

Sierra, Judy. *Counting Crocodiles.* *Illus. by Will Hillenbrand. Harcourt, 1997.* (PreK–Gr. 1)

Slobodkina, Esphyr. *Caps for Sale.* *Illus. by the author. HarperCollins, 1947.* (PreK–Gr. 1)

Vere, Ed. *Banana!* *Illus. by the author. Henry Holt, 2010.* (PreK–Gr. 1)

Verse

Chant or sing "Five Little Monkeys Jumping on the Bed" (to the tune of "Shortnin' Bread," located at www.kididdles.com/lyrics.

Activity

Play sounds and calls of monkeys, apes, gorillas, and other primates, which you can find at www.monkeymania.co.uk/sounds and www.soundboard.com/sb/Monkey_Sounds_audio.

PRINCES AND PRINCESSES

Read-Alouds

Dodds, Dayle Ann. *The Prince Won't Go to Bed!* *Illus. by Kyrsten Brooker. Farrar, 2007.* (PreK–Gr. 1)

Emmett, Jonathan. *The Princess and the Pig.* *Illus. by Poly Bernatene. Walker, 2011.* (PreK–Gr. 3)

Fleming, Candace. *Clever Jack Takes the Cake.* *Illus. by G. Brian Karas. Schwartz & Wade, 2010.* (PreK–Gr. 3)

Heide, Florence Parry. *Princess Hyacinth: (The Surprising Tale of a Girl Who Floated).* *Illus. by Lane Smith. Schwartz & Wade, 2009.* (PreK–Gr. 2)

LaRochelle, David. *The End.* *Illus. by Richard Egielski. Scholastic/Arthur A.* Levine, 2007. (PreK–Gr. 2)

Quindlen, Anna. *Happily Ever After.* *Illus. by James Stevenson. Viking, 1997.* (PreK–Gr. 1)

Verse

Let children listen to the song "There Was a Princess Long Ago" at www.nurseryrhymes4u.com/NURSERY_RHYMES/Page_48.html or see it acted out in various videos on YouTube. Cast parts of Princess, Fairy, and Prince, with costumes, if you wish, and sing and act out the song in a big circle as follows:

There was a princess
   (In a circle, everyone curtsies/bows to the princess in the middle).
Long ago, long ago, long ago;
There was a princess long ago,
Long, long ago.

And she lived in a big high tower,
   (Hold hands above head in "triangle" shape to make tower).
A big high tower, a big high tower;
And she lived in a big high tower,
Long, long ago.

A wicked fairy cast a spell,
   (Fairy chases princess in circle, then taps toward her head as if casting a spell. Everyone in the circle casts a spell with pretend or heavystock paper "wands.")
Cast a spell, cast a spell;
A wicked fairy cast a spell,
Long, long ago.

Other verses in same format:

The princess slept for a hundred years,
   (Princess lies in middle of circle, sleeping; others put heads on folded hands as if sleeping)
A great big forest grew around, *(Hold arms up, crossed at wrists)*
A handsome prince came riding by,
   (Prince gallops round circle; others gallop in place)
He chopped the trees down with his sword,
   (Prince pretend-chops each "trees" with arm; everyone puts arms down as they are "chopped")
He woke the princess with a kiss,
   (Prince gives the princess a pretend kiss; everyone else blows kisses to princess)
The wedding bells went ding dang ding
   (All pretend to ring bells; prince and princess dance in middle)
And everybody's happy now, *(All clap, dance, jump, etc.)*
Happy now, happy now;
And everybody's happy now,
Happy now.

Activity

Make paper crowns. For each hat, poke a hole in the center of a paper plate and cut a radius from that center, stopping before you get to the brim. Make six or seven more cuts (Pretend you're cutting a pizza starting in the middle, but stopping when you get to the crust.) When you put this it on your head, the little triangular spears stand up like the pointy ridges on a crown. Children can decorate their crowns with crayons, stick-on jewels, and glitter pens.

RABBITS AND HARES

Read-Alouds

Bate, Lucy. *Little Rabbit's Loose Tooth.* *Illus. by Diane deGroat. Crown, 1975.* (PreK–Gr. 1)

Brown, Margaret Wise. *The Runaway Bunny.* *Illus. by Clement Hurd. HarperCollins, 1942.* (PreK–Gr. 1)

Fleming, Candace. *Muncha! Muncha! Muncha!* *Illus. by G. Brian Karas. Atheneum, 2002.* (PreK–Gr. 1)

Horse, Harry. *Little Rabbit Goes to School.* *Illus. by the author. Peachtree, 2004.* (PreK–Gr. 1)

Knudsen, Michelle. *Big Mean Mike.* *Illus. by Scott Magoon. Candlewick, 2012.* (PreK–Gr. 1)

Lester, Helen. *Listen, Buddy.* *Illus. by Lynn Munsinger. Houghton Mifflin, 1995.* (PreK–Gr. 1)

McDermott, Gerald. *Zomo the Rabbit: A Trickster Tale from West Africa.* *Illus. by the author. Harcourt, 1992.* (PreK–Gr. 2)

Pilkey, Dav. *The Dumb Bunnies.* *Scholastic/Blue Sky, 1994.* (PreK–Gr. 1)

Potter, Beatrix. *The Tale of Peter Rabbit.* *Illus. by the author. Warne, 1902.* (PreK–Gr. 1)

Reynolds, Aaron. *Creepy Carrots!* *Illus. by Peter Brown. Simon & Schuster, 2012.* (PreK–Gr. 2)

Rohmann, Eric. *My Friend Rabbit.* *Illus. by the author. Roaring Brook, 2002.* (PreK–Gr. 1)

Rosenthal, Amy Krouse. *Duck! Rabbit!* *Illus. by Tom Lichtenheld. Chronicle, 2009.* (PreK–Gr. 6)

Stevens, Janet. *Tops & Bottoms.* *Illus. by the author. Harcourt 1995.* (PreK–Gr. 3)

Walton, Rick. *So Many Bunnies: A Bedtime ABC and Counting Book.* *Illus. by Paige Miglio. HarperCollins, 1998.* (PreK–Gr. 1)

Wells, Rosemary. *Bunny Cakes*. *Illus. by the author. Viking, 1997.* (PreK–Gr. 1)

Verse
Recite "I'm a Little Bunny" on page 113.

Activity
Using white construction paper for the headband and white and pink papers for the floppy ears, children can make rabbit headbands, and then do the "Bunny Hop" in a line around the room.

RAIN   (*See also* Water, Weather)

Read-Alouds

Beaumont, Karen. *Move Over, Rover!* *Illus. by Jane Dyer. Harcourt, 2006.* (PreK–Gr. 1)

Crum, Shutta. *Thunder-Boomer!* *Illus. by Carol Thompson. Clarion, 2009.* (PreK–Gr. 1)

Ginsburg, Mirra. *Mushroom in the Rain*. *Illus. by Jose Aruego and Ariane Dewey. Macmillan, 1974.* (PreK–Gr. 1)

Hesse, Karen. *Come On, Rain*. *Illus. by Jon J Muth. Scholastic, 1999.* (PreK–Gr. 1)

Hest, Amy. *In the Rain with Baby Duck*. *Illus. by Jill Barton. Candlewick, 1995.* (PreK–Gr. 1)

Martin, Bill, Jr., and John Archambault. *Listen to the Rain*. *Illus. by James Endicott. Henry Holt, 1988.* (PreK–Gr. 1)

Polacco, Patricia. *Thunder Cake*. *Illus. by the author. Philomel, 1990.* (PreK–Gr. 1)

Stojic, Manya. *Rain*. *Illus. by the author. Knopf, 2000.* (PreK–Gr. 1)

White, Dianne. *Blue on Blue*. *Illus. by Beth Krommes. Beach Lane, 2014.* (PreK–Gr. 2)

Wiesner, David. *Hurricane*. *Illus. by the author. Clarion, 1990.* (PreK–Gr. 1)

Willems, Mo. *Are You Ready to Play Outside?* *Illus. by the author. Hyperion, 2008.* (PreK–Gr. 2)

Wood, Audrey. *The Napping House*. *Illus. by Don Wood. Harcourt, 1984.* (PreK–Gr. 1)

Verse
Recite "Rain, Rain, Go Away":

> Rain, rain, go away,
> Come again some other day.
> We want to go outside and play;
> Come again some other day.

Activity

Make paper plate rainbows. After cutting paper plates in half, cut out the half circle centers to make rainbow forms. Have children color the arc of colors in order, starting with red at the top. (Teach them the mnemonic ROY G. BIV: Red, orange, yellow, green, blue, indigo, violet.) They can also glue cotton balls at either end of the rainbow for clouds.

RATS (*See* Mice and Rats)

READING (*See* Books and Reading)

REPTILES AND AMPHIBIANS
(*See also* Alligators and Crocodiles; Dinosaurs; Frogs and Toads; Snakes; Turtles)

Read-Alouds

Bishop, Nic. *Nic Bishop Lizards*. *Photos by the author. Scholastic, 2010.* (PreK–Gr. 3)

Carle, Eric. *The Mixed-Up Chameleon*. *Illus. by the author. HarperCollins, 1984.* (PreK–Gr. 1)

Cowley, Joy. *Chameleon, Chameleon*. *Photos by Nic Bishop. Scholastic, 2005.* (PreK–Gr. 1)

Wiesner, David. *Art & Max*. *Illus. by the author. Clarion, 2010.* (PreK–Gr. 2)

Verse

Recite "A Salamander":

> I saw a little creature that was slimy, smooth, and wet.
>
> I thought it was the oddest thing that I had ever met.
>
> It was something like a lizard, but it had no scales at all.
>
> It was something like a frog, but it didn't hop—it crawled.
>
> So I took it to my teacher and she told me right away,
>
> "I see you brought a salamander into class today."

Activity

Hand out an outline of a lizard for children to decorate with colorful hole-punched dots. Play "Spot the Chameleon" game. Hide pairs of tiny plastic sticky chameleons (which you can find on Amazon in packs of 48 or 60) around the room—a red one on a red book, a green one on a plant, etc.—for pairs of children to spot. Make sure each pair of children finds one pair of chameleons so each child can keep a chameleon as a prize. Then pass out some paper and have kids draw a colorful picture and camouflage the chameleon in a part of the picture that matches its color.

RESOURCEFULNESS

Read-Alouds

Agee, Jon. Terrific. *Illus. by the author. Disney-Hyperion, 2005.* (PreK–Gr. 2)

Crews, Nina. Below. *Photos by the author. Henry Holt, 2006.* (PreK–Gr. 1)

Fleischman, Paul. Weslandia. *Illus. by Kevin Hawkes. Candlewick, 1999.* (PreK–Gr. 3)

Fleming, Candace. Clever Jack Takes the Cake. *Illus. by G. Brian Karas. Schwartz & Wade, 2010.* (PreK–Gr. 3)

Joyce, William. George Shrinks. *Illus. by the author. HarperCollins, 1985.* (PreK–Gr. 1)

Medina, Meg. Tía Isa Wants a Car. *Illus. by Claudio Muñoz. Candlewick, 2011.* (PreK–Gr. 2)

Seeger, Pete. Abiyoyo. *Illus. by Michael Hays. Simon & Schuster, 1986.* (PreK–Gr. 2)

Thomson, Bill. Chalk. *Illus. by the author. Amazon, 2010.* (PreK–Gr. 3)

Verse

Sing "High Hopes" with music by Jimmy Van Heusen and lyrics by Sammy Cahn, ©1959. Listen to Frank Sinatra's classic version on YouTube; you can find the lyrics and guitar chords at www.theguitarguy.com/highhope.htm.

Activity

Give each small group a random item, such as an ice cube tray, a set of erasers, or an empty water bottle. Each group must then create a game that uses the object and share the rules with the whole group.

RESPONSIBILITY

Read-Alouds

Donaldson, Julia. Superworm. *Illus. by Axel Scheffler. Scholastic/Arthur A.* Levine, 2014. (PreK–Gr. 1)

Ernst, Lisa Campbell. Stella Louella's Runaway Book. *Illus. by the author. Simon & Schuster, 1998.* (PreK–Gr. 1)

Graham, Bob. April and Esme, Tooth Fairies. *Illus. by the author. Candlewick, 2010.* (PreK–Gr. 2)

Hesse, Karen. *Spuds.* Illus. by Wendy Watson. Scholastic, 2008. (K–Gr. 2)

Hoose, Philip, and Hannah Hoose. *Hey, Little Ant.* Illus. by Debbie Tilley. Tricycle, 1998. (PreK–Gr. 2)

Hutchins, Pat. *Don't Forget the Bacon!* Illus. by the author. Greenwillow, 1976. (PreK–Gr. 1)

Polacco, Patricia. *Chicken Sunday.* Illus. by the author. Philomel, 1992. (PreK–Gr. 1)

Seuss, Dr. *Horton Hatches the Egg.* Illus. by the author. Random House, 1940. (PreK–Gr. 3)

Soman, David. *Three Bears in a Boat.* Illus. by the author. Dial, 2014. (PreK–Gr. 2)

Stevens, Janet, and Susan Stevens Crummel. *The Great Fuzz Frenzy.* Illus. by Janet Stevens. Harcourt, 2005. (PreK–Gr. 3)

Woodson, Jacqueline. *Each Kindness.* Illus. by E. B. Lewis. Penguin/Nancy Paulsen, 2012. (K–Gr. 4)

Verse

Sing "When I First Came to This Land." Look for lyrics at mainlynorfolk .info/folk/songs/whenifirstcametothisland.html and listen to the many recordings of it on YouTube.com.

Activity

Sit in a big circle. Take out a raw egg and explain how we are all responsible for the well-being, happiness, and safety of each other. Carefully pass the egg to the person next to you, and have that person pass it on, gently and carefully, until it makes its way around the circle.

RIDDLES

(*See* Riddles and Jokes on page 127 for books, ideas, and jokes to tell)

ROCKS AND MINERALS

Read-Alouds

Aston, Dianna Hutts. *A Rock Is Lively.* Illus. by Sylvia Long. Chronicle, 2012. (PreK–Gr. 3)

Baylor, Byrd. *Everybody Needs a Rock.* Illus. by Peter Parnall. Scribner, 1974. (K–Gr. 3)

Christian, Peggy. *If You Find a Rock.* Photos by Barbara Hirsch Lember. Harcourt, 2000. (PreK–Gr. 1)

McGuirk, Leslie. *If Rocks Could Sing: A Discovered Alphabet*. *Illus. by the author. Tricycle, 2011.* (PreK–Gr. 1)

Steig, William. *Sylvester and the Magic Pebble*. *Illus. by the author. Windmill, 1969.* (PreK–Gr. 3)

Verse

Recite "Mountains into Boulders"; adapted by Judy Freeman. Have each child put a pinch of sand in his or her hand as the group repeats the poem with you.

> Mountains into boulders, all across the land;
>
> Boulders into rocks, everywhere I stand;
>
> Big rocks into stones, pebbles into sand;
>
> I hold a thousand tiny mountains in my little hand.

Activity

After reciting the poem above, astonish children with the Google images of sand they'll see when you look up the keywords "sand magnified" online. The pictures show sand magnified up to 250 times. Let the children make pet rocks out of round flat rocks using paint, googly eyes, markers, yarn for hair, and then some.

SCHOOLS   (*See also* Teachers)

Read-Alouds

Allard, Harry. *Miss Nelson Is Missing*. *Illus. by James Marshall. Houghton Mifflin, 1985.* (PreK–Gr. 2)

Baer, Edith. *This Is the Way We Go to School: A Book about Children around the World*. *Illus. by Steve Björkman. Scholastic, 1992.* (PreK–Gr. 2)

Bliss, Harry. *Bailey*. *Illus. by the author. Scholastic, 2011.* (PreK–Gr. 1)

Child, Lauren. *I Am Too Absolutely Small for School*. *Illus. by the author. Candlewick, 2004.* (PreK–Gr. 1)

Cox, Judy. *Carmen Learns English*. *Illus. by Angela Dominguez. Holiday House, 2010.* (PreK–Gr. 2)

Creech, Sharon. *A Fine, Fine School*. *Illus. by Harry Bliss. HarperCollins, 2001.* (K–Gr. 3)

Dewdney, Anna. *Llama Misses Mama*. *Illus. by the author. Viking, 2009.* (PreK–K)

Henkes, Kevin. *Wemberly Worried*. *Illus. by the author. Greenwillow, 2000.* (PreK–Gr. 1)

Hest, Amy. *Off to School, Baby Duck!* Illus. by Jill Barton. Candlewick, 1999. (PreK–K)

Jackson, Ellen. *It's Back to School We Go! First Day Stories from Around the World.* Illus. by Jan Davey Ellis. Millbrook, 2003. (K–Gr. 4)

McGhee, Alison. *Countdown to Kindergarten.* Illus. by Harry Bliss. Harcourt, 2002. (PreK–Gr. 1)

Murray, Laura. *The Gingerbread Man Loose in the School.* Illus. by Mike Lowery. Putnam, 2011. (PreK–Gr. 1)

Rodman, Mary Ann. *First Grade Stinks!* Illus. by Beth Spiegel. Peachtree, 2006. (PreK–Gr. 1)

Ryder, Joanne. *Panda Kindergarten.* Photos by Katherine Feng. Collins, 2009. (PreK–Gr. 2)

Seuss, Dr., and Jack Prelutsky. *Hooray for Diffendoofer Day.* Illus. by Dr. Seuss and Lane Smith. Knopf, 1998. (K–Gr. 3)

Shannon, David. *David Goes to School.* Illus. by the author. Scholastic, 1999. (PreK–Gr. 2)

Slate, Joseph. *Miss Bindergarten Gets Ready for Kindergarten.* Illus. by Ashley Wolff. Dutton, 1996. (PreK–Gr. 1)

Verse

Recite "Homework! Oh, Homework!" by Jack Prelutsky in *The New Kid on the Block* (Greenwillow, 1984) and sing "This Is the Way We Go to School" to the tune of "Here We Go Round the Mulberry Bush":

> This is the way we go to school, go to school, go to school;
> This is the way we go to school so early in the morning.
> This is the way we dress ourselves, dress ourselves, dress ourselves;
> This is the way we dress ourselves so early in the morning.
> *Other verses:* Wash our hands; Brush our teeth; Carry our books. *(Add new verses the children compose.)*

Activity

Over the course of a week, allow each child to have a turn at being the teacher. Each "teacher" will have up to five minutes to instruct the rest of the class in a chosen subject. Let each child know when his or her turn will be, and encourage all to plan an interesting and fun lesson. Introduce each child this way: "Today, Julia will be our teacher for five minutes. What are you going to teach us today, Julia?"

SCIENCE
(*See* Animals; Color; Deserts; Earth; Flowers and Plants; Fruits and Vegetables; Moon; Ocean and Seashore; Rain; Rocks and Minerals; Seasons; Space; Water; Weather)

SEASHORE   (*See* Ocean and Seashore)

SEASONS   (*See also* Weather; Winter)

Read-Alouds

Clifton, Lucille. *The Boy Who Didn't Believe in Spring*. *Illus. by Brinton Turkle. Dutton, 1973.* (PreK–Gr. 2)

Ehlert, Lois. *Leaf Man*. *Illus. by the author. Harcourt, 2005.* (PreK–Gr. 1)

Fogliano, Julie. *And Then It's Spring*. *Illus. by Erin E. Stead. Roaring Brook, 2012.* (PreK–Gr. 1)

Gourley, Robbin. *Bring Me Some Apples and I'll Make You a Pie: A Story about Edna Lewis*. *Illus. by the author. Clarion, 2009.* (K–Gr. 3)

Henkes, Kevin. *Old Bear*. *Illus. by the author. Greenwillow, 2008.* (PreK–Gr. 1)

Hunter, Anne. *Possum's Harvest Moon*. *Illus. by the author. Houghton Mifflin, 1996.* (PreK–Gr. 1)

Johnston, Tony. *Winter Is Coming*. *Illus. by Jim LaMarche. Simon & Schuster/Paula Wiseman, 2014.* (PreK–Gr. 2)

Peters, Lisa Westberg. *Cold Little Duck, Duck, Duck*. *Illus. by Sam Williams. Greenwillow, 2000.* (PreK–Gr. 1)

Sendak, Maurice. *Chicken Soup with Rice: A Book of Months*. *Illus. by the author. HarperCollins, 1962.* (PreK–Gr. 1)

Udry, Janice May. *A Tree Is Nice*. *Illus. by Marc Simont. HarperCollins, 1956.* (PreK–Gr. 1)

Willems, Mo. *City Dog, Country Frog*. *Illus. by the author. Hyperion, 2010.* (PreK–Gr. 3)

Verse
Sing "In the Good Old Summertime." For lyrics and tune, go to www .kididdles.com/lyrics/i075.html.

Activity
In summer or fall, bring in leaves from different trees for children to identify from pictures in books or online. Have children make seasonal leaf pictures or leaf stamps by painting a leaf and pressing it onto paper.

SEEDS   (*See* Flowers and Plants; Fruits and Vegetables; Gardens; Trees)

SHAPES

Read-Alouds

Carter, David A. *One Red Dot: A Pop-up Book for Children of All Ages*. *Illus. by the author. Little Simon, 2005.* (PreK–Gr. 1)

Hall, Michael. *Perfect Square*. *Illus. by the author. Greenwillow, 2011.* (PreK–Gr. 1)

Intriago, Patricia. *Dot*. *Illus. by the author. Farrar, 2011.* (PreK–Gr. 1)

Thong, Roseanne Greenfield. *Round Is a Tortilla: A Book of Shapes*. *Illus. by John Parra. Chronicle, 2013.* (PreK–Gr. 1)

Tullet, Hervé. *Press Here*. *Illus. by the author. Handprint, 2011.* (PreK–Adult)

Walsh, Ellen Stoll. *Mouse Shapes*. *Illus. by the author. Harcourt, 2007.* (PreK–Gr. 1)

Verse

Do the fingerplay "Draw a Little Circle in the Air" on page 117.

Activity

Hold a Shape Day. Each child signs up for a shape and is responsible for bringing in an object in that particular shape to show and display, such as ice cream cones for cone shapes or balls for spheres.

SHARING   (*See* Generosity)

SHOES   (*See* Boots and Shoes; Clothing and Dress)

SIBLINGS

Read-Alouds

Byars, Betsy. *My Brother Ant*. *Illus. by Marc Simont. Viking, 1996.* (PreK–Gr. 1)

Harris, Robie H. *Mail Harry to the Moon!* *Illus. by Michael Emberley. Little, Brown, 2008.* (PreK–Gr. 1)

Henkes, Kevin. *Sheila Rae, the Brave*. *Illus. by the author. Greenwillow, 1987.* (PreK–Gr. 1)

Hesse, Karen. *Spuds*. *Illus. by Wendy Watson. Scholastic, 2008.* (K–Gr. 3)

Kellogg, Steven. *Much Bigger than Martin*. *Illus. by the author. Dial, 1976.* (PreK–Gr. 2)

Khan, Rukhsana. *Big Red Lollipop*. Illus. by Sophie Blackall. Viking, 2010. (PreK–Gr. 3)

Kornell, Max. *Me First*. Illus. by the author. Penguin/Nancy Paulsen, 2014. (PreK–Gr. 2)

Lin, Grace. *Ling & Ting: Not Exactly the Same!* Illus. by the author. Little, Brown, 2010. (PreK–Gr. 1)

McKissack, Patricia C. *The All-I'll-Ever-Want Christmas Doll*. Illus. by Jerry Pinkney. Schwartz & Wade, 2007. (PreK–Gr. 3)

Muth, Jon J. *Zen Shorts*. Illus. by the author. Scholastic, 2005. (K–Gr. 3)

O'Neill, Catharine. *Annie and Simon*. Illus. by the author. Candlewick, 2008. (PreK–Gr. 1)

Polacco, Patricia. *My Rotten Redheaded Older Brother*. Illus. by the author. Simon & Schuster, 1994. (PreK–Gr. 3)

Schaefer, Lola M. *One Special Day (A Story for Big Brothers and Sisters)*. Illus. by Jessica Meserve. Disney-Hyperion, 2012. (PreK–Gr. 1)

Sheth, Kashmira. *Tiger in My Soup*. Illus. by Jeffrey Ebbeler. Peachtree, 2013. (PreK–Gr. 2)

Tucker, Kathy. *The Seven Chinese Sisters*. Illus. by Grace Lin. Albert Whitman, 2003. (PreK–Gr. 2)

Viorst, Judith. *I'll Fix Anthony*. Illus. by Ray Cruz. HarperCollins, 1969. (PreK–Gr. 1)

Verse

"Itty Bitty Box" is a satisfying song about fractious siblings. Sing it to the tune of "Polly Wolly Doodle," substituting the word "sister" for "brother" the second time around:

> Oh, I wish I had an itty bitty box to put my brother in;
> I'd take him out and twist his snout, then put him right back again!
> Take him out, twist his snout, then put him right back again,
> If I only had an itty bitty box to put my brother in!

Activity

With children sitting in a circle, go around the room and have each child add a line to this statement: "The best thing about my sister (*or* brother *or* cousin, *if the child is an only*) is . . ."

SICK

Read-Alouds

Rostoker-Gruber, Karen. *Rooster Can't Cock-a-Doodle-Doo*. *Illus. by Paul Rátz de Tagyos. Dial, 2004.* (PreK–Gr. 1)

Slate, Joseph. *Miss Bindergarten Stays Home from Kindergarten*. *Illus. by Ashley Wolff. Dutton, 2000.* (PreK–Gr. 1)

Stead, Philip C. *A Sick Day for Amos McGee*. *Illus. by Erin E. Stead. Roaring Brook, 2010.* (PreK–Gr. 1)

Thomas, Shelley Moore. *Get Well, Good Knight*. *Illus. by Jennifer Plecas. Dutton, 2002.* (PreK–Gr. 1)

Yolen, Jane. *How Do Dinosaurs Get Well Soon?* *Illus. by Mark Teague. Scholastic/Blue Sky, 2003.* (PreK–Gr. 1)

Verse

Recite "Sick" by Shel Silverstein from his book *Where the Sidewalk Ends* (HarperCollins, 1974). Follow up with "Miss Polly Had a Dolly":

> Miss Polly had a dolly who was sick, sick, sick. (*rock the "baby"*)
> So she called for the doctor to come quick, quick, quick.
> > (*dial a phone*)
> The doctor came with his bag and his hat
> > (*hold up a bag and take off a hat*)
> And he knocked on the door with a rat-a-tat-tat. (*knock on a door*)
> He looked at the dolly and he shook his head,
> > (*shake your head gravely*)
> And he said, "Miss Polly, put her straight to bed!" (*shake your finger*)
> He wrote on a paper for some pills, pills, pills (*write on your palm*)
> "I'll be back in the morning for my bill, bill, bill."
> > (*hold out a piece of paper*)

Activity

Show children how to sneeze into the crook of their elbow so they don't spread germs to the rest of the group. Mimic hand washing while singing a simple song (or reciting "Miss Polly" above); when the song is over the germs will be gone.

SISTERS

(*See* Siblings)

SLEEP   (*See* Themed Program: Time for Bed on page 280)

SNAKES

Read-Alouds

Bishop, Nic. *Nic Bishop Snakes*. Photos by the author. Scholastic, 2012. (PreK–Gr. 3)

Cannon, Janell. *Verdi*. Illus. by the author. Harcourt, 1997. (PreK–Gr. 3)

Kimmel, Eric A. *Little Britches and the Rattlers*. Illus. by Vincent Nguyen. Marshall Cavendish, 2008. (PreK–Gr. 1)

Noble, Trinka Hakes. *The Day Jimmy's Boa Ate the Wash*. Illus. by Steven Kellogg. Dial, 1980. (PreK–Gr. 2)

Ungerer, Tomi. *Crictor*. Illus. by the author. HarperCollins, 1958. (PreK–Gr. 1)

Willems, Mo. *Can I Play, Too?* Illus. by the author. Hyperion, 2010. (PreK–Gr. 2)

Verse

Recite "Slippery Slim" by Leroy F. Jackson, from *The Peter Patter Book of Nursery Rhymes*, ©1918:

> Slippery Slim, a garter snake,
>
> Leaned against a garden rake
>
> And smiled a sentimental smile
>
> At Tilly Toad, on the gravel pile,
>
> Till that bashful miss was forced to hop
>
> And hide her face in a carrot-top.

Activity

Give kids paper to color with magic markers and roll into a snake, or pass out some Model Magic to mold.

SNOW   (*See* Seasons; Weather; Winter)

SONGS
(*See* Music; see chapter 5: "Music" on page 202 for multiple booklists, songs, and activities)

SOUNDS   (*See* Noises)

| SOUP | (*See* Themed Program: I'm Hungry on page 299) |

| SPACE | (*See* also Earth, Extraterrestrial Beings, Moon) |

Read-Alouds

Burleigh, Robert. *One Giant Leap.* Illus. by Mike Wimmer. Philomel, 2009. (K–Gr. 3)

Cole, Joanna. *The Magic School Bus Lost in the Solar System.* Illus. by Bruce Degen. Scholastic, 1990. (K–Gr. 3)

Florian, Douglas. *Comets, Stars, the Moon, and Mars: Space Poems and Paintings.* Harcourt, 2007. (K–Gr. 4)

Hort, Lenny. *How Many Stars in the Sky?* Illus. by James E. Ransome. HarperCollins, 1991. (PreK–Gr. 2)

Kelly, Mark. *Mousetronaut: Based on a (Partially) True Story.* Illus. by C. F. Payne. Simon & Schuster/Paula Wiseman, 2012. (PreK–Gr. 2)

McCarthy, Meghan. *Astronaut Handbook.* Illus. by the author. Knopf, 2008. (PreK–Gr. 2)

McNulty, Faith. *If You Decide to Go to the Moon.* Illus. by Steven Kellogg. Scholastic, 2005. (PreK–Gr. 2)

Patricelli, Leslie. *Higher! Higher!* Illus. by the author. Candlewick, 2009. (PreK)

Pinkney, Jerry. *Twinkle, Twinkle, Little Star.* Illus. by the author. Little, Brown, 2011. (PreK–Gr. 1)

Ray, Mary. *Stars.* Illus. by Marla Frazee. Beach Lane, 2011. (PreK–Gr. 1)

Todd, Traci N. *A Is for Astronaut: Space Exploration from A to Z.* Chronicle, 2006. (PreK–Gr. 2)

Verse

Recite the call-and-response chant in this chapter, "Let's Go on a Space Trip," on page 259.

Activity

Make toilet paper tube rockets. First, have kids color or paint the cardboard rolls. Then help them make cones from construction paper circles. Cut a radius into each circle and fold it into a cone shape, which can be glued on top of the roll. Glue orange and red crepe paper or tissue paper streamers to the inside of the rolls so they dangle out like flames, and glue decorative stripes of aluminum foil around the roll. Get out a big beach ball and let children land their rockets on the "planet."

SPANISH LANGUAGE

Read-Alouds

Dorros, Arthur. *Abuela.* Illus. by the author. Dutton, 1991. Also see Abuelo (2014). (PreK–Gr. 2)

Elya, Susan Middleton. *Eight Animals on the Town.* Illus. by Lee Chapman. Putnam, 2000. (PreK–Gr. 1)

Elya, Susan Middleton. *Say Hola to Spanish.* Illus. by Loretta Lopez. Lee & Low, 1996. (K–Gr. 3)

Montes, Marisa. *Los Gatos Black on Halloween.* Illus. by Yuyi Morales. Henry Holt, 2006. (PreK–Gr. 1)

Mora, Pat. *Gracias / Thanks.* Illus. by John Parra. Lee & Low, 2009. (PreK–Gr. 2)

Mora, Pat. *A Piñata in a Pine Tree: A Latino Twelve Days of Christmas.* Illus. by Magaly Morales. Clarion, 2009. (K–Gr. 2)

Morales, Yuyi. *Just in Case: A Trickster Tale and Spanish Alphabet Book.* Illus. by the author. Roaring Brook, 2008. (K–Gr. 2)

Paul, Ann Whitford. *Mañana, Iguana.* Illus. by Ethan Long. Holiday House, 2004. Also see Tortuga in Trouble (2009). (PreK–Gr. 2)

Ryan, Pam Muñoz. *Mice and Beans.* Illus. by Joe Cepeda. Scholastic, 2001. (PreK–Gr. 1)

Thong, Roseanne Greenfield. *Round Is a Tortilla: A Book of Shapes.* Illus. by John Parra. Chronicle, 2013. (PreK–Gr. 2)

Vamos, Samantha R. *The Cazuela That the Farm Maiden Stirred.* Illus. by Rafael López. Charlesbridge, 2011. (PreK–Gr. 3)

Verse

Sing "Diez Gatitos Lindos" ("Ten Pretty Kittens") to the tune of "Ten Little Indians." Then substitute *perritos* (puppies) for *gatitos*. You can also sing the song backwards, counting down, starting with "Diez, nueve, ocho gatitos." ending with "uno gatito lindo" or "uno perrito lindo."

> Uno, dos, y tres gatitos,
> Cuatro, cinco, seis gatitos,
> Siete, ocho, nueve gatitos,
> Diez gatitos lindos,
>
> Uno, dos, y tres perritos,
> Cuatro, cinco, seis perritos,
> Siete, ocho, nueve perritos,
> Diez perritos lindos,

Activity

Using the vocabulary from one of the read-alouds above, make individual Spanish-English dictionaries for children to illustrate and take home.

SPIDERS

Read-Alouds

Bishop, Nic. *Nic Bishop Spiders.* Photos by Nic Bishop. Scholastic, 2007. (PreK–Gr. 3)

Carle, Eric. *The Very Busy Spider.* Illus. by the author. Philomel, 1984. (PreK–Gr. 1)

Cronin, Doreen. *Diary of a Spider.* Illus. by Harry Bliss. HarperCollins/Joanna Cotler, 2005. (PreK–Gr. 3)

Graham, Margaret Bloy. *Be Nice to Spiders.* Illus. by the author. HarperCollins, 1967. (PreK–Gr. 1)

Hoberman, Mary Ann. *The Eensy-Weensy Spider.* Illus. by Nadine Bernard Westcott. Little, Brown, 2000. (PreK–Gr. 1)

Kimmel, Eric A. *Anansi and the Moss-Covered Rock.* Illus. by Janet Stevens. Holiday House, 1988. (PreK–Gr. 2)

Verse

Recite "The Eensy-Weensy Spider" and "Little Miss Muffet."

Activity

Make little yarn and pipe cleaner spiders to act out the nursery rhymes. For each one, cut two black pipe cleaners in half. Holding the four pieces together, tie one end of a 12" piece of rug yarn around the middle and wind it tightly around the pipe cleaners to form the body. Tie off the other end. Arrange and bend the eight pipe cleaners in half, with four on each side, to form the legs. If you like, glue on googly eyes.

SPORTS

Read-Alouds

Corey, Shana. *Players in Pigtails.* Illus. by Rebecca Gibbon. Scholastic, 2003. (K–Gr. 4)

DeGroat, Diane, and Shelley Rotner. *Homer.* Illus. by the authors. Orchard, 2012. (PreK–Gr. 1)

Gutman, Dan. *Casey Back at Bat.* Illus. by Steve Johnson and Lou Fancher. Harper-Collins, 2007. (Gr. 1–4)

Isadora, Rachel. *Max.* *Illus. by the author. Macmillan, 1976.* (PreK–Gr. 1)

Kessler, Leonard. *Here Comes the Strikeout.* *Illus. by the author. HarperCollins, 1965.* (PreK–Gr. 1)

Meshon, Aaron. *Take Me Out to the Yakyu.* *Illus. by the author. Atheneum, 2013.* (PreK–Gr. 3)

Parish, Peggy. *Play Ball, Amelia Bedelia.* *Illus. by Wallace Tripp. HarperCollins, 1972.* (PreK–Gr. 2)

Stadler, John. *Hooray for Snail!* *Illus. by the author. HarperCollins, 1984.* (PreK–Gr. 1)

Sylvester, Kevin. *Splinters.* *Illus. by the author. Tundra, 2010.* (K–Gr. 4)

Tavares, Matt. *Becoming Babe Ruth.* *Illus. by the author. Candlewick, 2013.* (Gr. 1–4)

Vernick, Audrey. *Brothers at Bat: The True Story of an Amazing All-Brother Baseball Team.* *Illus. by Steven Salerno. Clarion, 2012.* (Gr. 1–4)

Verse

Sing "Take Me Out to the Ballgame," which was written by Jack Norworth in 1908. Find all the lyrics, including the verses about Katie Casey (a girl who is "baseball mad"), and a bit of history at www.baseball-almanac.com/poetry/po_stmo.shtml. Listen to a lovely rendition by Carly Simon at www.youtube.com/watch?v = kRqHM6dOUJI.

Activity

Make mini sports pennants of favorite teams out of straws, construction paper, and streamers. Then play catch with a real baseball.

SPRING   (*See* Rain; Seasons; Weather; Winter)

ST. PATRICK'S DAY

Read-Alouds

Balian, Lorna. *Leprechauns Never Lie.* *Illus. by the author. Abingdon, 1980.* (PreK–Gr. 1)

Bunting, Eve. *St. Patrick's Day in the Morning.* *Illus. by Jan Brett. Clarion, 1980.* (PreK–Gr. 1)

DePaola, Tomie. *Jamie O'Rourke and the Big Potato: An Irish Folktale.* *Illus. by the author. Putnam, 1992.* (PreK–Gr. 2)

Edwards, Pamela Duncan. *The Leprechaun's Gold.* *Illus. by Henry Cole. HarperCollins, 2004.* (PreK–Gr. 2)

McDermott, Gerald. *Tim O'Toole and the Wee Folk: An Irish Tale.* *Illus. by the author. Viking, 1990.* (PreK–Gr. 2)

Rockwell, Anne. St. *Patrick's Day.* *Illus. by Lizzy Rockwell. Harper, 2010.* (PreK–Gr. 2)

Wojciechowski, Susan. *A Fine St.* *Patrick's Day.* *Illus. by Tom Curry. Random House, 2004.* (K–Gr. 3)

Verse

Sing "I'm a Little Leprechaun" to the tune of "I'm a Little Teapot":

> I'm a little leprechaun dressed in green,
>
> The tiniest man that you've ever seen.
>
> If you ever catch me, so it's told,
>
> I'll give to you my pot of gold.

Activity

Hand out plastic gold coins (or pebbles spray-painted gold) to each child, along with a paper printed with the phrase, "If I had a piece of lepre-chauns' gold, I would . . ." Let the children finish the sentence and draw what they would wish for. For more ideas, check out pinterest.com/dsavs/preschool-st-patricks-day.

STARS (*See* Space)

STUFFED ANIMALS AND TOYS (*See also* Dolls)

Read-Alouds

Barton, Chris. *Shark vs. Train.* *Illus. by Tom Lichtenheld. Little, Brown, 2010.* (PreK–Gr. 2)

De Sève, Randall. *Toy Boat.* *Illus. by Loren Long. Philomel, 2007.* (PreK–Gr. 1)

Falconer, Ian. *Olivia . . . and the Missing Toy.* *Illus. by the author. Atheneum, 2003.* (PreK–Gr. 1)

Feiffer, Jules. *I Lost My Bear.* *Illus. by the author. HarperCollins, 1998.* (K–Gr. 2)

Freeman, Don. *Corduroy.* *Illus. by the author. Viking, 1968.* (PreK–Gr. 1)

Gravett, Emily. *Monkey and Me.* *Illus. by the author. Simon & Schuster, 2008.* (PreK–K)

Raschka, Chris. *A Ball for Daisy.* *Illus. by the author. Schwartz & Wade, 2012.* (PreK–Gr. 1)

Seeger, Laura Vaccaro. *Dog and Bear: Two Friends, Three Stories.* *Illus. by the author. Roaring Brook, 2007.* (PreK–Gr. 1)

Willems, Mo. *Hooray for Amanda and Her Alligator*. *Illus. by the author. Balzer + Bray, 2011*. (PreK–Gr. 1)

Willems, Mo. *I Love My New Toy*. *Illus. by the author. Hyperion, 2008*. (PreK–Gr. 2)

Willems, Mo. *Knuffle Bunny: A Cautionary Tale*. *Illus. by the author. Hyperion, 2005*. (PreK–Gr. 2)

Verse

Recite "Teddy Bear, Teddy Bear":

> Teddy Bear, Teddy Bear, turn around,
> Teddy Bear, Teddy Bear, touch the ground.
> Teddy Bear, Teddy bear, jump up high,
> Teddy Bear, Teddy Bear, touch the sky.
>
> Teddy Bear, Teddy Bear, bend down low,
> Teddy Bear, Teddy Bear, touch your toes.
> Teddy Bear, Teddy Bear, read the news,
> Teddy Bear, Teddy Bear, shine your shoes.
>
> Teddy Bear, Teddy Bear, go upstairs,
> Teddy Bear, Teddy Bear, say your prayers.
> Teddy Bear, Teddy Bear, turn off the light,
> Teddy Bear, Teddy Bear, say goodnight.

Activity

Children can draw pictures of or describe what they think their favorite stuffies are doing right now.

SUMMER   (*See* Rain; Seasons; Weather)

SUN   (*See* Space)

TEACHERS   (*See* also Schools)

Read-Alouds

Allard, Harry. *Miss Nelson Is Missing*. *Illus. by James Marshall. Houghton Mifflin, 1977*. (PreK–Gr. 2)

Brown, Peter. *My Teacher Is a Monster. (No, I Am Not.)* *Illus. by the author. Little, Brown, 2014*. (PreK–Gr. 2)

Finchler, Judy. *Miss Malarkey Doesn't Live in Room 10. Illus. by Kevin O'Malley. Walker, 1995.* (PreK–Gr. 1)

Henkes, Kevin. *Chrysanthemum. Illus. by the author. Greenwillow, 1991.* (PreK–Gr. 1)

Henkes, Kevin. *Lilly's Purple Plastic Purse. Illus. by the author. Greenwillow, 1996.* (K–Gr. 2)

Houston, Gloria. *My Great-Aunt Arizona. Illus. by Susan Conde Lamb. HarperCollins, 1992.* (K–Gr. 3)

Slate, Joseph. *Miss Bindergarten Gets Ready for Kindergarten. Illus. by Ashley Wolff. Dutton, 1996.* (PreK–Gr. 1)

Walton, Rick. *Mr. President Goes to School. Illus. by Brad Sneed. Peachtree, 2010.* (PreK–Gr. 2)

Verse

Sing "On My First Day" (to the tune of "Zip-a-dee-do-dah").

> Zip-a-dee-do-dah, Zip-a-dee-ay! I'm excited because it's my first day!
> I'm gonna learn and I'm gonna play; Zip-a-dee-do-dah, Zip-a-dee-ay!
> It is time for us to go, now.
> We're gonna ride the school bus—Our new teacher's waiting for us!
> Zip-a-dee-do-dah, Zip-a-dee-ay! Wonderful feeling, on my first day!

Activity

Play "Teacher Says" instead of "Simon Says." Everyone gets a turn at being the teacher and giving commands to the others, who must follow simple instructions except when the leader doesn't preface them with "Teacher Says."

TECHNOLOGY   (*See* Computers and Technology)

TEDDY BEARS   (*See* Stuffed Animals and Toys)

TEETH

Read-Alouds

Bate, Lucy. *Little Rabbit's Loose Tooth. Illus. by Diane deGroat. Crown, 1975.* (PreK–Gr. 1)

Clement, Rod. *Grandpa's Teeth. Illus. by the author. HarperCollins, 1998.* (PreK–Gr. 1)

Davis, Katie. *Mabel the Tooth Fairy and How She Got Her Job. Illus. by the author. Harcourt, 2003.* (PreK–Gr. 1)

Diakité, Penda. *I Lost My Tooth in Africa.* Illus. by Baba Wagué Diakité. Scholastic, 2006. (PreK–Gr. 3)

Graham, Bob. *April and Esme, Tooth Fairies.* Illus. by the author. Candlewick, 2010. (PreK–Gr. 2)

McGhee, Alison. *Mrs. Watson Wants Your Teeth.* Illus. by Harry Bliss. Harcourt, 2004. (PreK–Gr. 1)

Palatini, Margie. *Sweet Tooth.* Illus. by Jack E. Davis. Simon & Schuster, 2004. (PreK–Gr. 2)

Simms, Laura. *Rotten Teeth.* Illus. by David Catrow. Houghton Mifflin, 1998. (K–Gr. 2)

Steig, William. *Doctor De Soto.* Illus. by the author. Farrar, 1982. (K–Gr. 2)

Verse

Recite "My Wiggly Jiggly Loose Tooth" adapted by Judy Freeman:

My wiggly jiggly loose tooth was hanging by a thread,
So I yanked my loose tooth loose and fell back on the bed.

I wiped it with a tissue, wiping off the blood so red;
And I put it 'neath my pillow, and then I went to bed.

The fairy snatched my loose tooth and then away she sped;
And now I have a dollar and a hole inside my head.

Activity

Cut a paper plate in half. Have children draw huge smiling mouths filled with teeth, and outline them in black crayon or paste on Styrofoam peanuts. Attach a popsicle stick to the back of the creation to create a toothy mask.

THANKSGIVING

Read-Alouds

Allegra, Mike. *Sarah Gives Thanks.* Illus. by David Gardner. Albert Whitman, 2012. (K–Gr. 3)

Anderson, Laurie Halse. *Thank You, Sarah: The Woman Who Saved Thanksgiving.* Illus. by Matt Faulkner. Simon & Schuster, 2002. (K–Gr. 3)

Greene, Rhonda Gowler. *The Very First Thanksgiving Day.* Illus. by Susan Graber. Atheneum, 2002. (PreK–Gr. 2)

Jackson, Alison. *I Know an Old Lady Who Swallowed a Pie.* *Illus. by Judith Byron Schachner. Dutton, 1997.* (PreK–Gr. 1)

Mora, Pat. *Gracias / Thanks.* *Illus. by John Parra. Lee & Low, 2009.* (PreK–Gr. 2)

Pilkey, Dav. *'Twas the Night before Thanksgiving.* *Illus. by the author. Orchard, 1990.* (PreK–Gr. 2)

Spinelli, Eileen. *Thanksgiving at the Tappletons'.* *Illus. by Megan Lloyd. HarperCollins, 1982.* (PreK–Gr. 1)

Sweet, Melissa. *Balloons over Broadway: The True Story of the Puppeteer of Macy's Parade.* *Illus. by the author. Houghton Mifflin, 2011.* (K–Gr. 4)

Verse
Sing "Thanksgiving Song" in chapter 5, "Music," on page 184.

Activity
Sure, you can make the usual turkeys from cut-out handprints, but you can really get to the heart of the matter by simply asking kids to tell what they're most thankful for this year.

TIGERS   (*See also* Lions)

Read-Alouds

Brown, Peter. *Mr. Tiger Goes Wild.* *Illus. by the author. Little, Brown, 2013.* (PreK–Gr. 2)

Dowson, Nick. *Tigress.* *Illus. by Jane Chapman. Candlewick, 2004.* (PreK–Gr. 1)

Fleming, Candace. *Oh, No!* *Illus. by Eric Rohmann. Schwartz & Wade, 2012.* (PreK–Gr. 1)

LaRochelle, David. *It's a Tiger!* *Illus. by Jeremy Tankard. Chronicle, 2012.* (PreK–Gr. 1)

Lester, Julius. *Sam and the Tigers.* *Illus. by the author. Dial, 1996.* (PreK–Gr. 1)

Sheth, Kashmira. *Tiger in My Soup.* *Illus. by Jeffrey Ebbeler. Peachtree, 2013.* (PreK–Gr. 2)

Verse
Recite "Eenie, Meenie, Miney, Moe":

> Eenie, meenie, miney, moe, catch a tiger by the toe.
>
> If he hollers, let him go, eenie, meenie, miney, moe,
>
> My mother said to pick the very best one and you are IT.

Activity

Make handprint tigers. Children dip a hand in orange paint and press it onto a piece of construction paper. When they turn their paper upside down, their fingers become the tiger's legs and head. Paste googly eyes onto the thumb, draw a tail, and color black stripes, and, oh, no, it's a tiger!

TIME

Read-Alouds

Carle, Eric. *The Grouchy Ladybug*. *Illus. by the author. HarperCollins, 1977.* (PreK–Gr. 1)

Crummel, Susan Stevens. *All in One Hour*. *Illus. by Dorothy Donohue. Marshall Cavendish, 2003.* (PreK–Gr. 1)

Harper, Dan. *Telling Time with Big Mama Cat*. *Illus. by Barry Moser and Cara Moser. Harcourt, 1998.* (PreK–Gr. 1)

Hutchins, Hazel. *A Second Is a Hiccup: A Child's Book of Time*. *Illus. by Katy MacDonald Denton. Scholastic/Arthur A. Levine, 2007.* (PreK–Gr. 1)

Hutchins, Pat. *Clocks and More Clocks*. *Illus. by the author. Macmillan, 1970.* (PreK–Gr. 1)

Jenkins, Steve. *Just a Second: A Different Way to Look at Time*. *Illus. by the author. Houghton Mifflin, 2011.* (PreK–Gr. 4)

Lamb, Albert. *Tell Me the Day Backwards*. *Illus. by David McPhail. Candlewick, 2011.* (PreK–Gr. 1)

Rathmann, Peggy. *10 Minutes Till Bedtime*. *Illus. by the author. Putnam, 1998.* (PreK–Gr. 1)

Singer, Marilyn. *Nine O'Clock Lullaby*. *Illus. by Frané Lessac. HarperCollins, 1991.* (PreK–Gr. 1)

Verse

Recite "Hickory Dickory Dock."

Activity

Time children doing a variety of activities. How many times can they jump up and down, hop on one foot, or clap hands, etc. in one minute?

TOADS   (*See* Frogs and Toads)

TOYS (*See* Stuffed Animals and Toys)

TRAINS

Read-Alouds

Barton, Chris. *Shark vs. Train.* *Illus. by Tom Lichtenheld. Little, Brown, 2010.* (PreK–Gr. 2)

Bee, William. *And the Train Goes . . . Illus. by the author. Candlewick, 2007.* (PreK–Gr. 1)

Cooper, Elisha. *Train. Illus. by the author. Orchard, 2013.* (PreK–Gr. 1)

Crews, Donald. *Freight Train. Illus. by the author. Greenwillow, 1978.* (PreK–Gr. 1)

Eaton, Jason Carter. *How to Train a Train. Illus. by John Rocco. Candlewick, 2013.* (PreK–Gr. 2)

Floca, Brian. *Locomotive. Illus. by the author. Atheneum/Richard Jackson, 2013.* (PreK–Gr. 6)

Piper, Watty. *The Little Engine That Could. Illus. by Loren Long. Philomel, 2005.* (PreK–Gr. 1)

Rinker, Sherri Duskey. *Steam Train, Dream Train. Illus. by Tom Lichtenheld. Chronicle, 2013.* (PreK–Gr. 1)

Siebert, Diane. *Train Song. Illus. by Michael Wimmer. HarperCollins, 1990.* (PreK–Gr. 1)

Westcott, Nadine Bernard. *I've Been Working on the Railroad: An American Classic. Illus. by the author. Hyperion, 1996.* (PreK–Gr. 1)

Verse

Recite "Train!" on page 268 and "This Is a Choo Choo Train":

> This is a choo choo train (*squat*)
> Puffing down the track (*rotate your arms together, forward*)
> Now it's going forward, (*move forward*)
> Now it's going back. (*move back, rotating your arms backward*)
>
> Now the bell is ringing (*pull a rope*)
> Now the whistle blows
>   (*hold your fist near your mouth and say, "Toot, toot"*)
> What a lot of noise it makes (*cover your ears*)
> Everywhere it goes. (*stretch out your arms*)

Activity

Duplicate a drawing of a simple locomotive cab, facing left, one for each child, to color, cut out, and glue to the left-hand edge of a large piece of white drawing paper. Hand out red squares of paper. Have children write their names in marker or black crayon, in capital letters, with one letter per square. They then glue their squares in order, from left to right, to form their names as the cars of the train. Have children cut out and glue black construction paper wheels to the bottom. Choo choo!

TRANSPORTATION

(*See* Airplanes; Bicycles; Boats and Ships; Cars and Buses; Trucks; Trains)

TREES

Read-Alouds

Cherry, Lynne. *The Great Kapok Tree: A Tale of the Amazon Rain Forest.* Illus. by the author. Harcourt, 1990. (K–Gr. 3)

Chin, Jason. *Redwoods.* Illus. by the author. Roaring Brook/Flash Point, 2009. (PreK–Gr. 3)

Ehlert, Lois. *Leaf Man.* Illus. by the author. Harcourt, 2005. (PreK–Gr. 1)

Ehlert, Lois. *Pie in the Sky.* Illus. by the author. Harcourt, 2004. (PreK–Gr. 1)

Ehlert, Lois. *Red Leaf, Yellow Leaf.* Illus. by the author. Harcourt, 1991. (PreK–Gr. 1)

Gackenbach, Dick. *Mighty Tree.* Illus. by the author. Harcourt, 1992. (PreK–Gr. 1)

Hall, Zoe. *The Apple Pie Tree.* Illus. by Shari Halpern. Scholastic/Blue Sky, 1996. (PreK–Gr. 1)

Nivola, Claire A. *Planting the Trees of Kenya: The Story of Wangari Maathai.* Illus. by the author. Farrar, 2008. (K–Gr. 3)

Pfeffer, Wendy. *A Log's Life.* Illus. by Robin Brickman. Simon & Schuster, 1997. (PreK–Gr. 2)

Udry, Janice May. *A Tree Is Nice.* Illus. by Marc Simont. HarperCollins, 1956. (PreK–Gr. 1)

Verse

Sing "The Tiny Little Apple Seed" to the tune of "The Eentsy Weentsy Spider"

The tiny little apple seed was planted in the ground,

Down came the rain, falling all around,

Out came the sun, as bright as bright can be,

And the tiny little apple seed became an apple tree!

Activity

Tell the board story "The Ossopit Tree" on page 39.

TRUCKS (*See also* Cars and Buses; Trains)

Read-Alouds

Burton, Virginia Lee. *Mike Mulligan and His Steam Shovel.* *Illus. by the author. Houghton Mifflin, 1939.* (PreK–Gr. 1)

Crews, Donald. *Truck.* *Illus. by the author. Greenwillow, 1980.* (PreK–Gr. 1)

Floca, Brian. *Five Trucks.* *Illus. by the author. Atheneum/Richard Jackson, 2014.* (PreK–Gr. 1)

Lee, Mark. *20 Big Trucks in the Middle of the Street.* *Illus. by Kurt Cyrus. Candlewick, 2013.* (PreK–Gr. 1)

McMullan, Kate. *I Stink.* *Illus. by Jim McMullan. HarperCollins, 2002.* (PreK–Gr. 1)

Rinker, Sherri Duskey. *Goodnight, Goodnight, Construction Site.* *Illus. by Tom Lichtenheld. Chronicle, 2011.* (PreK–Gr. 1)

Savage, Stephen. *Supertruck.* *Illus. by the author. Roaring Brook, 2015.* (PreK–Gr. 1)

Sturges, Philemon. *I Love Trucks!* *Illus. by Shari Halpern. HarperCollins, 1999.* (PreK–Gr. 1)

Sutton, Sally. *Roadwork.* *Illus. by Brian Lovelock. Candlewick, 2008.* (PreK–Gr. 1)

Vestergaard, Hope. *Digger, Dozer, Dumper.* *Illus. by David Slonim. Candlewick, 2013.* (PreK–Gr. 1)

Verse

Sing "Five Big Dump Trucks." Listen to the tune at www.good-kids.net/songs/show_flash.php?flash = 31727.

Five big dump trucks rolling down the road

Five big dump trucks rolling down the road

One pulls off to unload

Four big dump trucks rolling down the road

(Continue counting down from four to three to two, ending with the last verse as follows.)

> One big dump truck rolling down the road
> One big dump truck rolling down the road
> It pulls off to unload
> No more dump trucks rolling down the road

Activity

With painter's tape (a one- or two-inch roll of the blue stuff that's easy to remove), make a series of roads on the floor. If you like, add traffic lights, cross streets, and even ramps. Children will have a great time steering their small toy trucks down the road.

TURTLES   *(See also* Reptiles and Amphibians)

Read-Alouds

Berger, Melvin. *Look Out for Turtles!* *Illus. by Megan Lloyd. HarperCollins, 1992.* (PreK–Gr. 2)

Cyrus, Kurt. *The Voyage of Turtle Rex.* *Illus. by the author. Harcourt, 2011.* (PreK–Gr. 2)

Falwell, Cathryn. *Turtle Splash!: Countdown at the Pond.* *Illus. by the author. Greenwillow, 2001.* (PreK–Gr. 1)

George, William T. *Box Turtle at Long Pond.* *Illus. by Lindsay Barrett George. Greenwillow, 1989.* (PreK–Gr. 1)

Gorbachev, Valeri. *Turtle's Penguin Day.* *Illus. by the author. Knopf, 2008.* (PreK–Gr. 1)

Guiberson, Brenda Z. *Into the Sea.* *Illus. by Alix Berenzy. Henry Holt, 1996.* (PreK–Gr. 1)

Hadithi, Mwenye. *Tricky Tortoise.* *Illus. by Adrienne Kennaway. Little, Brown, 1988.* (PreK–Gr. 1)

Paul, Ann Whitford. *Tortuga in Trouble.* *Illus. by Ethan Long. Holiday House, 2009.* (PreK–Gr. 2)

Pinkney, Jerry. *The Tortoise & the Hare.* *Illus. by the author. Little, Brown, 2013.* (PreK–Gr. 2)

Verse

Recite "There Was a Little Turtle":

> There was a little turtle, *(make a fist with your thumb sticking out)*
> He lived in a box. *(cup your hands together for a box)*

He swam in a puddle, *(wiggle your hand to represent swimming)*
He climbed on the rocks.
    (let your fingers climb up a fist you make with the opposite hand)

He snapped at a mosquito, *(snap your fingers)*
He snapped at a flea, *(snap your fingers)*
He snapped at a minnow, *(snap your fingers)*
And he snapped at me! *(snap your fingers)*

He caught the mosquito, *(clap your hands)*
He caught the flea, *(clap your hands)*
He caught the minnow, *(clap your hands)*
But he didn't catch me! *(wag your index finger back and forth)*

Activity

Stage a race between the tortoise and the hare—outside if you can, or in a hallway. Set up starting and finish lines. Half of the children can be hares, racing almost to the finish line but then stopping for a nap. The other half, the tortoises, should plod slowly but steadily and win the race.

UNITED STATES   (*See also* Earth)

Read-Alouds

Bates, Katharine Lee. *America the Beautiful: Together We Stand.* Illus. by Bryan Collier (and nine other artists). Orchard, 2013. (K–Gr. 2)

Borden, Louise. *America Is. . .* Illus. by Stacey Schuett. McElderry, 2002. (PreK–Gr. 2)

Guthrie, Woody. *This Land Is Your Land.* Illus. by Kathy Jakobsen. Little, Brown, 1998. (PreK–Gr. 2)

Keller, Laurie. *The Scrambled States of America.* Illus. by the author. Henry Holt, 1998. (PreK–Gr. 2)

Pattison, Darcy. *The Journey of Oliver K. Woodman.* Illus. by Joe Cepeda. Harcourt, 2003. (PreK–Gr. 2)

Priceman, Marjorie. *How to Make a Cherry Pie and See the U.S.A.* Illus. by the author. Knopf, 2008. (PreK–Gr. 2)

Talbott, Hudson. *United Tweets of America: 50 State Birds.* Illus. by the author. Putnam, 2008. (PreK–Gr. 2)

Yaccarino, Dan. *Go, Go America.* Illus. by the author. Scholastic, 2008. (PreK–Gr. 2)

Verse

Sing "America the Beautiful," "This Land Is Your Land," and "You're a Grand Old Flag." Find the lyrics for all at www.kididdles.com/lyrics/allsongs.html.

Activity

Set out a giant floor puzzle map of the U.S. for children to assemble. (You can find one at Staples and various places online.) Print out a black-and-white map of the U.S. for each child with instructions to color all the states they've visited with one color and the states they'd like to visit with another color. You can find several types of free reproducible U.S. maps at www.mrprintables.com/printable-map-of-the-united-states.html.

VALENTINE'S DAY

Read-Alouds

Bunting, Eve. *The Valentine Bears*. *Illus. by Jan Brett. Clarion, 1983.* (PreK–Gr. 1)

Carlson, Nancy. *Louanne Pig in the Mysterious Valentine*. *Illus. by the author. Carolrhoda Books, 2004.* (PreK–Gr. 1)

Hoban, Lillian. *Arthur's Great Big Valentine*. *Illus. by the author. HarperCollins, 1989.* (PreK–Gr. 1)

Samuels, Barbara. *Happy Valentine's Day, Dolores*. *Illus. by the author. Farrar, 2006.* (PreK–Gr. 1)

Spinelli, Eileen. *Somebody Loves You, Mr. Hatch*. *Illus. by Paul Yalowitz. Simon & Schuster, 1991.* (PreK–Gr. 2)

Verse

Recite the traditional "Roses Are Red," and the children's parody version:

Roses are red,

Violets are blue,

Sugar is sweet,

And so are you.

Rose are red, violets are blue

That's what they say but it just isn't true!

Roses are red and apples are too,

But violets are violet, violets aren't blue.

An orange is orange, but Greenland's not green;

A pinky's not pink, so what does it mean?

To call something blue when it's not, we defile it,

But what can you do? It's so hard to rhyme violet.

Activity

Make Valentines for your favorite book characters.

VALUES, ETHICS, AND CHARACTER EDUCATION

(*See* Compassion and Kindness; Cooperation; Courage; Apologies, Forgiveness, and Manners; Friendship; Generosity; Honesty; Perseverance; Resourcefulness; Responsibility)

VEGETABLES   (*See* Fruits and Vegetables)

VEHICLES

(*See* Airplanes; Bicycles; Boats and Ships; Cars and Buses; Trains; Trucks)

WATER   (*See also* Ocean and Seashore; Rain)

Read-Alouds

Adler, David A. *Things That Float and Things That Don't.* Illus. by Anna Raff. Holiday House, 2013. (K–Gr. 2)

Berry, Lynn. *What Floats in a Moat?* Illus. by Matthew Cordell. Simon & Schuster, 2013. (PreK–Gr. 2)

Cobb, Vicki. *I Get Wet.* Illus. by Julia Gorton. HarperCollins, 2002. (PreK–Gr. 2)

Dorros, Arthur. *Follow the Water from Brook to Ocean.* Illus. by the author. HarperCollins, 1991. (PreK–Gr. 2)

Kerley, Barbara. *A Cool Drink of Water.* Illus. with photos. National Geographic, 2002. (PreK–Gr. 2)

Kurtz, Jane, and Christopher Kurtz. *Water Hole Waiting.* Illus. by Lee Christiansen. Greenwillow, 2002. (PreK–Gr. 1)

Locker, Thomas. *Water Dance.* Illus. by the author. Harcourt, 1997. (PreK–Gr. 2)

Sayre, April Pulley. *Raindrops Roll.* Photos by the author. Beach Lane, 2015. (PreK–Gr. 3)

Verse

Recite "Water" by Leroy F. Jackson, from *The Peter Patter Book of Nursery Rhymes,* ©1918:

> There's water in the rain barrel,
> And water in the well,
> There's lots of water in the pond
> Where Hannah Hawkins fell.
>
> There's water in the ocean,
> And water in the skies,
> And when a fellow blubbers
> He gets water in his eyes.
>
> But in the Barca desert
> Where the hippodoodles play,
> The water in the rivers
> Just dries up and blows away.

Activity

Play "Will It Float" with a portable tub of water, bath toys, and other random objects. Children predict which ones will float and drop them into the tub.

WEATHER   (*See also* Rain; Seasons; Winter)

Read-Alouds

Barrett, Judi. *Cloudy with a Chance of Meatballs.* *Illus. by Ron Barrett. Atheneum, 1978.* (PreK–Gr. 4)

DePaola, Tomie. *The Cloud Book.* *Illus. by the author. Holiday House, 1975.* (PreK–Gr. 2)

Elliott, David. *Finn Throws a Fit.* *Illus. by Timothy Basil Ering. Candlewick, 2009.* (PreK–Gr. 1)

Sayre, April Pulley. *Raindrops Roll.* *Photos by the author. Beach Lane, 2015.* (PreK–Gr. 3)

Tresselt, Alvin. *Hide and Seek Fog.* *Illus. by Roger Duvoisin. Lothrop, 1965.* (PreK–Gr. 1)

Wiesner, David. *Hurricane.* *Illus. by the author. Clarion, 1990.* (PreK–Gr. 1)

Verse

Sing "What's the Weather" to the tune of "Clementine"

> What's the weather, what's the weather,
>> what's the weather like today?
>
> Tell us (*insert a child's name here*),
>> what's the weather, what's the weather like today?

> Is it sunny? (*hold your arms in big circle above your head*)
>
> Is it cloudy? (*cover your eyes with your hands*)
>
> Is it rainy out today? (*wave your fingers down like rain*)
>
> Is it snowy? (*shiver*)
>
> Is it windy? (*wave your arms*)
>
> Can we go outside and play?

Activity

Make an illustrated weather chart with your kids. Have the children predict and record what they think the weather will be during the next week or month and monitor how close they come.

WEDDINGS

Read-Alouds

Henkes, Kevin. *Lilly's Big Day*. *Illus. by the author. Greenwillow, 2006.* (PreK–Gr. 1)

Isaacs, Anne. *Meanwhile, Back at the Ranch*. *Illus. by Kevin Hawkes. Schwartz & Wade, 2014.* (K–Gr. 4)

Look, Lenore. *Uncle Peter's Amazing Chinese Wedding*. *Illus. by Yumi Heo. Atheneum, 2006.* (PreK–Gr. 1)

Soto, Gary. *Snapshots from the Wedding*. *Illus. by Stephanie Garcia. Putnam, 1997.* (PreK–Gr. 2)

Verse

Sing "Lavender's Blue, Dilly Dilly" You'll find the lyrics and chords at www.acousticmusicarchive.com/lavenders-blue-chords-lyrics, and listen to one of many recordings of it at YouTube.com.

> Lavender's blue, dilly dilly, lavender's green,
>
> When you are King, dilly dilly, I shall be Queen.

Who told you so, dilly dilly, who told you so?

'Twas my own heart, dilly dilly, that told me so.

Call up your friends, dilly, dilly, set them to work,

Some to the plough, dilly dilly, some to the fork,

Some to the hay, dilly dilly, some to thresh corn,

Whilst you and I, dilly dilly, keep ourselves warm.

Lavender's blue, dilly dilly, lavender's green,

When you are King, dilly dilly, I shall be Queen.

Who told you so, dilly dilly, who told you so?

'Twas my own heart, dilly dilly, that told me so.

Activity

Stage your own wedding with a decorated paper wedding cake, pipe cleaner wedding rings, and flower bouquets made of tissue paper and pipe cleaners.

WHALES

Read-Alouds

Barnett, Mac. *Billy Twitters and His Blue Whale Problem.* *Illus. by Adam Rex. Disney-Hyperion Books, 2009.* (PreK–Gr. 2)

Donaldson, Julia. *The Snail and the Whale.* *Illus. by Axel Scheffler. Dial, 2004.* (PreK–Gr. 2)

McCloskey, Robert. *Burt Dow, Deep-Water Man: A Tale of the Sea in the Classic Tradition.* *Illus. by the author. Viking, 1963.* (K–Gr. 4)

Pinkney, Andrea Davis. *Peggony Po: A Whale of a Tale.* *Illus. by Brian Pinkney. Hyperion, 2006.* (K–Gr. 2)

Verse

Recite "If You Ever Meet a Whale":

If you ever ever ever ever ever,

If you ever ever ever meet a whale,

You must never never never never never,

You must never never never touch its tail.

For if you ever ever ever ever ever,

If you ever ever ever touch its tail,

You will never never never never never,

You will never never meet another whale.

Activity

A blue whale can be more than one hundred feet long. Take your children outside or to a long hallway and have them count out and measure a hundred feet. Unwind a ball of string on the ground as they measure.

WIND   (*See* Rain; Seasons; Weather; Winter)

WINTER   (*See* also Seasons; Weather)

Read-Alouds

Aylesworth, Jim. *The Mitten.* *Illus. by Barbara McClintock. Scholastic, 2009.* (PreK–Gr. 1)

Brett, Jan. *The Hat.* *Illus. by the author. Putnam, 1997.* (PreK–Gr. 1)

Brett, Jan. *The Mitten.* *Illus. by the author. Putnam, 1989.* (PreK–Gr. 1)

Burton, Virginia Lee. *Katy and the Big Snow.* *Illus. by the author. Houghton Mifflin, 1943.* (PreK–Gr. 1)

Cassino, Mark, and Jon Nelson. *The Story of Snow: The Science of Winter's Wonder.* *Illus. by Nora Aoyagi. Photos by Mark Cassino. Chronicle, 2009.* (K–Gr. 3)

Fleming, Denise. *Time to Sleep.* *Illus. by the author. Henry Holt, 1997.* (PreK–Gr. 1)

Johnson, David A. *Snow Sounds: An Onomatopoeic Story.* *Houghton Mifflin, 2006.* (PreK–Gr. 1)

Keats, Ezra Jack. *The Snowy Day.* *Illus. by the author. Viking, 1962.* (PreK–Gr. 1)

Martin, Jacqueline Briggs. *Snowflake Bentley.* *Illus. by Mary Azarian. Houghton Mifflin, 1998.* (K–Gr. 4)

Neitzel, Shirley. *The Jacket I Wear in the Snow.* *Illus. by Nancy Winslow Parker. Greenwillow, 1989.* (PreK–Gr. 1)

O'Malley, Kevin. *Straight to the Pole.* *Illus. by the author. Walker, 2003.* (PreK–Gr. 1)

Peters, Lisa Westberg. *Cold Little Duck, Duck, Duck.* *Illus. by Sam Williams. Greenwillow, 2000.* (PreK–Gr. 1)

Rocco, John. *Blizzard.* *Illus. by the author. Disney-Hyperion, 2014.* (PreK–Gr. 3)

Rohmann, Eric. *A Kitten Tale*. Illus. by the author. Knopf, 2008. (PreK–Gr. 1)

Sabuda, Robert. *The Blizzard's Robe*. Illus. by the author. Atheneum, 1999. (K–Gr. 3)

Sakai, Komako. *The Snow Day*. Illus. by the author. Scholastic/Arthur A. Levine, 2009. (PreK–Gr. 1)

Steig, William. *Brave Irene*. Illus. by the author. Farrar, 1986. (K–Gr. 3)

Wilson, Karma. *Bear Snores On*. Illus. by Jane Chapman. McElderry, 2002. (PreK–Gr. 1)

Verse

Sing "Frosty the Snowman" by Walter "Jack" Rollins and Steve Nelson, which was first recorded by Gene Autry and the Cass County Boys in 1950. Find the lyrics and music at www.kididdles.com/lyrics.

Activity

Make snowflake shapes by squeezing school glue onto plastic wrap. When the shapes are dry, peel them off and hang them as window clings.

WISHES

Read-Alouds

Buehner, Caralyn. *Fanny's Dream*. Illus. by Mark Buehner. Dial, 1996. (K–Gr. 3)

Carle, Eric. *The Mixed-Up Chameleon*. Illus. by the author. HarperCollins, 1984. (PreK–Gr. 1)

Egan, Tim. *Burnt Toast on Davenport Street*. Illus. by the author. Houghton Mifflin, 1997. (PreK–Gr. 2)

Howe, James. *I Wish I Were a Butterfly*. Illus. by Ed Young. Harcourt, 1987. (PreK–Gr. 1)

Kraft, Erik. *Chocolatina*. Illus. by Denise Brunkus. Scholastic, 1998. (PreK–Gr. 2)

LeSieg, Theo. *I Wish That I Had Duck Feet*. Illus. by B. Tobey. Beginner Books, 1965. (PreK–Gr. 1)

Lionni, Leo. *Alexander and the Wind-up Mouse*. Pantheon, 1969. (PreK–Gr. 1)

Meddaugh, Susan. *The Witch's Walking Stick*. Houghton Mifflin, 2005. (K–Gr. 2)

Rosenthal, Amy Krouse. *Yes Day!* Illus. by Tom Lichtenheld. HarperCollins, 2009. (PreK–Gr. 1)

Steig, William. *Sylvester and the Magic Pebble*. Illus. by the author. Windmill, 1969. (PreK–Gr. 2)

Verse

Recite the traditional English nursery rhyme "Star Light, Star Bright"

> Star light, star bright,
> The first star I see tonight;
> I wish I may, I wish I might,
> Have the wish I wish tonight.

Activity

On black paper paste a small white or gray pom-pom and little pieces of white yarn blowing away from it (like a dandelion). Then using white crayon on the black paper, children can write (or dictate) their wishes.

WITCHES   (*See also* Ghosts; Halloween; Monsters)

Read-Alouds

Balian, Lorna. *Humbug Witch*. *Illus. by the author. Star Bright, 2003.* (PreK–Gr. 1)

DePaola, Tomie. *Strega Nona*. *Illus. by the author. Prentice-Hall, 1975.* (PreK–Gr. 4)

Leuck, Laura. *One Witch*. *Illus. by S. D. Schindler. Walker, 2003.* (PreK–Gr. 1)

McGhee, Alison. *A Very Brave Witch*. *Illus. by Harry Bliss. Simon & Schuster, 2006.* (PreK–Gr. 1)

Meddaugh, Susan. *The Witch's Walking Stick*. *Illus. by the author. Houghton Mifflin, 2005.* (K–Gr. 2)

Palatini, Margie. *Piggie Pie*. *Illus. by Howard Fine. Clarion, 1995.* (PreK–Gr. 1)

Wood, Audrey. *Heckedy Peg*. *Illus. by Don Wood. Harcourt, 1987.* (K–Gr. 2)

Verse

Have children recite the chant "Boiling Hot!" adding new ingredients each time.

> Boiling hot, boiling hot
> What will we put in the witch's pot?
> Boiling hot, boiling hot
> We'll put some spiders in the witch's pot.

Activity

Children will have fun making a witch's legs bookmark. First have them cut a bookmark-size white paper rectangle almost in two (the legs), adding red stripes in crayon or paint. Next, have them cut oval shoes from black construction paper and glue them to the ends of the legs.

WOLVES

Read-Alouds

Kulka, Joe. *Wolf's Coming!* Illus. by the author. Carolrhoda, 2007. (PreK–Gr. 1)

Palatini, Margie. *Bad Boys.* Illus. by Henry Cole. HarperCollins, 2003. (PreK–Gr. 1)

Palatini, Margie. *Piggie Pie.* Illus. by Howard Fine. Clarion, 1995. (PreK–Gr. 1)

Schwartz, Corey Rosen. *The Three Ninja Pigs.* Illus. by Dan Santat. Putnam, 2012. (PreK–Gr. 2)

Scieszka, Jon. *The True Story of the 3 Little Pigs!* Illus. by Lane Smith. Viking, 1989. (K–Gr. 6)

Trivizas, Eugene. *The Three Little Wolves and the Big Bad Pig.* Illus. by Helen Oxenbury. McElderry, 1993. (PreK–Gr. 2)

Wiesner, David. *The Three Pigs.* Illus. by the author. Clarion, 2001. (PreK–Gr. 1)

Verse

Sing "Who's Afraid of the Big Bad Wolf?" from the 1933 Disney cartoon *Three Little Pigs.* Find the lyrics at www.allmusicals.com/lyrics/disney/whosafraidofthebigbadwolf.htm and the cartoon segment with the song on YouTube.

Activity

To make a wolf picture, have children paste a maple leaf upside down onto construction paper; add a black paper oval for a nose, two googly eyes, and two paper triangles or two smaller leaves (honey locust would work) for ears. They can finish their pictures with crayons, adding background and/or the rest of the wolf's body.

ZOOS

Read-Alouds

Campbell, Rod. *Dear Zoo: A Lift-the-Flap Book.* Illus. by the author. Four Winds, 1982. (PreK–K)

Massie, Diane Redfield. *The Baby Beebee Bird.* Illus. by Steven Kellogg. HarperCollins, 2000, c1963. (PreK–Gr. 1)

Paxton, Tom. *Going to the Zoo.* Illus. by Karen Schmidt. Morrow, 1996. (PreK–Gr. 1)

Rathmann, Peggy. *Good Night, Gorilla.* Illus. by the author. Putnam, 1994. (PreK–Gr. 1)

Rex, Adam. *Pssst!* Illus. by the author. Harcourt, 2007. (PreK–Gr. 1)

Savage, Stephen. *Where's Walrus?* Illus. by the author. Scholastic, 2011. (PreK–Gr. 1)

Smith, Danna. *Two at the Zoo.* Illus. by Valeria Petrone. Clarion, 2009. (PreK–Gr. 1)

Stead, Philip C. *A Sick Day for Amos McGee.* Illus. by Erin E. Stead. Roaring Brook, 2010. (PreK–Gr. 1)

Verse

Sing Tom Paxton's "Going to the Zoo." You'll find lyrics and chords at songs2play.angelfire.com/goingtothezoo.htm and various covers of the song on YouTube.

Activity

Make your own zoo. Children can draw a zoo animal, filling a piece of 4-by-6-inch construction paper. Glue colored pipe cleaners in vertical lines (to mimic bars) over the animal pictures. (If they want their zoo animals "to get out," have them bend the pipe cleaners a bit before gluing them down.) Make a Zoo Wall in your room of all the animals.

BOOKLIST: PROFESSIONAL BOOKS FOR PRESCHOOL AND PRIMARY PROGRAMS

Bauer, Caroline Feller. *Celebrations: Read-aloud Holiday and Theme Book Programs.* H. W. Wilson, 1985. An anthology of stories, poems, and activities for toddler programs about Halloween, Spring, Grandparents' Day, and other special occasions.

Briggs, Diane. *Toddler Storytime Programs.* Scarecrow Press, 1993. A librarian's compendium of twenty-five themed programs, with books, fingerplays, and action rhymes, stories, puppetry, games, and crafts. Briggs's *Preschool Favorites: 35 Storytimes Kids Love* (American Library Association, 2007) is also filled with wonderful activities and books.

Cobb, Jane. *What'll I Do with the Baby-o? Nursery Rhymes, Songs, and Stories for Babies.* Black Sheep Press, 2007. Cobb talks about the need for reciting rhymes to our babies, and suggests 350 fingerplays, rhymes, songs, stories to tell, and books to read. Packaged with a CD of thirty-six of the songs.

Diamant-Cohen, Betsy. *Mother Goose on the Loose.* Neal-Schuman, 2006. In a loose-leaf binder with a CD, Diamant-Cohen offers ten multimedia storytime programs designed to build motor, music, social, and preliteracy skills in infants and toddlers, incorporating books, rhymes, fingerplays, flannelboard stories, music, and dance. A Spanish version is also available.

Diamant-Cohen, Betsy, and Melanie A. Hetrick. *Transforming Preschool Storytime: A Modern Vision and a Year of Programs.* Illus. by Celia Yitzhak. American Library Association/Neal-Schuman, 2013. Including up-to-date theory and research about child development, this book features eight "scripts" for extended story hours, with books and activity ideas.

Dietzel-Glair, Julie. *Books in Motion: Connecting Preschoolers with Books through Art, Games, Movement, Music, Playacting, and Props.* American Library Association/Neal-Schuman, 2013. Filled with storytime ideas, this book devotes one chapter to each area listed in the subtitle.

Ernst, Linda L. *Baby Rhyming Time.* Neal-Schuman, 2008. A great how-to about putting together library programs for newborns to two-year-olds, including twelve ready-to-go programs, an extensive themed booklist, and a CD-ROM of scripts, songs, patterns, and more.

Ghoting, Saroj Nadkarni, and Pamela Martin-Diaz. *Storytimes for Everyone! Developing Young Children's Language and Literacy.* American Library Association, 2013. The authors include up-to-date research on early literacy as well as enhanced literacy storytime ideas, including complete sample storytimes for infants and toddlers, two- and three-year-olds, and preschoolers.

Hopkins, Carol Garnett. *Artsy Toddler Storytimes: A Year's Worth of Ready-to-Go Programming.* American Library Association/Neal-Schuman, 2013. Fifty-two themed storytimes for ages one to three, include booklists, songs and rhymes, flannelboards with reproducibles, art activities, and links to downloadable "Artsy Helper Sheets."

MacMillan, Kathy, and Christine Kirker. *Storytime Magic: 400 Fingerplays, Flannelboards, and Other Activities.* American Library Association, 2009. A wealth of rhymes; songs; games and activities; plus flannelboard, puppet, and crafts ideas with patterns you can magnify and use. Find still more ideas for programs in *Baby Storytime Magic: Active Early Literacy through Bounces, Rhymes, Tickles and More* (2014), *Kindergarten Magic: Theme-Based Lessons for Building Literacy and Library Skills* (2012), *Multicultural Storytime Magic* (2012), and MacMillan's *A Box Full of Tales: Easy Ways to Share Library Resources through Story Boxes* (2008).

Marino, Jane. *Babies in the Library!* Scarecrow, 2003. Five programs for what Marino calls "prewalkers" and "walkers," with books, puppets, fingerplays, recordings, and videos.

Nicols, Judy. *Storytimes for Two-Year-Olds, Third Edition.* Illus. by Lori D. Sears. American Library Association, 2007. Fifty well-planned themed programs, with notes and an astute selection of books, fingerplays, and crafts.

Odean, Kathleen. *Great Books for Babies and Toddlers: More Than 500 Recommended Books for Your Child's First Three Years. Ballantine Books, 2003.* An excellent annotated booklist, divided into "Nursery Rhymes, Fingerplays and Songs" and "Picture-story Books for the Very Young."

Reid, Rob. *More Family Storytimes: Twenty-Four Creative Programs for All Ages. ALA, 2009.* In twenty-four themed, start-to-finish programs, Reid includes songs (usually with lyrics, some written by Reid to tunes you'll know); movement activities; games; poetry suggestions; and annotated picture-books and ways to use them. A tremendously fun follow-up to *Family Storytime* (1999) and a great companion to Reid's *Cool Story Programs for the School-Age Crowd* (2004).

Schiller, Pam, and Jackie Silberg. *The Complete Book of Activities, Games, Stories, Props, Recipes, and Dances for Young Children. Illus. by Richelle Bartkowiak and Deborah Wright. Gryphon House, 2003.* A comprehensive, valuable, well-indexed compendium of six hundred activities, stories, and ideas, with templates and patterns for puppets and crafts.

Scott, Barbara A. *The Holiday Handbook: 700+ Storytime Activities from Arbor Day to Yom Kippur ... from Diwali to Kwanzaa to Ramadan. Neal-Schuman, 2012.* Scott introduces more than thirty holidays and celebrations, including the history, annotated lists of children's poetry and books, activities, reproducible coloring pages, templates for flannelboards, and more.

Simpson, Martha Seif, and Lynne Perrigo. *Storycraft: 50 Theme-based Programs Combining Storytelling, Activities, and Crafts for Children in Grades 1–3. Illus. by Lynne Perrigo. McFarland, 2001.* Each of the fifty one-hour programs includes a bulletin board idea, an opener, suggestions for music and stories to read or tell, a craft, a group participation activity, and a related booklist.

Straub, Susan. *Reading with Babies, Toddlers and Twos; a Guide to Choosing, Reading and Loving Books Together. Sourcebooks, 2006.* Includes annotated booklists for children from birth to age three.

Zvirin, Stephanie. *Read with Me: Best Books for Preschoolers. Huron Street Press, 2012.* An intimate collection of more than five hundred annotated notable books published between 2001 and 2011, arranged into seven thematic chapters, that parents and caregivers can share with their children, from birth through preschool age.

WEBSITES: PRESCHOOL AND PRIMARY PROGRAMS

The Activity Idea Place *www.123child.com*

Toddler, preschool, and kindergarten teachers will find more than two hundred different lesson plan themes with extensive ideas for books, art, games, dramatic play, songs, and activities.

Iowa Library Services/State Library: Early Childhood Literacy

www.statelibraryofiowa.org/ld/t-z/youthservices/early-child-lit

Practical information, advice, and links on running lapsit and toddler programs.

Preschool Express *www.preschoolexpress.com*

Educator Jean Warren's free online educational activity resource, with art, games, songs, and other activities for parents, teachers and grandparents to use with young children, ages 1–5.

Teach Preschool *www.teachpreschool.org*

"Promoting Excellence in Early Childhood Education" is an extraordinarily comprehensive photo, book, and idea-filled blog by early childhood expert Deborah J. Stewart. For a random example, check out how she used the book *The Mitten* with the kids at her own preschool, Teach Preschool Children's Studio in Noblesville, Indiana, at www.teachpreschool.org/2012/01/retelling-our-own-version-of-the-mitten-book-in-preschool.

chapter 8

Programs for Upper Elementary and Middle School Children

Ages 8 to 14

*Their story, yours and mine—it's what we all carry with us on this trip we take,
and we owe it to each other to respect our stories and learn from them.*
—WILLIAM CARLOS WILLIAMS

O NE WONDERFUL ASPECT OF WORKING WITH TWEENS IS THEIR receptivity to more sophisticated ideas and activities. Though more and more tweens are being sucked into the vortex of technology (with their thumbs sometimes getting a better workout than their muscles and brains), many still have the time to savor a book, try out a new game, and actually play outside. That's why it's so satisfying to give them something so old fashioned it seems new: stories, books and reading-related activities that keep them involved, thinking, and laughing. There's quite a chasm between an eager eight-year-old and a fourteen-year-old whose hormones have kicked in, however, so you'll want to choose your material with that in mind.

Third graders don't have much interest in love or death; action and humor are more their cup of tea. Fourth and fifth graders seem to be maturing earlier, or at least they like to act more sophisticated than third graders. Many subjects appeal to sixth through eighth graders—ghost and horror stories, science fiction, classic "coming of age" stories, humor, biographies, and love stories are the most popular. You don't always need to plan an entire program of stories to tell with upper-grade kids. Sometimes telling a single story at the end of a class or after a library booktalk is a good shot in the arm for your group.

In a preschool story session, many storytellers prefer to remain seated, but we suggest standing when working with older boys and girls. We think standing appeals to tweens' instinctive sense of the dramatic. Moreover, with television and movies being the resident storytellers in most homes, we want to present the audience with a bit of "live" theater. In the end, do what feels right to you. No Storytelling Police will be checking to see whether you are standing or sitting.

When presenting a group of told stories, tell the longest one early in the program, while the audience is still fresh. A poem or riddle can bridge the gap to a second long story. Save the shortest selection or nonsense story for the end. When telling a story from a book, have the book on hand, along with a variety of related titles for your audience to see and—you hope—borrow to read at home. Know that the stories you tell will be retold to siblings, parents, and friends.

Poetry is popular with tweens. Narrative poems are particular favorites, as is the nonsense poetry of Douglas Florian, Alan Katz, Jack Prelutsky, Shel Silverstein, and Judith Viorst. Integrate a poem wherever possible. Recite a few riddles and tongue twisters, and then encourage the children to offer some they have heard. Try a story joke or a pair of think stories. You'll find the ones we've included below are good transitional material as well as great tales to conclude a program. A guitar and some folksongs will encourage a sing-along atmosphere, and a simple dramatization of a folktale can make a story hour special.

If you are meeting on a regular basis with the same children, you might try a series of myths from the folk history of a particular country. You can also travel around the world with folklore, pointing out each story on a map or globe, which is a pretty satisfying way to go. Finally, don't forget picture books. A picture-book story, either read or told, might be perfect for closing a program, as your audience calls out, "Just one more story, please!" Maurice Sendak's *Where the Wild Things Are* comes to mind: "The night Max wore his wolf suit and made mischief of one kind and another . . ."

We love and encourage activities and crafts in conjunction with book programs, although we must sometimes remind ourselves that they shouldn't overwhelm the stories. It's primarily the spoken and written word that we are trying to promote.

In the end, whether your program is twenty minutes, forty, or a full hour, fill it with stories you can't wait to share. In this chapter are many of our favorites—a veritable stories-to-tell bonanza filled with laughs, suspense, mystery, and even a tear or two—that we hope you'll love enough to add to your repertoire.

Mysterious Objects

We'll get started with a trio of winners to tell that middle graders (and older) will find compelling and remarkable. They can easily be linked together under the theme "Strange Goings-on" or "Mysterious Objects."

The Smuggler

Retold by Caroline Feller Bauer

Caroline first heard this story, which takes place after World War II, when she was living in Europe in 1962, at the time of the construction of the Berlin Wall. Now, of course, the Wall is gone, so the context for this story has changed entirely. Still, it's an old favorite of hers, and she liked to introduce it by saying: "Once upon a time, the city of Berlin was divided into two sections: East Berlin and West Berlin . . ."

In 1945, after the Second World War ended, Germany was occupied and divided into four sectors run by the British, Americans, French, and Russians. Berlin was divided into sectors, too. West Berlin was controlled by the US, Britain, and France; East Berlin was controlled by the Soviet Union. To pass from Western Berlin to Eastern Berlin, one had to go through control gates. Guards at the gates inspected identity cards and packages to guard against smuggling goods from one area to the other.

Each day, Peter arrived at "Checkpoint Charlie" riding his bicycle on the way to work. Resting on the handlebars each morning was a large muslin bag filled with sand. Every morning, Eric, the American guard, stopped Peter. "May I see your identity card, please?" he would ask. "Have you anything to declare?"

Peter always answered no, but still Eric was suspicious. Every morning he would eye the large bag of sand. And nearly every morning, but not every morning, he would dump the sand out onto a piece of burlap and run it through his fingers looking for something illegal. Eric was certain Peter was a smuggler, but he never found anything in the bag of sand, no matter how carefully he searched.

For three months, five days a week, Peter crossed through "Checkpoint Charlie" on his bicycle carrying a muslin bag of sand on the handlebars.

The search became a morning ritual.

"*Guten tag*, Herr Peter."

"*Grüss Gott*, Herr Eric."

"May I see your identity card, please?"

"Certainly."

"Anything to declare?"

"No, sir."

"What's in the bag?"

"Nothing, sir, only sand."

"Sand? I will empty it here and I will see for myself . . . Everything seems in order. You may pass. Have a good day."

"Thank you. *Auf Wiedersehen*."

The months passed. One day, Peter arrived on his bicycle carrying a large muslin bag on the handlebar. This time Eric talked to him in a low whisper. Eric was to leave that day to return to his home in the United States. He was to return to civilian life.

"Please," begged Eric, "before I leave, tell me what you have been smuggling all these months. I promise to tell no one."

"Certainly," answered Peter. "BICYCLES!"

The next story has all the ingredients to be an instant hit with this age group: a dab of inexplicable magic, humor, and the craziest ending ever. It's a variation on an old theme—what would you do if you could double everything you had?

The Wooden Box: A Chinese Folktale

Retold by Laura Simms

Judy heard Laura Simms tell this devastatingly funny story many years ago, and she still thinks of it whenever she eats potatoes. Find an interesting little wooden box as a prop, plus—of course—two nice potatoes, and you'll be all set for telling.

Pair it with the picture book Two of Everything: A Chinese Folktale, *retold and illustrated by Lily Toy Hong, (Albert Whitman, 1993). In that story, after digging up a large pot in his garden, poor old Mr. Haktak is astonished to find that whatever he throws in the pot automatically doubles, guaranteeing him and his wife instant wealth. Alas, when Mrs. Haktak falls into the pot, he must contend with two identical wives. While both stories hail from China, and both start off with a poor old husband and wife coming into great fortune, the outcomes are very different. You can start an interesting discussion as to how fortunes of the two couples diverge and why.*

Once upon a time there was a man and his wife who had nothing in the whole world to call their own but potatoes. Every day they used to dig in an old dry field for potatoes. Sometimes they'd find four; two potatoes they'd cook and two potatoes they'd sell at the market.

One day, while the man was digging for potatoes in that old dried field, he hit something hard. And he lifted up a wooden box. Well, if you're poor and you don't have very much, everything you find has a use. So he took it home and gave it to his wife. And she began to clean it. She cleaned the outside, and she lifted it up and she cleaned the inside.

When a red ribbon in her hair fell in the box, lo and behold, the box filled up with red ribbons. She took those red ribbons out of the box and it filled up with red ribbons again. She took those out of the box and it filled up with red ribbons again. Now they took all those red ribbons to the market and they sold them. They had a little bit of money, and they loved each other still.

One day, while the wife was coming back from the market (it was her turn to go to work—now they both didn't have to go every day), she decided to look inside the box and see all those red ribbons that had brought her such good luck.

When a gold coin she was holding in her hand fell in the box, lo and behold, the red ribbons disappeared and the box filled up with gold coins. She took those gold coins out of the box and it filled up with gold coins again. She took those gold coins out of the box; it filled up with gold coins again. She took those gold coins out of the box and it filled up with gold coins again. Why, they didn't have to go to the market anymore at all. All they had to do was stay at home and take the gold coins out of the box.

Well, they moved into a new house and they got servants. They began to be so rich they had anything at all they ever wanted. They grew greedy, and they grew lazy. And they didn't want to take those gold coins out of the box. And they weren't going to trust their servants. So they called their old grandfather, who was living up in the hills and was retired and hadn't worked for many years, to come on down and take the gold coins out of the box.

Poor old man, he didn't want to work—but it was family. So he came down and he took the gold coins out of the box. And he took the gold coins out of the box. And he took the gold coins out of the box. Poor old man, sometimes he was tired and he'd lean down and rest on his elbow. But the husband and wife would beat him and beat him and beat him and tell him to just keep taking the gold coins out of the box.

Poor old man. He was so tired and so old—one day he died . . . and he fell in the box. They took him outside. And, lo and behold, when they came back indoors, there was another dead grandfather in the box. They took him out and buried him and there was another grandfather and another grandfather and another grandfather. Well, they had to bury all those dead grandfathers and it cost them every single gold coin they had.

At last they had to get rid of their house and their servants and everything else they had. And the last gold coin was gone, and the last dead grandfather was buried, and the box disappeared. And they ended up with exactly what they began with . . . nothing but potatoes.

The next story basically tells itself. For simple props, find yourself an old green glass bottle and a pretty piece of cloth to represent the tablecloth. Tell your listeners that you found the bottle in a dusty corner of an antique store and you're pretty sure it could be a bottle from the story. Then tell them you don't want sweep the floor clean because you're not sure which of the two bottles it might be . . .

The Green Glass Bottle

Retold by Barbara Ker Wilson; from Fairy Tales of Ireland, *illus. by G. W. Miller, Casswell, 1959.*

Paddy O'Toole, his wife Bridget, and their three children lived in a little white farmhouse. Paddy rented the farmhouse and his few acres of ground from a landlord whose heart was as hard as a stone.

At first, all went well with Paddy. Then bad luck came to him. His chickens died and his oats were spoiled. Only his red cow was left. The three children went hungry, and Paddy knew that he could not afford to pay his rent when it was due. He was afraid the landlord would turn them out of the farm.

"What shall we do?" he asked Bridget.

"We must sell the cow in Cork market," she replied.

So the next morning Paddy set off early, walking behind the cow all the way across the hills to Cork. At midday he reached a hill just outside Cork. It was a small, round hill covered with rich green grass, and Paddy thought to himself that it was just the sort of place that the fairies, or Good People, were supposed to inhabit. For Paddy knew that there were plenty of the Good People living still in Ireland.

Suddenly he heard a shrill voice by his elbow. "Good morrow, Paddy O'Toole!"

Paddy started, and saw a little man standing beside him. He was dressed in a quaint green coat, with pointed red shoes on his feet, and a high black hat on his head.

"Good morrow," Paddy replied, wondering how the little man knew his name.

"Where are you going with that cow?"

"To Cork fair, to sell her."

"Will you sell her to me instead?"

"What will you give for her?" Paddy asked.

The little man fished in the pocket of his coat and produced a green glass bottle. "I'll give you this bottle," he said.

Paddy looked at the bottle, and could not help bursting into laughter. "Do you take me for such a fool that I would give away my good red cow for a green glass bottle—and an empty one at that?"

The little man frowned. "Take the bottle and give me the cow. You will not be sorry for it. When you get home, sweep out the room, spread a clean cloth on the table, put the bottle on the ground, and say these words: 'Bottle, do your duty.' Then you shall see what you shall see."

Paddy was so impressed by these words that he handed over the cow, and took the bottle in exchange.

"Good-bye, Paddy O'Toole; you are a rich man now!" cried the little man, as he disappeared over the hillside, driving the cow before him.

"God grant it so!" thought Paddy as he went home again.

"Why, Paddy, you're home early," Bridget greeted

him. "Did you sell the cow? And what's that bottle sticking out of your jacket?"

"That's what I got for the cow," said Paddy, putting the bottle on the table.

His poor wife was dumbfounded. "Are you telling me that all you got for our fine cow was that miserable green bottle?"

Then Paddy told her about his strange meeting, and by and by Bridget began to wonder whether there was some truth in the tale after all. So she got up, swept the floor, and spread a clean cloth on the table, as Paddy asked her to do.

Paddy put the bottle on the ground. "Bottle, do your duty," he said.

Before their astonished eyes, two tiny little fellows arose from inside the bottle. In an instant, they covered the table with dishes of gold and silver, piled high with all the good things you can think of. Then they went back into the bottle.

Paddy and Bridget were beside themselves with joy. They brought their three children to the table, and enjoyed the best meal they had ever had.

After this, Paddy sold the gold and silver dishes for a great deal of money— and since there was an endless supply of these dishes from the bottle, it seemed that they would not want for the rest of their days.

Now the landlord was very curious to know how Paddy had suddenly become a rich man. One day he came to visit him, and bothered him so much that at last Paddy told him the secret. At once the landlord wanted the magic bottle for himself, and he offered Paddy a sum of money for it. At first Paddy refused him, but when the landlord went on offering more and more money, at last he accepted his offer and gave him the bottle.

"After all, we have plenty of money now," he thought. "We shall be rich to the end of our days."

But Paddy was wrong. Gradually his money dwindled, and it was not long before he had to set out for Cork market to sell his cow, just as before. When he reached the round grassy hill where he had met the little man, you can imagine his surprise as he heard a shrill, well-remembered voice at his elbow say: "Well, Paddy O'Toole, I told you you would be a rich man!"

"Indeed, I was rich once—but it's poor I am now." Paddy answered sorrowfully.

Then the little man produced another green glass bottle, in appearance exactly the same as the first one. "Here is another bottle for you," he said. "You know what to do with it."

Paddy's face lit up with joy, and seizing the bottle, he hurried home.

"Luck's with us!" Bridget cried when she saw the second bottle; and without more ado she swept the floor and placed a clean white cloth on the table.

Paddy put the bottle on the floor. "Bottle, do your duty!" he said.

But to their dismay, two stout fellows with cudgels came out of the bottle, and belabored them until they were black and blue! When he had recovered from this beating, Paddy had an idea. He took the bottle and went to see the landlord.

"I have another bottle like the first one," he told him. "Would you like to buy it from me?"

"Oh ho! I would indeed." The landlord's eyes gleamed greedily. "Show it to me!"

Paddy set the bottle on the floor, and uttered the magic words; and in an instant the two stout fellows were out of the bottle, and beating the landlord with their cudgels.

"Help! Help!" cried the landlord. "Stop this at once, Paddy O'Toole!"

"They will not stop," said Paddy, "until you give me back the first bottle."

"Take it!" cried the landlord. "It's up there on the shelf."

Paddy took the first green bottle from the shelf; and as soon as he had it in his grasp, the two stout fellows with their cudgels returned to their own bottle.

So Paddy became a rich man once more, and he and his family never wanted for anything as long as they lived. And what became of the two bottles? Nobody knows, and for all I know, you may come across them yourself, one day.

Story Jokes

TIME FOR SCHOOL

Ramon's mother called upstairs: "Ramon, get up. You'll be late for school."

"I don't want to go to school. I don't like it there. The kids are mean to me. The teachers shout at me. I don't want to go to school."

"But darling, you have to go to school."

"Why?"

"Because you are fifty years old and you're the principal!"

Brief, self-contained story jokes like these make terrific fillers for this age group. Use them between longer stories or between more serious fare. In her travels to Middle East, Caroline collected many comical oft-told tales about the wise men/fools of the region: the Goha of Lebanon, Egypt, and Saudi Arabia; the Hodja (aka Nasreddin Hodja, also spelled Nasrettin Hoca, and pronounced something like "osha") of Turkish folklore; and the Rabbi from Israel.

When Judy was in Istanbul for a conference, she spent several hours winding through and getting lost in the Grand Bazaar. The Hodja was everywhere. (She now owns a little painting on an old Turkish manuscript page of the Hodja in his turban, riding backwards on his donkey, a common pose.) At one little shop they had flat, hand-carved leather stick puppets of the Hodja on his donkey. The merchant held one out to her and said, "Look, lady. Made of finest camel leather. You cannot burn it even if you want to." He flicked his cigarette lighter and held the flame against the leather. "You see?"

She shuddered and thought, "What would I do with that if I brought it home? Poor camel—look how he ended up." And she didn't buy it. Dumb, dumb, dumb. Of course, as soon as she got home, what was awaiting her but a copy of a witty new folktale picture book, *The Hungry Coat*, retold and illustrated by Demi (McElderry, 2004), all about Nasrettin Hoca and his encounter with snooty friends who ridiculed him when he went to a fancy dinner unavoidably dressed in smelly clothes. (See Caroline's retelling of that very story below, "The Hungry Clothes," which you can have listeners compare and contrast with Demi's exquisite picture book.) It's not like she could zip back to Istanbul, and you sure can't find indestructible-camel-leather Hodja puppets in your local toy store, that's for sure!

Once again, Judy learned the hard way her mother's wise adage, "If you see it, buy it. It won't be there when you go back. You never regret the things you do buy!"

At least you will now have a mini collection of these wonderful comic stories to tell.

THE GOHA

The Beautiful Dream
The Goha was sleeping in bed. Suddenly he sat up and called to his wife. "Quick, wife, hand me my glasses!"

"Here they are," she said. "Why do you want your glasses in the middle of the night?"

"I was having a very exciting dream," said the Goha, "but I couldn't see anything clearly."

The Goha put on his glasses and went back to sleep. He smiled and laughed as he slept.

The Fall
The Goha's next-door neighbors met him at the market.

"What was the noise we heard in your house last night?" they asked. "My cloak fell down the stairs," answered the Goha.

"A cloak doesn't make any noise."

"True," said the Goha, "but I was wearing it at the time."

THE HODJA

The Letter
A farmer brought the Hodja a letter. "Please read this for me," he said.

"I can't understand this letter," said the Hodja.

"Why not? You are wearing a turban of a wise and learned man."

"Here is the turban," said the Hodja. "If a turban makes a person wise, maybe now you'll be able to read the letter yourself."

The Lost Ring
The Hodja lost his gold ring in the house. His next-door neighbor saw him looking for it in the garden.

"Why are you looking for your ring out here in the garden if you lost it inside the house?"

"I am looking out here," said the Hodja, "because it is such a nice day, I thought I would enjoy the sunshine."

Where's the Fish?
The Hodja bought a kilo of fish at the market and brought it home. The next day, his wife cooked it and served it to her friends. When the Hodja came home for the evening meal, he asked his wife why she wasn't serving the fish.

"Very sad," said his wife. "The cat found it and ate it."

The Hodja went outside and found the cat looking his usual skinny self. He brought the cat inside and weighed it.

"The cat weighs exactly three kilos. If this is the cat, where's the fish? If this is the fish, where's the cat?"

The Hodja's Clothes
The Hodja was invited to dinner at the rich man's house. When he saw that he was going to be late, he decided not to go home to change his clothes and went to the rich man's house directly from the fields.

He arrived disheveled and out of breath. Through the window he could see that the rich man and his friends were already gathered around the dining table. They were all dressed in fine clothing. Some of the men's cloaks had gold and silver thread running through the cloth.

When the Hodja knocked on the door, a servant answered. The servant looked at the Hodja disdainfully.

"Who is it?" called the host.

"It is I," answered the Hodja.

The guests turned to look at the Hodja. They saw his dirty wrinkled clothes.

"Send him away," said the host, dismissing the man who obviously hadn't been invited to the party.

The Hodja hurried home and dashing in the door called to his wife, "Hurry, Fatima. I need a bath and my best clothes."

Soon, the Hodja was back at the rich man's house attired in his finest cloak and turban. He knocked on the door.

"Ah, greetings, Hodja" the servant bowed. "Our friend, the Hodja," announced the host. "Please be seated," he said, offering the Hodja a place next to him. The table was piled with trays of appealing food.

The Hodja picked up a fig from the tray in front of him and opening his cloak he said, "Here, cloak. A plump fig for you to eat. And here is some wine."

The guests stared at the Hodja. "What are you doing?" asked the rich man.

"I'm feeding my cloak. It is obvious that it is not I whom you wanted to invite, but my clothes."

THE RABBI

The Rabbi's Clothes

When the Rabbi and the student arrived at the inn in search of rooms, they were told that there was only one vacancy. They would have to share a room.

The student had to catch an early train to Warsaw the next day. He asked the innkeeper to wake him in time to get dressed and to get to the station in plenty of time.

When the knock sounded on the door the next morning, the student got up and dressed in the dark so as not to disturb the Rabbi.

As he ran out the door, he passed a mirror and saw that he was wearing the Rabbi's hat and coat.

"How awkward," exclaimed the student. "The innkeeper woke the Rabbi instead of me."

Think Stories

Think stories (also known as lateral puzzles or stories with holes) are built around an intriguing dilemma, a language trick, or a mystery that requires some creative thinking to solve.

After reading or telling the story, ask children to solve the dilemma, cautioning them, "Think before you answer." If they are stumped, read or tell the story again (as many times as they need you to). Then let your audience ask you questions as they work out the answer. Tell them that you will only respond with "Yes," "No," "Sorry, that is not relevant," or "That is not a yes-or-no question. Please rephrase it and try again." Then get ready for some lively discussion.

This is really another form of the game Twenty Questions and helps listeners narrow their search and sort through relevant clues to come up with a plausible answer. In fact, the training they get from conundrums like this will help them when they're working on a project or paper, trying to determine just what information is most important. It will also help them solve mysteries faced by Encyclopedia Brown in the wonderful and enduring series by Donald J. Sobol, not to mention the greatest deductive reasoner of them all, Mr. Sherlock Holmes.

Do one or two puzzlers at a session. Children adore figuring these out and get so excited when they unravel the final answer. Get ready for some very crazy questions and guesses. Try these little stories with older students and with adults, and you'll get the same types of responses. It's a great party game, too.

The first one, "John and Mary," is a classic that you might already know. (Don't assume your children will, though you should say, before someone can blurt out the answer, "If you've heard this story before and already know the solution, please do not raise your hand or tell anyone. The rest of us would love to figure out the answers for ourselves.")

JOHN AND MARY

The Story

John and Mary are found lying dead on the floor of a country house. There is broken glass on the floor and a puddle of liquid, too. No other people were in the house. How did John and Mary die? Think before you answer.

How It Works

After you read or tell the story (which you will need to memorize so you get all of the details just right), the kids will start asking you questions. "Were they murdered?" You'll say, "No." Someone will always ask a "why" question, like "Why is there broken glass?" a "what" question, like "What kind of liquid is on the floor?" or a "who" question, like "Who are John and Mary?" For each of those questions, you will answer, "That is not a yes-or-no question. Please rephrase it." Once the kids catch on, the question-answer dialog might go something like this:

"Is the broken glass a drinking glass?"
"No."
"Is the liquid blood?" *(They always ask that one.)*
"No."
"Is the liquid poison?" *(And that one.)*
"No."
"Is it water?"
"Yes."
"Are John and Mary married?"
"No."
"Are they related?"
"Sorry, that is not relevant."
"Do John and Mary know each other?"
"Yes."
"Did John and Mary have a fight?"
"Sorry, that is not relevant."
"Did John pull out a gun and shoot Mary and then shoot himself dead?"
"No"
"Did he stab her with the broken glass?" *(And the children will then say to each other, "No, he can't have shot her or stabbed her with the glass because the liquid is water, remember?" The questioner will say, "Oh, yeah. Right. I forgot that.")*
"Are John and Mary children?"
"Sorry, that is not relevant."
Someone will eventually come up with a brilliant question: "Are John and Mary human?"
"No."
"Are they animals?"

"Yes!"

"Are they birds?"

"No"

"Are they pets?"

"Yes!"

"Are they dogs?"

"No."

"Are they cats?"

"No."

At which point, someone comes up with:

"Are they fish?"

"Yes!"

"Who knocked over the fishbowl?"

"That is not a yes-or-no question. Please rephrase it."

Now, of course, kids must figure out how John and Mary came to be lying on the floor in a puddle of water with their fishbowl broken around them.

Answer: John and Mary are goldfish. Their bowl was broken when it was knocked to the floor by the family cat or dog.

Ready to give these a go? Some of them may be familiar. Remind kids again at the end not to blurt out the solution if they know it. The answers are at the end of the section. Some are ridiculously simple; others are trickier. Don't give in and read the answers to the kids; it's more satisfying for them if they figure things out for themselves.

You can find many more such stories on the Internet, looking up keywords like *lateral puzzles* or *stories with holes*, but many of the ones you'll find are inappropriate, since they're for adults. The many little "stories with holes" books by Nathan Levy, however, are far more kid-friendly. You can find them at Amazon.com or on Levy's own site, www.storieswithholes.com.

1. THE WINTER HIKER

A woman was hiking in the woods on a very cold night. She thought that she was lost until she saw an empty cabin through the trees and the snowdrifts. She knocked on the door. No one answered but the door was open. She went inside the cabin. She saw a candle, a kerosene lamp, and a woodstove. She reached inside her knapsack and discovered that she had only one match. What did she light first and why? Think before you answer.

2. APRIL, MAY, AND JUNE

Steven's mother had four children. The first was named April, the second was May, and the third was June. What was the name of her fourth child? Think before you answer.

3. THE PHOTO

Mr. Smith was showing his friends a photo of a young man. He said to them, "Brothers and sisters have I none. But this man's father is my father's son." How is Mr. Smith related to the man in the photo? Think before you answer.

4. THE DINNER

Mom, Dad, Daughter, Son, Aunt, Uncle, Sister, Brother, Niece, Nephew, and Cousin were all having dinner. But there were only four people at the table. Why? Think before you answer.

5. THE ACCIDENT

A boy and his father were in an automobile accident. Both were rushed to the hospital unconscious. The boy needed emergency surgery. When the boy was wheeled into the operating room, the surgeon looked at the child and declared, "I can't operate on this boy. He is my son!" How can this be? Think before you answer.

6. WHAT HAPPENED HERE?

On the ground are the following:

1. A carrot
2. A pile of pebbles
3. A pipe
4. And a big puddle of water

What happened here? Think before you answer.

7. HOME

Richard left home on a run and took three left turns. He wanted to run home again but couldn't, because the man with the mask was waiting for him there. Why? Think before you answer.

8. TIME FLIES

Make sense of this statement: "Time flies. I can't; they go too fast." Think before you answer.

9. WHAT IS IT?

The one who makes it doesn't keep it. The one who buys it doesn't use it. The one who uses it doesn't know it. What is it? Think before you answer.

10. THE SILVER CAR

A man stops his silver car by a hotel's property. The owner of the hotel demands hundreds of dollars from the man. The man agrees and pays in cash. Why is the owner demanding money, and why does the owner of the car pay it? Think before you answer.

Answers for Think Stories

1. *The Winter Hiker*: The hiker would light the match first, of course. Then she could light the candle with the match, and use the candle to light the lamp and the stove.
2. *April, May, and June*: Not, it wasn't July; it was Steven, of course.
3. *The Photo*: The man in the photo is Mr. Smith's son.
4. *The Dinner*: The son of the brother and the daughter of the sister are having dinner. The son and daughter are cousins. Now you can figure out the rest.
5. *The Accident*: The surgeon is the boy's mother. You would think children and adults would get this one right away, since it is no longer considered unusual for a woman to be a surgeon as it was when this little story first surfaced in the 1970s, but that's not the case. It's still a great puzzler to pose.
6. *What Happened Here?* The snowman melted.
7. *Home*: He was playing baseball and running for home plate; the man with the mask was the catcher hoping to tag him out.
8. *Time Flies*: Picture starting your stopwatch to time how fast the little flies are flying. They fly too fast to time them. Get it? It all depends on how you look at the words "time" and "flies"; "time" is the verb here and "flies" is the noun, which is hard for your brain to process at first.
9. *What Is It?* A coffin. This one comes from American folklore.
10. *The Silver Car*: This one's really tricky. Ready? They're playing Monopoly, and one player—the one with the little racecar—lands on other player's property and has to pay up.

Convoluted Logic Puzzlers

The first three of these five whimsical stories were told to Judy during dinner one night by her cousin, Farrell Fand, and three of his grandkids, Minka, then twelve, and eight-year-old twins, Shaiya and Noah. The first one is the simplest, though it tricks younger listeners. The second two demand creative thinking. The fourth is a puzzler Judy has known since she was their age. It stumped all three kids. The last one is just plain silly.

See if you can figure these out before reading the answers—share them with someone to see if they can help. Afterwards, see if your kids can solve them, by asking you only yes-or-no questions.

1. THE BUS

Pretend you're a bus driver. At your first stop, you pick up six passengers. At your next stop, you let off two of them. At the next corner, you pick up four and drop off one. At the next stop, you pick up five and drop off two. At the next stop, you pick up ten. How old is the bus driver? (Judy got this one. Easy!)

2. TRAPPED IN AN INDESTRUCTIBLE ROOM

You will be trapped for a week inside an indestructible room with a locked door and no other openings, and no food or water. You have only a calendar, a mattress, and a piano. How will you survive and escape? (Judy got this one.)

3. TRAPPED IN AN INDESTRUCTIBLE BOX

You are in an indestructible box with no openings, no doors, and no windows. All you have is a mirror and a table. How do you get out? (Judy didn't get this one.)

4. THE EGG

On a windy day, a rooster flew up to the top of the barn where the roof was very sharply slanted, sat on the peak in the middle of the rooftop, and laid an egg. Which way did the egg roll—down the left side of the roof or the right side?

5. THE GRASS IS ALWAYS GREENER

There was once a cow who lived by the river. She longed to cross the river where a field of green grass was growing. But she couldn't swim. She had no boat. There was no bridge across the river. She couldn't fly. So how did she get across the river to the nice green grass?

Oh, yes! You wanted the *ANSWERS*:

1. Well, how old are you?
2. You take the dates off the calendar and eat them. You get water from the springs in the mattress. Finally, you take the keys off the piano to unlock the door. You open the door and you are out.
3. You look through the mirror and see what you saw. You take the saw and you cut the table in half. Two halves make a whole. You climb through the hole and you are out.
4. Neither. Roosters don't lay eggs; hens do.
5. Give up? Don't feel badly—so did the cow!

Simiply Supernatural: Jump Stories and Other Chillers

A favorite interest of many tweens is the supernatural. Halloween is an obvious time to tell ghost stories, but it's just as much fun to hear a scary tale by the light of a May moon as it is when the harvest moon is glowing. Keep in mind that some adults object to young people reading and listening to any story that involves the supernatural. Most kids, however, enjoy a shiver now and then.

When you tell these tales, add some atmosphere to your classroom or library by setting up a campsite. First, make a campfire. Gather some small logs and put red, orange, and yellow tissue paper in their crevices for flames. Next, cut a giant full moon out of heavystock paper and hang it from the ceiling or tape it on a wall overlooking the campfire. Finally, bring in a sleeping bag or two, unzip them, and spread them on the floor in front of the "fire" for children to sit upon. Now you're ready to chill their spines with stories.

The best spooky stories are those that are believable. Tell your tale as though the experience actually happened to you or to someone you know, and act as though you believe every word that you are saying. A slow pace is usually more effective than the snappy pace you use to tell a humorous story. You'll know if you are being successful when you say something like "and here *it* comes now . . ." and point behind the audience, and your listeners give a little scream and turn around to see if *it* is coming!

"Jump stories" often rely on repetitive phrases that help to lull the listeners into a trance that lasts until the surprising conclusion makes them . . . *jump*! When telling such stories to younger tweens, don't underestimate how much even a simple story can scare them. Err on the side of humor, not horror with younger kids. You'll find many more suggestions for jump tales as well as scary stories and urban legends in our first volume of this series, *The Handbook for Storytellers*.

The Strange Visitor

Retold by Joseph Jacobs

"The Strange Visitor," from Joseph Jacobs's English Fairy Tales, *published in 1890, is popular at Halloween. You can draw it as you tell it or turn it into a flannelboard story, assembling the parts of the creature as you describe them—the broad broad soles; the small small legs; and so on, until you get to the orange jack-o'-lantern head. It's just right for third graders—not too scary and with a refrain that invites participation—but even older children will like it.*

A woman sat at her reel one night;
    And still she sat, and still she reeled, and still she wished for company.

In came a pair of broad broad soles, and sat down at the fireside;
    And still she sat, and still she reeled, and still she wished for company.

In came a pair of small small legs, and sat down on the broad broad soles;
    And still she sat, and still she reeled, and still she wished for company.

In came a pair of thick thick knees, and sat down on the small small legs;
    And still she sat, and still she reeled, and still she wished for company.

In came a pair of thin thin thighs, and sat down on the thick thick knees;
    And still she sat, and still she reeled, and still she wished for company.

In came a pair of huge huge hips, and sat down on the thin thin thighs;
    And still she sat, and still she reeled, and still she wished for company.

In came a wee wee waist, and sat down on the huge huge hips;
    And still she sat, and still she reeled, and still she wished for company.

In came a pair of broad broad shoulders, and sat down on the wee wee waist;
    And still she sat, and still she reeled, and still she wished for company.

In came a pair of small small arms, and sat down on the broad broad
    shoulders;
    And still she sat, and still she reeled, and still she wished for company.

In came a pair of huge huge hands, and sat down on the small small arms;
    And still she sat, and still she reeled, and still she wished for company.

In came a small small neck, and sat down on the broad broad shoulders;
    And still she sat, and still she reeled, and still she wished for company.

In came a huge huge head, and sat down on the small small neck.
    And still she sat, and still she reeled, and still she wished for company.

"How did you get such broad broad feet?" quoth the woman.
　　"Much tramping, much tramping." (*gruffly*)

"How did you get such small small legs?"
　　"Aih-h-h!-late–and wee-e-e–moul." (*whiningly*)

"How did you get such thick thick knees?"
　　"Much praying, much praying." (*piously*)

"How did you get such thin thin thighs?"
　　"Aih-h-h!–late–and wee-e-e–moul." (*whiningly*)

"How did you get such big big hips?"
　　"Much sitting, much sitting." (*gruffly*)

"How did you get such a wee wee waist?"
　　"Aih-h-h!–late–and wee-e-e–moul." (*whiningly*)

"How did you get such broad broad shoulders?"
　　"With carrying broom, with carrying broom." (*gruffly*)

"How did you get such small small arms?"
　　"Aih-h-h!–late–and wee-e-e–moul." (*whiningly*)

"How did you get such huge huge hands?"
　　"Threshing with an iron flail, threshing with an iron flail."
　　(*gruffly; hold an imaginary handle and swing it in an arc as if you're cutting hay*)

"How did you get such a small small neck?"
　　"Aih-h-h!–late–and wee-e-e–moul." (*pitifully*)

"How did you get such a huge huge head?"
　　"Much knowledge, much knowledge." (*keenly; point to your head*)

"And what do you come for?" (*meekly, breathlessly*)
　　"For **YOU**!" (*Lunge toward your audience with a wave of your arms and a stamp of the feet, yelling YOU at the top of your voice. If you do it right, your audience will really jump.*)

The Many Woes of Albert Varney

Retold by Judy Freeman

This tale has three scary parts, which will make listeners laugh after they scream. Try it on listeners in grades four and up.

WEB This script is available on ALA's Web Extras page at alaeditions.org/webextras.

Albert Varney was a mild-mannered, taciturn man, verging on grumpy. He lived in a small shack in the woods with his yellow dog, Sam. With his dog at his side, Albert was self-sufficient, hunting and trapping, growing his own vegetables, catching fish in the river. Once a week, he'd hike down to the general store for provisions. That's where he was one afternoon in October. He'd left Sam at home to guard the house. While buying this and that, he couldn't help but overhear three codgers talking about the old abandoned mansion on the edge of town.

"It's haunted," they were saying. "No one who goes in there stays for long. They get chased out by ghosts."

Albert snorted. "There's no such things as ghosts," he scoffed.

"That so?" said one. "You care to stay there tonight yourself and find out?"

And before Albert stopped to think what he had gotten himself into, he agreed to sleep all night in the master bedroom on the second floor of the old mansion.

The wind was blowing and the full moon rising when Albert opened the door to the old house. It creaked and squealed, the hinges were so rusty. Help me open that door, won't you? (*Listeners will make squeaky door noises as they pantomime opening the door with you.*)

Inside the floor was dusty, the foyer musty. Albert sneezed. Then he made his way up the dark, tall staircase to the second floor. The stairs creaked and cracked. Albert stopped and listened. Nothing. "Hmmph," snorted Albert. "No such things as ghosts."

He found the master bedroom. White sheets covered the furniture. A large four-poster bed sat in the middle of the room with white sheets and a pillow. Albert opened the window to get some fresh air and then hoisted himself up onto the bed. It was a warm night, so he only needed the sheet for a covering. Before he lay his head down on the pillow, though, he slipped his revolver underneath, just in case. "No point in taking any chances," he said to himself, and closed his eyes. Soon he was asleep.

Around about midnight, Albert's eyes flew open. He thought he heard something nearby and looked towards the door. "Who's there?" he demanded, but there was no reply.

"Hmmph. Probably just a squirrel or a mouse. No such things as ghosts."

Now he heard something scratching at the window. "Probably just a tree branch," he muttered, and he turned his head back towards the window where the moonlight was streaming in. And there, at the foot of the bed, in the middle of the bed, were two huge, white, ghostly eyes, staring back at him, unblinking.

Slowly and oh-so-quietly, Albert slid his hand under his pillow and grasped his revolver. He drew it out from under the pillow. He aimed it right between the two ghostly eyes. Slowly, he squeezed the trigger and *BLAM! AUUGGHHHH! (Scream loud enough to make everyone jump.)*

Well, you'd scream, too, if you just shot off your own big toe! His two big toenails, sticking out from under the covers, looked just like big, ghostly eyes, with the moonlight shining on them.

Poor Albert Varney. After he bandaged his sorry foot, he hobbled on home. When he arrived at the door, there was no Sam to greet him. "Hey, Sam," Albert called. "Here boy." No dog came running. The dog was gone. "That dern fool dog is probably off in the woods somewhere. Some guard dog he is," Albert grumbled and went back to bed.

The next morning, the dog was still gone. With his sore foot throbbing, Albert limped outside and called for his dog. "Heeeere, Sam. Come home, boy." But Sam didn't come home.

Albert went out to check his traps, and called for that dog, but Sam was nowhere to be seen. Albert came back home and went back to bed. He awoke around midnight. He thought he heard a noise, up in the attic.

Slowly and oh-so-quietly, Albert got out from under the covers. In his bare feet, he crept over to the fireplace and carefully took his shotgun down from the wall. Silently, he walked over to the steps leading up to the attic. He tiptoed up the attic steps. Halfway, he stopped to listen, but he didn't hear anything.

When he got to the top of the attic steps, he stopped again and listened. He didn't hear anything. He grasped the doorknob to the attic door with one hand. Slowly, he turned that knob and pushed open the door. Help me open that door, won't you? (*Listeners will make squeaky door noises as they pantomime opening the door with you.*) He took one step and *AUUGGHHHH!* (*Scream loud enough to make everyone jump.*)

Well, you'd scream, too, if you just stepped on a nail in your bare feet!

Poor Albert Varney. His dog was still gone and now he had two sore feet. But he needed to get some supplies from the general store. So the next morning, he started out, limping down the road. Unfortunately, no sooner was he halfway there when a huge thunderstorm blew in. Lightning flashed and thunder crashed all around him. There, on the side of the road, on the edge of town, stood that same old mansion. It didn't make sense to stay out in the storm, so Albert decided to seek shelter in that house again.

Albert opened the door to the old house. It creaked and squealed, the hinges were so rusty. Help me open that door, won't you? (*Listeners will make squeaky door noises as they pantomime opening the door with you.*)

Inside the floor was dusty, the foyer musty. Albert sneezed. Then he made his way to the living room. The floor creaked and cracked. Albert stopped and listened. Nothing. "Hmmph," snorted Albert. "No such things as ghosts anyway."

It was warm and dry in the house, and that was something. He sat on the living room floor to wait out the storm. As the lightning lit up the room, he looked around. There was not much in there anymore—just a few sticks of old furniture. And then he heard . . . a noise. It was faint at first, but soon grew a bit louder. It was a strange rapping noise. RAP RAP. (*Knock on a wooden surface or tap your foot on the floor to make this noise.*) It seemed to be coming from the other side of the room. RAP RAP.

At first Albert ignored the noise. It grew louder. RAP RAP. And more insistent. RAP RAP. He got up and walked over to the other side of the room. RAP RAP. It was louder over there. RAP RAP. The closer Albert got to the closet, the louder the noise became. RAP RAP. It seemed to be coming from inside of the closet. RAP RAP.

Albert didn't want to open that closet door. He'd had enough excitement already that week. RAP RAP. But he couldn't ignore that noise. It grew louder and more insistent. RAP RAP. He didn't want to open that door, but he had to open that door. He couldn't stand it one more minute. RAP RAP. He walked over to the closet, and he opened that door. Help me open that door, won't you? (*Listeners will make squeaky door noise as they pantomime opening the door with you.*)

RAP RAP. The noise was louder in the closet. In the closet, there was a shelf. *RAP RAP!* On the shelf, there was a box. *RAP RAP!* Albert lifted the box. He didn't want to open it, but he had to open it. Albert lifted the rusty latch. *RAP RAP!* He opened the box. Help me open that lid, won't you? (*Listeners will make squeaky noise as they pantomime opening the lid with you. If you have an actual box you can use, all the better.*)

Albert looked down and gasped. (*Gasp in horror, your eyes wide. Listeners will clutch the person sitting next to them.*)

Now he could see what was making that terrible rapping noise. He reached in the box, and pulled out a roll of . . . *WRAPPING PAPER!* Yes, it was a roll of *WRAPPING PAPER!* (*If you are using an actual box, you will want to pull out a roll of wrapping paper and hit it against the box so your listeners really get the wordplay joke and laugh in relief.*)

The Golden Arm

Retold by Caroline Feller Bauer

This is the quintessential jump story. Found in Joseph Jacobs's English Fairy Tales, *published in 1890, the original ending goes like this: "What hast thou done with thy Golden Arm?" "THOU HAST IT!" It loses something in old English, doesn't it? Caroline's version is best for older listeners, grade 6 and up.*

There was this man. He had a wife. The wife had a golden arm. It was made of real gold from the fingers of her hand right up to her shoulder. Pure gold.

Only she died. The wife died. There was a funeral and they buried the wife, golden arm and all, right there in the graveyard.

The man he went on home. He went to bed. In the middle of the night he got to thinking about the golden arm.

"Sure would be nice to have that golden arm. Must be worth a pack of money."

So along about midnight he gets up out of bed and goes to the graveyard with a shovel. He digs up his wife and he gets that golden arm. He comes on home.

By now it's about one o'clock in the morning and the man is in bed, but not asleep. He keeps thinking that he hears noises, and then he does hear a voice, all mixed up in the wind, saying real slow and creepy-like:

"Who's got my golden arm?

"Who's got my golden arm?"

The man he pulls the covers up over his head, but he can still hear the voice:

"Who's got my golden arm?

"Who's got my golden arm?"

The voice is inside the house now and coming up the stairs:

"Who's got my golden arm?

"Who's got my golden arm?"

The man puts the pillow over his head, but he can still hear the voice and something coming up the narrow stairs of his house:

"Who's got my golden arm?

"Who's got my golden arm?"

The man is lying still now, but he hears the voice and the something right in his room wailing:

"Who's got my golden arm?

"Who's got my golden arm?

WEB This script is available on ALA's Web Extras page at alaeditions.org/webextras.

"Who's got my golden arm?"

I GOT IT! (*Lunge menacingly towards the audience as you grab for the arm and say the final line in a loud, scary shout. There may be screaming.*)

The Ghost Catcher

By Caroline Feller Bauer

Tilly, the heroine, seems concerned only with her appearance (a trait with which many teenagers will readily identify), yet she successfully routs a ghost.

Tilly paid great attention to her appearance. She was always combing her hair and checking her looks in the mirror. Her clothes were always freshly pressed. She was chosen "Best Dressed" in her high school two years in a row. Her hobby was fashion; her avocation was cosmetology. She carried her cosmetics case with her wherever she went, even to the aerobics class that she attended twice a week at Gagny's Gym. When she left the exercise session, she always changed, showered, and primped.

One night as she left Gagny's, absorbed in the business of gracefully waving goodbye to the owner, she couldn't help but notice the glorious full moon, a harvest moon. "Bye, Til. Watch out for ghosts. It's almost Halloween," Jim Gagny warned.

"I don't believe in ghosts, Mr. Gagny," said Tilly as she glided out the door. She hadn't walked more than five yards when she took out her mirror to check her makeup. "Not bad," she thought to herself. "Here's hoping I meet the man of my dreams tonight."

Tilly's fantasy was that her predestined "knight in shining armor" would emerge one night from the shadows on Main Street and sweep her off her feet, marry her, and take her to live in a villa in the South of France. So far she had met only Old Man Bundy and his dog, and once Ms. Pritkin, her math teacher, on her way home.

Ghosts do exist, whether you believe in them or not, and two swooped down from the roof of MacArthur's hardware store and barred Tilly's way.

"WOOOOOO. HOOOOOOO," they wailed as they floated around Tilly's head. "WOOOOOOO. HOOOOOOO. Prepare for a voyage. We're taking you to the boss in the dungeon."

"Don't be ridiculous," said Tilly. "I'm not dressed for an audience with a ghost, even if he is your leader."

"WOOOOOOOO. HOOOOOOOO. Now we will seize you."

WEB This script is available on ALA's Web Extras page at alaeditions.org/webextras.

"Don't come any closer," screamed Tilly. "I have my ghost catcher here in my bag. I've caught two ghosts already tonight. Here they are." Tilly reached into her cosmetic case and pulled out her mirror. The ghosts looked in the mirror and saw themselves.

"WOOOOOOOOO. HOOOOOOOOO," screamed the ghosts. "Let's get out of here."

Tilly sat down on the curb in front of MacArthur's Hardware. She recombed her hair. She reapplied her lipstick. Then she put away her ghost catcher and went home to take a nice hot bath and to wash and blow-dry her hair for tomorrow.

BOOKLIST: SIMPLY SUPERNATURAL FICTION TITLES

Auxier, Jonathan. *The Night Gardener*. *Amulet, 2014*. Molly, fourteen, and her younger brother, Kip, have left the famine in Ireland for a job in England as servants on the Windsor estate, where a massive, sinister-looking tree is entwined in the very foundation of the house. (Gr. 5–8)

Black, Holly, and Tony DiTerlizzi. *The Spiderwick Chronicles, Book 1: The Field Guide*. *Illus. by Tony DiTerlizzi. Simon & Schuster, 2003*. Nine-year-old twins and their thirteen-year-old sister find a field guide to faeries in Great-Aunt Lucinda's creepy old mansion. (Gr. 2–5)

Dahl, Roald. *The Witches*. *Illus. by Quentin Blake. Farrar, 1983*. A young boy's Norwegian grandmamma warns him to be on his guard against witches, but they entrap him nevertheless. (Gr. 3–7)

DeKeyser, Stacy. *The Brixen Witch*. *Illus. by John Nickle. McElderry, 2012*. When he finds a golden guilder belonging to the witch of the mountain, Rudi Bauer unintentionally brings bad fortune to his village. (Gr. 3–6)

Delaney, Joseph. *The Revenge of the Witch*. *The Last Apprentice series, Book One. Greenwillow, 2005*. Twelve-year-old Thomas Ward, the left-handed seventh son of a seventh son, becomes the apprentice to the Spook, a man who walks the county protecting it from witches, boggarts, ghosts, and gasts. This is the first in the series, and it's not for the faint of heart. (Gr. 5–8)

Gaiman, Neil. *Coraline*. *Illus. by Dave McKean. HarperCollins, 2002*. Unlocking an old door in her family's new apartment, Coraline meets a strange couple who insist they are her "other" parents. (Gr. 4–7)

Gaiman, Neil. *The Graveyard Book*. *Illus. by Dave McKean. HarperCollins, 2008*. The night his family is murdered by a knife-wielding man, a toddler wanders into a nearby old English graveyard, where he is taken in and raised by ghosts. (Gr. 5–8)

Gaiman, Neil. *Wolves in the Walls.* *Illus. by Dave McKean. HarperCollins, 2003.* Lucy hears wolves inside the walls of her house, but her parents and brother don't believe her. A very spooky cover and chilling first half renders this picture book too dark for younger kids, but just right for older ones who like a little shiver and then a laugh. (Gr. 2–6)

Gidwitz, Adam. *A Tale Dark & Grimm.* *Dutton, 2010.* Royal children Hansel and Gretel journey through eight dangerous fairy tales (based on stories by the Brothers Grimm) in search of better parents and to save their kingdom. Follow up with the companion book, *In a Glass Grimmly* (2012). (Gr. 5–7)

Jinks, Catherine. *How to Catch a Bogle.* *Illus. by Sarah Watts. Harcourt, 2013.* In 1870, ten-year-old orphan, Birdie McAdam, is a proud apprentice to bogler Alfred Bunce, helping him rid London of foul and fearsome creatures that haunt houses and eat children. (Gr. 4–6)

Landy, Derek. *Skulduggery Pleasant.* *HarperCollins, 2007.* To solve her uncle's murder, twelve-year-old Stephanie Edgely teams up with Skulduggery Pleasant, a walking, talking skeleton and detective. (Gr. 5–8)

Oliver, Lauren. *Liesl & Po.* *Illus. by Kei Acedera. HarperCollins, 2011.* Three days after Liesl's father dies, two ghosts from the Other Side appear in her attic bedroom: a child named Po and a little, shadowlike ghost-pet named Bundle. (Gr. 4–7)

Riordan, Rick. *The Red Pyramid.* *Disney-Hyperion, 2010.* On Christmas Eve, fourteen-year-old Kane Carter and his twelve-year-old sister Sadie are with their Egyptologist dad when he unwittingly unleashes an ancient god and destroys the British Museum. (Gr. 5–9)

Schlitz, Laura Amy. *Splendors and Glooms.* *Candlewick, 2012.* After marionette master and magician Professor Grissini and his two young assistants perform their puppet show at Clara Wintermute's twelfth birthday party, Clara disappears. (Gr. 4–8)

Stanley, Diane. *The Silver Bowl.* *Harper, 2011.* Working as a scullery maid at Dethemere Castle, Molly has a horrifying vision of how Prince Mathias, heir to the throne, met his death. (Gr. 5–8)

Ursu, Anne. *Breadcrumbs.* *HarperCollins/Walden Pond, 2011.* Hazel heads into the snowy Minnesota woods to rescue her best friend, Jack, who has gone off with the White Witch on a sleigh drawn by wolves. (Gr. 4–7)

Vande Velde, Vivian. *Tales from the Brothers Grimm and the Sisters Weird.* *Illus. by Brad Weinman. Harcourt, 1995.* Retakes and remakes of thirteen well-known fairy tales. (Gr. 5–8)

Wooding, Chris. *Malice.* *Scholastic, 2009.* Say, "Tall Jake, take me away!" and he will. (Gr. 6–8)

BOOKLIST: SIMPLY SUPERNATURAL COLLECTIONS OF TALES

De Las Casas, Dianne. *Scared Silly: 25 Tales to Tickle and Thrill.* Libraries Unlimited, 2009. Silly, scary jump tales—most of them peppy rewrites of ones you know—just begging for a campfire or a darkened room. (Professional)

Half-Minute Horrors. *Ed. by Susan Rich. Harper, 2009.* Seventy little two-page jump stories you can read in thirty seconds, by major children's book authors, including Lane Smith, Neil Gaiman, Jack Gantos, James Patterson, and R. L. Stine. (Gr. 5–8)

Hamilton, Martha, and Mitch Weiss. *Scared Witless: Thirteen Eerie Tales to Tell.* Illus. by Kevin Pope. August House, 2006. Mostly funny jump tales, with tips for telling. (Gr. 4–6)

MacDonald, Margaret Read. *When the Lights Go Out: 20 Scary Tales to Tell.* Illus. by Roxane Murphy. H. W. Wilson, 1988. Twenty fun jump stories children will scream over; includes suggestions on how to tell them. (Professional)

Olson, Arielle N., and Howard Schwartz. *More Bones: Scary Stories from Around the World.* Illus. by E. M. Gist. Viking, 2008. Short and not terribly frightening, these twenty-two folktales are good for telling, as are the stories in the companion book, *Ask the Bones: Scary Stories from Around the World* (1999). (Gr. 4–7)

Parkhurst, Liz Smith. *The August House Book of Scary Stories: Spooky Tales for Telling Out Loud.* August House, 2009. Twenty chillers with a book cover that will give you pause. (Gr. 5–8)

San Souci, Robert D. *Short & Shivery: Thirty Chilling Tales.* Illus. by Katherine Coville. Doubleday, 1987. Ghastly little tales from all over the globe, featuring a nifty assortment of ghosts, skeletons, witches, wizards, and more. Follow up with *More Short & Shivery: Thirty Chilling Tales* (1994), *Even More Short & Shivery: Thirty Chilling Tales* (1997), and *Haunted Houses* (Henry Holt, 2010). (Gr. 4–8)

Schwartz, Alvin. *Scary Stories to Tell in the Dark.* Illus. by Brett Helquist. HarperCollins, 1981. These short, chilling jump tales work beautifully as transitions between longer selections, and you can't survive without the wickedly fun companion books: *More Scary Stories to Tell in the Dark* (1984) and *Scary Stories 3: More Tales to Chill Your Bones* (1991). These titles get banned a lot. (Gr. 4–8)

Stine, R. L., comp. *Beware! R. L. Stine Picks His Favorite Scary Stories.* HarperCollins, 2002. Twenty-three deliberately icky stories and poems from leading adult and children's book authors, including Ray Bradbury, Edward Gorey, William Sleator, and Alvin Schwartz. (Gr. 4–6)

Young, Richard, and Judy Dockrey Young. *Favorite Scary Stories of American Children.* Illus. by Don Bell. August House, 1999. The twenty-three scary stories in this eclectic, entertaining, and sometimes hair-raising collection are rated for ages five to six, seven to eight, and nine to ten. (K–Gr. 5)

Funny Stories

The stories above make listeners scream and then laugh. The stories below are simply comical, and they are great choices for ending a program with a lift.

The Magic Cap

By Johan Hart, from The Buried Treasure & Other Picture Tales from Holland, selected by Eulalie Steinmetz Ross. Lippincott, c1958

Don't you love it when the fool—also called the simpleton, the nitwit, the noodle-head, or the numbskull—turns out to get the last laugh? This is one of those. Of course, having a smart and clever wife helps, too.

There was once a farmer of whom his neighbors used to say that he had no more wits than he was born with, which were not very many. Although it was easy to get the best of him, he was fortunate in having for a wife a woman who was very smart and sharp as a needle. Hence Willem, as he was called, left all of the thinking to his wife and did whatever she told him to do.

One bright, sunny morning she said, "Willem, put on a clean smock and your Sunday clogs and take the cow with you to sell at the market. She is very fat and looks well; so you should get at least a hundred guilders for her."

So to the market went the farmer, pulling his cow behind him.

As he passed a certain inn, three ne'er-do-wells were standing in the doorway.

"There goes Willem, the simpleton," remarked one of them. "It should be easy enough to fool him."

The three put their heads together for an instant and straightaway agreed on a plan to get Willem's cow for little money. Then they took a shortcut across the fields and stood here and there along the road where Willem would pass.

As the farmer came towards him, the first scamp called out:

"Hi, Farmer, are you taking that donkey to market?"

"That is not a donkey; that is a cow," answered Willem.

"Ho, ho! Ha, ha! What kind of a farmer are you to think it is a cow?" And shaking with laughter, the scoundrel walked on.

Shortly afterwards Willem met the second rogue, who said:

"Why don't you ride that donkey instead of pulling him, Farmer?"

"That is not a donkey; that is a cow," replied Willem again.

"A cow? Why, Farmer, you must be blind to take that animal for a cow!" And the second scoundrel walked on.

Poor Willem turned around and looked at his cow doubtfully. Had he taken the wrong animal out of the stable? But no, there could be no mistake—this was their cow—the one his wife had told him to take to the market. Still his wife might be wrong too—they might both be mistaken, and perhaps he *was* leading a donkey, instead of a cow, to market.

Then he met the third scamp. "Good morning, Farmer. Is your donkey for sale?"

There! thought Willem. That was the third person to talk about a donkey; he and his wife *must* be wrong.

"Yes," he finally replied. "I am taking this donkey to market."

"In that case," said the other, "I will buy it from you for twenty guilders."

Now, twenty guilders was a good price for a donkey, so Willem agreed and went back to his farm, well satisfied that he had made a good sale.

When he got home his wife called him all kinds of an idiot, until he hung his head in shame. But she knew that it was not altogether his fault that he had gotten the worst of a bad bargain, so she put on her thinking cap and tried to find a way to get even with the three ne'er-do-wells.

Well, just before the next market day, the farmer's wife arranged to go to town and lay a trap for the three tramps. On market day itself she gave the farmer an old cap and told him exactly what he was to do with it.

As Willem was trudging along the road that led to town, he met the three ne'er-do-wells, who stopped to crow over the trick they had played on him.

"Oh, let bygones be bygones," said the farmer good-naturedly. "I have some money to spend today. Will you come and have a glass of cider with me?"

They gladly accepted and followed him to an inn. After they had all refreshed themselves, the farmer looked at the innkeeper and twirling his cap three times upon the forefinger of his right hand, asked, "Everything is paid for, is it not?"

"Yes, everything is paid for," the innkeeper repeated, as the farmer walked out, followed by his fair-weather friends.

As they were passing the next inn, Willem stopped and said aloud, as though talking to himself:

"It should work here, too," and asking the ne'er-do-wells to join him in another drink, he went inside. And again after they had had their fill, Willem spun his cap around his finger and walked out without paying a cent.

The rogues' eyes were by now fairly popping out of their heads, but no one spoke a word. When they came to the third inn, the farmer said, "Let's have dinner here; it won't cost a thing."

So the four went in and ordered a good dinner. When everyone had eaten and drunk his fill, the farmer picked up his cap and twirled it around his finger again, and lo and behold! once more the innkeeper said everything had been paid for.

By that time the three ne'er-do-wells could no longer hold back their curiosity and began questioning Willem. They wanted to know how he could eat and drink in every inn he went to without paying for anything.

The farmer told them that the secret lay in the cap. It was a magic cap, he said.

"How much do you want for your cap?" the first one asked. "I'll give you fifty guilders for it!" he added eagerly.

"I will give you eighty!" the second one cried.

"One hundred!" shouted the third, who was the greediest of all and whose mouth watered when he thought of all the good food and wine he would get if he had the cap in his possession.

"Sold!" said Willem.

The farmer ran all the way home with the hundred guilders in his hand; and how his wife chuckled when he gave her the money! "That's eighty guilders for our loss in the sale of the cow; ten guilders for the food and wine you and your fine friends feasted upon, which I paid for in advance yesterday, when I went to town; and ten guilders to teach those rascals a lesson," she counted, as she put the money in an old stocking and hid it on one of the low wooden beams above her head.

News

By Aidan Chambers, from Funny Folk: A Book of Comic Tales,
illustrated by Trevor Stubley. Heinemann, 1976

Take your time when you tell this tale so listeners can process each facet of the disastrous events. There are two distinct voices here—the urbane, wealthy landowner, increasingly appalled by what he is hearing, and his laconic steward who recounts the cause-and-effect story in reverse order.

A rich landowner was returning home from a journey when he met by the side of the road the steward he had left in charge of his estate while he was away.

"Ah, steward," hailed the returning gentleman cheerily, "how are you old fellow? And how are things at home?"

"Bad enough, sir," said the steward. "The magpie is dead."

"Well, well," said the gentleman. "Poor magpie. Gone at last, eh? And how did he die?"

"Over-ate himself, sir."

"Did he indeed! The greedy bird! What was it he liked so much?"

"Horseflesh. That's what got him, sir. Horseflesh."

"Never!" said the landowner. "How ever did he manage to find so much horseflesh that it killed him?"

"All your father's horses, sir."

"What! My father's horses! Are they dead too?"

"Aye, sir. Died of overwork."

"Why ever should they be overworked, steward?"

"Carrying all that water, sir."

"Carrying water! What were they carrying water for, man?"

"For sure, sir, to put the fire out."

"Fire! What fire?"

"Why, sir, the fire that burned your father's house to the ground."

"Good Lord, steward, is my father's house burnt down? How did that happen?"

"I reckon it were the torches, sir."

"What torches?"

"Them we used at your mother's funeral, sir."

"My mother is dead?"

"Aye, poor lady. She never looked up after it."

"After what, man, after what?"

"The loss of your father, sir."

"My father? Dead too?"

"Yes, poor gentleman. Took to his bed as soon as he heard of it."

"Heard of what?"

"Of the bad news, sir."

"More bad news! What bad news?"

"Well, sir, your bank has failed and all your money is lost, and you're not worth a penny in the world, sir. I thought I'd come and wait on you to tell you about it, sir, for I thought you'd like to hear the news."

The Giant Blueberry

Retold by Judy Freeman

"The Giant Blueberry" is a shaggy-dog story, a joke or story with a punch line twisted around an expression, aphorism, jingle, or nonsense word. You can find plenty of others online at sites like www.punoftheday.com. Here are a few of the endings:

WEB This script is available on ALA's Web Extras page at alaeditions.org/webextras.

"Pardon me, Roy. Is that the cat that chewed your new shoes?"

"A Benny shaved is a Benny urned."

"People who live in grass houses should not stow thrones."

For listeners to be in on the joke of this story, they must understand the context of the punch line. If they aren't acquainted with Mark Antony's quote from Shakespeare's play *Julius Caesar*, you can still tell the joke, but you'll need to prepare your audience beforehand. You remember the famous speech in *"Julius Caesar,"* right? It starts:

Friends, Romans, countrymen, lend me your ears;

I come to bury Caesar, not to praise him;

The evil that men do lives after them,

The good is oft interred with their bones,

So let it be with Caesar . . .

First, you'll need to find a reason to quote and explain the original speech and maybe talk about the play and who Julius Caesar was and what happened to him. Your kids will appreciate the gory details. Declaim the speech with great theatricality. Continue to quote the first two lines with your kids until they know them by heart.

Perhaps you were already planning to read aloud Aliki's stupendous non-fiction picture book, *William Shakespeare & the Globe* (HarperCollins, 1999), to introduce the bard to your third through eighth graders. Perfect timing!

Five minutes, an hour, a day, or even a week later, pull out a box of blueberries. "Look at these gorgeous berries," you exclaim. "I can't resist a delicious box of New Jersey blueberries. Hey, did I ever tell you the story about the world's biggest blueberry?" And you're off, telling the tale, to appreciative groans at the end, you hope. Then give each person a blueberry to eat.

Flip Wilson used to tell a version of the story. Here's how Judy and her friends told it in summer camp when she was a kid, with bits made up to fill in the parts she couldn't remember.

Long ago, in ancient Rome, there lived a poor farmer named Marcus who tried to make a living growing blueberries. It wasn't easy. One morning, he went outside to tend his blueberry bushes. There, hanging from the bush, was the hugest, most gorgeous berry that Marcus had ever seen. It was round and blue and simply gigantic. It was surely the most perfect berry that there ever was. Marcus ran into town and told everybody he saw about his amazing blueberry. People came from all over to view it. Marcus bragged, "Did I lie? Is this the most remarkable berry you've ever seen? Look how enormous it is!"

All day, people came by to remark on his prodigious berry. They said, "You weren't kidding. That's one big, fabulous berry."

Marcus was so proud. He said, modestly, "Yeah, well, if you take good care of your berries, your berries will take good care of you!"

Early the next morning, Marcus stepped outside to check on his blueberry bushes. Who did he spy but a disreputable-looking man lurking by the blueberry bushes. As soon as he saw Marcus, the man plucked the giant berry from the bush, hoisted it into his arms, and started to run away with it.

"Stop, thief! That's my magnificent, one-of-a-kind blueberry, the biggest and best blueberry I've ever grown. Where are you going with my beautiful blueberry?" Marcus cried.

Cradling the berry in his arms—this was one big piece of fruit—the man turned and hollered, "Hey, buddy, I've come to seize your berry, not to praise it!"

BOOKLIST: FUNNY STORIES

Angleberger, Tom. *The Strange Case of Origami Yoda.* *Illus. by the author. Amulet, 2010.* The Yoda finger puppet worn by Dwight, the weirdest kid at McQuarrie Middle School, offers life-changing advice to any student who asks. (Gr. 3–6)

Avi. *Romeo and Juliet, Together (and Alive) at Last.* *Orchard, 1987.* Laugh out loud as seventh-grader Pete Saltz organizes a disastrous student production of Romeo and Juliet. (Gr. 5–7)

Beaty, Andrea. *Dorko the Magnificent.* *Amulet, 2013.* Fifth-grader Robbie Darko thinks he's suffered enough disasters as an aspiring magician—but then his great-great-aunt, known as Grandma Melvyn, moves in. (Gr. 4–6)

Bruel, Nick. *Bad Kitty Gets a Bath.* *Illus. by the author. Roaring Brook, 2008.* Bad Kitty needs a bath? Uh, oh. Don't you know CATS HATE BATHS? (Gr. 1–4)

DePaola, Tomie. *Tomie dePaola's Front Porch Tales & North Country Whoppers.* *Illus. by the author. Putnam, 2007.* Told in the North Country dialect of New Hampshire, this is a droll compilation of eleven tales, dialogues, and wry asides, sorted by season. (Gr. 2–6)

Fleischman, Paul. *The Dunderheads.* *Illus. by David Roberts. Candlewick, 2009.* Miss Breakbone's students—misfits all, but each with a singular talent—are far smarter than she realizes. (Gr. 2–5)

Fleming, Candace. *The Fabled Fourth Graders of Aesop Elementary School.* *Schwartz & Wade, 2007.* Each Aesop's fable-based chapter features one of the fourth graders in Mr. Jupiter's rambunctious class. (Gr. 2–5)

Gaiman, Neil. *Fortunately the Milk.* *Illus. by Slottie Young. Harper, 2013.* A father claims he was abducted by aliens, held by pirates, rescued by a stegosaurus in a hot-air balloon, and then some . . . while going to buy milk for his children's cereal. (Gr. 3–6)

Howe, Deborah, and James Howe. *Bunnicula: A Rabbit-Tale of Mystery.* *Illus. by Alan Daniel. Atheneum, 1979.* Could the baby rabbit the Monroe family found at the Dracula movie really be a vampire bunny, sucking the juices out of unsuspecting vegetables? (Gr. 3–7)

Manes, Stephen. *Be a Perfect Person in Just Three Days.* *Illus. by Tom Huffman. Clarion, 1982.* When a library book falls on Milo Crinkley's head, the boy decides to follow its instructions on how to become a perfect kid. (Gr. 3–6)

McMullan, Kate. *School! Adventures at the Harvey N. Trouble Elementary School.* *Illus. by George Booth. Feiwel and Friends, 2010.* On Hotsy-Totsy Monday, Ron Faster, a very fast runner, starts his week by taking the school bus driven by Mr. Stuckinaditch, which gets stuck in a ditch. (Gr. 2–5)

Morris, Gerald. *The Adventures of Sir Gawain the True.* *Illus. by Aaron Renier. Houghton Mifflin Harcourt, 2011.* When King Arthur's nephew, Sir Gawain the Undefeated, saves a damsel from a fire-breathing dragon, he is too self-involved to accept her gift of gratitude. From The Knights' Tales series. (Gr. 3–5)

Peirce, Lincoln. *Big Nate: In a Class by Himself.* *Illus. by the author. HarperCollins, 2010.* Sixth-grader Nate Wright's fortune cookie fortune reads, "Today you will surpass all others," but the only thing he seems to be excelling at today is getting in trouble and getting detention. (Gr. 3–6)

Sachar, Louis. *Sideways Stories from Wayside School.* *Illus. by Julie Brinckloe. Morrow, 1998, c1978.* All about the class of kids on the thirtieth floor of a crazy school with one classroom on each floor. The sequel, *Wayside School Is Falling Down* (1989), is also priceless. (Gr. 3–6)

Scieszka, Jon, and Francesco Sedita. *Spaceheadz: SPHDZ, Book #1!* *Illus. by Shane Prigmore. Simon & Schuster, 2010.* New kid Michael K. is stuck sitting at the back of the classroom with two strange kids, who tell him they are Spaceheadz from another planet and need his help to save the world. (Gr. 3–5)

Spratt, R. A. *The Adventures of Nanny Piggins.* *Illus. by Dan Santat. Little, Brown, 2010.* A chocolate-loving four-foot pig—whose last job was as the flying pig at the circus—takes the job of nanny for Mr. Green's three children. (Gr. 3–7)

Taback, Simms. *Kibitzers and Fools: Tales My Zayda (Grandfather) Told Me.* *Illus. by the author. Viking, 2005.* Thirteen short, comical Jewish tales about a variety of fools, from nebbishes to schnooks. (Gr. 2–6)

Vernon, Ursula. *Dragonbreath: Curse of the Were-wiener.* *Dial, 2010.* In the school cafeteria, Danny Dragonbreath's weird hot dog bites Wendell's finger, and now Danny's iguana friend is growing hair on his back. (Gr. 3–5)

Reinventing Fairy Tales

Telling fairy tale parodies has several advantages. One, they're funny. There's nothing that raises the sprits like hearing someone tell or read a funny story. And two, they connect listeners with the original story. If your tweens don't know the "Little Red Riding Hood" story (and you should never assume that they do), telling a parody of it gives you a chance to rehash the original—or have your audience retell it, round robin.

You may already know James Thurber's short fable, "The Little Girl and the Wolf," where the girl shoots the figure in the bed, "for even in a night-cap a wolf does not look any more like your grandmother than the Met-ro-Goldwyn lion looks like Calvin Coolidge." The story is from Thurber's collection of original and satirical fables, *Fables from Our Times and Poems Illustrated* (Harper, 1940). You'll surely want to read his version aloud as an introduction to parody (and to Thurber's longer works, including uproarious short stories like "The Secret Life of Walter Mitty" and "The Night the Bed Fell"). Each fable ends with a moral; the one accompanying this story reads, "Moral: It is not so easy to fool little girls nowadays as it used to be."

You can continue your tour of "Red Riding Hood" take-offs with the title story in Patricia Santos Marcantonio's *Red Ridin' in the Hood, and Other Cuentos.* The author has reset and updated eleven well-known fairy tales, some in the barrio, and others in the Mexican countryside. The useful glossary at the back will help kids translate the many Spanish words and phrases. "Bianca Nieves and the Seven Vaqueritos," "Juan and the Pinto Beanstalk," and "Belleza y La Bestia" are three you'll recognize immediately. All the stories are fun to tell or read, and they are just right for groups to write up for reader's theater presentations.

You'll find more suggestions for parodies and fractured fairy tales in our first volume, *The Handbook for Storytellers* (American Library Association, 2015).

Red Ridin' in the Hood

Title story from the book Red Ridin' in the Hood, and Other Cuentos
by Patricia Santos Marcantonio (Farrar, 2005) (Gr. 5–8)

Inside a cardboard box, Mamá packed a tin of chicken soup, heavy on cilantro, along with a jar of peppermint tea, peppers from our garden, and a hunk of white goat cheese that smelled like Uncle José's feet.

That meant one thing.

"Roja, your *abuelita* is not feeling well," Mamá told me. "I want you to take this food to her."

"But Mamá, me and Lupe Maldonado are going to the movies," I replied, but felt guilty as soon as I said it.

"What's more important? Your grandmother or Lupe and the movies?" Mamá closed up the box.

"Wear your new dress, the one that Abuelita made for you. That will make her feel better," Mamá said.

I couldn't say no because I didn't want to feel guilty again, so I put on the red dress. It was long and old-fashioned, with a high collar. I looked like the kid on *Little House on the Prairie.*

"Go straight to Abuelita's apartment," Mamá said.

"Sí, Mamá," I answered.

"Here's bus fare."

"Sí, Mamá."

"And keep away from Forest Street. You know it means trouble."

"Sí, Mamá."

I waited for another order, but instead Mamá kissed my cheek.

The day was bright, so I put on my sunglasses, hoping none of my friends would see me carrying a cardboard box that smelled like Uncle José's feet and wearing a dress that made me look *estúpida.*

I decided to walk and keep the bus fare. I was saving change for a new shirt I had seen in the window of the Martínez clothing store—a shirt a whole lot cooler than the number I was wearing.

After a few blocks my arms grew tired carrying the box and I knew I needed to take a shortcut. I looked up. There it was.

FOREST STREET.

I could hear Mamá's voice telling me to stay away, but I didn't listen.

Forest Street got its name because it was lined with the biggest trees in the whole barrio, tall and thick and blocking out the sun, making even morning light seem like sunset. As I walked down the street, the city and home seemed far away. Birds whistled a delicate, carefree rhythm. Two skinny police officers nodded to me as they walked past.

"I don't know why Mamá says this block is trouble," I said to myself. "It's quiet and kinda peaceful."

But as I walked further, the trees grew thicker and Forest Street grew dark.

Then came a roar and the blare of loud salsa music.

Up rolled a glossy brown low-rider Chevy with licks of flame painted on the hood. It jolted up and down, the hydraulics making the driver's large, hairy ears bounce. His smile was broad and full of teeth. SUAVECITO was painted on the back windshield in blue and silver.

"*¡Hola!*" he greeted me.

I didn't stop. I remembered Mamá's advice about not talking to strangers, and this guy was strange.

"I say, *hola,* Red."

I stopped. "How'd you know my name?"

"You're wearing red, ain't you?" His smile and laugh were mixed with a growl. "My name is Lobo, Lobo Chávez."

I began walking again.

"Where you going?" He pushed his sunglasses to the top of his head. His eyes were orange hungry marbles.

"Not that it's any of your business, Lobo Chávez, but I'm going to visit my *abuelita.* She's not feeling so well today."

"You should be careful," he said. "Lots of bad dudes hanging around Forest Street."

"Like you?"

"Not me. I'm harmless." Lobo's gigantic tongue went all the way around his mouth and over his large black nose. "Hey, Roja, just a few doors down is the best *panadería* in town. Stop in and get your *abuelita* some empanadas with *calabaza.* She'll love 'em."

"Thank you, I will."

Lobo pulled down his sunglasses. "I hope your ol' grandma feels better, Red." He zoomed up the street, hydraulics in time to the beat of the music on his radio.

Lobo Chavez was right about the bakery. The *calabaza* empanadas were great. I bought two, one for Abuelita and one for me, which I ate as I walked slowly, enjoying the treat. But then I noticed the sun starting to go down, so I hurried.

Abuelita's apartment building was at the edge of Forest Street. I ran up the stairs and I knocked at her door.

No answer.

"Abuelita, it's Roja."

Inside, I heard scurrying.

"Abuelita, are you okay?"

"*Sí,* Roja. *Entra,*" a little voice said.

The room smelled of the lavender soap my grandma used. It also smelled like wet dog. That was unusual because Abuelita's landlord wouldn't let her have a pet.

"I'm in the bedroom, Roja," she called to me.

"Abuelita, you sound like you got a chest cold."

I opened the door. The shades were drawn and the room was dark. But there was enough light to see Lobo Chávez in Abuelita's bed, wearing her nightgown and glasses and smiling as if I didn't notice he was not my grandmother.

I knew then that this was one pretty dumb wolf.

Yet I worried he might have hurt my grandmother. I realized suddenly how much I really loved her, and how angry I was at this wolf in Abuelita's clothing. I decided to play along to find out what had happened to her.

"Abuelita, look at what Mamá sent you," I said, all cheery like the girl on *Little House,* and set the food on the table.

"That looks so good." Lobo rubbed his bloated stomach.

I wanted to laugh, but couldn't.

"Abuelita, I never noticed before, but what big *orejas* you have."

He put a hand to his ear. "The better to hear you with, *nieta.*"

"And what big *ojos* you have, Abuelita," I said.

"The better to see you with, Roja." Lobo opened his eyes so big I thought they would pop out of his head.

"And, Abuelita, what big *dientes* you have."

Lobo slobbered a little. He had been waiting for this one. He leaped out of my grandmother's bed. "The better to eat you with!"

But I had secretly grabbed a chunk of the goat cheese, and when Lobo opened his big mouth, I shoved in the whole smelly piece.

Lobo put his claws to his throat and groaned. "This tastes like someone's dirty feet. Yuck!"

I ran out the door and yelled, "POLICE!"

The two officers I had passed earlier ran up the stairs.

"That wolf has my grandmother," I told them.

The officers chased Lobo around the apartment, but the wolf tripped on Abuelita's long nightgown, and they easily caught him.

"Where is my grandmother, Lobo Chávez?" I yelled.

"She wasn't here. I was going to eat you and then eat her for dessert when she came home. I eat people. That's my job," Lobo confessed, his face still a little green from eating all that stinky cheese.

Just then, Abuelita walked in.

"Where have you been?" I hugged my grandmother. "A wolf was going to eat us."

"I was feeling better and went out for a quick game of bingo," she said.

Abuelita looked at Lobo. "Officers, please take my nightgown off that wolf. He's getting hair all over it."

"Yes, señora," the officers replied.

"Well, I am happy you are safe, Abuelita" I said.

"Well, I am happy you are safe," she said. "This is a dangerous world, and it's best to keep your eyes and ears wide open, even if they aren't as big as a wolf's."

"Good advice." One of the officers smiled. "We are taking this Lobo Chávez to jail for planning to eat people and impersonating a little old lady. We'll lock him up until his teeth fall out and the only thing he can eat is oatmeal."

The wolf howled.

"Here you go, young lady. You deserve this for your bravery." The officer threw me the keys to Lobo's low-rider.

The wolf howled again.

"Come on, you." The officers took Lobo Chávez away.

"Well, I'm hungry after all this excitement," Abuelita said. "What did you bring me?"

"Chicken soup and peppers, and the goat cheese that saved our lives," I said.

"Is that the *queso* that smells like your Uncle José's feet?"

"Yes."

Abuelita grabbed her sweater. "How about Chinese, Roja?"

"I'd love it, Abuelita. And I love you."

Off we went in my new low-rider. We both laughed as hydraulics bumped along, and I never had to walk down Forest Street again.

Prindella and the Since

By F. Chase Taylor, aka Colonel Stoopnagle

If you really want to have your audience laughing or at least looking at you with raised eyebrows, read aloud Taylor's "Prinderella and the Since." To be truly effective, this needs to be memorized so you can rattle it off, but once you have it, you'll know it for life. You'll find Judy's version of the story in her book Once Upon a Time: Using Storytelling, Creative Drama, and Reader's Theater with Children in Grades K–6 *(Libraries Unlimited, 2007).*

Here, indeed, is a story that'll make your cresh fleep. It will give you poose gimples. Think of a poor little glip of a surl, prairie vitty, who, just because

WEB This script is available on ALA's Web Extras page at alaeditions.org/webextras.

she had two sisty uglers, had to flop the moar, clinkle the shuvvers out of the stitchen cove and do all the other chasty nores, while her soamly histers went to a drancy bess fall. Wasn't that a shirty dame?

Well, to make a long shorry stort, this youngless hapster was chewing her doors one day, when who should suddenly appear but a garry fawdmother. Beeling very fadly for this witty prafe, she happed her clands, said a couple of waggic merds, and in the ash of a flybrow, Cinderella was transformed into a bavaging reauty. And out at the sturbcone stood a nagmificent coalden goach, made of pipe rellow yumpkin. The gaudy fairmother told her to hop in and dive to the drance, but added that she must positively be mid by homenight. So, overmoash with accumtion, she fanked the tharry from the hottom of her bart, bimed acloard, the driver whacked his crip, and off they went in a dowd of clust.

Soon they came to a casterful wondel, where a pransome hince was possing a tarty for the teeple of the pown. Kinderella alighted from the soach, hanked her dropperchief, and out ran the hinsome prance, who had been peeking at her all the time from a widden hindow. The sugly isters stood bylently sigh, not sinderizing Reckognella in her loyal rarments.

Well, to make a long shorty still storer, the nince went absolutely pruts over the provvly lincess. After several dowers of antsing, he was ayzier than crevver. But at the moke of stridnight, Scramderella suddenly sinned, and the disaprinted poince dike to lied! He had forgotten to ask the nincess her prame! But as she went stunning down the long reps, she slicked off one of the glass kippers she was wearing, and the pounce princed upon it with eeming glize.

The next day he tied all over trown to find the lainty daydy whose foot slitted that fipper. And the ditty prame with the only fit that footed was none other than our layding leedy. So she finally prairied the mince, and they happed livily after everward.

Judy's wonderful optometrist and dear friend, the late Raymond Taube, who was always ready with a punny riposte, handed her a copy of this next story back in the 1980s and said, "I thought you'd appreciate this." He was right. She's kept that piece of paper all these years. Along with the word-wacky "Prinderella and the Cince," above, it's a sidesplitting fractured fairy tale that takes some brain muscle to figure out. In 1940, Howard L. Chace, professor of Romance languages at Miami University, published "Ladle Rat Rotten Hut," a story that used "homophonic transformation," in the first issue of *Sports Illustrated* in 1954, and included it in his book *Anguish Languish* in 1956.

Perhaps you'd like to get started with a short warm-up. Read aloud Chace's well-known rewrite of the following nonsense verse and see if you can translate it from Anguish into English:

"Murder, mare argo art toe swarm?
"Yap, mar doling dodder,
Hank yore clues honor higglery larme
An dun gore norther warder!"

These are all actual words, though there may be a few (*argo*? *higglery*? *larme*?) you can't define off the top of your head. All the better for your readers to break out the dictionary and look them up. Did you recognize the verse? If not, it's a good one to learn and recite when your own kids want to go swimming:

Mother, may I go out to swim?
Yes, my darling daughter.
Hang your clothes on a hickory limb,
And don't go near the water!

In *Anguish Languish*, Chace states,

> People who are addicted to telling dialect stories, or chronically frus-
> trated because they can't tell them without Scotch brogue or Brook-
> lynese getting mixed up with Deep South, will be overjoyed with
> Anguish. Anguish is definitely not a dialect, since it consists only
> of unchanged English words that anyone can pronounce. . . . Read
> everything in this text aloud, and preferably in a group. Make a game
> of it. You'll find it easier to understand Anguish when you *hear* it than
> when you see it. If you have trouble, listen to someone else read it to
> you, preferably someone who doesn't quite know what he's reading.
> This often gives the best effect. Watch what happens when the listen-
> ers understand better than the reader.[1]

Now it's time to try an entire story with your kids, grades 5 and up. Read the first paragraph aloud and puzzle it out together. Then hand out copies to your children and have them read it aloud together and write down its English translation. It's best to divide it up and have two or three kids work on each paragraph, so it goes quicker. Then each group can read aloud its results. You can compile the complete English version of the story, based on your kids' translation and hand that out, too.

Ready?

Ladle Rat Rotten Hut

from Anguish Languish: Furry Tells *by Howard L. Chace, Prentice-Hall, 1956*

Wants pawn term dare worsted ladle gull hoe lift wetter murder inner ladle cordage honor itch offer lodge, dock, florist. Disk ladle gull orphan worry Putty ladle rat cluck wetter ladle rat hut, an fur disk raisin pimple colder Ladle Rat Rotten Hut.

Wan moaning Ladle Rat Rotten Hut's murder colder inset.

"Ladle Rat Rotten Hut, heresy ladle basking winsome burden barter an shirker cockles. Tick disk ladle basking tutor cordage offer groin-murder hoe lifts honor udder site offer florist. Shaker lake! Dun stopper laundry wrote! Dun stopper peck floors! Dun daily-doily inner florist, an yonder nor sorghum-stenches, dun stopper torque wet strainers."

"Hoe-cake, murder," resplendent Ladle Rat Rotten Hut, an tickle ladle basking an stuttered oft.

Honor wrote tutor cordage offer groin-murder, Ladle Rat Rotten Hut mitten anomalous woof.

"Wail, wail, wail!" set disk wicket woof, "Evanescent Ladle Rat Rotten Hut! Wares are putty ladle gull goring wizard ladle basking?"

"Armor goring tumor groin-murder's," reprisal ladle gull. "Grammar's seeking bet. Armor ticking arson burden barter an shirker cockles."

"O hoe! Heifer gnats woke," setter wicket woof, butter taught tomb shelf, "Oil tickle shirt court tutor cordage offer groin-murder. Oil ketchup wetter letter, an den—O bore!"

Soda wicket woof tucker shirt court, an whinny retched a cordage offer groin-murder, picked inner windrow, an sore debtor pore oil worming worse lion inner bet. Inner flesh, disk abdominal woof lipped honor bet, paunched honor pore oil worming, an garbled erupt. Den disk ratchet ammonal pot honor groin-murder's nut cup an gnat-gun, any curdled ope inner bet.

Inner ladle wile, Ladle Rat Rotten Hut a raft attar cordage, an ranker dough ball. "Comb ink, sweat hard," setter wicket woof, disgracing is verse.

Ladle Rat Rotten Hut entity bet rum, an stud buyer groin-murder's bet.

"O Grammar!" crater ladle gull historically, "Water bag icer gut! A nervous sausage bag ice!"

"Battered lucky chew whiff, sweat hard," setter bloat-Thursday woof, wetter wicket small honors phase.

"O, Grammar, water bag noise! A nervous sore suture anomalous prognosis!"

"Battered small your whiff, doling," whiskered dole woof, ants mouse worse waddling.

"0 Grammar, water bag mouser gut. A nervous sore suture bag mouse!"

Daze worry on-forger-nut ladle gull's lest warts. Oil offer sodden, caking offer carvers an sprinkling otter bet, disk hoard-hoarded woof lipped own pore Ladle Rat Rotten Hut an garbled erupt.

MURAL: Yonder nor sorghum stenches shut ladle gulls stopper torque wet strainers.

BOOKLIST: REINVENTING FAIRY TALES

Gidwitz, Adam. *In a Glass Grimmly.* *Dutton, 2012.* In the kingdom of Märchen, cousins Jack and Jill and a three-legged talking frog set off on a perilous quest to find and bring back "the most important and the most powerful looking glass in the history of the world." (Gr. 5–7)

Gidwitz, Adam. *A Tale Dark & Grimm.* *Dutton, 2010.* Royal children Hansel and Gretel journey through eight dangerous fairy tales (based on stories by the Brothers Grimm) in search of better parents and to save their kingdom. (Gr. 5–7)

Hanson, Mary. *How to Save Your Tail: If You Are a Rat Nabbed by Cats Who Really Like Stories about Magic Spoons, Wolves with Snout-Warts, Big, Hairy Chimney Trolls . . . and Cookies Too.* *Illus. by John Hendrix. Schwartz & Wade, 2007.* Snared by the castle's two cats, a rat named Bob bribes his way out with cookies and some well-told stories. (Gr. 2–5)

Jackson, Ellen. *Cinder Edna.* *Illus. by Kevin O'Malley. Lothrop, 1994.* Cinderella's next-door neighbor—take-charge Edna—has a ball at the ball with Prince Rupert, the fun younger brother of boring Prince Charming. (K–Gr. 6)

Levine, Gail Carson. *Ella Enchanted.* *HarperCollins, 1997.* Cursed at birth by the interfering fairy Lucinda's "gift" of obedience, fourteen-year-old Ella is shipped off to finishing school by her father. (Gr. 4–7)

Levine, Gail Carson. *The Fairy's Return and Other Princess Tales.* *Illus. by Mark Elliott. HarperCollins, 2006.* A compilation of all six of Levine's fairy-tale novellas that spoof well-known tales. (Gr. 4–7)

Marcantonio, Patricia Santos. *Red Ridin' in the Hood: And Other Cuentos.* *Illus. by Renato Alarcão. Farrar, 2005.* Eleven traditional fairy tales are reset in the barrio and given contemporary plot twists with Latino flavor. (Gr. 4–8)

Pullman, Philip. *I Was a Rat!* *Illus. by Kevin Hawkes. Knopf, 2000.* What is the connection between Roger, who insists he used to be a rat, and the Princess Aurelia? (Gr. 4–7)

Scieszka, Jon. *The Frog Prince Continued.* *Illus. by Steve Johnson. Viking, 1991.* Not content with his happily-ever-after life with his princess, the prince decides he'd like to be a frog again, and seeks out a witch to help him. (Gr. 2–5)

Scieszka, Jon. *The Stinky Cheese Man and Other Fairy Stupid Tales.* *Illus. by Lane Smith. Viking, 1992.* Funniest fairy-tale parody ever, and a Caldecott Honor winner, too. (K–Gr. 12)

Scieszka, Jon. *The True Story of the 3 Little Pigs!* *Illus. by Lane Smith. Viking Kestrel, 1989.* Alexander T. Wolf defends his actions towards the three little pigs, insisting he was framed. (Gr. 1–6)

Shirtliff, Liesl. *Rump: The True Story of Rumpelstiltskin.* *Knopf, 2013.* Orphaned twelve-year-old Rump—who does not know his own full name—relates how his magical ability to spin straw into gold comes with a twist: he must accept anything people offer him in exchange. (Gr. 3–6)

Stanley, Diane. *Rumpelstiltskin's Daughter.* *Illus. by the author. Morrow, 1997.* The now sixteen-year-old daughter of the miller's daughter from the story "Rumpelstiltskin" decides it's time to teach the gold-loving king a lesson. (Gr. 2–5)

Vande Velde, Vivian. *Tales from the Brothers Grimm and the Sisters Weird.* *Illus. by Brad Weinman. Harcourt, 1995.* Retakes and remakes of thirteen well-known fairy tales. (Gr. 5–8)

Love Stories

Around Valentine's Day, it's fun to introduce stories about love and like, crushes and breakups, to upper-elementary and middle-school kids, many of whom are going through the "he likes, she likes" phase and getting ready for dating. The two stories below prove that there's a match for every person and that while beauty is fleeting, love may be eternal. After a storytelling and booktalking session on love, hand out those little candy hearts with sayings on them. Sweet.

The Prince Who was a Rooster

Retold by Caroline Feller Bauer

Caroline first heard this story from her usually serious grandfather. She said it was always quite a sight to see her grandfather prancing around the room crowing. Of course, if you want to tell it with audience participation, alert your listeners to join in whenever you cackle or crow. If your style is less flamboyant, you can tell the story without the sound effects—it's still perfectly wonderful.

WEB This script is available on ALA's Web Extras page at alaeditions.org/webextras.

It was a pity. The prince was such a handsome young man. He had been well educated by tutors. He spoke three languages quite fluently and he rode a horse as well as any man. It was such a pity that he believed that he was a rooster.

It happened one day after a particularly grueling session with his mathematics professor. Prince Aaron was discouraged when the problem he was working refused to come out in a satisfactory manner. He chanced to look out the window and saw a rooster pecking about the yard. "What a fine life the rooster has," mused the prince. "All he has to do is peck and crow, peck and crow. His life is so much easier than mine. I would love to be a rooster. I will be a rooster."

The prince threw off his clothes, flapped his arms and crowed.

His family was astonished and saddened. Prince Aaron's mother and father wrung their hands and shook their heads. The servants averted their eyes and continued to serve the prince, but were shocked that the future ruler thought he was a rooster. How could the prince ever find a princess if he was a rooster?

Now Prince Aaron refused to eat the meals prepared by the castle kitchen and instead ate corn thrown on the floor. He refused to lay in his bed or sit in a chair. He was deaf to the pleas that he continue his studies. He strode around the castle completely naked, crowing and flapping his arms.

The queen was sure that the prince would tire of such strange behavior. But the king thought they better do something. He sent out a royal proclamation.

Anyone who could cure the prince would be given a fine prize. Several men came to the castle to try to plead with the prince, but he was difficult to talk to, crowing and flapping his arms.

After several discouraging weeks, the young girl who fed the royal hens and rooster asked for an audience with the king and queen.

"I think I can cure your son of his rooster behavior," she said, bowing before the royal couple.

"But how can you help?" lamented the king.

"Don't worry," said the henkeeper. "Just let me have some time with your son."

Pauline entered the room where the prince was happily flapping his arms. He crowed at Pauline. Pauline crawled under the desk where the Prince was nibbling on some kernels of corn. She cackled like a hen.

"Greetings, Rooster," she said.

"Who are you?" asked the prince.

"I am a hen come to join you," answered the girl.

"But why are you wearing clothes?"

"Shhh," cautioned Pauline. "I don't want anyone to know I'm a hen. Hens get eaten, you know."

The prince looked thoughtful. "Would you like some corn?" he offered.

"Thank you," said Pauline, "but first I will fetch a plate and a fork to eat it."

"If you are a chicken, why would you eat your corn like a human being?" asked Prince Aaron.

"Shhh," cautioned Pauline. "I don't want anyone to know I'm a hen. Hens get eaten, you know."

The prince looked thoughtful. He crowed and flapped his arms. Pauline cackled and flapped hers. They grinned at each other.

Pauline said, "I think I would like to read now. Where do you keep your books?"

"How can you read if you are a hen?" asked the prince.

"Shhh. It's boring to just cackle and peck all day, and anyway I don't want anyone to know I'm a hen. Hens get eaten, you know."

The prince looked thoughtful. He flapped his arms and crowed. Pauline flapped her arms and cackled. They grinned at each other.

He said, "I think I'll get dressed. I'm a bit cold wearing nothing. Since you are my guest, I think I'll join you at the dining-room table. And I happen to have a book with a very interesting mathematical problem. Perhaps you would enjoy working it with me."

As the afternoon drew to a close, the prince asked Pauline the henkeeper if she would like to be his bride. "Of course," said Pauline. The prince crowed with pleasure.

"Shhh," cautioned Pauline. "Roosters get eaten too." The parents of the prince were so delighted that they gave Pauline one-half of the kingdom.

The prince and Pauline were soon married. In time they became the rulers of the kingdom. The people were pleased with their new rulers.

Only King Aaron and Queen Pauline knew that they were really a rooster and a chicken.

The Very Pretty Lady

from The Devil's Storybook *by Natalie Babbitt (Farrar, 1974)*

There was a very pretty lady who lived all alone. She didn't have to live all alone; she was so pretty that there were many young men anxious to marry her. They hung about in her dooryard and played guitars and sang sweet songs and tried to look into the windows. They were there from dawn to dusk, always sad, always hopeful. But the very pretty lady didn't want to marry any of them. "It's no use being loved for the way one looks," she said to herself. "If I can't be loved in spite of my face, then I will never marry anyone at all."

This was wise no doubt, but no one can be wise all the time. For the truth is that the very pretty lady rather liked the fact that she was pretty, and sometimes she would stand in front of the mirror and look and look at herself. At times like that she would be pleased with herself and would go out to the dooryard and talk to all the young men and let them go with her to market and carry home her bags and packages for her. And for a long time afterward they would all look a good deal more hopeful than sad.

But most of the time the very pretty lady stayed inside her cottage, feeling lonely regardless of all the young men in the dooryard, longing for someone who would love her as she wanted to be loved.

Now, after a while, one way or another, the Devil heard about the very pretty lady and he decided that she was the very thing he needed to brighten up his days in Hell. So he packed a satchel of disguises and went up to have a look at her.

He had heard how very pretty she was, but no had told him that she never let anyone into her cottage. He went disguised as a beggar, but she wouldn't open the door. He tried appearing as a preacher and then as a king, but that didn't work either. So at last he simply disguised himself as one of her suitors and hung about with the others waiting for market day.

When the pretty lady came out at last, the Devil walked beside her all the way to town, looking at her every moment, and he carried back the heaviest package. By the time she had gone inside her cottage again, his mind was made up: she was indeed exactly what he needed in Hell, and he had waited long enough to get her.

When night came and the sad and hopeful young men had all gone home the Devil threw off his disguise and wished himself into the pretty lady's bedroom with a puff of red smoke and a noise like thunder. The pretty lady woke up at once, and when she saw him she shrieked.

"Don't be alarmed," said the Devil calmly. "It's only me. I've come to take you away to Hell."

"Never!" cried the pretty lady. "I shan't go and there's no way you can make me."

"That's true," said the Devil, "there isn't. You have to come of your own free will when you come before your time. But you'll like it so much down there. You'll be the prettiest thing in the place."

"I'm that already, right here," said the pretty lady, "for all the good it does me. Why should I go away to be the same thing somewhere else?"

"Ah, but in Hell," said the Devil, "your beauty will last forever and ever, whereas here it can only fade."

For the first time the pretty lady was tempted, and the Devil knew it. He fetched a mirror from her bureau and held it up in front of her so she could look at herself. "Wouldn't it be a shame," he coaxed, "to let such a pretty face go to waste? If you stay here, it can only last fifteen or twenty more years, but in Hell there is no time. You will look just as you do now till the stars fall and a new plan is made, and we all know that will never happen."

The pretty lady looked at herself in the mirror and felt, as she sometimes did, that it was rather nice to be pretty, but in the nick of time she remembered what it was she really wanted. "Tell me," she said, "is there any love in Hell?"

"Love?" said the Devil with a shudder. "What would we want with a thing like that?"

"Well then," said the pretty lady, pushing away the mirror, "I'll never agree to go. You can beg all you want from now till Sunday, but it won't be of any use."

At this the Devil grew very angry and his eyes glowed like embers. "Is this your final word?" he demanded.

"That is my final word," she answered.

"Very well!" he said. "I can't take you against your will, that's true. But I can take your beauty. I can, and I will." There was another clap of thunder and the Devil disappeared in a cloud of smoke. He went straight back to Hell and took all the pretty lady's beauty with him, and tacked it up in little fragments all over his throne room, where it sparkled and twinkled and brightened up the place very nicely.

After a couple of years, however, the Devil grew curious about the lady and went up to see how she was getting along. He arrived at her cottage at twilight and went to peer in through the window. And there she was, ugly as a boot, sitting down to supper. But candles lit the table and she was no longer alone. Sitting with her was a young man just as ugly as she, and in a cradle near her chair lay a very ugly baby. And the strange thing was that there was such love around the table that the Devil reeled back as if someone had struck him.

"Humph!" said the Devil to himself. "I'll never understand this if I live to be a trillion!"

So he went back to Hell in a temper and tore down all the lady's beauty from the walls of his throne room and threw it away, and it floated up out of Hell into a dark corner of the sky and made itself, more usefully, into a new star.

BOOKLIST: BOOKS ABOUT LOVE

Angleberger, Tom. *The Strange Case of Origami Yoda.* Amulet, 2010. The Yoda finger puppet worn by Dwight, the weirdest kid at McQuarrie Middle School, offers life-changing advice to any student who asks—including Tommy, who has finally decided to ask Hannah to dance. (Gr. 3–6)

Avi. *Romeo and Juliet Together (and Alive!) at Last.* Orchard, 1987. With his best friend secretly in love with fellow eighth-grader Anabell Stackpoole, Ed Sitrow spearheads a school production of Romeo and Juliet to bring the two together. (Gr. 5–7)

DiCamillo, Kate. *The Tale of Despereaux: Being the Story of a Mouse, a Princess, Some Soup, and a Spool of Thread.* Illus. by Timothy Basil Ering. Candlewick, 2003. Despereaux, a ridiculously small and sickly mouse with huge ears, falls madly in love with the Princess Pea, a human girl. (Gr. 4–8)

Henry, O. *The Gift of the Magi.* Illus. by P. J. Lynch. Candlewick, 2008. In this handsome picture book of the classic short story, a young husband and his wife each sell their most precious possession to buy one another special Christmas presents. (Gr. 6–Adult)

Jackson, Ellen. *Cinder Edna.* *Lothrop, 1994.* In a picture book for all ages, Cinderella's next-door neighbor, Edna, finds Prince Charming "borrring," but hits it off with his geeky younger brother, Rupert. Great for reading aloud or telling. (K–Gr. 6)

Kindl, Patrice. *Goose Chase.* *Houghton Mifflin, 2001.* Imprisoned in a tower, the Goose Girl must figure out a way to avoid marriage with two terrible suitors, both of whom care only for her diamond tears and gold-producing hair. (Gr. 5–8)

Kindl, Patrice. *Keeping the Castle.* *Viking, 2012.* In search of a wealthy husband to help support her mother and brother, spunky seventeen-year-old Althea Crawley of Yorkshire, England, hears that handsome Lord Boring has just arrived in town. A comedy of manners, reminiscent of Jane Austen's *Pride and Prejudice*, but more tongue-in-cheek. (Gr. 7–10)

Kindl, Patrice. *Owl in Love.* *Houghton Mifflin, 1993.* Fourteen-year-old Owl is in love with her science teacher. "I found out where he lives and every night I perch on a tree branch outside his bedroom window and watch him sleep." The catch? Owl is a wereowl: girl by day, owl by night. (Gr. 5–8)

Levine, Gail Carson. *Ella Enchanted.* *HarperCollins, 1997.* Cursed at birth by an interfering fairy's "gift" of obedience, fourteen-year-old Ella runs away from finishing school and gradually finds herself falling in love with her dearest friend, Prince Charmont. (Gr. 4–7)

McKinley, Robin. *Beauty: A Retelling of the Story of Beauty & the Beast.* *HarperCollins, 1978.* Because her father picks a rose for her from a stranger's castle garden, Beauty, the youngest and plainest of three sisters, must move in with the Beast. A novelized retelling of the old French fairy tale. (Gr. 6–10)

Napoli, Donna Jo. *The Prince of the Pond: Otherwise Known as De Fawg Pin.* *Dutton, 1992.* Jade—the frog narrator—aids, befriends, and falls in love with Pin, the new frog in the pond, formerly a human prince until his unfortunate encounter with a witch. (Gr. 4–7)

Schmidt, Gary D. *Okay for Now.* *Clarion, 2011.* In the companion to *The Wednesday Wars* (Clarion, 2007), twelve-year-old Doug Swieteck moves with his family to "stupid Marysville," New York, where the only saving graces are a girl named Lil and an elderly librarian, Mr. Powell, who gives him drawing lessons. (Gr. 6–9)

Spinelli, Jerry. *Stargirl.* *Knopf, 2000.* Sixteen-year-old Leo looks back on his junior year, when he fell for Stargirl, the iconoclastic, nonconformist new girl, who becomes popular and then is shunned by her classmates. (Gr. 6–9)

Stanley, Diane. *Bella at Midnight.* *HarperCollins, 2006.* In a new take on the Cinderella story, sixteen-year-old Bella is shattered when she must return to the unloving household of her father, Sir Edward. (Gr. 5–8)

Van Draanen, Wendelin. *Flipped.* *Knopf, 2001.* In alternating chapters, Bryce describes the six years he has spent avoiding his pesky, eccentric neighbor Julianna, who details her huge crush on blue-eyed Bryce. (Gr. 6–8)

At Death's Door

Not that death is any laughing matter, but some of these stories and suggested books give it a humorous spin, while others are more thoughtful or suspenseful. Fifth grade and up is the most appropriate audience for a storytelling session and booktalk on this subject.

The Calendar

By Barbara Ann Porte

Barbara Ann Porte's story "The Calendar," taken from Jesse's Ghost and Other Stories *(Morrow, 1983), is perfect for older kids who are impatient with chores and homework, and just can't seem to get themselves organized.*

There was a girl one time who never would do any of her chores, at least not well, and never in the proper order. It wasn't that she didn't try. She just couldn't seem to get things straight. She wasn't dumb, not by a long shot. She simply was not organized. Not a crime, of course, but inconvenient.

"You've got to get organized," that girl's mother told her over and over and over. Her mother, you see, was organized. Oh, she kept after her all right. After her and after her until she'd hear her own self shouting. "Hush," she would say then, glad they lived in the country with no neighbors to hear. There was just the girl's dad, and he was busy milking cows and shutting up his ears against the woman's sound, for it was high-pitched anytime that she was cranky, and having that girl for a daughter, she was very often cranky.

Well, such bickering and such reminding and such forgetting went on day in and day out, month in and month out, year after year until the girl was maybe twelve, perhaps thirteen, almost older than a girl.

Then when it was almost the New Year and snow was on the ground, the mother came home from town one day, lugging a heavy package wrapped up in bright paper. It was a gift, a calendar. It was a century calendar, and it was for the girl. For a hundred years she wouldn't need a new one.

"Here, have it," said the woman to her daughter. "Have and keep it. I will show you how." One thing about the girl's mother, you see, she was always willing to show how. She always knew the right and only way. The girl believed her. It was the only thing she had to go by.

So the girl's mother showed her how to write down her list of chores and other things to do neatly in the squares for the days she meant to do them and how to cross each one off in order when she'd done it. "List everything," her mother said, so she did.

On Monday she might write: "dusting, churning, clean the cobwebs from the barn, shell the beans for soup," and so on. She would cross off each chore when it was finished until she got to "brush my teeth" and "go to bed." Then she'd go to bed. Only sometimes, before she fell asleep, she'd look ahead to see what Tuesday held. Or, if she'd finished early on a Monday, she might do a Tuesday chore, then cross it off, leaving Tuesday free for Wednesday work. Now that she was better organized, this happened more and more. There came days when she was weeks, then weeks when she was months, before herself. Oh, was that girl's mother ever pleased. Why wouldn't she be? This went on for a long, long time until one day, the day I'm telling you about—on that day the girl came into the kitchen where her mother stood cooking.

"It's done," said the girl. "I have done it." She said it loud, in a proud, not girlish way.

And when the woman looked up from the pot that she was stirring, she did not see her daughter standing there in front of her. No, she didn't. Instead, she saw an old, old woman, older than herself, her voice old-woman high. It was the girl, you see. She'd finished up her life.

She stood there in the kitchen, older than her mother, holding out her calendar, and it was nearly all crossed out. That many years had the girl grown old.

(Caroline likes to end the story right here, with the sense of mystery. However, Porte's story continues on to a more macabre conclusion. What follows is the author's actual ending, which will appeal to sixth graders and up.)

The father of that girl took the calendar that day and buried it beside the rear barn wall. He was afraid, you see, although he didn't know why, to be rid of it completely. The girl, old woman, daughter, she stayed on, living on the farm, mostly keeping to her room.

Some years passed by. Then, one rainy night, a bolt of lightning stuck the barn, and fire burned it down, burned it to the ground. Afterward, when they went to the old woman's room to check on her, they found her dead. Some said she had suffocated. They buried her quick the next day. The casket was shut tight, shut tight, you see, so the rest wouldn't see, how that old woman's corpse was charred.

Bouki Cuts Wood

Retold by Harold Courlander, from The Piece of Fire and Other Haitian Tales

Uncle Bouki is the Haitian trickster, rascal, and fool, in the mold of Anansi the Spider from Africa, Coyote from the American Southwest, or Juan Bobo from Puerto Rico. He's a lazy man who always looks for the easy way out and the easy path to riches, which is why he gets tricked in turn most of the time by his wilier friend, Ti Malice. The late folklorist Harold Courlander collected many of these tales in Haiti and they are mighty funny. Here's one of our favorites, where Bouki is so clueless, he doesn't know if he is dead or not.

Bouki went out to cut wood in the pine forest. He climbed a tree, sat on a branch, and began to chop with his machete. A traveler came along and stopped to watch him. "Wye!" the man said. "Just look at that! He's sitting on the same branch that he's chopping. In a few minutes the branch will fall, and he'll be on the ground. How foolish can a person be?"

Bouki stopped chopping. "Who is the stupid man who calls me foolish?" He called down, "Are you trying to foretell the future? Only God knows what is going to happen."

The traveler said no more. He went on his way.

Bouki resumed his chopping. Just as the man predicted, the branch broke, and Bouki came down with it.

Bouki gave it some thought. "It was just as the man predicted," Bouki said. "He must be a *bocor*, a diviner."

He jumped on his donkey and rode after the man. When he caught up with him on the trail, he said, "*Bocor*, you told the truth. I didn't know you were a diviner. You predicted the future, and it came out just as you said. So tell me one more thing: When am I going to die?"

The traveler answered, "Who in his right mind wants to know that? But if you insist, I'll tell you." He thought for a moment. "You'll die when your donkey brays three times," he said, and continued on his way.

"Thank you, *bocor*, thank you," Bouki called after him. Then he said to himself, "Three times! This donkey is braying all the time!"

And as soon as they started back, the donkey opened is mouth and brayed.

"Stop! That's one already!" Bouki shouted.

The donkey brayed again.

"Stop! Stop! That's twice already!" Bouki shouted.

And as the donkey opened its mouth and stretched its neck to bray again, Bouki leaned over the animal's head and tried to push its jaws together. He struggled. The donkey struggled. Then it came—another bray.

"That's the end," Bouki said. "He brayed three times! Therefore, I must be dead!"

So he fell off the donkey and lay motionless at the side of the trail. He didn't try to get up, because dead men lie where they fall.

After a while, some farmers came along. "There is Bouki, sleeping on the trail," one of them said.

"No," another one said, poking Bouki with his hoe, "he must be dead."

They sat him up, but he fell down again.

"Yes," they said, "old Bouki is finished. We'll have to take him home."

They picked him up an carried him, feet first, head behind. As they walked, the donkey followed and sniffed at Bouki's face. Bouki sneezed. When the men heard that, they dropped Bouki on the ground and ran.

Bouki lay without moving. Some other farmers came along. "Look!" they said. "Old Bouki is dead!"

They also picked him up and carried him. After a little while they stopped. "Which trail goes to Bouki's house?" one of them asked.

"That one between the trees," another one said.

And another answered, "No, it's straight ahead."

They put Bouki on the ground while they argued. "This way," one said. "That way," another said.

Finally, without opening his eyes, Bouki moved his arm slowly until it pointed back the way they had come.

"It's not proper for the dead to argue," he said. "But all of you are wrong. We passed my trail way back there."

The farmers took a quick look at Bouki and began to run. Again he was alone. No one came. He lay patiently. After a while he felt a sensation in his stomach. "If I was alive," he thought, "that would mean that I am hungry. But as I'm dead, I must be mistaken."

After a while, he opened one eye slowly. He saw his donkey nuzzling an avocado that had fallen from a tree.

"Leave it!" Bouki shouted. He jumped to his feet and snatched the avocado away from the donkey. He opened it and ate.

Then he got on his donkey and started home. "Dead or not," he said, "I need a big bowl of rice and beans."

BOOKLIST: AT DEATH'S DOOR

Babbitt, Natalie. *Tuck Everlasting.* *Farrar, 1975.* Ten-year-old Winnie Foster meets the members of the Tuck family, who have discovered a fountain of youth. (Gr. 4–8)

Bragg, Georgia. *How They Croaked: The Awful Ends of the Awfully Famous.* *Illus. by Kevin O'Malley. Walker, 2011.* Gruesome but often funny tales about the deaths of nineteen historic figures. (Gr. 5–12)

Gaiman, Neil. *The Graveyard Book.* *Illus. by Dave McKean. HarperCollins, 2008.* After his family is brutally murdered, a toddler wanders into a nearby graveyard, where he is taken in and raised by ghosts. (Gr. 5–8)

Gantos, Jack. *Dead End in Norvelt.* *Farrar, 2011.* One memorable summer Jack becomes the scribe to the elderly Miss Volker, typing the obituaries she dictates for the old folks who are dropping like flies in their little town. (Gr. 5–8)

Morris, Gerald. *The Adventures of Sir Gawain the True: The Knights' Tales.* *Illus. by Aaron Renier. Houghton Mifflin, 2011.* When King Arthur's nephew, Sir Gawain the Undefeated, saves a damsel from a fire-breathing dragon, he is too self-involved to accept her gift of gratitude. (Gr. 3–5)

Oliver, Lauren. *Liesl & Po.* *Illus. by Kei Acedera. HarperCollins, 2011.* Three days after Liesl's father dies, two ghosts from the Other Side appear in her attic bedroom: a child named Po and a little, shadow-like ghost-pet named Bundle. (Gr. 4–7)

Peck, Richard. *A Long Way from Chicago: A Novel in Stories.* *Dial, 1998.* Starting in 1929, Joey and his kid sister spend August with their no-nonsense, whopper-spinning grandma in her small Illinois town. The relevant and hilarious stand-alone chapter to share is "Shotgun Cheatham's Last Night Above Ground." (Gr. 5–7)

Peck, Richard. *The Teacher's Funeral: A Comedy in Three Parts.* *Dial, 2004.* After the funeral of his teacher, Miss Myrt Arbuckle—of whom fifteen-year-old Russell Culver says, "She died of her own meanness"—he is stunned to discover that his older sister, Tansy, will be the new teacher at their one-room country schoolhouse. (Gr. 5–8)

Quicklist of Thematic Program Starters for Tweens, Ages 8 to 14

In this section, we provide you with thirty-five program ideas that we hope will engage you and your kids. For each program, we give you a brief overview of what you can do and, whenever relevant, a booklist of first-rate materials to read or tell aloud, booktalk, or simply put on display for kids to check out after your session. When we list books that seem to be for much younger children, fear not. These are fabulous picture books that even tweens and teens will enjoy. They will also be great fun to begin or end your program.

Other ideas will spring from the hottest new book or from the next movie based on a children's book. Think back to the over-the-top Harry Potter parties and the excitement surrounding the Hunger Games trilogy, the Wimpy Kid books, and the Percy Jackson and the Olympians series when they came out. Whatever that great new book or trend is this year, you'll no doubt come up with an inspiring, book-focused way to celebrate with your children.

Art Studio

Program description: Show illustrations of signature works by fine artists and children's book illustrators, or read aloud one of the books listed below to get everyone in the mood to make art. Put out a variety of materials and supplies—paints, crayons, markers, colored pencils, fabric scraps, glue, clay, construction paper. Instead of hewing to a pattern or a defined project, give children the freedom to create whatever they like.

BOOKLIST: ARTISTS

Carle, Eric. *The Artist Who Painted a Blue Horse*. *Illus. by the author. Philomel, 2011.* (PreK–Gr. 6)

Close, Chuck. *Chuck Close Face Book*. *Illus. with photos and reprods. Abrams, 2012.* (Gr. 3–8)

Colón, Raúl. *Draw!* *Illus. by the author. Simon & Schuster, 2014.* (PreK–Gr. 2)

Degen, Bruce. *I Gotta Draw*. *Illus. by the author. Harper, 2012.* (PreK–Gr. 3)

Gerstein, Mordicai. *The First Drawing*. *Illus. by the author. Little, Brown, 2013.* (PreK–Gr. 6)

Haseley, Dennis. *Twenty Heartbeats*. *Illus. by Ed Young. Roaring Brook, 2008.* (Gr. 1–6)

Look, Lenore. *Brush of the Gods*. *Illus. by Meilo So. Schwartz & Wade, 2013.* (K–Gr. 4)

Raczka, Bob. *Here's Looking at Me: How Artists See Themselves*. *Illus. with reprods. Millbrook, 2006.* (Gr. 3–6)

Raczka, Bob. *No One Saw: Ordinary Things through the Eyes of an Artist.* *Illus. with reprods. Millbrook, 2002.* (Gr. 3–6)

Saltzberg, Barney. *Beautiful Oops!* *Illus. by the author. Workman, 2010.* (K–Gr. 6)

Wiesner, David. *Art & Max.* *Illus. by the author. Clarion, 2010.* (PreK–Gr. 6)

Author/Illustrator Visits

Program description: Introducing children to an author or illustrator every year is a spectacular way to encourage an interest in that artist's works as well as writing and art in general. Sure, hosting a well-known author can be pricey, but it may make a difference in the way children regard literature. Your Friends of the Library or parent-teacher organizations may help foot the bill. Look locally for up-and-coming writers or artists, who may charge less in exchange for the opportunity to try out their stories on real kids. Many authors are doing visits by Skype or other face-to-face programs so they don't have to leave their writing desks. These are often inexpensive (sometimes even free). They may not be as personal as an in-building visit, but are certainly still worthwhile. To prepare for an author program, have children read, do projects on, and become very familiar with the books your speaker has written. Many schools and libraries decorate the walls with children's work related to the author or illustrator's work, and treat the day like a special holiday—which, of course, it is.

Babysitting Training

Program description: The American Red Cross gives many one-day babysitting training sessions in public libraries around the US for youth ages eleven to fifteen. They do charge a fee. For information visit their website, www.red cross.org. You could also invite a local day-care provider, a parent, or an experienced babysitter to do a session on how to care for children, change diapers, contact emergency services, and entertain children of varying ages (including, of course, how to read aloud to little ones).

BOOKLIST: BABYSITTING

Bertrand, Lynne. *Granite Baby.* *Illus. by Kevin Hawkes. Farrar, 2005.* (Gr. 1–4)

Fox, Mem. *Ten Little Fingers and Ten Little Toes.* *Illus. by Helen Oxenbury. Harcourt, 2008.* (PreK)

Frazee, Marla. ***The Boss Baby.*** *Illus. by the author. Beach Lane, 2010.* (PreK–Gr. 2)

Frazee, Marla. ***Walk On! A Guide for Babies of All Ages.*** *Illus. by the author. Harcourt, 2006.* (PreK–Gr. 2)

Harris, Robie. ***It's NOT the Stork! A Book about Girls, Boys, Babies, Bodies, Families, and Friends.*** *Illus. by Michael Emberley. Candlewick, 2006.* (K–Gr. 3)

Shea, Bob. ***Dinosaur vs. Bedtime.*** *Illus. by the author. Disney-Hyperion, 2010.* (PreK–Gr. 1)

Spratt, R. A. *The Adventures of Nanny Piggins. Illus. by Dan Santat. Little, Brown, 2010.* (Gr. 3–7)

Travers, P. L. ***Mary Poppins.*** *Illus. by Mary Shepard. Harcourt, 1934.* (Gr. 4–7)

Baseball Bash

Program description: In spring, celebrate baseball in poetry, prose, and song. Start with a chorus or two of "Take Me Out to the Ball Game." Read aloud a baseball story. Have two volunteers, a boy and a girl, perform the back-and-forth notes of "The Southpaw" by Judith Viorst (in Marlo Thomas's *Free to Be . . . You and Me*), in which best friends share barbs when Richard doesn't want Janet to play on his team. (Have them read this story—photocopied onto two colors of paper that you tear into scraps—as if they're actually reading from their notes to each other.) Read aloud Ernest Lawrence Thayer's "Casey at the Bat" (which most of today's children have never heard). Especially handsome is the Caldecott Honor Book *Casey at the Bat*, illustrated by Christopher Bing. Follow up with Dan Gutman's comical sequel, *Casey Back at Bat*. Talk about how baseball lingo has infiltrated the English language, using some of the examples in *Hey Batta Batta Swing! The Wild Old Days of Baseball* by Sally Cook and James Charlton. Then read aloud the following sentences and have listeners explain what they mean in baseball and in life.

Baseball Expressions

- Brendon was not exactly batting a thousand on his science test—he got every question wrong.
- The new school cost in the ballpark of two million dollars.
- Mrs. Vitali really threw her class a curveball when she announced a pop science quiz.
- When his parents couldn't find a babysitter, Abe stepped up to the plate and offered to stay home and take care of his little sisters, Molly and Julia.
- Talia invited Zoey to sleep over on Friday night, but said she'd have to take a rain check.
- Jake thought learning subtraction was hard, but division was a whole new ball game.
- Chris liked his new friend Kevin right off the bat.
- Sharron and Steve's social studies report on the Revolutionary War touched all bases.
- This year's school play was a smash hit.

BOOKLIST: BASEBALL (AND A FEW OTHER SPORTS)

Abbott & Costello. *Who's on First?* *Illus. by John Martz. Quirk, 2013.* (Gr. 2–6)

Adler, David A. *Lou Gehrig: The Luckiest Man.* *Illus. by Terry Widener. Harcourt, 1997.* (Gr. 2–5)

Burleigh, Robert. *Home Run: The Story of Babe Ruth.* *Illus. by Mike Wimmer. Harcourt, 1998.* (Gr. 2–4)

Burleigh, Robert. *Stealing Home: Jackie Robinson against the Odds.* *Simon & Schuster, 2007.* (Gr. 3–8)

Cline-Ransome, Lesa. *Satchel Paige.* *Illus. by James E. Ransome. Simon & Schuster, 2000.* (Gr. 2–5)

Cook, Sally, and James Charlton. *Hey Batta Batta Swing! The Wild Old Days of Baseball.* Illus. by Ross MacDonald. McElderry, 2007. (Gr. 1–8)

Coy, John. *Hoop Genius: How a Desperate Teacher and a Rowdy Gym Class Invented Basketball.* Illus. by Joe Morse. Carolrhoda, 2013. (Gr. 1–5)

Gutman, Dan. *Casey Back at Bat.* Illus. by Steve Johnson and Lou Fancher. Harper-Collins, 2007. (K–Gr. 8)

Gutman, Dan. *The Day Roy Riegels Ran the Wrong Way.* Illus. by Kerry Talbott. Bloomsbury, 2011. (Gr. 1–5)

Krull, Kathleen. *Lives of the Athletes: Thrills, Spills (and What the Neighbors Thought).* Illus. by Kathryn Hewitt. Harcourt, 1997. (Gr. 4–8)

Low, Alice. *The Fastest Game on Two Feet, and Other Poems about How Sports Began.* Illus. by John O'Brien. Holiday House, 2009. (Gr. 3–6)

Moss, Marissa. *Barbed Wire Baseball.* Illus. by Yuko Shimizu. Abrams, 2013. (Gr. 3–5)

Nelson, Kadir. *We Are the Ship: The Story of Negro League Baseball.* Illus. by the author. Hyperion/Jump at the Sun, 2008. (Gr. 3–12)

Piven, Hanoch. *What Athletes Are Made Of.* Illus. by the author. Atheneum, 2006. (Gr. 2–6)

Skead, Robert. *Something to Prove: The Great Satchel Paige vs. Rookie Joe DiMaggio.* Illus. by Floyd Cooper. Carolrhoda, 2013. (Gr. 2–6)

Tavares, Matt. *Becoming Babe Ruth.* Illus. by the author. Candlewick, 2013. (Gr. 1–5)

Tavares, Matt. *Henry Aaron's Dream.* Illus. by the author. Candlewick, 2010. (Gr. 2–6)

Thayer, Ernest Lawrence. *Casey at the Bat: A Ballad of the Republic Sung in the Year 1888.* Illus. by Christopher Bing. Handprint, 2000. (Gr. 2–Adult)

Thomas, Marlo. *Free to Be . . . You and Me.* Thirty-fifth anniversary edition. Developed and edited by Carole Hart and others; original volume, ed. by Francine Klagsbrun. Redesigned and illus. by Peter H. Reynolds. Running Press Kids, 2008, c1974. (Look up "The Southpaw" by Judith Viorst.) (K–Gr. 6)

Vernick, Audrey. *Brothers at Bat: The True Story of an Amazing All-Brother Baseball Team.* Illus. by Steven Salerno. Clarion, 2009. (K–Gr. 6)

Winter, Jonah. *You Never Heard of Sandy Koufax?!* Illus. by André Carilho. Schwartz & Wade, 2009. (Gr. 3–8)

Winter, Jonah. *You Never Heard of Willie Mays?!* Illus. by Terry Widener. Schwartz & Wade, 2013. (Gr. 3–8)

Battle of the Books

Program Description: Battle of the Books, a reading incentive program for students in grades three to twelve, got started in Alaska back in the 1970s by Roz Goodman, a wonderful school librarian. Each year, a school (or district or county or state) selects a list of about fifteen good books per grade level and develops questions about each book. Schools can also subscribe, for a fee, to America's Battle of the Books at www.battleofthebooks.org. Teams of five students compete to provide title and author for the book that answers each question. For the list of rules and a sample permission slip for the Manalapan-Englishtown (New Jersey) Middle School Media Center, go to www.mers.k12.nj.us and pull down the MEMS Media Center. Teams within a school or district compete, and in many places there is then a county or state competition. When Judy was a school librarian in New Jersey, she held an annual "In What Book" competition between the fifth-grade classes, where each student composed three questions, one per book, about fiction they had read and loved. You can have a more general contest using common titles and make up your own questions. The point is to get children excited about books and reading.

Ben Franklin, Renaissance Man

Program description: Introduce America's Renaissance man with a program of books, stories, and science. You'll get many ideas and games from The Electric Ben at www.ushistory.org/franklin/fun, as well as instructions on how to make bottle pipes reminiscent of Ben's musical invention, the Glass Armonica; a battery made from a lemon, which ties in with Ben's experiments with electricity; and letterpress stamps created from potatoes. You'll also find a link to his autobiography, *The Autobiography of Benjamin Franklin* (published posthumously in 1791), from which you can read an anecdote or two in his own words.

BOOKLIST: BEN FRANKLIN

Barretta, Gene. *Now & Ben: The Modern Inventions of Benjamin Franklin. Illus. by the author. Henry Holt, 2006.* (Gr. 1–4)

Byrd, Robert. *Electric Ben: The Amazing Life and Times of Benjamin Franklin. Dial, 2012.* (Gr. 2–6)

D'Aulaire, Ingri, and Edgar Parin D'Aulaire. *Benjamin Franklin.* Illus. by the authors. Doubleday, 1950. (K–Gr. 5)

Fleming, Candace. *Ben Franklin's Almanac: Being a True Account of the Good Gentleman's Life.* Illus. with paintings and reprods. Atheneum, 2003. (Gr. 5–Adult)

Franklin, Benjamin. *The Autobiography of Benjamin Franklin.* Dover, 1996. *(Or any other of many available editions.)* (Gr. 8–Adult)

Freedman, Russell. *Becoming Ben Franklin: How a Candle-Maker's Son Helped Light the Flame of Liberty.* Illus. with paintings and reprods. Holiday House, 2013. (Gr. 4–8)

Fritz, Jean. *What's the Big Idea, Ben Franklin?* Illus. by Margot Tomes. Coward, 1976. (Gr. 2–5)

Giblin, James Cross. *The Amazing Life of Benjamin Franklin.* Illus. by Michael Dooling. Scholastic, 2000. (Gr. 2–5)

Gutman, Dan. *Qwerty Stevens, Stuck in Time with Benjamin Franklin.* Simon & Schuster, 2002. (Gr. 3–6)

Harness, Cheryl. *The Remarkable Benjamin Franklin.* Illus. by the author. National Geographic, 2005. (Gr. 3–6)

Lawson, Robert. *Ben and Me: An Astonishing Life of Benjamin Franklin by His Good Mouse, Amos.* Illus. by the author. Little, Brown, 1939. (Gr. 4–8)

McDonough, Yona Zeldis. *The Life of Benjamin Franklin: An American Original.* Illus. by the author. Henry Holt, 2006. (Gr. 2–4)

Schanzer, Rosalyn. *How Ben Franklin Stole the Lightning.* Illus. by the author. HarperCollins, 2003. (Gr. 2–6)

St. George, Judith. *So You Want to Be an Inventor?* Illus. by David Small. Philomel, 2002. (Gr. 3–8)

Book Characters' Birthday Party

Program description: Have kids help you decorate the room with balloons and birthday-themed streamers, and set a birthday table with party favors and festive plates. Play party games like "Pin the Tail on the Rat" (from *The Tale of Despereaux*). Each child can decorate a book-themed cupcake to eat (though you'll want to ask about food allergies before doing this) complete with a red (unlit) candle they can pretend to blow out. For inspiration, look up *book cakes* online or on Pinterest. (Here's one set: pinterest.com/flamelauthor/book-cakes.) Combine it with a booktalk on books where characters celebrate a birthday, and sing the happy birthday song to them.

BOOKLIST: BIRTHDAYS

Cleary, Beverly. *Beezus and Ramona.* Illus. by Louis Darling. Morrow, 1955. (Gr. 2–5) (Read aloud Chapter 6: "Beezus's Birthday.")

Corbett, Sue. *12 Again.* Dutton, 2002. (Gr. 5–7)

Hurwitz, Johanna, ed. *Birthday Surprises: Ten Great Stories to Unwrap.* Morrow, 1995. (Gr. 3–7)

Lairamore, Dawn. *Ivy's Ever After.* Holiday House, 2010. (Gr. 4–7)

Law, Ingrid. *Savvy.* Dial, 2008. (Gr. 4–7)

Mass, Wendy. *11 Birthdays.* Scholastic, 2009. (Gr. 4–6)

Naylor, Phyllis Reynolds. *The Great Chicken Debacle.* Marshall Cavendish, 2001. (Gr. 3–6)

Urban, Linda. *A Crooked Kind of Perfect.* Harcourt, 2007. (Gr. 4–6)

Weeks, Sarah. *Oggie Cooder, Party Animal.* Illus. by Doug Holgate. Scholastic, 2009. (Gr. 2–4)

Book-Cover Rejuvenation

Program description: Have the dust jackets of some of your best books bit the dust, or do they look too old and ratty for anyone to pick up the book? Young artists to the rescue! Announce a Save-Our-Covers Rescue Program for Beleaguered Books. In the first session, booktalk a selection of great books with pitiful covers, emphasizing that these books are often rejected because their covers are worn and torn, old and outdated. Then show a handful of fabulous books with terrific, eye-catching covers and discuss the components that make each one work. (See our sample list below.) Have each child select one of the books you have booktalked (or one from a table covered with other sorry specimens) to take home to read. Give each child a piece of rough copy paper so they can sketch out a new cover. Remind them to include the title, author, spine, and front and back covers. They can even create book flaps with a blurb. In session two, the children go to work with assorted art materials (pens, pencil, markers, etc.) and create beautiful new dust jackets. Cover their final work with Mylar dust jacket covers, and have a book display of the newly finished books. Think about holding a reception for the artists and their rejuvenated books.

BOOKLIST: FABULOUS BOOKS WITH TERRIFIC COVERS

Angleberger, Tom. *The Strange Case of Origami Yoda*. Illus. by the author. Amulet, 2010. (Gr. 3–6)

Applegate, Katherine. *The One and Only Ivan*. Illus. by Patricia Castelao. Harper, 2012. (Gr. 3–7)

Auxier, Jonathan. *The Night Gardener*. Amulet, 2014. (Gr. 5–8)

Bell, Cece. *El Deafo*. Illus. by the author. Amulet, 2014. (Gr. 3–7)

Black, Holly. *Doll Bones*. Illus. by Eliza Wheeler. McElderry, 2013. (Gr. 5–8)

Boyce, Frank Cottrell. *Cosmic*. HarperCollins/Walden Pond, 2010. (Gr. 5–8)

Bruel, Nick. *Bad Kitty Gets a Bath*. Illus. by the author. Roaring Brook, 2008. (Gr. 1–4)

DiCamillo, Kate. *Flora & Ulysses: The Illuminated Adventures*. Candlewick, 2013. (Gr. 3–6)

DiCamillo, Kate. *The Miraculous Journey of Edward Tulane*. Candlewick, 2006. (Gr. 3–7)

Draper, Sharon M. *Out of My Mind*. Atheneum, 2010. (Gr. 4–8)

Erdrich, Louise. *Chickadee*. Illus. by the author. Hyperion, 1999. (Gr. 3–6)

Holm, Jennifer L. *The Fourteenth Goldfish*. Random House, 2014. (Gr. 4–6)

Korman, Gordon. *Swindle*. Scholastic, 2008. (Gr. 4–7)

Lin, Grace. *Where the Mountain Meets the Moon*. Illus. by the author. Little, Brown, 2009. (Gr. 2–6)

Mass, Wendy. *11 Birthdays*. Scholastic, 2009. (Gr. 4–6)

Palacio, R. J. *Wonder*. Knopf, 2012. (Gr. 4–8)

Peirce, Lincoln. *Big Nate: In a Class by Himself*. Illus. by the author. HarperCollins, 2010. (Gr. 3–6)

Phelan, Matt. *Bluffton: My Summers with Buster*. Illus. by the author. Candlewick, 2013. (Gr. 3–7)

Schmidt, Gary D. *Okay for Now*. Illus. with paintings by John James Audubon. Clarion, 2011. (Gr. 5–8)

Spinelli, Jerry. *Hokey Pokey*. Knopf, 2013. (Gr. 4–8)

Telgemeier, Raina. *Smile!* Illus. by the author. Graphix, 2010. (Gr. 5–8)

Weeks, Sarah. *Pie*. Scholastic, 2011. (Gr. 4–6)

Book Jigsaw Puzzles

Program description: Ask children to pick a favorite book and draw a book cover for it on white poster board with the title, author, and a full-page colorful illustration. Have them cut their covers into curvy pieces, jigsaw puzzle style. Store each puzzle in a labeled color envelope. Children can trade puzzles and assemble them. Have a variety of good books with good covers on hand.

Book Speed-Dating One

Program description: Spread out a hefty stack of marvelous books on your tables. Titles can be an eclectic assortment of newest or best books or books in a single genre—historical fiction, humorous fiction, graphic novel, free verse, nonfiction, etc. Ask each child to select one book from a table. Give them three to five minutes to read the blurb and the first several pages of their chosen title. When the timer goes off, readers tell one another about their book and why they liked it (or didn't). Each reader has first dibs on the book he or she sampled, but put a sign-up sheet Post-it note on the back cover of each book for others who may want to read it, too, and put

them on the reserve list. Students then move on to the next table and do the same thing with the books there. This activity also works with picture books, easy-to-read fiction, nonfiction, and poetry for the kindergarten-through-grade-2 set.

Book Speed-Dating Two

Program description: This is a student-generated version of book speed-dating. Students go to the shelves and locate one book they loved and would like to recommend to others. Back at the tables, each person in that group has one minute to "sell" that book to the rest of his or her tablemates. The seller puts a little sticky note on the book and takes down the names of each person who would like to read the book; the first person on the list has dibs; others get their names on the reserve list. Although students will do the final book selection, you should demonstrate how to select a book and then do two one-minute pep talks on it to model a few different ways to get everyone excited to read it.

Book Brags

Program description: At the end of the school year, have your students make a list of the best books they read during the year that they would recommend for the students coming into that grade in September. Have them make a large decorated poster, with titles and authors and spot illustrations, that you can laminate and put up when new kids arrive in the fall. You can call it something like, "Books the Fifth-Grade Class of 2016 Recommends for the Fifth-Grade Class of 2017" (or something much spiffier, which the kids can suggest). As inspiration, show them your own top-ten titles from the past year.

Book Love Notes

Program Description: What are your top-ten books ever? Do a presentation on your best books ever, whether they're picture books, fiction, informational, poetry, or a combination. Hand out neon-colored 5-by-8-inch sticky notes and some paper. Have children make a list of their favorites and pull as many as they can find from the library shelves. Then have them create and decorate book love notes, writing a personal message on the order of, "This is one of my favorite books ever because _____!" or something pithier. After they sign and date the note, they can stick it on the inside front or back cover for someone else to discover as a nice surprise.

Fantasy Book Club

Program description: Having a monthly fantasy book club will allow you to share and read novels based on folktales or folkloric themes, and to try out all different subgenres of fantasy, including high fantasy, animal fantasy, and fantasy set in other worlds. Some fantasies pull magic into our world, such as in Wendy Mass's *11 Birthdays,* in which Amanda keeps reliving her eleventh birthday and Rick Riordan's *The Lightning Thief,* in which a contemporary kid meets up with a cast of Greek gods and goddesses in modern dress. Some fantasies start in our world but end up somewhere else, such as Norton Juster's *The Phantom Tollbooth* and Lauren Oliver's *The Spindlers.* A third type of fantasy takes place in its own richly imagined world.

Let's say you choose to read one of a third type: *Rump: The True Story of Rumpelstiltskin* by Liesl Shirtliff, which provides a backstory to the Rumpelstiltskin tale, narrated by the eponymous guy himself. In discussing this book with your club members, you'll want to read aloud or tell the story of "Rumpelstiltskin" and show/read/discuss its many variants from various countries. You should also share picture-book parodies, such as *Rumpelstiltskin's Daughter* by Diane Stanley. Your club members can compare the reworkings of other fairy tale retellings and parodies, such as *Ella Enchanted* by Gail Carson Levine. Since the miller's daughter has to spin straw into gold, you might enlist a local weaver to demonstrate how to spin wool into yarn with a drop spindle or find a video that shows the process. From here your club can move on to explore other genres or start a genres book club.

BOOKLIST: FANTASY FICTION

Juster, Norton. *The Phantom Tollbooth. Illus. by Jules Feiffer. Random House, 1961.* (Gr. 5–8)

Levine, Gail Carson. *Ella Enchanted. HarperCollins, 1997.* (Gr. 4–7)

Harrold, A. F. *The Imaginary. Illus. by Emily Gravett. Bloomsbury, 2015.* (Gr. 3–6)

Mass, Wendy. *11 Birthdays. Scholastic, 2009.* (Gr. 4–6)

Oliver, Lauren. *The Spindlers. Illus. by Kei Acedera. HarperCollins, 2011.* (Gr. 4–7)

Riordan, Rick. *The Lightning Thief. (Percy Jackson & the Olympians, Book 1) Hyperion, 2005.* (Gr. 5–8)

Shirtliff, Liesl. *Rump: The True Story of Rumpelstiltskin.* *Knopf, 2013.* (Gr. 3–6)

Stanley, Diane. *Bella at Midnight.* *HarperCollins, 2006.* (Gr. 5–8)

Stanley, Diane. *Rumpelstiltskin's Daughter.* *Illus. by the author. Morrow, 1997.* (Gr. 2–6)

Ice Cream!

Program description: Did you know that July is National Ice Cream Month in the US? Read aloud an ice cream book or two, such as *Should I Share My Ice Cream?* by Mo Willems, which is a wonderful book for kids of all ages to act out as a soliloquy if you can project it on a screen. You play Piggie and your participants play Elephant trying to decide whether to share his cone. After dramatizing the story, hand out the words to the Shel Silverstein's poem "Eighteen Flavors" from *Where the Sidewalk Ends*, and Jack Prelutsky's "Bleezer's Ice Cream" from *The New Kid on the Block.* (There's a very cute animated video of this at www.youtube.com/watch?v = YuPlUQvViX8). Read the words as a group.

You know how Ben & Jerry's always comes up with interesting new flavors based on celebrities? There's Stephen Colbert's Americone Dream and the ridiculously delicious Cherry Garcia (vanilla ice cream, fudge flakes, and cherries), named after the late Grateful Dead singer, Jerry Garcia. Bring in a container of one of these to show. Then have children invent the flavor of their dreams, based on a larger-than-life book character. Using a Ben & Jerry's container as inspiration, make a template with a blank face for kids to design. They can paste these on actual pint containers.

As a grand finale, have the kids make ice cream! If you have access to an electric or hand-cranked ice cream maker, great. Hand-cranked is probably better, as everyone can take a turn. But children can make their own ice cream with a Ziploc bag, ice cubes, half-and-half, and some rock salt. With kids helping to hold, measure and pour, here's what you do:

1. For each child, fill a gallon-size Ziploc bag half full with ice cubes and ½ cup kosher or rock salt. (If you can, fill these bags in advance and put them in a freezer).
2. With each child, fill a pint-size Ziploc bag with one cup of half-and-half, two tablespoons sugar, and ½ teaspoon vanilla extract. Seal each bag carefully.
3. Insert the small sealed bag into the gallon-size bag. Seal the bigger bag carefully.

4. Ask the children to shake their bags for about five minutes or until the cream mixture hardens.

5. After they remove the small bag from the big one—and wipe it off with a paper towel—they can add chocolate chips, strawberries, or whatever mix-ins you provide. They can spoon their treats right out of the bag. Delish!

BOOKLIST: ICE CREAM

Prelutsky, Jack. *The New Kid on the Block.* *Illus. by James Stevenson. Greenwillow, 1984.* (Read aloud "Bleezer's Ice Cream" on page 48.) (K–Gr. 8)

Silverstein, Shel. *Where the Sidewalk Ends.* *Illus. by the author. HarperCollins, 1974.* (Read aloud "Eighteen Flavors" on page 116.) (K–Gr. 8)

Willems, Mo. *Should I Share My Ice Cream? Illus. by the author. Hyperion, 2011.* (PreK–Gr. 2)

Library Scavenger Hunt

Program description: Your goal is to familiarize children with the offerings of the library—including fiction, nonfiction, biography, picture books, poetry, and folklore—and help the children locate them on the shelves. A scavenger hunt with clues for your pirate-crew children is a fun way to do this. Do a pirate booktalk and then divide your group into teams. Give each team a different list of "treasures" to find. For example, they might be asked to find a fiction book about a dog, a photograph of an egret, a map of Thailand, a picture of the person on a hundred-dollar bill, a recipe for cookies, a poem about a tree, a picture book by Mo Willems, a fiction book by Kate DiCamillo, the year of Amelia Earhart's birth and death, and so on. Give teams a time limit, reminding them to use the library's catalog as well as their common sense to find items on their lists. Although you can also have children do an online hunt—looking up answers and recording them—a physical one is more fun. Ask players to bring their swag to their team's table. (If you fear the library's shelves will be disheveled, supply each team with shelf markers to use.) At the end, have each team read its list aloud, holding up their findings so everyone else can see what they came up with. If you like, give members of the winning team small prizes or give everyone a cute bookmark, a pirate eye-patch, or a Hershey's Kiss.

BOOKLIST: PIRATES

Florian, Douglas. *Shiver Me Timbers: Pirate Poems & Paintings*. *Illus. by Robert Neu-becker. Beach Lane, 2012.* (Gr. 1–6)

Gaiman, Neil. *Fortunately, the Milk*. *Illus. by Slottie Young. Harper, 2013.* (Gr. 3–6)

Helquist, Brett. *Roger the Jolly Pirate*. *HarperCollins, 2004.* (K–Gr. 3)

Long, Melinda. *How I Became a Pirate*. *Illus. by David Shannon. Harcourt, 2003.* (PreK–Gr. 2)

Mad Science

Program description: Do a science experiment with your group, and then send them off to one of several experiment stations you've set up with cool things to do. Visit "Science Bob" Pflugfelder's splendid website (www.sciencebob .com), which will help you come up with some awe-inspiring tricks. Pflug-felder provides easy-to-follow, printed instructions ("You Will Need," "What to Do," "How Does It Work") and questions to ask as kids practice "Random Acts of Science." Some of his experiments include "Blobs in a Bottle (The World's Easiest Lava Lamp)," "Chicken Sounds from a Cup," and "Make a Paperclip Float," all doable within the confines of a classroom or library. Print out the instructions for children, working in groups of three to five, and away they go. Show them the many tempting science experiment books on the 507 and 508 shelves in the library.

BOOKLIST: SCIENCE AND SCIENTISTS

Ardley, Neil. *101 Great Science Experiments*. *Illus. with photos. DK, 2006.* (Gr. 3–6)

Barnett, Mac. *Oh No! Or, How My Science Project Destroyed the World*. *Illus. by Dan Santat. Disney-Hyperion Books, 2010.* (PreK–Gr. 3)

Benton, Jim. *The Fran That Time Forgot*. *Illus. by the author. Simon & Schuster, 2005.* (And others in the Franny K. Stein, Mad Scientist series.) (Gr. 2–5)

Branzei, Sylvia. *Hands-on Grossology*. *Illus. by Jack Keely. Price Stern Sloan, 2003.* (Gr. 2–6)

Cobb, Vicky, and Kathy Darling. *We Dare You! Hundreds of Science Bets, Challenges, and Experiments You Can Do at Home*. *Illus. by True Kelly, Meredith Johnson, and Stella Orinai. Skyhorse, 2008.* (Gr. 3–7)

Cole, Joanna. *The Magic School Bus and the Science Fair Expedition*. *Illus. by Bruce Degen. Scholastic, 2006.* (Gr. 1–4)

Dowell, Frances O'Roark. *Phineas L. MacGuire . . . Erupts! The First Experiment. Illus. by Preston McDaniels. Atheneum, 2006.* (And others in the Phineas L. MacGuire series.) (Gr. 2–5)

Masoff, Joy. *Oh Yuck! The Encyclopedia of Everything Nasty. Illus.* by Terry Sirrell. *Workman, 2000.* (Gr. 4–8)

Mills, J. Elizabeth. *The Everything Kids' Easy Science Experiments Book: Explore the World of Science through Quick and Fun Experiments! Illus. by Kurt Dolber. Adams Media, 2010.* (Gr. 3–6)

Ofill, Jenny. *11 Experiments That Failed. Illus.* by Nancy Carpenter. *Schwartz & Wade, 2011.* (PreK–Gr. 4)

Robinson, Tom. *The Everything Kids' Science Experiments Book: Boil Ice, Float Water, Measure Gravity—Challenge the World around You! Adams Media, 2001.* (Gr. 3–6)

Scieszka, Jon. *Science Verse. Illus.* by Lane Smith. *Viking, 2004.* (Gr. 2–8)

Sierra, Judy. *The Secret Science Project That Almost Ate the School. Illus.* by Stephen *Gammell. Simon & Schuster, 2006.* (PreK–Gr. 3)

Movies: What's Playing?

Program description: Invite a local newspaper reviewer or someone on the news staff who regularly sees G or PG rated movies to meet with your group. Reproduce some movie reviews from online sources or from your local newspaper. Hold a movie-review session and discussion of the latest films, especially ones inspired by children's books. Have children make book-into-movie posters to display for a Book-into-Movie Night, during which you show a book-based film and lead a discussion comparing and evaluating the book and the movie. You might want to add a review section to your library, classroom, or school's website, "Books into Movies: What's New, What's Worth Reading and Seeing, and Why," showcasing kids' reviews.

BOOKLIST: MOVIES

Avi. *Silent Movie. Illus.* by C. B. Mordan. *Atheneum, 2003.* (Gr. 1–6)

DePaola, Tomie. *26 Fairmount Avenue. Illus.* by the author. *Putnam, 1999.* (Read aloud Chapter 3 where five-year-old Tomie goes to see Mr. Walt Disney's new movie, Snow White.) (Gr. 1–4)

Selznick, Brian. *Wonderstruck: A Novel in Words and Pictures. Illus.* by the author. *Scholastic, 2011.* (Gr. 4–8)

Mummies

Program description: What kid doesn't love to learn about mummies? Share a mummy book or two and then make 6- to 8-inch stick-figure people out of bendable wire or flexible garden ties. Wrap them with thin torn strips of white gauze, muslin, or old white sheets. Tie the ends so they don't come undone. Since they're bendable, children can arrange them in any way. Make little cat mummies, if the figures need a royal pet.

BOOKLIST: MUMMIES

Aliki. *Mummies Made in Egypt.* *Illus. by the author. Crowell, 1987.* (Gr. 3–6)

Clements, Andrew. *Temple Cat.* *Illus. by Kate Kiesler. Clarion, 1996.* (K–Gr. 4)

Cole, Joanna. *Ms. Frizzle's Adventures: Ancient Egypt.* *Illus. by Bruce Degen. Scholastic, 2005.* (Gr. 1–4)

Hall, Katy, and Lisa Eisenberg. *Mummy Riddles.* *Illus. by Nicole Rubel. Dial, 1997.* (Gr. 1–4)

Hawass, Zahi A. *Curse of the Pharaohs: My Adventures with Mummies.* *Illus. with photos. National Geographic, 2004.* (Gr. 4–8)

Hawass, Zahi A. *Tutankhamun: The Mystery of the Boy King.* *Illus. with photos. National Geographic, 2005.* (Gr. 3–7)

LaFevers, R. L. *Theodosia and the Serpents of Chaos.* *Illus. by Yoko Tanaka. Houghton Mifflin, 2007.* (Gr. 4–7)

Putnam, James. *Mummy. (Eyewitness Book)* *Photos by Peter Hayman. DK, 2009.* (Gr. 4–8)

Riordan, Rick. *The Red Pyramid.* *Disney-Hyperion, 2010.* (Gr. 5–9)

Scieszka, Jon. *Tut, Tut. (Time Warp Trio Series)* *Illus. by Lane Smith. Viking, 1996.* (Gr. 2–5)

Sloan, Christopher. *Mummies! Dried, Tanned, Sealed, Drained, Frozen, Embalmed, Stuffed, Wrapped, and Smoked . . . and We're Dead Serious.* *Illus. with photos. National Geographic, 2010.* (Gr. 3–6)

Weitzman, David. *Pharaoh's Boat.* *Illus. by the author. Houghton Mifflin, 2009.* (Gr. 4–8)

Mystery Party

Program description: Hold a Mystery Party for young sleuths in honor of book detectives like Encyclopedia Brown, Cam Jansen, and Precious Ramotswe. You can keep things simple or you can make fancy clues and hide them in sequence around your room. The post "How to throw a mystery party for kids, lazy Type B mom style" on the Mom-101 website (www.mom-101.com/2012/07/how-to-throw-a-mystery-party-for-kids-lazy-type-b-mom-style .html) gives you options and will make you laugh a lot. You can have older kids write and perform their own mystery play, an original one or one based on a children's book, like Marjorie Weinman Sharmat's *Nate the Great* or Margie Palatini's *The Web Files*. If kids write a script for and perform an Encyclopedia Brown story, the audience can try to solve the mystery.

BOOKLIST: MYSTERIES

Adler, David A. *Cam Jansen and the Mystery of the Dinosaur Bones.* *Illus. by Susanna Natti. Viking, 1981.* (Gr. 2–4)

Child, Lauren. *Utterly Me, Clarice Bean.* *Illus. by the author. Candlewick, 2003.* (Gr. 2–5)

Cronin, Doreen. *The Trouble with Chickens.* *Illus. by Kevin Cornell. Balzer + Bray, 2011.* (Gr. 2–5)

Ferraiolo, Jack D. *The Big Splash.* *Amulet, 2008.* (Gr. 5–7)

Landy, Derek. *Skulduggery Pleasant.* *HarperCollins, 2007.* (Gr. 5–8)

Palatini, Margie. *The Web Files.* *Illus. by Richard Egielksi. Hyperion, 2001.* (K–Gr. 3)

Reynolds, Aaron. *Joey Fly, Private Eye, in Creepy Crawly Time.* *Illus. by Neil Numberman. Henry Holt, 2009.* (Gr. 3–6)

Roberts, Willo Davis. *The View from the Cherry Tree.* *Atheneum, 1975.* (Gr. 5–8)

Sharmat, Marjorie Weinman. *Nate the Great.* *Illus. by Marc Simont. Coward, 1972.* (K–Gr. 3)

Smith, Alexander McCall. *The Great Cake Mystery: Precious Ramotswe's First Case.* *Illus. by Iain McIntosh. Random House/Anchor Books, 2012.* (Gr. 3–5)

Sobol, Donald J. *Encyclopedia Brown, Boy Detective.* *Illus. by Leonard Shortall. Nelson, 1963.* (Gr. 3–6)

Origami Operations

Program description: Demonstrate how to create various origami figures and let children create their own. Tie your session to Tom Angleberger's *The Strange Case of Origami Yoda*. You can have the kids make the "World's Simplest Origami Yoda" (instructions are on the author's website, www.origamiyoda.com), but if you have any proficiency with origami or know anyone else who does, give children the opportunity to do more complex folding. You'll find scores of videos and step-by-step illustrated instructions on Origami Instructions (www.origami-instructions.com); the diagrams and animated instructions on Origami Club (en.origami-club.com) will help make you look like a pro. Pick three or four figures and learn them by heart.

BOOKLIST: ORIGAMI

Angleberger, Tom. *The Strange Case of Origami Yoda*. *Illus. by the author. Amulet, 2010.* (Gr. 3–6)

George, Kristine O'Connell. *Fold Me a Poem*. *Illus. by Lauren Stringer. Harcourt, 2005.* (Gr. 1–4)

Meinking, Mary. *Easy Origami: A Step-by-Step Guide for Kids*. *Illus. with photos. Capstone, 2009.* Move up to *Not-Quite-So-Easy Origami*, then Chris Alexander's *Sort-of-Difficult Origami* and *Difficult Origami* (all 2009). (Gr. 2–6)

Paperback Swap

Program description: You don't always have to arrange a book fair to put new books into the hands of children. Try a paperback swap. You can do it with a group, a class, a grade level, or even a whole school. On a given week, ask participants to bring in one or more paperbacks in good condition. Log in the name of each participant on a database or chart, and write down how many books he or she has brought in. Return the books that seem to be family treasures or on their last legs. You may receive far more than you expect, so give yourself a day to set out everything on tables or carts. On the day of the swap, hand out tickets. Each child receives one less ticket than the number of books he or she brought in (if a girl brings in, say, four books, give her three tickets to spend). This will help ensure you have enough books for everyone. Let older children know it's OK to bring in picture books; other participants might want good books to read to younger siblings.

Plant a Garden; Harvest a Feast

Project Description: If your school or library has space outside for a small garden, have a cadre of kids help you prepare the soil and plant flowers, vegetables, or even a tree. Do you know a local landscaper or a forest ranger? Maybe he or she would do a workshop for you on how to plant and care for a garden or identify trees. If you have no outside space, window boxes might be just the thing.

BOOKLIST: GARDENS AND GARDENING

Aston, Dianna Hutts. *A Seed Is Sleepy*. *Illus. by Sylvia Long. Chronicle, 2007.* (PreK–Gr. 4)

Chine, Jason. *Redwoods*. *Illus. by the author. Roaring Brook/Flash Point, 2009.* (Gr. 1–4)

George, Kristine O'Connell. *Old Elm Speaks: Tree Poems*. *Illus. by Kate Kiesler. Clarion, 1998.* (Gr. 2–6)

Gourley, Robbin. *Bring Me Some Apples and I'll Make You a Pie: A Story about Edna Lewis*. *Clarion, 2009.* (Gr. 1–4)

Hopkins, H. Joseph. *Tree Lady: The True Story of How One Tree-Loving Woman Changed a City Forever*. *Illus. by Jill McElmurry. Beach Lane, 2013.* (Gr. 1–4)

Kadohata, Cynthia. *Weedflower*. *Atheneum, 2006.* (Gr. 5–8)

Nivola, Claire A. *Planting the Trees of Kenya: The Story of Wangari Maathai*. *Illus. by the author. Farrar, 2008.* (Gr. 1–4)

Stevens, Janet. *Tops & Bottoms*. *Illus. by the author. Harcourt, 1995.* (PreK–Gr. 2)

Poetry Slam

Program description: Hold a session where children are encouraged to read aloud or recite either their favorite published poems or ones they have written. In a formal slam, participants are expected to perform the poems they have composed. Have a microphone on a stand so each performer can face the group and be heard. This idea can be expanded to a series of workshops on writing and performing poetry and on the work of established poets. At globalwrites.org/student-work you can watch "Grand Slam," a video demonstrating how Global Writes, a Bronx-based nonprofit, inspires teens to write and perform their works. The following list includes books that introduce poetic forms, and/or contain information on how to write and/or perform poetry.

BOOKLIST: POETRY

Harley, Avis. *Fly with Poetry: An ABC of Poetry.* *Illus. by the author. Boyds Mills, 2000.* (Gr. 2–6)

Janeczko, Paul B. *A Kick in the Head: An Everyday Guide to Poetic Forms.* *Illus. by Chris Raschka. Candlewick, 2005.* (Gr. 5–8)

Janeczko, Paul B. *Poetry from A to Z: A Guide for Young Writers.* *Simon & Schuster, 1994.* (Gr. 4–8)

Janeczko, Paul B. *Seeing the Blue Between: Advice and Inspiration for Young Poets.* *Candlewick, 2002.* (Gr. 4–8)

Kennedy, X. J., comp. *Knock at a Star: A Child's Introduction to Poetry.* *Illus. by Karen Ann Weinhaus. Little, Brown, 1982.* (Gr. 3–6)

Prelutsky, Jack, ed. *Read a Rhyme, Write a Rhyme.* *Illus. by Meilo So. Knopf, 2005.* (Gr. 1–4)

Puppet-Making Workshop

Program description: In the first session, children can create puppets out of old socks or gloves, felt, paper bags, and other found materials. For session two, divide them into small groups to develop puppet shows based on a book, story, or their own collaborative imaginations. In session three, give them an opportunity to practice their plays, which they can present in session four, for an audience of younger children. See chapter 2, "Puppetry," p. 47, for books about poetry and stories to perform.

Reading Aloud to Young'uns

Program description: Tweens who look after younger siblings or who are starting to babysit can use a bit of cheering on to read to their young charges. Hold a session where you model read-aloud techniques, showcase the kinds of books young children like, and give participants an opportunity to practice reading aloud to each other with expression. Distribute an annotated booklist of great books for babies, toddlers, and preschoolers or duplicate our "Booklist: Best Picture Books for Babies and Toddlers" on page 269.

Say Cheese: Photography

Program description: Provide simple picture-taking pointers for amateur photographers. If your own photography skills are not up to par, ask a parent who is knowledgeable and experienced, a teacher of photography, or a professional photographer to help out. You'll want to cover how to shoot, save, manipulate, organize, and print using a smart phone, tablet, or digital camera. Take kids on a photo shoot around the building or outside. Print out pictures on a color printer and critique them as a group. Post the photos on a bulletin board—real or virtual—or make scrapbooks of digital photos on the computer. Showcase photography books, books illustrated with photographs (such as travel or animal books), biographies of famous photographers, and, if you have any tucked away in an attic somewhere, vintage photography equipment.

BOOKLIST: PHOTOGRAPHY

Armstrong, Jennifer. *Photo by Brady: A Picture of the Civil War*. *Atheneum, 2005.* (Gr. 6–12)

Bishop, Nic. *Nic Bishop Spiders*. *Photos by the author. Scholastic, 2007.* (PreK–Gr. 5)

Goldstone, Bruce. *That's a Possibility! A Book about What Might Happen*. *Photos by the author. Henry Holt, 2013.* (Gr. 1–5)

Hughes, Langston. *My People*. *Photos by Charles R. Smith. Atheneum, 2009.* (K–Gr. 12)

Kerley, Barbara. *One World, One Day*. *Illus. with photos. National Geographic, 2009.* (K–Gr. 4)

Lurie, Susan. *Swim, Duck, Swim!* *Photos by Murray Head. Feiwel and Friends, 2014.* (PreK–Gr. 2)

Martin, Jacqueline Briggs. *Snowflake Bentley*. *Illus. by Mary Azarian. Houghton Mifflin, 1998.* (Gr. 1–5)

Nau, Thomas. *Walker Evans: Photographer of America*. *Photos by Walker Evans. Roaring Brook/Neal Porter, 2007.* (Gr. 6–9)

Partridge, Elizabeth. *Restless Spirit: The Life and Work of Dorothea Lange*. *Photos by Dorothea Lange. Viking, 1998. (Gr. 6–12)*

Sing Out!

Program description: If you like to sing, organize a program of sing-along songs. or invite a musician friend/duo/band to conduct the session. Make a songbook of the songs being performed and give participants a copy. Children can add illustrations, if they like. For songs and great music-related book suggestions see chapter 5, "Music," on page 159.

Spelling Bee

Program description: Hold a spelling bee in your classroom, school, or library. Make a list of easy, medium, and hard words. You can hand out the list in advance if you like. Consider giving extra points if spellers can use the word in a sentence, and a bonus if the sentence is an interesting or clever one.

BOOKLIST: SPELLING

Best, Cari. *Beatrice Spells Some Lulus and Learns to Write a Letter.* *Illus. by Giselle Potter. Farrar/Margaret Ferguson, 2013.* (K–Gr. 2)

Clements, Andrew. *Frindle.* *Simon & Schuster, 1996.* (Gr. 4–7)

Ferris, Jeri Chase. *Noah Webster and His Words.* *Illus. by Vincent X. Kirsch. Houghton Mifflin, 2012.* (Gr. 2–5)

Frasier, Debra. *Miss Alaineus: A Vocabulary Disaster.* *Illus. by the author. Harcourt, 2000.* (Gr. 2–5)

Lichtenheld, Tom, and Ezra Fields-Meyer. *E-mergency!* *Illus. by Tom Lichtenheld. Chronicle, 2011.* (K–Gr. 3)

Rose, Deborah Lee. *The Spelling Bee before Recess.* *Illus. by Carey F. Armstrong-Ellis. Abrams, 2013.* (Gr. 1–4)

Take-Apart Day

Program description: Ask friends, family, and other adults give you small appliances, cameras, old phones and even DVD players, computers, and vacuum cleaners that no longer work. Obviously, you won't want anything with dangerous substances inside. Infinitely curious about how things work, children will have great fun taking these items apart to see how everything connects and goes together. You'll need screwdrivers of varying sizes, boxes to put the pieces in, paper towels, and plastic cloths to cover your tables. If you have friends who are scientists or engineers, ask them to join you and give the aspiring mechanics some background. You'll probably want to limit this to grades three and up, and you will need to have all participants swear on their lives that they won't take anything apart at home without a parent's permission.

BOOKLIST: HOW THINGS WORK

Love, Carrie, and Penny Smith, eds. *How Things Work Encyclopedia.* Illus. with photos. DK, 2010. (Gr. 2–7)

Macaulay, David. *The New Way Things Work.* Illus. by the author. Houghton Mifflin, 1998. (Gr. 5–12)

Macaulay, David. *Toilet: How It Works.* Illus. by the author. David Macaulay Studio, 2013. (Gr. 2–6)

Woodford, Chris, et. al. *Cool Stuff and How It Works.* Illus. with photos. DK, 2005. (Gr. 6–9)

Theater Arts Workshop

Program description: This should be an ongoing activity for anyone who loves to act. Pull in improvisation, reader's theater, pantomime, and acting exercises. The workshops do not have to end in a performance, but if the children are interested, they can put on plays for parents and younger children, at day-care centers, or videotape them for posterity.

BOOKLIST: THEATER

Aliki. *A Play's the Thing.* Illus. by the author. HarperCollins, 2005. (K–Gr. 3)

Aliki. *William Shakespeare & the Globe.* Illus. by the author. HarperCollins, 1999. (Gr. 2–8)

Avi. *Romeo and Juliet—Together and Alive at Last.* Orchard, 1987. (Gr. 5–7)

Blackwood, Gary L. *The Shakespeare Stealer.* Dutton, 1998. (Gr. 5–8)

Hoffman, Mary. *Amazing Grace.* Illus. by Caroline Binch. Dial, 1991. (K–Gr. 3)

Schmidt, Gary D. *Okay for Now.* Clarion, 2011. (Gr. 6–8)

Schmidt, Gary D. *The Wednesday Wars.* Clarion, 2007. (Gr. 6–8)

Schwartz, Amy. *Starring Miss Darlene.* Illus. by the author. Roaring Brook, 2007. (PreK–Gr. 2)

Tweens Tell Stories

Program description: Teach your group to be storytellers. Demonstrate how to tell simple stories. Have participants pick a story to learn and hold a story-telling festival for the tellers. You'll find more information on student story-tellers and loads of great strategies and stories to tell in our companion volume, *The Handbook for Storytellers* (American Library Association, 2015). Also visit Planet Esme (www.planetesme.com/storytelling.html), where you'll find author Esme Raji Codell's guidelines for teaching children how to tell stories.

Word Games

Program description: Set out Scrabble, Bananagrams, Big Boggle (with the 5-by-5 grid) and/or Super Big Boggle (with a 6-by-6 grid) and make a lotta words.

BOOKLIST: WORD GAMES

Agee, Jon. *Elvis Lives! And Other Anagrams.* *Illus. by the author. Farrar, 2000.* (Gr. 4–8)

Berlin, Eric. *The Puzzling World of Winston Breen.* *Putnam, 2007.* (Gr. 4–6)

Escoffier, Michaël. *Take Away the A.* *Illus. by Kris Di Giacomo. Enchanted Lion, 2014.* (Gr. 1–4)

Martin, Ann M. *Rain Reign.* *Feiwel & Friends, 2014.* (Gr. 4–6)

Raczka, Bob. *Lemonade, and Other Poems Squeezed from a Single Word.* *Illus. by Nancy Doniger. Roaring Brook, 2011.* (Gr. 2–6)

Steig, William. *CDB.* *Illus. by the author. Simon & Schuster, 2000, c1968.* (Gr. 1–6)

Wolitzer, Meg. *The Fingertips of Duncan Dorfman.* *Dutton, 2011.* (Gr. 5–8)

Writers and Artists Club

Program description: Some of your children might be eager to attend a creative writing program for aspiring writers (and illustrators, too). You can structure the program just like an adults' critique group. Children can write or draw during your sessions or at home and bring in their efforts to share aloud with the rest of the group. Participants should give positive feedback, and then helpful suggestions on how to strengthen/revise/expand the work, whether it's story, poem, memoir, essay, or picture. Put some of the submissions on your blog.

BOOKLIST: WRITERS AND ARTISTS

Ahlberg, Allan. *The Pencil.* Illus. by Bruce Ingman. Candlewick, 2008. (PreK–Gr. 3)

Allen, Susan, and Jane Lindaman. *Written Anything Good Lately?* Illus. by Vicky Enright. Millbrook, 2006. (K–Gr. 3)

Barnett, Mac. *Chloe and the Lion.* Illus. by Adam Rex. Disney-Hyperion, 2012. (K–Gr. 4)

Bruel, Nick. *Bad Kitty Drawn to Trouble.* Illus. by the author. Roaring Brook/Neal Porter, 2008. (Gr. 2–5)

Christelow, Eileen. *What Do Authors and Illustrators Do?* Illus. by the author. Clarion, 2013. Previously published separately as *What Do Authors Do?* (1995) and *What Do Illustrators Do?* (1999). (Gr. 1–4)

Colón, Raúl. *Draw!* Illus. by the author. Simon & Schuster, 2014. (PreK–Gr. 2)

Creech, Sharon. *Love That Dog.* HarperCollins, 2001. (Gr. 4–8)

DePaola, Tomie. *The Art Lesson.* Illus. by the author. Putnam, 1989. (K–Gr. 3)

Hanlon, Abby. *Ralph Tells a Story.* Illus. by the author. Amazon, 2012. (PreK–Gr. 2)

Hills, Tad. *Rocket Writes a Story.* Illus. by the author. Schwartz & Wade, 2012. (K–Gr. 2)

Kitchen, Alexa. *Drawing Comics Is Easy (Except When It's Hard).* Illus. by the author. DKP, 2006. (Gr. 2–6)

Klausmeier, Jesse. *Open This Little Book.* Illus. by Suzy Lee. Chronicle, 2013. (PreK–Gr. 4)

LaMarche, Jim. *The Raft.* Illus. by the author. HarperCollins, 2000. (K–Gr. 2)

Leedy, Loreen. *Look at My Book: How Kids Can Write & Illustrate Terrific Books.* Illus. by the author. Holiday House, 2004. (K–Gr. 5)

Reynolds, Peter. *The Dot.* Illus. by the author. Candlewick, 2003. (Gr. 1–6)

Rylant, Cynthia. *Mr. Putter and Tabby Write the Book.* Illus. by Arthur Howard. Harcourt, 2004. (PreK–Gr. 2)

Sturm, James, Andrew Arnold, and Alexis Frederick-Frost. *Adventures in Cartooning.* First Second, 2009. (Gr. 2–6)

Woodson, Jacqueline. *Locomotion.* Putnam, 2003. (Gr. 5–8)

Afterword: And, Finally . . .

O UR LAST STORY IS A FOND FAREWELL TO THIS VOLUME, WHICH we have stuffed to the gills with glorious nonsense, including many of our favorite songs, jokes, stories, children's books, and wordplay. We hope you have found some treasures and ideas here to help introduce your children to the delights and joys of the English language.

The Silly Farmer

Retold by Pleasant DeSpain

Pleasant DeSpain is a professional storyteller whose collections of stories are particularly useful for the teller in search of short humorous stories. "The Silly Farmer" is an Ethiopian tale from Twenty-Two Splendid Tales to Tell. *After reading or telling the story, you can have your group act it out in pairs (or trios, with one actor playing the wife, adding dialogue as needed) as a creative drama exercise.*

Once there was a silly farmer named Zaheed. One day his wife told him that she was going to have a baby. Zaheed asked her what kind of baby it would be, but she didn't know.

"Then," said Zaheed, "I will visit the wise old woman who lives at the base of the mountains. She has magic, both black and white, and she will be able to tell me."

He took a gold piece that he had hidden deep in his mattress and walked all morning until he reached the old witch's hut.

"I've come to ask you a difficult question," said Zaheed. "And if you can give me a satisfactory answer, I'll pay you with this piece of gold."

The old woman stared at him with dark eyes and nodded her agreement.

"My wife is going to have a child, but she doesn't know what kind it will be. Can you tell me?"

The old woman opened a small wooden chest and removed three ancient bones. She tossed them on the ground and studied the pattern they made. She shook her head and said, "Ehh."

Zaheed shook his head and said, "Ehh."

She tossed them again and studied the pattern. "Ahh!"

"Ahh!" repeated Zaheed.

Once more she tossed the bones and studied the pattern. "Of course!" she exclaimed.

"Of course!" shouted Zaheed.

"Your wife's child will be either a boy or a girl."

"How wonderful!" said Zaheed. He gave the witch the gold piece and ran home to tell his wife the good news.

Several months later his wife had a fat baby girl. "You see," Zaheed told all of his neighbors, "the old woman was right!"

Soon it was time to baptize the girl, but Zaheed and his wife couldn't think of a proper name for her.

"I'll go ask the old woman," said Zaheed. "She is wise and will tell me our daughter's name."

He took another piece of gold from the mattress and walked back to the witch's hut. After Zaheed explained the problem, the old woman took the bones from the chest and tossed them onto the floor. She shook her head and said, "Ehh."

Zaheed shook his head and said, "Ehh."

She tossed them again and studied the pattern. "Ahh!"

"Ahh!" said Zaheed.

Once more she tossed the bones. "Of course!"

"Of course!" repeated Zaheed.

"Give me the gold," said the witch, "and I will whisper the child's name into your hands."

Zaheed did as she said and extended his hands. She quickly whispered into them and said, "Now close your hands tight so that you won't lose it on the way home."

The farmer ran toward home with his hands clasped together. When he came to his neighbor's farm, he saw several of the men pitching hay into tall stacks. "I have it! I have it!" Zaheed cried. "The name of my daughter is here in my hands!"

Just then he slipped on some loose hay and fell to the ground. His hands came apart, and he yelled, "Now I've lost it! Quickly, help me find it again!"

Several of the men ran up and helped Zaheed search through the haystack with their pitchforks.

Soon after, a woman from the village walked by and asked what they were looking for. Zaheed explained how the witch had given him the name and how he had lost it.

"It is nonsense!" she declared. "Simply nonsense!"

"Oh, thank you!" said Zaheed. "I thought I had lost it forever."

When he got home, the silly farmer explained everything to his wife. "The witch whispered the name into my hands, but I lost it on the way home. The neighbor woman found it and told it to me. Our daughter's name is Nonsense! Simply Nonsense!"

And they call her Simply Nonsense, to this very day.

Simply nonsense. There's nothing wrong with that! Now go forth and tell stories, read stories, and spread some magic.

Credits

"Pockets" from *Blackberry Ink* by Even Merriam. Copyright (c) 1985 by Eve Merriam. Used by permission of Marian Reiner.

"The Silly Farmer" by Pleasant DeSpain from *Twenty-Two Splendid Tales to Tell*. Copyright © 1979, 1990, 1991 by Pleasant DeSpain. Published by August House, Inc. and reprinted by permission of Marian Reiner.

"The Goat Well" from *The Fire on the Mountain and Other Stories from Ethiopia and Eritrea* by Harold Courlander and Wolf Leslau © 1978 by Harold Courlander and Wolf Leslau. Reprinted by permission of the Emma Courlander Trust.

"When the Red, Red Robin Comes Bob-Bob-Bobbin' Along" by Harry M. Woods. Used by permission of David Woods.

"The Pancake Hat" © 1988 words by Sarah Pirtle. Discovery Center Music, BMI, music traditional. "Pancake Hat" is part of a collection of one hundred songs by Sarah Pirtle, who received the Magic Penny Award for lifetime achievement in children's music; the songs are recorded by A Gentle Wind in Albany, NY. (www.gentlewind.com).

"Red Ridin' in the Hood" from RED RIDIN' IN THE HOOD: AND OTHER CUENTOS © 2005 by Patricia Santos Marcantonio. Illustrations © 2005 by

Subject Index

Author Index

Title Index